Contents

List of Tables

List of abbreviations and points for the user

Points

1. Lists of words are in general alphabetical, though occasionally a deviation from this has seemed more helpful.
2. Where required, the plural of a noun is indicated in brackets after the noun, e.g. *das Lager* (–), i.e. *die Lager; der Hut* (¨e), i.e. *die Hüte*, etc. (–en, –en) or (–n, –n) indicates a weak masculine noun, cf. 1.3.2.
3. If necessary, the stressed syllable in a word is indicated by the mark ' placed before the stressed syllable, e.g. *die Dok'toren, unter'schreiben*. Where required, a stressed word in context is shown by underlining, e.g. *Wie bust denn <u>du</u> gekommen*?

Abbreviations

In principle, abbreviations have been kept to a minimum. The following have been used where required by considerations of space.

abbrev.	abbreviated		jdn.	jemanden
acad.	academic		lang.	language
acc.	accusative		lit.	literary
adj.	adjective		masc.	masculine
arch.	archaic		nom.	nominative
Austr.	Austrian		neut.	neuter
aux.	auxiliary		obs.	obsolete
Bav.	Bavarian		occ.	occasionally
ch.	chapter		o.s.	oneself
cl.	clause		part.	participle
coll.	colloquial		pej.	pejorative
conj.	conjunction		pl.	plural
dat.	dative		prep.	preposition
elev.	elevated		pres.	present
esp.	especially		pron.	pronounced
etw.	etwas		sb.	somebody
fem.	feminine		sg., sing.	singular
form.	formal		sub. cl.	subordinate clause
gen.	genitive		sth.	something
indic.	indicative		Switz.	Switzerland
inf.	informal		techn.	technical
jd.	jemand		vb.	verb
jdm.	jemandem		vulg.	vulgar

PREFACE to the second edition

Since the appearance of the first edition in 1971, Hammer's grammar has been an indispensable source of information about modern German grammar and usage for teachers and students of German. Its acknowledged strength lay above all in the wealth of well chosen examples, but also in its comprehensiveness and its sheer reliability. However, much has changed in the intervening twenty years, and it became clear that a thoroughgoing revision which retained the essential virtues of Mr Hammer's work had become necessary. For, if the basic structure of the language remains unaltered, the needs of language students and sixth-formers learning German are now rather different, as is the range of German with which they must cope and the methods by which they are taught, and it is these needs which this revised edition is intended to address.

In preparing the revision, I have attempted to bear a few central principles in mind, given that the work is intended to be a comprehensive descriptive grammar of standard German for the use of the foreign learner whose native or first language is English. First, if it is to be used by advanced learners of German in sixth forms and on university courses, it can no longer be taken for granted that they will be fully familiar with grammatical terminology and notions. I have thus added a certain amount of explanatory material to help the user to understand the points of grammar and usage being treated. In general, I have used familiar and traditional grammatical terminology where possible, and thus refer, for example, to 'subordinating conjunctions' rather than 'complementizers'. However, where I consider more recent and perhaps less familiar terms and ideas to be a help to the potential user in understanding the structures of the language, as is the case with 'determiners' (Chapter 5) or the 'valency' of verbs (Chapter 18), I have adopted them and explained them fully.

Secondly, I have retained the range of examples which constituted one of the principal strengths of the original edition. In practice, I have kept a large proportion of Mr Hammer's examples, but checked them again with native speakers to confirm that they fully reflect current usage. Where I have substituted new examples, it has been with the aim of extending the range of registers covered (in particular to represent everyday spoken usage more fully) or updating the material.

Thirdly, it is taken as a basic principle that the work should be as comprehensive as possible and serve as a reference work which may be consulted on any point of grammar and usage. To this end, all the individual sections have been checked to confirm that the information is as full as necessary for the English learner and that it is as accurate as possible. A substantial body of research has been completed in the last twenty years which has increased our knowledge and understanding of current usage in German – there have, for example, been two completely new editions of the standard DUDEN grammar since 1971 – and this has been consulted at every stage. The reviser's debt to this original research on the modern language may be seen in the bibliography.

Fourthly, the changed needs of the present-day learner have been borne in mind by including information on all forms of the modern language. Thus, more attention has been paid to registers other than formal writing or literature and details given on spoken usage to reflect the greater emphasis paid to communicative skills in modern language teaching. Thus, where spoken and written usage diverge, this is clearly explained, as are forms which, though they may be regarded as grammatically 'correct', are felt to be stilted outside the most formal written registers. Similarly, forms which are frequently heard in everyday speech but widely thought of as substandard or incorrect are included here, as the foreign learner will encounter them every day, but with a clear indication of their status. In general, the foreign learner is counselled to avoid such forms as they sound particularly unacceptable when spoken with a foreign accent. Important regional variants within standard German are also included and marked accordingly, but purely dialectal forms have been ignored.

Finally, the structure of the work has been totally recast to simplify the user's task in finding his or her way to the required information. In practice, this has meant that the bulk of the text is quite new to this revised edition. Although the basic sequence of chapters is much the same as in the original edition, the layout has been simplified, longer chapters have been split up (that on verbs, which constituted almost a quarter of the whole book, has been divided into seven separate chapters), related information which was scattered in different parts has been brought together (even where this has involved a certain amount of repetition) and cross-references have been radically simplified and eliminated where unnecessary. The index has been expanded to include as many words and topics as possible, and to facilitate access to the material it has been divided into a German word index, an English word index and a topic index.

Acknowledgements

It is with sincere gratitude that I acknowledge the assistance I have been fortunate enough to receive during the preparation of the revised edition, first and foremost to those German speakers, unfortunately too numerous to mention, who have answered questions, given advice and, often unwittingly, provided me with examples and other linguistic data. I am especially indebted to those friends and colleagues in Britain who have been kind enough to comment on draft chapters, provide me with material, let me see their own notes resulting from their use of the first edition and advise me in other ways, in particular Dr J.S. Barbour, Dr C. Beedham, Mr P.A. Coggle, Dr D. Duckworth, Dr J.L. Flood, Dr C. Hall, Mr W. Hanson, Mr P. Holgate, Mr D.H.R. Jones, Prof. W.J. Jones, Dr K.M. Kohl, Mr D.G. McCulloch, Dr G.D.C. Martin, Dr D. Rösler, Ms M. Schwab, Dr R.W. Sheppard, Prof. H.G. Siefken, Dr J.K.A. Thomaneck, Mrs A. Thompson, Dr B. Thompson, Mr M.R. Townson, Mr B.A. Watson, Dr J. West and Dr D.N. Yeandle. I must also express my thanks to the German Academic Exchange

Service, who made it possible for me to spend a month at the Institut für deutsche Sprache in Mannheim, where I was able to check many aspects of usage and points of grammar in its computerised corpus of modern spoken and written German and use its inestimable library facilities. I am very grateful to all colleagues there for their help, particularly to Mr Tobias Brückner, Prof. U. Engel, Prof. G. Stickel, Mrs Eva Teubert, Prof. R. Wimmer and Dr Gisela Zifonun. Last but not least, I must acknowledge my debt to Royal Holloway and Bedford New College, University of London, which granted me an invaluable term's leave of absence to work on this revision and to all my colleagues in the German Department at RHBNC for their continued support whilst I was engaged on this task.

Martin Durrell
1991

PREFACE to the third edition

The principal aim of the revised second edition of Hammer's grammar was to make the excellent material of the original version accessible to a new generation of students by providing more detailed explanations, improving the layout and presentation and providing a more comprehensive system of access to the material. In short, it was to be more up-to-date and user-friendly, whilst retaining the basic ordering of the original and much of its wealth of examples. Reactions from users and practical experience in working with the new edition suggest that these aims were welcome and that they were fulfilled to a certain extent, but that further improvements were possible and necessary. The present revised third edition is intended to achieve these.

After some hesitation, it was decided that the basic, relatively traditional lay-out based on the parts of speech should be retained. If there is much in favour of a presentation which systematically uses longer authentic texts as the basis for an account of grammatical structures and usage (like Weinrich (1993)), such an approach would probably be unfamiliar to most potential users and could detract from the usefulness of the work for everyday reference. Similarly, considerations of the user prevailed in the decision to retain a separate chapter on expressions of time, although consistency would suggest that the material dealt with there really belongs elsewhere, e.g. in the chapter on adverbs or the chapter on prepositions.

It was clear, though, that there was scope for the essential information in each chapter to be presented in the form of easily consulted tables. This has been done systematically in this new edition, so that almost every chapter or section has a table summarising basic points or presenting inflectional paradigms. Similarly, an innovation in the second edition was that each chapter has a short introduction explaining the subject matter of the chapter and any relevant grammatical terminology. These have been made more consistent and aim more deliberately to summarise the contents of each chapter so that the user can find his/her way more easily to the relevant material. In practice, all explanatory material has been subjected to close scrutiny from the point of view of the potential user and revised where necessary, with the aim of simplifying and clarifying explanations wherever possible. The opportunity was also taken to review all the language examples, substituting better or newer material where required.

Naturally, all information about specific points of grammar and usage was checked fully against my own database of modern German, the corpus of spoken and written German at the Institut für deutsche Sprache in Mannheim and the most recent academic research, as reflected (selectively) in the bibliography. This has resulted in substantial revision of some chapters and sections, notably the account of adverbs (Chapter 7), of the subjunctive mood (in particular the analysis of the *würde*-form in the light of Thieroff (1992)) and of the gender of foreign words in section 1.1. A number of sections have been added on points which were dealt with sketchily or inadequately in the second edition, for instance on verb agreement (section 12.1.4), on commands and the imperative (section 16.2) and on complement clauses (section 19.2). And, of course, information had to be given on the reformed spelling which will be implemented from summer 1998 onwards (section 23.7).

As for the second edition, I owe an immense debt of gratitude to a large number of friends, colleagues and acquaintances in the English- and German-speaking countries without whose help this revision would have been impossible. In addition to those who already helped me for the second edition, I must offer particular thanks to Dr Paul Bennett, Dr Carol Chapman, Dr Bruce Donaldson, Mr Piklu Gupta, Prof. Randall Jones, Dr John Manton, Ms Victoria Martin, Prof. Ulrike Meinhof, Dr Michael Minden, Prof. Hugh Ridley, Ms Susan Tebbutt and Dr Sheila Watts. I am particularly grateful, too, for the continuous collaborative help and support of Prof. David Brée and his colleagues and post-graduates at the Department of Computer Science, University of Manchester.

Martin Durrell
1996

1

Nouns

1.1 Gender

Every German noun is assigned to one of the three genders: masculine, feminine or neuter. Grammatical gender is distinct from natural gender (i.e. 'males', 'females' and 'things', as in English), and this classification appears quite arbitrary. For this reason, foreign learners are always recommended to learn German nouns together with their gender as shown by the relevant definite article, e.g.: masculine: *der Tisch*, feminine: *die Wand*, neuter: *das Fenster*. Unlike many languages, German only has gender differences in the singular, not in the plural, cf: *die Tische, die Wände, die Fenster*.

In practice, the meaning or the form (especially the ending) of a noun often gives a useful clue to its gender, as does the way the plural is formed. A knowledge of these, even if there are some exceptions, is a valuable assistance in learning genders and can help to eliminate random guesswork. Köpcke (1982) gives an illuminating account of the complexities of gender assignment in German. Corbett (1991) is a full and helpful survey of the role of gender in language and has good detail on German.

Table 1.1 summarises the most useful clues to gender in modern German.

1.1.1 Masculine by meaning

(a) Male persons and male animals
(See also 1.1.4.)

> der Arzt, der Ingenieur, der König, der Student, der Vater
> der Bock, der Eber, der Hahn, der Hengst, der Löwe

NB: Diminutives in -*chen* and -*lein*, including names, are neuter (cf. 1.1.7), e.g.: *das Büblein, das Karlchen, das Kerlchen*.

(b) Seasons, months and days of the week

> der Frühling, der Januar, der Mittwoch

NB: (i) Compounds, e.g. *das Frühjahr, die Jahreszeit*, have the gender of the second element, cf. 1.1.9.
> (ii) Exceptions: *die Nacht, die Woche, das Jahr*.

(c) Points of the compass and words referring to winds and kinds of weather

> der Norden, der Osten, der Süden, der Westen;
> der Föhn, der Passat, der Taifun, der Wind;
> der Frost, der Hagel, der Nebel, der Regen, der Schnee, der Sturm, der Tau

NB: Exceptions: *die Brise, das Eis, das Gewitter* (see 1.1.8c); *die Graupel, das Wetter, die Witterung* (see 1.1.6).

TABLE 1.1 *Gender assignment*

	Masculine	**Feminine**	**Neuter**
Gender linked to meaning	Male persons Male animals Seasons, months Days of the week Points of the compass Weather words Rocks and minerals Alcholic drinks Makes of cars Rivers outside Germany Monetary units Mountains	Female persons Female animals Aeroplanes Motor-bikes Ships German rivers Numerals	Young persons Young animals Metals Elements Chemicals Physical units Letters of the alphabet Nouns from other parts of speech Hotels Restaurants Cinemas Countries Towns
Gender linked to ending or form of noun	Nouns ending in *-ant, -ast, -ich, -ig,* *-ismus, -ling, -or,* *-us*	Nouns ending in *-a, -anz, -ei, -enz,* *-heit, -ie, -ik, -in,* *-keit, -schaft, -sion,* *-tät, -ung, -ur*	Nouns ending in *-chen, -icht, -il, -it,* *-lein, -ma, -ment, -tel,* *-tum, -um*
	Nouns from strong verbs	Nouns ending in *-t* from verbs	Nouns referring to things ending in *-al,* *-an, -ar, -är, -at, -ent,* *-ett, -ier, -iv, -o, -on*
	Nouns ending in *-er* from verbs		Nouns from infinitives Most words with prefix *Ge-* Most nouns ending in *-nis* and *-sal*

(d) Rocks and minerals

der Diamant, der Granit, der Lehm, der Quarz, der Ton

NB: Exceptions: *das Erz, die Kohle, die Kreide, das Mineral.*

(e) Alcoholic drinks and plant-based drinks

der Cocktail, der Gin, der Kirsch, der Schnaps, der Wein, der Wodka
der Kakao, der Kaffee, der Most, der Saft, der Tee

NB: Exception: *das Bier.*

(f) Makes of car

der Audi, der BMW (but cf. 1.1.2b), der Citroën, der Mercedes, der Polo, der Rolls-Royce, der Škoda, der Trabant

(g) Rivers outside Germany

(See 1.1.2c for those within Germany.)

> der Jordan, der Kongo, der Mississippi, der Po, der Shannon, der Severn

NB: Those ending in *-a* or *-e* are feminine, e.g.: *die Seine, die Themse* the Thames, *die Wolga.* Also *die Liffey.*

(h) Monetary units

> der Dollar, der Franken, der Pfennig, der Rappen, der Schilling

NB: There are several exceptions, notably: *die Mark, das Pfund.*

(i) Mountains and mountain ranges

> der Ätna, der Brocken, der Montblanc, der Mount Everest, der Säntis, der Balkan, der Harz, der Himalaja, der Jura, der Spessart, der Taunus

NB: There are some exceptions, e.g.:
> (i) Compounds: *das Erzgebirge, das Matterhorn, die Zugspitze.*
> (ii) *die Eifel, die Haardt, die Rhön, die Sierra Nevada.*

1.1.2 Feminine by meaning

(a) Female persons and animals

(See also 1.1.4.)

> die Frau, die Gans, die Henne, die Köchin, die Kuh, die Mutter, die Sau

NB: Exceptions: *das Weib, das Fräulein, das Mädchen* (and other diminutives in *-chen* and *-lein*, see 1.1.7).

(b) Aeroplanes, motor-bikes and ships

> die Boeing 767, die Cessna, die Tu-154;
> die BMW (but cf. 1.1.1f), die Honda;
> die „Bismarck", die „Bremen"

NB: Some aeroplane and ship names keep the grammatical gender of the word, e.g.: *der Airbus, der Storch; der „Albatros", das „Möwchen".*

(c) Native German names of rivers

> die Donau, die Elbe, die Ems, die Fulda, die Lahn, die Maas, die Memel, die Neiße, die Oder, die Ruhr, die Saale, die Spree, die Weichsel

NB: There are a number of exceptions, the most important being: *der Inn, der Lech, der Main, der Neckar, der Rhein.*

(d) Names of numerals

> die Eins, die Vier, die Tausend, die Million, die Milliarde

NB: As expressions of quantity, the following are neuter: *das Dutzend, das Hundert, das Tausend* (cf. 9.1.5b).

1.1.3 Neuter by meaning

(a) Young persons and animals
(See also 1.1.4.)

> das Baby, das Ferkel, das Fohlen, das Junge (but cf. 1.1.12), das Kalb, das Kind, das Lamm, das Pony (but cf. 1.1.12)

(b) Metals and chemical elements

> das Aluminium, das Blei, das Eisen, das Gold, das Kobalt, das Kupfer, das Messing, das Silber, das Uran, das Zinn

NB: Exceptions: *die Bronze, der Phosphor, der Schwefel, der Stahl* (and compounds such as *der Sauerstoff* 'oxygen', cf. 1.1.9).

(c) Physical units and entities

> das Ampère, das Atom, das Elektron, das Molekül, das Pfund, das Watt

NB: *Liter* and *Meter* may be masculine or neuter, see 1.1.11b.

(d) Letters of the alphabet and musical notes

> das A, ein großes D, das Ypsilon
> das hohe C, das Cis, das Ges

NB: In Swiss usage letters are masculine, e.g.: *der A.*

(e) Other parts of speech used as nouns
Note that this includes verb infinitives, colours, languages and English *ing*-forms, e.g.:

> das Ach, das Blau des Himmels, das vertraute Du, das In-Kraft-Treten, das Jenseits, das Kommen, sein ewiges Nein, das moderne Spanisch, das Doping, das Meeting

(f) Hotels, Cafés, Restaurants and Cinemas

> das Hilton, das „Kranzler", das „Roxy"

(g) Names of continents, countries, provinces and towns

> das gärende Afrika, das viktorianische England, das alte Bayern, das zerstörte Frankfurt, das historische Neustadt (but: **die** Stadt)

For the use of the article with these neuter names, see 4.4.1c.

Exceptions:

(i) A number of names of countries and provinces are feminine; they are always used with the definite article, cf. 4.4.1b. The commonest are:

> die Arktis, die Antarktis; die Lausitz, die Pfalz, die Schweiz and those in *-a, -e, -ei* and *-ie* (except *Afrika, China*), e.g.: die Riviera, die Bretagne, die Türkei, die Normandie

(ii) A few are masculine; they are also commonly used with the article, cf. 4.4.1a:

> der Irak, der Iran, der Jemen, der Kongo, der Libanon, der Sudan

1.1.4 The gender of nouns for humans and animals: some special cases

(a) Professions, occupations, nationality, etc.

(i) For many names denoting professions, occupations or nationality the basic designation is masculine, and a feminine may be formed from it with the suffix *-in* (see also 22.2.1f):

>der Engländer – die Engländerin
>der Koch – die Köchin
>der Lehrer – die Lehrerin
>der Türke – die Türkin

or by replacing *-mann* with *-frau*, e.g.:

>der Kaufmann – die Kauffrau
>der Amtmann – die Amtsfrau (the form *Amtmännin* is now obsolete)
>der Milchmann – die Milchfrau

(ii) These forms are normally used where appropriate to refer to female persons:

>Sie gilt als die beste **Kundin**   *She is considered our best customer*
>von unserem Geschäft
>Heute abend habe ich deine   *I saw your friend Anna this evening*
>**Freundin** Anna gesehen

On the other hand, the masculine form is often used in a general sense to refer to either sex, especially with titles and 'newer' professions (including those hitherto predominantly or exclusively male), or when the profession itself is emphasised, e.g.:

>der damalige Minister für Volksbildung Margot Honecker
>Frau Professor Dr. Hartmann, Frau Bundestagspräsident Rita Süßmuth
>(but the feminine form is usual if the title *Frau* is omitted, e.g.: Bundestagspräsidentin Rita Süßmuth)
>Sie ist Ingenieur, Autoschlosser, Informatiker

This usage is particularly common after the verb *sein*, and it was predominant in the former GDR.

(iii) However, usage is nowadays variable and uncertain, as recent surveys (e.g. Doleschal (1992)) have shown. The use of undifferentiated masculine nouns to refer to women (or men and women) may be seen as discriminatory, but it is quite common in practice, even with younger speakers. Indeed, some speakers (male and female) feel that terms like *Professorin* sound derogatory. In general, the feminine form is used if it is felt to be relevant in context:

>Die neue Lehrerin scheint sehr beliebt zu sein
>(*Der neue Lehrer* would be odd if a woman is referred to)

The feminine forms are usual to refer back to a woman (or women) already mentioned:

>Meine beiden Schwestern sind Ärzt**innen** (NOT Ärzte)
>Hanne Frisch, die Ärzt**in** (NOT der Arzt), die ihn behandelte
>Sie wurde die erste Professor**in** an einer deutschen Universität

In advertisements, both forms are now commonly given:

> Wir suchen ab sofort **eine(n)** — *We have an immediate vacancy for a*
> **Musiklehrer(in)** — *music teacher*
> Wir brauchen **eine/n** — *We have a vacancy for a social and*
> **Mitarbeiter/in** für Gemeinde- — *youth worker*
> und Jugendarbeit

When no feminine form is available, the masculine is used despite the anomaly:

> der Säugling hieß Anna; unser werter Gast, Frau Dr. Schilling;
> der Teenager war schwanger; der Inhaber dieses Passes ist Deutscher

In written German, the feminine form is sometimes used to refer to feminine nouns denoting things:

> Die Sowjetunion ist die größte — *The Soviet Union is the largest*
> Produzentin von Personenwagen — *producer of private cars in the*
> im Ostblock (NZZ) — *eastern block*

(iv) In the plural, to refer to both men and women, various possibilties are current. It is not uncommon for the masculine form to be used:

> Der Bürgermeister begrüßte **die Besucher** aus der Hauptstadt Wien

However, this may be regarded as discriminatory, especially where the feminine form is in common usage. Both forms may then be given:

> liebe Zuschauer und Zuschauerinnen; die Studenten und Studentinnen

A recent development is the use of the feminine form with a capital *I* (sometimes spoken as long [i:]) to indicate both sexes, e.g.:

> die **StudentInnen** der Westfälischen Wilhelmsuniversität Münster

(b) Animals

The names of species may be masculine, feminine or neuter:

> der Fisch, die Ratte, das Pferd, etc.

Many familiar or domesticated animals have different masculine and feminine forms:

> der Fuchs – die Füchsin   der Hahn – die Henne
> der Gänserich – die Gans   der Kater – die Katze

NB: **die** *Drohne* 'drone' – **der** *Weisel* 'queen bee'

In most cases one of these is selected to designate the species (e.g. **der** *Fuchs*, **die** *Gans*, **die** *Katze*) and the other is only used if the sex is known or relevant in context.

In the absence of a specific term, male or female animals and birds can be indicated by *das Männchen* or *das Weibchen*, e.g.:

> das Zebramännchen; das Froschweibchen

(c) Anomalous genders of names of human beings

die Geisel *hostage*	das Mündel *ward (in legal language masc.)*
das Genie *genius*	die Person *person*
das Haupt *head (of state, family)*	die Wache *sentry*
das Individuum *individual*	die Waise *orphan*
das Mannequin *mannequin*	das Weib *woman, wife (pej. or arch.)*
das Mitglied *member*	

In addition, *all* nouns in *-chen* and *-lein* are neuter, irrespective of sex, e.g.: **das Bübchen, das** *Fräulein*, etc. (see 1.1.7).

NB: (i) *zum Waisen machen* 'to orphan'
  (ii) Difficulties of agreement in contexts where grammatical and natural gender conflict are dealt with in 1.1.13.

1.1.5 Some nouns are masculine by form

(a) Nouns with the following endings

-ant	der Konsonant	**-ig**	der Honig	**-or**	der Motor
-ast	der Kontrast	**-ismus**	der Idealismus	**-us**	der Rhythmus
-ich	der Teppich	**-ling**	der Liebling		

NB: Common exceptions: *das Labor, das Genus* 'gender', *das Tempus* 'tense'.

(b) Nouns formed from strong verbs without a suffix

der Betrieb, der Biß, der Fall, der Gang, der Sprung, der Wurf, etc.

NB: Common exceptions: *das Band* (see 1.1.12), *das Grab,* das *Leid* 'harm', 'sorrow', *das Maß* 'measurement', *das Schloß, das Verbot.*

1.1.6 Some nouns are feminine by form

(a) Nouns with the following endings

-a	die Villa	**-ik**	die Panik	**-tion**	die Revolution
-anz	die Eleganz	**-in**	die Freundin	**-tät**	die Universität
-ei	die Bücherei	**-keit**	die Heiterkeit	**-ung**	die Bedeutung
-enz	die Existenz	**-schaft**	die Botschaft	**-ur**	die Natur
-heit	die Gesundheit	**-sion**	die Explosion		
-ie	die Biologie	**-sis**	die Basis		

NB: Common exceptions are words in *-ma* (see 1.1.7), chemical terms in *-in* (see 1.1.7) and the following: *das Sofa, das Genie, der Atlantik, der Katholik, das Mosaik, der Pazifik, das Abitur, das Futur, das Purpur.*

(b) Most nouns ending in *-t* from verbs

die Ankunft, die Fahrt, die Flucht, die Macht, die Schlacht, die Sicht

NB: There are several common exceptions, i.e. *der Dienst, der Durst, der Frost, das Gebot, das Gift, der Verdienst, der Verlust.*

1.1.7 Nouns with the following endings are neuter

-chen	das Mädchen	**-lein**	das Büchlein	**-tel**	das Viertel
-icht	das Dickicht	**-ma**	das Schema	**-tum**	das Eigentum
-il	das Ventil	**-ment**	das Appartement	**-um**	das Album
-it	das Dynamit				

and chemical terms in *-in*: das Benzin, das Protein

NB: Common exceptions: *der Kontinent, der Profit, der Granit, die Firma, der Zement, der Irrtum, der Reichtum, der Konsum.*

1.1.8 Endings as a clue to gender

Here we are dealing with tendencies rather than rules.

(a) Nouns in *-el*, *-er* and *-en*
(i) Nouns in *-er* (usually from verbs) denoting persons are masculine: *der Bäcker, der Bettler, der Lehrer, der Redner.*

(ii) All nouns from verb infinitives in *-en* are neuter (see 1.1.3e): *das Essen, das Kaffeetrinken, das Kommen.*

(iii) About 60 per cent of other nouns in *-el*, *-en* and *-er* are masculine: *der Flügel, der Schatten, der Fehler.*

(iv) About a quarter of those in *-el* and *-er* (**none** in *-en*) are feminine: *die Butter, die Regel, die Steuer* 'tax' (cf. 1.1.12), *die Wurzel.*

(v) The rest (some 15 per cent) are neuter: *das Fieber, das Segel, das Zeichen.*

(b) Nouns in *-e*
The vast majority of these (90 per cent) are feminine, e.g.:

die Blume, die Bühne, die Garage, die Liebe, die Sahne

There are five major groups of exceptions, i.e.:

(i) Names of male persons and animals (see 1.3.2), e.g.: *der Bote, der Junge, der Lotse* 'pilot' (of ship), *der Löwe.*

(ii) Eight irregular masculines (see 1.3.3), i.e.: *der Buchstabe, der Friede, der Funke, der Gedanke, der Glaube, der Name, der Same, der Wille.*

(iii) Two other masculine nouns, i.e.: *der Charme, der Käse.*

(iv) Most nouns with the prefix *Ge-* are neuter (see 1.1.8c), e.g.: *das Gebirge, das Gefälle, das Gemüse.*

(v) A few other neuter nouns, i.e.: *das Auge, das Ende, das Erbe* 'inheritance' (cf. 1.1.12), *das Image, das Interesse, das Prestige, das Regime, das Repertoire.*

(c) Nouns with the prefix *Ge-* [gə-]
The majority of these (over 90 per cent) are neuter, e.g.:

das Geäst, das Gebäude, das Gebot, das Gelübde, das Gesetz, das Gespräch

There are three groups of exceptions:

(i) A few names of male or female humans, e.g.:

> *der Gehilfe/die Gehilfin* 'assistant', *der Gemahl/die Gemahlin* (elev.) 'spouse', *der Genosse/die Genossin* 'comrade', *der Gevatter* (arch.) 'godfather'.

(ii) Eleven other masculines:

der Gebrauch	*use*	der Gehorsam	*obedience*	der Geschmack	*taste*
der Gedanke	*thought*	der Genuß	*enjoyment*	der Gestank	*stink*
der Gefallen	*favour*	der Geruch	*smell*	der Gewinn	*profit*
der Gehalt	*content*	der Gesang	*singing*		

NB: *Gefallen* and *Gehalt* are neuter in other meanings, see 1.1.12.

(iii) Eleven other feminines:

die Gebärde	*gesture*	die Gefahr	*danger*	die Gestalt	*figure*
die Gebühr	*fee*	die Gemeinde	*community*	die Gewähr	*guarantee*
die Geburt	*birth*	die Geschichte	*history;*	die Gewalt	*force,*
			story		*violence*
die Geduld	*patience*	die Geschwulst	*tumour*		

(d) Nouns with the suffixes -*nis* and -*sal*

These are mainly (about 70 per cent) neuter, e.g.:

> das Bedürfnis, das Ereignis, das Erlebnis, das Scheusal, das Schicksal

About 30 per cent are feminine, including:

(i) most in -*nis* from adjectives, e.g.: *die Bitternis, die Finsternis*.

(ii) most in -*nis* from verbs denoting a state, e.g.: *die Besorgnis, die Betrübnis*.

(iii) some other common feminines, e.g.: *die Erkenntnis, die Erlaubnis, die Kenntnis, die Mühsal, die Trübsal*.

(e) Nouns with the following endings are usually neuter if they refer to things

However, if they refer to persons they are masculine, see 1.1.1:

-al	das Lineal	-at	das Sekretariat	-iv	das Adjektiv
-an	das Organ	-ent	das Talent	-o	das Büro
-ar	das Formular	-ett	das Etikett	-on	das Mikrophon
-är	das Militär	-ier	das Papier		

NB: There are several exceptions, of which the most common are: *der Kanal, die Moral, der Skandal, der Altar, der Kommentar, der Apparat, der Automat, der Salat, der Senat, die Manier, der Kanton, die Person*

1.1.9 The gender of compound words and abbreviations

(a) Compound nouns usually have the gender of the last component

> **der** Fahrplan, **die** Bushaltestelle, **das** Hallenbad

Exceptions

(i) Some compounds of *der Mut* are feminine, i.e.: *die Anmut, die Armut, die Demut, die Großmut, die Langmut, die Sanftmut, die Schwermut, die Wehmut*.

(ii) For the compounds of *der/das Teil*, see 1.1.11c.

(iii) Others:

die Scheu	BUT der Abscheu	der Grat	BUT das Rückgrat
(cf. 1.1.11)		die Woche	BUT der Mittwoch
das Wort	BUT die Antwort	das Gift	BUT die Mitgift *dowry*

(b) The gender of abbreviations is determined by the basic word

der HSV (der Hamburger Sportverein)
die CDU (die Christlich-Demokratische Union)
das BAFöG (das Bundesausbildungsförderungsgesetz)

(c) Shortened words have the gender of the full form

der Akku (Akkumulator)
das Labor (Laboratorium)
der Krimi (Kriminalroman)
die Lok (Lokomotive)
die Uni (Universität)

NB: But note **das** *Foto* (despite: *die Fotographie*). However, in Switzerland **die** *Foto* is the norm.

1.1.10 The gender of recent English loan-words

Large-scale borrowing of words from English is a characteristic feature of modern German. These need to be assigned to a gender, and this is determined by a few chief principles (which sometimes conflict), cf. the survey by Gregor (1983). They may be summarised as follows:

(a) Many English words adopt the gender of the nearest German equivalent

der Air-bag	**(der** Sack)	die Band	**(die** Kapelle)
der Airport	**(der** Flughafen)	die Box	**(die** Büchse)
der Bob	**(der** Schlitten)	die Gang	**(die** Bande)
der Lift	**(der** Aufzug)	das Baby	**(das** Kind)
der Shop	**(der** Laden)	das Bike	**(das** Fahrrad)
der Smog	**(der** Nebel)	das Girl	**(das** Mädchen)

NB: This principle may result in a word having two genders in different meanings, e.g.: **der** *Service* 'service' (by analogy with **der** *Dienst*); **das** *Service* '(tea-/coffee-)service' (by analogy with **das** *Geschirr*).

(b) The ending or the form of some English words can determine the gender
(i) Words with suffixes similar to German suffixes adopt the gender associated with that suffix:

der Broiler, der Container, der Computer, der Dimmer (*-er* is masc.)
der Agitator, der Konduktor, der Rotor (*-or* is masc.)
die Animation, die Supervision (*-sion* and *-tion* are fem.)
die City, die Lobby, die Publicity, die Party, die Story (*-ie* is fem.)
das Klosett, das Pamphlet, das Ticket (*-ett* is neut.)
das Advertisement, das Realignment, das Treatment (*-ment* is neut.)

(ii) Monosyllabic nouns from verbs are often masculine (cf. 1.1.5b):

der Hit, der Look, der Raid, der Rock, der Streik, der Strip, der Talk

(iii) Nouns from phrasal verbs or English *ing*-forms are usually neuter, possibly because they are seen as infinitives or similar, cf. 1.1.3e:

> das Blow-up, das Check-up, das Handout, das Teach-in
> das Dumping, das Floating, das Meeting, das Merchandising

NB: There are some exceptions, e.g.: *der Fallout, die Holding* (company)

(c) If there is no other indication, monosyllabic nouns tend to be masculine

> der Chip, der Choke, der Lunch, der Sex, der Spot, der Trend

BUT:

> die Bar, die Couch, die Farm, das Match, das Steak, das Team

(d) No gender has yet become firmly established in a good number of cases
Common examples are:

der/das Blackout	der/das Deal	der/das Ketchup	der/das Plaid
der/das Break	der/die Forehand	der/das Looping	der/das Radar
der/das Cartoon	der/das Go-slow	der/die Parka	die/das Soda
der/das (coll. also: die) Joghurt			

1.1.11 Nouns with varying gender

The gender of a few nouns is not fixed, although the variation is often linked to regional or register differences.

(a) Some common examples

Abscheu *abhorrence*	**der** (occ. **die**)	Kompromiß *compromise*	**der** (Austr. **das**)
Aperitif *aperitif*	**der** (Switz. **das**)	Match *match*	**das** (Austr./Switz. **der**)
Backbord *port*	**das** (Austr. **der**)	Meteor *meteor*	**der** (astronom. **das**)
Barock *Baroque*	**der** or **das**	Mündel *ward*	**das** (legal **der**)
Dotter *yolk*	**der** or **das**	Puff *brothel* (vulg.)	**der** (Au. **das**)
Dschungel *jungle*	**der** (occ. **das**, obs. **die**)	Pyjama *pyjamas*	**der** (Austr./Switz. **das**)
Fakt *fact*	**das** (occ. **der**)	Radio *radio*	**das** (south German **der**)
Filter *filter*	**der** (techn. **das**)	Sakko *jacket*	**der** (Austr. **das**)
Foto *photo*	**das** (Switz. **die**)	Sims *(window-)sill, mantelpiece*	**der** or **das**
Gelee *jelly*	**das** or **der**	Soda *soda*	**die** or **das**
Gischt *spray* (*from waves*)	**der** or **die**	Spargel *asparagus*	**der** (Switz. **die**)
Katapult *catapult*	**das** or **der**	Steuerbord *starboard*	**das** (Austr. **der**)
Kehricht *sweepings*	**der** or **das**	Taxi *taxi* (NB: also **die** *Taxe* common)	**das** (Switz. **der**)
Keks *biscuit*	**der** (Austr. **das**)	Virus *virus*	**der** (medical **das**)
Knäuel *ball* (wool)	**der** or **das**	Zubehör *accessories*	**das** or **der**

(b) *Liter* and *Meter*

(i) Both these words (and their compounds, e.g. *Zentimeter*) are officially neuter, i.e. *das Liter,* *das Meter.*

(ii) However, they are regularly masculine in colloquial speech, and not infrequently in print, i.e. *der Liter, der Meter.* Written Swiss usage *always* prefers the masculine.

(c) *Teil*

(i) Nowadays *Teil* is usually masculine, i.e. *der Teil,* in all meanings:

dieser Teil von Deutschland, er behielt den größten Teil für sich.

(ii) However, it may be neuter in a few set phrases:

ich für mein (*or* meinen) Teil; das bessere (*or* den besseren) Teil wählen;
sie trug ihr (*or* ihren) Teil dazu bei; er hat sein (*or* seinen) Teil getan

(iii) The neuter *das Teil* is also usual in technical language, to refer to a detached part, cf. *jedes einzelne Teil, ein defektes Teil.*

(iv) Compounds of *Teil* are mostly masculine, with the following exceptions:

das Abteil *compartment*   das Gegenteil *opposite*
das (*legal* der) Erbteil *inheritance*   das/der Oberteil *upper part*
das Einzelteil *separate part*   das Urteil *verdict*
das Ersatzteil *replacement part*

1.1.12 Double genders with different meanings

There are many words whose meanings are distinguished by having a different gender. The most common are:

der Band ("e) *volume, book*   das Band ("er) *ribbon*
                                        das Band (-e) *bond, fetter* (cf. 1.2.8)

NB: Also: die Band (-s) (pron. [bɛnt]) *band, (pop) group.*

der Bulle (-n,-n) *bull; cop* (coll.)   die Bulle (-n) *(papal) bull*
der Bund ("e) *union; waistband*   das Bund (-e) *bundle, bunch*
der Ekel (no pl.) *disgust*   das Ekel (-) (coll.) *nasty person*
der Erbe (-n,-n) *heir*   das Erbe (no pl.) *inheritance, heritage*
der Flur (-e) *entrance hall* (north German) die Flur (-en) *meadow* (elev.)
der Gefallen (-) *favour*   das Gefallen (no pl.) *pleasure*
der Gehalt (-e) *content*   das Gehalt ("er) *salary*
    (Austr. also = *salary*)
der Golf (-e) *gulf*   das Golf (no pl.) *golf*
der Gummi (-s) *eraser*   das Gummi (no pl.) *rubber (as material)*
der Harz *Harz (mountains)*   das Harz (no pl.) *resin*
der Heide (-n) *heathen*   die Heide (-n) *heath*
der Hut ("e) *hat*   die Hut (no pl.) *guard*
                                        (e.g.: auf der Hut sein *be on one's guard*)
der Junge (-n,-n) *boy*   das Junge (adj.) *young (of animals)*
der Kiefer (-) *jaw*   die Kiefer (-n) *pine*
der Kunde (-n,-n) *customer*   die Kunde (no pl.) *knowledge, news* (elev.)
das Lama (-s) *llama*   der Lama (-s) *lama*
der Laster (-) *lorry* (coll.)   das Laster (-) *vice*
der Leiter (-) *leader*   die Leiter (-n) *ladder*

der Mangel (˙) *lack*
die Mark (-) *mark (coin)*
die Marsch (-en) *fen (north German)*
der Mensch (-en,-en) *human being*
der Messer (-) *surveyor; gauge*
der Militär (-s) *military man*
der Moment (-e) *moment*
der Otter (-) *otter*
   (also: der Fischotter)
der Pack (-e or ¨e) *package*
der Pony (no pl.) *fringe (of hair)*
der Schild (-e) *shield*
der See (-n) *lake*
die Steuer (-n) *tax*
der Stift (-e) *pen,*
   stripling (coll.)
der Tau (no pl.) *dew*
der Tor (-en,-en) *fool* (lit.)
der Verdienst (no pl.) *earnings*
die Wehr (no pl.) *defence*

die Mangel (-n) *mangle*
das Mark (no pl.) *marrow (bone)*
der Marsch (¨e) *march*
das Mensch (-er) *slut* (coll., pej.)
das Messer (-) *knife*
das Militär (no pl.) *the military*
das Moment (-e) *(determining) factor*
die Otter (-n) *adder*
   (also: die Kreuzotter)
das Pack (no pl.) *mob, rabble*
das Pony (-s) *pony*
das Schild (-er) *sign, plate*
die See (no pl.) *sea*
das Steuer (-) *steering-wheel, helm*
das Stift (-e) *foundation,*
   home (e.g. for aged)
das Tau (-e) *rope, hawser*
das Tor (-e) *gate, goal*
das Verdienst (-e) *merit, achievement*
das Wehr (-e) *weir*

1.1.13 Problems of gender agreement

Difficulty with gender agreement arises most often when grammatical gender and natural gender do not correspond, as in the nouns dealt with in 1.1.4.

(a) In formal written German, pronouns normally agree with the grammatical gender of the noun, irrespective of natural gender

Wir suchen eine männliche Fachkraft. **Sie** muß im Besitz eines Führerscheins sein	*We are looking for a skilled male worker. He must have a clean driving licence*
ein**es** der Mitglieder dieses Vereins	*one of the members of this club*
Ich kann mich jedoch an keine Person erinnern, **die** in dem so benannten Vorort wohnte (*Grass*)	*however, as I cannot remember any person who lived in the suburb of that name*
Dem Mädchen hat es sehr gefreut, daß **es seine** Großmutter wiedersehen konnte	*The girl was pleased that she could see her grandmother again*

This rule is rarely adhered to consistently. The relative pronoun does in practice almost always agree for grammatical gender. However, personal pronouns usually have the form appropriate to the natural gender of the person referred to (i.e. *sie* or *er*), especially in spoken German:

Das Mädchen da drüben? **Sie** hat doch <u>rotes</u> Haar!	*That girl over there? But she's got <u>red</u> hair!*

Even in writing natural gender tends to predominate if the pronoun is some distance from the noun it refers to, especially if it is in a different clause or sentence:

Das junge Mädchen ist gestern abend angekommen. **Sie** ist sehr liebenswürdig	*The young girl arrived last night. She's very kind*
Sie stürzten sich auf das Mädchen, **das** in der Ecke stand, und drohten **ihr** mit Erschießen (*Quick*)	*They rushed upon the girl standing in the corner and threatened to shoot her*

Fräulein is treated in this way, i.e. as a neuter noun, when it is used on its own, e.g. *das Fräulein, das ihn bediente*. But when followed by a name, feminine pronouns are used: *Fräulein Müller, die mich gestern bediente*.

(b) Neuter singular pronouns are used to refer to male and female persons

Sie stehen eine Weile schweigend, jedes die Hand auf der Schulter des anderen (*Fallada*)	*They stood silent for a while, each with their hand on the other's shoulder*

(c) Adjectives and determiners always agree with grammatical gender

ein junges Mädchen, **das** unartige Bübchen, eine männliche Person

This also applies with *Fräulein* followed by a name, for instance at the start of a letter: *Liebes Fräulein Müller*.

(d) Personal names in *-chen* and *-lein* are treated as neuter

Unser kleines Fritzchen spielt mit seiner Modelleisenbahn
Das Mariechen konnte gestern nicht schlafen. **Es** dachte an **seine** kranke Mutter

In speech the pronouns appropriate to natural gender are often used.

NB: In colloquial south German speech neuter pronouns can be used to refer to a younger girl, whatever her name. This is considered to be a mark of affection.

1.2 Noun plurals

1.2.1 Regular ways of forming noun plurals in German

There are no absolute rules which determine how a particular noun forms its plural, and recommended practice for foreign learners is to learn the plural of each noun separately with the noun. In practice, however, the gender and the form of a noun give helpful clues as to its plural form, and it is worth knowing these.

Table 1.2 shows the different ways in which nouns form plurals in German and how the gender and the form of the noun are related to this.

1.2.2 The plural of masculine nouns

(a) Most masculine nouns ending in *-el*, *-en* or *-er* form their plural without an ending or *Umlaut*

der Onkel – die Onkel	der Haken – die Haken
der Bäcker – die Bäcker	der Computer – die Computer

Exceptions are the words dealt with in section 1.2.2b and:

der Bauer (-n,-n)	*farmer, peasant*	der Pantoffel (-n)	*slipper*
der Bayer (-n,-n)	*Bavarian*	der Stachel (-n)	*thorn; sting*
der Charakter (-e)	*character*	der Vetter (-n)	*cousin*
der Muskel (-n)	*muscle*		

TABLE 1.2 *The plural of German nouns*

	Masculine	Feminine	Neuter
No ending, same form as the singular	most ending in -*el*, -*en*, -*er*	None	nearly all those ending in -*el*, -*en*, -*er* and all those ending in -*chen* and -*lein* All *Ge–e* words
No ending but Umlaut on stressed vowel	about 20 in -*el, en*	Only 2, *Mutter* and *Tochter*	Only 2, *Kloster* and *Wasser*
(er)/(¨er)	about 12	None	about 25% of those not in other groups
(-e)	about 50% of those not in other groups	only those ending in -*nis* and -*sal*	about 75% of those not in other groups
(-¨e)	about 50% of those not in other groups	about 30 mono-syllables	only 1, *Floß*
(-en)/(n)	all those in -*e* and some others, mainly denoting male living beings	over 90%	about 12

(b) About 20 masculine nouns in -*el*, -*en* or -*er* form their plural solely by umlauting the stressed vowel
These are:

der Acker	*field*	der Hafen	*harbour*	der Ofen	*stove*
der Apfel	*apple*	der Hammer	*hammer*	der Sattel	*saddle*
der Boden	*floor*	der Kasten	*box*	der Schaden	*damage*
der Bogen	*arch*	der Laden	*shop; shutter*	der Schnabel	*beak*
der Bruder	*brother*	der Magen	*stomach*	der Schwager	*brother-in-law*
der Faden	*thread*	der Mangel	*lack*	der Vater	*father*
der Garten	*garden*	der Mantel	*coat*	der Vogel	*bird*
der Graben	*ditch*	der Nagel	*nail*		

NB: (i) *der Bogen* and *der Kasten* may have the plural (-) in north German.
The compound *der Ell(en)bogen* always has (-).
(ii) *der Laden* sometimes has the plural (-) in north German usage in the meaning 'shutter'.
(iii) In spoken south German *der Kragen* and *der Wagen* may have the plural (¨). This usage appears to be spreading to the north, but it is considered incorrect in written German.

(c) About a dozen masculines have a plural in (¨er)/(-er)

Umlaut is used if possible. These are:

der Bösewicht	*villain*	der Mann	*man*	der Strauch	*shrub*
(arch.)					
der Geist	*spirit*	der Mund	*mouth*	der Wald	*forest*
der Gott	*god*	der Rand	*edge*	der Wiking	*Viking*
der Irrtum	*error*	der Reichtum	*wealth*	der Wurm	*worm*
der Leib	*body*	der Ski	*ski*		

NB: (i) For the plural of compounds in *-mann*, see 1.2.7.
    (ii) *Der Bösewicht* has an equally used alternative plural in (-e).

(d) Most other masculine nouns form their plural in (-e) or (¨e)

der Arm – die Arme	der Hund – die Hunde
der Punkt – die Punkte	der Versuch – die Versuche
der Bart – die Bärte	der Bock – die Böcke
der Fuß – die Füße	der Stuhl – die Stühle

Umlaut is found with about half the nouns where it would be possible.
The following list gives a selection of common masculines which have a plural
in (-e) without *Umlaut* even though the vowel could have *Umlaut*:

der Aal	*eel*	der Huf	*hoof*	der Schuh	*shoe*
der Arm	*arm*	der Hund	*dog*	der Star	*starling*
der Beruf	*profession*	der Laut	*sound*	der Stoff	*material*
der Besuch	*visit*	der Monat	*month*	der Tag	*day*
der Dolch	*dagger*	der Mond	*moon*	der Takt	*beat* (music)
der Dom	*cathedral*	der Ort	*place*	der Thron	*throne*
der Druck	*pressure*	der Pfad	*path*	der Verlag	*publishing house*
der Erfolg	*success*	der Punkt	*point*	der Verlust	*loss*
der Grad	*degree*	der Ruf	*call*	der Versuch	*attempt*
der Gurt	*belt*	der Schluck	*gulp*		

Nouns ending in stressed *-al, -an, -ar, -on* and *-or* also have the plural ending (-e),
without *Umlaut*:

der Bibliothekar – die Bibliothekare   der Major – die Majore

Exceptions:

der Altar – die Altäre	*altar*	der Kanal – die Kanäle	*canal*
der Kardinal – die Kardinäle	*cardinal*	der Tenor – die Tenöre	*tenor*

NB: (i) *der General, der Korporal* and *der Kran* have either (¨e) or (-e).
    (ii) *der Erlaß* has (-e) in German usage, but (¨e) in Austria and Switzerland.
    (iii) *der Rest* usually has the pl. (-e), but (-er) is frequent in colloquial speech and com-
        mercialese, and (-en) occurs in Swiss usage.
    (iv) *der Pastor* (usual pl. (-en)) may have (¨e) in north German usage.
    (v) The plural of *der Saal* is *die Säle*, cf. 23.4.2.

(e) A number of masculine nouns have the plural (-en)/(-n)

These fall into three groups, depending on the declension of the singular:

(i) The so-called 'weak' masculines which have *-(e)n* in the accusative, genitive and dative singular as well as in the plural, e.g.:

> der Affe – die Affen der Bär – die Bären
> der Mensch – die Menschen der Student – die Studenten

Full details about these are given in 1.3.2.

(ii) Some irregular masculines, cf. 1.3.3. The following occur in the plural:

> der Buchstabe *letter* der Funke *spark* der Name *name*
> (of alphabet)
> der Friede *peace* der Gedanke *thought* der Same *seed*

(iii) A few other masculines with a regular singular:

der Dorn	*thorn*	der Nerv	*nerve*	der Stachel	*prickle*
der Fasan	*pheasant*	der Pantoffel	*slipper*	der Strahl	*ray*
der Fleck	*spot*	der Pfau	*peacock*	der Typ	*bloke, guy*
der Lorbeer	*laurel*	der Schmerz	*pain*	der Untertan	*subject*
der Mast	*mast*	der See	*lake*	der Vetter	*cousin*
der Muskel	*muscle*	der Staat	*state*	der Zeh	*toe*

Words in unstressed *-on* and *-or* also belong to this group, but shift the stress in the plural, e.g.:

> der D<u>ä</u>mon – die Dä<u>mo</u>nen der Pro<u>fes</u>sor – die Profes<u>so</u>ren

NB: (i) *der Bau* 'building' and *der Sporn* 'spur' have the irregular plurals *die Bauten* and *die Sporen*.
(ii) *die Seen* is pronounced *See-en* [ze:ən].
(iii) *der Fleck* has an alternative singular form *der Flecken*.
(iv) *der Zeh* has the alternative (mainly north German) singular *die Zehe*.
(v) *der Typ* may have the 'weak' singular declension in colloquial speech, see 1.3.2c.

1.2.3 The plural of feminine nouns

(a) Over 90 per cent of all feminine nouns have the plural (-en)/(-n)

> die Arbeit – die Arbeiten die Bühne – die Bühnen
> die Last – die Lasten die Wiese – die Wiesen

NB: (i) Feminine nouns in *-in* double the consonant in the plural, e.g.:
die Studentin – die Studentinnen.
(ii) *die Werkstatt* has an irregular plural with *Umlaut* and the suffix *-en*: *die Werkstätten.*

(b) About a quarter of feminine monosyllables have a plural in (¨e)
The following are the most common:

die Angst	*fear*	die Haut	*skin*	die Nacht	*night*
die Axt	*axe*	die Kraft	*strength*	die Naht	*seam*
die Bank	*bench*	die Kuh	*cow*	die Not	*need, distress*
die Braut	*fiancée*	die Kunst	*art*	die Nuß	*nut*
die Brust	*breast*	die Laus	*louse*	die Sau	*sow*
die Faust	*fist*	die Luft	*air; breeze*	die Schnur	*string*
die Frucht	*fruit*	die Lust	*desire*	die Stadt	*town, city*
die Gans	*goose*	die Macht	*power*	die Wand	*wall*
die Gruft	*vault, tomb*	die Magd	*maid*	die Wurst	*sausage*
die Hand	*hand*	die Maus	*mouse*	die Zunft	*guild*

NB: (i) Compounds of *-brunst*, *-flucht* and *-kunft* also have the plural (¨e), e.g.: *die Feuersbrunst, die Ausflucht, die Auskunft.*
(ii) *die Sau* and *die Schnur* may have the pl. (-en) in technical usage.

(c) Feminine nouns in *-nis* and *-sal* have the plural (-e)

Few have plurals in use. Those in *-nis* double the consonant in the plural:

> die Kenntnis – die Kenntnisse   die Mühsal – die Mühsale

(d) Two feminine nouns have the plural (¨)

> die Mutter – die Mütter (cf. 1.2.8)   die Tochter – die Töchter

(e) No feminine nouns have plurals in (-) or (¨er)

1.2.4 The plural of neuter nouns

(a) Neuter nouns ending in *-el*, *-en*, *-er*, diminutives in *-chen* and *-lein* and words in *Ge. . .e* have the plural (-)

> das Segel – die Segel   das Kissen – die Kissen
> das Messer – die Messer   das Mädchen – die Mädchen
> das Büchlein – die Büchlein   das Gebäude – die Gebäude

NB: The only exceptions are the two nouns dealt with in 1.2.4b.

(b) Two neuter nouns have plurals in (¨)

> das Kloster – die Klöster   das Wasser – die Wässer

das Wasser has the alternative plural *die Wasser* (though neither plural form is common in practice). Its compounds, e.g. *das Abwasser* 'effluent' always have the plural with *Umlaut*, e.g. *die Abwässer*.

(c) About a quarter of neuter nouns have the plural (¨er)/(-er)

Umlaut is used if possible. The majority are monosyllabic, e.g.:

> das Blatt – die Blätter   das Dorf – die Dörfer
> das Kind – die Kinder   das Tal – die Täler

A few polysyllabic neuters have this ending. The following are common:

> das Gehalt   *salary*   das Gemüt   *mood*   das Gespenst *ghost*
> das Gemach *chamber*   das Geschlecht *sex*   das Regiment *regiment*
> (elev.)
>   das Gesicht   *face*   das Spital   *hospice*

In addition, all nouns in *-tum* take this plural, e.g.:

> das Altertum – die Altertümer

NB: (i) *das Roß* 'steed' (usual pl. *die Rosse*) commonly has the plural (¨er) in Austria and Bavaria, where it is the everyday word for 'horse'.
>   (ii) A number of words are used colloquially with an (-er/¨er) plural in a derogatory or facetious sense, e.g.: *die Dinger, die Scheusäler*.

(d) Roughly three-quarters of neuter nouns have the plural (-e)

> das Bein – die Beine   das Gefäß – die Gefäße
> das Jahr – die Jahre   das Schaf – die Schafe
> das Ventil – die Ventile   das Verbot – die Verbote

This group includes most neuters of more than one syllable, especially foreign words, with the exceptions listed under other groups.

NB: (i) Neuters ending in *-nis* double the consonant in the plural, e.g.: *das Zeugnis – die Zeugnisse.*

(ii) *das Knie* has the plural *die Knie*, pronounced *Knie-e* [kni:ə], cf. 23.4.1.

(e) *One* neuter noun has the plural (¨e)

das Floß *raft* – die Flöße

(f) A few neuter nouns have the plural (-en)/(-n)
The following are the most frequent:

das Auge *eye*	das Hemd *shirt*	das Juwel *jewel*	
das Bett *bed*	das Herz *heart*	das Ohr *ear*	
das Ende *end*	das Insekt *insect*	das Statut *statute*	
das Fakt *fact*	das Interesse *interest*	das Verb *verb*	

NB: (i) Scientific terms in *-on* also belong to this group, with a shift of stress in the pl., e.g.: *das Elektron – die Elektronen.*

(ii) *das Herz* has an irregular singular, i.e.: *das Herz, des Herzens, dem Herzen* (see 1.3.4).

(iii) *das Kleinod* 'jewel' has the unusual plural *die Kleinodien.*

1.2.5 The plural ending (-s)

das Auto – die Autos	die Oma – die Omas
das Baby – die Babys	der PKW – die PKWs
der Balkon – die Balkons	der Streik – die Streiks

(a) This ending is used with most recent loan-words from English or French

das Atelier – die Ateliers	der Scheck – die Schecks
der Chef – die Chefs	das Sit-in – die Sit-ins
das Detail – die Details	der Streik – die Streiks
das Hotel – die Hotels	das Team – die Teams
das Labor – die Labors	der Tunnel – die Tunnels
der Park – die Parks	der Waggon – die Waggons

This ending is increasingly common, cf. Bornstein and Butt (1987), but it has been frowned upon by purists as 'un-German'. Attempts have been made to foster the use of 'native' German plurals with foreign words, recommending forms like *die Parke, die Streike*, which many dictionaries still list. However, few such forms are widely used in practice. Only with English words in *-er* (e.g.: *der Computer – die Computer*) is a plural formation other than *-s* common with loan-words.

NB: English words in *-y* mostly have a plural in *-ys*, e.g.: *die Babys, die Rowdys*. However, some keep the usual English spelling, e.g.: *die Lobby – die Lobbies, die Party – die Partys* or *die Parties.*

(b) This ending is used with most words ending in a vowel other than unstressed *-e*

das Auto – die Autos	das Genie – die Genies
der Ossi – die Ossis	der Uhu – die Uhus

(c) (-s) is used with abbreviations and shortened words

    der PKW – die PKWs   die Lok – die Loks

NB: This ending may be omitted in speech, esp. in south German e.g.: *die PKW*.

(d) (-s) is used with some north German seafaring words
The most frequent are:

    das Deck – die Decks   der Kai – die Kais
    das Dock – die Docks   das Wrack – die Wracks

(e) (-s) is used in colloquial speech with some words referring to persons

    die Bengels, die Doktors, die Fräuleins, die Jungs (or die Jungens), die Kerls, die Kumpels, die Mädels, die Onkels

This usage is characteristic of substandard north German speech, where some of these (e.g. *Jung(en)s*, *Kumpels*, *Mädels*) are very frequent. The standard plural form (*die Jungen, die Kumpel, die Mädel*, etc.) is always preferred in writing.

(f) (-s) is used with family and other names

    die Müllers, die Buddenbrooks, zwischen den beiden Deutschlands (*Zeit*)

1.2.6 Unusual plural forms

A number of words, particularly those borrowed from the classical languages, have retained unusual plural forms. Some of the more unusual ones are in practice restricted to formal written language.

(a) Most words in *-us* or *-um* replace this by *-en* in the plural

    der Genius – die Genien   das Album – die Alben (coll. Albums)
    der Organismus – die Organismen   das Museum – die Museen
    der Rhythmus – die Rhythmen   das Visum – die Visen (or: Visa)
    der Zyklus – die Zyklen   das Zentrum – die Zentren

NB: There are a few exceptions, mainly of unusual words, but cf. *der Kaktus – die Kakteen*, pron. [kak`te:ən] (coll.: *die Kaktusse*); *das Tempus* tense – *die Tempora*; *der Terminus* term – *die Termini*.

Some words in *-us* have adopted a native plural, e.g.:

    der Bonus – die Bonusse   der Krokus – die Krokusse
                                  (rare die Krokus)
    der Bus – die Busse   der Zirkus – die Zirkusse
    der Globus – die Globusse
      (rare die Globen)

(b) Most words in *-ma* form the plural in *-men*

    das Aroma – die Aromen (or Aromas)   die Firma – die Firmen
    das Dogma – die Dogmen   das Paradigma – die Paradigmen
                                      (acad. Paradigmata)
    das Drama – die Dramen   das Thema – die Themen
                                      (acad. Themata)

A few have a plural in -*mata*:

das Dilemma – die Dilemmata
    (now commoner: Dilemmas)
das Komma – die Kommata
    (in speech: usually Kommas)

das Schema – die Schemata
    (also Schemen or Schemas)

(c) A few other words replace -*a* by -*en*

die Pizza – die Pizzen
    (or die Pizzas)
die Razzia – die Razzien
    (or die Razzias)
die Regatta – die Regatten

die Skala – die Skalen

die Veranda – die Veranden

die Villa – die Villen

(d) Other frequent words:

das Adverb – die Adverbien
der Atlas – die Atlanten
    (also coll. Atlasse)
das Epos – die Epen
das Examen – die Examina
    (now commoner: Examen)
der Espresso – die Espressi
    (or Espressos)
das Fossil – die Fossilien

das Fresko – die Fresken

der Index – die Indices
    (or Indexe)
das Konto – die Konten
    (also Konti, or coll. Kontos)
das Lexikon – die Lexika
    (also Lexiken, or coll. Lexikons)
das Material – die Materialien
das Mineral – die Mineralien
    (or Minerale)

der Mythos – die Mythen
die Praxis – die Praxen

das Prinzip – die Prinzipien
das Privileg – die Privilegien

das Reptil – die Reptilien

das Risiko – die Risiken
    (coll. Risikos)
der Saldo – die Salden
    (also Saldos or Saldi)
das Solo – die Soli (or Solos)

das Stadion – die Stadien

das Tempo – die Tempi
    (or Tempos)
das Textil – die Textilien
das Utensil – die Utensilien

1.2.7 The plural of words in -*mann*

Compounds of -*mann* usually replace this by -*leute* in the plural when they refer to the occupation as such or to the group as a whole, e.g.:

der Fachmann – die Fachleute   der Kaufmann – die Kaufleute

In cases where we think more in terms of individuals than a group, or where we are not dealing with persons, the plural is -*männer*, e.g.:

die Ehrenmänner, Froschmänner, Schneemänner, Staatsmänner

In one or two cases both are used without any clear difference of meaning:

die Feuerwehrleute/-männer   die Kameraleute/-männer

However, the following should be noted:

die Ehemänner *husbands* BUT die Eheleute *married couples*
die Seemänner *seamen* (as individuals), BUT die Seeleute *seafaring folk* (general)

1.2.8 A few words have two plurals with different meanings

The following are the most common:

der Abdruck – die Abdrucke *offprints*
die Abdrücke *impressions*
das Band – die Bande *bonds* (elev.)
die Bänder *ribbons*
die Bank – die Bänke *benches*
die Banken *banks*
das Ding – die Dinge *things*
die Dinger *things* (coll.); *girls* (coll.)
der Effekt – die Effekte *effects* (i.e. results)
die Effekten *effects* (i.e. valuables)
das Land – die Länder *countries, provinces*
die Lande *regions* (esp. in historical contexts)
der Mann – die Männer *men*
die Mannen *vassals* (hist.)
die Mutter – die Mütter *mothers*
die Muttern *nuts* (for bolts)
der Rat – die Räte *councils, officials*
die Ratschläge *pieces of advice*
der Stock – die Stöcke *sticks*
die Stockwerke *storeys* (sg. also: das Stockwerk)
der Strauß – die Strauße *ostriches*
die Sträuße *bunches* (of flowers)
das Wort – die Wörter *words* (in isolation)
die Worte *words* (connected words, i.e. sayings)

NB: The distinction between *die Wörter* and *die Worte* is rarely maintained in practice and many consider it unnecessary pedantry, cf. Sanders (1992: 52–5): 'Sogar sprachlich hoch gebildete Leute, denen kaum je ein Fehler unterläuft, scheitern am Unterschied zwischen *Worten* und *Wörtern*'. In practice *Wörter* is used in both senses.

1.2.9 In many instances the most usual equivalent of a German singular is an English plural

The following are frequent:

das Archiv *archives*
die Asche *ashes*
das Aussehen *looks*
das Benehmen *manners*
der Besitz *possessions*
der Bodensatz *dregs*
die Brille *spectacles*
der Dank *thanks*
das Fernglas *binoculars*
der Hafer *oats*
das Hauptquartier *headquarters*
die Hose *trousers*
der Inhalt *contents*
die Kaserne *barracks*
der Lohn *wages*
das Mittel *means*
das Mittelalter *the Middle Ages*

die Politik *politics*
das Protokoll *minutes* (of meeting)
der Pyjama *pyjamas*
der Reichtum *riches*
im Rückstand *in arrears*
der Schadenersatz *damages* (legal)
die Schere *scissors*
das Schilf *reeds*
die Treppe *(flight of) stairs, steps*
die Umgebung *surroundings*
die Waage *scales*
die Wahl *elections*
das Werk *works* (factory)
die Zange *tongs*
der Ziegenpeter *mumps*
der Zirkel *(pair of) compasses*

Naturally, many of these German words may also be used in the plural in appropriate contexts:

Die meisten Löhne sind erhöht worden   *Most wages have been raised*
Er wohnt zwei Treppen hoch   *He lives on the second floor*

1.2.10 Some German nouns are used only, or predominantly, in the plural

Usually, this corresponds to English usage, e.g.: *die Ferien* 'holidays', *die Leute* 'people'.

(a) In a few instances German and English usage differs

die Flitterwochen *honeymoon*   die Pocken *smallpox*
die Kosten *cost(s)*   die Ränke *intrigue* (elev.)
die Kurzwaren *haberdashery*   die Trümmer *rubble*
die Lebensmittel *food*   die Wirren *turmoil*
die Möbel *furniture*   die Zinsen *interest* (*on a loan*)

NB: (i) *die Eltern* has no commonly used singular to correspond to English 'parent' (*ein Elternteil* is officialese).
(ii) *die Geschwister* brothers and sisters.

(b) Usage with the names of festivals is different in German

Ostern, Pfingsten and *Weihnachten* are generally treated as plurals:

Frohe Weihnachten!   Sie hat uns letzte Ostern besucht

However, *Weihnachten* and *Ostern* may occur as neuter singulars, particularly with an indefinite article:

Wir haben ein stilles Weihnachten verbracht   *We had a quiet Christmas*
Hast du ein schönes Ostern gehabt?   *Did you have a nice Easter?*

All are followed by a verb in the singular:

Weihnachten steht vor der Tür   *Christmas is almost here*
Pfingsten fällt dieses Jahr spät   *Whitsun is late this year*

1.2.11 Some English nouns have plurals, but their German equivalents do not

In such cases a plural has to be expressed through other forms:

der Atem *breath*   die Atemzüge *breaths*
das Essen *meal*   die Mahlzeiten *meals* (occ. die Essen)
die Furcht *fear*   die Befürchtungen *fears*
der Käse *cheese*   die Käsesorten *cheeses* (occ. die Käse)
der Kohl *cabbage*   die Kohlköpfe *cabbages*
die Liebe *love*   die Liebschaften *loves* (occ. die Lieben)
der Luxus *luxury*   die Luxusartikel *luxuries*
das Obst *fruit*   die Obstsorten *fruits*
der Rasen *lawn*   die Rasenflächen *lawns*
der Raub *robbery*   die Raubüberfälle *robberies*
der Sport *sport*   die Sportarten *sports*
der Tod *death*   die Todesfälle *deaths* (occ. die Tode)
das Unglück *accident*   die Unglücksfälle *accidents*

The following words are used in the singular only in German, and this corresponds to both singular and plural in English:

> der Kummer *care(s)* die Sehnsucht *longing(s)* der Verdacht *suspicion(s)*

1.2.12 Some German nouns have normal singular and plural forms which have no real correspondence in English

die Auskunft *(piece of) information*	die Auskünfte *information*
das Brot *bread, loaf*	die Brote *loaves*
der Blitz *(flash of) lightning*	die Blitze *flashes of lightning*
der Fortschritt *advance*	die Fortschritte *progress*
die Hausaufgabe *(piece of) homework*	die Hausaufgaben *homework*
die Kenntnis *(piece of) knowledge*	die Kenntnisse *knowledge*
die Nachricht *(piece of) news*	die Nachrichten *news*
der Rat *(piece of) advice*	die Ratschläge *(pieces of) advice*
der Schaden *damage*	die Schäden *(instances of) damage*

1.2.13 German normally uses a singular noun for items of clothing and parts of the body if each individual only possesses one of each

Sie alle hoben **die rechte Hand**	*They all raised their right hands*
Ihnen klopfte **das Herz**	*Their hearts were beating*

The plural *die Herzen* in the last example could suggest that each person had more than one heart. Nevertheless, exceptions are not unknown, especially if the possessive is used rather than the definite article (see 4.6.1), e.g.:

> Die Passagiere drehten **ihre Köpfe** *The passengers turned their heads*
> (Frisch)

1.2.14 Masculine and neuter nouns of weight, measurement or value, preceded by a numeral or by an adjective indicating number, have the singular form

> zwei **Pfund** Kirschen, zwei **Sack** Kartoffeln, drei **Dutzend** Eier, zwei **Paar** Schuhe, zehn **Faß** Wein, zwanzig englische **Pfund**, um ein paar **Dollar** mehr

zwei, drei, mehrere **Glas** Bier	*two, three, several glasses of beer*
ein paar **Schluck** (Kaffee)	*a few mouthfuls (of coffee)*
Wir hatten zehn **Grad** Kälte	*We had ten degrees of frost*
zehn **Schritt**	*ten paces*
3 **Schuß** – zwei Mark 50	*3 shots for two marks fifty*

The singular is typically used when shopping or ordering in restaurants:

> Diese hier sind gerade das richtige. Geben Sie mir bitte drei **Stück**!
> Bringen Sie mir bitte drei **Erdbeereis** und zwei Glas **Bier**!

Masculine and neuter nouns of measurement do have plural endings if they are seen as individual objects:

> Auf dem Hof lagen zehn **Fässer** *There were ten barrels in the yard*

Feminine nouns of measurement do take the plural form:

> zehn **Flaschen** Wein zwei **Ladungen** Holz vier **Tassen** Kaffee

*Except that die Mark never has a plural ending: zwanzig **Mark**.*

NB: For the agreement of the verb with measurement phrases, see 12.1.4f.

1.3 Noun declension

Table 1.3 shows regular German noun declensions, with the definite article. Wegener (1995) is a comprehensive study of noun declension in modern German.

TABLE 1.3 *Declension of regular nouns*

	Masculine		Feminine		Neuter	
	Singular	Plural	Singular	Plural	Singular	Plural
Nom.	der Stuhl	die Stühle	die Frau	die Frauen	das Jahr	die Jahre
Acc.	den Stuhl	die Stühle	die Frau	die Frauen	das Jahr	die Jahre
Gen.	des Stuhles	der Stühle	der Frau	die Frauen	des Jahres	der Jahre
Dat.	dem Stuhl	den Stühlen	der Frau	die Frauen	dem Jahr	den Jahren

1.3.1 Case endings with regular nouns in German

The majority of German nouns only have two endings which signal case. These are added to the basic singular or plural forms, producing the regular declension patterns summarised in Table 1.3. These endings are:

(a) Masculine and neuter nouns add -*s* or -*es* in the genitive singular
For the use of -*s* and -*es* see 1.3.6. Examples:

> des Bahnhofs, des Busches, des Fensters, des Mann(e)s, des Tal(e)s

NB: For the occasional omission of this ending, see 1.3.7.

(b) -*n* is added in the dative plural if possible
i.e. if the nominative plural does not end in -*n* or -*s*, e.g.:

> den Kindern, den Fenstern, den Hunden, den Stühlen, den Töchtern

No ending is added if the basic plural form ends in -*n* or -*s*, e.g.:

> den Gärten, den Frauen, den Autos, den Müllers

Nouns of measurement often lack the -*n* after numerals, e.g.: *eine Entfernung von zweihundert Kilometer*(**n**). In some colloquial German, especially in the south, this dative plural -*n* is sometimes omitted, and one may even see notices such as *Eis mit Früchte*. This is regarded as substandard.

NB: No -*n* is used in the set phrase *aus aller Herren Länder* 'from the four corners of the earth'.

1.3.2 'Weak' masculine nouns

A small group of so-called 'weak' masculine nouns, most (but by no means all) of which denote living beings, have the ending -*n* or -*en* throughout the plural *and* in all singular cases except the nominative.

TABLE 1.4 *Declension of weak masculine nouns*

	Singular	Plural	Singular	Plural	Singular	Plural
Nom.	der Affe	die Affen	der Held	die Helden	der Herr	die Herren
Acc.	den Affen	die Affen	den Helden	die Helden	den Herrn	die Herren
Gen.	des Affen	der Affen	des Helden	der Helden	des Herrn	der Herren
Dat.	dem Affen	den Affen	dem Helden	den Helden	dem Herrn	den Herren

(a) The following masculine nouns belong to this group

(i) Those which end in *-e* in the nominative singular, e.g.:

> der Affe, der Bote, der Chinese, der Franzose, der Schwabe

A few masculine nouns in *-e* follow other declension patterns. *Der Käse* and *der Charme* are regular. The eight nouns which decline like *der Name* (see 1.3.3) are called 'mixed' masculine nouns.

(ii) A large number of foreign nouns, in particular, those ending in stressed *-and*, *-ant*, *-aph*, *-arch*, *-at*, *-ent*, *-et*, *-ist*, *-krat*, *-log*, *-nom*, *-on*, e.g.:

> der Diamant, der Monarch, der Automat, der Student, der Komet, der Komponist, der Demokrat, der Psycholog(e), der Astronom, der Dämon

Also a number with other endings, e.g.:

> der Barbar, der Chirurg, der Kamerad, der Katholik, der Prinz, der Tyrann

(iii) A few native nouns which do not end in *-e* in the nominative singular. The following are the most frequent:

der Bär	*bear*	der Graf	*count*	der Narr	*fool*
der Bauer	*peasant*	der Held	*hero*	der Oberst	*colonel*
der Bayer	*Bavarian*	der Herr	*gentleman*	der Ochs	*ox*
der Bub	*lad*	der Hirt	*shepherd*	der Papagei	*parrot*
(south German)					
der Fink	*finch*	der Mensch	*human being*	der Spatz	*sparrow*
					(south German)
der Fürst	*prince*	der Nachbar	*neighbour*	der Tor	*fool* (lit.)

Note that *der Herr* has the ending *-n* in the singular but *-en* in the plural:

> den Herrn, des Herrn, dem Herrn; die Herren, der Herren, den Herren.

(b) Weak masculine nouns have no ending in the singular if they are used without a determiner

This avoids the possibility of ambiguity between singular and plural:

> Die Situation war für Arzt und Patient kritisch
>
> *The situation was critical for doctor and patient alike*
>
> Ich schrieb an Herrn Schulze, Präsident des Gesangvereins
>
> *I wrote to Herr Schulze, the president of the choral society*

However, the noun *der Herr* always keeps the ending *-n* in the singular even if used without a determiner, e.g. (when addressing an envelope): *Herrn Alfred Bletzer*.

(c) The singular endings of weak masculine nouns are often dropped in colloquial German
They have the 'regular' forms: *den Bauer, des Bauers, dem Bauer.* In general, this usage is regarded as colloquial and substandard and avoided in formal writing. However, it is seen as acceptable with a small number of nouns in written German, i.e.:

> der Magnet, der Oberst, der Papagei, der Partisan, der Spatz
> (also, less commonly, with der Bauer and der Nachbar)

On the other hand, *der Typ* 'bloke', 'chap' (see 1.2.2e) sometimes has the 'weak' declension in colloquial speech: *den Typen, des Typen, dem Typen.*

NB: Adjectives which are used as nouns, e.g. *der Beamte, der Vorsitzende,* keep their adjectival declensions, see 6.4. They should **NOT** be confused with 'weak' masculine nouns.

1.3.3 Irregular (sometimes called 'mixed') masculine nouns

TABLE 1.5 *Declension of irregular masculine nouns*

	Singular	Plural
Nom.	der Name	die Namen
Acc.	den Namen	die Namen
Gen.	des Namens	der Namen
Dat.	dem Namen	den Namen

Eight masculine nouns with the plural (*-n*) have the ending *-n* in the accusative and dative singular, but *-ns* in the genitive singular (cf. Table 1.5). They are:

der Buchstabe *letter*	der Funke *spark*	der Name *name*
(of alphabet)	der Gedanke *thought*	der Same *seed*
der Friede *peace*	der Glaube *belief*	der Wille *will*

der Friede, der Funke, der Glaube and *der Same* have alternative forms with *-n* in the nominative singular as well, i.e. *der Frieden, der Funken, der Glauben, der Samen.* Of these *der Frieden, der Funken* and *der Samen* are now commoner in practice than the forms without *-n*, especially in speech, but *der Glaube* is far more usual than *der Glauben.*

1.3.4 The irregular neuter *das Herz*

The neuter noun *das Herz* has the ending *-ens* in the genitive singular and *-en* in the dative singular, i.e.: *das Herz, des Herzens, dem Herzen.* However, regular singular forms (*des Herzes, dem Herz*) often occur in colloquial speech and medical writing.

1.3.5 Dative singular in -e

In older German, regular masculine and neuter nouns, particularly those of one syllable, regularly added *-e* in the dative singular, e.g.:

> dem Flusse, dem Manne, dem Tage, dem Tale

This 'dative -*e*' is now uncommon. It is occasionally used in formal writing, and even there it can sound old-fashioned or facetious. However, it is still current in a few fixed phrases, e.g.:

das Kind mit dem Bade ausschütten	*throw out the baby with the bathwater*
im Falle, daß	*if*
bis zu einem gewissen Grade	*to a certain extent*
im Grunde genommen	*basically*
jdm. zum Halse heraushängen	*be sick of sth.*
jdm. im Halse steckenbleiben	*stick in one's throat*
aus vollem Halse	*at the top of one's voice*
nach Hause	*home*
zu Hause	*at home*
im Jahre 1995	*in 1995*
auf dem Lande	*in the country*
im Laufe des Tages	*in the course of the day*
bei Lichte betrachtet/besehen	*seen in the (cold) light of day*
in gewissem Maße	*to a certain extent*
jdn. zu Rate ziehen	*consult sb.*
in diesem Sinne	*in this sense*
am Tage	*by day*
unter Tage arbeiten	*work below ground*
jdn./etwas im Zaume halten	*keep sb./sth. in check*
(nicht) zum Zuge kommen	*(not) to get a look-in*

Many of these phrases are used equally commonly without the -*e*, e.g. *im Lauf des Tages, am Tag.*

1.3.6 Genitive singular in -es or -s?

Masculine and neuter nouns have the ending -*s* or -*es* in the genitive singular. The choice between these most often depends on style, rhythm and ease of pronunciation, cf. the account in Kohrt (1992). The ending -*es* is often felt to be more formal and tends to be preferred in monosyllabic words, words with a stressed final syllable and those ending in more than one consonant. However, in some cases usage is more fixed:

(a) -es must be used with nouns ending in -s, -ß, -x or -z

des Krebses, des Maßes, des Reflexes, des Kreuzes, etc.

It is also commonly used with nouns in -*sch*, -*st* or -*zt*:

des Tisches, des Dienstes, des Arztes, etc.

NB: (i)   Neuter nouns in -*nis* have genitive singular -*nisses*, e.g. *des Ereignisses.*
 (ii) Foreign nouns in -*s* and -*x* usually lack the ending (see 1.3.7f).

(b) -s is normal
(i) with polysyllabic words ending in an unstressed syllable:

des Abends, des Königs, des Lehrers, des Schicksals

(ii) with words ending in a vowel (or vowel + *h*):

des Schnees, des Schuhs, des Uhus

(iii) with names and foreign words:

>   Schillers Dramen, des Hotels, des Klubs

1.3.7 Non-inflection in the genitive singular

In some instances (apart from names, see 1.3.8) the ending -(e)s is omitted in the genitive singular of masculine and neuter nouns, i.e.:

(a) Frequently with the names of the months and seasons

>   am Morgen des zehnten Januar(s)
>   die kräftigste Zyklone des beginnenden Herbst (*NZZ*)

The months in -*er* more often keep the -*s*: *in den ersten Tagen des Oktobers*. The -*s* is also often omitted with the names of the weekdays, e.g. *am Morgen des folgenden Mittwoch*. This is considered incorrect.

(b) Often with names of artistic styles and epochs

>   des Barock(s), des Empire(s), des Rokoko(s), etc.

(c) Optionally, with abbreviations and other parts of speech used as nouns

>   ein Stück des eignen Ich(s)   meines Gegenüber(s)
>   eines gewissen Jemand(s)   des Lkw(s)

(d) With certain foreign nouns (and several native German words)

This is particularly prevalent with words seen as technical terms or specific names, e.g.:

>   des Dativ, des Dynamo, des Establishment, des Gulasch, des Holunder, des Interesse, des Islam, des Parlament, des Parterre, des Radar

This usage has increased notably in recent years. However, DUDEN (1995: 252) and (1985: 691) maintain that it is quite incorrect.

(e) Frequently after prepositions when the noun has no accompanying adjective or determiner

>   laut Bericht   wegen Schnee geschlossen   trotz Geldmangel

Compare (illustrating the absence and presence of -*s* dependent on the absence or presence of article or adjective):

>   eine Agrar-Reform, die aber wegen   *an agricultural reform which is only*
>   **Geldmangel** und **gebremsten Eifers**   *proceeding slowly because of a lack*
>   nur langsam vorankommt (*Zeit*)   *of money and moderated zeal*

However, usage is variable on this point, and the genitive ending is still by no means unusual in written German:

>   eine Strafuntersuchung gegen mehrere   *a criminal investigation against*
>   Stadtpolizisten wegen schwerer   *several city police officers for*
>   Körperverletzung und **Amtsmißbrauchs**   *grievous bodily harm and abuse of office*
>   (*NZZ*)

(f) Foreign nouns in -*s* and -*x* usually have no ending in the genitive

> des Atlas   des Chaos   des Index   des Globus   des Sozialismus   des Zirkus

However, a few foreign words like *der Bus* and *der Kongreß* have been fully assimilated and are treated as German words, e.g. *des Busses, des Kongresses*.

1.3.8 Declension of proper names and titles

(a) Proper names without titles and geographical names add -*s* in the genitive singular

> Helmut Kohls Politik   Elisabeths Bücher
> die Werke Johann Sebastian Bachs   der Tod Friedrichs des Großen
> die Straßen Deutschlands   Deutschlands Straßen

Personal names ending in -*s*, -*ß*, -*x*, -*z* do not add -*s* in the genitive. In writing an apostrophe may be used:

> Fritz' Schwester   Agnes' Hut   Perikles' Tod   Marx' Einfluß

In speech, a construction with *von* is usual and may also be used in writing as an alternative to the apostrophe:

> der Einfluß von Marx   der Tod von Perikles   der Hut von Agnes

With geographical names in -*s*, -*ß*, -*x*, -*z*, only *von* is possible:

> die Straßen von Paris   die Geschichte von Florenz

NB: In colloquial north German, the titles of members of the family are treated as names, e.g.: *Tantes Haus, Mutters Kleid, Vaters Anzug*.

(b) Proper names rarely have the ending -*s* in the genitive singular if they are used with an article

> die Rolle des Egmont   die Werke eines Johann Sebastian Bach
> die Gedichte des alten Goethe   die Briefe dieses Schmidt

(c) Geographical names used with an article

(i) With German names, the ending -(*e*)*s* is optional:

> eines vereinigten Europa(s)   die Einwohner des geteilten Berlin(s)

However, if the article is part of the name (e.g. with rivers), the ending is normally used, e.g. *an den Ufern des Rheins* (occ. *des Rhein*).

(ii) Foreign geographical names usually lack the ending -*s*:

> an den Ufern des Nil   die Berge des High Peak

(d) Proper names with titles in the genitive singular

(i) If there is no article, only the name is declined:

> König Heinrichs Politik   die Politik König Heinrichs
> Onkel Roberts Haus   Bundeskanzler Kohls Amtsantritt

(ii) If there is an article, only the title is declined:

> die Siege des Kaisers Karl   die Hauptstadt des Landes Niedersachsen

(iii) If the title is a weak masculine noun, the ending *-n* is optional:

Wir bedauern Genosse(n) Schmidts Versetzung nach Bautzen

However, *Herr* is *always* declined (see 1.3.2b), and a following title may then lack the ending *-s*: *der Vortrag des Herrn Generaldirektor(s) Kramer.*

(iv) *Doktor* and *Fräulein*, used as titles, are never declined:

die Erfolge unseres Doktor Meyer   die Mutter dieses Fräulein Sauer

(e) Titles and names of books, plays, newspapers, hotels, companies
(i) These are normally fully declined:

ein Lied aus Schillers **„Räubern"**, aus Brechts **„kaukasischem Kreidekreis"**
Sie las es in **der „Süddeutschen Zeitung"**, **im „Spiegel"**
Ich wohne **im „Goldenen Apostel"**

(ii) A full title between quotation marks remains in the nominative:

in Brechts Drama „Der kaukasische Kreidekreis", im Hotel „Goldener Apostel", in der Wochenzeitschrift „Der Spiegel"

(iii) A short title in the genitive with an article may drop the *-(e)s*:

in der letzten Strophe **des Erlkönig(s)**

(iv) Names of companies should always be declined in full:

der Überschuß bei **der Süddeutschen Zucker-AG**
die ehemalige Verwaltung **der Deutschen Reichsbahn**

2
Case

German has four cases, **nominative, accusative, genitive** and **dative**. They are indicated by inflections of the pronoun, noun or noun phrase. The function of the cases is to indicate the role of these in the clause or sentence and thus their relationship to other parts of the sentence. In English, which has lost its cases (apart from the possessive in -*s* and some pronouns like *I – me*, etc.), this is achieved in other ways, chiefly through word order (e.g. *My brother* [subject] *gave his friend* [indirect object] *the book* [direct object]) or by using prepositions (e.g. *My brother gave the book **to** his friend*).

Case marking plays an essential part in showing the structure of a German sentence; this becomes clear in particular in relation to verb valency (see Chapter 18) and word order (see Chapter 21).

All the German cases have a variety of uses, as summarised in Table 2.1. Details are given in the remainder of this chapter, with reference where necessary to fuller details elsewhere in the book. In particular, the use of cases with prepositions is treated comprehensively in Chapter 20. A full account of case in

TABLE 2.1 *The cases in German*

		Summary of chief uses	
Nom.	{	Nouns in isolation: The subject of the verb: Nouns after *sein* and *werden*:	*Dein Onkel, wann siehst du ihn wieder?* *Heute kommt der Zug etwas später an* *Horst ist sein bester Freund*
Acc.	{	The direct object of the verb: Conventional greetings: To denote length of time: To express distance covered: After some prepositions:	*Sie wirft einen Stein in den Bach* *Guten Tag!* *Ich bleibe den ganzen Tag in Bremen* *Sie geht den ganzen Weg zu Fuß* *Sie tat es für ihren Bruder*
Gen.	{	Linking nouns or noun phrases: After a few prepositions:	*die Hälfte seines Einkommens* *Er konnte wegen des Regens nicht kommen*
Dat.	{	The indirect object of the verb: The sole object of some verbs: The beneficiary of the action: To show possession: With many adjectives: After some prepositions:	*Ich gebe es meinem Bruder* *Sie hat ihrem Freund dabei geholfen* *Sie schrieb mir die Adresse auf* *Wir zogen dem Verletzten die Hose aus* *Das Gespräch war ihm sehr nützlich* *Sie ist mit ihrem Freund gekommen*

German is given by Helbig (1973). Blake (1994) is a recent general survey of case in language, with information on many languages besides German.

2.1 The nominative

2.1.1 The nominative is the neutral case

It is used with nouns or pronouns in isolation:

> **Ein schöner Tag** heute, nicht?
> Und **dein Onkel**, wann siehst du ihn wieder?
> Und **du**, was meinst du dazu?

Similarly for persons and things addressed and in exclamations:

> Was beunruhigt dich, **mein Lieber?** **Herr Müller**, Telefon für Sie!
> Ach **du liebe Zeit!** **Der unverschämte Kerl!**

It can be used in so-called 'absolute' phrases, where the noun phrase is placed outside the main framework of the clause;

> als er an den Mann dachte, zu dem er *when he thought of the man he now*
> jetzt gehen mußte, **dieser Mann aus** *had to go to, that man from Röder's*
> **Röders Abteilung** (*Seghers*) *company*
> Er saß am Feuer, **der Hund zu seinen** *He sat by the fire, the dog at his*
> **Füßen** *feet*

The type of absolute phrase seen in the last example is found mainly in formal, especially literary German; other registers generally prefer a construction with *mit*, e.g. *mit dem Hund zu seinen Füßen*.

2.1.2 The most important syntactic role of the nominative case is to mark the subject of the finite verb

For further details see 18.2. As the subject is shown through case marking it does not have to precede the verb, as it does in English, cf. 21.2.3:

> **Der Zug** war nicht pünktlich Heute war **der Zug** nicht pünktlich
> Heute war ausnahmsweise **der Mittagszug** nicht pünktlich

2.1.3 The nominative is used after the verbs *sein, werden, bleiben, heißen, scheinen* and with the passive of *nennen*

> Karl ist, wird, bleibt **mein Freund** Ich will **ein Schuft** heißen
> Er scheint **ein großartiger Turner** Er wurde **der Weise** genannt

Further details about these verbs is given in 18.8.

2.2 The accusative

2.2.1 The main function of the accusative is to mark the direct object of transitive verbs

> Ich habe **einen Stein** geworfen Die Putzfrau hat **den Fußboden** gebohnert
> Sie hat mir **den Inhalt** erklärt Er hat **die Tauben** im Park vergiftet

Full details are given in 18.3. A very few verbs, e.g. *kosten* and *lehren*, take two objects in the accusative, see 18.3.3.

2.2.2 Some intransitive verbs can be used with a 'cognate' accusative noun

This is a noun whose meaning is related to that of the verb and which thus repeats or explains more fully the idea expressed by the verb, e.g.:

Er starb **einen schweren Tod**   Sie schlief **den Schlaf** der Gerechten

2.2.3 Most conventional greetings and wishes are in the accusative:

Guten Morgen, Tag, Abend	Gute Nacht	Guten Rutsch (ins neue Jahr)
Schönen Sonntag	Besten Dank	Herzlichen Glückwunsch
Viel Vergnügen	Gute Besserung	Angenehme Reise

In effect this is an elliptical construction, with a verb such as *wünschen* being understood.

2.2.4 A few adjectives are used with the accusative

e.g. *etwas gewohnt sein*. Details are given in 6.5.2.

2.2.5 The accusative is used in a number of adverbial constructions

(a) To denote length of time or a point in time

Es hat **den ganzen Tag** geschneit   Ich war **einen Monat** in Stuttgart
Ich sah ihn **letzten Freitag**   Er kommt noch **diesen Monat** zurück

For further detail on usage, see 11.4.1. The accusative is also used in dates in letters: *Essen, den 4. August.*

(b) To express a measurement or value

This is particularly frequent with adjectives of measurement:

Das ist **keinen Pfennig** wert   Der Tisch ist **ein(en) Meter** breit
Das Kind ist **vier Jahre** alt   Der Sack wiegt **einen Zentner**

(c) To express distance with verbs and adverbs denoting motion

Ich bin **den ganzen Weg** zu Fuß gegangen   Sie kam **den Berg** herauf
Wir sind **die Straße** heruntergekommen

This adverbial accusative is particularly common with the direction adverbs formed with *hin-* and *her-* (see 7.2.4):

Wir stiegen **die Treppe** hinauf   Sie kam **die Treppe** herunter

2.2.6 The accusative is sometimes used in so-called 'absolute' phrases

This usage without a verb is mainly restricted to formal literary German:

Wilhelmine, **den Kopf geneigt,**   *Wilhelmine, her head bowed, lets*
erlaubt ihm, ihr Haar zu lösen   *him untie her hair*
(*Wolf*)
Den Bauch voller Fracht, fliegt der   *Its belly full of freight, the jet*
Jet nach Fernost (*Spiegel*)   *flies to the Far East*

This construction is uncommon even in literary German, and a construction with *mit* is often used, as is usual in other registers, e.g.: *mit dem Bauch voller Fracht.*

2.2.7 The accusative is used with a number of prepositions

(a) Some prepositions are always followed by the accusative

e.g. *bis, durch, für, gegen, ohne, um*. See section 20.1 for details.

(b) Ten prepositions are followed by the accusative if they express movement in a particular direction

i.e. *an, auf, entlang, hinter, in, neben, über, unter, vor, zwischen*
See section 20.3 for details.

2.3 The genitive

In modern German the genitive case is mainly restricted to formal (especially written) registers. This section outlines its current uses with this general proviso. In some contexts a phrase with *von* may be preferred to a genitive, especially in colloquial speech (see 2.4). For the genitive of personal pronouns see 3.1.2; for the genitive of the relative pronoun, see 5.4.1c.

2.3.1 The main role of the genitive is to link nouns or noun phrases

For this, English typically uses the preposition *of*. We often think of the genitive as the 'possessive' case, but its range is wider, since it occurs:

(a)	**to express possession:**	das Haus meines Bruders
(b)	**as a partitive:**	die Hälfte des Kuchens
(c)	**for the subject of a verbal noun:**	die Abfahrt des Zuges
(d)	**for the object of a verbal noun:**	der Umbau des Hauses
(e)	**to qualify a noun:**	ein Strahl der Hoffnung
(f)	**to define a noun:**	die Pflicht der Dankbarkeit

For the genitive in measurement phrases, see 2.7.

2.3.2 The genitive usually follows the noun on which it depends

    die Gefahr **eines Erdbebens**   das Rauschen **der Bäume**

The only exception is that proper names in the genitive may come first:

Karls Freund	**Manfreds** Stereoanlage	**Frau Benders** Haus
Heinrich Bölls Werke	**Deutschlands** Grenzen	

However, in written German, personal names without a title, and geographical names may also follow:

    ein Freund **Karls**   die Werke **Heinrich Bölls**   die Grenzen **Deutschlands**

Otherwise, the genitive comes first only in old-fashioned literary style or set phrases:

seiner Vorfahren großes altes Haus	*the large old house of his ancestors*
(*Th. Mann*)	
Undank ist **der Welt** Lohn	*Never expect thanks for anything*

In other contexts it sounds facetious:

da wir **des Postministers**	*as we reject the post minister's*
Kabelpläne verwerfen (*Zeit*)	*plans for cable television*

2.3.3 A few verbs take an object in the genitive

e.g. *bedürfen, gedenken, sich ermächtigen.* For details on this construction, see 18.5.

2.3.4 The genitive may be used as the predicate complement of the verb *sein*

This is restricted in practice to a few set expressions, e.g.:

Wir sind gleichen Alters	*We are of the same age*
Ich bin der Ansicht, daß ...	*I am of the view that ...*
Ich bin der Auffassung, daß ...	*I am of the opinion that ...*
Hier ist meines Bleibens nicht (lit.)	*I cannot remain here*
Er ist guter Dinge	*He is in good spirits*
Wir waren guter Laune	*We were in a good mood*
Sie ist der Meinung, daß ...	*She is of the opinion that ...*
Er wurde anderen Sinnes (lit.)	*He changed his mind*
Dann sind wir des Todes	*Then we are doomed*
Sie sind der festen Überzeugung, daß ...	*They are firmly convinced that ...*
Das Wort ist griechischen Ursprungs	*The word is of Greek origin*

2.3.5 The genitive is found in a few adverbial phrases

In the main these are set expressions or fixed idioms.

(a) The genitive can denote habitual or indefinite time
(see also 11.4.2 for further details):

eines Tages, eines schönen Sommers, eines Sonntagmorgens
montags, abends, wochentags, werktags

(b) Other adverbial genitives

unverrichteter Dinge	*without achieving anything*
letzten Endes	*after all*
meines Erachtens (abbrev. m.E.)	*in my view*
allen Ernstes	*in all seriousness*
stehenden Fußes (lit.)	*immediately*
gesenkten/erhobenen Hauptes	*with one's head bowed/raised*
leichten/schweren Herzens	*with a light/heavy heart*
Hungers sterben (lit.)	*to die of starvation*
Sie fährt erster Klasse	*She is travelling first class*
aller Orten (lit.)	*everywhere*
seines Weges gehen (lit.)	*to go on one's way*
meines Wissens (abbrev. m.W.)	*to my knowledge*

2.3.6 A few adjectives govern the genitive

A frequent English equivalent is a construction with *of*, e.g.:

Er ist **einer solchen Tat** nicht fähig   *He is not capable of such a deed*

Full details are given in 6.5.3.

2.3.7 A number of prepositions govern the genitive

e.g. *statt, trotz, während, wegen.* Full details of these are given in 20.4.

2.4 Genitive or *von*?

A prepositional phrase with *von* is often used rather than a genitive. The genitive is widely used in writing, especially in technical and non-literary registers, but, except with names, it tends to be avoided entirely in colloquial speech, where a paraphrase with *von* is usually preferred, e.g.: *das Dach vom Haus, der Ring von seiner Frau* (for usual written German: *das Dach des Hauses, der Ring seiner Frau*).

However, even in written German there are contexts where the genitive is not possible and where the paraphrase with *von* **must** be used. There are other written contexts where this paraphrase **may** be used, i.e. where it is an acceptable alternative to the genitive. Pfeffer and Lorentz (1979) and Lauterbach (1993) give details on current usage.

This section outlines those contexts where the paraphrase with *von* must or may be used in written German rather than a genitive. Elsewhere, the paraphrase with *von* is normally used in colloquial speech only.

2.4.1 The genitive is *not* usual in written German

(a) If a noun stands by itself or is used with an indeclinable word

der Bau von Kraftwerken	*the building of power stations*
die Wirkung von wenig Wein	*the effect of a little wine*
der Preis von fünf Fahrrädern	*the price of five bicycles*
ein Strahl von Hoffnung	*a ray of hope*

(b) With a descriptive phrase

eine Frau von bezaubernder Höflichkeit	*a woman of enchanting politeness*
ein Ereignis von weltgeschichtlicher Bedeutung	*an event of global historical significance*

(c) With personal pronouns

The genitive forms of personal pronouns are rarely used, cf. 3.1.2:

fünf von euch	*five of you*
ein Freund von ihr	*a friend of hers*

(d) In partitive constructions with *viel, wenig* and indefinites

viel/wenig von dem, was sie sagte	*much/little of what she said*
etwas von ihrem Charme	*something of her charm*
welches von diesen Büchern?	*which of those books?*
nichts von diesem Zauber	*nothing of this magic*

2.4.2 A paraphrase with *von* *may* be used as an alternative to the genitive in written German

(a) To avoid consecutive genitives in -(e)s

der Turm von dem Palast des Königs }
der Turm des Palastes des Königs } *the tower of the king's palace*

Consecutive genitives are considered stylistically poor, but they are not unknown, cf. *die Existenz eines Verdachts eines Verstoßes gegen den Atomsperrvertrag (SZ).*

(b) If a noun is qualified by an adjective alone

der Bau von modernen Kraftwerken ⎫
der Bau moderner Kraftwerke ⎭   *the building of modern power stations*

There is a clear preference for *von* in these contexts if the first noun is qualified by an indefinite article, e.g. *ein fader Geruch von aufgewärmten Speisen* (*Zweig*).

(c) With nouns qualified by indefinites, etc.

die Ansicht von vielen Politikern ⎫
die Ansicht vieler Politiker ⎭   *the view of many politicians*

(d) Most partitive constructions
(except those listed at 2.4.1d above):

eines von den wenigen alten Häusern ⎫
eines der wenigen alten Häuser ⎭   *one of the few old houses*

viele von meinen Freunden ⎫
viele meiner Freunde ⎭   *many of my friends*

zwei von seinen Kindern ⎫
zwei seiner Kinder ⎭   *two of his children*

(e) With geographical names which have no article:

die Zerstörung von Dresden ⎫
die Zerstörung Dresdens ⎭   *the destruction of Dresden*

die Hauptstadt von Deutschland ⎫
die Hauptstadt Deutschlands ⎭   *the capital of Germany*

2.5 The dative

The dative has the widest range of all the German cases, with many idiomatic uses, cf. the detailed account in Wegener (1985). It can mark the indirect or sole object of a verb (2.5.1–2). It is also used as a so-called 'free dative' with other verbs where it is not a grammatical requirement (2.5.3), and it can mark possession (2.5.4). In all these contexts it typically marks a person (rather than a thing) in some way concerned or affected, if not necessarily very directly, by the action or the event expressed through the verb. Finally, it is widely used with adjectives.

2.5.1 The dative marks the indirect object of transitive verbs

For full details see 18.4.2. It is used typically with verbs of giving and receiving, etc., and it often corresponds to an English indirect object indicated by the word order or a phrase introduced by *to* or *for*:

Ich zeigte dem Polizisten meinen Führerschein   *I showed the policeman my driving-licence/I showed my driving-licence to the policeman*

Ich habe meinem Freund ein Buch gebracht   *I brought my friend a book/I brought a book to/for my friend*

2.5.2 Many verbs govern a sole object in the dative

e.g.: *danken, dienen, folgen, gratulieren, helfen, schmeicheln*. These are treated fully in 18.4.1.

2.5.3 The dative often marks a person affected in some way by the action or event expressed by the verb

Here, unlike the constructions dealt with in 2.5.1 and 2.5.2, the dative is not nec-essarily a grammatical requirement of the verb and is often referred to as a 'free' dative. For an alternative view, see Eisenberg (1994: 298–307). These uses are often idiomatic and lack a clear English equivalent. Various sub-groups of 'free' dative have been identified, but there are similarities between them all (and between them and the possessive dative, cf. 2.5.4). These 'free' datives are most common with verbs expressing an activity, especially moving and making things, or a change of state.

(a) The dative can indicate a person on whose behalf the action is done
(i) This is sometimes referred to as the 'dative of advantage' or 'benefactive' dative and often corresponds to an English phrase with *for*:

Sie schrieb **mir** seine Adresse auf	*She wrote his address down for me*
Ich öffnete **ihr** die Tür	*I opened the door for her*
Er füllte **meinem** Vater das Glas	*He filled the glass for my father/my father's glass*

(ii) It is sometimes used with things, especially things being altered:

Sie setzt **dem Auto** einen neuen Motor ein	*She's putting a new engine in the car*

(iii) In this 'benefactive' sense a dative reflexive pronoun is common in idio-matic colloquial speech if a physical action is involved:

Ich will **mir** das Buch anschauen	*I want to go and look at that book*

(iv) A phrase with *für* is a frequent alternative to the dative in this sense, espe-cially in spoken German:

Er will **mir/für mich** Blumen kaufen	*He's going to buy some flowers for me*
Ich habe **ihm die Tür/die Tür für ihn** geöffnet	*I opened the door for him*

The construction with *für* may be preferable if the dative is ambiguous. For instance, *Er hat seinem Vater einen Brief geschrieben* could mean 'to his father' or 'for his father', whereas *Er hat für seinen Vater einen Brief geschrieben* is quite clear.

(b) The dative may indicate a person who is disadvantaged by the action
This 'dative of disadvantage' characteristically indicates a person who is affected by something undesirable happening to the person or thing which is the subject or direct object of the verb:

Mir ist Großmutters Vase kaputtgegangen	*Grandmother's vase broke on me*

(c) The dative may mark a person from whose standpoint an action or event is judged or in respect of whom the statement holds good
This usage typically involves an adjective qualified by *zu* or *genug*:

Mir verging die Zeit zu schnell	*As far as I was concerned, the time passed too quickly*
Fährt sie **dir** schnell genug?	*Is she going fast enough for you?*

A similar dative of the person concerned is frequently used with the verb *sein* and a noun. In such cases, English uses a phrase with *to* or *for*:

Das Wiedersehen mit dir war **mir** ein Vergnügen	*It was a pleasure for me to see you again*
Dem Schüler war diese Zensur ein Trost	*This mark was a consolation to/for the schoolboy*

(d) The 'ethic dative' shows the speaker's emotional involvement

It is most common with the first person in commands or exclamations:

Dann soll **mir** mal so einer vorbeikommen!	*Just let me catch one like that coming past!*
Seid **mir** doch nett!	*Be nice, for my sake!*

2.5.4 The dative of possession

(a) The dative often indicates possession

This is especially frequent with parts of the body or articles of clothing, but it is also found with close relatives and prized possessions (like vehicles or houses). The definite article is used rather than a possessive, cf. 4.6; the dative usually precedes the item possessed:

Einem Mann ist das Bein gebrochen worden (*FR*)	*One man's leg was broken*
Mir muß der Mund offengeblieben sein (*Borst*)	*My mouth must have hung open*
Dem Alten ist gerade die Frau gestorben	*The old man's wife has just died*
Das Kind ist **mir** vors Auto gelaufen	*The child ran in front of my car*

If the possessor is the subject of the sentence, a reflexive pronoun in the dative is used. This may be optional if no ambiguity is involved:

Er wischte **sich** den Schweiß von der Stirn	*He wiped the sweat from his brow*
Willst du (**dir**) den grünen Pullover anziehen?	*Are you going to put your green pullover on?*

It is difficult to give hard and fast rules as to when the possessive dative *must* be used and when it *cannot* be used. In general the following tendencies may be observed:

(i) It is *not* used if no-one else could possibly do it to or for one:

Er machte die Augen auf	*He opened his eyes*
Sie hob den Arm	*She raised her arm*
Er nickte mit dem Kopf	*He nodded*

(ii) It *must* be used if the body part or article of clothing is used with a preposition (other than *mit*):

Ich habe **mir** in den Finger geschnitten	*I've cut my finger*
Die Mütze fiel **mir** vom Kopf	*The cap fell off my head*
Regen tropfte **mir** auf den Hut	*Rain was falling on my hat*

(iii) It *must* be used where reference is not to the subject of the sentence:

Die Mutter wäscht **ihm** die Hände	*His mother is washing his hands*
Wir zogen **dem Verletzten** die Hose aus	*We took the injured man's trousers off*

(b) If the dative is used rather than a possessive construction, the person is seen as affected by the action as well

Possession can be indicated by a genitive phrase or a possessive like *sein* or *mein*. However, these often have a different meaning to the possessive dative. Compare:

Regen tropfte **ihm auf den Hut**	(he was wearing it and getting wet)
Regen tropfte **auf seinen Hut**	(he wasn't necessarily wearing it)
Sie strich **dem Jungen übers Gesicht**	(normal for: 'she ran her hand over the boy's face')
Sie strich **über das Gesicht des Jungen**	(only possible if the boy is dead or unconscious)
Er zog **ihr die** Jacke an	*He helped her on with her jacket*
Er zog **sich ihre** Jacke an	*He put her jacket on*

(c) With some verbs the accusative is used rather than the dative

The effect of this is that the whole person is seen as more directly affected, rather than simply the body part, e.g.:

Der Hund biß **ihm/ihn** ins Bein   Ich klopfte **ihm/ihn** auf die Schulter

In practice, accusative and dative are equally common and usual with the following verbs:

beißen   küssen   stechen   stoßen   zwicken

With some verbs, the accusative occurs, but the dative is more common:

hauen   klopfen   schießen   schlagen   schneiden   treten

(d) In colloquial speech a dative may be used rather than a genitive to indicate possession

This construction is common but it is universally regarded as substandard and only found in written German to indicate colloquial speech:

Das ist **meiner Mutter** ihr Hut	*That's my mother's hat*
Meinem Onkel sein Garten ist ganz groß	*My uncle's garden is quite big*
Dem Huck Finn sein Vater (*Andersch*)	*Huck Finn's father*

The use of the dative with *sein* to show possession is a substandard regionalism, mainly heard in the west and south-west:

Ist der Hut **dir**?   *Is that your hat?*

Standard German would use: *Gehört der Hut dir?*

2.5.5 The dative with adjectives

(a) The dative is the most common case governed by adjectives

e.g.: *Er ist seinem Bruder sehr ähnlich.* Full details are given in section 6.5.1.

(b) Adjectives with *zu* or *genug* may govern a dative or a phrase with *für*

The latter may come before or after the adjective, whereas the dative always precedes:

Diese Uhr ist **mir** zu teuer/**für mich** zu teuer/zu teuer **für mich**	*That watch is too expensive for me*
Dieser Mantel ist **mir** nicht warm genug/**für mich** nicht warm genug/nicht warm genug **für mich**	*That coat is not warm enough for me*

(c) A personal dative is used in impersonal constructions with *sein* and *werden* with certain adjectives expressing sensations

The person in the dative is experiencing the sensation; it corresponds to a simple subject in English:

Es ist **mir** kalt/**Mir** ist kalt   *I am cold*

For the omission of *es*, see 18.2.4e. This construction occurs with the following adjectives:

bange	heiß	schlecht	übel	unwohl
gut	kalt	schwindlig	warm	

2.6 Apposition

A noun phrase is said to be 'in apposition' to another noun phrase if it immediately follows and expands it by giving some additional information about it, e.g. *Wilhelm, **der letzte deutsche Kaiser**; Berlin, **die Hauptstadt der Bundesrepublik Deutschland***. There is usually no explicit linking word, but comparative phrases introduced by *als* and *wie* are also commonly considered to be 'in apposition' to the noun they qualify, e.g. *ein Tag **wie jeder andere**; er gilt **als großer Staatsmann**; Jürgen ist größer **als du**.*

NB: Apposition in measurement phrases is dealt with in section 2.7.

2.6.1 A noun phrase in apposition usually has the same case as the noun which it follows

Es spricht Herbert Werner, **der** Vorsitzende des Vereins	*The speaker is Herbert Werner, the chairman of the society*
6,8 Prozent der Frauen empfinden die Arbeitslosigkeit als **einen** Makel (*LV*)	*6.8 per cent of the women feel that being unemployed is a stigma*
der „Mythos der Schweiz" als **eines** Landes mit vier Landessprachen (*NZZ*)	*The 'myth of Switzerland' as a country with four national languages*
in Michelstadt, **einem** kleinen Städtchen im Odenwald	*in Michelstadt, a little town in the Odenwald*
für Heinrich Böll als gläubi**gen** Katholiken	*for Heinrich Böll as a devout Catholic*
nach einem Tag wie **diesem**	*after a day like this*

2.6.2 There are some exceptions to this rule

The rule given in 2.6.1 is followed in over 90 per cent of cases in both spoken and written German. However, a few exceptions are found:

(a) In two contexts the exception is common

(i) After a genitive, an unqualified noun in apposition is usually in the nominative:

nach dem Tode meines Onkels, **Bürgermeister** der Stadt Krefeld	*after the death of my uncle, the mayor of the city of Krefeld*

(ii) In dates a weekday introduced by *am* may be followed by the date in the dative or the accusative:

am Montag, **dem** 3. Juli 1989   or   am Montag, **den** 3. Juli 1989

(b) Occasionally other exceptions to the general rule are encountered

These are in practice much less common alternatives, i.e.:

(i) nominative or dative after a genitive noun:

> nach dem Tode meines Onkels, **der/dem** früheren Bürgermeister dieser Stadt
> die Wirtsleute des „Birnbaumes", **einem** kleinen Dorfhaus (*BZ*)

(ii) genitive after a phrase with *von*:

> die Hauptstadt von Kalifornien, des reichsten Bundesstaates

These and similar exceptions are neither common nor becoming more frequent, cf. the survey by Bergenholtz (1985).

2.6.3 German often uses appositional constructions with geographical names

e.g.: *die Insel Rügen; die Universität Hamburg; die Stadt Bremen*. In most such constructions English has *of*: *the University of Hamburg*, etc.

NB: German uses *bei* with battles, e.g. *die Schlacht bei Lützen* 'the battle of Lützen'.

2.7 Measurement phrases: genitive, *von* or apposition?

There is much variation and uncertainty in respect of case usage in measurement phrases, cf. Hentschel (1993). This survey presents the most widely accepted current usage.

NB: For the use of singular nouns in measurement phrases, e.g. *zwei Pfund Kirschen*, see 1.2.14.

2.7.1 Nouns and noun phrases after a noun of measurement are most commonly in the same case as the noun of measurement

The two phrases are in apposition, cf. 2.6:

eine Flasche **Wein**	*a bottle of wine*
eine Flasche **deutscher Wein**	*a bottle of German wine*
er kauft zwei Flaschen **deutschen Wein**	*he is buying two bottles of German wine*
mit einer Tasse **heißem Tee**	*with a cup of hot tea*
von vier Kilo **grünen Erbsen**	*of four kilograms of green peas*

NB: In spoken German it is not uncommon to hear datives for accusatives and vice versa, e.g. *Er kauft zwei Flaschen deutschem Wein, mit einer Tasse heißen Tee*. This is considered incorrect in writing.

2.7.2 The genitive is sometimes used after a noun of measurement

eine Flasche **sommerabendlichen Dufts** (*Süßkind*)	*a bottle of the perfume of a summer evening*
zehn Jahre **treuer Mitarbeit**	*ten years faithful service*

In practice this alternative only occurs in the sequence: noun of measurement + adjective + noun. In the masculine and neuter singular it can sound stilted and is restricted to formal writing, but it is not uncommon in the plural.

2.7.3 Usage with words of rather vague quantity

e.g.: *die Anzahl, die Gruppe, der Haufen, die Schar, die Reihe, die Sorte*. Usage with these varies according to whether the following noun has an adjective with it, i.e.:

(a) If the following noun has an adjective with it (or is an adjective used as a noun)

In these contexts the following noun may be in the genitive or (especially in speech) in a phrase with *von*:

zwei Gruppen junger Arbeiter	*or* zwei Gruppen von jungen Arbeitern
große Mengen neuer Platten	*or* große Mengen von neuen Platten
eine Reihe ernsthafter Probleme	*or* eine Reihe von ernsthaften Problemen
die wachsende Anzahl Ausreisewilliger	*or* von Ausreisewilligen

(b) If these words are followed by a single noun

Normal usage is a phrase with *von*, although simple apposition is also possible (cf. 2.7.1):

eine Art (von) Museum	eine Menge (von) Schallplatten
eine Anzahl (von) Touristen	

2.7.4 Usage with nouns of number

i.e.: *das Dutzend, das Hundert, das Tausend, die Million, die Milliarde*. Used in the plural without a preceding numeral, these are followed by a phrase with *von*, or, if the following noun has an adjective with it, by a phrase in the genitive or in apposition:

Dutzende von Anfragen   Tausende von Briten   Millionen von Menschen
Tausende von jungen Arbeitern *or* Tausende junger Arbeiter
or Tausende junge Arbeiter

If they are used in the singular or the plural with a numeral the following noun is usually in apposition, less commonly in the genitive:

zwei Millionen hungernde(r) Menschen	*two million starving people*
ein Dutzend Eier	*a dozen eggs*
Allein im Bahnhof kam es im Februar	*In the station alone there were more*
diesen Jahres zu mehr als einem	*than a dozen pickpocket thefts*
Dutzend Taschendiebstählen (MM)	*in February this year*

2.7.5 Usage in contexts where the noun of measurement is in the dative

The following alternatives are current:

(a) With nouns of measurement in *-er*

e.g.: *Zentner* 'hundredweight' (i.e. 500 kilos), *Liter, Meter*, etc. These may take the dative plural ending *-n* rather than the following noun:

mit zwei Zentnern Äpfel *or* mit zwei Zentner Äpfeln

(b) If the following noun is plural, it may be in the nominative

i.e. it may lack the usual -*n* of the dative plural:

mit einem Haufen **Butterbrote(n)**	*with a pile of sandwiches*
mit einem Dutzend **Kühe(n)**	*with a dozen cows*
mit einem Dutzend **saure(n) Äpfel(n)**	*with a dozen sour apples*

However, the dative should be used if the case is not otherwise clear from the measurement noun or its articles, adjectives, etc.:

von drei Kilo **Äpfeln**	*of three kilos of apples*
mit zwei Tüten **Nüssen**	*with two bags of nuts*

(c) An adjective preceding the second noun may have the 'weak' adjective ending -*en*

von einem Pfund **gekochten** Schinken ⎫
von einem Pfund **gekochtem** Schinken ⎭   *of a pound of cooked ham*

2.7.6 Usage in contexts where the noun of measurement is in the genitive

In practice such constructions are avoided, even in written German, most commonly by using the paraphrase with *von*. For example, *der Preis von einem Pfund gekochtem/gekochten Schinken*, etc. is preferred to stilted constructions like *der Preis eines Pfundes gekochten Schinkens*.

3

Personal pronouns

Pronouns are a limited ('closed') set of short words which stand for or replace nouns or noun phrases. In particular they stand for nouns or noun phrases which have already been mentioned or which are so well known to the speaker and the listener that they do not need to be repeated in full. Pronouns are used in the same grammatical environments as nouns or noun phrases and thus, in German, they usually change their form in the same way to indicate case, number or gender.

The so-called 'personal' pronouns are used to refer to the speaker(s) (the 'first person'), the person(s) addressed (the 'second person') and other person(s) or thing(s) just mentioned (the 'third person'). The forms and uses of these are treated in detail in this chapter.

Other pronouns are dealt with in Chapter 5, i.e. the demonstrative pronouns (the 'this' and 'that' words, see 5.1), the possessive pronouns (e.g. *meines* and *seines*, see 5.2), the interrogative pronouns (used to ask questions, see 5.3), the relative pronouns (the 'who' and 'which' words, see 5.4) and the indefinite pronouns (e.g. the 'some' and 'any' words, see 5.5).

3.1 The forms of the personal pronouns

The personal pronouns have distinct forms to indicate number, case and, in the third person, gender. All these forms are given in Table 3.1.

TABLE 3.1 *Personal pronouns*

	First person		Second person (familiar)		Second person (polite)	Third person			
	Singular	Plural	Singular	Plural	Singular/plural	Masc.	Fem.	Neut.	Plural
Nom.	ich	wir	du	ihr	Sie	er	sie	es	sie
Acc.	mich	uns	dich	euch	Sie	ihn	sie	es	sie
Gen.	meiner	unser	deiner	euer	Ihrer	seiner	ihrer	seiner	ihrer
Dat.	mir	uns	dir	euch	Ihnen	ihm	ihr	ihm	ihnen

3.1.1 The declension of the personal pronouns: additional notes

(a) **In everyday speech, personal pronouns are reduced and weakly stressed**

'ch soll's 'm geben	*for*	ich soll es ihm geben
Jetzt kannste'n sehen	*for*	jetzt kannst du ihn sehen

These reductions are seldom used in written German, with the exception of 's for *es*, which is quite common in written dialogue and poetry.

(b) In rapid colloquial speech, the subject pronouns *ich, du* and *es* are often omitted entirely

> (Ich) Weiß es nicht   Kannst (du) morgen kommen?   (Es) Scheint zu klappen

(c) In south Germany *mir* is commonly heard for *wir*

> **Mir** gehen jetzt ins Kino   *for*   **Wir** gehen jetzt ins Kino

This usage, though very frequent, is universally regarded as substandard.

3.1.2 The genitive of the personal pronouns

(a) The genitives of the personal pronouns are only used in formal registers
They practically never occur in everyday speech, but only in writing:

> mittels einer Paßbildaufnahme **seiner** selbst (*Grass*)
> *by means of a passport photograph of himself*
> Ist die Politik erst einmal auf die Straße verlegt, dann wird sich die Straße **ihrer** annehmen (*OH*)
> *If politics is moved onto the streets, the streets will take it over*

Even in writing, they can sound rather stilted and awkward, and their use can be avoided in a number of ways:

(i) With verbs, an alternative construction or a different verb can be used (for further information, see 18.5):

> Erinnern Sie sich **an mich** (rarely: meiner)
> Er braucht **mich** nicht (rarely: Er bedarf meiner nicht)

(ii) After most prepositions the dative is used in speech and is now acceptable in writing:

> wegen **uns**, trotz **ihnen**, statt **ihm** (*or* an seiner Stelle)

To refer to things, the adverbs *statt dessen, trotzdem, währenddessen* and *deswegen* are normally used rather than the preposition with a pronoun.

(iii) After the prepositions which have alternative constructions with *von* (cf. 20.4.2b) the prepositional adverb *davon* (cf. 3.5) is used rather than a pronoun in the genitive, e.g.: *innerhalb* **davon**, *unweit* **davon**
    Alternatively, the prepositions may be used on their own, as adverbs: *außerhalb* 'outside (it)', *jenseits* 'on the other side (of it)'.

(iv) In other contexts, *von* is used (see 2.4.1c):

> sechs **von ihnen**, drei **von euch**, ein Freund **von mir**

(b) The genitive personal pronouns usually only refer to persons or animals

> Ich bedarf **seiner** nicht   *I don't need him*

The demonstratives *dessen* or *deren* are used to refer to things:

> Ich bedarf **dessen** nicht   *I don't need it*

Nevertheless, this usage is not absolutely fixed:

Er läßt seinen Autoschlüssel im Küchenschrank, so daß andere Familienmitglieder sich **seiner** bedienen können (*MM*)	*He leaves his car key in the kitchen cupboard so that other members of the family can use it*

(c) Special forms (in -(e)t-) of the genitive pronouns are used with the prepositions *wegen*, *um ... willen* and *-halben*
(See also 20.4.)

They are compounded with the preposition as illustrated:

meinetwegen, deinetwegen, um ihretwillen, um unsertwillen, seinethalben

(d) The genitives *mein*, *dein* and *sein* are archaic
They are occasionally used for stylistic effect:

Man gedachte **sein** (*for* seiner) nicht mehr

3.2 Reflexive and reciprocal pronouns

3.2.1 Forms of the reflexive pronoun

The reflexive pronoun *sich* is used for the third person (singular and plural), and for the 'polite' second person, in the accusative and dative cases. For the other persons and cases, the personal pronouns given in Table 3.1 are used reflexively.

To show the accusative and dative reflexives we give below the present tense and the imperative of the reflexive verbs *sich setzen* 'sit down' and *sich (etwas) einbilden* 'imagine (something)':

ich	setze	mich		ich	bilde mir	(etwas) ein
du	setzt	dich		du	bildest dir	(etwas) ein
er	setzt	sich		er	bildet sich	(etwas) ein
wir	setzen	uns		wir	bilden uns	(etwas) ein
ihr	setzt	euch		ihr	bildet euch	(etwas) ein
Sie	setzen	sich		Sie	bilden sich	(etwas) ein
sie	setzen	sich		sie	bilden sich	(etwas) ein
	setze	dich!			bilde dir (das) ein!	
	setzt	euch!			bildet euch (das) ein!	
	setzen	Sie sich!			bilden Sie sich (das) ein!	

3.2.2 The genitive pronoun is sometimes used reflexively in formal German

It mainly occurs in conjunction with certain adjectives (see 6.5.3). To avoid ambiguity, it always occurs with *selbst*:

Er ist **seiner selbst** sicher	*He is sure of himself*
Sie war **ihrer selbst** nicht mehr mächtig	*She had lost control of herself*

3.2.3 The reflexive pronoun is used after a preposition to refer back to the subject of the sentence

Er hatte kein Geld **bei sich**	*He had no money on him*
Sie schlossen die Tür **hinter sich**	*They closed the door behind them*

3.2.4 Usage in infinitive constructions without *zu*

It is not always clear in these constructions who the reflexive pronoun refers to, cf. Grewendorf (1984) and Hentschel and Weydt (1994: 221). Normal usage is as follows:

(a) A reflexive pronoun is normally taken as referring back to the object of the finite verb

Er hörte **seinen Freund sich** tadeln	*He heard his friend blaming himself*
Er ließ **den Gefangenen sich** ausziehen	*He made the prisoner get undressed*

(b) A non-reflexive pronoun refers back to the subject of the finite verb

Er hörte seinen Freund **ihn** tadeln	*He heard his friend blaming him*
Er ließ den Gefangenen **ihn** ausziehen	*He made the prisoner undress him*

(c) A reflexive pronoun after a preposition refers back to the subject

Peter sah eine dunkle Gestalt vor **sich** auftauchen	*Peter saw a dark shape appear in front of him*
Eva ließ mich bei **sich** wohnen	*Eva let me live at her place*

3.2.5 In infinitive clauses with *zu*, the choice of pronoun depends on who is understood to be the subject of the infinitive

The following examples are taken from DUDEN (1995: 329):

Karl versprach Peter, **sich** zu entschuldigen	(Karl is to apologize)
Karl versprach Peter, **ihn** zu entschuldigen	(Karl is excusing Peter)
Karl bat Peter, **sich** zu entschuldigen	(Peter should apologize)
Karl bat Peter, **ihn** zu entschuldigen	(Peter is asked to excuse Karl)

(See 13.2.4b.)

3.2.6 Emphatic 'myself', 'yourself', etc. is rendered by using the appropriate pronoun with the addition of *selbst* or *selber*

These are always stressed:

Ich habe **selbst/selber** mit dem Minister darüber gesprochen	*I spoke to the minister about it myself*
Er hat **selbst/selber** den Brief gelesen	*He's read the letter himself*

NB: Unstressed *selbst* has the meaning 'even' and always precedes the pronoun (or noun) which it qualifies, e.g.: **Selbst er** hat den Brief gelesen.

3.2.7 The reciprocal pronoun (= English 'each other')

As an equivalent to 'each other', German uses either the plural of the reflexive pronoun or *einander*. The latter is less common in speech than writing, but it is the only possible alternative after prepositions, in which case it is written together with the preposition (*durcheinander, miteinander*, etc.):

Sie sahen sich (*or* einander) oft	*They often saw each other*
Wir gehen uns (*or* einander) aus dem Wege	*We avoid each other*
Wir verlassen uns aufeinander	*We rely on each other*
Sie sprachen voneinander	*They were talking about each other*
BUT Sie sprachen von sich	*They were talking about themselves*

If the reflexive pronoun could be ambiguous, *selbst* can be added to confirm that the sense is reflexive or *gegenseitig* to show that it is reciprocal:

Sie widersprachen sich selbst	*They contradicted themselves*
Sie widersprachen sich gegenseitig	*They contradicted each other*
(*or* Sie widersprachen einander)	

3.3 Pronouns of address

For English 'you', German distinguishes between the 'familiar' pronouns *du* and *ihr*, and the 'polite' pronoun *Sie*. English lacks this distinction, and English-speaking learners of German need to establish which is appropriate in context. Since the late 1960s the use of *du* and *Sie* (commonly referred to by the verbs *duzen* and *siezen*) has shifted with changing social attitudes. The use of *du* has become more widespread, particularly among younger people, and Germans nowadays sometimes feel insecure about which one to use in unfamiliar sur-roundings. However, consciousness of the need to use the 'right' one is still strong.

Essentially, *du* signals intimacy, affection and solidarity. People who use *du* to one another are conscious of belonging to the same group or standing together, whereas *Sie* signals a degree of social distance (rather than simply 'politeness'). Thus, in the 'wrong' situation *du* will sound familiar and signal a lack of respect (it can be such a gross insult that people have been fined for slander for using it), whilst *Sie* in the 'wrong' situation will sound standoffish or pompous. Good accounts of current usage are Clyne (1995: 130–7) and Kretzenbacher and Segebrecht (1991).

Outside school or university, when addressing fellow pupils or fellow stu-dents, non-native speakers are advised to let native speakers take the initiative in proposing the use of *du*. It is very important for English speakers to be aware that the use of *du* (and first names) is still *much* less frequent or acceptable between adults than the use of first names in the English-speaking countries, especially between colleagues at work and casual acquaintances.

3.3.1 The uses of *du, ihr,* and *Sie*

(a) *du* is used

(i) When speaking to children (up to about fourteen – in schools to the 10th class), to animals and inanimate objects, to oneself and to God.

(ii) Between relatives and close friends, between schoolchildren and students, predominantly between blue-collar workmates, between non-commissioned soldiers and between members of clubs, interest groups and (especially left-wing) political parties.

The use of *du* to persons regarded as of lower status – with the expectation that they should use *Sie* back – is now obsolete. When it resurfaces it is offensive, often deliberately so; it is particularly reprehensible (and racist) when used indiscriminately to non-Europeans.

(b) *ihr* **is used to address two or more people whom the speaker would individually call** *du*

As *ihr* is unambiguously plural, whereas *Sie* can be singular *or* plural, it is often used to address a group, even if one is not *per du* with every single one of them, e.g. (at work):

> Ich wollte **euch** doch alle zum Kaffee einladen

Occasionally, *ihr* may be used to any group to stress plurality, even if all would normally be addressed individually as *Sie. ihr* can sometimes function as a kind of neutral compromise to mask the speaker's uncertainty about whether to use *du* or *Sie.*

(c) *Sie* **is used in all other cases**

It is used especially to adult strangers and generally in middle-class professions (e.g. to colleagues in an office or a bank).

Usually, the use of *du* is linked to that of first names, that of *Sie* to formal titles (*Herr Engel, Frau Kallmeyer*, etc.). However, the use of *Sie* and first names is not uncommon from adults to older teenagers and in 'trendy' circles (in the latter case possibly in imitation of American usage).

3.3.2 *du* **and** *ihr* **and their forms (***dich, dein, euch***, etc.) are spelled with initial capitals in letter-writing**

> Ich danke **Dir** recht herzlich für **Deinen** Brief

NB: This use of capitals will be eliminated in the reformed spelling, cf. 23.7.3.

(See also 23.1.3b.)

3.3.3 Other forms of address

(a) Titles are often used in shops, restaurants, etc. to address customers

> Was wünscht **der Herr**?   Was möchten **die Herrschaften** zu Mittag essen?

NB: The use of singular titles of rank with a plural verb (e.g. *Was wünschen gnädige Frau, Herr Major?*) is now archaic or facetious.

(b) In older German the singular pronouns *Er* **and** *Sie* **(spelled with capitals) were used to address people of a lower social standing**

This usage is now obsolete (except facetiously), but it persisted into the early twentieth century, especially in Austria.

3.4 Third person pronouns

3.4.I The third person singular pronouns agree in gender with the noun to which they refer

For things, *er, sie* or *es* can thus all correspond to English *it*:

> Dein Bleistift? Ach, **er** lag vorhin
> auf dem Tisch, aber ich muß **ihn**
> jetzt verloren haben
> Er hörte meine Meinung und stimmte
> **ihr** bei
>
> *Your pencil? Oh,* **it** *was lying on
> the table a little while ago, but
> I must have lost* **it** *now*
> *He heard my opinion and agreed with
> it*

Darf ich Ihr Buch noch eine Woche
behalten? Ich habe **es** noch nicht
gelesen

*May I keep your book another week?
I haven't read it yet*

NB: Possible conflicts between grammatical and natural gender are explained in 1.1.13.

3.4.2 In informal colloquial speech, the demonstrative pronouns *der,* *die, das* are often used rather than a third person personal pronoun

der kommt wohl nicht mehr	*for*	**er** kommt wohl nicht mehr
ich hätt' **die** nicht wieder erkannt	*for*	ich hätte **sie** nicht wieder erkannt

Although common, this usage is considered substandard, and even in speech it
is avoided (and considered rude) if the person referred to is present. It is usually
avoided in written German, especially to refer to people, but it may occur if there
is a possible ambiguity or a need for emphasis, cf. Bethke (1990):

Sie hatte die Fernsehanstalten . . .
massiv unter Druck gesetzt, als **die**
sich in Gibraltar umtaten (*Zeit*)

*She had put massive pressure on
the television companies, when
they were nosing around in
Gibraltar*

3.4.3 Third person pronouns are used in comparative clauses with *wie*

This makes it absolutely clear what is being compared:

Das waren Reichtümer, wie **sie**
Fürsten nicht besaßen (*Süßkind*)
Ein Kuchen, wie **ihn** deine Mutter
backt, ist was Besonderes

*These were riches such as princes
did not possess
A cake like your mother makes is
something special*

3.5 Third person pronoun or prepositional adverb?

The prepositional adverb (sometimes called the 'pronominal adverb') is formed
by prefixing *da(r)-* to the preposition, e.g. *damit, daran, darüber.*

3.5.1 To refer to things, the prepositional adverb is often used rather than the preposition followed by a third person pronoun

Modern usage, as detailed by Engel (1991: 755-60), is broadly as follows:

(a) The pronoun *es* is not normally used after prepositions

Da steht mein neues Auto. Ich habe
lange **darauf** (NOT auf es) warten
müssen

*There's my new car. I had to wait
a long time for it*

NB: (i) *ohne* can be used with a following *es*, cf. 3.5.2.
    (ii) The use of *es* with prepositions is not unknown, but DUDEN (1995: 367) considers
the prepositional adverb to be preferable.

(b) Preposition plus personal pronoun is always used to refer to individual persons

This does not apply to groups of people, cf. 3.5.1d:

Du darfst nicht **mit ihr** spielen
Ich kann mich nicht **an ihn** erinnern

*You mustn't play with her
I can't remember him*

(c) When reference is to a specific concrete object (or objects), either preposition plus pronoun or the prepositional adverb may be used

Ich habe diese Geschirrspülmaschine seit drei Wochen und bin sehr zufrieden **damit** *or* **mit ihr**	*I've had this dishwasher for three weeks and am very satisfied with it*

In practice, the prepositional adverb is the rather more frequent of these alternatives.

(d) The prepositional adverb is used to refer to abstracts and groups of people

Wie findest du den Vorschlag? Bist du **damit** einverstanden?	*What do you think of the suggestion? Do you agree with it?*
Ich erwarte zehn Gäste, **darunter** einige sehr alte Bekannte	*I am expecting ten guests, among them some very old acquaintances*

(e) The prepositional adverb is always used to refer to whole sentences

Ihr Mann hat eine neue Stelle gekriegt. **Darüber** freut sie sich sehr	*Her husband has got a new job. She's very pleased about it*

(f) If motion is involved, separable prefixes with *hin-* or *her-* are used rather than the prepositional adverb
(cf. 7.2.4):

Wir fanden eine Hütte und gingen **hinein**	*We found a hut and went into it*
Sie kam an einen langen Gang und eilte **hindurch**	*She came to a long passage and hurried through it*

3.5.2 Four common prepositions do not form a prepositional adverb

These are *außer, gegenüber, ohne, seit*. They are used with pronouns with reference to people *or* things:

Außer ihm ist keiner gekommen	*Nobody came apart from him*
Vor uns ist das Rathaus, und **ihm gegenüber** liegt der Dom	*In front of us is the town hall and opposite it is the cathedral*
Ohne es wäre unser Erfolg nicht möglich gewesen	*Without it our success wouldn't have been possible*

With reference to things, the pronoun is usually omitted after *gegenüber* and *ohne*, e.g.: *(ihm)* **gegenüber** *liegt der Dom,* **ohne** *(es) wäre es nicht möglich gewesen.*

With reference to things, it is more usual to use the adverbs *außerdem* and *seither* rather than *außer* and *seit* plus a pronoun. In practice this means that *seit* is rarely used with a pronoun at all.

NB: The prepositions which govern the genitive do not form prepositional adverbs. For the use of pronouns with them, see 3.1.2a.

3.5.3 Further notes on the use of the prepositional adverb

(a) In colloquial speech the prepositional adverb is often split:

Da weiß ich nichts von	Da kann ich nichts mit anfangen

This usage was originally typical of north Germany, but, as Glück and Sauer (1990: 69) report, it has recently become more widespread.

(b) When the prepositional adverb replaces preposition plus pronoun, the second syllable is usually stressed

da<u>durch</u>, da<u>mit</u>, da<u>ran</u>

In spoken German the first syllable may be reduced, e.g.: *dran, drin*. However, if the prepositional adverb is a replacement for preposition plus demonstrative, (i.e. = 'with <u>that</u>', 'in <u>that</u>', etc., cf. 5.1.1i), then the *first* syllable is stressed, e.g.: <u>da</u>durch, <u>da</u>mit, <u>da</u>ran.

(c) The prepositional adverb is often used to anticipate a following daß-clause or infinitive phrase

Ich verlasse mich **darauf**, daß sie rechtzeitig kommt

For details of this usage, see 6.6.2, 18.6.14 and 19.2.5.

3.6 Special uses of the pronoun es

The pronoun *es* has an extended range of uses beyond simply referring back to a neuter noun. In many constructions it functions as a grammatical particle (sometimes called a 'clitic'). Buscha (1988) and Askedal (1990) give detailed accounts.

es cannot be given heavy stress. If emphasis is needed *es* is replaced by *das* for most of the uses given in this section, e.g.:

Sind **das** Ihre Handschuhe?   **Das** bist du   Ich mache **das** schon

3.6.1 es can refer to elements other than neuter nouns

(a) *es* **can refer to a whole phrase, sentence or situation**

Willst du die Brötchen holen?	*Will you get the rolls?*
Angela macht **es** schon	*Angela is already doing it*
Ich weiß, daß sie gestorben ist,	*I know that she is dead, but Uwe*
aber Uwe weiß **es** noch nicht	*doesn't know it yet*

(b) *es* **can refer back to a noun or adjective complement of** *sein* **or** *werden*
In English nothing equivalent or a different equivalent is required:

Er soll zuverlässig sein, und ich	*He is said to be reliable and I am*
bin sicher, daß er **es** ist	*sure he is*
Ist Jürgen ein guter Schwimmer?	*Is Jürgen a good swimmer?*
Ja, er ist **es**	*Yes, he is (one)*
Sein Vater ist Arzt, und er wird **es**	*His father is a doctor and he's*
auch	*going to be one, too*

3.6.2 Impersonal and other uses of es as the subject of a verb

(a) *es* **is used as a formal subject in many impersonal constructions**
(i) With all kinds of impersonal verbs or verbs used in impersonal constructions, e.g.:

es regnet   es klingelt   es fehlt mir an Geld   es bedarf noch einiger Mühe

Details on the use of *es* as an impersonal subject are given in 18.2.4.

(ii) As an indefinite subject, communicating the idea of a vague, impersonal agent:

Ringsum war alles still, dann **schrie es**	*Round about everything was quiet, then there was a cry*
Ihn **trieb es** in die schottischen Hochlande (*Zeit*)	*He felt a desire to go the Highlands of Scotland*

(iii) In impersonal reflexive constructions, often with the force of a passive, cf. 15.4.3b:

Es schreibt sich so leicht mit diesem Filzstift	*It's so easy to write with this felt-tip pen*

es can be omitted in this construction if it is not in first position in a main clause, e.g.: *eine Stadt, in der (es) sich gut lebt.*

(iv) In impersonal passive constructions and in passive constructions with verbs which do not govern the accusative (see 15.1.3–4):

Es wurde in dieser Zeit viel gearbeitet	*A lot of work was done at this time*
Es wurde im Nebenzimmer geredet	*There was talking in the next room*
Es kann ihm doch nicht geholfen werden	*He can't be helped, though*

es is always omitted in this construction if it is not in first position in a main clause, e.g.: *In dieser Zeit wurde viel gearbeitet. Wir wissen doch, daß in dieser Zeit viel gearbeitet wurde.*

(b) *es* can be used as an indeterminate subject with the verbs *sein* and *werden* followed by a noun or an adjective
(i) This usually corresponds to the English use of *it*:

Es ist der Briefträger, ein Polizist	*It's the postman, a policeman*
Es wurde spät	*It got late*
Es ist Mittag	*It's midday.*
Es ist Sonntag heute	*It's Sunday today*

es can be omitted in non-initial position in time phrases, e.g.: *Jetzt ist (es) Mittag. Er weiß, daß (es) heute Sonntag ist.*

(ii) *es* can be used with a *plural* verb, corresponding to English 'they':

Es sind Ausländer	*They're foreigners*
Sind es Ihre Handschuhe?	*Are they your gloves?*
Was sind es?	*What are they?*

(iii) In this indeterminate function, *es* can refer back to a non-neuter or plural noun, as an alternative to the expected masculine, feminine or plural pronoun:

Seine Mutter lebt noch. **Es/Sie** ist eine alte Frau	*His mother is still alive. She's an old woman*
Siehst du die Kinder dort? **Es/Sie** sind meine	*Do you see the children there? They're mine*

(c) *es* with *sein* and a personal pronoun (= English 'It's me', etc.)

(i) The German construction differs from the English one, with *es* following the verb:

Du bist es. Ich bin es	*It's you. It's me*
Seid ihr es gewesen?	*Was it you?*
Sie werden es wohl sein	*It will probably be them*

(ii) 'Cleft sentence' constructions with relative clauses are based on this construction in German: (cf. English: 'It was you who rang the bell'):

Er war es, der es mir sagte	*It was him who told me*
Du warst es also, **der** geklingelt hat	*So it was you who rang the bell*

Other cleft sentence constructions, especially those corresponding to the English type 'It was this morning that I saw her', are unusual in German (see 21.2.3a).

(d) *es* is often used as a 'dummy subject' in initial position in order to permit the 'real' subject to occur later in the sentence

(i) This construction is particularly frequent if the 'real' subject is indefinite. It gives more emphasis to the 'real' subject, cf. 21.2.2d. With *sein*, this *es* corresponds to 'there' in 'there is/are', see 18.2.5b:

Es ist ein Brief für Sie da	*There's a letter for you*
Es waren viele Wolken am Himmel	*There were a lot of clouds in the sky*

This *es* is omitted if it is not in first position in a main clause, e.g.: *Viele Wolken waren am Himmel. Ich weiß, daß ein Brief für mich da ist.*

NB: For *es ist/sind* and *es gibt* for English 'there is/are', see 18.2.5.

(ii) *es* may be used in this construction with *any* verb in German. The verb agrees with the 'real' subject, not with the *es*:

Es saß eine alte Frau am Fenster	*There was an old woman sitting at the window*
Es hatte sich auch ihr Verhältnis zu den Nachbarn verändert	*Their relationship to their neighbours had changed, too*
Es liegen zwei Briefe für Sie auf dem Schreibtisch	*There are two letters for you lying on the desk*

This construction is particularly frequent with verbs of happening:

Es ist gestern ein schwerer Unfall **passiert**	*A serious accident happened yesterday*

In spoken German *da* is a common alternative to *es* in this function:

Da hat eine alte Frau am Fenster gesessen.

(e) *es* can be used to anticipate a following subordinate or infinitive clause which is the real subject of the verb

Es freut mich, daß du dein Examen bestanden hast	*I am pleased that you have passed your exam*
Es fällt mir ein, daß ich ihn schon gesehen haben muß	*It occurs to me that I must already have seen him*
Es war mir nicht möglich, früher zu kommen	*It wasn't possible for me to come earlier*
Es liegt mir fern, Schwierigkeiten zu machen	*The last thing I want is to make difficulties*

If the clause precedes the verb there is no need for the *es*, e.g.: *Daß du dein Examen bestanden hast, freut mich.*

This 'anticipatory' *es* is often omitted if it is not in first position in a main clause:

Dann fiel (es) auf, daß er kein weißes Hemd trug	*Then it was noticed that he wasn't wearing a white shirt*
Ihm steht (es) nicht zu, ein Urteil zu fällen	*It's not up to him to pass judgement*

Usage is variable on this point and no hard and fast rules for the omission of *es* can be given, cf. the survey by Marx-Moyse (1983). Nevertheless, the following regularities may be noted:

(i) The omission of *es* is especially common with the following verbs:

auffallen	sich erweisen	gelten 'be valid'	hinzukommen
aufgehen	sich ergeben aus	sich herausstellen	vorschweben
dazukommen	feststehen	hervorgehen	sich zeigen
einfallen	folgen aus		

(ii) With many verbs, especially those expressing feelings and emotions, *es* can be omitted before a following *daß*-clause if the main clause begins with a pronoun:

Ihn interessiert (es) nur, daß ihr Vater viel Geld hat	*The only thing that interests him is that her father's got a lot of money*
Damit hängt (es) natürlich zusammen, daß er im Gefängnis sitzt	*Of course, that's connected with the fact that he's in prison*

(iii) *es* can be omitted with the verb *sein*, if the main clause begins with the noun or adjective complement of *sein*:

Wichtig ist (es), daß er es weiß	*It's important for him to know it*
Wichtig ist (es), diesen Satz richtig zu verstehen	*It is important to understand this sentence correctly*
Ein Glück ist (es), daß du kommst	*It's fortunate you're coming*

With *klar, leicht, möglich, schwer* and *wichtig, es* can be omitted in such constructions if the main clause begins with a pronoun:

Ihm war (es) völlig klar, daß er jetzt springen mußte	*It was quite clear to him that he had to jump now*

NB: *es* is not omitted before *wenn*-clauses: *Mir ist es recht, wenn sie jetzt kommt.*

3.6.3 es as the object of a verb

(a) An accusative *es* is often used to anticipate a following infinitive or *daß*-clause which is the object of the verb

Ich konnte **es** kaum ertragen, ihn so leiden zu sehen	*I could hardly bear to see him suffer like that*
Ich habe **es** erlebt, daß Riemann die beste Rede gehalten hat	*I have known Riemann to give the best speech*

(i) The use of this 'anticipatory' object *es* is variable, and hard and fast rules are impossible to give, cf. the survey by Ulvestad and Bergenholtz (1983). However, it is particularly common with the following verbs:

ablehnen	erleben	leiden	verantworten
angewöhnen	ermöglichen	leisten	verdienen
aufgeben	ertragen	leugnen	vergessen
aushalten	fertigbringen	lieben	vermeiden
bedauern	genießen	merken	versäumen
begrüßen	gönnen	mögen	vertragen
bemerken	halten für	schaffen	verzeihen
bereuen	hassen	schätzen	wagen
betrachten als	hindern	übelnehmen	zulassen
dulden	hinnehmen	überlassen	
erfahren	lassen	unterlassen	

The phrases *nicht erwarten können* and *nicht wahrhaben wollen* are also usually found with an anticipatory *es*, as is *finden* followed by an adjective, e.g.: *Ich finde es schön, daß du da bist.*

(ii) Verbs of saying, thinking and knowing, e.g.: *ahnen, denken, erzählen, fühlen, glauben, hören, sagen, wissen* are also often used with an anticipatory *es* in conjunction with certain adverbs and particles, in particular *bereits, deutlich, doch, genug, ja, oft* and *schon,* or when there is an appeal to the listener's prior knowledge, e.g.:

Ich habe (es) ihm deutlich gesagt, daß er schreiben muß	*I've told him clearly enough that he's got to write*
Ich ahnte (es) schon, daß sie schwanger ist	*I already suspected she was pregnant*
Sie wissen (es) ja selber, daß die Ampel rot war	*You know yourself that the lights were red*

(b) *es* corresponds to English 'so' as the object of a few verbs, especially *sagen* 'to say' and *tun* 'to do'

Er hat es gesagt	*He said so*
Warum hast du es getan?	*Why did you do so?*

However, *es* is not essential with *glauben* and *hoffen*:

Kommt sie? – Ich glaube/hoffe (es)	*Is she coming? – I think/hope so*

(c) *es* is used as an object in a number of idiomatic verbal phrases

es auf etwas absehen	*be after sth.*
es auf etwas ankommen lassen	*take a chance on sth.*
es jdm. antun	*appeal to sb.*
sie hat es ihm angetan	*he fancies her*
es mit jdm./etwas aufnehmen können	*be a match for sb./sth.*
es bei etwas belassen	*leave it at sth.*
es weit bringen	*go far*
es zu etwas bringen	*attain sth. (esp. a position)*
er hat es zum Oberst gebracht	*he got to be a colonel*
es an etwas fehlen lassen	*be lacking in sth.*
es eilig haben	*be in a hurry*
es gut haben	*be fortunate*
es schlecht haben	*be unfortunate*
es in sich haben	*be a tough nut to crack*
es mit jdm./etwas halten	*trust sb./sth.*
es sich leicht/schwer machen	*make it easy/difficult for o.s.*

es gut mit jdm. meinen   *mean well with sb.*
es mit etwas genau nehmen   *be punctilious with sth.*
es mit jdm. zu tun haben   *have to deal with sb.*
es sich mit jdm. verdorben haben   *have fallen out with sb.*
es mit etwas (dat.) versuchen   *try (one's hand at) sth.*

3.6.4 *es* is used with a few adjectives in constructions with the verb(s) *sein* and/or *werden*

In particular with adjectives which govern the genitive of nouns (cf. 6.5.3), e.g.:
Ich bin es nun überdrüssig. The following adjectives occur in this construction:

    los   müde   satt   teilhaftig   überdrüssig   wert   würdig   zufrieden

Also: *Ich bin es gewohnt* 'I am used to it'
       Ich wurde es gewahr (lit.) 'I became aware of it'

NB: When *gewohnt sein* and *wert sein* are used with a following *daß*-clause, the *es* may
optionally be used to anticipate the subordinate clause: *Ich bin (es) nicht mehr gewohnt,
am frühen Morgen aufzustehen.*

4

The articles

German, like English, has a definite and an indefinite article. The articles belong
to a closed set of words known as 'determiners', which are used with a noun to
link it to a particular context or situation. Besides the articles, the determiners
include all those words, like the demonstratives (*dieser, jener*, etc.), the possessives (*mein, sein*, etc.) and indefinites (*einige, etliche*, etc.), which are used to determine nouns and typically occur first in the noun phrase, before any adjectives.
The articles differ from the other determiners in that they are only used in conjunction with a noun, whilst the other determiners may also be used as pronouns. Because of their importance the articles are treated here in a separate
chapter; the other determiners are dealt with, in all their uses, in Chapter 5. Bisle-
Müller (1991) is a good recent survey of the meaning and use of articles and
determiners in German.

The definite and indefinite articles change their form in accordance with the
case, gender and number of the following noun. In grammatical terminology,
they are said to 'decline' in 'agreement' with the noun. In practice the form of the
article is the principal way in which these grammatical categories of the noun, in
particular case and gender, are identified in German.

The forms of the articles are given in Table 4.1 and Table 4.2. Section 4.1 gives
further details on these forms and sections 4.2 to 4.9 deal with the uses of the articles. In most instances (85 per cent) German and English agree on the use of definite, indefinite or no ('zero') articles with nouns. However, as the articles are
very frequent words, the instances where the two languages do not correspond
are by no means insignificant, in particular where German uses a definite article
when English has none. We attempt to give general and simple indications of
where usage differs in the two languages, principally on the basis of the excellent surveys by Grimm (1986 and 1987).

TABLE 4.1 *Declension of the definite article*

	Masculine	Feminine	Neuter	Plural
Nom.	der	die	das	die
Acc.	den	die	das	die
Gen.	des	der	des	der
Dat.	dem	der	dem	den

4.1 The declension of the articles

The declension of the definite and indefinite articles is given in full in Table 4.1 and Table 4.2. The remainder of this section provides additional information on these forms.

4.1.1 The definite article

(a) In spoken German the definite article is relatively unstressed and reduced forms are usual

der [dɐ]	*die* [dɪ]	*das* [d(ə)s] or [s]
den [d(ə)n] or [n]	*dem* [d(ə)m] or [m]	*des* [d(ə)s]

These reductions are rarely reflected in writing except in the contractions used with some prepositions, cf. 4.1.1c. However, they are the norm in unaffected everyday speech, since the full forms, e.g. [de:m], have the force of a demonstrative, i.e. = 'this' or 'that', cf. 5.1.1. Compare:

Ich habe 'n Tisch gekauft	*I bought the table*
Ich habe <u>den</u> [de:n] Tisch gekauft	*I bought that table*

(b) The definite article cannot be omitted in pairs of words if a different gender or number is involved

In English we can say 'the house and garden(s)' or 'the son(s) and daughter(s)', with the definite article being understood to refer to the second noun as well. This is only possible in German if the two nouns have the same gender or number; in other contexts the second article, with its different form, *must* be included, e.g.:

> **das** Haus und **der** Garten/**die** Gärten
> **der** Sohn und **die** Tochter/**die** Töchter

On the other hand, *die Söhne und Töchter* is correct, since both nouns are plural and would have the same article.

NB: This rule naturally applies to all the other determiners, and to adjectives used with nouns, e.g.: *sein Sohn und seine Töchter* BUT *seine Söhne und Töchter*; *guter Wein und gutes Bier* BUT *alte Männer und Frauen*.

(c) Contracted forms of the definite article are used with some prepositions

(i) Contractions which are usual in speech and writing are:

ans = an + das	**am** = an + dem	**beim** = bei + dem	**ins** = in + das
im = in + dem	**vom** = von + dem	**zum** = zu + dem	**zur** = zu + der

With these the uncontracted forms are only used if the article is relatively stressed. This often depends on style and sentence rhythm, with many Germans considering the uncontracted forms to be 'better style' in formal writing. However, uncontracted forms are particularly frequent to refer back to something recently mentioned in order to make it clear that it is the one meant. Note the difference between:

> Er ging **zu der** Hütte (i.e. the one we were just talking about)
> Er ging **zur** Hütte (i.e. the one we all know about).

Where the force of *der* is demonstrative (i.e. = 'that', cf. 5.1.1), only the uncontracted form is possible, e.g.:

Einer der Affen war besonders lebhaft. Klaus wollte unbedingt eine Aufnahme von **dem** Affen machen	*One of the monkeys was particularly active. Klaus really wanted to take a picture of that monkey*

Similarly, where the noun is particularised, e.g. by a following relative clause, the uncontracted form is usual:

an dem Nachmittag, an dem sie anrief	*on the afternoon when she called*
Er geht **zu der** Schule, wo sein Vater früher war	*He goes to the school where his father used to be*

On the other hand, only the contracted forms are used in set phrases and expressions, e.g.:

am Dienstag	am 10. Mai	im Frühling	zur Zeit	am einfachsten
im Freien	im Vertrauen	im Gang	zum Frühstück	
Ich nahm ihn beim Wort		Sie war beim Kochen		

Compare:

Am Dienstag kam er spät zur Arbeit	*On Tuesday he came to work late*
An dem Dienstag kam er spät zur Arbeit	*That Tuesday he came to work late*

(ii) Contractions which are common in speech and sometimes used in writing.

aufs = auf + das	**durchs** = durch + das	**fürs** = für + das
übers = über + das	**ums** = um + das	**unters** = unter + das

Written German prefers the uncontracted forms of these, using the contracted ones chiefly only in set phrases, e.g.:

aufs Land fahren	fürs Leben gern
übers Herz bringen	ums Leben kommen

(iii) Contractions which are usual in spoken German, but only very occasionally found in writing, usually in set phrases. These are:

außerm	hinterm	hintern	hinters	überm
übern	unterm	untern	vorm	vors

(iv) Other contractions are regular in everyday colloquial speech but not normally used in writing, e.g.:

an'n   bei'n   durch'n   in'n   mit'm   nach'm   seit'm

TABLE 4.2 *Declension of the indefinite article*

	Masculine	Feminine	Neuter
Nom.	ein	eine	ein
Acc.	einen	eine	ein
Gen.	eines	einer	eines
Dat.	einem	einer	einem

4.1.2 The indefinite article

(a) The indefinite article has no plural

Indefinite plural nouns are used without an article, as in English:

Hier gibt es gute Weine   *There are good wines here*

The negative indefinite article *kein*, which declines like *ein* in the singular, has the plural forms nominative/accusative *keine*, genitive *keiner*, dative *keinen*, cf. 5.5.16, e.g.:

Hier gibt es keine guten Weine   *There are no good wines here*

(b) In spoken German the indefinite article is relatively unstressed and reduced forms are frequent

ein [n]	*eine* [nə]	*einen* [nən]
einem [nəm]	*einer* [nɐ]	*eines* [nəs]

These reductions are rare in writing (except to render the flavour of colloquial dialogue) but they are the norm in unaffected speech, where the full forms, e.g. [aɪn], [aɪnən], etc., would be interpreted as the numeral *ein* 'one'. Compare:

Ich habe **'n** Buch gekauft   *I bought a book*
Ich habe **ein** [aɪn] Buch gekauft   *I bought one book*

4.2 Use of the articles with abstract nouns

4.2.1 German frequently uses the definite article with abstract nouns where English usually has no article

This is particularly the case where the reference is to a specific and definite whole, known and familiar to the speaker and listener, e.g.:

(a) Abstract nouns

Er fürchtet **das Alter**	*He is afraid of old age*
Er liebte **die Demokratie** (*K. Mann*)	*He loved democracy*
Wir hängen von **der Industrie** ab	*We depend on industry*
Die Zeit vergeht	*Time passes*
Das Volk lebt **im Elend** (*Spiegel*)	*The people are living in misery*
Die Menschheit braucht nichts	*Humanity needs nothing more*
nötiger als **den Frieden**	*urgently than peace*

(b) Infinitives used as nouns

Er hat **das Schwimmen** verlernt	*He has forgotten how to swim*
Das Kaffeetrinken kam im 17.	*Coffee-drinking came to Europe*
Jahrhundert nach Europa	*in the seventeenth century*

4.2.2 In some contexts, by contrast, abstract nouns are used with no article in German

Clear rules are difficult to formulate precisely, but the following generalisations are broadly valid:

(a) Where the idea is referred to not as a whole, but in a vaguely general, indefinite and partial sense, which comes as a new idea in the context

In such contexts *some* or *any* can often be inserted in the English sentence without changing the essential meaning of the sentence:

Zu dieser Aufgabe gehört **Mut**	*This task demands (some) courage*
Es war nicht das erstemal, daß **Verrat** seinen Lebensweg gekreuzt hatte (*Hermlin*)	*It was not the first time that (some) treachery) had crossed his path*
Unentschlossenheit wäre jetzt verhängnisvoll	*(Any) indecision now would be fatal*
Bewegung ist gesund	*(Any) exercise is healthy*

Compare the two following sentences:

Unter seinen Anhängern entstand **Mißtrauen**	*(Some) distrust arose among his followers*
Das **Mißtrauen** wächst unter seinen Anhängern	*Distrust is growing among his followers*

In the second sentence 'distrust' is a specific notion, already known and familiar from the context. In the first it is a new concept of a rather vague, general and indefinite nature.

In practice such a partial or indefinite sense is often present when an abstract noun, particularly one denoting a human quality or emotion, is used with an adjective, e.g.:

Ich verachte **kleinliche Eifersucht**	*I despise (any) petty jealousy*
Im Heer wuchs **neuer Mut**	*In the army new courage was growing*
Er neigt zu **unnötiger Verschwendung**	*He tends to unnecessary extravagance*

(b) In proverbs, sayings and set phrases

Alter schützt vor **Torheit** nicht	*There's no fool like an old fool*
Not kennt kein Gebot	*Necessity knows no law*
Stolz ist keine Tugend	*Pride is not a virtue*

(c) In a number of other contexts

(i) In general statements, cf. 4.3.1.

(ii) In some constructions with the verbs *sein* and *werden*, cf. 4.8.2.

(iii) In pairs of words and enumerations, cf. 4.8.1.

(iv) In many phrasal verbs, cf. 4.2.3.

4.2.3 Article use with abstract nouns in phrasal verbs

Abschied nehmen, in Druck geben, in Erfahrung bringen

The use of a definite or zero article with these is often a matter of individual idiom, cf.: *zum Abschluß bringen* BUT *zu Ende bringen*. However, the following general rules usually apply:

(a) Infinitives as nouns have a definite article in phrasal verbs with prepositions

ins Rollen kommen, zum Kochen bringen

(b) Feminine nouns in phrasal verbs with *zu* have a definite article

> zur Kenntnis bringen, zur Verfügung stehen

(c) All phrasal verbs with *außer* and *unter*, and most of those with *in* have no article

> außer Gefahr sein, jdn unter Druck setzen, jdn in Verlegenheit bringen

NB: Those with *in* plus an infinitive used as a noun have an article, cf. (a) above.

(d) Most phrasal verbs with *gehen*, *halten* and *setzen* have no article

> in Erfüllung gehen, in Gang halten, in Brand setzen

(e) Abstract nouns used with *haben* have no article

> Aufenthalt haben, Angst haben, Durst haben, Geduld haben, Mut haben

(f) Phrasal verbs consisting of a verb and an object noun as a unit usually have no article

> Anspruch erheben, Antwort geben, Abschied nehmen, Rücksicht üben, Krieg führen, Not leiden, Zeit sparen

(g) An article is used with phrasal verbs if the noun is qualified by an adjective

This applies even if the phrasal verb normally lacks an article, e.g.:

jdn. in Gefahr bringen	*lead sb. into danger*
jdn. in (eine) große Gefahr bringen	*lead sb. into great danger*
jdn. in die größte Gefahr bringen	*lead sb. into the greatest danger*

4.2.4 The use of the article with some other groups of nouns is similar to that with abstract nouns

(a) Names of substances

These have a definite article if they are understood as general concepts, but no article if they are used in an indefinite or partial sense:

Die Butter kostet sechs Mark das Pfund	*Butter costs six marks a pound*
Faraday hat **die Elektrizität** erforscht	*Faraday investigated electricity*
Die Bauern bauen hier **Roggen** an	*The farmers grow rye here*
Wir importieren **Kaffee** aus Afrika	*We import coffee from Africa*

NB: (i) A definite article also occurs in some set phrases, e.g.:
> *beim Bier sitzen; Das steht nur auf dem Papier; Man kann nicht von der Luft leben.*

(ii) Usage is optional in generalisations, cf. 4.3, e.g.:
> *(Die) Elektrizität ist eine wichtige Energiequelle.*

(b) Names of meals

A definite article is used if they are referred to as known quantities, but the article is optional if the reference is indefinite or partial:

Das Mittagessen wird um 13 Uhr eingenommen	*Lunch is taken at 1 p.m.*
Wir sollen uns vor **dem Frühstück** treffen	*We are to meet before breakfast*
Ich habe (**das**) **Mittagessen** bestellt	*I have ordered lunch*
Wann bekommen wir (**das**) **Frühstück?**	*When are we getting breakfast?*

(c) Names of sicknesses and diseases

These have a definite article when they are referred to in general as known quantities, but there is no article when they are referred to in an indefinite or partial sense, or as a new idea in the context, particularly after *haben*:

Er ist an **der Schwindsucht** gestorben	*He died of consumption*
Sie ist an **den Masern** erkrankt	*She fell ill with measles*
Die Grippe hat Tausende weggerafft	*Influenza carried off thousands*
Ich habe **Kopfschmerzen, Gelbsucht**	*I've got a headache, jaundice*

Singular names of specific illnesses are used with the indefinite article to refer to a bout of that disease. This is particularly the case when the noun is modified by an adjective:

Er ist an **einer Lungenentzündung** gestorben	*He died of (a bout of) pneumonia*
Er hat **einen Schnupfen, eine Erkältung**	*He's got a cold*

(d) Names of languages

These nouns from adjectives (see 6.4.6a) have two forms:

(i) An inflected one, always used with the definite article, which refers to the language in a general sense:

Das Spanische ist **dem Portugiesischen** sehr nahe verwandt	*Spanish is very closely related to Portuguese*
eine Übersetzung aus **dem Russischen** ins **Deutsche**	*a translation from Russian into German*

(ii) An uninflected form, which refers to the language in a specific context. With this, article use is similar to that in English:

das **Deutsch** des Mittelalters	*the German of the Middle Ages*
Luthers **Deutsch**	*Luther's German*
Sie kann, lernt, versteht **Deutsch**	*She knows, learns, understands German*
Sie kann **kein Deutsch**	*She doesn't know any German*
Sie spricht **ein** akzentfreies **Deutsch**	*She speaks German without an accent*
eine Zusammenfassung in **Deutsch**	*a summary in German*

4.2.5 A definite article is usual in German with some other groups of mainly abstract nouns which often lack an article in English

(a) Historical periods, literary and philosophical movements, religions

Marx begreift **den Feudalismus** als notwendige Stufe der historischen Entwicklung (*Knaur*)	*Marx sees feudalism as a necessary stage in the process of history*
der deutsche **Expressionismus**	*German Expressionism*
Diese Auffassung ist charakteristisch für **den Islam**	*This view is characteristic of Islam*

(b) Arts and sciences

Ich erwarte von **der Literatur** mehr	*I expect more stimulus from*
Anregung als **vom Leben** (*Grass*)	*literature than from life*
Darüber schweigt **die Geschichte**	*History is silent about that*
ein Lehrbuch **der Astronomie**	*a textbook of astronomy*
Sie liebt **die Musik**	*She loves music*

NB: No article is used for school or university subjects, e.g.:

Sie hat eine Zwei in **Geschichte** *aber eine Vier in* **Mathe**.
Else studiert **Astronomie** *in Göttingen.*

(c) Institutions, company titles and buildings

Sie geht in **die Schule**	*She goes to school*
Er wurde **ins Parlament** gewählt	*He was elected to parliament*
Die Bundesrepublik gehört **der NATO** an	*The Federal Republic is part of NATO*
Er arbeitet bei **der BASF**	*He works for BASF*
im Kölner **Dom**, das Ulmer **Rathaus**	*in Cologne cathedral, Ulm town hall*

NB: No article is used with names of buildings with a proper name in apposition, e.g.:
Schloß Sanssouci, Burg Gibichstein, Kloster Beuron.

4.3 Use of articles in generalisations

4.3.1 Both German and English can express generalisations about people and things in a number of different ways

(a) Die Tanne ist ein Nadelbaum	*The fir is a conifer*
(b) Die Tannen sind Nadelbäume	
(c) Eine Tanne ist ein Nadelbaum	*A fir is a conifer*
(d) Tannen sind Nadelbäume	*Firs are conifers*

German tends to use constructions like (a) above, whereas English has a clear preference for sentences like (d), so that the following example illustrates a very common type of equivalence:

Das Auto ist der Fluch **der**	*Cars are the curse of modern*
modernen Stadt (*Zeit*)	*cities*

Construction (b), with a definite article and a plural noun, is quite common in German, but it is only used in English with a limited number of nouns (especially nouns of nationality). Compare:

Die Beschwerden vermehren sich	*Complaints are increasing*
Die Steuern waren drückend (*Brecht*)	*Taxes were oppressive*
Die Italiener lieben die Musik	*The Italians love music*

English *man* in the sense 'human being' is usually found with no article, whilst *der Mensch*, with a definite article, is regular in German in general statements of type (a) above, e.g.:

Der Mensch ist ein seltsames	*Man is a strange animal*
Geschöpf	

4.3.2 In general statements with nouns which have no plural, the definite article and zero article are alternatives in German

This applies in particular to abstract nouns and names of substances:

(Der) Frieden ist das höchste Gut der Menschen	*Peace is man's greatest good*
(Das) Rauchen schadet der Gesundheit	*Smoking is injurious to health*
(Das) Eisen ist ein Metall	*Iron is a metal*

4.4 Use of articles with geographical and other proper names

4.4.1 Usage with geographical and astronomical names

(a) Masculine names of countries
With these, the definite article is usual, but optional:

> (der) Libanon   (der) Iran   in/im Sudan

With masculine names of regions or provinces the use of the definite article is the norm, e.g.: *der Balkan, der Bosporus*.

(b) Feminine and plural names of countries and regions
These are always used with a definite article:

die Schweiz	die Türkei	die Ukraine	die Lausitz
die USA	die Niederlande	die Normandie	

(c) Neuter names of countries and cities
No article is used with most of these:

> Deutschland Norwegen Spanien Leipzig London Stockholm Ulm

However, a few neuter names of regions and provinces are normally used with the article:

das Elsaß	das Engadin	das Ries	das Wallis *Valais*
das Rheinland	das Vogtland (and all others in -*land*)		

The article *is* always used with neuter nouns from adjectives for German regions. These are frequent in colloquial German: *Jetzt kommen wir **ins Bayrische**; Das Dorf liegt **im Thüringischen**.*

NB: Use of the article is optional with *Tirol: in/im Tirol.*

(d) Other geographical and astronomical names have a definite article
This is so even where English has no article:

der Bodensee	*Lake Constance*	der Genfer See	der Mont Blanc
der Mars	der Venus	der Jupiter	

(e) The definite article is used to refer to street names

> Ich wohne in **der Goethestraße** Wir treffen uns auf **dem Schloßplatz**
> **Der Alexanderweg** ist die zweite Querstraße zur **Humboldtstraße**

NB: No articles are used in addresses:
Frau Gerlinde Haarmann, Weserstraße 247, 34125 Kassel
Herr Andreas Wernli, Kellergasse 7, CH-3014 Bern.

4.4.2 In standard German there is usually no article with personal names

There are, however, some exceptions to this, i.e.:

(a) In colloquial speech a definite article is frequent with names

Ich sehe die Monika   Gestern war ich bei der Frau Schmidt

(b) To clarify case or gender
(see also 4.7.1):

der Vortrag des Klaus Müller   Das hat Klaus dem Wolfgang Pedersen gesagt
Ich habe eben mit der Rupp (i.e. Frau Rupp, NOT Herr Rupp) gesprochen

(c) To individualise the person concerned more strongly

Der Lehmann hat einen ausgezeichneten Vortrag gehalten
die Briefe Leopold Mozarts an das Nannerl (*Hildesheimer*)

NB: The use of the article is almost regular with performing artists and other 'stars', e.g.:
die Callas, der Karajan, die Garbo.

(d) To refer to characters in plays

Er hat in der vorigen Saison den Hamlet gespielt

4.4.3 All geographical and proper names are used with a definite article when qualified by an adjective

das heutige Deutschland   das viktorianische England
das zerstörte Dresden   das kalte Moskau
der junge Heinrich   der alte Doktor Schulze

This applies also to saints' names: *der heilige Franziskus* 'Saint Francis'.

4.5 Use of articles in time expressions

4.5.1 Names of months and seasons usually have the definite article

Der April war verregnet   Wir fahren **im August** nach Italien
Der Frühling war dieses Jahr spät   **Im Winter** friert der Bach zu

The names of the months have no article after prepositions other than *an, bis zu* and *in*, cf. 4.5.3, or after *Anfang, Mitte, Ende*:

Es war kalt für April   Der Fahrplan gilt von Mai bis Oktober
Ende Februar hat es geschneit   Er kommt erst Anfang Mai

No article is used after *sein* and *werden*, cf. 4.8.2c, e.g.: *Es ist, wird Sommer; Es ist Januar*, or when the name is qualified by *nächsten, letzten, vorigen, vergangenen*: *nächsten Oktober, letzten Herbst.*

4.5.2 The major festivals have no article

Weihnachten   Silvester   Neujahr   Pfingsten   Ostern

NB: *der Heilige Abend* 'Christmas Eve'; *der Karfreitag* 'Good Friday'.

4.5.3 All time nouns are used with the definite article after the prepositions *an*, *bis zu* and *in*

am Mittwoch	am 27. Januar	bis zum Montag im Jahre 1945
am Tag *by day*	in der Nacht *at night*	in der vorigen Woche
in der Gegenwart *at present*		

After other prepositions in time expressions there is normally no article, see 11.5.

4.6 Definite article or possessive?

4.6.1 The definite article is used to refer to parts of the body and articles of clothing

(a) **This is usual in German, whereas in English the possessive is the rule**

Hast du **die Zähne** geputzt?	*Have you cleaned your teeth?*
Sie hat **das Bein** gebrochen	*She has broken her leg*
Sie strich **den Rock** glatt	*She smoothed her skirt*

Das Mädchen zog **den** rötlichen Kamm aus **dem** Haar, nahm ihn in **den** Mund und fing an, mit **den** Fingern **die** Frisur zurechtzuzupfen (*Böll*)

A possessive dative is frequent in such constructions, and essential when the relevant person is not the subject of the verb, cf. 2.5.4, e.g.:

Sie nahm es (**sich**) in **den** Mund	*She put it in her mouth*
Die Mütze fiel **mir vom** Kopf	*My cap fell off my head*
Wir zogen **dem Verletzten die** Hose aus	*We took the injured man's trousers off*

(b) **However, a possessive is normal in German rather than the definite article in a few contexts**

(i) When the owner has been named in a previous sentence, or when the part of the body or article of clothing is the first element in the sentence:

Ein Fremder erschien. **Seine Stirn** glänzte. **Sein Anzug** war altmodisch	*A stranger appeared. His forehead glistened. His suit was old-fashioned*
Meine Beine sind nicht krumm (*Brecht*)	*My legs aren't crooked*

(ii) When the owner must be specified, but the verb does not permit the use of a possessive dative:

Ich erblickte eine Wespe auf **meinem Ärmel**	*I caught sight of a wasp on my sleeve*
Sie legte **ihre Hand** auf **seine Hand** (*Wendt*)	*She put her hand on his hand*

(iii) To emphasise the owner or avoid ambiguity:

Langsam hob sie **ihre rechte Hand**	*Slowly, she raised her right hand*
Hast du **deine Zähne** geputzt?	*Have you cleaned your teeth?*
Zieh (**dir**) lieber **deinen Mantel** an!	*Put **your** coat on (i.e. not mine!)*
Ich zog **mir seine Hose** an	*I put his trousers on*

4.6.2 The definite article is used rather than a possessive with some abstract nouns

This is particularly frequent with nouns denoting human attributes and emotions, which are thus seen as 'part' of the person concerned. A possessive dative may occur under the same conditions as with body parts:

Du mußt versuchen, **die/deine Angst** zu überwinden — *You must try to overcome your fear*
Ich werde ihm **die Faulheit** austreiben — *I shall rid him of his laziness*
Der Appetit ist mir vergangen — *I've lost my appetite*

4.6.3 The definite or indefinite article, as appropriate, are commonly used rather than a possessive with the adjective *eigen*

Er hat **den/seinen eigenen** Sohn erschlagen — *He has killed his own son*
Jetzt haben wir **eine eigene** Wohnung — *We've got our own flat/a flat of our own now*

But, as a set phrase with no article:

Das haben wir **mit eigenen Augen** gesehen — *We saw it with our own eyes*

4.7 Miscellaneous uses of the definite article

4.7.1 The definite article is sometimes used, even where it would not otherwise be required, to make the case of a noun clear

This applies in particular in respect of the genitive and dative cases.

(a) Examples of the definite article used to mark genitive case

der Geruch des Seetangs — *the smell of seaweed*
ein Ausdruck des Erstaunens — *an expression of surprise*

In practice it is not possible for a noun (other than a proper name) to be used in the genitive without a determiner or an adjective to show the case, cf. Lauterbach (1993). In this way, the article is essential in the first of the following sentences to indicate the case:

Sie bedarf **der Ruhe** ⎫
Sie braucht **Ruhe** ⎭ *She needs rest*

If ambiguity could arise from the use of a definite article, then the paraphrase with *von* must be used, cf. 2.4. Thus 'the smell of seaweed' can only be *der Geruch von Seetang*, if *der Geruch des Seetangs* could be taken to mean 'the smell of the seaweed'.

(b) Examples of the definite article used to mark dative case

Ich ziehe Kaffee **dem Tee** vor — *I prefer coffee to tea*
Dieses Metall gleicht **dem Gold** — *This metal resembles gold*
Er hat sich **der Physik** gewidmet — *He devoted himself to physics*

4.7.2 The definite article may be used in a distributive sense

In such contexts English commonly uses the indefinite article or *per*:

Die Butter kostet sechs Mark **das Pfund**	*The butter costs six marks a/per pound*
Sie kommt zweimal **die Woche** (*or* zweimal in der Woche)	*She comes twice a week*
Wir fuhren 80 Kilometer **die Stunde**	*We were doing 50 miles per hour*

pro or (with measurements) *je*, both without an article, are common alternatives to the definite article:

Wir zahlten 15 Pfennig **pro/je Meter**	*We paid 15 pfennigs a/per metre*
Es kostet 12 Mark **pro Stunde**	*It costs 12 marks an hour*

4.7.3 The definite article is always used with *meist*

Er hat **das meiste Geld**	*He has (the) most money*
die meisten Jungen	*most of the boys*
die meisten meiner Freunde	*most of my friends*

4.8 Miscellaneous uses of the zero article

4.8.1 Nouns used in pairs or enumerations often lack the definite article even when a single noun in the same construction would require one

In many cases these are conventional or set phrases:

(in) Form und Inhalt	*(in) form and content*
Tag und Nacht	*day and night*
mit Müh und Not	*with great difficulty*
Es geht um Leben und Tod	*It's a matter of life and death*
in Hülle und Fülle	*in plenty*
Rhein, Main und Donau sind schiffbare Flüsse	*The Rhine, the Main and the Danube are navigable rivers*
Sie ließ Schale und Rest im Eßzimmer liegen (*Baum*)	*She left the skin and the remains lying in the dining-room*
In Industrie und Handwerk bleiben Tausende von Arbeitsplätzen unbesetzt (*Spiegel*)	*In industry and trade thousands of job vacancies remain unfilled*

4.8.2 No article is used in some constructions with the complement of the verbs *sein, werden, bleiben*

(a) With nouns denoting professions, nationality, origins or classes of people in general

Er ist **Arzt, Bäcker, Installateur**	*He is a doctor, a baker, a plumber*
Ich bin **Deutscher, Engländer, Schwede**	*I am a German, an Englishman, a Swede*
Franz ist **gläubiger Katholik**	*Franz is a devout Catholic*
Helmut blieb **Junggeselle**	*Helmut remained a batchelor*
Danach wurde er **Marxist**	*After that he became a Marxist*

The indefinite article *is* used if the noun does not refer to a class:

Sie ist **eine bekannte Anwältin**	*She is a well-known lawyer*
Er ist **ein richtiger Schauspieler**	*He's a real actor*

However, the *indefinite* article is used in descriptive constructions with professions and positions, e.g.:

Er hatte die Stelle **eines** **Untersuchungsrichters**, den Titel **eines Professors**	*He had the position of examining magistrate, the title of professor*

(b) With certain nouns used mainly in formal writing
i.e. *Bedingung, Fakt, Gegenstand, Grundlage, Sache, Schwerpunkt, Tatsache, Voraussetzung, Ziel*. These usually precede the verb:

Tatsache ist, daß ...	*It is a fact that ...*
Bedingung dafür ist, daß er den Vertrag unterschreibt	*The condition for this is that he signs the contract*
Grund meines Schreibens ist der Artikel „Unser Garten" (*HA*)	*The reason I am writing is the article 'Our Garden'*

(c) With names of months and seasons, and abstract nouns used in a general sense
This runs counter to usual practice with these, cf. 4.2 and 4.5:

Es war schon **April**	*It was already April*
Jetzt ist **Sommer**	*It's summer now*
Heute abend ist **Tanz**	*There's a dance on tonight*
Das ist **Geschmackssache**	*That is a matter of taste*
Donnerstags ist **Sitzung**	*On Thursdays there is a meeting*

4.8.3 The indefinite article is commonly lacking in phrases introduced by *als* 'as'

Ich kannte ihn **als Junge**	*I knew him when I was a boy*
Er sprach **als Franzose**	*He spoke as a Frenchman*
die Bedeutung des Passes als **wichtige(r) Handelstraße**	*the significance of the pass as an important trade route*
Als überzeugter Demokrat kann ich das nicht gutheißen	*As a convinced democrat, I cannot approve of that*
Er gilt als **bester Tenor** der Neuzeit	*He is reckoned to be the best tenor of modern times*

NB: (i) With verbs which are usually followed by *als*, e.g. *ansehen, betrachten, fühlen, gelten* the appropriate article is a permissible alternative, e.g.: *Er gilt als (der) beste Tenor der Neuzeit.*
(ii) The article is commonly used in the genitive, e.g.: *mit der Verhaftung des Generals als (des) eigentlichen Putschführers.*

4.8.4 The article can be omitted in appositional phrases in formal German

Zunächst kamen wir nach Florenz, **(der) Hauptstadt der Toskana**	*First we arrived at Florence, the capital of Tuscany*
dieses Zürich, **Treffpunkt der Kaufleute** (*Frisch*)	*this Zurich, the meeting place of businessmen*
Neil Armstrong, **amerikanischer Astronaut**, betrat als erster Mensch den Mond (*Zeit*)	*Neil Armstrong, the American astronaut, was the first man to set foot on the moon*

4.8.5 No article is used in a few formulaic expressions referring to people

This usage is restricted to formal, especially official registers, e.g.:

Angeklagter hat gestanden, daß …	*The accused confessed that …*
Unterzeichneter bittet um rasche	*The undersigned requests a speedy*
Entscheidung seiner Angelegenheit	*decision in the matter concerning him*
Verfasser behauptet, das Problem	*The author claims to have solved the*
gelöst zu haben	*problem*

4.8.6 Articles are often omitted for stylistic effect in headlines and advertisements, etc.

Verbrechen gestanden. Münchner	*Crime admitted. Munich businessman*
Kaufmann vom Geschäftspartner	*killed by partner*
erschlagen (*HA*)	
Wohnung mit Bad gesucht möglichst	*Flat with bathroom required as close*
nahe Stadtzentrum	*as possible to city centre*

4.8.7 The zero article is the most usual equivalent in German for the English indefinite determiners *some* or *any*

Ich möchte **Suppe**	*I should like some soup*
Brauchen Sie **Marken**?	*Do you need any stamps?*
Ich habe (rote) **Äpfel** gekauft	*I bought some (red) apples*
wenn du noch **Schwierigkeiten** hast	*if you have any more difficulties*
Hast du **Geld** bei dir?	*Have you got any money on you?*

For further information on German equivalents for 'some' and 'any', see 5.5.9b.

4.8.8 No article is used with adverbial genitives

e.g.: *schweren Herzens* 'with a heavy heart', see 2.3.5b.

4.9 Article use with prepositions

Article use with prepositions is to a considerable degree idiomatic. Use in phrasal verbs and time phrases is dealt with in sections 4.2.3 and 4.5.3, and more detail, in particular concerning differences between English and German use of articles in set phrases with prepositions, may be found in Chapter 20 under the individual prepositions. In this section we deal with those special cases where general rules can be stated.

4.9.1 The indefinite article is often omitted in adverbial or adjectival phrases consisting of preposition, adjective plus noun

This is particularly common where a set phrase is extended by an adjective and is characteristic of formal registers:

… einen Virtuosen **mit italienischem**	*a virtuoso with an Italian name*
Namen (*Th. Mann*)	
ein Mann, der solchem Rat nicht	*a man who failed to follow such*
folgte und **zu schrecklichem Ende**	*advice and met a terrible end*
kam (*Hildesheimer*)	
Wir erhielten den Betrag **in frei**	*We received the sum in a freely*
konvertierbarer Währung	*convertible currency*

This usage is also the norm in phrases with *mit* which are alternatives to adverbial genitives, cf. 2.3.5b:

Sie ging **mit schnellem Schritt** (= schnellen Schrittes) über die Straße	*She crossed the road at a fast pace*

4.9.2 The definite article can be omitted in prepositional phrases if the following noun is qualified by a genitive or another prepositional phrase

This is very frequent in set formulae in formal registers:

auf Anraten des Arztes	*on the advice of a doctor*
in Gegenwart von zwei Kollegen	*in the presence of two colleagues*
die Studie, die Smith noch **in Diensten** der Bank verfaßte, ... (*Spiegel*)	*the study which Smith wrote in the service of the bank ...*
unter Ausnutzung aller Möglichkeiten	*by exploiting all possibilities*

4.9.3 A few prepositions are used with a zero article in some or all of their uses

The most noteworthy (because of the differences to English) are:

(a) *mit* is often used with no article when a part–whole relationship is involved

ein Zimmer **mit Bad**	ein Hut **mit breitem Rand**
ein Opel **mit Schiebedach**	eine Suppe **mit Wursteinlage**

(b) *ohne* is used with no article in German in cases where English has an indefinite article

Sie trat **ohne Brille** auf
Er geht gern **ohne Hut**
Ich übersetzte den Text **ohne Wörterbuch, ohne Mühe**
Wie hast du die Tür **ohne Schlüssel** aufgemacht?

(c) A number of other prepositions, mainly belonging to formal written registers, are used without a following article

More information is given under the individual prepositions in Chapter 20:

ab	ab ersten/erstem Mai, Preise ab Fabrik *ex works*, ab Bahnhof
gemäß	Die Angelegenheit wurde gemäß Verordnung entschieden

NB: An article is normally used if *gemäß* comes after rather than before the noun, e.g.: *den geltenden Verordnungen gemäß*.

infolge	Die Straße ist infolge schlechten Wetters gesperrt
kraft	Er handelte kraft Gesetzes
laut	Der Fahrer wurde laut Gesetz verurteilt
mangels	Der Angeklagter wurde mangels Beweises freigesprochen
per	per Einschreiben *by registered mail*, per Anhalter fahren *to hitch-hike*
pro	pro Stück, pro Tag, pro männlichen Angestellten
von ... wegen	Diese Angelegenheit muß von Amts wegen geklärt werden
zwecks	Junge Dame möchte netten, gebildeten Herrn zwecks Heirat kennenlernen (*FAZ*)

5

Other determiners and pronouns

Determiners are a limited ('closed') set of words used with nouns to relate them to a particular context or situation. The German determiners include the articles (which are dealt with in Chapter 4), the demonstratives (e.g. *dieser, jener, solcher*), the possessives (e.g. *mein, unser*), interrogatives (e.g. *welcher*) and the quantifiers and indefinites (e.g. *alle, einige, manche, viele*). Most of these are also used as pronouns, i.e. to refer back to a noun already mentioned.

Traditional German terminology often fails to distinguish between the use of these words as determiners and as pronouns, using the term 'pronoun' for both, cf. Hentschel and Weydt (1994: 214). However, the distinction is useful for the English learner, as these words often have different sets of endings when they are being used as determiners or pronouns.

All these words and their uses are treated in this chapter, together with those of the relative and other pronouns not dealt with in Chapter 3. Sections 5.1–4 deal with the demonstratives, the possessives, the interrogatives and the relative pronouns, and section 5.5 gives details on the remaining indefinites, quantifiers and other determiners and pronouns.

All but a very few of these determiners and pronouns express case, number and gender in agreement with the noun which they qualify or to which they refer, or according to their role in the sentence. A characteristic feature of determiner endings to mark these categories in German is that they differ from those of a following adjective (see Chapter 6).

5.1 Demonstratives

5.1.1 *der* 'that'

der is the most frequent demonstrative in spoken German. It can be used, like French *ce*, to point in a general way to something distant or something near at hand. In this way, it may be the equivalent of both *this* and *that*.

(a) *der*, when used as a determiner, has exactly the same written forms as the definite article
i.e. as given in Table 4.1. It differs from the definite article in speech because it is stressed, e.g. *den* [de:n], *der* [de:ʀ], etc. It is thus quite distinct from the definite article, whose spoken forms are always unstressed and reduced, e.g. *'n, d'n* or *d'r*, etc., cf. 4.1.1. Compare:

Ich möchte ein Stück von d'r Wurst	*I would like a piece of the sausage*
Ich möchte ein Stück von **der** [de:ʀ] Wurst	*I would like a piece of this/that sausage*

In written German the demonstrative force of *der* may sometimes be clear from the context, especially when a relative clause follows, e.g:

Ich kann dir **die** Hefte der Zeitschrift schicken, die dir noch fehlen	*I can send you those issues of the journal which you haven't got yet*
Bei **der** Lehrerin würde ich auch nichts lernen	*I wouldn't learn anything from that teacher either*

Usually, though, it would be difficult to tell the demonstrative *der* apart from the definite article in writing, and *dieser* is usually preferred (for both English *this and that*, see 5.1.2).

(b) The declension of demonstrative *der* used as a pronoun

This is the same as the declension of the determiner, *except* in the genitive and the dative plural. The full forms are given in Table 5.1.

NB: The genitive forms *dessen* and *deren* are compounded with a following *-halben, -wegen* or *-willen*, with a *-t-* inserted, e.g. *dessentwegen, um derentwillen.*

(c) Typical examples of the use of *der* as a pronoun

Note that it often corresponds to English *the/this/that one*:

mein Wagen und **der** meines Bruders	*my car and my brother's*
Die Sache ist nämlich **die**: er ist schon verheiratet	*It's like this: he's already married*
Diese Seife ist besser als **die**, die ich gebrauche	*This soap is better than the one I use*
Wir können **dem** nicht so viel Bedeutung beimessen	*We cannot attach so much importance to that*
Die sind mir zu teuer	*Those are too expensive for me*
Das Buch liegt auf dem Tisch. Ja, auf **dem** da drüben	*The book's lying on the table. Yes, on that one over there*

TABLE 5.1 *Declension of demonstratives*: der, dieser, derjenige

	Masculine	Feminine	Neuter	Plural
Nom.	der	die	das	die
Acc.	den	die	das	die
Gen.	dessen	deren	dessen	deren
Dat.	dem	der	dem	denen
Nom.	dieser	diese	dieses	diese
Acc.	diesen	diese	dieses	diese
Gen.	dieses	dieser	dieses	dieser
Dat.	diesem	dieser	diesem	diesen
Nom.	derjenige	diejenige	dasjenige	diejenigen
Acc.	denjenigen	diejenige	dasjenige	diejenigen
Gen.	desjenigen	derjenigen	desjenigen	derjenigen
Dat.	demjenigen	derjenigen	demjenigen	denjenigen

(d) Pronominal *der* is often used instead of a third person pronoun

This usage is mainly colloquial, especially to refer to persons, see 3.4.2:

Ist der Teller kaputt? Ja, **den** hat Astrid fallen lassen	*Is the plate broken? Yes, Astrid dropped it*
Keine Möwen. **Die** waren weiter draußen (*Grass*)	*No gulls. They were further offshore*

(e) *der* can be strengthened by the addition of *da* or *hier*

This makes it more clear whether *this* one (here) or *that* one (there) is being referred to. This usage, with either the determiner or the pronoun *der*, is limited to informal colloquial speech:

das Buch da *that book*	das Buch hier *this book*
das da *that one*	das hier *this one*

(f) The genitive of the pronoun *der* can be used for a possessive pronoun to avoid ambiguity

Sie war die Tochter des Schriftstellers Thomas Mann und **dessen** viertes Kind (*Spiegel*)	*She was the daughter of the writer Thomas Mann and his fourth child*
Dennoch wurden sie alle geprägt von ihrer Stadt und **deren** geistiger Tradition	*Nevertheless they were all moulded by their city and its intellectual tradition*
Erboste Bauern nahmen britische LKW-Fahrer gefangen und plünderten **deren** Konvois (*Zeit*)	*Angry farmers held some British lorry-drivers captive and plundered their (i.e. the lorry-drivers') convoys*

In colloquial German, the genitive of *der* can appear instead of a possessive for emphasis, e.g.: *Ich kann* **deren** *Mann nicht leiden.*

(g) In the genitive plural *derer* occurs rather than *deren* to refer forwards

It is most frequent with a following relative clause:

die Zahl **derer**, die seit 1950 die Westzone verlassen haben (*ND*)	*the number of those who have left the Western zone since 1950*

(h) The pronoun *das* is used as an emphatic form of *es*

Like *es*, it can be used with either singular or plural forms of the verb *sein*. In the corresponding English constructions we distinguish between *that* and *those* (see 3.6):

Das sind meine Bücher	*Those are my books*
Das ist mein Arm, meine Hand, mein Knie	*That is my arm, my hand, my knee*

(i) A form of the prepositional adverb is normally used rather than a preposition followed by the demonstrative pronoun

e.g. *da̲mit* 'with that', *da̲rin* 'in that'. The stress is on the first syllable, cf. 3.5.3b:

Da̲mit kann man die Büchse doch nicht aufmachen, oder?	*You can't open the can with that, can you?*

To refer to something near or something just mentioned, a prepositional adverb with *hier-* can be used, e.g. *hiermit* 'with this', *hierin* 'in this':

Hierüber läßt sich nichts mehr sagen	*There is nothing more to be said about this*

The prepositional adverb is not used in written German before a following relative clause (although it may sometimes be heard in speech), cf. 5.4.3c:

Ich richtete meine ganze Aufmerksamkeit **auf das**, was er erklärte	*I focused my whole attention on what he was saying*

5.1.2 *dieser* 'this'

The declension of *dieser* is the same whether it is used as a pronoun or as a determiner; it is given in full in Table 5.1. Note that there is an increasing tendency to use the form *diesen* in the genitive singular masculine and neuter of the determiner rather than *dieses* if the noun has the ending -(e)s, e.g. *im Februar diesen Jahres* (MM) (for *dieses Jahres*). DUDEN (1985: 185) considers this usage to be substandard.

(a) As a determiner and a pronoun *dieser* refers to something near at hand, corresponding to English *this*

However, it is frequently used simply to point to something in contexts where the difference between near and distant is not crucial. In such contexts it often corresponds to English *that*.

As a determiner, *dieser* occurs in both spoken and written German, but as a pronoun it is mainly restricted to writing:

Diese Erklärung ist unbefriedigend	*This explanation is unsatisfactory*
Dieser Junge arbeitet aber gut	*That boy really does work well*
Er kaufte den roten Wagen nicht,	*He didn't buy the red car, because*
weil ihm **dieser** (spoken: der hier)	*he liked this one much better*
viel besser gefiel	

(b) The short pronoun form *dies* is commonly used for *dieses*

It refers to something close by or recent and its use corresponds closely to English *this*:

Dies geschieht nicht oft	Gerade **dies** hatte ich vergessen

dies, like *das*, can be used irrespective of gender or number, with a plural verb where appropriate: *Dies sind meine Schwestern; Dies ist meine Frau.*

NB: In formal writing, *dies* is occasionally used as a determiner for *dieses*, e.g. **Dies** Werk malte Konrad Witz aus Basel (Borst).

5.1.3 *jener* 'that'

jener declines like *dieser*, cf. Table 5.1. As a determiner or a pronoun it is largely restricted to a few special uses in formal written German, i.e.:

(a) To contrast with *dieser*

Herr Schröder wollte nicht dieses Bild verkaufen, sondern **jenes**	*Mr Schröder did not want to sell this picture, but that one*
Wir sprachen über dieses und **jenes** (less formal: über dies und das)	*We talked about this and that*

(b) To refer to something distant, but well known

Werfen wir einen kurzen Blick über den Eisernen Vorhang **jener** Zeit (*Sonnenberg*)	*Let us cast a short glance at the Iron Curtain of those times*

(c) With a following relative clause

Sein linker Arm war mit dicken Tüchern umwickelt, wie es bei **jenen** Brauch ist, die Hunde zum Anpacken einüben (*Dürrenmatt*)	*His left arm had thick material wrapped round it, as is the custom with those who train dogs to attack*

NB: DUDEN (1985: 370) labels this use incorrect, prescribing *derjenige* rather than *jener* in such contexts (see also 5.4.5b).

5.1.4 *derjenige* 'that'

Both parts of *derjenige* decline, see Table 5.1. It is an emphatic demonstrative determiner or pronoun and is almost exclusively used with a following restrictive relative clause, corresponding to English 'that (one), which/who'. It is now quite frequent in spoken registers as well as in writing.

Wir wollen **diejenigen** Schüler herausfinden, die musikalisch begabt sind	*We want to find those pupils who are musically gifted*
Dieses neue Denken ist für **denjenigen**, der ein bißchen Bildung hat, ein sehr altes Denken gewesen (*Heuss*)	*This new way of thinking was an old way for those who have a little education*

5.1.5 *derselbe* 'the same'

Both parts of *derselbe* decline, like *derjenige* (see Table 5.1). However, unlike *derjenige*, it may be used with a contracted preposition, e.g. *am selben Tag, zur selben Zeit*. It corresponds to English 'the same':

Er besucht **dieselbe** Schule wie dein Bruder	*He goes to the same school as your brother*
Sind das **dieselben**?	*Are those the same?*
Sie wohnt im **selben** Haus	*She lives in the same house*
Es läuft auf (ein und) **dasselbe** hinaus	*It all comes to the same thing*

NB: The difference between *derselbe*, i.e. 'the very same' and *der gleiche*, i.e. 'one which is similar' (cf. *Er trägt den gleichen Hut* 'He is wearing the same (i.e. a similar) hat') is often ignored in spoken German, *derselbe* being used in both senses. It is widely felt, though, that this distinction should be upheld, at least in writing.

5.1.6 *solch-* 'such'

solch- occurs in a number of forms, i.e.:

- inflected *solcher*, which declines like *dieser* (Table 5.1), except that in the genitive singular masculine and neuter it usually has the ending *-en*, not *-es*, if the noun has the ending *-(e)s*, e.g. *Der Vorzug solchen Spieles* (*Th. Mann*).
- endingless *solch*, used with an indefinite article: *solch ein Unsinn*.
- *solch-* used after the indefinite article *ein* or another determiner, with the endings of an adjective: *ein solches Buch, jeder solche Gedanke*.

The use of these various forms may be summarised as follows:

(a) The commonest variants for the determiner are *ein solcher* in the singular and *solche* in the plural

This applies both to written and spoken German:

Eine solche Auflockerung könnte dem politischen Diskurs gut bekommen (*Zeit*)	*Such a relaxation of tension could benefit the political debate*
Einen solchen Wagen würde ich nie kaufen	*I would never buy a car like that*
Solchen Leuten kann man alles erzählen	*You can tell people like that anything*
solche großen Häuser	*such big houses*

NB: In colloquial speech, *so ein* is also current in the singular for 'such a', e.g. *in so einer Stadt, so ein Geschenk*. In the plural, simple *so* may be used, e.g. *Das sind so Sachen*, but this is clearly considered substandard.

(b) Inflected *solcher* as a determiner in the singular is found principally in formal, especially literary registers

bei **solchem** Wetter	*in such weather*
ein Mann, der **solchem** Rat nicht folgte (*Hildesheimer*)	*a man who failed to follow such advice*

(c) Usage as a determiner with a following adjective

(i) The most usual equivalent with singular count nouns for English *such a* followed by an adjective is *ein so* (more colloquial *so ein*):

ein so großes Haus ⎱ **so ein** großes Haus ⎰	*such a big house*

(ii) In spoken German *so* is also used with plural count nouns and singular mass nouns, but the written language prefers inflected *solcher*:

so große Häuser (spoken) **solche** großen Häusern (written) ⎰	*such big houses*
bei **so** gutem Wetter (spoken) bei **solchem** guten Wetter (written) ⎰	*in such good weather*

(iii) In literary registers uninflected *solch* is not uncommon if an adjective follows. It also occurs in a few set phrases:

Der Westen ließ sich von **solch** verfehlter Ablehnung allen Verhandelns leiten (*Zeit*)	*The West allowed itself to be guided by such a mistaken rejection of any negotiations*
mit **solch** unermüdlichem Eifer	*with such tireless enthusiasm*
Solch dummes Gerede!	*Such stupid gossip!*

(d) Uninflected *solch* can be used in formal registers with a following indefinite article

This is more emphatic than if the article comes first:

Solch einem Experten sollte das nicht passieren	*That shouldn't happen to **such** an expert*

NB: Uninflected *solch* is sometimes used without *ein* before a singular neuter noun, e.g.: *solch Wetter*. This sounds old-fashioned.

(e) Pronoun usage

(i) The most usual variants are *solche* (plural) and *so einer* (singular):

Ich habe **solche** oft gesehen	*I've often seen ones like that*
So eines kann ich mir nicht leisten	*I can't afford one like that*

(ii) Singular *solcher* is used after *als*:

Der Fall als **solcher** interessiert mich	*The case as such interests me*

(iii) Singular *(k)ein solcher* is restricted to literary registers. In the singular it sounds rather stilted:

Sie hatte auch **einen solchen**	*She had one like that, too*
Leider haben wir **keine solchen** mehr	*I'm afraid we haven't got any more like that*

(f) The adjective *derartig* is a common, more emphatic alternative to *solch*

It is used with *ein* in the singular, or a zero article in either singular or plural:

Er fuhr mit einer **derartigen** Geschwindigkeit gegen die Mauer, daß ...	*He drove into the wall at such a speed, that ...*
Erfahrung im Umgang mit **derartiger** Kälte hat niemand (*Bednarz*)	*Nobody has experience in dealing with that degree of cold*
Derartige Gerüchte hören wir oft	*We often hear rumours like those*

If another adjective follows, *derartig* may be uninflected, e.g.: *Er fuhr mit einer derartig(en) hohen Geschwindigkeit gegen die Mauer, daß ...* In some contexts, though, there can be a difference in meaning. Compare *ein derartig dummes Geschwätz* (i.e. 'gossip which is stupid to such an extent') and *ein derartiges dummes Geschwätz* (i.e. 'such gossip which is stupid').

(g) *dergleichen* and *derlei*

dergleichen and *derlei* do not decline. They are used as determiners or pronouns meaning 'suchlike', 'that kind/sort of':

Dergleichen Behauptungen stören mich	*Assertions like that bother me*
nichts **dergleichen**	*nothing of the kind*
und **dergleichen** mehr (abbrev. u.dgl.m.).	*and so forth*
Er hatte ein langes Messer oder **dergleichen** in der Tasche	*He had a long knife or something of the kind in his pocket*
Die rotblonde Miß Leclerc hatte **derlei** Tricks nicht nötig (*BILD*)	*The strawberry blonde Miss Leclerc didn't need tricks like that*
Sie sah **derlei** nicht ungern (*Jacob*)	*She wasn't averse to that kind of thing*

5.2 Possessives

5.2.1 The possessives have distinct base forms for each of the persons

These are given in Table 5.2 together with the personal pronoun to which they relate.

NB: (i) To refer back to indefinites, the masculine form *sein* is used: *Wer hat **seine** Zahnbörste vergessen? Niemand hatte **sein** Heft mit.*

(ii) A demonstrative is sometimes used instead of a third person possessive to avoid ambiguity, cf. 5.1.1f.

TABLE 5.2 *Form of the possessives*

Base form for each person	
ich	mein
du	dein
er	sein
sie	ihr
es	sein
wir	unser
ihr	euer
Sie	Ihr
sie	ihr

5.2.2 When used as determiners the possessives have the same endings as the indefinite article

Table 5.3 gives the forms of *mein* 'my'. The following is to be noted in relation to the declension of the possessive determiners:

TABLE 5.3 *Declension of the possessive determiner*

	Masculine	Feminine	Neuter	Plural
Nom.	mein	meine	mein	meine
Acc.	meinen	meine	mein	meine
Gen.	meines	meiner	meines	meiner
Dat.	meinem	meiner	meinem	meinen

(a) The *-er* of *unser* and *euer* is part of the stem and *not* an ending
The endings are attached to this stem e.g. *unseres, euere*.

(b) When *unser* and *euer* have an ending, the *-e-* of the stem is often dropped
e.g. *unsrer, unsren, eurer, euren*. Alternatively, the *-e-* of the endings *-en* or *-em* may be dropped, e.g. *unsern, unserm, euern, euerm*.

With *unser*, the full forms are the more usual ones in written German, although the reduced forms, which are the norm in speech, are quite permissible.

With *euer*, the forms with no *-e-* in the stem, i.e. *euren, eurer, eures, eurem*, are by far the most common in both spoken and written German.

5.2.3 Used as pronouns, the possessives have the endings of *dieser*

Table 5.4 gives the full forms of *meiner* 'mine'.

(a) The forms of the possessive pronouns
(i) Note in particular the endings in the nominative singular masculine and the nominative/accusative singular neuter (*meiner, meines*, etc.) which differ from the endingless forms of the possessive determiner. Compare:

Das ist nicht **mein** Hut, sondern **deiner**
Hast du **dein** Fahrrad? Ich sehe **mein(e)s** nicht
Ihr Garten ist größer als **uns(e)rer**
Er sprach mit **meinen** Eltern, ich mit **seinen**
Ich nehme **uns(e)ren** Wagen. In **seinem** habe ich immer Angst

TABLE 5.4 *Declension of the possessive pronoun*

	Masculine	Feminine	Neuter	Plural
Nom.	meiner	meine	meines	meine
Acc.	meinen	meine	meines	meine
Gen.	meines	meiner	meines	meiner
Dat.	meinem	meiner	meinem	meinen

(ii) The *-e-* of the nominative/accusative neuter ending *-es* is often dropped in writing and almost always in speech, i.e. *meins, deins*. With *unseres* and *eueres* the *-e-* of the stem is dropped, i.e. *unsers, euers*. Otherwise, *unserer* and *euerer* can drop the *-e-* of the stem or the ending as with the possessive determiner, cf. 5.2.2 above.

(iii) Endingless forms of the possessive are occasionally found in set phrases, archaic expressions or poetic language:

> Er kann **mein** und **dein** nicht unterscheiden   **Dein** ist mein Herz!
> Die Welt ist **unser**   Die Rache ist **mein**

(b) Alternative forms of the possessive pronoun
The following forms occur as alternatives to *meiner, deiner, unserer*, etc.:

(i) *der meinige* 'mine', *der deinige* 'yours', *der uns(e)rige* 'ours', etc.

(ii) *der meine* 'mine', *der deine* 'yours', *der uns(e)re* 'ours', etc.

In these, the possessive forms are used as adjectives and have adjective endings. They are less common than *meiner*, etc., being found mainly in formal written German. Type **(ii)** is rather more emphatic than *meiner*, etc., whilst type **(i)** is current mainly in set phrases, e.g.: *die Deinigen* 'your people' (i.e. your family); *Ich habe das Meinige getan* 'I've done my bit'.

5.2.4 Differences between German and English in the use of the possessives

(a) A definite article is often used rather than a possessive to refer to parts of the body and articles of clothing
e.g.: *Sie hat sich **den** Arm gebrochen.* Details are given in 4.6.

(b) Some idiomatic equivalents

Das gehört mir. Gehört das dir?	*That's mine. Is that yours?*
ein Freund von mir einer meiner Freunde }	*a friend of mine*
Freunde von mir	*friends of mine*
Das ist eins von meinen Büchern	*That's a book of mine*
Mein Vater und meine Mutter (cf. 4.1.1b)	*My father and mother*

5.3 Interrogatives

5.3.1 *welcher* 'which'

(a) *welcher* **has the same endings as** *dieser*

The forms are the same whether it is used as a determiner or a pronoun and are as given in Table 5.1. Further notes on the forms of *welcher*:

(i) Before an adjective the endingless form *welch* is sometimes used, in formal written German only, as an alternative to the declined form:

> **Welch** berühmter Schriftsteller hat diesen Roman geschrieben?
> Die Künstler zeigten, **welch** reiches Kulturgut sie mitbrachten (*MM*)

(ii) In the genitive singular masculine and neuter the determiner can have the ending *-en* rather than *-es* if the following noun has the ending *-(e)s*:

> Welchen/Welches Kindes Buch ist das?
> Innerhalb welchen Zeitraumes müssen nicht bestandene Prüfungen wiederholt werden? (*Uni Innsbruck*)

In practice, the genitive tends to be avoided if possible.

(iii) *welcher* may have the neuter singular form *welches* when it is used as a pronoun in an indefinite sense with the verb *sein*, irrespective of the gender and number of the noun it refers to, e.g.:

> **Welches** ist die jüngere Schwester?   **Welches** sind die besten Zeitungen?
> **Welches** ist der längste Fluß in Amerika?

Welche(r), in agreement with the following noun, would be equally possible in the above examples, e.g.: *Welche ist die jüngere Schwester?* etc.

(b) *welcher* **can be used as a determiner or a pronoun**

Welches Bier willst du trinken?	*Which beer do you want to drink?*
Welchen Zug nehmen wir denn?	*Which train shall we take?*
Aus **welchem** Land kommt sie denn?	*Which country does she come from?*
Welcher berühmte Schriftsteller hat diesen Roman geschrieben?	*Which famous author wrote this novel?*
Hier sind zwei gute Romane. **Welchen** möchtest du zuerst lesen?	*Here are two good novels. Which one would you like to read first?*
Er fragte mich, **welchen** (Roman) ich zuerst lesen wollte	*He asked me which (novel) I wanted to read first*

(c) *welcher* **is used in exclamations (= 'What (a) ...!)**

> Welcher Unterschied!   Welche Überraschung!   Welcher schöne Tag!
> Welchen unglaublichen Unsinn hat er geredet!

Endingless *welch* is an alternative to the declined form *welcher* in exclamations if *ein* or an adjective follows:

> **Welch** eine Überraschung!   **Welch** ein Unterschied!
> **Welch** unglaublichen Unsinn hat er geredet!   **Welch** (ein) schöner Tag!

Der Smogalarm machte erneut deutlich, in **welch** hohem Maße die Luft mit Giftstoffen verseucht ist (*MM*)	*The smog alarm made it clear once again to what high degree the air is polluted with poisonous substances*

This exclamatory use of *welch(er)* is mainly found in formal German. *was für (ein)*, cf. 5.3.2, is more current in speech.

NB: The form *welcher* has a number of other uses, i.e.:
    (i) as a relative pronoun (= 'who', 'which'), see 5.4.2.
    (ii) as an indefinite (= 'some', 'any'), see 5.5.26.

5.3.2 *was für (ein[er])* 'what kind of (a)'

(a) *was für (ein[er])* can be used as a determiner or a pronoun

(i) Used as a determiner, *ein* in *was für ein* declines like the indefinite article, see Table 4.2. It is absent in the plural and before mass nouns in the singular:

Aus **was für einer** Familie stammt er?	*From what kind of a family does he come?*
Sie können sich denken, in **was für einer** schwierigen Lage ich mich befand	*You can imagine in what an awkward situation I found myself*
Was für ausländische Marken haben Sie?	*What kinds of foreign stamps do you have?*
Was für Käse soll ich kaufen?	*What kind of cheese shall I buy?*

Note that the case of *ein* depends on the role of the phrase in the sentence, i.e. it is *not* dependent on *für*.

(ii) The form *was für einer* 'what kind (of a one)' is used as a pronoun, with *einer* having the endings of the pronoun *meiner*, see Table 5.2. In the plural *was für welche* is used:

Er hat sich ein neues Auto gekauft.	*He has bought a new car*
Was für ein(e)s?	*What kind?*
Ich habe ihr Blumen gebracht.	*I took her some flowers*
Was für welche?	*What kind?*

NB: (i) *was für welcher* is used in place of *was für einer* in the singular in colloquial north German speech, e.g.: *Er hat einen neuen Wagen gekauft. – Was für welchen?*
    (ii) *was für (ein)* is also used in concessive clauses, see 19.6.2c.

(b) *was* is often separated from *für (ein[er])*

This is especially frequent in speech, but the construction is also used in writing:

Was hast du denn **für ein** Auto gekauft?	**Was** sind das **für** Vögel?

(c) *was für (ein[er])* is used in exclamations (= 'What (a)...!')

It is in practice commoner than *welcher*, cf. 5.3.1c, especially in less formal registers. In this usage the separated form is more frequent:

Was für eine Chance!	*What a chance!*
Was für herrliche Blumen!	*What lovely flowers!*
Er ist ein Schauspieler – und **was für einer!**	*He's an actor – and what an actor!*
Was sind das **für** wunderschöne Häuser!	*What lovely houses these are!*

If there is a verb in these exclamations, it may, alternatively, go to the end, like in a subordinate clause: *Was für wunderschöne Häuser das **sind!***

(d) In speech *was für* (*ein*[*er*]) is often used for *welcher* 'which'
cf. 5.3.1. This usage is considered substandard:

Was für ein Kleid ziehst du an?   *Which dress are you going to wear?*

5.3.3 *wer, was* 'who', 'what'

(a) *wer* **and** *was* **are used only as pronouns**
(i) *wer*, like English *who*, only refers to persons. It does not distinguish gender
and it has the following case forms:

Nom. wer
Acc. wen
Gen. wessen
Dat. wem

Examples of use:

Wer hat diesen Brief geschrieben?   *Who wrote this letter?*
Wen hast du heute gesprochen?   *Who(m) did you speak to today?*
Wem wollten sie vorhin helfen?   *Who(m) did they want to help just now?*
Mit **wem** hast du gespielt?   *Who(m) did you play with?*
Wessen Bücher sind das?   *Whose books are those?*
Ich kann Ihnen sagen, **wer** spielte   *I can tell you who was playing*

(ii) *was*, like English *what*, refers only to things. Its only case form is the genitive
wessen:

Was bewegt sich dort im Gebüsch?   *What is moving there in the bushes?*
Was hat sie dir zum Geburtstag   *What did she give you for your*
geschenkt?   *birthday?*
Wessen schämst du dich?   *What are you ashamed of?*
Weißt du, **was** er getan hat?   *Do you know what he did?*

wessen, whether referring to people or things, is felt to be clumsy and tends to be
avoided, even in written German. Thus *Wem gehören diese Bücher?* is used rather
than *Wessen Bücher sind das?* and *Warum schämst du dich?* rather than *Wessen
schämst du dich?*

As *was* has no dative, a paraphrase has to be used in constructions where it
would be needed, e.g.:

Welcher Ursache kann man seinen   *To what can one ascribe his success?*
Erfolg zuschreiben?   *(Literally 'To what cause . . .?')*

(b) **Nominative** *wer* **and** *was* **are usually followed by a singular verb**
(i) Compare the examples in (a) above and the following:

Wer **kommt** denn morgen?   *Who's coming tomorrow?*
Was **liegt** dort in der Ecke?   *What's that lying there in the corner?*

(ii) However, with *sein* the appropriate singular or plural form of the verb is
used, as in English:

Wer **ist** das an der Tür?   *Who's that at the door?*
Wer **sind** diese Leute?   *Who are those people?*
Was **ist** der Vogel da?   *What's that bird there?*
Was **sind** die längsten Flüsse der Welt?   *What are the longest rivers in the world?*

(iii) To emphasise quantity, *alles* is often added to sentences with *wer* and *was*. This usage is chiefly colloquial, e.g.:

Wer kommt denn morgen alles?	*What people are coming tomorrow?*
Wen kennen Sie hier alles?	*What people do you know here?*
Was hat er denn alles gefragt?	*What were the things he asked?*

(c) *was* is not used in combination with most prepositions

(i) The compound forms *wo(r)* + preposition, e.g. *woran, womit, wozu*, etc., are used instead. These forms are a sub-type of the prepositional adverb, cf. 3.5:

Womit schreibst du?	*What are you writing with?*
Worauf soll ich mich setzen?	*What shall I sit on?*
Worüber sprechen Sie?	*What are you talking about?*
Ich habe gehört, **worum** er gebeten hat	*I heard what he was asking for*

NB: The following prepositions are *not* used in the form with *wo(r)*-: *außer, gegenüber, hinter, neben, ohne, seit, zwischen*.

(ii) The forms *wodurch, wonach, wovon* and *wozu* can only be used if there is no idea of movement involved, e.g.:

Wodurch weiß er das?	*How is it that he knows that?*
Wonach soll man sich denn richten?	*By what is one to be guided?*
Wovon sollen wir leben?	*What are we to live on?*
Wozu gebraucht man das?	*What is that used for?*

Compare: *durch was?* 'through what?', *von wo?* or *woher?* 'where ... from?', *wohin?* 'where ... to?'.

(iii) In colloquial German *was* (irrespective of case) is often heard with a preposition instead of *wo(r)* + preposition, e.g.: *Von was sollen wir leben?* This usage is considered substandard.

(d) *wer* and *was* are commonly used in exclamations

Wer hätte so was erwartet!	*Who would have expected such a thing!*
Wem hat er nicht alles geholfen!	*Who(m) hasn't he helped!*
Was <u>haben</u> wir gelacht!	*How we laughed!*
Was er nicht alles tut!	*The things he does!*

(e) *was* can be followed by an adjective used as a noun, with the neuter ending *-es*

See 6.4 for further details on these forms. The adjective is separated from *was* and placed later in the sentence:

Was haben sie **Wichtiges** besprochen?	*What important matters did they discuss?*
Was ist **Komisches** dran?	*What's funny about it?*
Was könnt ihr hier **anderes** erwarten?	*What else can you expect here?*
(Fallada)	

(f) *was* can be used in the sense of 'why?' or 'what for?'

This usage is restricted to colloquial German:

Was sitzt ihr da rum?	*What are you doing just sitting around?*

was in this usage often carries a tone of reproach.

(g) Idiomatic differences between German and English

In a few contexts German has *wie* where English uses *what*, i.e.:

Wie ist Ihr Name, bitte?	*What is your name, please?*
Wie heißt Ihr Bruder?	*What's your brother called?*
Wie ist das Buch?	*What's the book like?*

(h) Other uses of *wer* and *was*

(i) *wer* and *was* are used as relative pronouns (= 'who', 'which', 'that') in some contexts, see 5.4.3 and 5.4.5a.

(ii) *wer* and *was* are used in some concessive clauses (i.e. = 'whoever', 'whatever'), see 19.6.2.

(iii) For the colloquial use of *wer* as an indefinite (i.e. = 'someone'), see 5.5.27.

5.4 Relative pronouns

5.4.1 *der* 'who', 'which', 'that'

(a) *der* is the most commonly used relative pronoun in German

The relative pronoun *der* declines like the demonstrative pronoun *der*, see Table 5.1. *der* agrees in **gender** and **number** with the noun it refers to (called the 'antecedent'), and takes its **case** from its function within the clause which it introduces. Unlike English, the relative pronoun is *never* omitted in German:

Das Buch, **das** ich lese, ist recht interessant	*The book I am reading is very interesting*
Ich kannte den Mann, **der** gestern gestorben ist	*I knew the man who died yesterday*
Mein Balkon, **den** ich endlich einmal nutzen konnte, erwies sich als sehr praktisch	*My balcony, which I was at last able to use, proved very convenient*
Der Mann, **dem** ich helfe, ist sehr alt	*The man I am helping is very old*
ein Zwischenfall, **dessen** Butkus sich ein Leben lang schämen sollte (*Surminski*)	*an incident which Butkus was to be ashamed of all his life*
Wir kamen an die Straße, an **deren** anderem Ende er wohnt	*We came to the street, at the other end of which he lives*

NB: If a relative pronoun refers back to two (or more) nouns linked by *oder*, it agrees in gender and number with the nearest, e.g.: *das Loch oder der Graben, in **den** er gestürzt ist.*

(b) Relative clauses are less frequent in spoken German than in writing

In speech a construction with a main clause (and the verb in second place) and the demonstrative pronoun *der* is often used rather than a dependent relative clause (with the verb at the end). Although not unknown, this is felt to be poor style in writing, unless colloquial speech is being imitated, as in the following examples:

Er trug ein Heft bei sich, **in dem** standen die Namen der fünfzig Verräter (*E.W. Heine*)	*He had a little book with him in which the names of the fifty traitors were written down*
Es gibt Leute, **die** freuen sich über die Fahrt (*Bichsel*)	*There are people who are pleased about the trip*

(c) The genitive of *der*

(i) The genitive of *der* corresponds to English 'whose' or 'of which':

die Frau, **deren** Name ich immer vergesse	*the woman whose name I always forget*
Sie blickten auf das Mietshaus gegenüber, in **dessen** Erdgeschoß sich eine Schreibwarenhandlung befand	*They looked out on the apartment house opposite, on the ground floor of which there was a stationer's*

(ii) In the genitive plural and the genitive singular feminine *derer* may be used rather than *deren*:

ein Zusammenhang ausgebildeter Verfahrensweisen, innerhalb **derer** der einzelne Wissenschaftler seine besondre Aufgabe erfüllt (*Bollnow*)	*a framework of established procedures within which the individual scientist carries out his own particular task*
die ungewöhnliche Autorität, **derer** sich die katholischen Bischöfe in Polen erfreuen (*Spiegel*)	*the extraordinary authority which is enjoyed by the Catholic bishops in Poland*

This usage is labelled 'incorrect' by DUDEN (1995: 340), but *derer* is in practice more frequent than *deren*, especially in the plural. However, *deren* is preferred if a noun follows: *die Frau, deren Tochter du kennst.*

(iii) After prepositions, the shorter form *der* also occurs for *deren*:

eine lange Übergangszeit von sechs Jahren, innerhalb **der** die Länder die Juristenausbildung umstellen können (*Zeit*)	*a long transitional period of six years, within which the Länder can reorganise the training of lawyers*

(iv) Constructions of the type *one of whom, most of which, some of which* correspond to constructions with *von denen* in German, e.g.:

die Studenten, **von denen** ich **einen** nicht kenne	*the students, one of whom I don't know*
eine Anzahl Jungen, **von denen** ich **die meisten** kenne	*a number of boys, most of whom I know*
viele Bilder, **von denen einige** ganz gut sind	*a lot of pictures, some of which are quite good*

(v) It is incorrect (though a common mistake by Germans) to decline *dessen* and *deren*, i.e.: *ein Mann, von dessen* (not *dessem*) *Erfolg ich hörte.*

(vi) *dessen* and *deren* are compounded with *-halben, -wegen* and *-willen* with the insertion of a *-t-*, e.g. *derentwegen, um dessentwillen*:

das Außenhandelsgesetz, **dessentwegen** Nixon so lange mit dem Kongreß kämpft (*Welt*)	*The foreign trade bill, because of which Nixon has been battling so long with Congress*

(d) Relative pronouns with first and second person personal pronouns

Normally, the pronoun is repeated in the relative clause, e.g.:

du, der/die **du** ja nicht alles wissen kannst für mich, die **ich** noch gar nicht ordentlich lesen konnte (*Dönhoff*)	*you, who cannot know everything for me, who couldn't read properly yet*

The alternative construction with a third person verb, e.g.: *ich, der seit 20 Jahren seinem Volke dient (FAZ)*, is possible, but less frequent in practice, cf. Freund (1989).

5.4.2 *welcher* 'who', 'which', 'that'

(a) *welcher* is chiefly used as a stylistic variant of *der*
It has the same endings as *dieser*, see Table 5.1, but it is not normally used in the genitive. It is restricted to formal written German, and even there it is much less frequent than *der*. DUDEN (1985: 755) considers it clumsy and advises against its use. Examples:

die Gerüchte, **welche** über die wirtschaftliche Lage meines Vaters am Orte umgelaufen waren (*Th. Mann*)	*The rumours which had been circulating in the town about my father's financial situation*
Der Herr tat doch immer so, als umgäbe ihn eine vielköpfige Familie, **welcher** er Anweisungen zu geben hätte (*Grass*)	*The gentleman always acted as if he was surrounded by a large family to which he had to give instructions*

It is most frequent (although never necessary) to avoid repeating forms of *der*:

Die, **welche** zuletzt kamen, waren erschöpft

Compare, though, as perfectly acceptable (cf. 5.4.5b):

Die, **die** gingen, haben in der DDR mehr verändert, als die, **die** geblieben sind (*FR*)

(b) *welcher* is used in formal German before a noun which refers back to part or whole of the preceding clause
This use corresponds to that of English *which*. In this construction *welcher* agrees with the following noun for case, number and gender:

Er wurde zum Stadtdirektor ernannt, **welches Amt** er gewissenhaft verwaltete	*He was appointed town-clerk, which office he administered conscientiously*
Er sagte ihr, sie müsse den Betrag sofort zurückzahlen, **welcher Forderung** sie dann auch nachging	*He told her she had to repay the amount immediately, which request she then complied with*

5.4.3 *was* is used as a relative pronoun in some contexts

The only case form of *was* in this usage is the genitive *wessen*, which tends to be avoided. After prepositions, forms of *was* are replaced by the prepositional adverb in *wo(r)-*, see 5.4.4b. *was* is used:

(a) After neuter indefinites
i.e. *alles, einiges, etwas, folgendes, manches, nichts, vieles, weniges*:

Nichts/Etwas/Alles, **was** er sagte, war mir neu	*Nothing/Something/Everything (that) he said was new to me*
Sie mieden alles, **was** ihre Unabhängigkeit einschränken könnte (*Walser*)	*They avoided anything which could restrict their independence*

After *etwas*, *das* may be used as an alternative to *was* if something specific is referred to:

Gerade in diesem Moment fiel ihr etwas ein, **das** sie erstarren ließ: Die Gasrechnung (*Baum*)	*Just then she remembered something that made her go rigid: the gas bill*
Ich erinnere mich an etwas Merkwürdiges, **das** er sagte	*I remember something strange that he said*

das is occasionally found after other indefinites, but this usage is considered incorrect, cf. DUDEN (1985: 37).

NB: *was* is often heard for *das* to refer to a neuter noun, e.g.: *das Buch,* **was** *er mir geliehen hat.* This usage is considered substandard.

(b) After a neuter adjective used as a noun referring to something indefinite

This usage is particularly frequent with superlatives:

Das Richtige, **was** man sich ansehen müßte, finden wir nie (*Fallada*)	*The right things [in museums] that one ought to look at, we never find*
Das erste, **was** Evelyn sah, waren Mariannes Augen (*Baum*)	*The first thing Evelyn saw was Marianne's eyes*

If the adjective refers to something specific, *das* can be used: *Das Gute,* **das** *er getan hat, wird ihn überdauern*, although the difference in meaning can be very slight. However, *was* is *always* used after superlatives.

(c) After the indefinite demonstrative *das*

Eben das, **was** uns fehlte, hat er uns verweigert	*He denied us just what we were lacking*

If *das* is in the genitive or dative, or after a preposition, it cannot be omitted. In English, by contrast, only *what* may be needed. Compare:

Ich hörte nichts von **dem, was** er mir sagte	*I didn't hear anything of what he said to me*
eine Antwort auf **das, was** er gerade dachte (*Walser*)	*an answer to what he was just thinking*
ein eifriger Leser dessen, **was** neu auf den Markt kommt (*Zeit*)	*a keen reader of what is new on the market*

(d) To refer back to a whole clause

Er hat sein Examen bestanden, **was** mich sehr erstaunt	*He has passed his examination, which surprises me very much*
Er sagte, er hätte mich damals gesehen, **was** ich nicht glauben konnte	*He said he had seen me then, which I couldn't believe*

5.4.4 Relative pronouns after prepositions

(a) Normal usage is the appropriate form of *der* after the preposition

The construction corresponds more closely to that of written English than to that with a 'stranded' preposition typical of spoken English. Compare the alternative renderings for the first example:

die Frau, **auf die** Sie warten	*the woman for whom you are waiting*
	the woman (who) you are waiting for
der Stuhl, **auf den** du dich setzen wolltest	*the chair you wanted to sit down on*
der Stuhl, **auf dem** du sitzt	*the chair you are sitting on*
der Bleistift, **mit dem** sie schreibt	*the pencil she is writing with*
die Stadt, **in der** ich wohne	*the town I live in*

(b) The form *wo(r)* + preposition as a relative pronoun

The forms of the prepositional adverb in *wo(r)*- (e.g. *worauf, woran, wovon*, etc., cf. 5.3.3c) are used as relative pronouns in some constructions.

(i) The form *wo(r)* + preposition is used in all contexts where *was* is used as a relative pronoun (cf. 5.4.3), as a substitute for preposition plus *was*, which does not occur:

Das, **woran** du denkst, errate ich nie	*I'll never guess what you're thinking of*
Es kam etwas, **womit** kein Mensch auf der Welt hätte rechnen können (*Süßkind*)	*Something came which nobody on earth could have reckoned with*
Er hat sein Examen bestanden, **worüber** ich mich freue	*He has passed his examination, which I am very pleased about*

If *etwas* refers to something specific, preposition + *das* can be used instead of *wo(r)* + preposition: *Ich spürte, daß noch etwas geschehen war ... etwas, **für das** sich nur ein Anlaß ergeben hatte* (*Lenz*).

(ii) *wo(r)* + preposition used to be a common alternative to the preposition followed by *der* to refer to things, e.g.: *das Heim, **worin** ich geboren wurde* (*Th. Mann*). It is now much less usual even in formal writing.

The use of prepositional adverb with *da(r)*- (e.g. *darauf, daran*, cf. 3.5) as a relative pronoun to refer to things, e.g.: *das Heim, **darin** ich geboren wurde*, is now obsolete.

5.4.5 'the one who', 'he/she who', 'that which'

There are a number of German equivalents for these English constructions.

(a) *wer* and *was* may be used in generalisations as compound relatives

Wer viele Freunde hat, ist glücklich	*He who has many friends is happy*
Wer wagt, gewinnt	*Who dares wins*
Und **was** noch schlimmer ist, er merkt es selber nicht	*And what is worse, he doesn't realise it himself*
Was du sagst, stimmt nicht	*What you say is not right*

If there is a difference in case or construction between the two clauses, an appropriate form of the demonstrative will normally be added to begin the main clause:

Wem du traust, **der** wird dir auch trauen	*He whom you trust will also trust you*
Was wir getan haben, **darüber** müssen wir auch Rechenschaft ablegen	*What we have done we shall also have to answer for*

However, cases where such a clarifying demonstrative is not used are by no means rare. For details see Leirbukt (1995):

Wen es zum Lehrerberuf hinzieht, bevorzugt eher die philosophischen Fächer (*Zeit*)	*Those who are attracted to the teaching profession favour arts subjects*

(b) Where a demonstrative pronoun is followed by a relative pronoun, the following alternatives are found

(i) Demonstrative *der* followed by relative *der*. Despite the repetition, this is the commonest alternative in practice:

Die, die gingen, haben in der DDR mehr verändert, als **die, die** geblieben sind (*FR*)	*Those who left have changed more in the GDR than those who stayed*

(ii) Demonstrative *der* followed by relative *welcher*. This alternative is restricted to more elevated styles:

Die, welche ich kaufen wollte, waren mir zu teuer	*The ones I wanted to buy were too expensive for me*

(iii) Demonstrative *derjenige* followed by relative *der* or (in elevated style) *welcher*. This is frequent in both speech and writing:

Diejenigen, die (welche) in den hinteren Reihen saßen, konnten nichts sehen	*Those who were sitting on the back rows couldn't see anything*

(iv) Demonstrative *jener* followed by relative *der* (or *welcher*). This is not uncommon in formal writing, although DUDEN (1985: 370) calls it 'incorrect':

Der deutsche Zug darf nicht aufgehalten werden von **jenen, die** sich hinter Europa verstecken, um Deutschland zu verhindern (*ARD*)	*The train called Germany mustn't be held up by those people who are hiding behind Europe in order to prevent a (united) Germany*

(v) *der* can be used as a compound relative (e.g. 'he who'). This is common in speech:

Die hier sitzen, sind Verfluchte (*Wolf*)	*Those who are sitting here are cursed*
Der ihm Brötchen und Bockwurst verkaufte, kam aus Winsen an der Luhe (*Surminski*)	*The man who sold him rolls and sausage came from Winsen an der Luhe*

5.4.6 Other forms of the relative

(a) To refer to a place, *wo* can be used as a relative as an alternative to *der* with a preposition

die Stadt, **wo** (*or* in der) ich wohne	*the town where I live*

If motion to or from a place is involved, *wohin* or *woher* are used:

die Stadt, **wohin** (*or* in die) ich ging	*the town to which I went*
das Dorf, **woher** (*or* aus dem) er kam	*the village from which he came*

NB: The use of *wo* as a general relative pronoun (e.g.: die Frau, **wo** jetzt kommt) is a substandard regionalism.

(b) Usage with time words

In such contexts English often uses *when* as a relative. A number of alternatives exist in German, depending on register:

(i) Preposition with *der* is the most widely accepted form for writing:

Den Tag, **an dem** er ankam, werde ich nie vergessen	*I shall never forget the day when he arrived*
in einer Zeit, **in der** die Jugend immer unabhängiger wird	*at a time when youth is becoming more and more independent*

(ii) *als* (for past time) or *wenn* (for present or future time) are possible alternatives. In formal (especially literary) German *da* is often used:

In dem Augenblick, **als** der Hund aufsprang, schrie er (*Valentin*)	*At the moment when the dog jumped up, he shouted*
an seinem nächsten Geburtstag, **wenn** er volljährig wird	*on his next birthday, when he comes of age*
Ach, wo sind die Zeiten, **da** Pinneberg sich für einen guten Verkäufer hielt? (*Fallada*)	*Alas, where are the days when Pinneberg considered himself a good salesman?*

(iii) The use of *wo* as a relative indicating time is common, especially in speech. Although it is widely used in writing, many Germans consider it to be colloquial and prefer other alternatives in formal registers:

im Augenblick, **wo** er die Tür aufmachte	*at the moment when he opened the door*
Wir leben in einer Zeit, **wo** Verkaufen arm macht (*Remarque*)	*We live in times when selling makes one poor*
jetzt, **wo** ich das weiß	*now that I know that*

(c) *wie* **is used to indicate manner, principally after** *die Art*

die Art, wie er zu mir sprach	*the manner in which he spoke to me*
so, wie ich es gewohnt bin	*just as I am used to*

(d) *warum* **is used to indicate cause, chiefly after** *der Grund*

weshalb is an alternative in formal registers:

der Grund, warum (weshalb) ich nach Breslau ging	*the reason why I went to Wrocław*

5.5 Indefinites, quantifiers and other determiners and pronouns

This section explains the meaning and use of the remaining determiners and pronouns. A list of them is given in Table 5.5.

NB: For the declension of adjectives after these determiners see 6.2.3.

TABLE 5.5 *Indefinites, quantifiers and other pronouns*

aller, alle	irgend(-)	meinesgleichen
ander	jeder	nichts
beide(s)	jedermann	niemand
einer	jedweder, jeglicher	sämtlich
ein wenig, ein bißchen	jemand	unsereiner
ein paar	kein, keiner	viel, viele
einige(r)	lauter	wenig, wenige
etliche	man	welcher
etwas	manch, mancher	wer
folgende(r)	mehrere	

5.5.1 *aller, alle* 'all (the)'

(a) *all-* 'all (the)', used as a determiner, has various alternative forms

(i) Inflected *aller*, with the endings of *dieser* (see Table 5.1), used on its own:

Alle Kinder spielen gern	*All children like playing*
Alle Schüler waren gekommen	*All the pupils had come*
mit **allen** denkbaren Mitteln	*with all conceivable means*
alles Glück dieser Erde	*all the happiness of this world*

This is the commonest alternative in the plural, especially in the nominative and accusative. In the singular it is largely restricted to formal registers and set phrases.

NB: (i) In the genitive singular masculine and neuter, the ending *-en* is now preferred to *-es* if the noun has the ending *-(e)s*, e.g.: *solch verfehlte Ablehnung allen* (less frequent: *alles*) *Verhandelns* (*Zeit*).

(ii) Plural *alle* may correspond to English 'all' or 'all (of) the'. *alle* is <u>never</u> followed by a genitive, so that *alle Schüler* is the equivalent of 'all the pupils' or 'all of the pupils'.

(ii) Inflected *aller* followed by the definite article:

alle die Bücher	*all the books*
alle die Mühe	*all the trouble*

This is quite common, especially in colloquial speech, in the plural, and with feminine nouns in the nominative and accusative singular.

(iii) Uninflected *all* followed by the definite article:

all das schlechte Wetter	*all the bad weather*
all die Schüler	*all the pupils*
mit **all dem** Geld	*with all the money*

This is the most frequent alternative in the singular, and it is quite frequent in the plural. Attempts to establish a consistent difference of meaning between inflected and uninflected forms, e.g. DUDEN (1995: 345), are unconvincing.

NB: The most idiomatic equivalent of English *all* with a singular noun is often a phrase with *ganz*, see (g) below.

(b) *all-* **is often used in conjunction with another determiner**
In the plural both inflected and uninflected forms are found, in the singular only uninflected *all*:

> **all mein** Geld von **all diesem** Brot
> **all/alle meine** Brüder nach **all ihrer** Mühe
> mit **all/allen diesen** Schwierigkeiten

NB: Only the inflected form is used before *solch*, which then has the endings of an adjective, e.g.: *alle solchen Frauen*.

(c) *all-* **used as a pronoun declines like** *dieser*
(see Table 5.1), but it has no genitive singular forms. The neuter singular *alles* is used for 'everything', the plural *alle* for 'everyone':

> **Alles** ist bereit *Everything is ready*
> Ich bin mit **allem** einverstanden *I agree to everything*
> **Alle** waren anwesend *Everybody was present*
> Sind das **alle**? *Is that all (of them)?*

(d) Plural *alle* **'all' is often used with a personal pronoun**

> Sie hat uns **alle** beleidigt *She insulted us all*
> Ich habe mit ihnen **allen** gesprochen *I have spoken to all of them*
> Das ist unser **aller** Hoffnung *That is the hope of all of us*

alle usually follows the pronoun, but in the nominative it can be separated from it. In this case it has slightly less emphasis. Compare:

> Sie **alle** sind gekommen }
> Sie sind **alle** gekommen } *They have all come*

(e) Uninflected *all* **and inflected** *alles* **are commonly used with the demonstratives** *das* **and** *dieses*
This corresponds to English 'all that' or 'all this'. Uninflected *all* always precedes the demonstrative, but inflected *alles* may precede or follow the demonstrative or, with less emphasis, be separated from it:

> Ich habe **all das/alles das/**
> **das alles** schon gesehen } *I've already seen all that*
> **Das** habe ich **alles** schon gesehen }
> Ich bin mit **all dem/dem allen/** *I agree to all that*
> **allem dem** einverstanden
> Mit **all diesem** werde ich nicht *I can't cope with all this*
> fertig

NB: In the dative singular, when *all-* follows the demonstrative, it may have the ending *-en* as an alternative to *-em*, e.g.: *dem/diesem allen* or *dem allem*.

(f) A noun can be qualified by a following inflected *all-*
all- follows the verb if the noun comes first. This usage is most common in the plural:

> **Die Kinder** spielen **alle** im Garten
> **Die Semmeln** sind **alle** trocken

In the singular this construction is typical of colloquial speech and is restricted to the nominative and accusative singular feminine and neuter:

> **Das Brot** ist **alles** trocken
> Ich habe **die Milch alle** verschüttet

Singular *alles* is often used with a plural noun after the verb *sein* in the sense 'nothing but', e.g.: *Das sind alles Lügen.*

(g) The use of *ganz* for English 'all'

In practice, the adjective *ganz* is often the most idiomatic equivalent of English 'all', particularly with singular nouns. Thus, English 'all my money' may correspond in German to *mein ganzes Geld* or *all mein Geld*, with the former being used rather more frequent. Compare also:

Der **ganze** Wein war schlecht	*All the wine was bad*
diese **ganze** Unsicherheit	*all this uncertainty*
mit seiner **ganzen** jugendlichen Energie	*with all his youthful energy*

With collective nouns, time expressions and geographical names *ganz* is often the only possible equivalent for English 'all':

Die **ganze** Familie kommt	*all of the family is coming*
den **ganzen** Tag (lang)	*all day (long)*
der **ganze** Januar war kalt	*all January it was cold*
ganz Europa, **ganz** Schweden,	*all (of) Europe, all (of) Sweden,*
ganz München	*all (of) Munich*
in der **ganzen** Schweiz	*in all of Switzerland*

The use of *ganz* with a plural noun is colloquial, e.g.: *Nach dem Sturm waren die ganzen Fenster kaputt.* In such cases *sämtliche* (see 5.5.23) is a common alternative in formal registers, e.g.: *Nach dem Sturm waren **sämtliche** Fenster* ('all the windows') *kaputt.*

(h) Other uses of *all-*

(i) *alles* can be used to emphasise a large number of people or things with the interrogatives *wer* and *was*, cf. 5.3.3b, e.g.:

> Wer kommt denn **alles**?   Was hast du dort **alles** gekauft?

(ii) In regional colloquial speech in the south and west, *all(e)s* (often spelled *als*) is used to emphasise the continuous nature of an action (= English 'keep on doing sth.'):

> Er hat **als** geflucht   *He kept on cursing*

(iii) In colloquial north German *alle* is used in the sense of 'all gone':

> Die Butter ist jetzt **alle**
> Meine Geduld ist **alle**

(iv) *alle* is compounded with the demonstrative pronoun in the phrases *bei alledem* 'for all that', *trotz alledem* 'in spite of all that'.

(v) *alles* occurs frequently with an adjective used as a noun, cf. 6.4.5, e.g.: *alles Wichtige* 'all (the) important things'.

5.5.2 *ander* 'other'

(a) *ander* is in most contexts used as a simple adjective

However, it has a few special forms and uses which resemble those of a determiner or a pronoun. The following examples illustrate the range of its most common uses:

der **and(e)re** Student	*the other student*
mein **anderes** Pferd	*my other horse*
der **and(e)re**	*the other one*
irgendein **and(e)rer**	*some/any other one*
die drei **anderen**	*the three others*
alle **anderen**	*all the others*
alles **and(e)re**	*everything else*

(b) Notes on the spelling and forms of *ander*

(i) The first *-e-* is often dropped in writing, e.g. *andre, andrer, andres*. With the endings *-en* and *-em*, though, it is more usual to drop the second *-e-*, e.g. *ander(e)m, ander(e)n* (less common: *andrem, andren*).

(ii) When used without a following noun, i.e. as a noun or pronoun, it differs from other adjectives in *never* being spelled with a capital letter, as the above examples show.

(iii) When *ander* is used without a preceding article or other determiner, a following adjective has the same ('strong') endings as those of *ander*, *except* that *-en* is the norm in the dative singular masculine and neuter:

anderes dummes Gerede	mit anderer moderner Musik
andere italienische Maler	aus anderem wertvollen Material

NB: (i) 'another cup of tea' = *noch eine Tasse Tee*.
  (ii) For the adverb *anders* 'else', cf. 7.3.5.

5.5.3 *beide* 'both'

(a) *beide* 'both' can be used as a determiner or a pronoun

It has the same endings as the plural of *dieser* (see Table 5.1):

Ich habe **beide** Bücher gekauft	*I bought both books*
Beide Brüder sind gekommen	*Both brothers came*
Seine Brüder sind **beide** gekommen	*His brothers both came*
Beide sind gekommen	*Both came*

beide, used as a pronoun, can be strengthened by *alle*:

Alle beide sind gekommen	*The two of them came*

(b) *beide* can also be used as a simple adjective

This occurs after a definite article or another determiner. It then has the endings of an adjective ('weak' declension) and often corresponds to English 'two':

Seine **beiden** Brüder sind gekommen	*His two brothers came*
Die **beiden** Brüder sind gekommen	*The two brothers came*

(c) Used with a personal pronoun, *beide* usually has the endings of *dieser*

wir beide, sie beide, von euch beiden, unser beider

There is some variation in usage with *wir* and *ihr*:

(i) In isolation *wir beiden* can used rather than *wir beide*. It is generally less common, but it is usual if a noun follows, e.g.: *wir beiden Freunde*.

(ii) *ihr beiden* is more usual than *ihr beide* in isolation, e.g.: *Ihr beiden, wollt ihr mitkommen?* Within a clause both are possible, e.g.: *Wollt ihr beide(n) schon mitkommen?*

(iii) If *beide* is separated from the pronoun, only the ending *-e* is usual:

Wir wollen beide schon mitkommen.	Ihr wolltet wohl **beide** mitkommen, oder?
Beide halten sie ein Wahlergebnis für möglich, das eine große Koalition erzwänge (*Zeit*)	They *both* consider an election result possible . . .

(d) The neuter singular *beides* is used collectively to refer to two things:

Sie hatte einen Hut und einen Regenschirm mit und ließ **beides** im Zug liegen	She had a hat and an umbrella with her and left both on the train
Sprechen Sie Deutsch oder Englisch?	Do you speak German or English?
– **Beides**	– Both
Beides ist möglich	Either is possible

If *beides* is the subject of *sein*, the verb can be singular or plural:

Das Hotel und die Landschaft: **beides** ist/sind schön	The hotel and the scenery: both are lovely

NB: The use of *beides* to refer to people is purely colloquial, e.g.: *Ich habe mit den Brüdern Schmidt zu Mittag gegessen. Beides ist/sind* (in writing: *Beide sind*) *Vegetarier*.

(e) Other uses of *beide* and other equivalents of English 'both'

Einer von beiden könnte uns helfen	One/Either of the two could help us
An beiden Enden des Ganges hängt ein Bild	At either end of the corridor there is a picture
in beiden Fällen	in either case
Keiner von beiden ist gekommen	Neither of them came
Sowohl seine Frau als (auch) seine Tochter sind krank	Both his wife and his daughter are sick

5.5.4 *einer* 'one'

(a) The pronoun *einer* declines like the possessive pronoun *meiner*
The endings are given in Table 5.4. Note that *einer* has different endings from those of the indefinite article *ein* in the nominative singular masculine (*einer*) and the nominative/accusative singular neuter (*eines*).

Genitive forms of *einer* are rarely used (see DUDEN 1985: 204–5). The paraphrase with *von* (see 2.4) is usually preferred, e.g.: *die Empfehlung von einem ihrer Freunde*, rather than: *die Empfehlung eines ihrer Freunde* 'the recommendation of one of her friends'.

NB: (i) *eines* may be written *eins*, reflecting its usual pronounciation.
(ii) For the use of *eins* as a numeral 'one', see 9.1.2.

(b) *einer* corresponds to English pronoun 'one'

einer der Männer, **eine** der Frauen, **ein(e)s** der Kinder	*one of the men, one of the women, one of the children*
Ein Fenster war offen und **ein(e)s** war zu	*One window was open and one was shut*
Ich sprach mit **einer** der Damen	*I spoke to one of the ladies*
eines der Themen, die der slowenische Außenminister angesprochen hat (*Presse*)	*one of the topics which the Slovenian Foreign Minister touched on*

Unstressed *einer* has the negative *keiner*, cf. 5.5.16, stressed *einer* has the negative *nicht einer*. Compare: *Ich habe keinen gesehen* 'I haven't seen one' and *Ich habe nicht einen gesehen* 'I haven't seen <u>one</u>'.

(c) *einer* often has the sense of 'someone', 'anyone'

Einer muß es getan haben	*Someone must have done it*
einer, der ihn kannte	*a person/someone who knew him*
Mit so **einem** will ich nichts zu tun haben	*I don't want anything to do with anyone like that*
Da kam **einer** durch die Glastür	*Someone came through the glass door*

This is common in spoken German. It is often equivalent to *jemand*, see 5.5.15, although this more clearly refers to an indefinite 'somebody' whose identity is quite unknown, cf. Engel (1991: 668–9). *jemand* is also generally more polite, where *einer* can sound offensive, particularly in the feminine, cf.: *Da war gerade eine mit sechs Kindern.*

As a substitute for *man*, nominative *einer* is restricted to colloquial speech (e.g.: *Und das soll einer wissen!*). However, the other masculine case forms of *einer* may substitute for those which *man* lacks, see 5.5.18.

(d) *ein-* can be used as an adjective with the definite article, the demonstratives or the possessives
It then has the 'weak' adjective endings (see Table 6.1):

Der eine deutsche Tourist beschwerte sich	*One German tourist complained*
Das eine Gute ist, daß er Mut hat	*The one good thing is that he has courage*
das eine, das ich brauche	*the one thing I need*
Mein einer Sohn ist gestorben (coll.)	*One of my sons has died*
Mit dieser einen Hand konnte er Wunder tun	*With this one hand he could perform miracles*

Particularly common is *der eine* linked to a following *der andere*, corresponding to English '(the) one ... the other', etc. In German, though, the definite article is usually present, whereas it may be lacking in English, and the plural *die einen* may occur, in the meaning 'some':

Das eine Buch habe ich gelesen, das andere aber noch nicht	*I've read one of the books, but not the other one yet*
Die einen sangen, die anderen spielten	*Some were singing, others were playing*

(e) Some idiomatic uses of *einer*, and other equivalents of English 'one'

Das ist aber einer!	*He's quite a lad*
Du bist mir einer!	*You're a nice one!*
Eins wollte ich noch sagen	*There's one more thing I wanted to say*
Trinken wir noch eins?	*Shall we have another (drink)?*
Es ist mir alles eins	*It's all the same to me*
Er redet in einem fort	*He talks without stopping*

5.5.5 *ein wenig, ein bißchen* 'a little'

(a) *ein wenig* corresponds to English 'a little'

The *ein* does *not* decline. *von* (see 2.4) is used rather than a genitive:

Ich hatte noch **ein wenig** deutsches Geld	*I still had a little German money*
Der Zug hatte sich **ein wenig** verspätet	*The train had got a little late*
Der Saal war **ein wenig** ruhiger geworden	*The room had become a little more quiet*
mit **ein wenig** männlicher Eitelkeit	*with a little male vanity*

(b) *ein bißchen* can replace *ein wenig* in most contexts

It could be used in all the examples in (a) without any difference in meaning, but it can sound more colloquial. Unlike *ein wenig*, it can, optionally, be declined in the dative singular, e.g. *mit ein(em) bißchen Geld*. This is normal when it is used as a pronoun, e.g. *Mit einem bißchen wäre ich schon zufrieden*. It also differs from *ein wenig* in that it can occur with a preceding adjective:

ein winziges bißchen Käse	*a tiny little bit of cheese*
mit einem ganz kleinen bißchen gesundem Verstand	*with a very little bit of common sense*

NB: In spoken south German usage the form *ein bisse(r)l* is a frequent variant for northern *ein bißchen*.

(c) *bißchen* may also be used with a demonstrative, a possessive or *kein*

mit dem bißchen Verstand, den er hat	*with that little sense he has*
mit ihrem bißchen Talent	*with her bit of talent*
Er hat kein bißchen Humor	*He hasn't got the least sense of humour*

5.5.6 *ein paar* 'a few'

The *ein* of *ein paar* does not decline. *von* (see 2.4) is used rather than a genitive. *ein paar* is close in meaning to *einige*, cf. 5.5.7, but it sounds more colloquial:

Ein paar Flaschen Wein haben wir noch im Keller	*We've still got a few bottles of wine in the cellar*
Willst du **ein paar** haben?	*Do you want a few?*
mit der Hilfe von **ein paar** alten Freunden	*with the help of a few old friends*

The *ein* can be replaced by another determiner, which is declined. Such combinations can sound pejorative:

Was soll ich mit den **paar** Mark anfangen?	*What am I supposed to do with these lousy few marks?*
der Wert meiner **paar** Möbel	*the value of my few bits of furniture*
Die Straßenbahn kommt alle **paar** Minuten	*The tram comes every few minutes*

NB: *ein paar* should not be confused with *ein Paar* 'a pair'. Compare *ein paar Schuhe* 'a few shoes' but *ein Paar Schuhe* 'a pair of shoes'.

5.5.7 *einiger, einige* 'some'

einig- refers to a limited amount or number. It corresponds to English unstressed 'some', (or 'a few', as it is close in meaning to *ein paar*, see 5.5.6). It declines like *dieser* (see Table 5.1) except that the genitive singular masculine and neuter form (which is little used) is *einigen*.

(a) The use of *einiger* in the singular is limited

The usual German equivalents of English unstressed *some* in the singular are *etwas* (see 5.5.9), or, most commonly, simply the zero article (see 4.8.7), e.g.: *Ich habe heute (etwas) Butter gekauft* 'I bought some butter today'.

When *einig-* is used in the singular it implies a rather unusual or unexpected quantity and often comes close to English 'no little'. It is most frequent with mass and abstract nouns (especially *Entfernung* and *Zeit*), adjectives used as nouns and collectives:

mit **einigem** Glück	*with some degree of luck*
bei **einigem** guten Willen (*Th. Mann*)	*with a certain degree of good will*
vor ihm in **einiger** Entfernung	*some distance in front of him*
vor **einiger** Zeit schon	*some time ago now*
nach **einigem** Überlegen	*after some consideration*
Diese Schlangen, die ihr Gift spucken, zielen bis drei Meter weit noch mit **einiger** Treffsicherheit (*Grzimek*)	*These snakes which spit their venom can aim up to three metres with no little accuracy*

Singular *einig-* is mainly used as a determiner rather than as a pronoun, but the neuter singular *einiges* does occur as a collective indefinite pronoun:

einiges davon	*some of it*
Ich habe noch **einiges** zu tun	*I've still got a few things to do*

(b) *einige* is widely used both as a determiner and a pronoun in the plural

Sie wollte **einige** Ansichtskarten von Rothenburg kaufen	*She wanted to buy some postcards of Rothenburg*
In der Stadt gibt es **einige** Friseure	*There are a few hairdressers in the town*
unter Verwendung **einiger** technischer Mittel	*by using some technical methods*
Einige mußten stehen	*Some/A few had to stand*
Sie hat schon **einige** mitgebracht	*She's already brought some/a few*

German often uses a zero article where English uses unstressed *some* to refer to a number of things. Thus, a common alternative to the first example above would be: *Sie wollte Ansichtskarten von Rothenburg kaufen.*

NB: *einige* is often used with numerals to mean 'a few', e.g. *einige tausend Bücher* 'a few thousand books'.

5.5.8 *etliche* 'some'

etliche is similar in meaning to *einige*. However, it typically implies 'more than the expected number'. In this way, it can approach the meaning of English 'several' or 'a fair number of'. It declines like *dieser* (see Table 5.1) and it is used almost exclusively in the plural, as a determiner (much less commonly as a pronoun).

It is by no means as obsolete or old-fashioned as some authorities maintain, e.g. Engel (1991: 543), but is quite widely used, with its special meaning, in both spoken and written German:

Warum ist die Bahn so unpünktlich geworden? Da gibt es **etliche** Ursachen (*Spiegel*)	*Why have the railways become so unpunctual? There are several/a (good) number of reasons for this*
Etliche dieser Stücke sind auch für Anfänger relativ leicht zu bewältigen (*SWF*)	*Some/A number of these pieces are relatively easy to manage, even for a beginner*

5.5.9 *etwas* 'something', 'anything'

etwas is used as an indefinite pronoun, to qualify nouns, and as an adverb. It has no case forms and is not used in genitive constructions, the paraphrase with *von* (see 2.4) being used if necessary.

(a) As an indefinite pronoun, *etwas* corresponds to English 'something' or 'anything'

Etwas störte mich	*Something bothered me*
Ich habe **etwas** für Sie	*I've got something for you*
Hast du **etwas** gesagt?	*Did you say anything?*

In this use, *etwas* is commonly reduced to *was* in colloquial speech unless it occupies first place in the sentence. Note: *etwas* is often used with *von* in a partitive sense, i.e. 'some (of)':

Ich möchte etwas von diesem Kuchen *I would like some of this cake*

etwas can be omitted in such contexts: *Ich möchte von diesem Kuchen.*

(b) Qualifying a noun, *etwas* has the sense of 'some', 'any' or 'a little'

It is used chiefly with mass and abstract nouns in the singular. However, as an equivalent to unstressed English 'some' or 'any', German very commonly uses the zero article (see 4.2.2a, 4.8.7 and 5.5.7b), and *etwas* could be omitted in *all* the examples given below:

Ich brauche **etwas** frisches Fleisch	*I need some fresh meat*
Er hat kaum **etwas** Geld	*He has hardly any money*
Bringen Sie mir bitte **etwas** Brot	*Please bring me some bread*
Sie muß **etwas** Geduld haben	*She needs a little patience*
Etwas mehr Aufmerksamkeit wäre nützlich gewesen	*A little more attentiveness would have been useful*

etwas is commonly used with a following adjective used as a noun (see 6.4.5). The adjective has the strong endings:

etwas ganz Neues	*something quite new*
Er hat von etwas ganz Neuem gesprochen	*He spoke of something quite new*

(c) As an adverb, *etwas* means 'somewhat', 'a bit'

Er ist etwas nervös	*He is somewhat/rather/a bit nervous*
Es geht ihm etwas besser	*He is somewhat/a bit better*
Er zögerte etwas	*He hesitated somewhat/a bit*

5.5.10 *folgend*

folgend can be used as a simple adjective, but it has some special forms and uses which resemble those of a determiner or pronoun. Unlike English 'following', it is often used without a preceding article or other determiner. In these contexts a following adjective usually has 'weak' endings in the singular and 'strong' endings in the plural, see 6.2.3:

alle **folgenden** Bemerkungen	*all the following remarks*
Sie machte **folgende** Bemerkungen	*She made the following remarks*
Sie machte **folgende** treffende Bemerkungen	*She made the following apposite remarks*
folgender interessante Gedanke	*the following interesting thought*
mit **folgender** nachdrücklichen Warnung	*with the following firm warning*
Sie sagte mir **folgendes**: ...	*She said the following to me: ...*
Im **folgenden** wird diese Frage näher erläutert	*In the following this question will be clarified more precisely*
Aus **folgendem** läßt sich schließen, daß ...	*From the following it may be deduced that ...*

When *folgend* is used as a pronoun meaning 'the following', as in the last three examples, it begins with a small letter.

5.5.11 *irgend*

(a) The principal use of *irgend* is to emphasise indefiniteness
It occurs in combination with a large number of indefinite pronouns, adverbs and determiners, giving them the sense of 'some ... or other' or 'any ... at all'. DUDEN (1985: 365) prescribes that it should be written as a separate word with *etwas*, *jemand* and *solche*, but compounded with other words, e.g. *irgendwer*, *irgendwas*, *irgendeiner*, *irgendwo*, etc. However, this ruling is by no means systematically adhered to.

NB: In the reformed spelling, see 23.7.2, all compounds of *irgend* will be written together, i.e. *irgendetwas*, *irgendjemand*.

(b) *irgend* can be compounded with most interrogative adverbs to form indefinite adverbs
(See 7.5 for the basic forms of these interrogative adverbs), i.e.:
irgendwann 'sometime or other', 'any time'; *irgendwie* 'somehow', 'anyhow'; *irgendwo* 'somewhere', 'anywhere'; *irgendwohin* '(to) somewhere', '(to) anywhere'; *irgendwoher* 'from somewhere', 'from anywhere'. Examples of use:

Du mußt es **irgendwie** machen	*You'll have to do it somehow*
Er fährt heute nachmittag **irgendwohin**	*He's going somewhere this afternoon*
Gehst du heute abend **irgendwohin**?	*Are you going anywhere tonight?*

(c) With *einer, (et)was, jemand* and *wer, irgend* stresses indefiniteness

irgendeiner, irgend jemand and *irgendwer* correspond to English 'somebody', 'anybody', *irgend etwas* to 'something', 'anything'. In practice, *irgendeiner* and *irgendwer* are commoner than simple *einer* and *wer* (see 5.5.4 and 5.5.27) to mean 'somebody', 'anybody':

Irgendwann wurden von **irgendwem** diese Briefe aus dem Kasten genommen (*Böll*)	*At some time or other someone (or other) took these letters out of the letter-box*
Versteht er **irgend etwas** vom Wein?	*Does he know anything (at all) about wine?*
irgend so etwas	*something/anything like this*
Irgendeiner soll es gesagt haben	*Someone (or other) is supposed to have said it*
Hat denn **irgend jemand** angerufen?	*Did anybody phone?*

Note that only *irgend jemand* and *irgend etwas*, not simple *jemand* or *etwas*, are possible in response to a question, cf. Heidolph *et al.* (1981: 666f.):

Wer hat eben geklopft? – **Irgend jemand**	*Who just knocked? – Someone or other*
Was willst du denn kaufen? – **Irgend etwas**	*What are you going to buy, then? – Something or other*

In colloquial north German, *irgend* can be compounded with the prepositional adverb with *wo(r)-* (see 5.3.3c), in place of *irgend etwas* with a preposition:

Ich habe mich **irgendworan** gestoßen (written: an irgend etwas)	*I knocked against something or other*

(d) *irgendein(er)* and *irgendwelcher*

These correspond to 'some (or other)', 'any (whatsoever)', often with the sense of 'no matter which/who'. They are used as determiners or pronouns:

(i) The determiner *irgendein* has the endings of the indefinite article *ein*, see Table 4.2. It is used in the singular with countable nouns:

Er zeigte mir **irgendeine** Broschüre	*He showed me some brochure or other*
Hat er **irgendeine** Bemerkung gemacht?	*Did he make any remark (at all)?*
Die Selbstmordquote soll höher sein als in **irgendeinem** anderen Ort der Welt (*Bednarz*)	*The suicide rate is supposed to be higher than in any other place in the world*

(ii) The pronoun *irgendeiner*, which declines like *meiner* (see Table 5.4) only has singular forms. It can only refer to countable nouns. The masculine and feminine are used in the sense of 'somebody', 'anybody':

Irgendeiner muß dich gesehen haben	*Someone or other must have seen you*
Wenn du wirklich einen neuen Tisch suchst, mußt du hier im Geschäft **irgendeinen** gesehen haben, der dir gefällt	*If you're really looking for a new table, you must have seen one here in the shop which you like*
Ich habe ein paar Bücher über Berlin. Sie können sich **irgendeins** ausleihen	*I've got a few books on Berlin. You can borrow any one you like*

(iii) *irgendwelcher*, which declines like *dieser* (see Table 5.1), is used as a determiner in the singular with mass and abstract nouns, and in the plural. The genitive is rarely used in the singular:

Er zeigte mir **irgendwelche** neue Bücher	*He showed me some new books or other*
Er redete **irgendwelches** dumme(s) Zeug	*He was talking some stupid rubbish or other*
Wenn Sie **irgendwelche** Probleme haben, wenden Sie sich an uns (*Bednarz*)	*If you have any problems (at all), turn to us*

NB: Colloquially, *irgendwelcher* is often used for *irgendein*, e.g. *Er zeigte mir irgendwelche Broschüre* (cf. (i) above).

(e) *irgend so ein* **(plural:** *irgend solche***) corresponds to English 'one/some of those', 'any/some such'**
It often has a pejorative tone:

Wer war es? – Es war **irgend so ein** Vertreter für Doppelfenster	*Who was it? – It was one of those men who sell double glazing*
Er machte **irgend solche** komische Bemerkungen	*He made some such odd remarks*

(f) *irgend* **is used as an independent adverb with the sense of** *irgendwie*
i.e. 'somehow, anyhow, in some way':

wenn **irgend** möglich	*if at all possible*
Wenn es **irgend** geht, wäre ich froh	*If it's somehow possible, I would be happy*

5.5.12 *jeder* 'each', 'every'

(a) *jeder* **is only used in the singular, as a determiner or a pronoun**
jeder declines like *dieser* (see Table 5.1), but *jeden* is as frequent as *jedes* in the genitive singular masculine and neuter, *if* the following noun has the ending -(*e*)*s*, e.g. *am Ende jeden/jedes Abschnitts*. It is not used in the genitive as a pronoun. As a determiner it corresponds to English 'each', 'every', as a pronoun to English 'everyone', 'everybody':

Sie hat **jedem** Kind einen Apfel gegeben	*She gave each child an apple*
nach **jedem** solchen Versuch	*after each such attempt*
Er kam **jeden** Tag zur selben Zeit	*He came every day at the same time*
In diesem kleinen Ort kennt **jeder** **jeden**	*In this little place everyone knows everybody else*

jeder often has an individualising sense (i.e. 'no matter which/who'), in which case it can be the equivalent of English 'any':

Das weiß doch **jeder** gebildete Bürger	*Any/Every educated citizen knows that, though*
Die industrielle Revolution verwandelte die Lebensbedingungen der Menschen radikaler als **jeder** andere Ereigniszusammenhang der neueren Geschichte (*Jaeger*)	*The Industrial Revolution changed people's living conditions more radically than any other set of events in recent history*

NB: The neuter *jedes* can refer back to both sexes: *Seine Eltern waren sehr tüchtig, jedes auf seine Weise.*

(b) The combination *ein jeder* is more emphatic than *jeder*

It is used chiefly as a pronoun and is particularly frequent in the individualising sense of stressed 'any', i.e. 'no matter which/who'. In this combination, *jeder* has the same endings as a simple adjective:

Ein jeder wollte was sagen	*Everyone wanted to say something*
Das könnte doch **ein jeder** machen	*Everybody/Anybody (at all) could do that*
Das kannst du doch nicht **einem jeden** erzählen	*But you can't tell that to just anybody*
Die Wünsche **eines jeden** werden berücksichtigt	*The wishes of every individual are taken into account*

5.5.13 *jedermann* 'everybody', 'everyone'

jedermann is restricted in modern German to elevated, formal registers and set phrases. Its meaning is the same as that of *jeder*, which is much more commonly used. Its only case form is the genitive *jedermanns*.

Jedermann wußte, daß Michael den Wehrdienst verweigert hatte	*Everyone knew that Michael had refused to do military service*
Das ist nicht jedermanns Sache	*That's not everyone's cup of tea*

5.5.14 *jedweder*, *jeglicher* 'each', 'every'

jedweder and *jeglicher* are both alternatives to *jeder* as determiners or pronouns. Both decline like *jeder*, but are largely restricted to formal written language.

(a) *jedweder* is rather more emphatic than *jeder*

Though by no means totally obsolete, it has a rather old-fashioned ring and is used sparingly, even in very formal registers:

Er weist seine Sekundanten an, auf **jedwede** Bedingung der Gegenseite einzugehen (*Frevert*)	*He instructs his seconds to agree to each and every condition of his opponent*

(b) *jeglicher* stresses the individuality of the items in question

It is most often used in the sense of stressed *any* (i.e. 'no matter who/what'). It is most frequent nowadays with abstract nouns and in negative contexts. Unlike *jeder*, it can also be used in the plural:

Verständlichkeitsstörungen, die **jegliche** Deutung nahezu **jeglicher** Szene zulassen (*HA*)	*lapses in intelligibility which allow any interpretation of almost every scene*
Gorbatschow lehnte **jegliche** Änderung der Grenzziehungen in der Sowjetunion ab (*FR*)	*Gorbachov turned down any alteration of the frontiers in the Soviet Union*
Das entbehrt **jeglicher** Grundlage	*That is completely unfounded*
die vollkommen unbefangene Ablehnung **jeglicher** demagogischer Attraktionen (*Pörtner*)	*the completely natural rejection of all kinds of attractive demagogery*

5.5.15 *jemand* 'somebody', 'someone', *niemand* 'nobody', 'no-one'

(a) Declension and use of *jemand* and *niemand*

jemand 'somebody', 'someone' and *niemand* 'nobody', 'no-one' have the following case forms:

Nom.	jemand	niemand
Acc.	jemand(en)	niemand(en)
Gen.	jemand(e)s	niemand(e)s
Dat.	jemand(em)	niemand(em)

In the accusative and dative, the endingless forms are rather more common in practice in both spoken and written German:

Ich habe **niemand** (less frequent: **niemanden**) gesehen
Ich habe **jemand** (less frequent: **jemandem**) das Paket gegeben

The genitive forms tend to be avoided by paraphrasing, i.e. *Hat jemand diese Aktentasche liegenlassen?* rather than: *Ist das jemands Aktentasche?* Pronouns and determiners referring back to *jemand* and *niemand* have the masculine singular form:

Niemand, **der** es weiß   Jemand hat **seine** Tasche vergessen

NB: (i) In colloquial spoken German, *einer* and *wer* are common alternatives to *jemand*, see 5.5.4 and 5.5.27, as is *keiner* for *niemand*, see 5.5.16.

(ii) The indefiniteness of *jemand* may be emphasised by combining it with *irgend*, cf. 5.5.11c.

(b) *jemand* and *niemand* with a following adjective
When followed by an adjective, *jemand* and *niemand* are usually endingless in the accusative and dative. The adjective is treated as a noun (cf. 6.4), and spelled with a capital letter (except *ander*, cf. 5.5.2). It may have the ending *-es* in *all* cases, or, alternatively, *-en* in the accusative and *-em* in the dative:

Jemand Fremd**es**, Jemand anders ist gekommen
Ich habe jemand Fremd**es** (**-en**), jemand anders (ander**en**) gesehen
Ich habe mit jemand Fremd**em** (**-es**), jemand anders (ander**em**) gesprochen

NB: The south German use of the ending *-er* in the nominative, e.g. *jemand Bekannter, jemand anderer* is considered non-standard by DUDEN (1985: 370).

5.5.16 *kein, keiner* 'no, not . . . any, none'
(a) *kein* is the negative form of the indefinite article
It declines like the possessive determiner *mein*, see Table 5.3. It is used in the main where a corresponding positive sentence would have an indefinite or a zero article, and it is thus usually the equivalent of English 'not a', 'not . . . any' or 'no':

Es war ein angenehmer Anblick	Es war **kein** angenehmer Anblick
Kennst du einen Arzt?	Kennst du **keinen** Arzt?
Wir haben frische Brötchen	Wir haben **keine** frischen Brötchen
Ich habe Geld	Ich habe **kein** Geld

(b) *kein* or *nicht* in negation?
The selection of *kein* or *nicht* in negation is not always straightforward for English learners. In general, *kein* is used to negate an indefinite noun (whether this has the indefinite article or a zero article), as in the examples given under (a) above, whereas *nicht* is used in other cases, notably to negate a whole sentence, e.g. *Sie will heute mitkommen. Sie will heute **nicht** mitkommen.* However, there are contexts where the choice seems less clear-cut, i.e.:

(i) German phrases with an indefinite noun (and thus negated with *kein*) which have rather different English equivalents:

Ich bin Deutscher	Ich bin **kein** Deutscher
Ich habe Angst, Hunger	Ich habe **keine** Angst, **keinen** Hunger
Ich spreche Deutsch	Ich spreche **kein** Deutsch
Ich habe Lust, etwas zu tun	Ich habe **keine** Lust, etwas zu tun
ein Problem von großer Bedeutung	ein Problem von **keiner** großer Bedeutung

(ii) Phrasal verbs with nouns, e.g. *Atem holen, sich Mühe geben, Freude empfinden* and all those with *haben*, e.g. *Angst, Durst, Hunger haben*, etc. are generally negated with *kein*:

Er hat sich **keine** Mühe gegeben	Ich habe **keinen** Durst, Hunger
Dabei hat er **keine** Freude empfunden	Sie hatten **keine** Angst

Phrasal verbs with *nehmen* have *kein* or *nicht*:

Er hat **keine/nicht** Rücksicht auf mich genommen
Sie wollen **keine/nicht** Rache nehmen
Sie hat **keinen/nicht** Abschied von ihm genommen

nicht occurs with phrasal verbs where the noun is so closely linked to the verb that it is felt as the equivalent of a separable prefix:

Er spielt **nicht** Klavier	Sie läuft **nicht** Schi
Sie haben in Berlin **nicht** Wurzel gefaßt	Er hat **nicht** Wort gehalten
Er kann **nicht** Auto fahren	Sie schreibt **nicht** Maschine

Similarly: *Schritt fahren, Gefahr laufen*, etc.

(c) *kein* **and** *nicht ein*

kein is the usual equivalent of English 'not a' (and the use of *nicht ein* for *kein* is a typical English learners' mistake in German). Nevertheless, there are a few contexts where *nicht ein* is used:

(i) If *ein* is stressed, i.e. 'not one/a (single)':

Die TAP besitzt **nicht ein** Flugzeug,   *TAP doesn't own a single aeroplane,*
denn alle 38 Maschinen sind geleast   *as all 38 machines are leased*
(NZZ)

(ii) For direct contrasts:

Das ist eine Ulme, **nicht eine** Eiche   *That's an elm, not an oak*

(iii) *nicht ein* is more usual than *kein* after *wenn* 'if': *Man hätte ihn kaum bemerkt, wenn ihm **nicht ein** Schnurrbart etwas Distinguiertes verliehen hätte.*

(d) Some idiomatic uses of *kein* as a determiner

Sie ist noch **keine** zehn Jahre alt	*She's not yet ten years old*
keine zwei Stunden vor meiner Abreise	*within two hours of my departure*
Es ist noch **keine** fünf Minuten her	*It is less than five minutes ago*
Sie ist schließlich **kein** Kind mehr	*After all, she's no longer a child*

(e) The form *keiner* is used as a pronoun

It declines like *meiner*, see Table 5.4, with, similarly, the endings *-er* in the nominative singular masculine and *-(e)s* in the nominative/accusative singular neuter. It is rarely used in the genitive:

> **Keiner** von uns hat es gewußt
> **Keiner** im Büro wollte was sagen
> Zum Schluß hat sie **kein(e)s** der Bücher gekauft
> Haben Sie einen Farbfernseher? – Nein, wir haben **keinen**
> In **keinem** dieser neuen Häuser möchte ich wohnen
> **kein(e)s** von beiden *neither of them*

NB: (i) The neuter form *kein(e)s* is used to refer to people of different sex: *Ich fragte meine Eltern, aber **keins** (von beiden) wußte es.*
(ii) The use of *keiner* for *niemand* to mean 'no-one', 'nobody' (see 5.5.15a) is frequent in speech but considered to be substandard.

5.5.17 *lauter* 'only', 'nothing but'

lauter is indeclinable. It is used only as a determiner, i.e. before nouns:

Dort lag **lauter** Eis und Schnee	*Nothing but ice and snow lay there*
Es kamen **lauter** junge Leute	*Only young people came*
Er hat **lauter** solchen Unsinn geredet	*He only spoke rubbish like that*

5.5.18 *man* 'one'

(a) The indefinite pronoun *man* corresponds to English 'one'

However, unlike 'one', it is not restricted to elevated speech. Rather, it corresponds to the general use of 'you' in spoken English, or, frequently, to 'we', 'they' or 'people' (and the overuse of *Leute* in contexts where *man* would be appropriate, is typical of English learners' German). It is also often used in contexts where English would most naturally use a passive construction, e.g. *Man sagt* 'It is said', cf. 15.4.1. The corresponding pronouns are possessive *sein* and reflexive *sich*:

Als **man** sich zum Abendessen setzte, fehlte der alte Herr	*When they/we sat down to dinner the old gentleman was missing*
Man hat sich nach dir erkundigt	*People were asking after you*
Man sollte seinen Freunden helfen	*One ought to help one's friends*
Hier spricht **man** meistens Plattdeutsch unter sich	*People mainly speak Low German here amongst themselves*

man is sometimes used, for reasons of politeness, to refer to the speaker, e.g.: *Darf man fragen, wohin Sie fahren?* In certain situations this can acquire a note of sarcasm. This is always so when it is used to refer to the listener, e.g.: *Hat man schon wieder zu tief ins Glas geguckt?*

NB: (i) *man* should never be referred back to with *er*, e.g.: *Wenn man müde ist, muß **man** (not er) sich setzen.*
(ii) The form *frau* has recently gained some currency in feminist circles as a substitute for *man*, calling attention to the gender discrimination felt to be inherent in the form *man*.

(b) *man* **only has a nominative case form**
In the accusative and dative *einen* and *einem* (see 5.5.4) are used:

Man weiß nie, ob er **einen** erkannt hat	*You never know whether he has recognised you*
So leid es **einem** tut, man muß manchmal hart sein	*However much you regret it, you have to be hard sometimes*

NB: The use of the nominative form *einer* for *man* (see 5.5.4) is generally considered to be a substandard colloquialism.

5.5.19 *manch* 'some', 'many a'

manch always has the rather special sense of stressed 'some', i.e. 'a fair number, but by no means all'. This may be equivalent to English 'many a' and in certain contexts comes close to the sense of English 'several'. *manch* has a number of alternative forms, as follows.

(a) As a determiner, *manch* is most often used in the inflected form *mancher* i.e. with the endings of *dieser*, see Table 5.1.

In the genitive singular masculine and neuter, the form *manchen* is occasionally found besides the more frequent *manches* if the following noun has the ending -(e)s, (e.g. *manches Mannes* or *manchen Mannes*)

mancher can be used in the singular or the plural. The singular form (like English 'many a') may put more emphasis on the individual items, whereas the plural (like English stressed 'some') stresses the collectivity. In practice, however, the difference between, for example, *mancher schöne Tag* and *manche schöne Tage* is slight. Examples of usage:

der Stoßseufzer **mancher** deutschen Frau, die von der bisherigen Pille enttäuscht ist (*BILD*)	*the deep sigh of many a German woman who has been disappointed by the present pill*
An **manchen** Tagen blieb er lange im Bett	*Some days he stayed in bed a long time*
ein überhöhter Preis, wie er in **manchen** Reparaturwerkstätten seit Jahren üblich ist (*BILD*)	*an exorbitant price, such as has been usual in some garages for years*

(b) **Uninflected** *manch* **is also quite commonly used as a determiner**
(i) Before the indefinite article *ein*. This is a less common alternative to inflected *manch*, and it is mainly used in formal written German. The individual items are emphasised rather more strongly:

Da gibt es mancherlei Grund zum Zweifeln – **manch ein** Zeitgenosse wird sagen: zum Verzweifeln (*Zeit*)	*There are many kinds of reasons for doubt – many a contemporary will say: for despair*

(ii) Before an adjective, where the uninflected form is a widespread and frequent alternative to the inflected one, especially in the singular:

Sie konnten dem Kanzler **manch** guten Tip geben (*MM*)	*They were able to give the Chancellor many a good tip*
. . . um neben **manch** Komischem auch etliches Entlarvende bieten zu können (*MM*)	*. . . to be able to present quite a few revealing things besides much that is comical*

(iii) Before neuter nouns. This alternative sounds rather old-fashioned, but it has become rather fashionable again recently, cf. Engel (1991: 546):

manch Wörtchen der Verwunderung (*Th. Mann*)	*many a word of amazement*

(c) As a pronoun *mancher* declines like *dieser*

See Table 5.1. It is not used in the genitive:

Mancher hat es nicht geglaubt	*Not many believed it*
Das ist schon **manchem** passiert	*That has happened to quite a few people*
Manche trinken Tee, andere lieber Kaffee	*Some people drink tea, others prefer coffee*
manche meiner Bekannten	*a fair number of my acquaintances*

manch einer is a fairly frequent alternative to inflected *mancher*:

Manch einer mußte auf die Mittagspause verzichten (*MM*)	*Some had to give up their lunch hour*

5.5.20 *mehrere* 'several'

mehrere is used, in the plural only, as a determiner or a pronoun. It has the same endings as *dieser*, see Table 5.1:

Ich habe **mehrere** Bücher darüber gelesen	*I have read several books about it*
Es ist doch viel spannender, mit **mehreren** Jungen auszugehen, als immer an einem zu kleben (*BILD*)	*But it's much more exciting to go out with several boys than always to stick with one*
Mehrere standen draußen und warteten	*Several people were standing outside waiting*

5.5.21 *meinesgleichen* 'people like me'

meinesgleichen is indeclinable. Parallel forms can be formed for the other persons, i.e. *deinesgleichen, seinesgleichen, ihresgleichen, unsresgleichen, euresgleichen*. They sound rather old-fashioned nowadays:

Ich und **meinesgleichen** interessieren uns für so etwas nicht	*I and people like me aren't interested in things like that*
Euresgleichen hat es wirklich leicht	*People like you really have it easy*
Dieser Wagen hat nicht **seinesgleichen**	*This car has no equal*

5.5.22 *nichts* 'nothing'

nichts does not decline:

Aus **nichts** wird **nichts** (proverb)	*Nothing comes of nothing*
Nichts gefiel ihr dort	*She didn't like anything there*
nichts als Schwierigkeiten	*nothing but difficulties*

nichts is often used with a following adjective used as a noun, which has the strong endings, cf. 6.4.5:

nichts Neues	*nothing new*
Er hat von **nichts** Neuem gesprochen	*He didn't speak of anything new*

It is also common with *von* in partitive constructions, i.e. 'nothing (of)':

Ich möchte **nichts** von dem Essen	*I don't want any of the food*
nichts von alledem	*nothing of all that*

NB: In colloquial speech *nichts* is almost invariably pronounced *nix*.

5.5.23 *sämtlich* 'all (the)'

sämtliche inflects like *dieser*, see Table 5.1, and can be used as a determiner or a pronoun. It only occurs in the plural and is an emphatic alternative to *alle*:

Wir haben nicht den Ehrgeiz, **sämtliche** Pflanzen zu sammeln, die in der Serengeti vorkommen (*Grzimek*)	*We have no ambition to collect all the plants which occur in the Serengeti*
die Anschriften **sämtlicher** neuen Mitglieder	*the addresses of all the new members*

sämtliche is rather more limited than *alle*, since it can refer to all the members of a subgroup of persons or things, but not to all those which are in existence. Thus, one can say *Sämtliche* (or *Alle*) *Bäume in diesem Wald wurden gefällt*, but only: *Alle* (not *Sämtliche*) *Menschen sind sterblich*.

sämtliche can also be used with a preceding definite article or other determiner, in which case it has the endings of an adjective:

Meine **sämtlichen** Verwandten haben mir geschrieben	*All my relatives wrote to me*

As an adverb, *sämtlich* is used in the meaning 'without exception':

Sämtlich waren sie dem Staat eigen (*Johnson*)	*They all belonged to the state*

5.5.24 *unsereiner* 'someone like me', 'one of us'

unsereiner declines like *dieser*, see Table 5.1. There are parallel forms for the other persons, i.e. *eurereiner, ihrereiner*, although these are less frequent in practice:

Unsereiner kann das nicht wissen	*Someone like me can't know that*
Mit **unsereinem** spricht sie nie	*She doesn't talk to the likes of us*

NB: In the nominative and accusative, the neuter form *unsereins* is a common alternative to the masculine, especially in colloquial speech.

5.5.25 *viel* 'much', *viele* 'many', *wenig* 'a little', *wenige* 'a few'

The various forms and uses of *viel* 'much', 'many', 'a lot of' and *wenig* '(a) little', '(a) few', 'not many' are broadly similar. Both occur as a determiner, a pronoun or an adverb. Both have alternative uninflected and inflected forms, in the latter case with the endings of *dieser* (see Table 5.1). In certain constructions and uses the uninflected forms are more usual, in others the inflected, without any identifiable difference in meaning.

NB: (i) *ein wenig* 'a little' is invariable, see 5.5.5.
(ii) For the comparatives of *viel* and *wenig*, see 8.2.4.

(a) Used as pronouns, *viel* and *wenig* are most often uninflected in the singular, but inflected in the plural
They are not used in the genitive singular:

Er hat **viel/wenig** erzählt	Er will **viel/wenig** haben
Viel/Wenig von dem Kuchen	Sie hat **viel/wenig** verraten
Ich bin mit **viel/wenig** von dem einverstanden, was du sagst	
Viele/Wenige von diesen Büchern	Ich habe **viele/wenige** gesehen

The inflected singular forms nominative/accusative *vieles*, dative *vielem* are occasionally used, chiefly in formal writing:

Sie hat **vieles** versucht	*She has tried a lot of things*
Mit **vielem** bin ich nicht einverstanden	*There's much I don't agree with*

Inflected forms of *wenig* (i.e. *weniges*, *wenigem*) are rare.

(b) Used as determiners, *viel* and *wenig* are usually uninflected in the singular, but inflected in the plural
The genitive singular is scarcely ever used, the paraphrase with *von* being preferred:

Dazu ist **viel** Mut nötig	*Much courage is needed for that*
Ich trinke **wenig** Milch	*I don't drink much milk*
Er handelte mit **viel** Geschick	*He acted with a lot of skill*
Sie ist mit **wenig** Geld ausgekommen	*She managed with little money*
die Wirkung von **wenig** Wein	*the effect of not much wine*
der Genuß von **viel** Obst	*eating a lot of fruit*
Viele Probleme wurden besprochen	*Many problems were discussed*
Gestern waren **wenige** Zuschauer im Stadion	*There weren't many spectators at the ground yesterday*
Er hat **viele/wenige** Freunde	*He has a lot of/few friends*
die Reden **vieler** Politiker	*the speeches of a lot of politicians*
mit **vielen/wenigen** Ausnahmen	*with a lot of/few exceptions*

There are some common exceptions to the usage outlined above:

(i) Inflected singular forms are not unusual in formal registers with a following adjective used as a noun (cf. 6.4.5), e.g.: *Er hat **vieles/weniges** Interessante gesagt* (for everyday *Er hat **viel/wenig** Interessantes gesagt*).

(ii) Inflected forms are quite common in the dative singular masculine and neuter, e.g.: *Mit **viel/vielem** Zureden konnten wir einiges erreichen.*

(iii) Uninflected plural forms are occasionally found, mainly in colloquial speech: *Im Grunde interessieren mich furchtbar **wenig** Dinge außer meiner eigenen Arbeit (Langgässer).*

(iv) Inflected singular forms are found in a few set phrases, notably *vielen Dank*.

(c) *viel* and *wenig* can be used with a preceding definite article or other determiner
They then have the usual adjective endings:

Ich staunte über das **viele** Geld, das er ausgab	*I was amazed at the large amount of money that he spent*
der Mut dieser **vielen/wenigen** Frauen	*the courage of these many/few women*
Sie hat ihr **weniges** Geld verloren	*She lost her little bit of money*
die **wenigen**, die ihn erkannten	*the few who recognised him*

(d) *wenig* in constructions like *wenig gutes Fleisch* **can be ambiguous**

It could mean 'not much good meat' or 'not very good meat'. If the context does not resolve the ambiguity, the first meaning can be made clear by replacing *wenig* by *nicht viel*, i.e. *nicht viel gutes Fleisch*, the second by using *nicht sehr*, i.e. *nicht sehr gutes Fleisch*.

Similarly, *weniger gutes Fleisch* could mean 'meat which was less good' or 'a smaller amount of good meat' (English 'less good meat' shows similar ambiguity). This ambiguity can also be resolved if necessary by paraphrasing, i.e. *nicht so gutes Fleisch* or *nicht so viel gutes Fleisch*.

(e) The spelling of *soviel, wieviel, zuviel,* **etc.**

The following account follows the rulings given in DUDEN (1985).

(i) *soviel, sowenig* are spelled as single words when used as adverbs or conjunctions, e.g.:

soviel wie möglich	ich bin **sowenig** schuldig wie du
soviel ich weiß	**sowenig** du auch gelernt hast

However, they are spelled as separate words if *so* is qualifying *viel* or *wenig* used as determiners or pronouns, i.e. in the meanings 'so much', 'so many', 'so little', 'so few', e.g.:

so viel Fleiß	**so viele** Schätze	**so wenig** Geld	**so wenige** Häuser

(ii) *wieviel* is written as a single word, *wie viele* and *wie wenig* as two:

Wieviel Geld hast du bei dir?	**Wie viele** Computerspiele hast du?
Wie wenig er davon wußte!	

(iii) *zuviel* and *zuwenig* are usually written as single words:

Er gab mir **zuviel/zuwenig** vom Eisbein	Im Tee ist **zuviel/zuwenig** Zucker

They are written as separate words if *zu* is particularly stressed or if *viel* or *wenig* is inflected:

Sie haben für diese Stelle **zu wenig** Erfahrung
Er hat **zu viele** Eier gekauft

NB: In the reformed spelling, see 23.7.2, *all* compounds with *viel* and *wenig* will be written separately, e.g. *so viel, wie viel, zu wenig*.

5.5.26 *welcher* 'some', 'any'

welcher has the endings of *dieser*, see Table 5.1, when it is used as an indefinite pronoun. It is typical of colloquial speech, other alternatives (i.e. *einige, manche, etwas*) usually being preferred in formal registers.

It is used without restriction in the plural, but in the singular it can only refer to a mass noun. It refers back to a noun which has just been mentioned or for 'some people' identified by a following relative clause:

Hast du Käse? – Ja, ich habe **welchen**	*Have you got any cheese? Yes, I've got some*
Wenn kein Wein da ist, hole ich uns **welchen**	*If there's no wine left, I'll get us some*

Ich brauche Marken. Kannst du mir **welche** geben?	*I need some stamps. Can you give me some/any?*
Hier sind **welche** vom Westfernsehen (*Bednarz*)	*Here are some people from Western television*

NB: For the use of *welcher* as an interrogative, see 5.3.1, as a relative pronoun, see 5.4.2.

5.5.27 *wer* 'someone', 'somebody'

wer is used as a pronoun in colloquial speech, where formal registers prefer *jemand* (see 5.5.15):

Dich hat wieder **wer** angerufen	*Someone's been on the phone for you again*
Die hat wohl wieder **wen** angelächelt	*It looks as if she's picked some bloke up again*
Hast du wenigstens **wem** Bescheid gesagt?	*Have you at least told someone about it?*

NB: For the use of *wer* as an interrogative pronoun, see 5.3.3.

6

Adjectives

Adjectives are usually defined as words which describe, modify, or qualify nouns and pronouns. They can do this in two principal ways, i.e.:

- by being placed immediately before the noun they qualify:

  der **helle** Tag   *eine* **hohe** Wand   **reines** Gold

  This is termed the **'attributive'** use of the adjective. In German, as in English (but unlike, say, French or Italian), the adjective normally comes in front of the noun, after any determiners.

- by being used as a complement to a noun which is the subject or object of a verb:

  Hiltrut ist aber **klein**   Das Mädchen lag **krank** im Bett
  Er ißt die Würstchen **warm**   Sie strich die Wand **gelb**

This is termed the **'predicative'** use of the adjective.

In German, attributive adjectives (and *only* attributive adjectives) inflect. Like determiners, they have endings which show the case, number and gender of the noun and are said to be 'in agreement' with it. There are two main sets of adjective endings in German, the so-called 'strong' and 'weak' declensions. Which one is used depends on whether a determiner precedes the adjective and what kind of ending it has (if any). These endings are illustrated in Table 6.1 and explained in sections 6.1–3.

Adjectives can be used as nouns in German much more readily than is the case in English (e.g. *der Alte* 'the old man', *die Fremde* 'the foreign woman', *das Wichtige* 'the important thing'). Section 6.4 treats these in detail. Finally, sections 6.5–6 deal with the use of cases and prepositions after adjectives.

We can compare the extent to which a particular person or thing possesses the quality expressed by an adjectives by using special endings, e.g. *schön – schöner – schönst*. This is called the 'comparison' of adjectives, using the so-called 'comparative' and 'superlative' degrees. The comparison of adjectives and adverbs is treated in Chapter 8.

6.1 Declension of adjectives

6.1.1 German adjectives are only inflected when they are used attributively

ein **guter** Mensch   diese **schönen** Tage   frisches Brot

When used predicatively, or in phrases separated from the noun, they have no endings:

Der Mensch war **gut**   Er trat **ungeduldig** in das Zimmer
Er fühlte sich **gesund**   Wir essen die Möhren **roh**
Mein Vater, in Hamburg **tätig,** ...   Das Klima machte ihn **krank**
Sie hielt ihn für **dumm**   Das gilt als **sicher**

Optimistisch wie immer, sie ließ sich von ihrem Vorhaben nicht abhalten
ein erstklassiger Kellner, **rasch**, nicht **schwerhörig** (*Wohmann*)
Das Gewehr gehörte zu ihm wie eine Frau zu einem Mann, **schweigsam, schön** und **zuverlässig** (*E.W. Heine*)

The use of an uninflected adjective after the noun is poetic, e.g.: *O Täler weit*, *o Höhen!* (*Eichendorff*). However, it has become frequent as a stylistic device in advertising and technical language, cf. DUDEN (1995: 256), e.g.:

Henkel **trocken**   Schrankwand in Eiche **rustikal** oder Kiefer **natur**
Whisky **pur**   700 Nadelfeilen **rund** nach DIN 8342

6.1.2 The two basic declensions of adjectives in German

These are usually called the **STRONG** and **WEAK** declensions. The various endings are shown in Figure 6.1 below and illustrated in full, with articles and nouns, in Table 6.1. The tables are arranged with the neuters next to the masculines to show the overlap between the endings more clearly.

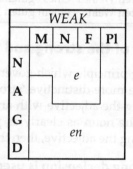

FIG 6.1 *Endings for adjective declensions*

(a) The strong declension has relatively more distinctive endings

They are identical to those of *dieser* (see Table 5.1), *except* that the genitive singular masculine and neuter ends in *-en*:

ein Stück international**en** Gewässers (*Presse*)
ein Desaster riesig**en** Ausmasses (*ARD*)
die Perfektion rein**en** Klanges (*Hi-Fi ad*)

However, with weak masculine nouns which have the ending *-en* in the genitive singular (cf. 1.3.2), the strong adjective has the ending *-es*, e.g. *obiges Adressaten.* This form rarely occurs in practice.

(b) The weak declension has only two endings, *-e* and *-en*

-e is used in the nominative singular of all genders and the accusative singular feminine and neuter. *-en* is used for *all* other combinations of case, number and gender.

NB: The nominative and accusative plural have the ending *-en*, e.g. *die guten Kinder.*

TABLE 6.1 *Adjective declension*

STRONG endings, used with no determiner

	Masculine	Neuter	Feminine	Plural
Nom.	guter Wein	gutes Brot	gute Suppe	gute Weine
Acc.	guten Wein	gutes Brot	gute Suppe	gute Weine
Gen.	guten Weines	guten Brotes	guter Suppe	guter Weine
Dat.	gutem Wein	gutem Brot	guter Suppe	guten Weinen

WEAK endings, illustrated with the definite article

	Masculine	Neuter	Feminine	Plural
Nom.	der gute Wein	das gute Brot	die gute Suppe	die guten Weine
Acc.	den guten Wein	das gute Brot	die gute Suppe	die guten Weine
Gen.	des guten Weines	des guten Brotes	der guten Suppe	der guten Weine
Dat.	dem guten Wein	dem guten Brot	der guten Suppe	den guten Weinen

'MIXED' endings, illustrated with the indefinite article

	Masculine	Neuter	Feminine
Nom.	ein guter Wein	ein gutes Brot	eine gute Suppe
Acc.	einen guten Wein	ein gutes Brot	eine gute Suppe
Gen.	eines guten Weines	eines guten Brotes	einer guten Suppe
Dat.	einem guten Wein	einem guten Brot	einer guten Suppe

6.2 The use of the strong and weak declensions

The underlying principle which governs the use of the strong and weak declensions is that the more distinctive 'strong' endings are used if there is no determiner preceding the adjective with an ending which indicates the case, gender or number of the noun as clearly as possible. If there is a determiner with an ending preceding the adjective, then the less distinctive 'weak' endings are used.

6.2.1 The strong declension is used, in line with the above principle

(a) When no determiner precedes the adjective

frische Milch   frisches Obst   schöne Tage   durch genaue Beobachtung
mit neuem Mut   das Niveau französischer Filme   aus deutschen Landen

Naturally, this also applies to adjectives used after simple numerals used on their own (including the genitives *zweier* and *dreier*, cf. 9.1.3a), after preceding genitives and after the genitive of the relative pronoun:

zwei schöne Pfirsiche	*two fine peaches*
Karls unermüdlicher Eifer	*Karl's tireless zeal*
in Astrids kleinem Arbeitszimmer	*in Astrid's little study*
mein Freund, dessen ältester Sohn	*my friend, whose eldest son was ill*
krank war	

(b) When a determiner preceding the adjective is endingless

ein älterer Herr	mein neues Kleid	unser kleines Kind
kein schöner Tag	manch reiches Land	viel indischer Tee
ein paar grüne Äpfel	lauter faule Äpfel	welch herrliches Wetter!
bei solch herrlichem Wetter	mit was für englischen Büchern?	

This means that the strong endings are used after the endingless forms of the indefinite articles *ein* and *kein* and after the possessives (i.e. *mein, dein, unser,* etc.) in the nominative singular masculine and the nominative/accusative singular neuter, as the relevant examples above show. The adjective declension with these determiners is often referred to as the 'mixed' declension; it is illustrated in full in Table 6.1.

6.2.2 The weak declension is used after most determiners with endings which clearly indicate the case, gender and number of the noun

This rule applies after all the major determiners, i.e.:

(a) The definite article and demonstrative *der*

der weiße Wein	den weißen Wein	des weißen Weines	die weißen Weine

(b) The indefinite articles *ein* and *kein* and the possessives if they have an ending
i.e. except in the nominative singular masculine and the nominative/ accusative singular neuter, cf. 6.2.1b:

einen weißen Wein	seinem weißen Wein	ihrer weißen Weine

(c) *dieser, jener, jeder* and *welcher*

dieser weiße Wein	diesen weißen Wein	diesen weißen Weinen
jenes weißen Weines	jedem weißen Wein	von welchem weißen Wein?

6.2.3 After most other determiners, adjectives have the weak endings

This is in accordance with the general principle given in 6.2. However, there are some variations and exceptions. The following summary represents modern usage with the quantifiers and indefinites treated in 5.5.

NB: For adjective endings after *ander*, see 5.5.2.

(a) In the singular, weak endings are used

mancher brave Mann	solches dumme Gerede	einiges Interessante
durch irgendwelchen puren Unsinn	mit folgender nachdrücklichen Warnung	
mit allem möglichen Fleiß	mit einigem bühnentechnischen Aufwand (*Zeit*)	
von vielem kalten Wasser	us wenigem schlechten Wein	

NB: *jeglicher* is frequently followed by strong endings, e.g. *jegliches organisches Leben* (Grzimek).

(b) In the plural there is some uncertainty and variation
(i) After *alle, beide* and *sämtliche* the weak endings are usual:

alle fremden Truppen	sämtliche schönen Bücher
beide bekannten Politiker	aller interessierten Zuschauer

NB: Strong endings are occasionally found, especially with *beide*, e.g. *beide deutsche Staaten*.

(ii) After *irgendwelche* and *solche* either weak or strong endings are used. The weak endings are more frequent:

> solche schönen (less common: schöne) Tage
> irgendwelcher interessierten (less common interessierter) Zuschauer

(iii) After *manche* either strong or weak endings occur. The strong endings are more frequent:

> manche schöne (less common: schönen) Aussichten

(iv) After *einige, etliche, folgende, mehrere, viele, wenige* strong endings are the rule:

> einige neue ICE-Verbindungen   etliche fremde Besucher
> folgende bezeichnende Beispiele   mehrere große Städte
> vieler kleiner Zimmer   weniger günstiger Zeiten

NB: Weak endings are occasionally found, most often in the genitive plural, e.g. *einiger großen ausländischen Firmen* for (much more frequent) *einiger großer ausländischer Firmen.*

(c) Some of these indefinites and quantifiers may themselves be preceded by one of the major determiners

i.e. by a definite or indefinite article, by one of the demonstratives *dieser* or *jener*, or by one of the possessives *mein, dein*, etc. They are then treated like adjectives and have a weak or strong adjective ending, as appropriate:

> eine solche interessante Nachricht   aller solchen guten Wünsche
> mit der folgenden krassen Behauptung   diese vielen alten Dörfer
> mit seinem wenigen deutschen Geld   mein sämtliches kleines Vermögen

(d) Some of the above determiners have alternative endingless forms

The conditions under which these occur are explained under the relevant determiner in section 5.5. These endingless forms are followed by adjectives with strong endings, following the principle explained above:

> viel deutsches Geld   manch schöner Tag   solch dummes Gerede

6.2.4 A series of adjectives preceding a noun all have the same (weak or strong) ending

> dieser schöne, große Garten   mein lieber alter Vater
> gutes bayrisches Bier   die Lösung wichtiger politischer Probleme

One occasional deviation from this rule is that in the dative singular masculine or neuter, a second (or subsequent) adjective may, optionally, have the weak ending *-en* rather than the strong ending *-em*:

> mit dunklem bayrischem/bayrischen Bier
> nach langem beunruhigendem/beunruhigenden Schweigen
> nach wochenlangem politischen Tauziehen (*Presse*)

-en is used less than *-em* in such cases in modern German, and DUDEN (1985: 24) labels it incorrect. However, it is common in all kinds of written German, and it is the norm with adjectives used as nouns, see 6.4.2b.

6.2.5 The adjective is still declined if a the noun is understood

'One' often has to be supplied in the equivalent English construction:

Welches Kleid hast du gewählt? –	*Which dress did you choose? –*
Das rote	*The red one*
Ich habe mein Taschenmesser verloren.	*I've lost my penknife. I'll have*
Ich muß mir ein neues kaufen	*to buy myself a new one*
Deutsche Weißweine sind süßer als	*German white wines are sweeter than*
französische	*French*

6.2.6 Determiners and adjectives governing nouns of different genders cannot be understood

In English an adjective (with or without a determiner) can be understood in a series of two (or more) nouns, e.g. *my old aunt and uncle, dear Ruth and Martin, the new table and chairs.* This is not possible in German if the nouns involved are of a different gender or number. The determiner and/or adjective must be repeated, with the appropriate different endings:

mein alter Onkel und meine alte Tante	liebe Ruth, lieber Martin
der neue Tisch und die neuen Stühle	

6.2.7 In a few special cases an attributive adjective has no ending

(a) In older German adjectives sometimes lacked the strong ending *-es* before a neuter singular noun in the nominative or accusative
This usage is retained in a few idioms and set phrases, e.g.:

etwas auf gut Glück tun	*to take a chance*
sich lieb Kind machen	*to ingratiate oneself*
Gut Ding will Weile haben	*Nothing good is done in a hurry*
Ruhig Blut bewahren!	*Keep calm!*
Kölnisch Wasser	*eau de Cologne*
ein gehörig/gut Stück	*a substantial/good piece*
ein gut Teil	*a large proportion*
ein ander Mal	*another time*
(more usual ein anderes Mal)	

(b) Some foreign adjectives ending in a vowel do not take endings
Most of these are colour terms, i.e.: *beige, lila, orange, rosa*:

ein beige Rock	ein lila Mantel	die orange Farbe (*MM*)
ein rosa Kleid	eine prima Ware	

In writing a suffix such as *-farben* or *-farbig* is an acceptable alternative for the colour terms, e.g. *ein rosafarbenes Kleid.* In substandard speech, an *-n-* is often inserted as a base for the usual endings, e.g. *ein rosanes Kleid.* This is unacceptable in standard written German.

(c) An adjective used as an adverb to qualify a following adjective has no ending
Compare the difference between *ein unheilbarer, fauler Junge* 'an incurable lazy boy' and *ein unheilbar fauler Junge* 'an incurably lazy boy'. However, this distinction is not always clear-cut, and the first of a pair of adjectives is sometimes left

uninflected even if it is not being used as an adverb. This is a common stylistic device in modern prose:

ein reingebürtiger Pole von **traurig** edler Gestalt (*Grass*)	*a pure-bred Pole with a sad, noble figure*
seine **hochrot** abstehenden Ohren (*Grass*)	*his deep red, protuberant ears*

einzig may regularly have no ending if it can be considered as qualifying a following adjective e.g. *die einzig(e) mögliche Lösung*.

NB: For similar usage with *derartig*, see 5.1.6f.

(d) Adjectives in *-er* from town names do not inflect

die Leipziger Messe, die Lüneburger Heide, der Kölner Dom

(e) Adjectives in *-er* from numerals do not inflect

die neunziger Jahre 'the nineties'

(f) Uninflected adjectives are used with names of letters and numerals

groß *A*, klein z, römisch *IV*, arabisch 4

(g) *halb* and *ganz* are not declined before geographical names used without an article

halb Berlin, ganz Deutschland, ganz Europa

NB: See 9.3.2 for details on the use of *halb*.

6.2.8 The declension of adjectives after personal pronouns

(a) Adjectives used after a personal pronoun usually have strong endings

ich armer Deutscher   Wer hat dich dummen Kerl gesehen?
Wer konnte euch treulosen Verrätern helfen?
Wer kümmert sich um uns frühere Kollegen?

(b) Weak endings are found in a few contexts

(i) In the (rarely used) dative singular, weak **or** strong endings can be used in the masculine and neuter, e.g.: *mir mittellosem/mittellosen Mann*, but the feminine almost always has weak endings, e.g.: *Er hat mir alten* (rarely *alter*) *Frau geschmeichelt*.

(ii) Weak endings are more usual in the nominative plural:

wir jungen Kollegen   ihr hilflosen Kerle
ihr Deutsche (less usual ihr Deutschen)

However, for 'we Germans' *wir Deutsche* and *wir Deutschen* are equally common.

6.3 Irregularities in the spelling of some adjectives

6.3.1 The spelling of inflected adjectives in *-el, -en, -er*

(a) Adjectives in *-el* always drop the *-e-* when the adjective is inflected

> ein dunkler Wald, eine respektable Leistung

NB: When used as a noun, *dunkel* drops the *-e-* of the ending, e.g. *im Dunkeln* 'in the dark'.

(b) Adjectives in *-en* may drop the *-e-* when the adjective is inflected

This is the norm in everyday speech, but is less usual in writing: *eine metallene* (rarely written: *metallne*) *Stimme, ein seltener* (rarely written: *seltner*) *Vogel*.

(c) Adjectives in *-er*

Foreign adjectives and those with *-au-* or *-eu-* before the *er always* drop the *-e-*:

> eine makabre Geschichte   mit teuren Weinen   durch saure Milch

The others usually keep it in written German, though it is dropped in speech: *eine muntere* (rarely written: *muntre*) *Frau*.

NB: (i) The *-e-* of the comparative ending *-er* (cf. 8.1) is rarely omitted in writing, e.g.: *eine bessere* (rarely in writing: *beßre*) *Lösung*.
(ii) For the spelling of declined *ander*, see 5.5.2.

(d) The *-e-* is quite often left out in *-el-* or *-er-* in the middle of a word

> neb(e)lige Tage, eine wäss(e)rige Suppe

6.3.2 *hoch* 'high'

hoch has the special stem form *hoh-* to which the usual endings are added:

> der Berg ist **hoch** BUT ein **hoher** Berg   mit einem **hohen** Grad

6.3.3 A few adjectives have alternative base forms with or without final *-e*

e.g.: *Er ist* **feig** or **feige** 'He is cowardly'. They are:

blöd(e)	bös(e)	fad(e)	irr(e)	leis(e)	mild(e)
müd(e)	öd(e)	träg(e)	trüb(e)	vag(e)	zäh(e)

With all except *blöd(e)*, *mild(e)* and *zäh(e)* the alternative with *-e* is more common in written German. The form without *-e* is more frequent in spoken German unless the adjective is stressed.

NB: These have the same inflected forms, with the endings being added to the stem without *-e*, e.g.: *ein feiger Junge*.

6.4 Adjectives used as nouns

6.4.1 All adjectives and participles can be used as nouns in German

They are then usually written with a capital letter (but cf. 23.1.1a):

> der Alte *the old man*   die Alte *the old woman*
> das Alte *old things*   die Alten *the old people*

English cannot turn adjectives into nouns as easily, except in a few restricted cases (*the young, the old, the Dutch, the good, the bad and the ugly*, etc.). and we usually have to supply a dummy noun like *man, woman, thing(s), people* to be used with the adjective. The over-use of the corresponding German words like *Ding* or *Leute* is a characteristic feature of the German of English learners.

Idiomatic German exploits fully the possibilities of concise expression offered by the fact that adjectives can readily be used as nouns. In particular, they are often used where full clauses would be needed in English:

Die Farbe dieser Vögel war das für mich **Interessante**	*The colour of these birds was what interested me*
Er hat sich über das **Gesagte** aufgeregt	*He got annoyed about what had been said*
Das **Erschreckende** an diesem Vorfall war seine scheinbare Unabwendbarkeit	*What was terrifying about this occurrence was its apparent inevitability*
Die gerade **Eingestiegenen** waren ein älterer Herr und eine elegante Dame	*The people who had just got in were an elderly man and an elegant lady*
ein Ort, wo das irgendwie zu denkende **Konkrete** unwiederbringlich in **Abstraktes** umschlägt	*a point where concrete reality, however it may be imagined, becomes irrevocably abstract*

6.4.2 The declension of adjectives used as nouns

(a) Adjectives used as nouns decline like attributive adjectives
i.e. they have weak or strong endings according to the rules given in 6.2. They thus have the same endings as any preceding adjective, e.g.: *ein zuverlässiger Angestellter, von einer unbekannten Fremden*. The declension with the definite and indefinite articles of a typical masculine adjective used as a noun, *der Angestellte* 'employee', is given in Table 6.2.

NB: *der Angestellte* is naturally only used of a male employee. A female employee will be *die Angestellte, eine Angestellte*, with the appropriate endings, see 6.4.3.

Adjectives used as nouns in this way are not to be confused with 'weak' masculine nouns, whose declension looks quite similar, see Table 1.4. Note the difference between the endings of adjectives being used as nouns and 'weak' masculine or other regular nouns:

Adjective used as noun	*'Weak' masculine (or other) noun*
der Deutsche, des Deutschen, note: ein Deutscher	der Franzose, des Franzosen, BUT: ein Franzose
das Junge 'young of an animal' note: ein Junges	der Junge 'boy' BUT: ein Junge
die Fremde 'female stranger' dat. sing.: der Fremden	die Fremde 'foreign parts' BUT: in der Fremde 'abroad'

(b) In a few contexts adjectives used as nouns decline in a different way from other adjectives
(i) In the dative singular the adjective used as a noun usually has the ending *-en* if preceded by an adjective with the strong endings *-em* or *-er*:

Ich sprach mit Karls altem Bekannten, mit Helmuts englischer Bekannten

TABLE 6.2 *Adjective used as a noun*

	Declension with definite article	Declension with indefinite article
Singular		
Nominative	der Angestellte	ein Angestellter
Accusative	den Angestellten	einen Angestellten
Genitive	des Angestellten	eines Angestellten
Dative	dem Angestellten	einem Angestellten
Plural		
Nominative	die Angestellten	Angestellte
Accusative	die Angestellten	Angestellte
Genitive	der Angestellten	Angestellter
Dative	den Angestellten	Angestellten

(ii) In apposition (see 2.6), the weak ending is used in the dative singular even if there is no determiner:

> Er sprach mit Karl Friedrichsen, Angestell**ten** (rarely: Angestell**tem**) der BASF in Ludwigshafen
> Er sprach mit Heike König, Angestell**ten** (never: Angestell**ter**) der BASF in Ludwigshafen

(iii) The neuters *das Äußere*, *das Ganze* and *das Innere* may have the weak *or* the strong endings in the nominative/accusative singular after the indefinite article or the possessives *if* another adjective comes first:

> sein schlichtes Äußere(s)   ein einheitliches Ganze
> mein eigenes Innere(s)

6.4.3 Masculine and feminine adjectival nouns usually refer to people

(a) The sex is indicated by using the appropriate article
e.g. *der Fremde* 'the (male) stranger', *die Fremde* 'the (female) stranger'. A large number of those in common use correspond to simple nouns in English:

der Adlige	*aristocrat*	der Heilige	*saint*
der Abgeordnete	*representative*	der Industrielle	*industrialist*
der Angestellte	*employee*	der Jugendliche	*young person*
der Beamte	*civil servant*	der Obdachlose	*homeless person*
der Bekannte	*acquaintance*	der Reisende	*traveller*
der Deutsche	*German*	der Staatsangehörige	*citizen*
der Erwachsene	*adult*	der Überlebende	*survivor*
der Freiwillige	*volunteer*	der Verlobte	*fiancé*
der Fremde	*stranger*	der Verwandte	*relative*
der Gefangene	*prisoner*	der Vorgesetzte	*superior*
der Geistliche	*clergyman*	der Vorsitzende	*chairman*
der Gesandte	*emissary*		

(b) A few feminine adjectival nouns represent special cases
(i) A few referring to things are always feminine, i.e.:

> die Elektrische 'tram' (mainly south German)   die Gerade 'straight line'
> die Rechte, die Linke 'right', 'left' (hand); (political) 'right', 'left'

e.g.: *überdrüssig des Terrors einer revolutionären **Linken*** (SDZ).

(ii) Some feminines which were originally adjectival nouns are now treated as regular feminine nouns:

> die Brünette 'the brunette', die Vertikale 'the vertical',
> die Parallele 'the parallel (line)', die Horizontale 'the horizontal',
> aus der Horizontale (no longer: Horizontalen)

After a numeral, though, *drei Parallele* is still used beside the more usual *drei Parallelen*.

(iii) *die Illustrierte* 'the magazine' is usually still treated as an adjectival noun, e.g.: *in dieser Illustrierten*. In the plural, though, it may have the endings of an adjective or of a regular feminine noun, e.g.: *Wir haben zwei Illustrierte/Illustrierten gekauft.*

(iv) Exceptionally, the feminine form corresponding to *der Beamte* is *die Beamtin*. This is treated as a regular feminine noun, with the plural *die Beamtinnen.*

6.4.4 Neuter adjectival nouns usually denote abstract or collective ideas

Es ist schon **Schlimmes** passiert	*Bad things have already happened*
Er hat **Hervorragendes** geleistet	*He has achieved outstanding things*
der Schauer des **Verbotenen** und	*the frightening fascination of what*
Versagten (*Zweig*)	*is forbidden or denied*
... zugleich immer aufbauend auf das	*... at the same time always building*
Erreichte (*Mercedes advert*)	*on what has been achieved*

NB: *das Junge* 'the young' (of an animal), cf. 1.1.12.

Especially in spoken German, the names of regions within the German-speaking countries often take the form of neuter adjectival nouns, e.g.:

> Jetzt kommen wir ins **Hessische**   Hier sind wir im **Thüringischen**
> Der Baron von Münchhausen kam im **Braunschweigischen** zur Welt (*Kästner*)

6.4.5 Neuter adjectival nouns are frequently used after indefinites

e.g. *alles, nichts, viel(es), wenig,* cf. 5.5. They have weak or strong endings depending on whether the indefinite itself has an ending, e.g.:

> alles Gute   von allem Guten   nichts Neues   von nichts Neuem
> weiteres Interessante   folgendes Neue   lauter Neues
> viel/wenig Interessantes   von viel Interessantem
> (BUT: vieles Interessante, von vielem Interessanten, cf. 5.5.25b)

6.4.6 Words denoting languages and colours have the form of neuter adjectival nouns

(a) Names of languages
For further detail on the use of the article with these nouns, see 4.2.4d.

(i) The most common form, used to refer to the language in a specific context, or when an adjective precedes, is a neuter adjective. It is usually endingless, but may have the ending *-s* in the genitive:

> Wir lernen **Spanisch, Französisch, Russisch, Englisch**
> Die Aussprache des modernen **Deutsch(s)**

(ii) To refer to the language in a general sense, an inflected adjectival neuter noun is used. It *always* has the definite article and can *never* be used with a preceding adjective, e.g.:

> **Das Englische** ist **dem Deutschen** verwandt
> eine Übersetzung aus **dem Tschechischen**
> BUT: eine Übersetzung aus **dem amerikanischen Englisch**

(b) Names of colours

These usually have the form of a neuter adjectival noun which does not decline except for the addition of *-s* in the genitive singular. The plural is also endingless in written German, though an *-s* may be used in speech:

> das **Grün** der Wiesen   von einem glänzenden **Rot**   in **Schwarz** gekleidet
> dieses häßlichen **Gelbs**   die beiden **Blau** (spoken only: **Blaus**)

In a few set phrases with the definite article this noun is declined:

> ins **Grüne** fahren   ins **Schwarze** treffen   Es ist das **Gelbe** vom Ei
> das **Blaue** vom Himmel herunter versprechen

6.5 Cases with adjectives

Many adjectives can be used with a noun dependent on them. The case of the noun depends on the particular adjective.

6.5.1 Adjectives which govern the dative

(a) The dative is the most common case used with adjectives

Er ist **seinem Bruder** sehr ähnlich	*He's very much like his brother*
Sie waren **ihrem Freund** beim Umzug behilflich	*They helped their friend when he moved house*
Dieses Gespräch war **mir** sehr nützlich	*This conversation was very useful for me*
Er war **seinem Gegner** überlegen	*He surpassed his opponent*
Ein **ihr** unbekannter Mann trat herein	*A man she didn't know walked in*

The following list gives a selection of frequent adjectives which govern the dative. The adjective usually follows the noun (or pronoun) dependent on it, but those marked with an asterisk in the following list may come first. Those marked with † may alternatively be used with *für* (before or after the adjective), e.g.: *Das war für mich unangenehm/unangenehm für mich* (see also 6.6). *böse* may also be used with *auf* or *mit* (see 6.6):

ähnlich*	*like, similar*	ergeben	*devoted, attached*
angenehm†	*agreeable*	erwünscht	*desirable*
begreiflich	*comprehensible*	fern	*distant*
behilflich	*helpful*	fremd	*strange*
bekannt	*known, familiar*	gefährlich†	*dangerous*
bequem	*comfortable*	gefällig	*obliging*
bewußt	*known*	nicht geheuer	*scary*
beschwerlich†	*arduous*	gehorsam	*obedient*
böse	*angry*	geläufig	*familiar*
dankbar	*grateful*	gemeinsam	*common*
eigen	*peculiar*	gerecht	*just*
entbehrlich†	*unnecessary*	gesinnt	*inclined*

gewogen (lit.)	*well-disposed*	schuldig	*owing*
günstig	*favourable*	schwer	*difficult*
heilig	*holy, sacred*	teuer	*expensive*
hinderlich	*awkward*	treu*	*faithful*
klar	*obvious*	überlegen	*superior*
lästig†	*troublesome*	verhaßt	*hateful*
leicht†	*easy*	verständlich†	*comprehensible*
möglich†	*possible*	wichtig†	*important*
nahe*	*near, close*	widerlich	*repugnant*
nötig	*necessary*	willkommen	*welcome*
nützlich†	*useful*	zugänglich†	*accessible*
peinlich†	*embarrassing*	zuträglich	*beneficial*
schädlich†	*injurious, harmful*		

(b) Some adjectives which govern the dative are only used predicatively

e.g.: Sie ist **mir** zugetan   *She is well-disposed towards me*

These are:

abhold (arch., lit.)	*ill-disposed*	untertan	*subordinate*
feind (arch., lit.)	*hostile*	zugetan	*well-disposed*
gram (lit.)	*angry (with)*	zuwider	*repugnant*
hold (arch., lit.)	*favourably disposed*		

This group also contains all the adjectives meaning 'all the same', e.g.: *Das ist mir gleich* 'That's all the same to me', namely, *einerlei*, *egal* (coll.), *gleich*, *piepe* (coll.), *wurs(ch)t* (coll.).

6.5.2 Adjectives which govern the accusative

They occur mainly in verbal constructions with *sein* or *werden*:

jdn./etwas *gewahr werden (lit.)	*become aware of sb./sth.*
Wir wurden unseren Irrtum gewahr	*We realised our mistake*
etwas gewohnt sein (cf. 6.6.1)	*be used to sth.*
Ich bin den Lärm nicht gewohnt	*I'm not used to the noise*
etwas/jdn. los sein/werden	*be/get rid of sth./sb.*
Endlich bin ich den Schnupfen los	*At last I've got rid of the cold*
etwas/jdn. *satt sein/haben	*be sick of sth./sb.*
Er ist/hat es gründlich satt	*He's thoroughly sick of it*
jdm. etwas schuldig sein	*owe sb. sth.*
Sie ist ihm eine Erklärung schuldig	*She owes him an explanation*
etwas *wert sein	*be worth sth.*
Es ist das Papier nicht wert, auf	*It's not worth the paper it's*
dem es steht (*MM*)	*printed on*

NB: (i) The adjectives asterisked can be used with a genitive in formal registers, see 6.5.3; in the case of *satt* this is only possible in conjunction with *sein*, not with *haben*.

(ii) *schuldig* is used with a genitive in the sense of 'guilty', e.g.: *Er ist des Verbrechens schuldig* 'He is guilty of the crime'.

6.5.3 Adjectives which govern the genitive

(a) The genitive with adjectives is mainly restricted to formal German

A number of the adjectives concerned have alternative constructions in less formal registers. With the exception of *bar*, they follow the noun:

bar *devoid of*	Seine Handlungsweise war bar **aller Vernunft**
	His action was devoid of all reason
bewußt *conscious of*	Ich war mir **meines Irrtums** bewußt
	I was conscious of my mistake
fähig *capable of*	Er ist **einer solchen Tat** nicht fähig
(or with *zu* + noun)	*He is not capable of such a deed*
froh *pleased at*	Sie war **seines Erfolges** froh
(usually: *über*)	*She was pleased about his success*
gewahr *aware of*	Wir wurden **unseres Irrtums** gewahr
(more often with acc.)	*We became aware of our mistake*
gewiß *certain of*	Sie können **meiner Unterstützung** gewiß sein
	You can be certain of my support
mächtig *master of*	Sie ist **des Deutschen** absolut mächtig
	She has a complete command of German
müde *tired of*	Sie waren **des langen Streites** müde (*Döblin*)
	They were tired of the long quarrel
schuldig *guilty of*	Der Angeklagte ist **des Hochverrats** schuldig
(cf. 6.5.2)	*The accused is guilty of high treason*
sicher *sure of*	Er ist **seiner Sache** noch nicht sicher (*Zeit*)
	He is not quite sure of his ground
überdrüssig *tired of*	Er war **des Herumhockens** überdrüssig (*Pinkwart*)
(or, rarely, with acc.)	*He was tired of sitting around*
wert *worthy of*	etwas, das **jeder Anstrengung** wert ist (*Th. Mann*)
(often with acc.)	*something which is worth any effort*
würdig *worthy of*	Er ist **dieser Ehre** nicht würdig
	He is not worthy of this honour

(b) *voll* **is used in a number of alternative constructions**

(i) It is used with the genitive in formal written (mainly literary) language:

Das Theater war voll **aufmerksamer Zuschauer**.

(ii) With a noun standing alone, *voll* or *voller* is used with a nominative:

ein Korb **voll(er) Obst, voll(er) Äpfel**.

(iii) With a noun qualified by an adjective, *voll von* is used:

ein Korb voll **von herrlichem Obst, roten Äpfeln**.

(iv) *voll mit* is also frequent, particularly in spoken registers:

ein Korb voll **mit herrlichem Obst, roten Äpfeln**.

(c) A few adjectives governing the genitive are restricted to predicate use after *sein* and/or *werden*

These are used only in the most formal (particularly legal) written German:

| ansichtig | bedürftig | eingedenk | geständig | gewärtig | habhaft |
| (un)kundig | ledig | teilhaftig | verdächtig | verlustig | |

An example from official legal language:

| Er ist **der Bürgerrechte** für | *He has been deprived of his civic* |
| verlustig erklärt worden | *rights* |

6.6 Adjectives with prepositions

6.6.1 Many adjectives can be linked to a noun by means of prepositions

Das ist **von dem Wetter** abhängig   die **um ihre Kinder** besorgte Mutter
Er war **mit meinem Entschluß** einverstanden

Which preposition is used depends on the individual adjective, and as with prepositions used in the prepositional object of some verbs, (cf. 18.6), the preposition often retains little of its full meaning. Detailed information is available in Sommerfeldt and Schreiber (1977). We give below a selection of adjectives governing prepositional constructions, concentrating on those which are most frequent and those with constructions which differ from their usual English equivalents.

The prepositional phrase may precede or follow the adjective. If it contains a noun it commonly comes first but may come second; if it contains a pronoun it almost invariably comes second, i.e.:

either: Er ist **über den neuen Lehrling** verärgert
or (rather less usual):   Er ist verärgert **über den neuen Lehrling**
but always: Er ist verärgert **über ihn**

However, *arm* and *reich* usually precede the phrase with *an*, even if it contains a noun, e.g. *Das Land ist arm/reich an Bodenschätzen.*

(a) Frequently used adjectives governing prepositions

NB: *auf* and *über* always take the accusative when dependent on adjectives.

abhängig von	*dependent on*
angewiesen auf etwas/jdn. sein	*have to rely on sth./sb.*
Wir waren **auf uns selber** angewiesen	
ärgerlich auf/über	*annoyed with*
arm an	*poor in*
aufmerksam auf	*aware of*
Sie machte mich **auf meinen Irrtum** aufmerksam	
begeistert von/über	*enthusiastic about*
berechtigt zu	*justified in*
Sie sind **zu diesem Vorwurf** berechtigt	
bereit zu	*ready for*
Die Truppen waren **zum Einsatz** bereit	
besorgt um	*anxious about*
bezeichnend für	*characteristic of*
blaß, bleich vor	*pale with*
Er war völlig blaß/bleich **vor Entsetzen**	
böse auf/mit	*cross with*
Bist du böse **auf mich/mit mir**? (Or Bist du mir böse?, cf. 6.5.1)	
charakteristisch für	*characteristic of*
dankbar für	*grateful for*
Ich war ihm **für seine gütige Hilfe** dankbar	
durstig nach	*thirsty for*
eifersüchtig auf	*jealous of*
einverstanden mit	*in agreement with*
Bist du **mit diesem Vorschlag** einverstanden?	
empfänglich für	*susceptible to, receptive to*
Sie ist sehr empfänglich **für Schmeichelei**	

empfindlich gegen	*sensitive to*
Sie ist sehr empfindlich **gegen Kälte**	
ersichtlich aus	*obvious from, clear from*
Das ist **aus seiner letzten Bemerkung** ersichtlich	
fähig zu	*capable of*
Sie ist **zu einer solchen Tat** nicht fähig (or genitive, cf. 6.5.3a)	
fertig mit etwas sein	*have finished sth*
Bist du **mit dem Essen** schon fertig?	
geeignet für/zu	*suitable for*
Er ist **für diese/zu dieser Arbeit** nicht geeignet	
gefaßt auf	*ready for, prepared for*
Mach dich gefaßt **auf seine Reaktion!**	
gespannt auf	*extremely curious about*
Ich bin **auf diesen Film** sehr gespannt 'I am dying to see that film'	
gewöhnt an	*accustomed/used to*
Ich bin jetzt **an diesen Kaffee** gewöhnt	
(i.e. 'I have made myself accustomed to this coffee'. Compare: *Ich bin diesen Kaffee gewohnt*, cf. 6.5.2, 'This is the coffee I am used to')	
gierig nach	*greedy for*
gleichgültig gegen/gegenüber	*indifferent to(wards)*
höflich zu/gegenüber	*polite to(wards)*
hungrig nach	*hungry for*
interessiert an	*interested in*
müde von	*tired from*
Er war müde **von der schweren Arbeit**	

NB: *müde* governs a genitive in the sense 'tired of', see 6.5.3a.

neidisch auf	*envious of*
neugierig auf	*curious about*
reich an	*rich in*
scharf auf (coll.)	*keen on*
Er ist scharf **auf seine Rechte**	
schuld an etwas sein/haben	*be blamed for sth.*
Wer war/hatte **an dem Streit** schuld?	
sicher vor	*safe from*
stolz auf	*proud of*
typisch für	*typical of*
überzeugt von	*convinced of*
unabhängig von	*independent of*
verheiratet mit	*married to*
verliebt in	*in love with*
Sie ist **in den Bruder** ihrer Freundin verliebt	
verschieden von	*different to/from*
versessen auf	*(very, mad) keen on*
Er ist versessen **auf alte Sportwagen**	
verwandt mit	*related to*
vorbereitet auf	*prepared for*
wütend auf	*mad at, furious with*
Er war wütend **auf seine Chefin**	
zornig auf	*angry with*
zuständig für	*responsible for*

(b) *über* **(with the accusative) is used with many adjectives to mean 'about'**
(see also 20.3.12e), e.g.: *aufgebracht* 'outraged', *beschämt* 'ashamed', *bestürzt, betroffen* 'full of consternation', *empört, entrüstet* 'indignant', *entzückt* 'delighted', *erbittert* 'bitter', *erbost* 'infuriated', *erfreut* 'delighted', *erstaunt* 'amazed', *froh* 'glad' (cf. 6.5.3a), *glücklich* 'happy', *traurig* 'sad', *verwundert* 'astonished'.

(c) *vor* **is used with a number of adjectives expressing a cause**
(see also 20.3.15d), e.g.: *angst* 'fearful', *elend* 'miserable', *starr* 'stiff', *stumm* 'speechless'.

6.6.2 Many adjectives governing prepositions may be used with a *daß*-clause or an infinitive clause with *zu*

The dependent clause is commonly anticipated by the prepositional adverb (i.e. *da(r)* + preposition, e.g. *daran, damit*, cf. 3.5):

Er ist **davon** abhängig, daß ihm sein Bruder hilft	*He is dependent on his brother helping him*
Er ist **davon** abhängig, das Geld zu erhalten	*He is dependent on receiving the money*
Wir sind **dazu** bereit, Ihnen darüber Auskünfte zu geben	*We are prepared to give you some information about this*
Sie war **darüber** froh, daß sie ihn noch sehen würde	*She was pleased that she would still see him*

It is impossible to give clear rules for when the prepositional adverb is used in such constructions and when it is not. Usage is inconsistent and subject to variation. With a number of the adjectives given in section 6.6.1 it is quite optional and pairs of sentences like the following can be equally acceptable and grammatical:

Ich bin gewöhnt, jeden Tag eine Stunde zu üben
Ich bin daran gewöhnt, jeden Tag eine Stunde zu üben

In particular the prepositional adverb is wholly optional with the following adjectives: *begierig, bereit, böse, einverstanden, gespannt, gewöhnt, neugierig, stolz, überzeugt, vorbereitet* and those in 6.6.1b with *über*. If it is used with these it tends to focus emphasis on the content of the dependent clause or infinitive phrase. In practice, though, it is more commonly inserted than omitted, even where it is optional, especially in written German.

6.6.3 Phrases with some adjectives and prepositions can be used attributively

i.e. a whole extended adjectival phrase can be used before a noun. This 'extended epithet' construction is frequent in formal, especially technical and official German, and many of the adjectives listed in 6.6.1 (and others) can be used in this way:

zum **Einsatz bereite** Truppen	*troops ready to be deployed*
eine **von rhetorischen Effekten freie** Rede	*a speech free of rhetorical devices*
eine **für sie ganz typische** Haltung	*an attitude quite typical of her*

This construction is also very frequent with participles, see 13.5.3.

7
Adverbs

The traditional term 'adverb' covers a range of words with a variety of uses. Typically, adverbs are words which do not inflect and which serve to express relations of time, place, manner and degree. They can be used to qualify verbs, e.g. *Sie hat ihm **höflich** geantwortet*, or adjectives, e.g. *ein **natürlich** eleganter Stil*, and they very often relate to the sentence as a whole, e.g. *Er hat ihr **sicher** geholfen*. Their diversity means that it is not easy to define them satisfactorily or to distinguish them from adjectives on the one hand and other indeclinable words such as particles and verb prefixes on the other. Well presented recent accounts are to be found in Eisenberg (1994: 204–9) and Weinrich (1993: 547–608). In practice, though, every authority differs, sometimes quite radically, on what are to be considered as adverbs in German and how they are to be classified systematically. We have adopted here a simplified classification for practical purposes on the basis of these more extensive accounts, and this is summarised in Table 7.1.

Phrases, often with a preposition, can have the same function as an adverb in a sentence. Compare:

Sie hat **heute** gearbeitet – Sie hat **den ganzen Tag** gearbeitet
Sie ist **trotzdem** gekommen – Sie ist **trotz des Regens** gekommen
Sie blieb **dort** – Sie blieb **in der alten Stadt am Rhein**

The term 'adverbial' is commonly used to refer to both single words (i.e. 'adverbs') and phrases like the above (traditionally called 'adverbial phrases') which function adverbially.

This chapter only deals with adverbs proper (i.e. single words) and concentrates

TABLE 7.1 *Main types of adverbs*

Adverbs	Use	Examples
of time	Indicate point in time, duration or frequency	damals, lange, oft
of place	Indicate position or direction	dort, oben, herein
of attitude	Comment on what is said	sicher, wahrscheinlich
of viewpoint	Indicate point of view	finanziell, psychologisch
of reason	Indicate cause, condition, consequence or purpose	deshalb, dennoch, trotzdem
of manner	Answer the question '*wie?*'	fleißig, zufällig
of degree	Emphasise, amplify or tone down another word	sehr, genug, außerordentlich
Interrogative	Used to ask questions	wie?, wann?, warum?

on those adverbs of German and their uses which present significant differences from their most usual English equivalents, in particular adverbs of place (7.1), of direction (7.2), of manner, viewpoint, attitude and cause (7.3), adverbs of degree (7.4) and interrogative adverbs (7.5). Adverbs of time are dealt with in Chapter 11 with other time expressions (specifically in section 11.6), and modal particles in Chapter 10. The comparative and superlative forms of adverbs are treated in Chapter 8.

7.1 Adverbs of place

In this section we deal with those adverbs which indicate *position*.

7.1.1 *hier, dort, da*

(a) *hier* **refers to a place close to the speaker**
(= English *here*), e.g.:

> Ich habe deine Tasche **hier** im Schrank gefunden

(b) *dort* **refers to a place away from the speaker**
(= English *there*), e.g.:

> Ich sah deine Schwester **dort** an der Ecke stehen

(c) *da* **is a less emphatic alternative to** *dort*
It is used more frequently than *dort* and usually refers to a place away from the speaker, e.g.:

> Ich sah ihn **da** an der Ecke stehen

However, *da* is often used to point in a general, unemphatic way when the difference between 'here' and 'there' is not crucial. In such contexts it can in some contexts correspond to English *here*:

> Herr Meyer ist momentan nicht **da**   *Mr Meyer is not here at the moment*

7.1.2 *oben, unten*

German lacks noun equivalents for 'top' and 'bottom' and often uses phrases with *oben* and *unten* in contexts where they would be used in English:

oben auf dem Turm	*at the top of the tower*
Sie stand ganz **oben** auf der Treppe	*She was standing right at the top of the stairs*
unten auf dem Bild	*at the bottom of the picture*
Bis unten sind es noch zwei Stunden zu Fuß	*It's another two hours' walk to the bottom*
Die Säule wird **nach unten hin** breiter	*The column broadens out towards the bottom*
Sein Name steht **unten** auf der Liste	*His name is at the bottom of the list*
ganz **unten** im Kasten	*right at the bottom of the chest*
auf Seite 90 **unten**	*at the bottom of page 90*
von **oben** bis **unten**	*from top to bottom*

7.1.3 The adverb *mitten* is the most usual equivalent for the English noun 'middle'

It is usually followed by a preposition. In some contexts *mitten* has other English equivalents:

Mitten im Garten ist ein Teich	*In the middle of the garden there is a pond*
Sie stellte die Vase **mitten** auf den Tisch	*She put the vase in the middle of the table*
mitten in der Nacht	*in the middle of the night*
mitten in der Aufregung	*in the midst of the excitement*
Er war **mitten** aus seinem Urlaub zu der Konferenz gekommen	*He had come back to the conference in the middle of his holidays*
Ich war **mitten** unter den Leuten auf der Straße (*Zuckmayer*)	*I was in the midst of the people in the street*
Er bahnte sich **mitten** durch die Menge einen Weg	*He forced his way through the middle of the crowd*
mitten auf der Leiter	*halfway up/down the ladder*

7.1.4 *außen, draußen, innen, drinnen*

außen and *innen* mean 'on the outside', 'on the inside', i.e. they refer to the outer or inner surface of the object. *draußen* and *drinnen*, on the other hand, mean 'outside' and 'inside', i.e. away from the object or contained within it:

Die Tasse ist **außen** schmutzig	*The cup is dirty on the outside*
Ich mußte **draußen** warten	*I had to wait outside*
Die Äpfel sind **innen** faul	*The apples are rotten inside*
Drinnen ist es aber schön warm	*Indoors it's nice and warm, though*
Dieses Fenster geht **nach innen** auf	*This window opens inwards*
Wir kommen **von draußen**	*We are coming from outside*
Er schloß die Tür **von außen** zu	*He shut the door from the outside*
von außen/innen gesehen	*seen from the outside/inside*

NB: The use of *außen* and *innen* for 'outside' and 'inside' is now archaic or regional (especially Austrian).

7.1.5 Indefinite place adverbs

i.e. the equivalents of English 'somewhere', 'anywhere', 'everywhere', 'nowhere'.

(a) *irgendwo* corresponds to 'somewhere' or, in questions, 'anywhere'

Ich habe es **irgendwo** liegenlassen	*I've left it somewhere*
Hast du Paula **irgendwo** gesehen?	*Have you seen Paula anywhere?*

In spoken German simple *wo* is commonly used for *irgendwo* if unstressed, e.g.: *Ich habe ihn wohl wo liegenlassen.*

(b) *überall* corresponds to 'everywhere', or to 'anywhere' in the sense of 'no matter where'

Erika hat dich **überall** gesucht	*Erika was looking for you everywhere*
Sie dürfen hier **überall** parken	*You can park anywhere here*

(c) *nirgendwo, nirgends* correspond to 'nowhere', 'not ... anywhere'

Er war **nirgendwo/nirgends** zu sehen	*He was nowhere to be seen*
Ich habe dich gestern **nirgends** gesehen	*I didn't see you anywhere yesterday*

(d) *anderswo, woanders* **correspond to 'somewhere else', 'elsewhere'**
(in questions also = 'anywhere else'):

Sie müssen ihn **anderswo/woanders** suchen	*You'll have to look for him somewhere else*
Hast du ihn **anderswo/woanders** gesehen?	*Have you seen him somewhere/anywhere else?*

7.2 Adverbs of direction: *hin* and *her*

By using the adverbs *hin* and *her*, German can express direction away from or towards the speaker in a more systematic and consistent way than is usual or possible in English. These adverbs have a wide range of use and can occur alone or linked with another word. In general, *hin* denotes motion *away from* the speaker (or the person concerned), *her towards* the speaker.

7.2.1 *hin* and *her* are compounded with the position adverbs to form direction adverbs

By using these compound forms, German differentiates consistently between 'position', 'movement away from the speaker' and 'movement towards the speaker'. This can be illustrated by the interrogative adverbs:

Wo wohnen Sie?	*Where do you live?*
Wohin gehen Sie?	*Where are you going (to)?*
Woher kommen Sie?	*Where are you coming from?*

The other adverbs of position given in sections 7.1.1 and 7.1.5 compound in a similar way with *-hin* and *-her* to indicate direction to/from:

Sie wohnt **hier**	*She lives here*
Sie kommt **hierher**	*She's coming here*
Leg das Paket **hierhin**!	*Put the parcel down here!*
Sie wohnt doch **da/dort**	*She lives there*
In den Ferien fahren wir **dorthin/ dahin**, wo wir voriges Jahr waren	*In the holidays we're going where we were last year*
Dorther kommt sie	*That's where she comes from*
Ich komme gerade **daher**	*I've just come from there*
Er stand **dort** an der Ecke	*He was standing there on the corner*
Wie wollen wir **dorthin** kommen?	*How are we going to get there?*
Er geht heute nachmittag **irgendwohin**	*He's going somewhere this afternoon*
Sie geht **überallhin**	*She goes everywhere*
Morgen fahren wir **anderswohin**	*We're going somewhere else tomorrow*

wohin, woher, dahin and *daher* are often split, especially in spoken German, with *hin* and *her* being placed at the end of the clause:

Wo gehört dieses Buch **hin**?
Wo kommt deine Mutter **her**?
ein kleines, gutes Restaurant, **wo** keine Amerikaner **hin**kamen (*Baum*)
Da gehe ich praktisch nie **hin**
Da kommt er doch nicht **her**, oder?

This is not possible if these words are used in an extended sense, for example *woher* in: ***Woher** weißt du das?* 'How do you know that?' and *daher* in the meaning 'that is why', e.g.: ***Daher** hat sie sich aufgeregt.*

NB: (i) *von wo* and *von da/dort* are common alternatives to *woher, daher/dorther*, e.g.: **Von wo** *kommt er? Er kommt* **von da/dort**.

(ii) *dahin* is used with *sein* in the meaning 'finished', 'lost', e.g.:
Sein Leben ist **dahin***; Mein ganzes Geld war* **dahin**.

7.2.2 *hin-* and *her-* combine with many verbs as a separable prefix

(a) With most verbs they indicate the direction of movement

In such contexts they do not need a specific 'here' or 'there' element. The English equivalents (if any) can be idiomatic, especially if the verb does not primarily denote movement:

Heute ist eine Wahlversammlung, und ich gehe **hin**	*There's an election meeting today and I'm going there/to it*
Ich hielt ihm die Zeitung **hin**	*I held out the newspaper to him*
Ich hörte einen Ruf und sah **hin**	*I heard a cry and looked over in that direction*
Komm mal **her**!	*Come here!*
Gib den Schlüssel **her**!	*Give me the key!*
Er hat mich mit dem Auto **hergefahren**	*He drove me here*
Halt den Teller **her**!	*Hold out your plate*
Setz dich **her** zu mir!	*Come and sit down over here by me*

(b) Some verbs compounded with *hin-* and *her-* have a derived, abstract or figurative meaning

Those with *hin-* usually retain a directional meaning, but those with *her-* tend to be purely idiomatic. Selected examples:

sein Leben für etwas **hingeben**	*sacrifice one's life for sth.*
Das wird schon **hinhauen** (coll.)	*It'll be OK in the end*
Nach dem Interview **war** ich völlig **hin**	*After the interview I was shattered*
Die Burschen **fielen** über ihn **her**	*The youths attacked him*
Das Thema **gibt** doch nicht viel **her**	*There's not a lot to this topic*
Es **ging** recht lustig **her**	*It was good fun*
Sie hat ein Zimmer für ihn **hergerichtet**	*She got a room ready for him*
Mit der Qualität der Abiturienten **ist** es nicht mehr weit **her** (*Spiegel*)	*The quality of school-leavers isn't up to much any more*

7.2.3 *hin* and *her* can be used to emphasise direction with a preceding prepositional phrase

(a) With a preceding prepositional phrase they are usually optional

Wir wanderten bis zu den Bergen (**hin**)	Er blickte zur Decke (**hin**)
Wir fuhren nach Süden (**hin**)	Er ging zum Fenster (**hin**)
Wir wanderten durch das Tal (**hin**)	Sie flogen über den Berg (**hin**)
Eine Stimme kam von oben (**her**)	Rings um ihn (**her**) tobte der Sturm

NB: (i) The combination *an . . . hin* (see 20.3.2a) means 'alongside', e.g.:
Der Weg führt **an** *der Wiese* **hin** 'along the meadow'.

(ii) *von . . . her* is commonly used to mean 'in respect of', e.g.: *Das war schon verfehlt* **von** *der Zielsetzung* **her** (see 20.2.8a).

(b) With *hinter, neben, vor* and *zwischen, her* is used to indicate movement in relation to another person or thing

The noun in this construction is always in the dative case, cf. 20.3:

Er ging **hinter** ihr **her**	*He was walking behind her*
Der Hund lief **neben** mir **her**	*The dog was running beside me*
Ein deutscher Wagen fuhr **vor** ihm **her**	*A German car was driving in front of him*
Sie ging **zwischen** uns **her**	*She was walking between us*

The adverbs *hinterher* and *nebenher* are used in a similar sense, e.g.: *Er lief hinterher, nebenher* 'He was running behind, alongside'.

(c) Phrases with *auf* giving reasons or causes can be strengthened by *hin*
See also 20.3.5d:

Das tat er **auf** meinen Vorschlag **hin**	*He did it at my suggestion*
auf die Gefahr **hin**, erkannt zu werden	*at the risk of being recognised*

7.2.4 *hin-* and *her-* combine with prepositions to form directional adverbs

e.g. *hinab, herab, hinzu, herbei*, etc. These occur chiefly as separable verb prefixes. In general they link the direction indicated by the preposition with the notion 'away from' or 'towards' the speaker.

(a) Six prepositions form pairs of compounds with *hin-* and *her-*:

hinab, herab	*down*	hinein, herein	*in*
hinauf, herauf	*up*	hinüber, herüber	*over*
hinaus, heraus	*out*	hinunter, herunter	*down*

They are characteristically used in conjunction with a preceding prepositional phrase or a phrase in the accusative case (cf. 2.2.5c):

Wir stiegen die Treppe **hinauf**	*We climbed up the stairs*
Wir kamen die Treppe **herab/herunter**	*We came down the stairs*
Er ging in das Haus **hinein**	*He went into the house*
Er kam in das Zimmer **herein**	*He came into the room*

NB: (i) *hin-, herab* and *hin-, herunter* have identical meanings. Those with *-unter* are more usual in spoken registers.

(ii) *hinaus* and *heraus* are used with a preceding phrase with *zu* to indicate movement or vision out of or through doors, windows etc., e.g.: *Er blickte zur Tür hinaus; Sie warf es zum Fenster heraus.*

(b) Other prepositions or adverbs combine with only one of *hin-* or *her-*:

With *hin-*:	hindurch *through*	hinweg *away*	hinzu *in addition*
With *her-*:	heran *along; up (to)*	herbei *along*	herum *round*
	hervor *forth, out*		

Er drang durch die Menge **hindurch**	*He pushed through the crowd*
Die Rollbahn sauste unter uns **hinweg**	*The runway sped away beneath us*
Sie legte einige Papiere **hinzu**	*She put down some papers in addition*
Sie trat an den Tisch **heran**	*She stepped up to the table*
Einige Polizisten kamen **herbei**	*A few policemen came along*
Er kam um die Ecke **herum**	*He came round the corner*
Die Bücher lagen auf dem Tisch **herum**	*The books were lying around on the table*
Er zog einen Revolver unter dem Tisch **hervor**	*He pulled a revolver out from under the table*

NB: Formal German used to make a distinction between *herum* 'round in a circle' and *umher* 'criss-crossing'; 'higgledy-piggledy'. *herum* is now common in both senses in both speech and writing.

(c) The adverb with *hin-* or *her-* often repeats the direction given by a previous preposition

Der Vogel flog in das Zimmer **hinein**	Er kam **um** die Ecke **herum**
Wir kamen **aus** dem Wald **heraus**	Sie gingen **durch** das Tal **hindurch**

These constructions can seem tautologous or unnecessary to English learners. However, if the adverb is omitted, the effect is usually that the verb is emphasised rather than the direction and the adverb should thus be used *unless* the verb is to be stressed. Compare:

Der Vogel ist in das Zimmer **geflog**en (i.e. it flew rather than hopped)
Der Vogel ist in das Zimmer **hineingeflog**en (i.e. it didn't fly out)
Wir wollen die Truhe in dein Zimmer **trag**en (i.e. carry, not push)
Wir wollen die Truhe in dein Zimmer **hinübertragen**

If another word in the sentence bears the main stress, the adverb is optional, e.g.:

Der **Vogel** ist in das Zimmer (hinein)geflogen
Wir wollen die **Truhe** in dein Zimmer (hinüber)tragen

(d) Verbs with the simple prefixes, e.g. *ab-*, *an-*, *auf-*, etc. usually have a derived, extended or other non-literal sense

(see also 22.5.1) This is because simple direction is indicated by using the forms in *hin-* or *her-*. Compare:

Er ist (in das Zimmer) **hineingegangen**	*He went in(to the room)*
Die Zeitung ist **eingegangen**	*The newspaper closed down*
Er hat den Koffer **hereingebracht**	*He brought the suitcase in*
Das **bringt** nichts **ein**	*That's not worth it*
Er **kam** (aus dem Haus) **heraus**	*He came out (of the house)*
Mit 100 Mark **kommen** wir nicht **aus**	*We won't manage on 100 marks*
Ich **ging** zu ihm **hinüber**	*I went over to him*
Er ist zur SPD **übergegangen**	*He went over to the SPD*

(e) Some verbs with *hin-* and *her-* compounds have figurative meanings

sich zu etwas herablassen	*condescend to (do) sth.*
Er gibt eine Zeitschrift heraus	*He edits a journal*
Es kommt auf dasselbe heraus	*It all comes to the same thing*
Er leierte die Predigt herunter	*He reeled off the sermon*
Die Verhandlungen zogen sich hinaus	*The negotiations dragged on*

(f) In colloquial German, both *hin-* and *-her* are often reduced to *'r-* in compound forms, irrespective of the direction involved

This is especially frequent in north German usage, e.g.:

Wollen wir jetzt **'raus**gehen (written: hinausgehen)
Wollen wir die Jalousien **'runter**lassen? (written: herunterlassen)

These forms are occasionally found in writing if informal usage is being suggested, e.g.: *Ich ging morgens Bahnhofstreppen **rauf** und **runter** und nachmittags Bahnhofstreppen **runter** und **rauf** (Böll).*

7.2.5 Some special meanings and uses of *hin-* and *her-*

hin- often has the sense 'down':

> Sie legte sich **hin**   Der Junge fiel **hin**   Er setzte den Stuhl **hin**

vor sich hin means 'to oneself' (see 20.3.16b):

> Das murmelte er so **vor sich hin**   Sie las **vor sich hin**

hin und her means 'to and fro', 'back and forth':

> Er ging auf der Straße **hin und her**   *He was walking back and forth along*
> *the street*
> Ich habe es **hin und her** überlegt   *I've considered it from every point of view*

hin und wieder means 'now and again':

> **Hin und wieder** sehe ich ihn in der Stadt

her is used in the sense of 'ago' in time phrases (see also 11.5.13):

> Zwei Jahre **her** zogen wir nach Duisburg um   Das ist schon lange **her**
> Wie lange ist es **her**, daß du in Gießen studiert hast?

7.3 Adverbs of manner, viewpoint, attitude and reason

A large number of adverbs fall into these categories, or into related sub-groups which are not dealt with specifically. It is convenient to deal with them all together here.

7.3.1 Adverbs of manner and viewpoint

(a) Adverbs of manner typically answer the question *Wie?*

> Wie ist sie gefahren?   Sie ist **schnell** gefahren
> Wie hat sie gesungen?   Sie hat **gut** gesungen
> Wie hat er es gemacht?   Er hat es **anders** gemacht

When they occur in a sentence with *nicht*, the *nicht* always refers specifically to the manner adverb:

> Sie hat **nicht deutlich** gesprochen (she did speak, but not clearly)
> Werder Bremen hat gestern abend in Leverkusen **nicht gut** gespielt
> (they played, but not well)

(b) Adverbs of viewpoint indicate a context in which the statement is to be understood

They can be paraphrased by 'seen from a ... point of view' or '... speaking', e.g.:

> Die Stadt liegt **verkehrsmäßig** ungünstig
> (i.e. in terms of road and rail communications)
> **Finanziell** war diese Entscheidung eine Katastrophe
> (i.e. financially speaking)
> Deutschland ist **wirtschaftlich** stärker geworden
> (i.e. from an economic point of view)

(c) Most adjectives (and participles) can be used as adverbs

Most of these are in practice adverbs of manner or viewpoint. In English such adverbs are commonly marked by the suffix -*ly*, but German has no such ending, and these words have exactly the same form whether they are being used as adjectives or adverbs. Compare:

Er hat die Sache **überraschend schnell** erledigt	*He settled the matter surprisingly quickly*
Ein Dokument zeigt doch, daß er **mäßigend** und **bremsend** zu wirken versuchte (*Zeit*)	*A document nevertheless shows that he tried to exercise a moderating and calming influence*

An adverb qualifying an adjective before a noun is marked as such by having no ending. Compare:

ein **schön** geschnitzter Schrank	*a beautifully carved cupboard*
ein **schöner**, geschnitzter Schrank	*a beautiful carved cupboard*

NB: This distinction is not always maintained in practice, see 6.2.7c.

These adjective–adverbs can be very widely and flexibly used in German, often with compounding, in a way which lacks a direct English equivalent:

Er hat mir **brieflich** mitgeteilt, daß er anderer Meinung sei	*He informed me by letter that he was of a different opinion*
Widerrechtlich geparkte Fahrzeuge werden **kostenpflichtig** abgeschleppt	*Illegally parked vehicles will be removed at the owner's expense*
Das Mitbringen von Hunden ist **lebensmittelpolizeilich** verboten	*Bringing dogs (into the shop) is forbidden by order of the food inspectorate*

7.3.2 Adverbs of attitude

Adverbs of attitude express the speaker's comment on the content of the statement, i.e. whether he or she thinks it is probable, likely, welcome, well known or the like. In many ways their function overlaps with that of the modal particles (see Chapter 10). Because they relate to the sentence as a whole they are sometimes called *Satzadverbien* in German. Examples:

Anscheinend ist sie erst um sieben gekommen
(i.e. it appears to the speaker that she only arrived then)
Er fährt **leider** schon heute ab
(i.e. the speaker thinks it is unfortunate that he's going)
Natürlich/Selbstverständlich darfst du das machen
(i.e. the speaker's opinion is that it goes without saying)
Sie wird uns **sicher(lich)** helfen
(i.e. the speaker thinks that it is certain)

These adverbs of attitude have a number of characteristic features. In particular, although they can occur in a negative sentence, they cannot themselves be negated, e.g.:

Sie kommen **hoffentlich** noch heute
(but one can't say … *nicht hoffentlich*)
Er fährt **leider** nicht weg
(but … *nicht leider* is not possible)
Sie ist **wahrscheinlich** nicht gekommen
(but … *nicht wahrscheinlich* … does not make sense)

Unlike adverbs of manner, they cannot answer the question *Wie?*, but they **can** be used to answer a yes/no question:

> Singt sie heute? Ja, **bestimmt/leider/vielleicht/zweifellos**, etc.
> (but none of these words can answer the question *Wie singt sie?*)

7.3.3 Adverbs of reason

A large group of adverbs indicate cause, circumstance, condition, purpose or reason. The most frequent members of this group are:

allenfalls	*at most*	deswegen	*therefore*
andernfalls	*otherwise*	folglich	*consequently*
dabei	*at the same time*	gegebenenfalls	*if necessary*
dadurch	*thereby*	gleichwohl (elev.)	*nevertheless*
daher	*therefore*	infolgedessen	*consequently*
dann	*in that case*	jedenfalls	*in any case*
darum	*therefore*	mithin (elev.)	*consequently*
dazu	*to that end*	nichtsdestoweniger	*nevertheless*
demnach	*therefore*	somit	*consequently*
demzufolge (elev.)	*therefore*	sonst	*otherwise* (see 7.3.5b)
dennoch	*nevertheless*	trotzdem	*nevertheless*
deshalb	*therefore*		

7.3.4 Many German adverbs have a verb or a subordinate clause construction as their only or most natural idiomatic English equivalent

This applies principally to adverbs of manner, viewpoint or attitude. For instance, the most frequent equivalent of the English verb 'to like' is to use the German adverb *gern* with *haben* or another appropriate verb, e.g.: *Ich esse **gern** Käsekuchen* 'I like cheesecake'; *Sie hat Ihren Lehrer ganz **gern*** 'She quite likes her teacher'. A selection of these is given below. In some cases a construction with a verb is also possible in German, so that 'It must be admitted that it isn't easy' could correspond to *Man muß zugeben, daß es nicht einfach ist* or to *Es ist freilich nicht einfach*. But, in general, the equivalents with adverbs sound more idiomatic and concise:

Das Problem ist **allerdings** schwierig	*I must admit that the problem is difficult*
Er wurde **allmählich** rot im Gesicht	*He began to get red in the face*
Er hat **andauernd** gespielt	*He kept on playing*
Er ist **angeblich** arbeitslos	*He claims to be unemployed*
Er ist **anscheinend** nicht gekommen	*He seems not to have come*
Wir können Ihnen **bedauerlicherweise** nicht weiter behilflich sein	*We regret that we can be of no further assistance to you*
Er ist **bekanntlich** ein hervorragender Linguist	*Everyone knows that he is an outstanding linguist*
Hier können Sie **beliebig** lange bleiben	*You can stay here as long as you wish*
Am besten behalten Sie das für sich	*You'd better keep that to yourself*
Thomas kommt **bestimmt** mit	*I'm sure Thomas is coming with us / Thomas is sure to be coming with us*
Wir haben **erfreulicherweise** das Spiel gewonnen	*I'm glad to say that we won the game*
Es ist **freilich** nicht einfach	*It must be admitted that it isn't easy*
Gegebenenfalls kann man auch eine andere Taste wählen	*If the need should arise, another key may be selected*
Im Sommer spielt er **gern** Tennis	*He likes playing tennis in summer*
Hoffentlich erreichen wir die Hütte vor Sonnenuntergang	*I hope we shall reach the cabin before sunset*

Sie kann **leider** nicht kommen	*I'm afraid she can't come*
Im Winter spielt er **lieber** Fußball	*He prefers playing football in the winter*
Ich habe Reiten **lieber** als Radfahren	*I prefer riding to cycling*
Er kommt **möglicherweise** noch vor dem Abendessen	*It is possible that he will be coming before dinner*
Sie erschien **nicht**	*She failed to appear*
Die Firma stellt diese Ersatzteile **nicht mehr** her	*The company has ceased/stopped making these spare parts*
Nimm dir **ruhig** noch etwas zu trinken	*Don't be afraid to help yourself to another drink*
Alle Insaßen sind **vermutlich** ums Leben gekommen	*It is presumed that all the passengers lost their lives*
Er las **weiter**	*He continued to read/went on reading*
Ich habe sie **zufällig** in der Stadt gesehen	*I happened/chanced to see her in town*
Zweifellos wird auch dieses Jahr sehr wenig Schnee im Allgäu fallen	*There is no doubt that very little snow will fall in the Allgäu this year either*

7.3.5 *anders* and *sonst*

(a) *anders* means 'else' or 'differently'

In origin, *anders* is the genitive of the adjective *ander*, cf. 5.5.2. It usually has the written form *anders* (very occasionally *anderes*), which differentiates it from the nominative/accusative singular neuter of *ander*, which is normally written *andres* or *anderes*. It is used as follows:

(i) In the meaning 'else' with *jemand* and *niemand*:

Es ist jemand anders gekommen	*Somebody else came*
Der Schirm gehört jemand anders	*The umbrella belongs to somebody else*
Ich habe mit niemand anders gesprochen	*I didn't talk to anybody else*
Sie hat niemand anders als dich gesucht	*She wasn't looking for anyone else but you*

In standard German, *jemand, niemand* do not inflect in combination with *anders*, cf. 5.5.15b. In south German usage, inflected forms of *ander* sometimes occur rather than invariable *anders*, most commonly in the accusative and dative, e.g. *jemand/niemand anderer* (rare), *jemand/niemand anderen, jemand/niemand anderem.*

(ii) *anders* is used in the meaning 'else' with *wo, wohin, woher, (n)irgendwo*. Note the various alternative combinations:

woanders/anderswo/irgendwo anders	*somewhere else/elsewhere*
Ich gehe irgendwo anders hin/ woandershin/anderswohin	*I'm going somewhere else*
Er kommt anderswoher, nicht aus Hamburg	*He comes from somewhere else, not from Hamburg*
nirgendwo anders	*nowhere else*
Ich gehe nirgendwo anders hin	*I'm not going anywhere else*

(iii) *anders* also means 'different(ly)', 'in a different way':

Er ist ganz anders als sein Bruder	*He is quite different from his brother*
Du mußt es irgendwie anders anpacken	*You'll have to tackle it differently*
Es ist etwas anders	*It is rather different*
cf.: Es ist etwas and(e)res	*It is something else*
Das klingt jetzt anders	*That sounds different now*

(b) *sonst* **means 'else' or 'otherwise'**

(i) In some senses *sonst* can overlap with *anders* 'else' or *ander* 'other', 'different' (see (a) above). The following are thus possible alternatives:

Kannst du etwas anderes/sonst etwas vorschlagen?	*Can you suggest anything else?*
War noch jemand anders/sonst noch jemand da?	*Was anyone else here?*
Niemand anders/Niemand sonst hat mir geholfen	*Nobody else helped me*
sonstwo/sonst irgendwo/irgendwo sonst/anderswo, etc.	*somewhere/anywhere else*
Ich muß noch sonstwohin/anderswohin	*I've got to go somewhere else*
Wenn noch andere Probleme/sonst noch Probleme auftauchen, ...	*If any other problems arise, ...*
Wer anders kann es gesagt haben? (more common:) Wer kann es sonst gesagt haben?	*Who else can have said it?*

(ii) However, if the sense is clearly 'different' or 'other', only *ander* or, where appropriate, *anders*, can be used. Compare:

Da ist Professor Niebaum und niemand anders	*That's Professor Niebaum and nobody else* (i.e. not a different person)
Da ist Professor Niebaum und sonst niemand	*That's Professor Niebaum and nobody else* (i.e. he's the only one there)

(iii) If the meaning is clearly 'in addition', 'apart from that', 'otherwise', then only *sonst* is possible:

Wer kommt sonst noch?	*Who else is coming?*
Mit wem haben Sie sonst noch gesprochen?	*Who else did you talk to?*
Was hat sie sonst noch gesagt?	*What else did she say?*
sonst irgendwann	*some/any other time*
Sonst geht alles gut	*Otherwise all is well*
Wir müssen uns beeilen, sonst verpassen wir den Zug	*We'll have to hurry, otherwise we'll miss the train*
länger als sonst	*longer than usual*

7.3.6 Adverbs in *-weise*

The suffix *-weise* is very productive for the formation of adverbs of manner or attitude. It is most often added to nouns or adjectives.

(a) Adverbs formed from a noun or a verb + *-weise* are in the main manner adverbs with the meaning 'by way of', 'in the form of'

andeutungsweise	*by way of a hint*	paarweise	*in pairs*
ausnahmsweise	*by way of exception*	pfundweise	*by the pound*
beispielsweise	*by way of example*	probeweise	*on approval*
beziehungsweise	*or, as the case may be* (see 19.1.3b)	ruckweise	*by jerks*
		schrittweise	*step by step*
bruchstückweise	*in the form of fragments*	stückweise	*piecemeal*
		stundenweise	*by the hour*
dutzendweise	*by the dozen*	teilweise	*partly*
familienweise	*in families*	versuchsweise	*tentatively*
gruppenweise	*in groups*	zeitweise	*temporarily*
massenweise	*on a massive scale*	zwangsweise	*compulsorily*

Die Flüchtlinge strömten **massenweise** über die ungarische Grenze	*The refugees were flooding in hordes across the Hungarian border*
Sein neues Buch ist **stellenweise** ganz gut	*His new book is quite good in places*
Er wird **stundenweise** bezahlt	*He is paid by the hour*

These forms, which were originally exclusively adverbial, are more and more often used as adjectives as well, e.g.:

eine **probeweise** Anstellung	die **teilweisen** Verbesserungen
eine **ruckweise** Bewegung	eine **stundenweise** Bezahlung
der **stückweise** Verkauf	die **stufenweisen** Fortschritte
eine **schrittweise** Verminderung der Streitkräfte in Europa (*SZ*)	

Predominantly, though, they are used with nouns which denote a process, chiefly those which are derived from verbs, as in the examples above. Combinations like *der stückweise Preis* or *eine auszugsweise Urkunde* are not (yet?) generally regarded as acceptable.

(b) Adverbs of attitude are very commonly formed from adjectives or participles with the suffix *-weise* and the linking element *-er-*
e.g. *möglicherweise* from *möglich*, *bezeichnenderweise* from *bezeichnend*.

bedauerlicherweise	*regrettably*	liebenswürdigerweise	*obligingly*
begreiflicherweise	*understandably*	möglicherweise	*possibly, perhaps*
dummerweise	*foolishly*	natürlicherweise	*of course*
erstaunlicherweise	*astonishingly*	normalerweise	*normally*
fälschlicherweise	*erroneously*	überflüssigerweise	*superfluously*
glücklicherweise	*fortunately*	unglücklicherweise	*unfortunately*
interessanterweise	*interestingly*	unnötigerweise	*unnecessarily*
komischerweise	*funnily*	unvermuteterweise	*unexpectedly*

As these are adverbs of attitude, indicating a comment by the speaker on the statement, their meaning is different from that of the adjective–adverb of manner from which they are derived, and from that of the corresponding phrase with *Weise*, e.g.:

Er war **merkwürdig** müde	*He was strangely tired*
Er war **merkwürdigerweise** müde	*Strange to say, he was tired*
Er war **in merkwürdiger Weise** müde	*He was tired in an unusual way*
Er hat **vernünftig** geantwortet	*He replied sensibly*
Er hat **vernünftigerweise** geantwortet	*Sensibly enough, he replied*
Er hat **auf vernünftige Weise** geantwortet	*He replied in a sensible way*

NB: These adverbs in *-erweise* are never used as adjectives.

7.4 Adverbs of degree

7.4.1 Adverbs of degree (or 'intensifiers') are used to emphasise, amplify or tone down another part of speech

Their main use is to modify adjectives or other adverbs.

(a) A selection of the most frequent adverbs of degree in German

außerordentlich	*extraordinarily*	mäßig	*moderately*
äußerst	*extremely*	nahezu	*virtually*
beinahe	*almost, nearly*	recht	*really*
besonders	*especially*	relativ	*relatively*
durchaus	*absolutely, thoroughly*	sehr	*very* (cf. 7.4.3)
etwas	*a little*	überaus	*extremely*
fast	*almost, nearly*	verhältnismäßig	*relatively*
ganz	*quite*	völlig	*completely*
genug	*enough*	vollkommen	*completely*
geradezu	*absolutely, virtually*	wenig	*little*
höchst	*extremely, highly*	ziemlich	*fairly*
kaum	*hardly, scarcely*	zu	*too*

The above is by no means an exhaustive list; many more occur, particularly in colloquial speech (e.g. *echt, enorm, ungeheuer, unheimlich, verdammt*).

eine **durchaus** selbstkritische Einsicht	*a thoroughly self-critical understanding*
Der Kaffee ist **etwas** süß	*The coffee is a little sweet*
Er fährt schnell **genug**	*He's driving fast enough*
Das ist **geradezu** lächerlich	*That is little short of ridiculous*
Die Suppe war nur **mäßig** warm	*The soup was (only) moderately warm*
eine **nahezu** optimale Lösung des Problems	*a virtually optimal solution to the problem*
Er arbeitet **recht** gut	*He works really well*
ein **überaus** ehrliches Geschäft	*a thoroughly honest transaction*
Dieser Schriftsteller ist **wenig** bekannt	*This author is little known*

(b) *hoch* 'highly' is used with a small number of abstract adjectives

It is usually compounded with them, e.g *hochempfindlich, hochfrequent, hochinteressant, hochgeschätzt, hochqualifiziert*.

(c) *lange* and *längst*, usually preceded by *noch*, are used before a negative to indicate a considerable difference in degree

Das ist **noch lange nicht** gut genug	*That is not nearly good enough*
Dieses Buch ist **lange/längst nicht** so gut wie sein letztes	*This book isn't nearly as good as his last one*

7.4.2 Some adverbs of degree are used only or principally with adjectives in the comparative or superlative

bedeutend *significantly*
   Die Donau ist **bedeutend** länger als der Rhein
beträchtlich *considerably*
   Die Zugspitze ist **beträchtlich** höher als die anderen Gipfel in den bayrischen Alpen
denkbar *possible*
   Sie hat den **denkbar** schlechtesten Eindruck gemacht
entschieden *decidedly*
   Er hat **entschieden** schlechter gespielt als vor einem Jahr
viel *much*
   Diese Schule ist **viel** größer als meine

weit *far*
  Der Wagen ist **weit** schneller, als ich dachte
bei weitem (*by*) *far*
  Er ist **bei weitem** besser als Jochen
  Er ist **bei weitem** der beste in der Klasse
weitaus (*by*) *far*
  Isabella ist **weitaus** reifer, als man ihrem Alter nach schließen dürfte
  Der neueren Geschichte ist das **weitaus** größte Gewicht beizumessen
wesentlich *substantially*
  Er hat heute **wesentlich** besser gespielt

7.4.3 *sehr* is chiefly used as an adverb of degree (= 'very')

Er weiß es **sehr** gut   Das ist **sehr** nett von dir.

However, it has a wider range of use than English *very*:

(a) It can modify a verb or phrase, corresponding to English 'very much'

Ich bewundere sie **sehr**   Er ist **sehr** dafür   Das interessiert mich **sehr**
Das ist **sehr** nach meinem Geschmack   Er hat sich **sehr** verändert

(b) After *so*, *wie* or *zu*, it can denote degree, like English 'much'

Nicht **so sehr** die Handlung wie der Stil hat mich gefesselt
Wie sehr ich es bedaure, daß sie durchgefallen ist!
Er hat es sich **zu sehr** zu Herzen genommen

7.5 Interrogative adverbs

The German interrogative adverbs correspond to the English '*wh*-words'. They
fall into similar groups to other adverbs, i.e.:

Time

  wann? 'when?': **Wann** kommt der Zug in Gelsenkirchen an?
  bis wann? 'until when?', 'how long?': **Bis wann** bleibt ihr hier?
    'by when?': **Bis wann** seid ihr damit fertig?
  seit wann? 'since when?','how long?': **Seit wann** spielen Sie Tennis?
  wie lange? 'how long?': **Wie lange** wollt ihr heute noch spielen?
  wie oft? 'how often?': **Wie oft** fährt ein Bus nach Eberbach?

Place and direction (see also 7.2.1)

  wo? 'where?': **Wo** steckt die Angelika jetzt?
  wohin? 'where (to)?': **Wohin** fahrt ihr heute?/**Wo** fahrt ihr heute **hin**?
  woher? 'where from?': **Woher** kommt der Wagen?/**Wo** kommt der Wagen **her**?
  von wo? 'where from?': **Von wo** kommt der Wagen?

Manner

  wie? 'how?': **Wie** habt ihr das nur gemacht?

Cause

  warum? 'why?': **Warum** wollt ihr nicht gehen?
  was? 'why?' (coll.): **Was** rennst du denn so schnell? (cf. 5.3.3f)
  wieso? (coll.) 'why?': **Wieso** wollt ihr nicht gehen?
  weshalb? (formal) 'why?': **Weshalb** wollt ihr nicht gehen?
  wozu? 'what ... for?': **Wozu** benutzt man das?

The above interrogative adverbs can introduce indirect questions (cf. 16.6.4a and 19.2.4), e.g.:

> Er hat mich gefragt, **wann** ich morgen komme
> Ich habe dir doch gesagt, **wie** man das macht

NB: For the interrogative pronouns *was* and *wer*, see 5.3.3. For the interrogative determiner *welcher*, see 5.3.1.

8

Comparison of adjectives and adverbs

By using 'comparative' and 'superlative' forms we can indicate the degree to which a noun possesses the quality expressed by that particular adjective or adverb. Thus:

'positive' degree:	Mein Haus ist **groß**	*My house is big*
'comparative' degree:	Dein Haus ist **größer**	*Your house is bigger*
'superlative' degree:	Sein Haus ist **das größte**	*His house is the biggest*

Naturally, some adjectives or adverbs, such as *sterblich*, *einmalig* or *absolut*, have a meaning which excludes the possibility of comparison, and there are a number of other ways of indicating degree, for example by modifying the adjective or adverb by an adverb of degree, cf. 7.4.

The comparative is normally used to compare two items, the superlative more than two:

> der **größere** der beiden Brüder
> Von den zwei Büchern über Berlin hat er das **billigere** gekauft
> der **größte** von acht Jungen
> Von diesen vielen Büchern hat er das **billigste** gekauft

As in English, this rule is not universally observed in everyday speech.

This chapter deals with the formation and use of the comparative and superlative degree of adjectives and adverbs, and other various forms of comparison in German. Regular formation of comparatives and superlatives is treated in 8.1, with exceptions and irregularities dealt with in 8.2. Full examples are shown in Table 8.1. The use of the comparative (and other means of comparison) is treated in 8.3, that of the superlative in 8.4.

8.1 Regular formation of the comparative and superlative

8.1.1 The comparative and superlative of adjectives are formed by adding the endings -er and -st- to the positive form

> klein – kleiner – das kleinste

Table 8.1 gives further examples for the regular formation of comparatives and superlatives. As the superlative almost always occurs in an inflected form, with the definite article, *das* is included in our examples.

In English we can form comparatives and superlatives in two ways. With short

TABLE 8.1 *Formation of comparatives and superlatives*

	Positive	Comparative	Superlative
Regular formation of comparative and superlative	langsam schnell tief unwiderstehlich	langsamer schneller tiefer unwiderstehlicher	das langsamste das schnellste das tiefste das unwiderstehlichste
Adjectives in -el, -en, -er	dunkel trocken bitter teuer	dunkler trock(e)ner bitt(e)rer teurer	das dunkelste das trockenste das bitterste das teuerste
Adjectives in -d, -haft, -s, -sch, -sk, -ß, -t, -x and -z	süß sanft stolz	süßer sanfter stolzer	das süßeste das sanfteste das stolzeste
Adjectives ending in a long vowel or diphthong	früh treu	früher treuer	das früh(e)ste das treu(e)ste
Comparative and superlative formed with *Umlaut*	arm dumm grob	ärmer dümmer gröber	das ärmste das dümmste das gröbste
Adjectives with *Umlaut* in the comparative and superlative	alt grob arg hart arm jung dumm kalt	klug schwarz krank rot kurz scharf lang schwach	stark warm
Irregular comparatives and superlatives	bald gern groß gut hoch nah viel	eher lieber größer besser höher näher mehr	am ehesten am liebsten das größte das beste das höchste das nächste das meiste

adjectives, we use the endings *-er* and *-est*, with longer adjectives *more* and *most*. In German, the endings *-er* and *-st-* are used irrespective of the length of the adjective (but see 8.2.7).

Comparative and superlative forms inflect in the same way as any adjective when used before a noun:

> ein schnellerer Zug, der schnellste Zug, in der tiefsten Schlucht der Erde

There are a number of slight irregularities in the formation of some comparatives and superlatives. These are treated in detail in section 8.2.

8.1.2 For the superlative of adverbs, a phrase is used formed by using the stem in -st-, with the ending -en, together with the contraction *am*

Schumacher fährt **am schnellsten**	*Schumacher drives fastest*
Von der Burg aus sieht man es **am klarsten**	*You can see it most clearly from the castle*

For further details about the form *am ... sten*, which is sometimes also used in predicates after *sein*, see 8.4.1.

The comparative of adverbs is formed in *-er*, in an identical way to that of adjectives, e.g.: *Schuhmacher fährt aber schneller.*

8.2 Irregularities in the formation of comparatives and superlatives

The most important forms are summarised in Table 8.1.

8.2.1 Adjectives in *-el, -en, -er* may drop the *-e-* of the stem in the comparative

(a) Those in *-el* regularly drop the *-e-*

dunkel – dunkler   edel – edler

(b) Those in *-en* and *-er* usually drop the *-e-* if they have an inflectional ending

trocken – der trock**nere** Wein   bitter – ein bitt**rerer** Geruch

If there is no inflectional ending, the *-e-* is usually retained in writing, though it often drops in speech:

Dieser Wein ist trock**ener**   Dieser Geruch war bitt**erer**

If the *-er* is preceded by a diphthong, the *-e-* is always lost:

teuer – Diese Tasche ist teu**rer**   die teu**rere** Tasche

8.2.2 Some adjectives add *-est* in the superlative

(a) Those whose stem ends in *-haft, -s, -sk, -ß, -x* and *-z* always have *-est*

boshaft – der boshaft**este**   lieblos – der lieblos**este**
brüsk – der brüsk**este**   süß – der süß**este**
fix – der fix**este**   stolz – der stolz**este**

(b) Those whose stem ends in *-d, -t* and *-sch* most often have *-est unless* they have more than one syllable and the last syllable is unstressed

mild – der mild**este**   sanft – der sanft**este**
rasch – der rasch**este**   berühmt – der berühmt**este**

BUT spannend – der spannend**ste**, komisch – der komisch**ste**, etc.

(c) Those whose stem ends in a long vowel or diphthong have *-est* or *-st*

früh – der früh**ste**/früh**este**   treu – der treu**ste**/treu**este**

8.2.3 A number of frequently used adjectives and adverbs have *Umlaut* in the comparative and superlative, in addition to the ending

e.g. arm – ärmer – der ärmste. See also Table 8.1.

(a) The following always have *Umlaut*

alt	grob	klug	oft	schwarz
arg	hart	krank	rot	stark
arm	jung	kurz	scharf	warm
dumm	kalt	lang	schwach	

NB: (i) *groß, hoch* and *nah* also always have *Umlaut*, but are otherwise irregular, see 8.2.4.
(ii) *am häufigsten* is more often used than *am öftesten* to mean 'most often'.

(b) The following have alternative forms with or without *Umlaut*
e.g.: naß – nässer/nasser – der nässeste/nasseste:

bang	fromm	glatt	krumm	schmal
blaß	gesund	karg	naß	zart

In general, the forms without *Umlaut* are more frequent in writing, whereas those with *Umlaut* are more typical of spoken German, especially in the south. However, *Umlaut* is more usual in writing with *fromm* and *gesund*.

8.2.4 Some adjectives and adverbs have irregular comparative and superlative forms

bald	**eher**	am **ehesten**	*soon*
gern	**lieber**	am **liebsten**	*willingly, gladly*
groß	**größer**	das **größte**	*big, large*
gut	**besser**	das **beste**	*good*
hoch	**höher**	das **höchste**	*high*
nah	**näher**	das **nächste**	*near*
viel	**mehr**	das **meiste**	*much, many*
wenig	**weniger/**	das **wenigste/**	*little, few*
	minder	das **mindeste**	
wohl	**wohler/**	am **wohlsten/**	*well*
	besser	am **besten**	

Further notes on the use of some of these irregular comparative and superlative forms:

(a) *mehr* and *weniger*
These do not inflect, even when used with a following noun, e.g.: *Er hat **weniger** Geld als ich; Sie hat **mehr** Verstand als du; der Verlust von **weniger** Stunden*.

(b) *minder* and *mindest*
minder is restricted to formal written German. It is only used to qualify adjectives, most commonly with a preceding *nicht*: *Anderswo zwischen Ostsee und Erzgebirge ist die Lage der Denkmalpflege nicht **minder** prekär* (*Spiegel*).
    mindest tends to be used for 'least' in the sense 'slightest', e.g.:
*Er hatte nicht die **mindesten** Aussichten zu gewinnen.*

(c) *wohl*
wohl has the comparative and superlative forms *wohler* and *am wohlsten* in the meaning 'at ease', '(physically) well', e.g. *sich wohler fühlen. besser* and *am besten* are used in the meaning 'well', i.e. the adverb from 'good'.

(d) *nichts weniger als* **normally means 'anything but'**
i.e. the same as *alles andere als*:

>   Er ist **nichts weniger als** klug   *He is anything but clever*

For 'nothing less than', German often uses a positive statement: *Das ist wirklich katastrophal* 'That is nothing less than catastrophic'. However, some Germans do now use *nichts weniger als* in the sense of 'nothing less than', and ambiguity is possible.

8.2.5 Eight adjectives denoting position only have comparative and (in most cases) superlative forms

das äußere	*outer, external*	das äußerste	*outermost, utmost*
das innere	*inner, internal*	das innerste	*innermost*
das obere	*upper*	das oberste	*uppermost*
das untere	*lower*	das unterste	*lowest, bottom*
das vordere	*front*	das vorderste	*foremost, front*
das hintere	*back*	das hinterste	*back(most)*
das mittlere	*central, middle; medium*	das mittelste	*central, middle*
das niedere	*low, inferior*	(superlative not used)	
(mainly of social rank)			

These adjectives are only used attributively, i.e. before a noun, e.g.:

>   seine **äußere** Erscheinung   mit der **äußersten** Höflichkeit
>   seine **innersten** Gedanken   in der **vorderen**, **vordersten** Reihe

äußerlich and *innerlich* can be used as equivalents of English 'external(ly)' and 'internal(ly)' predicatively after *sein*, or as adverbs:

>   Seine Verletzungen sind nicht **äußerlich**, sondern **innerlich**,
>   Sie blieb **äußerlich**, **innerlich** ganz ruhig

8.2.6 The comparative and superlative of compound adjectives

(a) In general, compound adjectives are treated as single words and form their comparative and superlative in the usual way

altmodisch *old-fashioned*	– altmodischer	– das altmodischste
vielsagend *meaningful*	– vielsagender	– das vielsagendste
vielversprechend *promising*	– vielversprechender	– das vielversprechendste
weittragend *far-reaching*	– weittragender	– das weittragendste

(b) However, if both parts are considered to retain their original meaning, the first has the comparative or superlative form
Some commonly used combinations are written as compounds, less frequent ones are not, whilst with a few both alternatives are possible. There is in practice considerable variation in the forms actually used and a selection of the most frequent are given, following DUDEN (1985: 713–14), which gives a little more detail:

>   ein schwerverständlicher Text   *a text which is difficult to understand*
>   ein **schwerer verständlicher** Text – der **am schwersten verständliche** Text
>
>   eine dichtbevölkerte Stadt   *a densely populated city*
>   eine **dichter bevölkerte**/**dichterbevölkerte** Stadt
>   – die **am dichtesten bevölkerte**/**dichtstbevölkerte** Stadt

ein hochgelegener Ort   *a place situated high up*
ein **höhergelegener** Ort – der **höchstgelegene** Ort

naheliegende Gründe   *obvious reasons*
näherliegende Gründe – **nächstliegende** Gründe

(c) With a few adjectives the combination may be treated as a single word or as separate words

In the latter case the first word has the comparative or superlative form, which is compounded with some adjectives:

schwerwiegende Gründe   *serious, weighty reasons*
schwerer wiegende Gründe or **schwerwiegendere** Gründe
– die **am schwersten wiegenden** Gründe or die **schwerwiegendsten** Gründe

weitgehende Beschränkungen   *extensive limitations*
weitergehende Beschränkungen (Austr.) or **weitergehendere** Beschränkungen
– **weitestgehende** Beschränkungen or die **weitgehendsten** Beschränkungen

8.2.7 *mehr* and *meist* in comparison

(a) A very few adjectives form their comparative and superlative by means of a preceding *mehr* or *am meisten*

This is restricted to use with participles which are not normally used as adjectives, a few adjectives which are only used predicatively, like *zuwider* (see 6.5.1b), and unusually long and complex adjectives like *bemitleidenswert*:

Er verrichtet jetzt eine ihm **mehr zusagende** Tätigkeit	*He is now performing a job which appeals to him more*
Dresden ist die durch den Krieg **am meisten zerstörte** deutsche Stadt	*Dresden is the German city to have been most completely destroyed in the war*
Er ist mir noch **mehr zuwider** als sein Bruder	*He is even more repugnant to me than his brother*
Er ist der **am meisten bemitleidenswerte** Kranke	*He is the most to be pitied of all the patients*

With past participles a prefixed *meist-* can be used rather than *am meisten*, e.g.: *die meistzerstörte Stadt, der meistgekaufte Geschirrspülautomat Deutschlands.*

(b) *mehr* is also used if two qualities of the same object are being compared

i.e. in the sense 'rather', e.g.: *Diese Arbeit ist **mehr** langweilig als schwierig.* In rather more formal German, *eher* is an alternative to *mehr* in this meaning.

8.3 The use of the comparative and other types of comparison

8.3.1 The comparative particle is usually *als* (= 'than')

Peter ist älter **als** Thomas   Mein Wagen fährt schneller **als** deiner

(a) Alternatives to *als*

wie (or *als wie*) is common for *als* in colloquial speech, e.g. *Peter ist älter (als) wie Thomas.* These alternatives are regarded as substandard.

The use of *denn* in place of *als* is in general now archaic, but it can be used in formal registers to avoid the sequence *als als*:

Die Mauer erscheint eher als Kunstwerk **denn** als Grenze (*Schneider*)	*The wall appears rather as a work of art than as a frontier*

NB: *denn* is commonly used in a couple of set phrases: *mehr denn je* 'more than ever', *Geben ist seliger denn nehmen* 'It is more blessed to give than to receive'.

(b) Degree of difference is expressed by *um ... als*, or simply by a noun in the accusative

Eine Fahrt im TGV-Atlantique kann **um** bis zu 50 Prozent teurer kommen **als** in einem herkömmlichen Schnellzug (*FR*)	*A trip on the TGV-Atlantique can work out up to 50% more expensive than in an ordinary express train*
Er ist (**um**) **einen Monat** jünger **als** ich	*He is a month younger than me*

(c) To express a greater degree (= 'even') *noch* is used with the comparative

London ist eine **noch schmutzigere** Stadt als Amsterdam	*London is an even dirtier city than Amsterdam*
Er hat gestern **noch weniger** gearbeitet	*He worked even less yesterday*
Es regnete **noch stärker**	*It was raining even harder*

8.3.2 Lower degrees of comparison are expressed by *weniger*, *am wenigsten*

These correspond to English 'less tall than', 'least tall', etc.:

Er war **weniger optimistisch** als sein Bruder	*He was less optimistic than his brother*
Er arbeitet **weniger fleißig** als ich	*He works less hard than me*
der **am wenigsten talentierte** Spieler	*the least talented player*
Er arbeitet **am wenigsten fleißig** von allen	*He works the least hard of all*

In practice, *am wenigsten* is little used for 'least', and other constructions tend to be preferred wherever possible. Compare:

die **uninteressanteste** Rede	*the least interesting speech*
der **billigste/preiswerteste** Wagen	*the least expensive car*
die **einfachste** Methode	*the least difficult method*
möglichst geringe Kosten	*the least possible expenditure*

NB: In formal German, *minder* is an occasional alternative to *weniger*, cf. 8.2.4b, e.g.: *Angesichts der Aktenlage eine nicht **minder** verwegene Behauptung* (*Spiegel*).

8.3.3 The 'absolute comparative'

The comparative of a few common adjectives or adverbs is used not to signal a direct comparison, but to indicate a fair degree of the relevant quality, e.g. *ein älterer Herr* 'an elderly gentleman', *eine größere Stadt* 'a fair- sized town'. This is possible with the following:

alt	dick	dünn	gut	jung	kurz	neu
bekannt	dunkel	groß	hell	klein	lang	oft

Examples:

eine **bessere** Wohngegend	*a fairly good neighbourhood*
seit **längerer** Zeit	*for a longish time now*
ein **neueres** Modell	*a fairly new model*
Kommen Sie **öfter** (coll. also: öfters) hierher?	*Do you come here quite often?*

8.3.4 Progression is expressed by using *immer* with the comparative

This corresponds to English 'more and more':

Er lief **immer schneller**	*He ran faster and faster*
Das Benzin wird **immer teurer**	*Petrol is getting dearer and dearer*
Meine Arbeit wird **immer schwieriger**	*My work is getting more and more difficult*

NB: A construction like that of English, e.g. *Er lief schneller und schneller*, is occasionally found, but it is much less frequent than that with *immer*.

8.3.5 Proportion (i.e. 'the more … the more')

Proportion is expressed in German by using a subordinate clause introduced by the conjunction *je*, followed by a main clause beginning with *um so* or (especially in formal written German) *desto*:

Je länger man Deutsch lernt, **desto/um so** leichter wird es	*The longer you learn German, the easier it gets*
je eher, **desto/um so** besser	*the sooner the better*
Je besser das Wetter, **desto/um so** mehr können wir wandern	*The better the weather, the more we can go hiking*

NB: (i) In older German, a second *je* could be used rather than *desto* or *um so*. This survives in a few set phrases such as *je länger, je lieber* and *je länger, je mehr*.
(ii) As an equivalent to 'all the more because', German uses *um so mehr, als/da/weil* … (cf. 19.4.3b).
(iii) In colloquial German the combination *um so … um so* is common, e.g. *um so größer, um so besser* 'the bigger, the better'.

8.3.6 Equality is expressed by *so … wie* (= 'as … as')

Er arbeitet **so** fleißig **wie** ich
Peter ist **so** alt **wie** Thomas
Mein neuer Wagen fährt nicht **so** schnell **wie** deiner
Er ist nur halb **so** alt **wie** seine Schwester

A number of variations of this construction occur:

(a) In colloquial German, *als* is often used for *wie*

Peter ist **so** alt **als** Thomas   Ich bin doch **so** groß **als** du

This is not usually acceptable in written registers, but DUDEN (1985: 42) considers it acceptable in the following contexts:

(i) 'as well as' may be *sowohl wie* or *sowohl als* (see also 19.1.4b), e.g.:
*Ich will sowohl Anna **als/wie** (auch) Helga einladen.*

(ii) 'as soon/little as possible' may be *so bald/wenig wie möglich* or *so bald/wenig als möglich*.

(iii) 'twice as ... as' may be *doppelt so ... wie* **or** *doppelt so ... als*:
Die Ernte ist doppelt so groß als/wie im vorigen Jahr.

NB: The combination *als wie*, e.g. *Ich bin doch so groß als wie du* is common in speech, but
generally considered substandard.

(b) *so* can be omitted in some common phrases and idioms

    Er ist (so) hart wie Stahl   Er ist (so) schlau wie ein Fuchs

(c) 'just as ... (as)' is expressed by *ebenso ... (wie)* or *genauso ... (wie)*

    Peter ist **ebenso/genauso** alt **wie** Thomas
    Dort können wir **genauso** gutes Fleisch kaufen

(i) *ebenso* is also used to indicate equivalence between two qualities:

    Er ist **ebenso** fleißig wie geschickt   *He is (just) as industrious as he is*
                                        skilful

(ii) *ebensosehr* is used adverbially to indicate degree (= 'just as much'):

    Die Brücke ist **ebensosehr** ein Teil   *The bridge is just as much part of*
    der Landschaft wie der Fluß   *the scenery as the river*

(iii) *nicht so sehr ... wie* is used for 'not so much ... as':

    Er ist **nicht so sehr** dumm **wie** faul   *He is not so much stupid as lazy*

(d) *gleich* can be used to indicate equality

    Peter und Thomas sind **gleich** alt   *Peter and Thomas are the same age*
    Diese Städte sind etwa **gleich** groß   *These towns are about the same size*

8.4 Types and uses of the superlative

8.4.1 The superlative form *am ... sten*

This form (see 8.1.2) is used in the following contexts:

(a) Always for adverbs

    Von allen Gästen sprach er am   *Of all the guests he spoke least*
    wenigsten
    Ich arbeite am besten nachts   *I work best at night*
    Am einfachsten faxen Sie es ihr   *The simplest thing is to fax it to*
    durch   *her*
    Helmut läuft am schnellsten   *Helmut runs fastest*
    Das hasse ich an den Schulmeistern   *That's what I hate most about*
    am meisten (*Valentin*)   *schoolmasters*

(b) After the verb *sein*

Both superlative forms are found predicatively after *sein*, e.g. *Wer von euch ist **am
stärksten**?* and *Wer von euch ist **der stärkste**?*

(i) If a noun is understood, either can be used:

Diese Blume ist **die schönste/am schönsten**	*This flower is the most beautiful*
Unter den deutschen Flüssen ist die Donau **der längste/am längsten**	*Of the German rivers the Danube is the longest*

(ii) Only the form with *am* is used if there is no noun to be be understood or if something is being compared with itself (= 'at its most . . .'):

Ein Mercedes wäre **am teuersten**	*A Mercedes would be the dearest*
Für meinen Geschmack ist eine Nelke schöner als eine Tulpe, aber eine Rose ist natürlich **am schönsten**	*For my taste a carnation is nicer than a tulip, but a rose is the nicest*
Hier ist die Donau **am tiefsten**	*The Danube is (at its) deepest here*
Der Garten ist **am schönsten** im Juni	*The garden is (at its) nicest in June*

NB: In the reformed spelling, see 23.1.1f, superlatives used with an article after *sein* will be spelled with a capital, e.g. *Wer von euch ist der Stärkste?*

8.4.2 Any superlative may be used in an absolute sense

i.e. not as a comparison but in the sense 'extremely'. This is known as the 'elative' use of the superlative:

in **höchster** Erregung	*in great excitement*
mit **größter** Mühe	*with the greatest difficulty*
Es ist **höchste** Zeit, daß . . .	*It is high time that . . .*
Es herrschte das **rauheste** Wetter	*The weather was extremely raw*
Modernste Kureinrichtungen stehen zu Ihrer Verfügung (*FAZ*)	*You will have the use of the most up-to-date spa treatment*

8.4.3 An absolute adverbial superlative can be formed in *aufs . . . ste*

e.g. *aufs heftigste, aufs genaueste, etc.* It is common in formal writing:

Der große runde Tisch war **aufs festlichste** geschmückt (*Dürrenmatt*)	*The large round table was decorated in a most festive way*
Herr Naumann war **aufs äußerste** gereizt (*MM*)	*Mr Naumann was exceedingly irritated*
Sie protestierten **aufs schärfste** gegen die Verurteilung Max Reimanns (*ND*)	*They protested most strongly against the conviction of Max Reimann*

NB: In the reformed spelling, see 23.7.3 it will be permissible to spell these forms with a small or a capital letter, e.g *aufs heftigste* or *aufs Heftigste*.

8.4.4 Some adverbial superlatives are formed in *-st, -stens* and *zu . . . st*

Generally, only a few of each type are common, usually with an absolute or idiomatic meaning. New formations on these patterns are fairly limited.

(a) Adverbial superlatives in -*st*

These consist simply of the superlative stem, whether regular or irregular. Some are in common use in speech and writing, often with special meanings:

äußerst	*extremely*	meist	*mostly*
höchst	*highly, extremely*	möglichst	*as . . . as possible; if at all possible*
jüngst (elev.)	*recently*	unlängst	*recently*
längst	*for a long time; a long time ago*		

Some examples of usage:

Die Situation ist **höchst** problematisch	*The situation is highly problematical*
Er ist **längst** gestorben	*He died a long time ago*
Du mußt einen **möglichst** guten Eindruck machen	*You must make the best possible impression*
Sie ist **unlängst** zurückgekehrt	*She got back recently*

Others are quite frequent in formal registers, often in formulaic idioms:

eiligst	*as quickly as possible*	höflichst	*respectfully*
freundlichst	*friendly*	schleunigst	*as promptly as possible*
gefälligst	*kindly*	sorgfältigst	*most carefully*
gütigst	*kindly*	tunlichst	*absolutely*
herzlichst	*most cordially*		

Examples:

Ich danke Ihnen **herzlichst**	*I thank you most cordially*
Sie werden **höflichst** gebeten, diesen Irrtum ohne Verzug zu berichtigen	*You are respectfully requested to rectify this mistake without delay*
Wir machten uns **schleunigst** aus dem Staube (*Dönhoff*)	*We quickly got up off the floor*
Jeder Lärm ist **tunlichst** zu vermeiden	*Any noise is absolutely to be avoided*

These forms are coming to be increasingly widely used in both writing and speech. Some stylists, e.g. Götze and Hess-Lüttich (1989: 244), regard them as inflated and advise against using them. Although they can sound overdone or stilted, they are now common, and new formations on this model are often encountered, especially in journalism, e.g.:

Die Böhmendeutschen sind nicht ausgesiedelt, sondern **brutalst** vertrieben worden (*Presse*)	*The Germans of Bohemia were not resettled, but driven out in the most brutal fashion*

Some forms in -*st*, i.e. *best-, größt-, höchst-, kleinst-, kürzest-* can be compounded with *möglich* to mean 'the best possible', etc.:

die **bestmögliche** Lösung	der **größtmögliche** Schaden
die **kleinstmögliche** Summe	der **kürzestmögliche** Weg

(b) A few in -*stens* are still widely used

The majority are idiomatic:

bestens	*very well*	schnellstens	*as quickly as possible*
frühstens	*at the earliest*	spätestens	*at the latest*
höchstens	*at the most*	strengstens	*strictly*
meistens	*mostly*	wärmstens	*most warmly*
mindestens	*at least*	wenigstens	*at least*
nächstens	*shortly, soon*		

Selected examples in context:

Es kommen **höchstens** dreißig Gäste	*At most thirty guests are coming*
Ich stehe **meistens** früh auf	*I mostly get up early*
(more formal: meist)	
Ich brauche **mindestens** dreitausend Mark für diese Reise	*I need at least three thousand marks for this trip*
Wir kommen **spätestens** um sechs an	*We'll arrive at six at the latest*
Rauchen ist **strengstens** verboten	*Smoking is strictly prohibited*
Er könnte **wenigstens** anrufen	*He might at least ring up*

NB: *wenigstens* and *mindestens* are often interchangeable, but *mindestens* emphasizes the idea of the absolute minimum possible rather more strongly. It is used less often when no actual figure is mentioned, in which case *zumindest* (cf. (c) below) is a possible, rather more emphatic alternative to *wenigstens*.

(c) A few forms in *zu ... st* are still current, with idiomatic meanings

zumindest	*at (the very) least*	zuoberst	*(right) on top*
zunächst	*at first, in the first place*	zutiefst	*(very) deeply*
		zuvorderst	*(right) at the front*

Some examples of use in context:

Er hätte uns **zumindest** grüßen können	*He could at least have said hello*
Das Angebot sah **zunächst** verlockend aus	*The offer looked attractive at first*
Sie nahm das Buch, das **zuoberst** lag	*She took the book which was lying on top*
In seinem Brief erklärt Solschenizyn, er sei **zutiefst** bewegt von dem Angebot der schwedischen Akademie *(FR)*	*In his letter Solzhenitsyn declares that he was deeply moved by the Swedish Academy's offer*

9

Numerals

9.1 Cardinal numbers

The formation of the cardinal numbers is shown in Table 9.1.

9.1.1 Notes on the forms of the cardinal numbers

(a) Long numbers are rarely written out in full
i.e. those with more than one element, like *zweiunddreißig, hundertzwanzig*. In practice, complex numbers are rarely written fully except on cheques, and, in general, figures are used in written German more often than is usual in English.

(b) Numbers higher than a thousand are written with spaces every three digits
i.e. **not** commas as in English, i.e. 564 297, *not* 564,297. The comma is used in German for the English decimal point (see 9.3.3).

TABLE 9.1   *Cardinal numbers*

0 null	10 zehn	20 zwanzig
1 eins	11 elf	21 einundzwanzig
2 zwei	12 zwölf	22 zweiundzwanzig
3 drei	13 dreizehn	23 dreiundzwanzig
4 vier	14 vierzehn	24 vierundzwanzig
5 fünf	15 fünfzehn	25 fünfundzwanzig
6 sechs	16 se**chz**ehn	26 sechsundzwanzig
7 sieben	17 sie**bz**ehn	27 siebenundzwanzig
8 acht	18 achtzehn	28 achtundzwanzig
9 neun	19 neunzehn	29 neunundzwanzig
30 dreißig	100 hundert	1000 tausend
40 vierzig	101 hundert(und)eins	1001 tausend(und)eins
50 fünfzig	102 hundertzwei	1099 tausend(und)neunundneunzig
60 se**chz**ig	151 hunderteinundfünfzig	1100 tausendeinhundert/elfhundert
70 sie**bz**ig	200 zweihundert	
80 achtzig	535 fünfhundertfünfunddreißig	
90 neunzig		

564 297 fünfhundertvierundsechzigtausendzweihundertsiebenundneunzig
1 000 000 eine Million
2 000 000 zwei Millionen
5 276 423 fünf Millionen zweihundertsechsundsiebzigtausendvierhundertdreiundzwanzig
1 000 000 000 eine Milliarde

(c) *hundert* or *einhundert*?
There is a difference between *hundert* 'a hundred', *tausend* 'a thousand' and *einhundert* '**one** hundred', *eintausend* '**one** thousand'. However, *ein* is normally inserted in complex numbers, e.g. 101 100 *hunderteintausendeinhundert*.

(d) *und* may be used between *hundert* and *eins*
This is wholly optional, e.g. *hundert(und)eins, zweihundert(und)eins*, as also between *tausend* and tens or units, e.g. *tausend(und)eins, viertausend(und)elf, zwanzigtausend(und)zweiunddreißig*.

(e) *eine Million* and *eine Milliarde* are treated as separate nouns
They have a plural ending where necessary, e.g.:

    zwei Millionen   fünf Millionen vierhunderttausend

Numbers higher than *eine Milliarde* are rare in normal everyday use, so that, for instance, *tausend Milliarden* is more usual than *eine Billion*.

NB: The plural form is used when *one* million is followed by a decimal: *1,4 Millionen Mark*. This is spoken as *einskommavier Millionen Mark*.

(f) The old form *zwo* is often heard for *zwei*
This helps to avoid the possibility of confusion with *drei*. This usage is particularly frequent on the telephone, but it has become common in other spoken contexts and is extended to 2 in complex numbers, e.g.: *zwounddreißig*, and the ordinal *der zwote*.

(g) The numbers from 2 to 12 have alternative forms with an additional -*e*
e.g. *sechse, neune, elfe*. These are common in spoken colloquial German (especially in the south) for emphasis, particularly when stating the time, e.g.: *Ich bin um fünfe aufgestanden*.

(h) Longer numbers are often stated in pairs
e.g. *4711* (a brand of eau de Cologne), spoken *siebenundvierzig elf*. This usage is regular with telephone numbers (but not the dialling code), e.g. (*0621*) *54 87 23*, which is usually given as *null sechs zwo eins – vierundfünfzig siebenundachtzig dreiundzwanzig*.

(i) Years are usually stated in hundreds
e.g. *1996: neunzehnhundertsechsundneunzig*.

(j) *beide* is used in some contexts where English uses the numeral 'two'
This is particularly the case where it is a question of 'two and only two' of the relevant items, cf. 5.5.3b, e.g. *Ich möchte diese beiden Hemden* 'I would like these two shirts'.

(k) *fünfzehn* and *fünfzig*
These are usually pronounced *fuffzehn* and *fuffzig* in colloquial speech.

(l) As an indefinite large number, corresponding to English 'umpteen', colloquial German uses *zig*

> Ich kenne sie schon **zig** Jahre   *I've known her umpteen years*
> Die ist mit **zig** Sachen in die Kurve gefahren   *She took the bend at a fair old speed*

Compare also the compounds *zigmal* 'umpteen times', *zigtausend* 'umpteen thousand', etc.

(m) Cardinal numbers used as nouns
Where these refer to the numeral as such, they are feminine and have a plural in *-en* if required, e.g.:

> Die Sieben ist eine Glückszahl   In Mathe habe ich nie eine Fünf gehabt
> Die Hundert ist eine dreistellige Zahl
> Beim Abitur hat er drei Zweien und eine Eins gekriegt

Note that the feminine nouns *die Hundert* and *die Tausend*, referring to the numbers as such, as illustrated above, are to be distinguished from the neuters *das Hundert* and *das Tausend*, which refer to quantities, cf. 9.1.5b.

(n) The numeral 7 is usually written in handwriting with a stroke
i.e. 7. This helps to distinguish it from 1, which Germans write with an initial sweep, i.e. 1.

9.1.2 *eins, ein, einer* 'one'

(a) The form *eins* is used in isolation as a numeral
i.e. in counting and the like, cf. also:

> Wir müssen mit der (Linie) eins zum   *We've got to take the number one*
> Bahnhof fahren   *(i.e. tram, bus) to the station*

This form is also used with decimals (see also 9.3.3): *einskommasieben*.

(b) The form *ein* is used with a following noun
It agrees with the following noun for case and gender and has the same endings as the indefinite article, see Table 4.2.

> **ein** Tisch *one table*   **eine** Kirche *one church*   **ein** Buch *one book*
> durch **einen** Fehler *by one mistake*   aus **einem** Grund *for one reason*

The numerical sense of *ein* (i.e. 'one') is distinguished from the indefinite article *ein* (i.e. 'a', 'an') in speech by *ein* always being pronounced in full, cf. 4.1.2b. In writing, if there is a possibility of ambiguity in context, the numerical sense can be made clear typographically, e.g.:

> éin Buch   *ein* Buch   <u>ein</u> Buch   e i n Buch

In practice this is only necessary in exceptional cases.

After *hundert* and *tausend*, e.g. *301, 2001*, there is considerable uncertainty as to how or whether to decline forms of *ein*. The combinations *hundertundeine Mark* and *Tausendundeine Nacht* 'The 1001 Nights' are well established idiomatically. However, few Germans are sure whether this construction can be used in other contexts, i.e. *ein Buch mit dreihundertundeiner Seite*. However, the alternative of undeclined -*ein*, with a plural noun, e.g. *ein Buch mit dreihundertein Seiten*, offered by DUDEN (1995: 266), is felt by many speakers to be odd.

(c) The form *einer* is used as a pronoun
It declines like *meiner* (see Table 5.2):

> Wir haben einen Rottweiler, und ihr habt auch **einen**, nicht?
> **einer** der Männer *one of the men*   **ein(e)s** der Häuser *one of the houses*

Further details on the use of *einer* are given in 5.5.4.

(d) After a determiner *ein*- declines like an adjective
e.g. *der eine* ... 'the one ...'

> Das Dorf hatte bloß **die eine** Straße
> Mit **seinem einen** Auge sieht er schlecht

(e) *ein* has no ending in a few constructions
(i) When followed by *oder* or *bis* and another number, e.g. *ein oder zwei, ein bis zwei*:

> Ich pflückte **ein oder zwei** Rosen   Wir müssen **ein bis zwei** Tage warten
> Er kam vor **ein oder zwei** Wochen   Ich sprach mit **ein oder zwei** anderen

NB: *ein* is declined in these contexts with *Mark*, e.g. *eine bis fünf Mark.*

(ii) When linked with *andere* or *derselbe*, the alternatives of declining *ein* or leaving it endingless are equally acceptable:

> **Ein(er)** oder der andere machte eine   *One or other made a brief remark*
> kurze Bemerkung
> An **ein(em)** und demselben Tag machten   *On one and the same day three*
> drei Firmen Pleite   *firms went bankrupt*

With *mehrere*, *ein* is more commonly inflected:

> vor einem (rarely: ein) oder mehreren   *one or more months ago*
> Monaten

(iii) *ein* is not inflected in *ein Uhr* 'one o'clock', cf. 11.1.1. (Compare *eine Uhr* 'a/one clock').

9.1.3 Inflection of cardinal numbers
Apart from *ein* 'one', which is declined as explained in 9.1.2, cardinal numbers do not decline in German. Thus:

> gegen sechs Kinder   mit sechs Kindern   wegen sechs Kindern
> die sechs Kinder   mit den sechs Kindern   wegen der sechs Kinder

However, endings are found in one or two special contexts:

(a) *zwei* and *drei* have the genitive forms *zweier* and *dreier*
These are quite frequent in formal written German, e.g.:

> Der Taufe **zweier** Kinder aus der Ehe   *He agreed to the baptism of two*
> stimmte er zu (*MM*)   *children of the marriage*
> die vielerlei Eindrücke **dreier**   *the various impressions from three*
> anstrengender Tage (*Zeit*)   *strenuous days*

Note that a following adjective has the 'strong' ending *-er* (see 6.2.1b). In less formal German the paraphrase with *von* is used, e.g. *der Taufe von zwei Kindern, die Eindrücke von drei anstrengenden Tagen.*

(b) The numbers from 2 to 12 may have a dative in *-en* when used in isolation i.e. when no noun follows:

> Nur einer von **zweien** ist als gesund zu bezeichnen (*Zeit*)
> als sich die Tür hinter den **dreien** geschlossen hatte (*Welt*)

This is a common alternative to the endingless form (i.e. *einer von zwei*, etc.), even in spoken German, especially with the numbers 2, 3 and 4. It is most frequent for added emphasis and in set phrases such as *auf allen vieren* 'on all fours', *mit dreien* 'with three (Jacks)' (in the card game *Skat*), and in the formula *zu zweien, dreien, vieren* etc. 'in twos, threes, fours', e.g.:

> dieser Spaziergang **zu zweien** (*Th. Mann*)

A rather more frequent alternative here is the form in *-t* (using the stem of the ordinal, cf. 9.2.1), e.g. *zu zweit, zu dritt, zu viert*. However, as DUDEN (1995: 267) points out, a distinction can be made between *zu zweien* 'in pairs' and *zu zweit* 'as a pair' (i.e. when there are only two). Compare:

> Sie gingen **zu zweien** über die Straße   *They crossed the road in pairs*
> Sie gingen **zu zweit** über die Straße   *The two of them crossed the road together*

9.1.4 Cardinals have an adjectival form in -er

e.g. *fünfer, zehner*. This is used to denote value and measurement, or with reference to years. When they are used as adjectives, they do not decline (see 6.2.7e). When they are used as nouns, they have the dative ending *-n*:

Ich habe zwei Zehner und einen Hunderter	*I've got two ten mark notes and a hundred mark note*
zwei Fünfziger	{ *two fifty pfennig pieces* { or *two fifty mark notes*
zehn achtziger Marken	*ten 80 pfennig stamps*
eine Achtziger	*an 80 pfennig stamp*
die Zehner und die Einer	*tens and units*
eine Sechserpackung	*a six-pack*
in den neunziger Jahren dieses Jahrhunderts	*in the nineties of this century*
ein Mann in den Vierzigern	*a man in his forties*
eine Mittfünfzigerin	*a woman in her mid-fifties*
ein Dreitausender	*a mountain (over) 3000 metres high*
ein vierundneunziger Heppenheimer Krötenbrunnen	*a '94 Heppenheimer Krötenbrunnen* (i.e. a wine vintage 1994)

9.1.5 *hundert, tausend, Dutzend*

(a) *hundert* and *tausend* are used as normal numerals
They are not declined and can be preceded by quantifiers such as *einige, mehrere, viele*, etc.:

hundert, zweihundert Häuser	*a hundred, two hundred houses*
viele hundert Kisten	*many hundreds of cases*
mit mehreren hundert Kisten	*with several hundred cases*
einige tausend Bücher	*a few thousand books*

(b) *das Hundert, das Tausend* and *das Dutzend* are used as nouns of quantity
They have a plural in *-e*:

das zweite Dutzend	*the second dozen*
Hunderttausende von Menschen	*hundreds of thousands of people*
Die Menschen verhungerten zu	*People were starving in hundreds and*
Hunderten und Tausenden	*thousands*

In the genitive plural, they have the ending *-er if* no determiner precedes. A following adjective has the 'strong' endings:

eine Dokumentation in der Form	*a documentation in the form of*
Hunderter ausschließlich deutscher	*hundreds of exclusively German*
Zeugnisse (*Spiegel*)	*pieces of evidence*
die Flucht **Tausender** DDR-Bewohner	*the flight of thousands of*
(*Spiegel*)	*inhabitants of the GDR*

However, they retain the simple ending *-e* if preceded by a determiner in the genitive plural, e.g.: *die Ersparnisse vieler Tausende*.

NB: (i) *Dutzend* does not take the plural ending when used as a measurement noun in constructions such as *drei Dutzend* (*Eier*) 'three dozen (eggs)', cf. 1.2.14.

(ii) For the use of the genitive, apposition or a phrase with *von* after the nouns *Dutzend, Hundert, Tausend* see 2.7.4.

9.1.6 Qualification of cardinal numbers

Numerals may be modified by a number of adverbs of degree, e.g.:

bis zu *up to*	knapp *barely*	über *over*
unter *under*	zwischen *between*	
gegen, rund, um, ungefähr, circa/zirka (abbrev. ca.) *about, approximately*		

bis zu, gegen, über, um, unter and *zwischen* do not influence the case of a following noun when used adverbially with a numeral, i.e. in cases where the sentence would still be grammatically correct if they were omitted:

Bis zu zehn Kinder können mitfahren	*Up to ten children can come with us*
Sie ist zwischen 30 und 40 Jahre alt	*She is between 30 and 40 years old*

However, when they are used as prepositions, *gegen, über* and *um* take the accusative, *bis zu, unter* and *zwischen* the dative when used with numerical expressions. In such cases the sentence ceases to be grammatically correct if they are omitted, as in the following examples:

Kinder unter sieben Jahren zahlen	*Children under seven years old pay*
die Hälfte	*half-price*
Kinder über sechs Jahre zahlen voll	*Children over six years old pay*
	the full price
geeignet für Kinder zwischen sieben	*suitable for children between the*
und zwölf Jahren	*ages of seven and twelve*

Other adverbials used with numbers:

Es dauert gut drei Stunden	*It lasts a good three hours*
Er gab mir **ganze** fünf Mark	*He gave me all of five marks*

9.2 Ordinal numbers

9.2.1 The formation of ordinal numbers

Ordinal numbers are given in Table 9.2. Most ordinal numbers are formed by adding the suffix *-te* to the cardinals 2–19 and *-ste* to the cardinals from 20 upwards. The few exceptions to this pattern are shown in bold print in Table 9.2. All ordinal numbers are used and declined like adjectives. A few special forms and uses need to be noted.

(a) *der x-te* and *der zigste* **are used as indefinite ordinals**
i.e. as equivalents of English 'the umpteenth', e.g.:

> Das war mein **x-ter/zigster** Versuch

NB: *x-te* is pronounced [ɪkstə]. For the form *zig*, see 9.1.1l.

(b) The ordinal stems can be compounded with superlatives

> die **zweitbeste** Arbeit   die **drittgrößte** Stadt   der **vierthöchste** Berg

(c) Ordinal numbers are indicated in writing by using a full stop after the numeral

> am 14. Mai   das 275. Regiment   die 12. Klasse

This is nowadays the only usual means of indicating ordinal numbers; abbreviations (e.g. *am 5ten Mai*) are no longer current.

(d) Ordinal numbers can be used as nouns
In this respect they are like other adjectives, cf. 6.4, but they are written with a small initial letter, e.g:

> jeder dritte   Er kam als erster   Wer ist der zweite?

TABLE 9.2 *Ordinal numbers*

1 der **erste**	20 der zwanzigste
2 der zweite	21 der einundzwanzigste
3 der **dritte**	27 der siebenundzwanzigste
4 der vierte	
5 der fünfte	30 der dreißigste
6 der sechste	40 der vierzigste
7 der sie**bte**	50 der fünfzigste
8 der **achte**	60 der sechzigste
9 der neunte	70 der siebzigste
10 der zehnte	80 der achtzigste
11 der elfte	90 der neunzigste
12 der zwölfte	
13 der dreizehnte	100 der hundertste
14 der vierzehnte	101 der hundert(und)erste
15 der fünfzehnte	117 der hundertsiebzehnte
16 der sechzehnte	
17 der siebzehnte	1000 der tausendste
18 der achtzehnte	1 000 000 der millionste
19 der neunzehnte	

5437 der fünftausendvierhundertsiebenunddreißigste

NB: In the reformed spelling, cf. 23.7.3, ordinal numbers used as nouns will be spelled with capital letters, e.g. *jeder Dritte*.

9.2.2 Equivalents for English 'to be the first to'

For 'to be the first to', German uses either *als erster*, or *der erste* followed by a relative clause:

Die Russen **waren die ersten**, die einen künstlichen Erdsatelliten um den Globus schickten; sie brachten **als erste** einen Menschen in den Weltraum (*Zeit*)	*The Russians were the first to send an artificial satellite round the earth; they were the first to put a man into space*
Dann mußte Konstantin **als erster** über den Graben (*Dönhoff*)	*Then Konstantin had to be the first to cross the ditch*

9.2.3 Equivalents for English 'first(ly)', 'secondly' etc.

For these, German uses the stem of the ordinal with the suffix *-ens*, e.g. *erstens* 'first(ly)', *zweitens* 'secondly', *drittens* 'thirdly', etc. Alternatively, the forms *zum ersten, zum zweiten, zum dritten*, etc. are used.

9.3 Fractions

9.3.1 Fractions (*die Bruchzahlen*) are formed by adding *-el* to the ordinal stem

(with the exception of 'half', cf. 9.3.2):

ein **Drittel**   ein **Viertel**   ein **Fünftel**   ein **Achtel**   ein **Zehntel**

Fractions are neuter nouns. They have an endingless plural, e.g. *zwei Drittel*, and often lack *-n* in the dative plural:

Die Prüfung wurde von **vier Fünftel(n)** der Schüler bestanden

If a fraction is the subject of a verb, it takes a singular or plural ending as appropriate:

Ein Drittel **ist** schon verkauft   Zwei Drittel **sind** schon verkauft

When followed by a noun they are spelled with a small letter and an accompanying indefinite article takes its case and gender from the noun:

mit einer **drittel** Flasche   mit einem **viertel** Liter

They are often written together with common measurement words, e.g. *ein Viertelliter, fünf Achtelliter, vier Zehntelgramm* and (especially) *eine Viertelstunde*. The following alternative usages are thus all possible:

Er verfehlte den Rekord um **drei Zehntel einer Sekunde**
Er verfehlte den Rekord um **drei zehntel Sekunden**
Er verfehlte den Rekord um **drei Zehntelsekunden**

dreiviertel is normally treated as a single word, e.g. *dreiviertel der Klasse*. It is compounded with *Stunde*, e.g. *in einer Dreiviertelstunde* 'in three-quarters of an hour'.

When used with full integers, fractions are read out as written, with no *und*, e.g.: 3⅝ *drei fünfachtel*, 1⁷⁄₁₀ *eins siebenzehntel*.

9.3.2 'half' corresponds to the adjective *halb* and the noun *die Hälfte*

(a) 'half', used as a noun, is normally *die Hälfte*

Er hat mir nur **die Hälfte** gegeben	*He only gave me half*
die größere **Hälfte**	*the bigger half*

However, the form *das Halb*, from the adjective, is used to refer to the number as such:

(Ein) **Halb** ist mehr als ein Drittel	*Half is more than a third*

(b) *half a*: the usual equivalent is the indefinite article with *halb*

Ich aß einen **halben** Apfel	*I ate half an apple*
ein **halbes** Dutzend	*half a dozen*
ein **halbes** Brot	*half a loaf*

(c) *half the/this/my*

The usual equivalent is *die Hälfte* with a following genitive, but the appropriate determiner can be used with *halb* if the reference is to a whole thing which can be divided cleanly in two:

Die Hälfte der/dieser Äpfel ist schlecht	*Half the/these apples are bad*
die Hälfte meines Geldes	*half my money*
Ich aß **die Hälfte** des Kuchens ⎫ Ich aß **den halben Kuchen** ⎭	*I ate half the cake*

NB: The use of *halb* with a plural noun in such cases, i.e. *die halben Äpfel* 'half the apples' is considered substandard colloquial.

(d) English adverbial 'half' corresponds to German *halb*

halb angezogen	*half dressed*
Er weiß alles nur **halb**	*He only half knows things*

(e) German equivalents for English 'one and a half'

German uses either *eineinhalb* or (in more informal usage) *anderthalb*.
2½, 3½, etc. are *zweieinhalb, dreieinhalb*, etc. These are not declined:

Bis Walldürn sind es noch **eineinhalb/anderthalb** Stunden	*It's another hour and a half to Walldürn*
Sie wollte noch **sechseinhalb** Monate bleiben	*She wanted to stay another six and a half months*

(f) Some other phrases and idioms:

Er hatte halb soviel wie ich	*He had half as much as me*
Kinder fahren zum halben Preis	*Children travel half price*
Er ist mir auf halbem Wege entgegengekommen	*He met me half-way* (literal and figurative sense)
Ich nehme noch ein Halbes	*I'll have another half*
Das ist nichts Halbes und nichts Ganzes	*That's neither flesh nor fowl*
Die Besucher waren zur Hälfte Deutsche	*Half the visitors were German*
nach der ersten Halbzeit	*after the first half* (sport)
halb Europa, halb München (cf. 6.2.7g)	*half Europe, half Munich*

9.3.3 In German, decimals are written with a comma

i.e. *not* with a point, e.g.:

0,7	*nullkommasieben*	4,75	*vierkommasiebenfünf*
1,25	*einskommazweifünf*	109,1	*hundertneunkommaeins*
3,426	*dreikommavierzweisechs*		

In colloquial speech, two places of decimals may be read out in terms of tens and units, e.g. 4,75 *vierkommafünfundsiebzig*.

9.4 Other numerical usages

9.4.1 Numerically equal distribution is expressed by *je*

Ich gab den Jungen **je** zehn Mark	*I gave each of the boys ten marks*
A. und B. wurden zu **je** drei Jahren verurteilt	*A. and B. were each sentenced to three years*
Sie erhielten **je** fünf Kilo Reis	*They each received five kilograms of rice*

9.4.2 Multiples

(a) German adds suffixes *-fach* to the cardinal to form multiples

e.g. *einfach* 'single', *zweifach* 'twofold', *dreifach* 'threefold', etc.:

eine **einfache** Karte	*a single ticket*
ein **vierfacher** Olympiasieger	*a fourfold gold-medal winner*
... stiegen die Grundstückspreise	*... the price of land went up tenfold*
zunächst aufs **Zehnfache** (Böll)	*in the first instance*

(b) *zweifach* and *doppelt*

zweifach is sometimes interchangeable in meaning with *doppelt* 'double', but more often refers to two *different* things, whilst *doppelt* refers to two of the same, cf. DUDEN (1985: 191), e.g.: *ein zweifaches Verbrechen* 'two kinds of crime' but *Der Koffer hat einen doppelten Boden* 'the suitcase has a false bottom'. *zweifach* has the variant form *zwiefach* in older literary usage.

(c) *-fach* is also suffixed to a few indefinites

e.g. *vielfach* or *mehrfach* 'manifold', 'frequent(ly)', 'repeatedly', *mannigfach* 'varied', 'manifold'.

(d) Forms in *-fältig* can also be used as multiples

e.g. *zweifältig*, *dreifältig*, *vielfältig*, etc. These are rather less common than forms in *-fach*. Note too, (without *Umlaut!*), *mannigfaltig*, which is more frequent than *mannigfach*, and *die (heilige) Dreifaltigkeit* 'the (Holy) Trinity'. *einfältig* most often has the meaning 'simple(-minded)'.

(e) Equivalents for English 'single'

When it is used in the sense 'individual', 'separate', 'single' corresponds to *einzeln*, e.g. *Die Bände werden einzeln verkauft* 'The volumes are sold singly/separately'. In the sense 'sole', it corresponds to *einzig*, e.g. *Er hat keinen einzigen Freund* 'He hasn't got a single friend'.

9.4.3 *einmal, zweimal* etc.

(a) Adverbs made up from *-mal* suffixed to the cardinals express the number of occasions

e.g. *einmal* 'once', *zweimal* 'twice', *dreimal* 'three times', *zehnmal* 'ten times', *hundertmal* 'a hundred times', etc.:

Ich habe ihn diese Woche **dreimal** gesehen	*I've seen him three times this week*
Ich habe es **hundertmal** bereut	*I've regretted it a hundred times*
Also, Herr Ober, **zweimal** Gulasch, bitte	*Right, waiter, goulash for two, please*
anderthalbmal so groß wie das erste	*one and a half times as big as the first*

Adjectives are formed from these adverbs by suffixing *-ig*, e.g. *einmalig, zweimalig*:

eine einmalige Gelegenheit	*a unique opportunity*
nach dreimaligem Durchlesen seines Briefes	*after reading his letter three times*

Formed in a similar way is *mehrmalig* 'repeated(ly)'.

(b) Forms and phrases with *-mal* and *Mal*

A number of phrases with *Mal* have variant spelling forms. In principle *Mal* (plural *Male*) is a noun, and it is written separate from any preceding adjectives or determiners:

das erste **Mal**, das ich ihn sah	Das letzte **Mal** war das schönste
kein einziges **Mal**	ein um das andere **Mal** *time after time*
Ich werde es nächstes **Mal** tun	Das vorige **Mal** war es schöner
Beide **Male** bin ich durchgefallen	viele (hundert) **Male**
Ich habe ihn oft besucht; das eine **Mal** zeigte er mir seine Sammlung	
Dieses **Mal** wird sie mich anders behandeln müssen	
Die letzten paar **Male** war sie nicht zu Hause	

However, there is a common alternative of compounding *-mal* with the preceding adjective or determiner instead of using *Mal* as a separate word. This alternative is limited to the following set phrases:

diesmal	jedesmal	ein **paarmal**
das (über)nächstemal	das (vor)letztemal	zum **wievieltenmal?**
ein **andermal**	hundertemal	
ein **dutzendmal**	dutzendemal	
als er das **erstemal/letztemal** hier war, ...		
Ich tue es **zum erstenmal**, zum zweitenmal, zum drittenmal, zum letztenmal		

NB: *x-mal, zigmal* 'umpteen times'.

These forms are used if *Mal* is hardly stressed and not really felt to be a separate noun. In practice, however, the difference in usage between the compounded and the uncompounded forms is very slight.

vielmals 'many times' is used in a few set constructions, i.e.:

Ich danke Ihnen **vielmals** ⎫	
Danke **vielmals** ⎭	*Many thanks*
Ich bitte **vielmals** um Entschuldigung	*I do apologise*
Sie läßt Sie **vielmals** grüßen	*She sends you her kindest regards*

NB: *erstmals* 'for the first time'.

9.4.4 The suffix *-erlei*

-erlei is added to the cardinal numbers to give forms which mean 'x kinds of', e.g. *zweierlei* 'two kinds of', *dreierlei* 'three kinds of', *vielerlei* 'many kinds of', etc. They can be used as nouns or adjectives and do not decline:

Ich ziehe zweierlei Bohnen	*I grow two kinds of beans*
Er hat hunderterlei Pläne	*He's got hundreds of different plans*
Ich habe ihm dreierlei vorgeschlagen	*I suggested three different things to him*

einerlei is most often used in the sense 'all the same' (i.e. = *egal, gleich*, etc.), e.g. *Das ist mir alles einerlei.*

9.4.5 Mathematical terminology

The common arithmetic and mathematical functions are expressed as follows in German. In some cases the symbols used in Germany differ from those current in the English-speaking countries:

$4 + 5 = 9$	*vier und/plus fünf ist/gleich neun*
$8 - 6 = 2$	*acht weniger/minus sechs ist/gleich zwei*
$\left.\begin{array}{l} 3 \times 4 = 12 \\ 3 . 4 = 12 \end{array}\right\}$	*drei mal vier ist/gleich zwölf*
$8 : 2 = 4$	*acht (geteilt) durch zwei ist/gleich vier*
$3^2 = 9$	*drei hoch zwei (drei zum Quadrat) ist/gleich neun*
$3^3 = 27$	*drei hoch drei ist/gleich siebenundzwanzig*
$\sqrt{9} = 3$	*Quadratwurzel/zweite Wurzel aus neun ist/gleich drei*
$5 > 3$	*fünf ist größer als drei*

9.5 Addresses

These are typically written in the following form:

Herrn	Frau
Dr. Ulrich Sievers	Maria Jellinek
Sichelstraße 17	Maximiliansgasse 34
54290 Trier	1084 Wien
Familie	Herrn und Frau
Karl (und Ute) Schuhmacher	Peter und Eva Specht
Königsberger Straße 36	Steinweg 2½
64711 Erbach/Odw.	35037 Marburg/Lahn
Firma	An das
Eugen Spengel	Katasteramt Westfalen
Roßgasse 7-9	Bismarckallee 87
07973 Greiz	48151 Münster

When writing from outside the country, the appropriate country code, i.e. **D** (Germany), **A** (Austria), **CH** (Switzerland) is prefixed to the post code. On private letters the sender's name and address are written in a single line on the back of the envelope, preceded by *Abs.* (i.e. *Absender*), e.g.: *Abs.: Indermühle, Strohgasse 17, CH - 8600 Düsendorf*.

10

Modal particles

Modal particles express the speaker's attitude to what is being said. These words, such as *aber, doch, ja, mal, schon*, etc., (called in German *Abtönungspartikeln* or *Modalpartikeln*) are a typical feature of German, especially, if not exclusively, of everyday colloquial speech. By using them one may alter the tone of what is being said and, for example, appeal for agreement, express surprise or annoyance, soften a blunt question or statement or sound reassuring. They act as a kind of lubrication in dialogue, making sure that the speaker's intentions and attitudes are not misunderstood. German has a far richer repertoire of such words than English, which tends to use different means (notably intonation, tag questions like *isn't it?* and so forth) to the same end.

There is no agreement as to which words can be classified as 'modal particles' in German. Their function is very similar to that of adverbs of attitude (see 7.3.2), and like them they cannot be negated. But, as a general rule, modal particles are less independent and, in particular, most cannot normally be used on their own in first position in a main clause statement, before the main verb. Modal particles proper, which relate to the clause or sentence as a whole, are usually distinguished from 'scalar' or 'focus' particles (called *Gradpartikeln* in German), like *sogar*, which focus attention on a particular word or phrase in the sentence. However, these distinctions are rarely clear-cut, and many of these words can be used in more than one way. *auch* and *nur*, for example, can be used both as 'modal' and as 'scalar' particles, and *eigentlich* and *freilich*, among others, can function as adverbs of attitude as well as modal particles.

Such unresolved difficulties of definition and classification are beyond the scope of this book; illuminating recent discussions of the problems involved may be found in Eisenberg (1994: 204–9) and Hentschel and Weydt (1994: 279–93). This chapter aims to give a practical account of the use in modern German of all those words which have some claim to being considered as modal particles, and these are listed on Table 10.1. Since many of these words have other functions and it is not always straightforward (or useful in practice) to determine which uses of these words can be considered as those of 'modal particles', *all* the uses of the words included are dealt with here.

Much has been written on the meaning and use of the German modal particles. Useful, practically orientated recent books are Helbig (1988), Weydt *et al.* (1983) and, in English, West (1993). Much of the detail and many of the examples in this chapter are based on these accounts and they can be consulted with profit for further information.

TABLE 10.1 *Modal particles*

aber	etwa	nun
allerdings	freilich	nur
also	gar	ohnehin
auch	gleich	ruhig
bloß	halt	schließlich
denn	immerhin	schon
doch	ja	sowieso
eben	jedenfalls	überhaupt
eh	lediglich	übrigens
eigentlich	mal	vielleicht
einfach	man	wohl
erst	noch	zwar

10.1 *aber*

10.1.1 In statements, *aber* expresses a surprised reaction

In effect, it converts such statements to exclamations:

Das war aber eine Reise!	*That was quite a journey, wasn't it?*
Der Film war aber gut!	*The film was good*
Der Kaffee ist aber heiß!	*Oh! The coffee is hot*

aber can be given greater emphasis by adding *auch*. Compare:

Das war aber auch eine Reise!	*That really was some journey!*

ja is also used to express surprise (cf. 10.19.2), but surprise resulting from a difference in kind, where *aber* indicates a difference in degree. Compare:

Der Kaffee ist **aber** heiß	(i.e. hotter than you had expected)
Der Kaffee ist **ja** heiß!	(you had expected *cold* coffee)

In this sense, *aber* can be replaced by *vielleicht* (cf. 10.34.1): *Der Tee ist vielleicht heiß!*

10.1.2 *aber* can be used within a clause to express a contradiction

In such contexts, it has much the same sense it would have at the beginning (i.e. = English 'but', see 19.1.1). This sense is very close to that of *doch* (cf. 10.7.1):

Mein Freund kam aber nicht	*My friend didn't come, though*
Sie muß uns aber gesehen haben	*But she must have seen us*
Jetzt kannst du etwas schneller fahren ... Paß aber bei den Ampeln auf!	*You can go a bit quicker now ... Look out at the lights, though!*

Used with *oder*, *aber* has the sense of 'on the other hand':

Seine Befürwortung könnte der Sache helfen oder aber (auch) schaden	*His support might help the affair or, on the other hand, it might harm it*

10.1.3 When used initially in exclamations, *aber* adds emphasis to the speaker's opinion

It can sound scolding or reassuring, depending on the context:

Hast du was dagegen? – Aber nein!	*Have you any objection? – Of course not!*
Aber Kinder! Was habt ihr schon wieder angestellt?	*Now, now, childen! What have you been doing?*
Aber, aber! Was soll diese Aufregung?	*Oh now! What's all the excitement about?*

10.1.4 *aber* is also used as a co-ordinating conjunction

i.e. corresponding to English 'but', see 19.1.1.

10.2 *allerdings*

allerdings most often expresses a reservation about what has just been said. It usually corresponds to English 'admittedly', 'of course', 'to be sure', 'all the same', etc. *freilich* has a very similar meaning, see 10.14.

10.2.1 Within a sentence, the sense of *allerdings* is close to that of *aber*

However, it is rather less blunt:

Es ist ein gutes Buch, allerdings gefallen mir seine anderen etwas besser	*It's a good book. Even so, I like his others rather better*
Wir haben uns im Urlaub gut erholt, das Wetter war allerdings nicht sehr gut	*The holiday was a good rest for us. All the same, the weather wasn't very good*
Ich komme gern, allerdings muß ich zuerst der Rita Bescheid sagen	*I want to come, of course I'll have to tell Rita first*

10.2.2 Used in isolation in answer to a question, *allerdings* expresses a strongly affirmative answer

There can be a slight hint of a reservation or qualification of some kind which the speaker isn't making explicit:

Kennst du die Angelika? – Allerdings!	*Do you know Angelika? – Of course!* (I know what she's like, too!)
Ist der Helmut schon da? – Allerdings!	*Is Helmut here yet? – Oh, yes!* (and you should see who he's come with!)

10.3 *also*

10.3.1 *also* confirms something as the logical conclusion from what has just been said

It often corresponds to English 'so', 'thus' or 'then':

Du wirst mir also helfen können	*You're going to be able to help me, then*
Wann kommst du also genau?	*So, when are you coming precisely?*
Sie meinen also, daß wir uns heute entscheiden müssen	*So you think we're going to have to make a decision today*

10.3.2 Used in isolation, *also* links up with what has just been said

It can introduce a statement or a question:

Also, jetzt müssen wir uns überlegen, wie wir dahinkommen	*Well then, now we've got to think about how we're going to get there*
Also, besuchst du uns morgen?	*So, are you going to come to see us tomorrow?*
Also, gut!	*Well all right then!*
Also, so was!	*Well I never!*

10.4 *auch*

10.4.1 In statements, *auch* stresses the reasons why something is or is not the case

It can be used to correct a false impression and is often used with *ja*:

Günther sieht heute schlecht aus	*Günther's not looking well today*
– Er ist (ja) auch lange krank gewesen	*– Well, he's been ill for a long time*
Jetzt möchte ich schlafen gehen	*I'd like to go to bed now*
– Es ist (ja) auch spät	*– Well, after all, it is late*
Das hättest du nicht tun sollen	*You ought not to have done that*
– Ich habe es (ja) auch nicht getan	*– But I didn't do it, you know*

10.4.2 In yes/no questions, *auch* asks for confirmation of something which the speaker thinks should be taken for granted

The English equivalent is very often a tag question:

Kann ich mich auch darauf verlassen?	*I can rely on that, can't I?*
Hast du auch die Rechnung bezahlt?	*You **did** pay the bill, didn't you?*
Bist du auch glücklich mit ihm?	*You're happy with him, aren't you?*

10.4.3 *auch* turns w-questions into rhetorical questions

It confirms that nothing else could be expected:

Was kann man auch dazu sagen?	*Well, what can you say to that?*
Ich bin heute sehr müde – Warum gehst du auch immer so spät ins Bett?	*I'm very tired today – Well, why do you always go to bed so late?*

These questions can be turned into exclamations which emphasize the speaker's negative attitude:

Was war das auch für ein Erfolg?!	*Well, what sort of success do you call that?!*
Wie konnte er auch so schnell abreisen?!	*How **could** he have left as quickly as that?!*

10.4.4 *auch* reinforces commands

This is similar to the use of English 'Be/Make sure . . .!':

Bring mir eine Zeitung und vergiß es auch nicht!	*Bring me a paper and be sure you don't forget!*
Sei auch schön brav!	*Be sure you behave!*

10.4.5 Further uses of *auch*

(a) Before a noun *auch* has the force of English 'even'
It is an alternative to *sogar* or *selbst* as a scalar particle:

Auch der beste Arzt hätte ihr nicht helfen können	*Even the best doctor wouldn't have been able to help her*
Auch der Manfred kann sich ab und zu mal irren	*Even Manfred can be wrong now and again*
Und wenn auch!	*even so, no matter*

NB: The usual equivalent for English 'not even' is *nicht einmal*.

(b) As an adverb, *auch* has the meaning 'too', 'also', 'as well'

Der Peter will auch mit	*Peter wants to come too*
Die Gisela ist auch nett	*Gisela's nice as well*
In Potsdam sind wir auch gewesen	*We also went to Potsdam*

(c) The combination *auch nur* expresses a restriction
It corresponds to English 'even', 'as/so little/much as', etc.:

wenn ich auch nur zwei Freunde hätte	*if I only had just two friends*
ohne auch nur zu fragen	*without even so much as asking*
Es war unmöglich, auch nur Brot zu kaufen	*You couldn't buy so much as a loaf of bread*

(d) *oder auch* has the sense 'or else', 'or even'

Du kannst Birnen kaufen oder auch Pfirsiche	*You can buy pears or else peaches*

(e) *auch nicht*, *auch kein* and *auch nichts* are often used for 'nor', 'neither', etc.
See 19.1.3d for details on German equivalents of 'neither' and 'nor':

Ich habe nichts davon gewußt – Ich auch nicht	*I didn't know anything about it – Nor me/Neither did I*
Sie kann nicht nähen und stricken kann sie auch nicht	*She can't sew, and neither can she knit*
Das wird ihm auch nichts helfen	*That won't help him either*
Er liest keine Zeitungen und auch keine Bücher	*He doesn't read any newspapers or books*

(f) *auch* occurs in many concessive constructions
Its force is similar to that of English 'ever', e.g.: *Wer es auch sein mag* 'Whoever that may be'. Full details are given in 19.6.2.

10.5 *bloß*

bloß usually has a restrictive sense (= English 'only', 'simply', 'merely')
In all its uses it is a rather less formal alternative to *nur*, see 10.26:

Störe mich bloß nicht bei der Arbeit	*You'd better not disturb me while I'm working*
Wie spät ist es bloß?	*I wonder just what the time is*
Wenn er bloß bald käme!	*If only he would come soon!*
Sie hatte bloß 100 Mark bei sich	*She only had 100 marks on her*
Sollen wir Tante Mia einladen? –	*Shall we invite Aunt Mia? –*
Bloß nicht!	*Good heavens no!*

10.6 *denn*

10.6.1 As a modal particle, *denn* is used exclusively in questions

(a) *denn* **most often serves to tone down the question**

It refers back to what has just been said, or to the general context, and makes the question sound rather less blunt and more obliging. In practice it is almost automatic in *w*-questions:

Hast du denn die Renate gesehen?	*Tell me, have you seen Renate?*
Geht der Junge denn heute nicht in die Schule?	*Isn't the boy going to school today, then?*
Ach, der Bus hält. Sind wir denn schon da?	*Oh, the bus is stopping. Are we already there, then?*
Warum muß er denn in die Stadt?	*Tell me, why has he got to go to town?*
Wie bist denn <u>du</u> gekommen?	*Tell me, how did <u>you</u> get here?*
Wie geht es dir denn?	*How are you then?*

NB: In colloquial speech, *denn* is often reduced to *'n* and suffixed to the verb as a clitic, e.g. *Hast'n du die Renate gesehen? Wie bist'n du gekommen?*

(b) **If there is a negative element in the question,** *denn* **signals reproach**

The negative element may not be explicit. The question itself expects a justification rather than an answer:

Hast du denn keinen Führerschein?	*Come on, haven't you got a driving licence?*
Bist du denn blind?	*Come on now, are you blind?*
Wo bist du denn so lange geblieben?	*Where on earth have you been all this time?*
Was ist denn hier los?	*What on earth's going on here?*

(c) *denn* **can convert** *w*-**questions into rhetorical questions**

A negative answer is expected:

Wer redet denn von nachgeben?	*Who's talking of giving in?* (prompting the answer: nobody!)
Was haben wir denn damit erreicht?	*And what have we achieved by that?* (prompting the answer: nothing!)

Adding *schon* makes it absolutely clear that the question is rhetorical:

Was hat er denn schon damit gewonnen?	*And what did he gain by that?* (prompting the answer: nothing!)

(d) **Yes/no questions with** *denn* **can be used as exclamations of surprise**

They often begin with *so*:

Ist das Wetter denn nicht herrlich!	*How lovely the weather is!*
So hat er denn die Stellung erhalten!	*So he did get the job!*

(e) The combination *denn noch* is used to recall a fact

Wie heißt er denn noch?   *What is his name again?*

NB: The force of *denn noch* is similar to that of *doch gleich*, see 10.7.4.

10.6.2 Further uses of *denn*

(a) The combination *es sei denn, (daß)* is a conjunction meaning 'unless'
e.g.: *Sie kommt gegen ein Uhr, es sei denn, sie wird aufgehalten.* It is used chiefly in formal German; for further details see 16.5.3d.

(b) *geschweige denn* means 'let alone', 'still less':

Er wollte mir kein Geld leihen,   *He wouldn't even **lend** me any money,*
geschweige denn schenken   *let alone give me any*

(c) *denn* is often used in place of *dann* 'then'
e.g.: *Na, **denn** geht es eben nicht.* This usage is common in colloquial north German speech, but is considered to be substandard.

(d) *denn* is used as a coordinating conjunction indicating a cause or reason
It corresponds to English 'for', 'because', e.g.: *Er kann uns nicht verstehen, **denn** er spricht kein Deutsch.* For details, see 19.1.2.

(e) *denn* is sometimes used in formal German and set phrases for *als* 'than'
e.g. *mehr denn je* 'more than ever'. For details, see 8.3.1a.

10.7 *doch*

doch is used typically in an attempt to persuade the listener of the speaker's point of view. It usually expresses a contradiction or disagreement and often corresponds to English 'though' or a tag question. The element of persuasion can be given more force if *doch* is stressed.

10.7.1 In statements, *doch* indicates disagreement with what has been said

If it is stressed, it clearly contradicts, and its meaning is close to that of *dennoch* or *trotzdem*. If it is unstressed, it appeals politely for agreement or confirmation:

Gestern hat es <u>doch</u> geschneit   *All the same, it <u>did</u> snow yesterday*
Gestern hat es doch geschneit   *It snowed yesterday, didn't it?*
Ich habe <u>doch</u> recht gehabt   *Nevertheless, I <u>was</u> right*
Ich habe doch recht gehabt   *I was right, wasn't I?*
Wir müssen <u>doch</u> morgen nach Bremen   *All the same, we <u>have</u> got to go to*
     Bremen tomorrow

Ich habe ihm davon abgeraten, aber er   *I advised him against it, but he did*
hat es <u>doch</u> getan   *it all the same*
Du hast doch gesagt, daß du kommst   *You did say you were coming, didn't you?*

Unstressed *doch* may also mildly point out a reason for disagreement. In such contexts it is interchangeable with *aber*, see 10.1.2:

Wir wollten doch heute abend ins   *Surely we were going to go to the*
Theater gehen   *theatre tonight(, weren't we?)*
Die Ampel zeigt doch rot, wir   *But the lights are red, we can't go yet*
dürfen noch nicht gehen

In literary German *doch* may be used with the verb first in the clause. This is used principally to explain a preceding statement:

War ich doch so durch den Lehrbetrieb beansprucht, daß ich keine Zeit dafür fand (*Grass*)	*After all, I was so busy with my lessons that I didn't have any time for that*

NB: For the difference in meaning between *doch* and *ja* in statements appealing for the listener's agreement, see 10.19.1b.

10.7.2 Unstressed *doch* can turn a statement into a question expecting a positive answer

It is then the equivalent of a following *oder?* or *nicht (wahr)?*, and one of these may be used as well:

Den Wagen kann ich mir doch morgen abholen?	*I can collect the car tomorrow, can't I?*
Du kannst mir doch helfen(, oder)?	*You can help me, can't you?*
Du glaubst doch nicht, daß ich esgetan habe?	*Surely you don't think I did it?*

10.7.3 *doch* in commands

The force of *doch* in commands can vary depending on the context. Sometimes it adds a note of impatience or urgency, and in this sense it can be strengthened by *endlich* or, in a negative sentence, by *immer*:

Reg dich doch nicht so auf!	*For heaven's sake, don't get so excited*
Bring den Wagen doch (endlich) in die Werkstatt!	*For goodness' sake, take the car to the garage*
Mach doch nicht (immer) so ein Gesicht!	*Don't keep making faces like that*
Freu dich doch!	*Do cheer up*

In other sentences, it can moderate the force of the command, making it sound more advisory or encouraging. This can be made even more clear by adding *mal* or *ruhig*:

Lassen Sie mich doch (mal) das Foto sehen!	*Why don't you just let me see the photograph?*
Kommen Sie doch (ruhig) morgen vorbei!	*Why not drop by tomorrow?*

10.7.4 In *w*-questions, *doch* asks for confirmation of an answer or the repetition of information

It can be strengthened by adding *gleich* (see 10.16), and its force is then similar to that of *denn noch*, see 10.6.1e:

Wie heißt doch euer Hund?	*What did you say your dog is called?*
Wer was das doch (gleich)?	*What was that again?*
Wohin fahrt ihr doch auf Urlaub?	*Where did you say you were going on holiday?*

10.7.5 In exclamations, *doch* emphasises the speaker's surprise

In such sentences the force of *doch* is close to that of *ja*, cf. 10.19.2:

Wie winzig doch alles von hier oben aussieht!	*But how tiny everything looks from up here!*
Du bist doch kein kleines Kind mehr!	*You're not a baby any more, you know!*
Das ist doch die Höhe!	*That really is the limit!*

10.7.6 In wishes expressed with *Konjunktiv II*, *doch* emphasises the urgency of the wish

See also 16.7.6b. In such sentences *doch* is the equivalent of *nur* and may be used together with it, cf. 10.26.1c:

Wenn er doch jetzt käme!	*If only he would come now!*
Wäre ich doch zu Hause geblieben!	*If only I'd just stayed at home!*

10.7.7 Further uses of *doch*

(a) In reply to a question, *doch* contradicts a negative or emphasises an affirmative reply

Bist du nicht zufrieden? – Doch!	*Aren't you satisfied? – Yes, I am*
Kommt er bald? – Doch!	*Is he coming soon? – Oh, yes*
Er hat nie etwas für uns getan –	*He's never done anything for us –*
Doch, er hat mir einmal 100 Mark	*Oh, yes he has, he once lent me*
geliehen	*a hundred marks*

When used with *nein* or *nicht*, *doch* emphasises a negative reply:

Mutti, kann ich ein Stück Schokolade	*Mummy, can I have a piece of*
haben? – Nein doch, du hast jetzt	*chocolate? – Certainly not, you've*
genug gegessen	*had enough to eat*

(b) As a conjunction, *doch* is an alternative to *aber* 'but'

e.g.: *Sie wollten baden gehen, **doch** es hat geschneit.* Further details are given in 19.1.1.

10.8 *eben*

10.8.1 As a modal particle, *eben* typically expresses a confirmation that something is the case

It often corresponds to English 'just'.

(a) In statements, *eben* emphasises an inescapable conclusion

Das ist eben so	*But there, that's how it is*
Ich kann ihn nicht überreden. Er ist	*I can't convince him. He's just obstinate*
eben hartnäckig	
Er zeichnet ganz gut – Nun, er ist	*He draws quite well – Well, he is an artist*
eben ein Künstler	
Ich mache es, so gut ich eben kann	*I'll do it as well as I can*
	(given the circumstances)

(b) In commands, *eben* emphasises that there is no real alternative

These commands are often introduced by *dann*:

(Dann) bleib eben im Zug sitzen!	*Well, just stay on the train, then*
(Dann) fahr eben durch die	*Well, just drive through the town centre, then*
Stadtmitte!	

halt is a frequent alternative to *eben*. It was originally restricted to south Germany, but it has become more widely used in recent years.

10.8.2 Further uses of *eben*

(a) *eben* **can be used in the sense of 'exactly', 'precisely', 'just'**
In this meaning it can be used as a scalar particle before another word, or as a response to a statement or a question. *genau* is a common alternative:

Eben dieses Haus hatte mir zugesagt	*It was just this house which attracted me*
Das wäre mir eben recht	*That would be just what I'd like*
Eben daran hatte ich nie gedacht	*That's the one thing I hadn't thought of*
Das wird sie doch kaum schaffen –	*She won't manage it, will she?*
Eben!	*– Precisely!*

(b) **Used with** *nicht* **before an adjective,** *eben* **lessens the force of** *nicht*
gerade is a common alternative:

Sie ist nicht eben fleißig	*She's not exactly hard-working*
Der Zug war nicht eben pünktlich	*The train wasn't what you'd call on time*

(c) As an adverb, *eben* **means 'just (now)'**
gerade is a common alternative:

Wir sind **eben** (erst) angekommen	**Eben** geht mir ein Licht auf
Mit zweitausend Mark im Monat kommen wir **eben** (noch) aus	

(d) As an adjective, *eben* **means 'level'**
e.g.: *Die Straße ist hier nicht eben.*

10.9 *eh*

eh is an alternative to *ohnehin* or *sowieso*

Like them, it is an equivalent of English 'anyway' or 'in any case', but it is used predominantly in colloquial south German, especially in Austria and Bavaria, although its use is spreading to other areas:

Wenn ich arbeite, brauche ich eh immer mehr zum Essen (*Kroetz*)	*When I'm working I need more to eat anyway*
Für eine Markenpersönlichkeit wie Sie ist das neue Magazin der Süddeutschen eh ein Muß (*SZ*)	*It goes without saying that the new magazine of the 'Süddeutsche Zeitung' is a must for a person of quality like yourself*

10.10 *eigentlich*

eigentlich emphasises that something is actually the case, even if it appears otherwise. It is often used to change the topic of conversation.

10.10.1 *eigentlich* in questions

(a) *eigentlich* **can tone a question down and makes it sound more casual**
In such cases it is relatively lightly stressed. It comes close to the sense of English 'actually' and is often used in conjunction with *denn*:

Sind Sie eigentlich dieses Jahr schon im Urlaub gewesen ?	*Tell me, have you been on holiday yet this year?*
Wohnt die Eva eigentlich schon lange in Hameln?	*Has Eva actually been living a long time in Hameln?*
Wie spät ist es (denn) eigentlich?	*What time is it, actually?*

(b) In *w*-questions, *eigentlich* can imply that the question has not yet been answered fully or satisfactorily

In such contexts it is rather more heavily stressed and very close in meaning to *im Grunde genommen*, *tatsächlich* or *wirklich*, with the sense of 'at bottom', 'in actual fact', 'in reality':

Hast du eigentlich überhaupt keine Ahnung, wo sie ist?	*Do you really have absolutely no idea where she is?*
Wie heißt er eigentlich?	*What's his real name?*
Warum besuchst du mich eigentlich?	*Why, basically, did you come to visit me?*

10.10.2 *eigentlich* in statements

(a) *eigentlich* indicates that something actually is the case, despite appearances

It moderates a refusal, an objection or a contradiction by indicating how strong the reasons are:

Er scheint manchmal faul, aber er ist eigentlich sehr fleißig	*He appears lazy sometimes, but in actual fact he's quite hard-working*
Ich wollte eigentlich zu Fuß gehen	*In actual fact, I did want to walk*
Ich trinke eigentlich keinen Kaffee mehr	*Well, actually, I don't drink coffee now*

(b) Sometimes *eigentlich* can signal that the matter is still a little open

Wir haben eigentlich schon zu	*Well, actually, we're already closed* (hinting that an exception might not be wholly out of the question)
Das darf man hier eigentlich nicht	*Strictly speaking, that's not allowed here* (but, possibly, . . .)

10.10.3 As an adjective, *eigentlich* means 'real', 'actual', 'fundamental'

Was ist die **eigentliche** Ursache?   Er nannte nicht den **eigentlichen** Grund

10.11 *einfach*

einfach emphasises that alternative possibilities are excluded

It usually corresponds to English 'simply' or, especially in commands, 'just'. In commands it is frequently used in conjunction with *doch* and/or *mal* and in exclamations with *ja*:

Ich bin einfach weggegangen	*I simply walked away*
Ich werde ihm einfach sagen, daß es nicht möglich ist	*I'll simply tell him it's not possible*
Warum gehst du nicht einfach ins Bett?	*Why don't you just go to bed?*
Leg dich (doch) einfach hin!	*Why don't you just go and lie down?*
Geh doch einfach mal zum Zahnarzt!	*Why not just simply go to the dentist?*
Heute ist das Wetter (ja) einfach herrlich!	*The weather is simply lovely today!*

einfach is used as a true adverb, as well as a particle, but there is a clear difference in meaning between the two uses, As an adverb, *einfach* is always stressed and means 'in a simple manner'. Compare:

Sie macht es **ein**fach	*She is doing it simply*
	(in an uncomplicated way)
Sie **macht** es einfach	*She's simply doing it*
	('just', 'without further ado')
Du mußt **ein**fach anfangen	*You have to begin simply*
Du mußt einfach **an**fangen	*You simply have to begin*

10.12 erst

10.12.1 As a modal particle, *erst* has intensifying force

(a) In statements and exclamations

Here *erst* implies that something really is the absolute limit and perhaps more than expected or desirable. It is often strengthened by adding *recht*:

Dann ging es erst (recht) los	*Then things really got going*
Das konnte sie erst recht nicht	*That she really couldn't manage*
Das macht es erst recht schlimm	*That really does make it bad*
Sie hat schon Hunger, aber das Kind erst (recht)!	*She may be hungry, but that's nothing to how hungry the kid is*

(b) In wishes

Here, *nur* or *bloß* are alternatives to *erst* (and may be used with it):

Wäre er doch erst zu Hause! (*Fallada*)	*If only he were at home!*
Wenn er (bloß) erst wieder arbeiten könnte!	*If only he could start work again!*

10.12.2 As a scalar particle, *erst* indicates that there are/were less or fewer than expected

(a) Before a number or an expression of quantity it corresponds to 'only'

Ich habe erst zehn Seiten geschrieben	*I've only written ten pages*
Er ist erst sieben Jahre alt	*He's only seven years old*
Ich habe erst die Hälfte fertig	*I've only got half of it finished*

Before other nouns the sense is 'nothing less than':

Erst mit einem Lehrstuhl in Bonn wird er sich zufriedengeben	*He'll only be satisfied with a professorship in Bonn*

(b) In time expressions, *erst* implies that it is later than expected or desirable

It usually corresponds to English 'only', 'not before', 'not until' or, in certain contexts, 'as late as':

Er kommt erst (am) Montag	*He's not coming till Monday* / *He's only coming on Monday*
Es ist erst acht Uhr	*It's only eight o'clock*
Ich kam erst im Sommer nach Heidelberg	*I didn't get to Heidelberg until the summer*
erst wenn/als (see 19.3.2b)	*not until, only when*
wenn er erst zu Hause ist, ...	*once he's home ...*
Es hatte eben erst zu schneien aufgehört (*Jünger*)	*It had only just stopped snowing*
Ich kann den Wagen erst Anfang nächster Woche abholen	*I shan't be able to collect the car till the beginning of next week*

(c) *erst* 'only' should be carefully distinguished from *nur*

(cf. 10.26.2.)

(i) With numbers (cf. (a) above), *erst* implies that more are to follow. In English this may be made clear by adding 'as yet' to the sentence. *nur*, on the other hand, sets a clear limit, i.e. that number and no more. Compare:

Ich habe **erst** drei Briefe bekommen	*I've only received three letters (as yet)* (more are expected)
Ich habe **nur** drei Briefe bekommen	*I've only received three letters* (i.e. three and no more)

(ii) Whereas *erst* in time expressions (cf. (b) above) has the sense 'not before', etc., *nur* means 'on that one occasion'. Compare:

Sie ist erst (am) Montag gekommen	*She only came on Monday* (i.e. not before Monday)
Sie ist nur (am) Montag gekommen	*She only came on Monday* (i.e. on no other day)

NB: (i) The opposite of *erst* 'only' as a scalar particle is *schon*, cf. 10.30.5.
　　(ii) The distinction between *erst* and *nur* is not always consistently maintained in substandard colloquial speech.

10.13 *etwa*

10.13.1 In yes/no questions, *etwa* implies that something is undesirable and suggests that the answer ought to be *nein*

A common English equivalent is a negative statement followed by a positive tag question or an exclamation beginning with *Don't tell me . . .*:

Hast du die Zeitung etwa schon weggeworfen?	*You haven't thrown the paper away already, have you?*
Ist das etwa dein Wagen?	*That's not your car, is it?*
Habt ihr etwa geschlafen?	*Don't tell me you've been asleep!*

Such questions with *etwa* can be in the form of statements, in which case they also contain *doch nicht*:

Sie wollen doch nicht etwa nach Paderborn umziehen?	*You don't want to move to Paderborn, do you?*

10.13.2 In negative sentences, *etwa* intensifies the negation

Sie müssen nicht etwa denken, daß ich ihn verteidigen will	*Now don't go and think I want to defend him*
Komm nicht etwa zu spät zum Flughafen!	*Make sure you don't get to the airport too late!*

10.13.3 In conditional sentences *etwa* stresses the idea of a possibility

Wenn der Zug etwa verspätet sein sollte, so werden wir den Anschluß nach Gera verpassen	*If the train should be delayed we'll miss our connection to Gera*
Wenn das Wetter etwa umschlagen sollte, müssen wir die Wanderung verkürzen	*If the weather should change, we'll have to shorten our walk*

10.13.4 Uses of *etwa* before a noun or noun phrase as a scalar particle

(a) Before a number or expression of size or quantity, *etwa* expresses approximation

Ich komme etwa um zwei	*I'll come at about two*
Es kostet etwa dreißig Mark	*It costs about thirty marks*
Er ist etwa so groß wie dein Vater	*He is about as tall as your father*
Wir haben es uns etwa so vorgestellt	*We imagined it to be something like that*

(b) Before a noun or list of nouns, *etwa* suggests a possibility

It is often close in meaning to English 'for instance' or 'for example':

Er begnügte sich mit etwa folgender Antwort	*He was satisfied with, say, the following answer*
Bist du sicher, daß du den Jürgen gesehen hast, und nicht etwa seinen Bruder Thomas?	*Are you sure you saw Jürgen, and not perhaps his brother Thomas?*
Er hat viele Hobbys, (wie) etwa Reisen, Musik und Sport	*He has a lot of hobbies, for example travelling, music and sport*
Willst du etwa (am) Sonntag kommen?	*You're not thinking of coming on Sunday, are you?*

10.14 *freilich*

freilich usually has a concessive sense and its force is very similar to that of *allerdings*, see 10.2. It was originally typically south German, but it is coming to be used more widely.

10.14.1 Within a clause *freilich* means 'admittedly', 'all the same'

Es scheint freilich nicht ganz so einfach zu sein	*Admittedly, it doesn't appear to be that simple*
Wir nehmen ihn mit, freilich muß er pünktlich am Treffpunkt sein	*We'll take him with us, even so he'll have to get to the meeting place on time*

10.14.2 In answer to a question, *freilich* stresses that the answer is yes

It is often used in conjunction with *ja*. It lacks the hint that there is some kind of reservation or qualification to the answer which is sometimes present with *allerdings*:

Kennst du die Angelika? – (Ja,) freilich (kenne ich sie)!	*Do you know Angelika? – Of course (I know her)!*
Kannst du auch alles besorgen? – (Ja,) freilich!	*Can you see to it all? – Certainly I can!*

NB: *freilich* can *never* mean 'freely', which is *frei* in most contexts.

10.15 *gar*

gar is used in a number of ways with an intensifying sense.

10.15.1 The commonest use of *gar* is to intensify a negative

In these contexts it is an alternative to *überhaupt*:

Sie hatte gar nicht gewußt, ob er abfahren wollte (*Johnson*)	*She hadn't even known whether he wanted to leave*
Ich habe doch heute gar keine Zeit	*I really haven't got any time at all today*

Less commonly, it can intensify *so* or *zu* with an adjective (*allzu* is a more frequent alternative):

Du darfst das nicht gar so ernst nehmen	*You really mustn't take that quite so seriously*
Es waren gar zu viele Leute auf der Straße	*There were far too many people in the street*

10.15.2 *gar* can be used to emphasise the following word and indicate surprise

In such contexts it is the equivalent of English 'even' or 'possibly' and is a less frequent alternative to *sogar*, used mainly in literary registers:

Eher würde ich einem Habicht oder gar Aasgeier eine Friedensbotschaft anvertrauen als der Taube (*Grass*)	*I would rather entrust a message of peace to a hawk or even a vulture than to a dove*

10.16 *gleich*

As a modal particle *gleich* is used in *w*-questions to politely request the repetition of information

It is often used with *doch*, cf. 10.7.4:

Wie war Ihr Name (doch) gleich?	*What was your name again?*
Was hast du gleich gesagt?	*What was it you said?*

gleich is also used as a time adverb in the sense of 'immediately', e.g.: *Ich werde ihn **gleich** fragen*, or to mean 'at once' or 'at the same time', e.g. *Er hat **gleich** zwei Hemden gekauft*.

10.17 *halt*

halt is an alternative to *eben* in some senses

(See 10.8.) It was originally characteristic of south German speech, but its use has recently become more widespread:

Da kann man halt nichts machen	*There's just nothing to be done*
Dann nimm halt die U-Bahn!	*Just take the underground, then!*

10.18 *immerhin*

immerhin indicates that something might not have come up to expectations, but is acceptable at a pinch

It corresponds most often to English 'all the same' or 'even so' and can be used within a sentence or (very frequently) as a response:

Du hast immerhin tausend Mark gewonnen	All the same, you won a thousand marks
Wir haben uns immerhin ein neues Videogerät anschaffen können	Even so, we were able to buy a new video recorder
Das Wetter war miserabel, aber wir hatten ein schönes Zimmer – (Na,) immerhin!	The weather was lousy, but we did have a nice room – Well, that was something, at least!

10.19 *ja*

10.19.1 In statements, *ja* appeals for agreement

(a) By using it the speaker insists that what s/he is saying is correct

A common English equivalent is the *do*-form of the verb:

Wir haben ja gestern davon gesprochen	We did talk about that yesterday (you know)
Ihr habt ja früher zwei Autos gehabt	Of course, you used to have two cars
Ich komme ja schon	It's all right, I'm on my way
Der katastrophale Zustand des Landes ist ja gerade das Erbe der Diktatur (*Spiegel*)	Of course, the catastrophic state of the country is precisely the legacy of dictatorship

(b) *ja* has a distinct meaning from *doch* when used to appeal for agreement

doch (see 10.7.1) implies that the listener may hold a different opinion, but *ja* always presupposes that speaker and listener are in agreement. Compare:

Du könntest dir **ja** Karls Rad leihen	You could borrow Karl's bike, of course (we both know you can)
Du könntest dir **doch** Karls Rad leihen	Surely, you could borrow Karl's bike (you might have thought you couldn't)
Das ist es **ja** eben	Why, of course, that's the point
Das ist es **doch** eben	Don't you see, that's just the point
Er kann unmöglich kommen, er ist **ja** krank/	He can't possibly come, he's ill, as you know
er ist **doch** krank	he's ill, don't you know

10.19.2 In exclamations, *ja* expresses surprise

Heute ist es ja kalt!	Oh, it is cold today!
Er hat ja ein neues Auto!	Why, he's got a new car!
Das ist ja unerhört!	That really is the limit!
Da kommt ja der Arzt!	Oh (good), here comes the doctor!

By using *ja*, the speaker can express surprise that something *is* the case at all, unlike *aber* or *vielleicht*, by which surprise is expressed at the *extent* of a quality, cf. 10.1.1 and 10.34.1. Thus *die Milch ist ja sauer!* would be said if the milk had been expected to be fresh, whilst *die Milch ist **aber/vielleicht** sauer* expresses surprise at *how* sour the milk is. On the other hand, the force of *doch* in exclamations (see 10.7.5) is very similar to that of *ja*.

10.19.3 *ja* intensifies a command

There is often an implied warning or threat, especially if *ja* is stressed:

Bleib ja hier!	*Be sure to stay here!*
Geht ja nicht auf die Straße!	*Just don't go out onto the street!*
Er soll **ja** nichts sagen	*He really must not say anything (or else)*

NB: *nur* is an alternative to *ja* to intensify commands and sound a note of warning, cf. 10.26.1a.

10.19.4 *ja* can be used as a scalar particle

In a string of nouns, verbs or adjectives, *ja* (sometimes in combination with *sogar*) emphasizes the importance of the one (usually the last) before which it is placed. This often corresponds to English 'indeed', 'even' or 'nay':

Es war ein Erfolg, ja ein Triumph	*It was a success, indeed a triumph*
Es war ein unerwarteter, ja ein sensationeller Erfolg	*It was an unexpected, indeed a sensational success*
Sie konnte die Aussage bestätigen, ja (sogar) beeiden	*She was able to confirm the testimony, even on oath*

10.19.5 *ja* is the affirmative particle

i.e. corresponding to English 'yes', e.g.: *Kommst du morgen? – **Ja!*** It can also be used as a tag, e.g.:

Es geht um acht los, ja?	*We're starting at eight, aren't we?*

10.20 *jedenfalls*

The phrases *auf jeden Fall* and *auf alle Fälle* are possible alternatives to the particle *jedenfalls*.

10.20.1 In statements *jedenfalls* stresses the reason why something should be the case (or why something is not as bad as it may seem)

In these contexts, *jedenfalls* corresponds to 'at least' or 'at any rate':

Vielleicht ist er krank, er sieht jedenfalls schlecht aus	*Perhaps he's ill, at least he doesn't look well*
Er ist nicht gekommen, aber er hat sich jedenfalls entschuldigt	*He didn't come, but at least he did apologise*

wenigstens or *zumindest* are alternatives to *jedenfalls*, see 8.4.4b.

10.20.2 In commands *jedenfalls* indicates that something should be done in any event

It corresponds to English 'anyhow' or 'in any case':

Bei schönem Wetter gehen wir morgen baden. Bring jedenfalls deinen Badeanzug mit	*If it's fine we'll go swimming tomorrow. Bring your costume along anyhow*

10.21 *lediglich*

lediglich is used before another word to indicate a restriction or a limit

It is an emphatic alternative to *nur* in the sense 'only', 'no more than'. It is used mainly in formal registers and can sound stilted:

Er hat lediglich zwei Semester in Münster studiert	*He only studied two terms in Münster*
Ich verlange lediglich mein Recht	*I am only asking for what's due to me*

10.22 *mal*

10.22.1 *mal* moderates the tone of a sentence, making it sound less blunt

It is frequent in commands, requests and questions. It can correspond to English *just*, (although in practice this is used less than German *mal*):

Lies den Brief mal durch!	*Just read the letter through (will you?)*
Hol mal schnell den Feuerlöscher!	*Just quickly go and get the fire-extinguisher*
Das sollst du mal probieren	*You just ought to try that*
Ich will sie schnell mal anrufen	*I just want to ring her up quickly*
Würden Sie mir bitte mal helfen?	*Could you just help me?*
Hältst du mir mal die Tasche?	*Just hold my bag for me, will you?*

mal is almost automatically added to a command in colloquial speech, especially if there is nothing else in the sentence apart from the verb:

    Sieh mal her!   Hör mal zu!   Komm mal herüber!   Sag mal!

The tone of a request or a command may be moderated further by adding *eben*:

Reich mir eben mal das Brot!	*Just pass me the bread, would you?*
Lies den Brief eben mal durch!	*Won't you please just read the letter through?*

The combination *doch mal* makes a command sound more casual:

Nimm doch mal ein neues Blatt!	*Why don't you get another piece of paper?*
Melde dich doch mal beim Chef!	*Why not just arrange to see the boss?*

10.22.2 The particle *mal* is quite distinct from the adverb *einmal* 'once'

(see 9.4.3). *einmal* cannot replace *mal* in any of the contexts dealt with in 10.22.1. However, *einmal* is sometimes shortened to *mal* in colloquial speech, especially in the following combinations:

(a) *noch einmal* '(once) again', 'once more'

    Ich habe ihn noch (ein)mal gewarnt   *I warned him once again*

(b) *nun einmal* 'just'
This combination emphasises the lack of alternatives. It is a rather more forceful equivalent to *eben* or *halt*, cf. 10.8.1a:

    Es wird nun (ein)mal lange dauern   *It's just going to take a long time*

(c) *nicht einmal* 'not even':

    Er hat sie nicht (ein)mal gegrüßt   *He didn't even say hello to her*

10.23 *man*

man is a colloquial north German equivalent to mal in commands and requests

Geh du man vor!	*You just go ahead*
Seien Sie man bloß ruhig! (*Fallada*)	*Just keep calm*

10.24 *noch*

10.24.1 *noch* indicates something additional

In this sense it can be used as a scalar particle preceding a noun or pronoun, or as a modal particle within the clause:

Er hat noch drei Stunden geschlafen	*He slept another three hours*
Ich trinke noch eine Tasse Kaffee	*I'll have another cup of coffee*
Das wird sich noch herausstellen	*That will remain to be seen, too*
Wer war noch da?	*Who else was there?*
Und es hat auch noch geregnet!	*And apart from that, it rained too*

10.24.2 *noch* in time expressions

(a) *noch* can indicate that something is going on longer than expected
It can be strengthened by *immer* and corresponds to English *still* or *yet*:

Angela schläft (immer) noch	*Angela's still asleep*
Franz ist (immer) noch nicht gekommen	*Franz hasn't come yet/Franz still hasn't come*
Sie wohnen noch in Fritzlar	*They're still living in Fritzlar*
Ich habe sie noch nie gesehen	*I've never seen her (yet)*
Sie ist doch noch jung	*She's still young, isn't she?*

(b) If a particular point in time is indicated, *noch* indicates that an event took place or will take place by then
The implication may be that this is contrary to expectations:

Ich habe ihn noch vor zwei Tagen gesehen	*I saw him only two days ago*
Noch im Mai hat sie ihre Dissertation abgegeben	*She managed to hand her thesis in by the end of May*
Ich werde noch heute den Arzt anrufen	*I'll ring the doctor before tomorrow*

In this sense, *noch* can come after short time words and phrases rather than before them, e.g. *Ich werde* **heute noch** *den Arzt anrufen.*

10.24.3 Further uses of *noch*

(a) In *w*-questions, *noch* asks for the listener to jog the speaker's memory
i.e. suggesting that something has just slipped his/her mind:

Wie hieß er noch?	*Oh now, what* **was** *his name?*
Wann war das Spiel noch?	*Oh now, when* **was** *the game?*

(b) *noch* is used with comparatives in the sense of 'even'
e.g.: *Er ist noch größer als du.* For further details, see 8.3.1c.

(c) *noch* is used with *weder* as the equivalent of English 'neither . . . nor'
e.g.: *Er liest weder Bücher noch Zeitungen* (see 19.1.3d).

(d) *noch* is used with *so* and an adjective in a concessive sense
e.g.: *Wenn sie (auch) noch so fleißig ist, sie wird die Prüfung doch nicht bestehen* (see 19.6.2b).

10.25 *nun*

10.25.1 In questions, *nun* signals dissatisfaction with a previous answer

By using it the speaker insists that the correct or complete information should be provided:

Wann kommt der Zug nun an?	When **does** this train get in, now?
Stimmt es nun, daß sie verheiratet ist?	Now, is it really true that she's married?

nun is commonly used on its own as a question to push the other speaker to give more information, cf. *Nun?* 'Well?', *Nun . . . und?* 'And then what?'

10.25.2 *nun* signals that the speaker considers the topic exhausted

In this sense it occurs characteristically in isolation at the beginning of a sentence. It often corresponds to English 'well':

Nun, das ist alles schon wichtig, aber ich glaube, wir müssen zunächst das Wahlergebnis besprechen	Well, of course that's all very important, but I think we've got to discuss the election results first
Nun, natürlich hat er die besten Erfahrungen	Well, of course he's got the widest experience
Nun, wir werden ja sehen	Well, we shall see
Nun, meinetwegen!	All right then

10.25.3 *nun* is used as an adverb of time to mean 'now'

It is rather less definite than *jetzt* and it is used less frequently to refer simply to the present moment as such:

Nun wollen wir umkehren	Now we'll turn back
Nun hat er mehr Zeit als früher	Now he's got more time than he used to have
Geht es dir nun besser?	Are you better now?
als es nun Winter wurde, . . .	now when it turned to winter . . .

10.26 *nur*

nur is used as a modal particle with an intensifying sense and as a focusing particle with a restrictive sense (= 'only'). *bloß*, cf. 10.5, is a frequent alternative to *nur* in all its uses except where indicated below; it tends to be slightly more emphatic, and more colloquial.

10.26.1 As a modal particle, *nur* usually has intensifying force

(a) In a command, *nur* intensifies the basic meaning
Depending on the sense of the command, i.e. whether it is an urgent instruction or a request, it can make it sound more of a threat or more reassuring respectively.

(i) 'Threatening' or 'warning' *nur* is more common in negative commands or when *nur* is stressed. This sense is similar to that of *ja* (see 10.19.3):

Komm nur nicht zu spät!	*You'd better not be late!*
Nimm dich nur in acht!	*You'd better be careful!*
Geh nur nicht in diesen Laden!	*Whatever you do, don't go into that shop!*
Sehen Sie nur, was Sie gemacht haben!	*Just look what you've done!*

In this sense, *nur* (but **not** *bloß*) can be used initially in a positive or negative command using the infinitive or with no verb at all:

Nur nicht so schnell laufen!	*Just don't run so fast!*
Nur aufpassen!	*Just be sure to look out!*
Nur immer schön langsam!	*Take it nice and slow!*

(ii) The 'reassuring' sense of *nur* is close to that of *ruhig* (see 10.28):

Laß ihn nur reden!	*Just let him speak, do!*
Kommen Sie nur herein!	*Do come in!*
Hab nur keine Angst!	*Don't be afraid, will you!*
Nur weiter!	*Just carry on!* (implying: *It's all right so far*)

bloß is not used in this 'reassuring' sense, and commands with *bloß* always have a 'warning' tone. Compare *Laß ihn bloß reden!* 'Just let him speak (and you'll suffer the consequences)' with the first example in (ii) above.

(b) *nur* intensifies *w*-questions and makes them sound more urgent

Wie kann er nur so taktlos sein?	*How on earth can he be so tactless?*
Was können wir nur tun, um ihr zu helfen?	*Whatever can we do to help her?*
Wo bleibt sie nur?	*Where on earth is she?*

Such questions can be used as exclamations of reproach or astonishment, as no real answer is possible or expected:

Wie siehst du nur wieder aus?!	*What on earth do you look like?!*
Warum mußte er nur wegfahren?!	*Why on earth did he have to go away?!*

(c) *nur* intensifies a wish in the form of a *wenn*-clause

See also 16.7.6b. Its force is similar to that of *doch*, cf. 10.7.6, and they are often used together to add an even greater intensity to the wish:

Wenn sie (doch) nur anrufen würde!	*If only she would phone!*
Hätte ich nur mehr Zeit!	*If only I had more time!*
Wenn er mir nur geschrieben hätte!	*If only he had written me!*

10.26.2 *nur* is used as a scalar particle to express a restriction

i.e. with the force of English 'only'. It is used in all kinds of sentences to qualify nouns, verbs or adjectives:

Ich wollte nur Guten Tag sagen	*I only/just wanted to say Hello*
Die Mittelmeerküste ist sehr schön, sie ist leider nur etwas dreckig	*The Mediterranean coast is very nice, only I'm afraid it's rather dirty*
Er geht nur bei schönem Wetter spazieren	*He only goes for a walk when it's fine*
Ich vermute nur, daß er gestern in Urlaub gefahren ist	*I'm only assuming that he went on holiday yesterday*
Man kann es nur dort kaufen	*You can only buy it there*
Dort kann man nicht nur Bücher kaufen, sondern auch allerlei Zeitschriften	*You can not only buy books there, but also magazines of all kinds*

NB: (i) For the difference between *erst* and *nur* as an equivalent of English 'only', see 10.12.2c.

(ii) *nur daß* is used as the equivalent of the English conjunction 'only' (cf. also 19.7.6), e.g. *Die Zimmer waren in Ordnung, nur daß die Duschen fehlten.*

(iii) *lediglich*, cf. 10.21, is a more formal alternative to *nur*.

10.27 *ohnehin*

ohnehin indicates that something is correct irrespective of any other reasons given or implied

A typical English equivalent is 'anyway' or 'in any case'. It is a more formal alternative to (southern) colloquial *eh* (see 10.9), or *sowieso* (see 10.31):

Er trinkt ohnehin zu viel	*He drinks too much anyway*
Der Zug hat ohnehin Verspätung	*The train's late anyway*
Du mußt sofort zum Arzt – Ich hätte ihn ohnehin morgen besucht	*You'll have to go to the doctor right away – I would have gone to see him tomorrow in any case*

10.28 *ruhig*

ruhig lends a reassuring tone to what the speaker is saying

This meaning is clearly related to that of the adjective *ruhig* 'quiet'. It is used in commands (where it is an alternative to *nur*, cf. 10.26.1a), and in statements, especially with a modal auxiliary:

Bleib ruhig sitzen!	*Don't get up for me*
Arbeite ruhig weiter!	*Just carry on* (i.e. don't let me disturb you)
Auf dieser Straße kannst du ruhig etwas schneller fahren	*It's all right, you can go a bit faster on this road*
Sie dürfen ruhig hier im Zimmer bleiben	*You can stay here in this room, I don't mind*

10.29 *schließlich*

schließlich indicates that the speaker accepts the validity of a reason

It usually corresponds to English 'after all':

Es liegt schließlich nicht genug Schnee auf der Piste	*After all, there's not enough snow on the piste*
Wir wollen ihn schließlich nicht zu sehr reizen	*We don't want to annoy him too much, after all*
Schließlich kann das einem jeden passieren	*After all, it can happen to anybody*

10.30 *schon*

schon has perhaps the widest range of any of the German particles, and it is particularly difficult to make generalisations about its meaning.

10.30.1 The use of *schon* as a modal particle in statements

(a) In statements generally, *schon* expresses agreement or confirmation in principle, but with slight reservations

This sense is in practice concessive; it often has (or implies) a following *aber, nur* or the like, and *zwar* or, especially in north Germany, *wohl* are possible alternatives, cf. 10.35.3 and 10.36.1:

Das ist schon möglich(, aber ...)	*That's quite possible (but ...)*
Ich wollte schon kommen	*Well, I did want to come*
Das stimmt schon, aber es könnte auch anders kommen	*That may be true, but things might turn out differently*
Ja, ich glaube schon(, aber ...)	*Well, I think so(, but ...)*
Der Film hatte schon wunderschöne Aufnahmen, nur war er etwas langweilig	*The film may have had some lovely shots, only it was a bit boring*

In a response, *schon* corrects what has just been said and indicates why it was wrong:

Niemand fährt über Ostern weg – Mutter schon!	*Nobody's going away over Easter – But mother is!*
Heute waren keine deiner Freunde da – Der Kurt aber schon!	*None of your friends came today – But Kurt did!*
Er hat da ein sehr schönes Haus gekauft – (Das) schon, aber ...	*He's bought himself a nice house there – Well yes, but ...*

(b) In statements referring to the future, *schon* emphasises the speaker's confidence that something will happen

It usually sounds reassuring, but in some contexts and situations it may take on a more threatening tone. English 'all right' has similar force:

Er wird uns schon helfen	*He'll help us all right*
Es wird schon gehen	*It'll be all right, don't worry*
Ich krieg's schon hin	*I'll manage it all right*
Dem werde ich's schon zeigen!	*I'll show him all right!*

10.30.2 *schon* gives persuasive force to a *w*-question which expects a negative answer or where the speaker has a negative attitude

Was sagt die Regierung zu Ungarn? Nichts. Was sollen sie schon sagen? (*Horbach*)	*What does the government say about Hungary? Nothing. But then, what are they to say?*
Wer kann diesem Angebot schon widerstehen?	*Who can refuse this offer? (i.e. 'nobody')*
Warum kommt er schon wieder?	*What's he coming for again? (implying: 'he's up to no good')*
Na, und wenn schon?	*So what?*

10.30.3 In conditional sentences *schon* emphasises the condition

In addition it may point to the inescapability of the conclusion. It is normally used only in open conditions, with the indicative, see 16.5.2:

Wenn ich das schon mache, dann muß ich über alle Probleme informiert sein	*If I am going to do it, I'll need to be told about all the problems*
Wenn du schon ein neues Auto kaufst, dann aber keinen so teuren	*If you are going to buy a new car, then don't get one that's as expensive*
Wenn sie schon ans Meer fährt, dann will sie auch baden	*If she's going to the seaside, she will want to go swimming*

10.30.4 In commands, *schon* adds an insistent note

The sentence often begins with *nun*:

(Nun,) beeile dich schon!	*Do hurry up(, then)!*
Fang schon an!	*Do make a start!*
Sag mir schon, was du denkst! Ich	*Do tell me what you think. I shan't*
werde es dir nicht übelnehmen	*take it amiss*

10.30.5 *schon* is used as a scalar particle to express a restriction

erst is the opposite of *schon* in the contexts dealt with under (a) and (b) below, see 10.12.2:

(a) Referring to time, *schon* indicates that something is happening or has happened sooner than expected or desirable

In some contexts, it can stress that something actually *has* happened. In this meaning, it can correspond to English 'already', but its use is wider:

Er war schon angekommen	*He had already arrived*
schon am nächsten Tag	*the very next day*
Da bist du ja schon wieder	*There you are back again*
Sind Sie schon einmal in Köln gewesen?	*Have you been to Cologne before?*
Ich habe ihn auch schon in der Bibliothek gesehen	*I've sometimes seen him in the library*
Das habe ich schon 1961 geahnt	*I suspected that as early as 1961*
Es war schon 7 Uhr, als sie aufstand	*It was already 7 o'clock when she got up*

(b) Before a number or an expression of quantity, *schon* indicates that this is more than expected or desirable

Sie hat schon drei Briefe bekommen	*She has already received three letters*
Ich habe schon die Hälfte des Buches gelesen	*I've already read half the book*
Er wartet schon eine Stunde auf dich	*He's already been waiting for you for an hour*

(c) When used to qualify most nouns, *schon* expresses a restriction

It can occasionally be used to qualify another part of speech:

Schon der Gedanke ist mir unsympathisch	*The very thought is repugnant to me*
schon ihrer Kinder wegen	*if only because of their children*
Das geht schon daher nicht, weil …	*That's impossible, not least because …*
Schon vor dem Krieg war die Eisenbahn in Schwierigkeiten geraten	*Even before the war the railways had run into difficulties*

10.31 sowieso

sowieso indicates that something is correct irrespective of any other reasons given or implied

It usually corresponds to English 'anyway' or 'in any case'. It is a rather more colloquial alternative to *ohnehin*, cf. 10.27:

Ich kann heute sowieso nicht arbeiten	*I can't work today anyway*
Der ist sowieso scharf auf sie	*He fancies her anyway*
Ich wäre sowieso nach Nürnberg gefahren	*I would have gone to Nuremberg in any case*

10.32 überhaupt

10.32.1 überhaupt makes statements and commands more general

The English equivalent is often 'at all' or 'anyhow':

Duisburg ist überhaupt eine gräßliche Stadt	*Duisburg is a dreadful city anyhow*
Das ist überhaupt eine gefährliche Angelegenheit	*That's a risky business in any case*
Er liebte die italienische Sprache, ja die Sprachen überhaupt (*Goes*)	*He loved the Italian language, indeed, languages in general*
Seinen Mut müßte man haben, dachte ich. Oder überhaupt Mut (*Walser*)	*One ought to have his courage, I thought. Or any courage at all*
Ihr sollt überhaupt besser aufpassen!	*You ought anyway to pay more attention*

10.32.2 In questions, überhaupt casts doubt on the basic assumption

Er singt nicht besonders gut – Kann er denn überhaupt singen?	*He doesn't sing particularly well – Can he sing at all?*
Wie konntest du überhaupt so was tun?	*How could you do such a thing at all?*
Der Brief ist nicht da. Wo kann er überhaupt sein?	*The letter's not there. Wherever can it be?*
Was will er denn überhaupt?	*What the dickens does he want?*

10.32.3 überhaupt intensifies a negative

gar is a frequent alternative, see 10.15:

Du hättest es überhaupt nicht tun sollen, und besonders jetzt nicht	*You ought not to have done it at all, and particularly not now*
Sie hat überhaupt keine Ahnung	*She's got no idea at all*
Ich weiß überhaupt nichts von seinen Plänen	*I don't know anything about his plans*

10.33 übrigens

übrigens is used in statements and questions to indicate a casual remark which is incidental to the main topic of conversation

It corresponds to English 'by the way', etc.:

Ich habe übrigens erfahren, daß er eine neue Stelle bekommen hat	*Incidentally, I've found out he's got a new job*
Sie hat übrigens vollkommen recht	*She's perfectly right, by the way*
Wo wollt ihr übrigens dieses Jahr hin?	*By the way, where are you going this year?*

10.34 *vielleicht*

10.34.1 In exclamations unstressed *vielleicht* expresses surprise

These exclamations can have the form of statements or questions.

Siehst du vielleicht schlecht aus! Du siehst vielleicht schlecht aus! }	*Oh, you really do look awful!*
Die Kiste ist vielleicht schwer!	*How heavy the crate is!*
Du bist vielleicht ein Idiot!	*You really are stupid!*
Das hat vielleicht gegossen!	*It really did pour!*
Ich habe vielleicht gestaunt!	*I wasn't half surprised!*

Like *aber* (see 10.1.1), *vielleicht* expresses surprise at a difference in **degree** from the speaker's expectation, whereas *ja* (see 10.19.2) relates to a difference in **kind**.

10.34.2 In yes/no questions, *vielleicht* signals that the speaker expects a negative answer

Its sense is close to that of *etwa*, see 10.13.1. The English equivalent is often an exclamation beginning with *Don't tell me ...* or a negative statement followed by a positive tag question:

Willst du mir vielleicht erzählen, daß ...?	*You don't mean to tell me that ..., do you?*
Soll ich vielleicht bis 7 Uhr abends hier sitzen?	*I'm not supposed to sit here till seven at night, am I?*
Arbeitet er vielleicht?	*Don't tell me he's working?*

10.34.3 *vielleicht* is used as an adverb of attitude, (= English 'perhaps')

Sie ist vielleicht 30 Jahre alt	*She is perhaps thirty years old*
Sie wird vielleicht morgen kommen	*She may come tomorrow*
Wird sie uns vielleicht morgen besuchen?	*Will she come to see us tomorrow, perhaps?*

There is a clear difference in meaning between the use of *vielleicht* as an adverb and as a particle:

Die Kiste ist vielleicht schwer	*Perhaps the case is heavy*
Die Kiste ist vielleicht schwer!	*How heavy the case is!*

In requests in the form of a question, *vielleicht*, like English 'perhaps', expresses polite reserve on the part of the speaker:

Könnten Sie mir vielleicht sagen, wo es zum Bahnhof geht?	*Could you perhaps tell me the way the way to the station?*
Würden Sie mir vielleicht helfen?	*Would you perhaps help me?*

10.35 *wohl*

10.35.1 In statements, *wohl* signals a fair degree of probability

Its force is very similar to that of the future tense, cf. 14.4.3, and it is often used in conjunction with it. It corresponds to the English future tense or a positive statement followed by a negative tag question, or to formulae like 'I suppose', 'probably':

Das wird wohl der Briefträger sein	*That'll be the postman*
Sie sind wohl neu hier	*You're new here, aren't you?*
Sie hat wohl ihr Auto schon verkauft	*I suppose she's already sold her car*
Diese Probleme versteht er wohl nicht	*He probably doesn't understand these problems*
Ich habe ihn nie gesprochen, wohl aber oft gesehen	*I've never spoken to him, but I have often seen him*

The combination *ja wohl* sounds rather more certain, corresponding to English '(pretty) certainly' or 'no doubt':

Sie wird ja wohl noch in Potsdam sein	*She's pretty certainly still in Potsdam*
Das weißt du ja wohl	*No doubt you know that*

The combination *wohl doch* (or, for some speakers, *doch wohl*) sounds rather less certain, though the speaker hopes that it is the case:

Er hat wohl doch noch einen Schlüssel	*Surely he's got another key, hasn't he?*
Die Antje wird doch wohl noch das Abitur schaffen	*Antje's surely going to get through her Abitur, isn't she?*

10.35.2 In questions *wohl* signals uncertainty on the part of the speaker

It can make the question sound tentative, as if the speaker doubts whether the other can give a clear answer. The question can be in statement form:

Wer hat den Brief wohl geschrieben?	*Who can possibly have written the letter?*
Wie spät ist es wohl?	*I wonder what time it is*
Ist der Peter wohl schon zu Hause?	*Peter is at home, isn't he?*
Darf ich wohl bei Ihnen telephonieren?	*Might I use your telephone?*
Horst ist wohl gestern abend angekommen?	*Horst arrived last night, didn't he?*

10.35.3 In statements, stressed *wohl* has a concessive sense

It expresses agreement or confirmation in principle, but tinged with a slight reservation. It often has (or implies) a following *aber*, *nur* or the like. *zwar* or, especially in southern Germany, *schon* are possible alternatives, see 10.30.1a and 10.36.1:

Er ist wohl mein Freund, aber ich kann ihm nicht helfen	*He may be my friend, but I can't help him*
Das ist wohl möglich(, aber ...)	*That may be possible(, but ...)*
Herbert ist wohl nach Basel gefahren, aber nur für eine Woche	*Herbert did go to Basle, but only for a week*

10.35.4 *wohl* intensifies a command, making it sound urgent, insistent and rather abrupt

It is often used with *werden* or *wollen*:

Hebst du wohl das Buch wieder auf!	*Pick that book up again right away!*
Wirst du wohl sofort wieder ins Bett gehen!	*Will you go straight back to bed!*
Wollt ihr wohl endlich still sein!	*Once and for all, will you be quiet!*

10.35.5 As an adverb, usually stressed, *wohl* has the sense 'well', 'fully'

It often strengthens an affirmative response (i.e. *jawohl!* 'yes, indeed'):

Ich fühle mich wohl	*I feel well*
Er hatte es sich wohl überlegt	*He had considered it fully*
Er weiß sehr wohl, daß er unrecht hat	*He knows full well that he's wrong*
Schlaf wohl! Leb wohl!	*Sleep well! Farewell!*
Und er war so geartet, daß er solche Erfahrungen wohl vermerkte (Th. Mann)	*And his nature was such that he took full note of such experiences*

10.36 *zwar*

10.36.1 *zwar* can be used in a concessive sense

It is normally followed by a clause with *aber* (or one is implied), and the combination *zwar ... aber* can have the force of English '(al)though', cf. also 19.6.1b:

Er ist zwar krank, aber er kommt heute abend noch mit	*Although he's ill, he's still coming with us tonight*
Er stand nach Kinkels Aussage „zwar in der Mitte, aber doch mehr nach rechts als nach links" (Böll)	*According to Kinkel he was 'politically in the centre, but tending all the same to the right rather than the left'*

In north Germany *wohl* is a possible alternative to *zwar* in this concessive sense, cf. 10.35.3, whilst in southern and central Germany *schon* is used, cf. 10.30.1a.

10.36.2 *und zwar* is used in the sense of English 'namely' to specify what has just been mentioned

Mein Entschluß fiel auf dem neuen Flugplatz in Mexico-City, und zwar im letzten Augenblick (Frisch)	*My decision was taken at the new airport in Mexico-City, (in actual fact) at the very last minute*
Ich habe die wichtigsten Museen besucht, und zwar das kunsthistorische, das naturhistorische und die Albertina	*I visited the most important museums, namely the Museum of Art History, the Museum of Natural History and the Albertina*

11

Expressions of time

Usage in time expressions is characteristically idiomatic in all languages, involving special uses and meanings. German usage can differ quite markedly from that of English in the way in which various aspects of time are referred to, and particular attention is paid to these aspects in this chapter. Specifically, clock time ('telling the time') is treated in section 11.1, the names of the days of the week, months and public holidays in 11.2, and the way in which dates are expressed in 11.3. The use of cases (notably the accusative and the genitive) in time adverbials is explained in section 11.4, the main prepositions occurring in time adverbials are dealt with in 11.5 and simple time adverbs in 11.6.

11.1 Times of the clock

11.1.1 In everyday speech the twelve-hour clock is the norm

i.e. in normal conversation, when reference is not being made to public events, official timetables and the like. The relevant forms are all given in Table 11.1.

TABLE 11.1 *Clock times*

1.00	Es ist ein Uhr/eins	*It is one (o'clock)*
3.00	Es ist drei (Uhr)	*It is three (o'clock)*
3.05	fünf (Minuten) nach drei	*five (minutes) past three*
3.07	sieben Minuten nach drei	*seven minutes past three*
3.10	zehn (Minuten) nach drei	*ten (minutes) past three*
3.15	Viertel nach drei viertel vier (esp. S. & C. Ger.)	*quarter past three*
3.20	zwanzig nach drei zehn vor halb vier (not Switz.)	*twenty past three*
3.25	fünf vor halb vier	*twenty-five past three*
3.30	halb vier (sometimes written ½4)	*half past three*
3.35	fünf nach halb vier	*twenty-five to four*
3.40	zwanzig vor vier zehn nach halb vier (not Switz.)	*twenty to four*
3.45	Viertel vor vier dreiviertel vier (esp. S. & C. Ger.)	*quarter to four*
3.47	dreizehn Minuten vor vier	*thirteen minutes to four*
3.50	zehn (Minuten) vor vier	*ten (minutes) to four*
3.55	fünf (Minuten) vor vier	*five (minutes) to four*

11.1.2 In official contexts the twenty-four-hour clock is used

i.e. for timetables, television and radio programmes, theatrical performances, official meetings, business hours, etc. Examples:

0.27 null Uhr siebenundzwanzig	*12.27 a.m.*
5.15 fünf Uhr fünfzehn	*5.15 a.m.*
10.30 zehn Uhr dreißig	*10.30 a.m.*
13.07 dreizehn Uhr sieben	*1.07 p.m.*
21.37 einundzwanzig Uhr siebenunddreißig	*9.37 p.m.*
24.00 vierundzwanzig Uhr	*12.00 midnight*

In speech, *Uhr* is only omitted in giving the full hours between 1 a.m. and noon, e.g. *Ihr Zug kommt um 9.00 an* (spoken: *um neun (Uhr)*). Otherwise the full forms, with *Uhr*, are used, e.g. *Die Vorstellung beginnt um 20.00* (spoken: *um zwanzig Uhr*), *um 20.15* (*zwanzig Uhr fünfzehn*), etc.

Even in conversation it is quite common for such 'official' times to be given using the twenty-four-hour clock. Thus one would say *Mein Zug fährt um 19.35* (i.e. *um neunzehn Uhr fünfunddreißig*), but it would be odd to say *Tante Emilie hat uns für fünfzehn Uhr dreißig zum Kaffee eingeladen*.

11.1.3 Selected further phrases with clock times

Wieviel Uhr ist es? Wie spät ist es? (coll.) }	*What's the time?*
Wieviel Uhr haben Sie?	*What time do you make it?*
Um wieviel Uhr kommt sie?	*What time is she coming?*
Sie kommt um halb drei	*She's coming at half-past two*
um drei Uhr nachts	*at three in the morning*
um neun Uhr vormittags	*at nine in the morning*
um zwölf Uhr mittags	*at twelve noon*
um drei Uhr nachmittags	*at three in the afternoon*
um sieben Uhr abends	*at seven in the evening*
um Mitternacht	*at midnight*
Es ist Punkt/genau neun (Uhr)	*It is exactly nine (o'clock)*
Es ist gerade halb	*It is just half-past*
Es ist ungefähr neun (Uhr)	*It's about nine (o'clock)*
Es ist (schon) neun Uhr vorbei	*It's gone nine o'clock*
Er kommt ungefähr um neun Uhr	*He's coming at about nine o'clock*
Er kam gegen neun (Uhr) an	{ *He came at about nine* { *He came towards nine*

NB: (i) *gegen* is ambiguous with clock times, see 11.5.6.
    (ii) Notice the difference when referring to the half hour between German and English: *halb drei* 'half-past **two**'.

11.2 Days of the week, months and public holidays

11.2.1 The days of the week

Sonntag	*Sunday*
Montag	*Monday*
Dienstag	*Tuesday*
Mittwoch	*Wednesday*
Donnerstag	*Thursday*
Freitag	*Friday*
Samstag Sonnabend }	*Saturday*

As the equivalent for 'Saturday', *Samstag* was originally the southern word and *Sonnabend* northern (roughly to the north of Frankfurt am Main). Since 1949 *Samstag* has come to be known and used more widely, especially in the former West Germany, cf. Eichhoff (1977: 41).

NB: For English 'on Sunday', etc. German uses *am Sonntag*, etc., see 4.5.3 and 11.5.1.

11.2.2 The months

Januar	*January*	Mai	*May*	September	*September*
Februar	*February*	Juni	*June*	Oktober	*October*
März	*March*	Juli	*July*	November	*November*
April	*April*	August	*August*	Dezember	*December*

NB: (i) In Austria, *Jänner* and *Feber* are commonly used for *Januar* and *Februar*.
    (ii) *Juni* and *Juli* are sometimes pronounced *Juno* and *Julei* to avoid confusion, especially on the telephone.
    (iii) For English 'in January', etc., German has *im Januar*, etc., see 4.5.3 and 11.5.7.

11.2.3 The major public holidays and religious festivals

Neujahr(stag)	*New Year's Day*
Rosenmontag	*Carnival Monday*
	(the day before Shrove Tuesday)
Aschermittwoch	*Ash Wednesday*
Gründonnerstag	*Maundy Thursday*
Karfreitag	*Good Friday*
Ostersonntag	*Easter Sunday*
Ostern	*Easter*
Ostermontag	*Easter Monday*
Fronleichnam	*Corpus Christi*
Pfingsten	*Whitsun*
Pfingstsonntag	*Whit Sunday*
Pfingstmontag	*Whit Monday*
(Christi) Himmelfahrt	*Ascension Day*
Mariä Himmelfahrt	*Assumption of the Virgin Mary*
	(15th August)
Tag der Deutschen Einheit	*Day of German Unity* (3rd October)
Allerheiligen	*All Saints' Day* (1st November)
Buß- und Bettag	*Day of Penitence and Prayer*
	(Wednesday before the last Sunday
	before Advent)
der Heilige Abend *or* Heiligabend	*Christmas Eve*
Weihnachten	*Christmas*
Erster Weihnachts(feier)tag	*Christmas Day*
Zweiter Weihnachts(feier)tag	*Boxing Day*
Silvester	*New Year's Eve*

NB: *Ostern*, *Pfingsten* and *Weihnachten* are usually treated as plurals, see 1.2.10b.

11.3 Dates

11.3.1 Ordinal numbers are used for the days of the month

i.e. as in English. In practice numbers are always used for them in writing, i.e. they are never written out as words:

Der wievielte ist heute?
Den wievielten haben wir heute? } *What's the date today?*

Heute ist der 8.(spoken: achte) Mai
Wir haben heute den 8. (achten) Mai } *Today is the eighth of May*

Er kam am 5.(spoken: fünften) Juni, 1993   *He came on the fifth of June, 1993*
am 5.6.93 (spoken: am fünften,   *on 5.6.93*
sechsten, dreiundneunzig)

11.3.2 Usage where the day of the week precedes the date

There are three alternatives. The day of the week and the date may be in the accusative, or the day of the week may be preceded by *am* followed by the date in the accusative or the dative, i.e.:

Wir kommen Montag, den 5. Juni(,) um 15.30 Uhr in Hamburg an
Wir kommen am Montag, den 5. Juni um 15.30 Uhr in Hamburg an
Wir kommen am Montag, dem 5. Juni, um 15.30 Uhr in Hamburg an

The last alternative given is the most formal. The use of commas in the written form is given as prescribed by DUDEN (1985: 174).

11.3.3 Usage in letter headings

In private correspondence (i.e. where the address is not printed on the notepaper), the writer's address is not usually written out in full at the head of the letter, as is usual English practice. Instead, just the town is given, followed by the date, which may be written in various ways, i.e.:

Siegen, (den) 5.6.89   Siegen, (den/d.) 5. Juni 1989
Siegen, am 5.6.89   Siegen, im Juni 1989

When writing a formal letter to an unknown person, especially for the first time, some Germans put their full name and address in the top *left-hand* corner of the letter *and* the town and date, as given above, in the top *right-hand* corner.

11.4 The accusative and genitive cases used in time adverbials

The accusative and genitive cases of nouns denoting time can be used adverbially, without a preposition, in certain contexts.

11.4.1 Adverbial time phrases with the accusative

A noun denoting time can be used in the accusative case to express duration of time or a specific point in time or period of time.

(a) The accusative can be used to indicate a length of time

The period of time lies entirely in the past, present or future, and the accusative usually corresponds to English *for* (see 11.5.5b). The word or phrase in the accusative may optionally be followed by *lang*, or, emphasising the duration, *über* or *hindurch*:

Ich war einen Monat/drei Monate (lang) in Kassel	*I was in Kassel for a month/for three months*
viele Jahre (lang)	*for many years*
Jahre hindurch blieb er im Gefängnis	*He stayed in prison for years (on end)*
Ich bin jede Woche einen Tag (lang) in Kaiserslautern	*I am in Kaiserslautern one day every week*
Er lag den ganzen Tag (lang/über) im Bett	*He lay in bed the whole day/all day (long)*
den ganzen Sommer (lang)	*all summer, for the whole of the summer*
den ganzen Winter hindurch/über	*throughout the winter*
sein ganzes Leben (lang)	*all his life/for his whole life*
Wo warst du die ganze Zeit?	*Where were you the whole time?*
eine ganze Weile	*for quite a while*

(b) The accusative can be used to indicate a specific time

(i) Particularly in phrases denoting a period of time, corresponding to English 'last week', 'next year', etc. In many contexts, as shown in the examples below, a prepositional phrase is an alternative to the accusative:

Einen Augenblick zuvor hätte sie ihn noch retten können	*A moment before she could still have saved him*
Er kommt jeden Tag, jede Woche	*He comes every day, every week*
Sie fährt alle vierzehn Tage/alle paar Jahre in die Schweiz	*She goes to Switzerland every two weeks/every few years*
Jede halbe Stunde kommt er vorbei	*Every half hour he comes past*
Wir besuchen sie (am) nächsten Dienstag/ (am) kommenden Dienstag	*We are visiting her next Tuesday*
Wir besuchen sie kommende/nächste Woche/ in der kommenden/nächsten Woche	*We are visiting her next week*
Wir werden dieses Jahr/in diesem Jahr nicht verreisen	*We're not going away this year*
Sie ist 1987/im Jahre 1987 wieder zur Vorsitzenden des Vereins gewählt worden	*In 1987 she was elected chair of the society again*
Ich sah sie (am) letzten Freitag/ (am) vorigen Freitag/ (am) vergangenen Freitag	*I saw her last Friday*
Ich sah sie letzte/vorige/vergangene Woche/ in der letzten/vorigen/vergangenen Woche	*I saw her last week*
den 5. Juni/am 5. Juni	*on the 5th of June (see 11.3.2)*

The variants with the accusative are more frequent in everyday speech, whereas those with a preposition are rather commoner in writing. Further examples, with other prepositions:

> Ich bin **Mittag** (for um Mittag)
> wieder zu Hause *I'll be back home at noon*
> Fährst du **Ostern** (for zu Ostern)
> zu deinen Eltern? *Are you going to your parents' at Easter?*
> Sind Sie **das erste Mal** (for zum
> ersten Mal) hier? *Is this the first time you've been here?*

(ii) *Anfang*, *Mitte* and *Ende*, unlike their English equivalents, are used without a preposition, i.e. in the accusative, in time phrases:

> Er ist **Anfang Januar**, **Mitte Januar**, *He died at the beginning of January,*
> **Ende Januar** gestorben *in the middle of January, at the*
> *end of January*
>
> Ich fahre schon **Anfang, Ende** *I'm leaving at the beginning, at the*
> **nächster Woche** *end of next week*
> **Anfang 1990** fanden in der DDR die *At the beginning of 1990 the first*
> ersten freien Wahlen statt *free elections took place in the GDR*

NB: When *Anfang* and *Ende* are used without a following time phrase, they are preceded by *am*, e.g. *am Anfang* 'at the beginning', *am Ende* 'at the end'.

11.4.2 Adverbial time phrases with the genitive

The genitive of nouns denoting time can refer to indefinite or habitual time. These are mainly set expressions, and only in literary German are they commonly extended by adjectives:

> eines Tages *one day*
> eines schönen Tages *one fine day*
> eines schönen Sommers (*Frisch*) *one fine summer*
> eines Sonntags *one Sunday*
> eines Morgens *one morning*
> eines Sonntagmorgens *one Sunday morning*
> eines nebligen Morgens (*Kolb*) *one foggy morning*
> eines Nachts *one night*
> dieser Tage *in the next/last few days*

NB: Note the form *eines Nachts*, although *die Nacht* is feminine.

Some genitives have become simple adverbs. They are written with a small initial letter:

> morgens, vormittags *in the mornings*
> nachmittags, abends *in the afternoons, in the evenings*
> tags, nachts *by day, at night*
> dienstags, freitags *on Tuesdays, on Fridays*
> wochentags, werktags *on weekdays, on working days*
> Donnerstag abends/donnerstags abends *on Thursday evenings*
> von morgens bis abends *from morning till night*
> morgens und abends *morning and evening*

These adverbs are sometimes used to refer to single occasions, (e.g. *nachmittags* for *am Nachmittag*), especially in south German usage:

> Wir kamen dort sonntags auf dem *We came past there on Sunday during*
> Spaziergang vorüber (*Gaiser*) *our walk*

The simple forms *morgens*, *abends*, etc. originated from noun phrases in the genitive with the definite article, e.g. *des Morgens*, *des Abends*. These full phrases are still sometimes used in formal written German.

NB: In the spelling reform, see 23.7.3, forms with the weekdays will be spelled as a single adverb, e.g. *donnerstagabends*.

11.5 Adverbial time phrases with prepositions

This section treats the most common prepositions used with nouns denoting time. Further uses of all prepositions are explained fully in Chapter 20.

11.5.1 *an* (+ dative)

an is used with nouns denoting days and parts of the day. It is always followed by a noun in the dative case when referring to time, and the definite article is *always* used with nouns in the singular, see 4.5.3. In most contexts it corresponds to English 'in' or 'on':

am Tag	*in the daytime*
am Montag, am Dienstag, ...	*on Monday, on Tuesday, ...*
an Wochentagen	*on weekdays*
an besonderen Tagen	*on particular days*
am Morgen, am Nachmittag,	*in the morning, in the afternoon,*
am Abend	*in the evening*
am 31. Oktober (cf. 11.3)	*on the 31st of October*

NB: (i) *in* is used with *Nacht*, see 11.5.7a.
(ii) An accusative time phrase is often an alternative to a phrase with *an*, especially in spoken German, see 11.4.1b.
(iii) In the spelling reform, see 23.7.3, combinations of the days of the week and nouns denoting parts of the day in phrases with *am* will be written together, e.g. *am Donnerstagabend*.

an occurs with *Tag*, etc. even in contexts where English has no preposition:

am Tag nach seinem Tod	*the day after his death*
An diesem Morgen war er schlecht gelaunt	*That morning he was in a bad mood*
am anderen Tag, am anderen Morgen	*the next day, the next morning*

an occurs in a few other phrases:

Es ist an der Zeit, daß ...	*It is about time that ...*
am Anfang, am Ende (see 11.4.1b)	*at the beginning, at the end*
gleich am Anfang	*at the very beginning*

11.5.2 *auf* (+ accusative)

auf (+ accusative) indicates a period of time from 'now', corresponding to English 'for'. In this sense it is a less common alternative to *für*, see 11.5.5, found mainly in formal registers and set phrases:

Sie fährt auf vier Monate in die Schweiz	*She is going to Switzerland for four months*
auf unbestimmte Zeit	*indefinitely*
auf ewig, auf immer	*for ever, for good*

NB: *auf* is used idiomatically in *auf die Minute (genau)* '(precisely) to the minute'.

11.5.3 *bei*

bei is used chiefly with nouns which do not of themselves express time to indicate the 'time when x took/was taking/will take place':

bei seiner Geburt	*at his birth*
bei dieser Gelegenheit	*on this occasion*
bei der Probe	*during the rehearsal*

It is also used in a similar meaning in a few set phrases with nouns expressing time:

Paris bei Tag, London bei Nacht	*Paris by day, London by night*
bei Tagesanbruch	*at daybreak*
bei Einbruch der Nacht	*at nightfall*
bei Sonnenuntergang	*at sunset*

11.5.4 *bis*

bis indicates an end-point in time and can correspond to English 'until' or 'by'. It can only be used on its own with adverbs and simple time phrases like dates and the days of the week, and it is *never* followed by a definite article:

Bis 1945 lebte er in Wien	*Until 1945 he lived in Vienna*
Das Geschäft ist von 9 Uhr bis 18.30 Uhr durchgehend geöffnet	*The shop is open continuously from 9 a.m. until 6.30 p.m.*
Ich werde es bis heute abend, bis Montag fertig haben	*I'll have it finished by tonight, by Monday*
bis nächste Woche, nächstes Jahr	*until next week, next year*
bis dahin/bis dann	*by then, until then*
bis jetzt, bis anhin (Swiss)	*up to now*
Bis dahin bin ich längst zurück	*I'll be back long before then*

With days of the week, months and dates, *bis* can be used with or without a following *zu* (*and* the definite article):

bis (zum) Freitag	*by/until Friday*
bis (zum) 11. Juni	*by/until the 11th of June*
Bis (zum) kommenden Montag kannst du mich hier erreichen	*You can reach me here till next Monday*

In other contexts *bis must* be followed by *zu* with the definite article (or by another appropriate preposition):

bis zum 18. Jahrhundert	*until/by the 18th century*
bis zu seinem Tode	*until his death*
bis zu den Ferien	*until the holidays*
bis vor kurzem	*until recently*
Bis vor zwei Wochen war er hier	*He was here until two weeks ago*
Ich arbeite bis gegen Mittag im Büro	*I'm working at the office until about noon*
Wir wollen es bis auf weiteres verschieben	*We'll postpone it for the present*
bis auf weiteres	*until further notice*
bis tief/spät in die Nacht hinein	*till late at night*
bis in den Herbst hinein	*right into autumn*

A date following a phrase with *bis* and a weekday is in the accusative, e.g. *bis Montag,* **den** *5. September.* In other contexts, the date is in the dative, e.g. *bis morgen,* **dem** *11. November.*

NB: (i) *erst* is used for 'not until', e.g. *Er kommt erst am Montag*, cf. 10.12.1.
(ii) *bis* is frequently used in colloquial leave-taking phrases, e.g. *Bis gleich! Bis bald! Bis morgen! Bis nächste Woche!*

11.5.5 *für* and English 'for'

(a) *für* indicates a period of time extending from 'now'

In this sense, it corresponds to English 'for':

Ich habe das Haus für sechs Monate gemietet	*I've rented the house for six months*
Am nächsten Tag fuhren wir für einen Monat in den Schwarzwald	*The next day we went to the Black Forest for a month*

NB: (i) *auf* (+ accusative) is a less common alternative in this meaning, used chiefly in formal registers and set expressions, see 11.5.2.
(ii) The use of *für* is idiomatic in *Tag für Tag* 'day by day'.

(b) English 'for' has the following main German equivalents

(i) An accusative phrase, used to denote a period of time lying entirely in the past or future, e.g. *Er blieb einen Monat (lang) in Berlin* 'He remained in Berlin for a month'. See 11.4.1a for further details.

(ii) *seit* refers to a period of time which began in the past and extends up to the present, e.g. *Ich warte seit einer Stunde auf dich* 'I've been waiting for you for an hour'. See 11.5.9 for further details.

(iii) *für* (or more formal *auf*) to refer to a period of time extending from the present, as illustrated in (a) above.

In colloquial speech a phrase in the accusative is sometimes used instead of *für* to refer to a period of time extending from the present, e.g.: *Ich gehe eine halbe Stunde (lang) ins Cafe*. On the other hand, *für* is not unknown in the place of an accusative phrase to refer to a period of time lying entirely in the past or future, e.g. *Nur während der Wintermonate blieb er für längere Zeit an einem Ort* (Bumke).

11.5.6 *gegen*

gegen means 'about' or 'towards'. It can be ambiguous, especially with clock times, as some Germans understand *gegen zwei Uhr* to mean 'at about two o'clock', whilst others interpret it as 'getting on for two o'clock'. In other phrases it usually has the meaning 'towards'. It is normally used without an article in time expressions:

gegen Mittag, gegen Abend	*towards noon, towards evening*
gegen Monatsende	*towards the end of the month*
gegen Ende des Jahrhunderts	*towards the end of the century*

11.5.7 *in* (+ dative)

in (+ dative) can refer to a specific period of time or a length of time.

(a) It is used with most words denoting periods of time

It is used with all such words except those with which *an* is used (see 11.5.1), i.e. with the names of the months and seasons (*always* with a definite article, cf.4.5.3), e.g. *im Juli* 'in July', *im Sommer* 'in the summer' and with the following nouns:

der Augenblick	das Jahrhundert	der Monat	die Woche
die Epoche	die Minute	die Nacht	das Zeitalter
das Jahr			

im Augenblick, im letzten Augenblick	*at the moment, at the last moment*
in der Frühe (S. Ger.)	*early in the morning*
im Jahre 1996 (or: 1996)	*in 1996*
in den letzten paar Jahren	*in the last few years*
in letzter Minute	*at the last moment*
im Mittelalter	*in the Middle Ages*
in der Nacht	*at night*
in der Nacht von Sonntag auf Montag	*during the night from Sunday to*
in der Nacht zum/auf Montag	*Monday*
zweimal in der Woche	*twice a week*
in der Woche vor Weihnachten	*in the week before Christmas*
in der Vergangenheit	*in the past*
in Zukunft	*in future*

Most Germans consider that the only correct way of saying 'in 1996' in German is either *im Jahre 1996* or just *1996*, with no preposition. However, the form *in 1996* is increasingly common, in imitation of English usage.

NB: (i) For the use of *in* or *zu* with *Zeit* and *Stunde*, see 11.5.15b.
(ii) *im voraus* 'in advance'.

(b) *in* indicates a period of time within which something happens

Ich habe die Arbeit in zwei Stunden gemacht	*I did the work in two hours*
In zwei Jahren ist der Umsatz um 40% gestiegen	*In two years the turnover rose by 40 per cent*
im Lauf(e) der Zeit	*in the course of time*
Das kann man in zwei Tagen schaffen	*You can do that in two days*

NB: Das kann man **an** einem Morgen, Nachmittag, Abend schaffen

(c) *in* may indicate the time after which something happens or is done

Er kommt in einer halben Stunde zurück	*He's coming back in half an hour*
heute in acht Tagen	*a week today, in a week's time*
Sie fliegt in ein paar Tagen nach Sydney	*She's flying to Sydney in a few days' (time)*

NB: *in* can be ambiguous, like English 'in'. Thus, *in drei Tagen* can mean 'in the course of three days' or 'in three days' time'.

11.5.8 *nach*

nach usually corresponds to English 'after' or 'later':

Nach vielen Jahren ließen sie sich scheiden	*After many years they got divorced*
Einen Monat nach seiner Verhaftung wurde er freigelassen	*A month after his arrest he was released*
Nach Ostern studiert sie in Erlangen Chemie	*After Easter she's going to study chemistry in Erlangen*
bald nach Anfang des 17. Jahrhunderts	*soon after the beginning of the 17th century*
nach einer Weile	*after a while*
nach Wochen, Jahren	*weeks, years later*

11.5.9 *seit*

seit marks a period of time beginning in the past and continuing to the present or a more recent point in the past. It corresponds to English 'since' or 'for', see 11.5.5b:

Er ist seit drei Wochen hier	*He's been here for three weeks*
Ich wartete seit einer halben Stunde auf dem Marktplatz	*I had been waiting on the market-place for half an hour*
Seit wann bist du wieder zu Hause?	*Since when have you been back home?*
Seit seiner Krankheit habe ich ihn nicht mehr gesehen	*I haven't seen him again since his illness*
Erst seit kurzem gibt es Sondertarife nach Spanien	*There have only been special fares to Spain for a short while*
Ich kenne ihn seit langem, seit jeher	*I've known him for a long time, for ages*

NB: (i) For the use of tenses with *seit* 'for', see 14.2.2 and 14.3.4a.
(ii) An accusative phrase with *schon* is a possible alternative to *seit* 'for', e.g. *Er ist schon drei Wochen hier*, see 10.30.5a.

11.5.10 *über* (+ accusative)

über (+ accusative) occurs in a few time expressions in the sense of 'over':

Sie ist **über** Nacht, **übers** Wochenende geblieben	*She stayed overnight, over the weekend*
über kurz oder lang	*sooner or later*

It can be used *after* a noun in the accusative (see 11.4.1a) to emphasise duration:

Sie blieb die ganze Nacht **über**	*She stayed the whole night*
die Schwäne, die den Winter **über** geblieben waren (*Surminski*)	*The swans which had stayed the whole winter*

11.5.11 *um*

um is used with clock times and to express approximation.

(a) *um* corresponds to English 'at' with clock times
e.g. *um vier Uhr* 'at four o'clock', etc., see 11.1.3.

(b) With other time words *um* expresses approximation

It corresponds to English 'around' or 'about' and is often used with *herum* following the noun:

um Mitternacht (herum)	*around midnight*
um Ostern (herum)	*round about Easter time*
um 1890 (herum)	*around 1890*
die Tage um die Sommersonnenwende (herum)	*the days either side of the summer solstice*

NB: *um diese Zeit* is ambiguous. It can mean 'at this time' or 'around this time'. Adding *herum*, i.e. *um diese Zeit herum*, makes it clear that the second meaning is intended.

(c) Idiomatic time phrases with *um*

Stunde um Stunde	*hour after hour*
einen Tag um den anderen	*one day after the other*

11.5.12 *von*

von indicates a starting-point in time. It corresponds to English 'from' and is often linked with a following *an*:

Von 1976 an lebte sie in Rostock	*From 1976 she lived in Rostock*
Von kommendem Montag an kostet das Benzin 10 Pfennig mehr pro Liter	*From next Monday petrol will cost 10 pfennigs a litre more*
von Anfang an	*(right) from the start*
von neun Uhr an	*from nine o'clock (on)*
von nun an	*from now on*
von der Zeit an	*from then on*
von Anfang bis Ende	*from beginning to end*
von heute auf morgen	*from one day to the next, overnight*
von vornherein	*from the outset, from the first*
von jeher von alters her	*from time immemorial, always*
von Jugend auf	*from his (my, etc.) youth on*
von Zeit zu Zeit	*from time to time*

NB: *ab* can be used in the sense 'from' in time expressions, e.g. *ab Montag den/dem 5. August, ab nächste(r) Woche,* see 20.2.10a.

11.5.13 *vor*

vor (+ dative) corresponds to English 'ago' or 'before':

vor einem Jahr, vor mehreren Jahren	*a year ago, several years ago*
vor langer Zeit, vor einiger Zeit	*a long time ago, some time ago*
vor kurzem	*not long ago, recently* (cf. 11.6.5)
gestern vor acht Tagen	*a week ago yesterday*
die Verhältnisse vor der Krise	*the conditions before the crisis*

(See also 7.2.5.)

11.5.14 *während*

während usually corresponds to English 'during':

Sie hat während der Aufführung geschlafen	*She slept during the performance*
während der Wintermonate (*Bumke*)	*during the winter months*
während des letzten Urlaubs, den sie in Italien verbracht hatten (*Walser*)	*during the last holiday which they had spent in Italy*

However, unlike English 'during', *während* is not used with time words like *Tag*, *Abend*, *Nacht* or *Jahr* if these simply have a definite article with them. Compare:

am Tag, am Abend, in der Nacht	*during the day, during the evening, during the night*

während is possible if one of these nouns is qualified by something other than, or in addition to, a simple definite article:

Während der letzten Nacht ist der Junge zweimal aufgewacht	*During the previous night the boy woke up twice*
während eines einzigen Tages	*during/in the course of a single day*

In effect, *während* indicates a *period* rather than *duration*, and it can be used in this sense in contexts where 'during' is not possible or is unusual in English:

während der ganzen Nacht	*throughout the night*
Andere Vogelarten wie der Star können während mindestens zweier Jahre Neues dazulernen (NZZ)	*Other species of birds like starlings can learn new things over the course of at least two years*
Während dreier Jahre verbrachten sie den Urlaub auf Sylt	*Three years running they spent their holidays on Sylt*

11.5.15 *zu*

zu is used with a number of time words, i.e.:

(a) with the major festivals

zu Weihnachten	zu Ostern	zu Pfingsten	zu Neujahr

In south German, *an* is often used rather than *zu* with these festivals. In colloquial speech, there may be no preposition, e.g. *Sie kommt Weihnachten*.

(b) Both *zu* and *in* are used with *Zeit* and *Stunde*

(i) *zu* occurs in contexts denoting one or more specific points or limited periods of time:

zur Zeit	*at present, at the moment, at the time*
zur Zeit der letzten Wahlen	*at the time of the last election*
zu der Zeit, zu dieser Zeit	*at that time*
zu der Zeit, als du hier warst	*at the time when you were here*
zu einer anderen Zeit	*at some other time*
zu jeder Zeit (*or* jederzeit)	*at all times, at any time*
zu jeder Tageszeit	*at any time of the day*
zu gewissen Zeiten	*at certain times*
zur gewohnten Zeit	*at the usual time*
gerade noch zur rechten Zeit	*in the nick of time*
zu gleicher Zeit (*or* zugleich, gleichzeitig)	*at the same time, simultaneously*
Zu meiner Zeit war das alles anders	*In my time that was all different*
zu dieser Stunde	*at this hour*
zu jeder Stunde	*at any time*
zur selben Stunde	*at the same hour*
zu später Stunde (lit.)	*at a late hour*

NB: (also) *zu diesem Zeitpunkt* 'at this point in time'.

(ii) *in* is used to denote a period within or after which something occurs, or in phrases which are felt to denote duration rather than a point or limited period in time:

In all <u>der</u> Zeit (*or* In der ganzen Zeit) haben wir sie nicht gesehen	*In all that time we didn't see her*
In kurzer Zeit war er wieder da	*In a short time he was back again*
In unserer Zeit tut man das nicht mehr	*In our times that is no longer done*
in einer Zeit, in der die Städte wachsen	*at a time when towns are growing*
in einer solchen Zeit wie heute	*at a time like the present*
in früheren Zeiten	*in earlier times*
in künftigen Zeiten	*in times to come*
in der ersten Zeit	*at first*
in ruhigen Stunden	*in peaceful hours*
in elfter Stunde	*at the eleventh hour*

(c) *zu* **is used with** *Mal*

e.g.: *zum ersten Mal (zum erstenmal), zum zehnten Mal*, etc. (see 9.4.3).

11.6 Adverbs of time

Adverbs of time can indicate a point in time (e.g. *damals*), duration (e.g. *lange*) or frequency (e.g. *oft*). A selection of commonly used German time adverbs listed in terms of these categories is given in 11.6.1; the remainder of this section deals with a few time adverbs where German and English usage does not correspond.

11.6.1 Commonly used adverbs of time

Further information on some of these adverbs is given where indicated. Note that the 'present' in terms of time adverbs can sometimes be a point of reference in the past or future rather than the actual present moment.

(a) Indicating a point in time

(i) Referring to the present:

augenblicklich	*at the moment*	heutzutage	*nowadays*
derzeit	*at present*	jetzt	*now*
gegenwärtig	*at present, currently*	momentan	*at present*
gleichzeitig	*at the same time*	nun (10.25)	*now*
heuer (south German)	*this year*	vorerst	*for the moment*
heute (11.6.2)	*today*	zugleich	*at the same time*

(ii) Referring to the past (or 'previously'):

damals (11.6.3a)	*then, at that time*	kürzlich (11.6.5)	*a short time ago*
ehedem (arch.)	*formerly*	neuerdings, neulich (11.6.5) }	*recently*
ehemals (form.)	*formerly*	seinerzeit	*at the time*
einst	*once*	soeben	*just (now)*
früher	*formerly, previously*	unlängst (11.6.5)	*recently*
		vordem (lit.)	*in olden times*
gerade	*just (now)*	vorher (11.6.4)	*before(hand)*
gestern (11.6.2)	*yesterday*	vorhin	*just now*
jüngst (elev.)	*lately*	zuvor (11.6.4)	*before(hand)*

(iii) Referring to the future (or 'subsequently'):

alsbald (lit.)	*straightway*	hernach (form.)	*after(wards)*
augenblicklich	*at once*	morgen (11.6.2)	*tomorrow*
bald	*soon*	nachher (11.6.4)	*after(wards)*
danach (11.6.4)	*afterwards*	nächstens (8.4.4b)	*shortly*
darauf (11.6.4)	*after that*	sofort	*at once,*
daraufhin	*after that*	sogleich	*immediately*
demnächst	*soon*	später	*later*
einst	*once*	vorher	
gleich (10.16)	*at once*	zuvor	(11.6.4) *before(hand)*

(b) Indicating duration

bisher	*up to now,*	nunmehr (elev.)	*from now/then on*
bislang	*hitherto*	seither, seitdem	*since then*
fortan (elev.)	*henceforth*	solange	*meanwhile*
indessen (form.)		unterdessen	*in the meantime*
inzwischen	*meanwhile*	vorerst	*temporarily, for*
künftig	*in future*	vorläufig	*the time being,*
kurz	*for a short time*	vorübergehend	*for the moment*
lange	*for a long time*	währenddem (inf.)	
längst (8.4.4a)	*for a long time*	währenddessen	*meanwhile*
mittlerweile	*in the meantime*	zeitweilig	*temporarily*
momentan	*for an instant*		

lang can be suffixed to other time words to indicate duration, e.g. *stundenlang*, *monatelang, jahrelang* 'for hours, months, years (on end)', see also 11.4.1a.

(c) Indicating frequency

abermals	*once more*	nochmals	*again*
bisweilen (elev.)	*now and then*	oft	*often*
gelegentlich	*occasionally*	öfters	
häufig	*frequently*	selten	*seldom, rarely*
immer	*always*	ständig	*continually*
irgendwann (5.5.11b)	*sometime*	stets	*always*
je	*ever*	unaufhörlich	*incessantly*
jederzeit	*at any time*	wieder	*again*
manchmal	*sometimes*	wiederum (elev.)	
mehrmals	*repeatedly*	zeitweise	*at times*
meistens (8.4.4b)	*mostly*	zuweilen	*from time to time*
mitunter	*now and then*	zwischendurch	*in between times*
nie			
niemals	*never*		
nimmer (lit.)			

11.6.2 *gestern, heute* and *morgen*

These are used in conjunction with words indicating periods of the day to give the equivalent of English 'last night', 'this afternoon', etc.:

gestern morgen	*yesterday morning*
gestern abend	*last night* (before bedtime)
vorgestern	*the day before yesterday*
heute nacht	*last night* (after bedtime)
	tonight (after bedtime)
heute morgen/heute früh	*this morning*

heute vormittag	*this morning* (after breakfast)
heute nachmittag	*this afternoon*
heute abend	{ *this evening,* { *tonight* (before bedtime)
morgen früh	*tomorrow morning*
morgen vormittag	*tomorrow morning* (after breakfast)
übermorgen	*the day after tomorrow*

NB: In the reformed spelling, see 23.7.3, the noun denoting the part of the day in these combinations will be spelled with a capital, e.g. *gestern Morgen, heute Abend.*

11.6.3 German equivalents of English 'then'

(a) *damals* refers to past time
i.e., meaning 'at that time':

Sie war **damals** sehr arm	*She was very poor, then*
damals, vor dem großen Kriege (*Roth*)	*at that time, before the Great War*

(b) *dann* is used for other meanings of 'then' referring to time
especially in the sense of 'after that' with a series of actions or events:

Dann fuhr er weg	*Then he left*
Erst bist du an der Reihe, **dann** ich	*First it's your turn, then mine*
Wenn er dir schreibt, **dann** mußt du es deiner Mutter sagen	*If he writes to you, then you'll have to tell your mother*
Und wenn sie kommt, was machst du **dann**?	*And if she comes, what will you do then?*

dann is not used after a preposition, cf.: *bis dahin* 'till then', 'by then', *seither, seitdem* 'since then', *von da an* 'from then on', *vorher, zuvor* 'before then' (see also 11.6.4a).

(c) To intensify a question, the German equivalent is *denn*
e.g. *Was ist* **denn** *daran so komisch?* See 10.6.1 for further details.

11.6.4 German equivalents of English 'before' and 'after'

(a) *vorher* and *zuvor* are the commonest equivalents of 'before'
Both can be used with reference to past or future time:

Ich war ein Jahr **vorher/zuvor** da gewesen	*I had been there a year before*
Ich muß **vorher/zuvor** noch telephonieren	*I've got to make a phone call before then*
Er hatte uns am Tag **vorher/zuvor** besucht	*He had been to visit us the day before*
einige Zeit **vorher/zuvor**	*some time previously*

Referring to time up to the present moment, *früher* or *zuvor* are used (or, in a negative context, *noch*):

Sie hätten es mir **früher/zuvor** sagen sollen	*You ought to have told me before*
Ich habe sie **nie zuvor/noch nie** gesehen	*I've never seen her before*

(b) *danach* or *nachher* are the usual equivalents for 'after' (or 'later')
darauf is also often used after words expressing a period of time:

Ich habe sie einen Monat **danach/nachher** gesehen	*I saw her a month after/later*
Kurz **danach**/Kurz **nachher**/ Kurz **darauf** sah ich sie wieder	*I saw her again a short time after/shortly afterwards*
Am Tag **darauf/danach** gingen wir ins Theater	*The day after we went to the theatre*
Das werde ich dir **nachher** erzählen	*I'll tell you that afterwards*

NB: *im nachhinein* and *hinterher* are also frequently used for 'afterwards'.

11.6.5 German equivalents for English 'recent(ly)'

German has no single word with the range of meaning of English 'recent(ly)'.
The following are the main equivalents, and the choice depends on the precise
meaning to be expressed:

kürzlich/vor kurzem/unlängst	*a short time ago*
neulich/neuerdings	*the other day*
letzthin/in letzter Zeit/seit kurzem	*latterly* (i.e. during the last few weeks or months)

As the above are all adverbs, they have to be used in paraphrases, etc. to give
German equivalents for the English adjective *recent*, e.g.:

auf der **kürzlich stattgefundenen** Konferenz	*at the recent conference*
bei unserer Begegnung **neulich**	*at our recent meeting*
als er **vor kurzem** krank war	*during his recent illness*
eine **erst kürzlich eingeführte** Neuerung	*a (very) recent innovation*
sein **neuestes** Buch	*his most recent book*

Other selected equivalents:

bis vor kurzem	*until recently*
Ich habe ihn noch später gesehen als Sie	*I have seen him more recently than you*
Kurt hat sie zuletzt gesehen	*Kurt has seen her most recently/ just recently*

12

Verbs: Conjugation

The various forms of a verb express different grammatical ideas like tense, mood, person and number, which are known as 'grammatical categories'. All the forms of a verb make up its 'conjugation', as explained in 12.1. This chapter gives details on the conjugation of regular and irregular verbs in German in the simple present and past tenses (12.2), the compound future and perfect tenses (12.3), the passive (12.4) and the subjunctive (12.5). The forms of all strong and irregular verbs are given in Table 12.9.

12.1 Verb conjugation

12.1.1 The forms and grammatical categories of the German verb

German verbs are given in most dictionaries in the 'infinitive' form, ending in *-en* or *-n*, e.g. *kaufen, singen, wandern*. By deleting this *-(e)n*, we obtain the essential core of the verb, which is called the 'stem', e.g. *kauf-, sing-, wander-*. The stem carries the basic 'lexical' meaning of the verb (i.e. 'buy', 'sing' 'wander', etc.). By altering this stem, i.e. by adding prefixes or endings, or by changing the vowel (and in a few cases the consonants, too) we can show different grammatical categories, i.e.:

(a) Indicate the person and number of the subject of the verb

The verb in German is linked through its endings with the subject of the verb and is said to 'agree with' the subject. The form of the verb which agrees with the subject in this way is known as the 'finite verb'.

ich kaufe	du singst	er/sie/es wandert
wir kaufen	ihr singt	sie/Sie wandern

See 12.1.4 for further details on the agreement between subject and verb.

(b) Indicate the time of the action, process or event expressed by the verb

ich kaufe	(present)	–	ich kaufte	(past)
du singst	(present)	–	du sangst	(past)
er wandert	(present)	–	er wanderte	(past)

The various forms of the verb which express time relationships are known as the 'tenses' of the verb. German, like English, has two simple (i.e. one-word) tenses, the 'present' and the 'past' tense, as illustrated above. The formation of these simple tenses is explained in section 12.2.

The other tenses are 'compound' tenses, formed by using one (or more) of the 'auxiliary' verbs *haben*, *sein* or *werden* with the past participle or the infinitive, e.g.:

> ich **habe** gekauft, ich **habe** gesungen, ich **bin** gewandert (perfect)
> er **hatte** gekauft, er **hatte** gesungen, er **war** gewandert (pluperfect)
> sie **werden** kaufen, sie **werden** singen, sie **werden** wandern (future)

The formation of the compound tenses is explained in section 12.3, and the use of the tenses in German is treated in detail in Chapter 14.

(c) Show whether we are dealing with a fact, a possibility or a command

This is shown by the 'mood' of the verb. German has three moods:

(i) The 'indicative' mood states a fact:

> sie kauft   sie singt   sie ist gewandert

(ii) The 'subjunctive' mood indicates a possibility or a report:

> sie kaufe   sie sänge   sie würde wandern

(iii) The 'imperative' mood expresses a command:

> kaufe!   singt!   wandern Sie!

The formation of the subjunctive in German is explained in section 12.5, and its use is dealt with in Chapter 16. The use of the imperative is explained in section 16.2, together with other ways of expressing commands.

(d) Change the relationship between the elements in the sentence

Using a different 'voice' of the verb, i.e. the 'active' or the 'passive' voice, permits different elements to appear as the subject of the verb:

> active voice: Er **kaufte** das Buch
> passive voice (with *werden*):   Das Buch **wurde gekauft**
> passive voice (with *sein*):   Das Buch **war gekauft**

German has two types of passive, both of which are compound, using the verb *werden* or *sein* and the past participle. The formation of the passives is treated in section 12.4, and their uses are explained in Chapter 15.

(e) Construct the 'non-finite' forms of the verb

The non-finite forms of the verb are the 'infinitive', e.g. *kaufen, singen, wandern*, the 'present participle', e.g. *kaufend, singend, wandernd* and the 'past participle', e.g. *gekauft, gesungen, gewandert*. They are known as 'non-finite' since they do not show agreement with the subject of the verb, unlike the 'finite' forms (see (a) above).

These non-finite forms can be combined with auxiliary verbs to form the compound tenses and the passive voice (see 12.3–4). They have some other uses which are treated in detail in Chapter 13.

12.1.2 How a verb is conjugated depends on whether it is WEAK or STRONG

The main difference between these types of conjugation (sometimes called 'inflectional classes') is the way in which the past tense is formed:

(a) WEAK verbs form their past tense by adding *-te* to the stem

kauf-en – kauf-**te**   mach-en – mach-**te**   wander-n – wander-**te**

(b) STRONG verbs form their past tense by changing the vowel of the stem

beiß-en – biß   fließ-en – floß   sing-en – sang

Most German verbs are 'weak', and they can be considered as 'regular' verbs. Although there are relatively few 'strong' verbs, most of them are very common. There is no way of telling from the infinitive of a verb whether it is 'weak' or 'strong'. This means that the foreign learner needs to remember which verbs are 'strong' and learn their main forms, in particular their so-called 'principal parts', i.e. the infinitive, the past tense and the past participle (e.g. *bleiben – blieb – geblieben, fahren – fuhr – gefahren*). These are all given in full in Table 12.9.

In practice, the vowel changes in the strong verbs (called *Ablaut* in German) fall into a small number of recurrent patterns. It is useful to be aware of these patterns, which are shown in Table 12.1.

TABLE 12.1 *Vowel changes in strong verbs*

Vowel change	Example
ei – ie – ie	bleiben – blieb – geblieben
ei – i – i	beißen – biß – gebissen
i – a – u	singen – sang – gesungen
i – a – o	schwimmen – schwamm – geschwommen
ie – o – o	fliegen – flog – geflogen
e – a – o	helfen – half – geholfen
e – a – e	geben – gab – gegeben
e – o – o	fechten – focht – gefochten
a – u – a	fahren – fuhr – gefahren
a – ie – a	fallen – fiel – gefallen

12.1.3 There are also a small number of 'irregular' verbs

These fall into four main groups:

(a) A few irregular weak verbs have vowel changes (and sometimes also consonant changes) in the past tense and the past participle

kennen – kannte – gekannt   rennen – rannte – gerannt
bringen – brachte – gebracht   denken – dachte – gedacht

The main forms of these irregular weak verbs are given in Table 12.9.

(b) A few irregular strong verbs have consonant changes as well as vowel changes in the past tense and the past participle

geh-en – ging – gegangen   leid-en – litt – gelitten
steh-en – stand – gestanden   zieh-en – zog – gezogen

The main forms of these irregular strong verbs are given in Table 12.9.

(c) The 'modal auxiliary' verbs and *wissen*

The six modal auxiliary verbs *dürfen, können, mögen, müssen, sollen, wollen* and the verb *wissen* 'to know' have an irregular present tense with no *-t* in the third person singular and, in most cases, a different vowel in the singular and plural. Most also have a different vowel in the past tense and the past participle, e.g.:

> können – er kann, wir können – konnte – gekonnt
> müssen – er muß, wir müssen – mußte – gemußt
> wissen – er weiß, wir wissen – wußte – gewußt

All the forms of these verbs in the indicative are given in Table 12.4.

(d) The verbs *haben, sein* and *werden*

These three verbs are wholly irregular. Aside from their basic meanings, i.e. *haben* 'to have', *sein* 'to be', *werden* 'to become', they are used as auxiliaries to form the compound tenses and the passives. All the indicative forms of these verbs are given in Table 12.3.

12.1.4 Agreement of subject and finite verb

In German, the 'finite' verb (i.e. the main verb in the simple present and past tenses and the auxiliary verb in compound tenses) has endings which link it with the subject. We usually say that, through these endings, the verb 'agrees' with the subject for person (i.e. first, second or third person) and number (i.e. singular or plural), e.g.:

	Singular	Plural
First person	ich sing**e**	wir sing**en**
Second person	du sing**st**	ihr sing**t**
Third person	er/sie/es sing**t**	sie sing**en**

NB: In the 'polite' form of the second person (with *Sie*) the verb always has the the the ending of the third person plural, e.g. *Sie singen*.

In some constructions there can be uncertainty about what the verb agrees with. These are summarised below, following the survey by Jaeger (1992).

(a) If the subject of the verb is a clause, the verb has the third person singular endings

The clause can be a subordinate clause (see 19.2) or an infinitive clause (see 13.2.3):

> Daß sie nichts tut, **ärgert** mich sehr   *I'm very annoyed that she isn't doing anything*
> Sie wiederzusehen **hat** mich gefreut   *I was pleased to see her again*

(b) If the predicate complement of *sein* is plural and the subject singular, the verb is in the plural

> Mein Lieblingsobst **sind** Kirschen   *My favourite fruit is cherries*

This is in particular the case with *es, das* and other neuter pronouns (see 3.6.2b, 5.1.1h and 5.3.1a):

> Was **sind** das für Vögel? –   *What kind of birds are those? –*
> Es **sind** Storche   *They are storks*
> **Sind** es deine Handschuhe?   *Are they your gloves?*
> Welches **sind** deine Handschuhe?   *Which are your gloves?*

(c) With coordinated nouns as subject, the verb is usually plural

Helmut und sein Bruder **sind** gekommen	*Helmut and his brother have come*
Vater, Mutter, Tochter **saßen** beim Essen	*Father, mother and daughter were sitting down eating*

In some constructions a singular verb is possible (although less common than the plural), i.e.:

(i) If the subject follows the verb:

Im Osten **winkte** das Völkerschlacht-denkmal, die Türme und die Essen von Leipzig	*In the east, the war memorial, the towers and chimneys of Leipzig beckoned*

(ii) If the parts of the subject are seen as distinct (especially if the nouns are qualified by *jeder* or *kein*):

Wenig später **wurde** heiße Suppe und Weißbrot ausgeteilt	*A little later hot soup and white bread were distributed*
Ihm **konnte** kein Arzt und kein Apotheker mehr helfen	*No doctor and no chemist could help him now*

(iii) If the linked nouns are felt to form a single whole:

Diese Haltung und Miene **war** ihm eigentümlich (*Th. Mann*)	*This attitude and facial expression were peculiar to him*

(iv) With the conjunctions *sowie* and *sowohl . . . als/wie (auch)*:

Sowohl Manfred als auch seine Frau **war** einverstanden	*Both Manfred and his wife agreed*

(d) If the subject consists of nouns linked by a disjunctive conjunction the verb is usually in the singular

(i) This applies in particular to (*entweder . . .*) *oder* and *nicht (nur) . . ., sondern (auch)*

Entweder Hans oder Karl **wird** mir helfen	*Either Hans or Karl will help me*
Mit dieser Lösung **wäre** nicht nur die Mehrheit der Partei sondern auch Erhard selbst zufrieden gewesen (*Spiegel*)	*Not only the majority of the party but Erhard too would have been satisfied with this solution*

A plural verb is sometimes used with these, especially if the nearest noun is plural, e.g.: *Entweder Karl oder seine Brüder **werden** mir helfen.*

(ii) With *weder . . . noch*, either singular or plural is possible, but the plural is more frequent:

In Bonn **waren** sich weder Kabinett noch Regierungsfraktionen einig (*Zeit*)	*In Bonn neither the cabinet nor the governing parties were agreed*

(e) If a coordinated subject includes a pronoun, the verb has the ending which corresponds to the combination

(i) This applies in particular with the conjunction *und* and its synonyms:

Mein Mann und ich (= wir) **trennten** uns im Frühjahr (*Spiegel*)	*My husband and I separated in the spring*
Du und sie (= ihr) **könntet** damit zufrieden sein	*You and she can be satisfied with that*
Sowohl sie als auch er (= sie) **haben** sich darüber gefreut	*Both she and he were pleased about it*

These combinations can sound artificial, especially if the second person plural is involved, and they are often avoided by adding the appropriate plural pronoun, e.g.: *Ihr könnt damit zufrieden sein, du und sie.*

(ii) With disjunctive conjunctions, the verb usually agrees with the nearest pronoun, whether this precedes or follows:

Entweder du oder ich **werde** es ihnen sagen
Nicht nur die anderen, sondern auch du **sollst** es ihnen sagen
Dann **werden** nicht nur sie, sondern auch ihr es ihnen sagen
Nicht ich, sondern ihr **sollt** es ihnen sagen
Ich, nicht du, **sollst** es ihnen sagen

These, too, can sound unnatural, and can be avoided by repeating the verb or splitting one pronoun off, e.g.:

Entweder du **sagst** es ihnen, oder ich **sage** es ihnen
Entweder du **sollst** es ihr sagen **oder ich**

(f) Usage with expressions of measure or quantity

(i) With singular nouns of indefinite quantity followed by a plural noun, the verb is normally in the plural:

Ein Dutzend Eier **kosten** DM2,30	*A dozen eggs cost DM 2,30*
Es **waren** eine Menge Leute da	*There were a lot of people there*
Eine Gruppe von Studenten **standen** vor dem Bahnhof	*A group of students were standing in front of the station*
Die Hälfte meiner Gedanken **waren** bei ihr (*Grass*)	*Half my thoughts were with her*

Although this is the dominant usage in speech and common in writing, many authorities, e.g. DUDEN (1985: 415–16), continue to insist that the use of the singular (e.g. *ein Dutzend Eier* **kostet** *DM2,30*) is still current.

(ii) With singular measurement words followed by a plural noun, the verb may be either singular or plural:

Ein Kilogramm Kartoffeln **reicht/reichen** aus
Ein Kubikmeter Ziegelsteine **wiegt/wiegen** fast zwei Tonnen

(iii) With nouns of measure used with a numeral or a plural determiner, the verb is normally in the plural. In such cases, masculine and neuter nouns of measurement have no ending to show that they are plural (cf. 1.2.14):

Mehrere Liter Benzin waren verschüttet	*Several litres of petrol were spilled*
Fünf Kilo kosten dreißig Mark	*Five kilograms cost thirty marks*
Dafür wurden mir tausend Mark angeboten	*I was offered a thousand marks for it*

However, especially in spoken German, the verb may be in the singular, as the quantity is envisaged as a single whole: *Zwanzig Mark ist/sind zu viel*.

(g) Singular collective nouns are always used with a singular verb
This contrasts strongly with English usage, where the plural is the norm or at least quite frequent:

Die ganze Familie **ist** verreist	*The whole family have/has gone away*
Unsere Mannschaft **hat** wieder verloren	*Our team have/has lost again*
Die Polizei **kommt** gleich	*The police are coming straight away*
Die Regierung **hat** es beschlossen	*The government have/has decided it*

12.2 The simple present and past tenses, the non-finite forms and the imperative

These constitute the basic conjugation of the German verb. They are all single words, formed by adding different affixes to the verb stem or by changing the form of the stem in some way.

12.2.1 Weak and strong verbs

Weak and strong verbs differ mainly in the way in which they form the past tense and the past participle (their 'principal parts'). Weak verbs have the ending *-te* in the past tense and *-t* in the past participle, whilst strong verbs change the vowel of the stem in the past tense and have the ending *-en* (sometimes with a further change of vowel) in the past participle. Otherwise, weak and strong verbs have the same endings in the two simple tenses, the non-finite forms, and in the imperative mood (which is similar to the present tense).

Table 12.2 gives these forms for typical weak and strong verbs. The principal parts of all strong and irregular verbs are given in Table 12.9. However, there are a few regular variations to the general pattern of endings for strong and weak verbs as given in Table 12.2. These are:

(a) Verbs whose stem ends in *-d* or *-t*, or in *-m* or *-n* after a consonant
These verbs add *-e-* before the endings *-t*, *-st* and the *-te* of the past of weak verbs, e.g *du arbeitest, er arbeitet, er arbeitete, gearbeitet*, etc. The full forms of *warten* 'wait' are given in Table 12.2 as further illustration. Other examples:

> *finden* 'find': du findest, er findet, ihr findet; du fandest, ihr fandet
> *regnen* 'rain': es regnet, es regnete, geregnet
> *atmen* 'breathe': du atmest, sie atmet, ihr atmet, ich atmete, geatmet

NB: (i) Verbs with *l* or *r* before *m* or *n* do not need the linking *-e-*: *sie filmt* 'she is filming', *er lernt* 'he is learning'.
(ii) Strong verbs with a vowel change do not add *-t* in the third person singular, see (e) and (f) below.

(b) Verbs whose stem ends in *-s*, *-ß*, *-x* or *-z*
These have the ending *-t* in the second person singular, present tense:

> *rasen* 'race' – du rast   *grüßen* 'greet' – du grüßt
> *faxen* 'fax' – du faxt   *setzen* 'put' – du setzt

TABLE 12.2 *Simple forms of strong and weak verbs*

	Weak			Strong
Infinitive	kaufen	warten	wandern	singen
Present part.	kaufend	wartend	wandernd	singend
Past part.	gekauft	gewartet	gewandert	gesungen
Present tense	ich kaufe	ich warte	ich wand(e)re	ich singe
	du kaufst	du wartest	du wanderst	du singst
	es kauft	es wartet	es wandert	es singt
	wir kaufen	wir warten	wir wandern	wir singen
	ihr kauft	ihr wartet	ihr wandert	ihr singt
	Sie kaufen	Sie warten	Sie wandern	Sie singen
	sie kaufen	sie warten	sie wandern	sie singen
Past tense	ich kaufte	ich wartete	ich wanderte	ich sang
	du kauftest	du wartetest	du wandertest	du sangst
	es kaufte	es wartete	es wanderte	es sang
	wir kauften	wir warteten	wir wanderten	wir sangen
	ihr kauftet	ihr wartetet	ihr wandertet	ihr sangt
	Sie kauften	Sie warteten	Sie wanderten	Sie sangen
	sie kauften	sie warteten	sie wanderten	sie sangen
Imperative singular	kaufe!	warte!	wand(e)re!	singe!
pl. (familiar)	kauft!	wartet!	wandert!	singt!
pl. (polite)	kaufen Sie!	warten Sie!	wandern Sie!	singen Sie!

The use of the ending *-est* instead of *-t*, e.g. *du setzest*, is archaic in the present tense, except in Swiss usage, but it is still current in the past tense of strong verbs with stems ending in these consonants:

> du las**est** 'you read'   du ließ**est** 'you let'   du wuchs**est** 'you grew'

NB: Adding *-e-* in the second person plural of these strong verbs, e.g. *ihr laset, ihr aßet*, is archaic. The usual forms are *ihr last, ihr aßt*, etc.

(c) Verbs whose stem ends in *-el* and *-er*

These verbs have some differences from the general pattern of endings, and all the forms of *wandern* are given in Table 12.2 to illustrate such verbs.

(i) They have the ending *-n*, not *-en*, in the infinitive and the first and third person plural of the present tense, e.g. *klingeln* 'ring', *wandern* 'wander'.

(ii) In the first person singular of the present tense and the imperative singular, the *-e-* of the stem is always dropped with verbs in *-el* and occasionally with verbs in *-er* (more commonly in speech than in writing), e.g.: *ich klingle, ich wand(e)re*.

NB: In speech one can hear forms where the *-e-* of the stem is kept, but the *-e* of the ending dropped, e.g. *ich klingel, ich wander*, etc.

(d) Verbs whose stem ends in a long vowel or diphthong

Sometimes these lack *-e-* in their endings, in particular:

(i) The present tense and infinitive of *tun* 'do':

> ich tue, du tust, es tut, wir tun, ihr tut, sie tun

(ii) The present tense of *knien* [kniːən] 'kneel' is as follows:

> ich knie [kniːə], du kniest [kniːst], er kniet [kniːt],
> wir knien [kniːən], ihr kniet [kniːt], sie knien [kniːən]

The past tense of the strong verb *schreien* 'shout, scream' is similar, i.e.: *ich/er schrie, wir/sie schrien* [ʃriːən]. The past participle is *geschrieen* or *geschrien*.

(iii) Other such verbs generally lose the -*e*- of the ending -*en* in spoken German, and these forms are occasionally found in writing, e.g *schaun, gehn, gesehn* (for *schauen, gehen, gesehen*, etc.).

(e) Most strong verbs with -*e*- in the stem change this to -*i*- or -*ie*- in the second and third person singular present, and in the imperative singular
In general, verbs in short -*e*- change this to -*i*-, whilst those in long -*e*- usually change this to -*ie*-. These verbs never add the ending -*e* in the imperative singular. Examples:

essen	'eat':	du ißt, es ißt, iß!
helfen	'help':	du hilfst, es hilft , hilf!
lesen	'read':	du liest, es liest, lies!
stehlen	'steal':	du stiehlst, es stiehlt, stiehl!

There are some exceptions and further irregularities with these verbs, and full details are given for each verb in Table 12.9. However, the following general points may be noted:

(i) The following strong verbs in -*e*- do *not* change the vowel:

bewegen 'induce'	*gehen* 'go'	*genesen* 'recover'	*heben* 'lift'
melken 'milk'	*scheren* 'shear'	*stehen* 'stand'	*weben* 'weave'

(ii) *erlöschen* 'go out' (of lights, fires) changes -*ö*- to -*i*-, e.g. *es erlischt*.

(iii) Three strong verbs in long -*e*- change this to short -*i*-, i.e.:

> *geben* 'give' – du gibst, es gibt, gib!
> *nehmen* 'take' – du nimmst, es nimmt, nimm!
> *treten* 'step' – du trittst, es tritt, tritt!

(iv) Verbs with this vowel change whose stem ends in -*d* or -*t* do *not* add -*et* in the third person singular (cf. (a) above), e.g.:

> *gelten* 'be worth' – es gilt   *treten* 'step' – es tritt

(v) In non-standard colloquial speech, a regular imperative, without the vowel change, is common, e.g. *eß!, geb!, nehm!*

(f) Most strong verbs with -*a*- or -*au*- in their stem have *Umlaut* in the second and third person singular of the present

fahren 'go' : du fährst, es fährt	*lassen* 'let' : du läßt, es läßt
wachsen 'grow': du wächst, es wächst	*laufen* 'run' : du läufst, es läuft

There are some exceptions and further irregularities with these verbs, and full details are given for each verb in Table 12.9. However, the following general points may be noted:

(i) *stoßen* 'push' has *Umlaut* of *-o-*, e.g.: *du stößt, es stößt.*

(ii) *schaffen* 'create' and *saugen* 'suck' do *not* have *Umlaut*: *du schaffst, saugst; er schafft, saugt.*

(iii) Verbs with this *Umlaut* whose stem ends in *-d* or *-t* do *not* add *-et* in the third person singular (cf. (a) above), e.g.:

> *halten* 'hold' – es **hält**   *laden* 'load' – es **lädt**   *raten* 'advise'- es **rät**

NB: In spoken south German, *Umlaut* is often lacking, and one hears, e.g., *sie schlaft* instead of *sie schläft.* This is considered substandard.

(g) The ending -e of the imperative singular is usually dropped in speech:

> Komm in den Garten!   Setz dich!   Stör mich nicht!

This is not unusual in writing, too, but a few verbs *always* keep the *-e*, i.e. those with stems in *-d, -t, -ig*, and *-m* or *-n* after another consonant:

> Antworte mir sofort!   Rede nicht so laut!   Entschuldige bitte!
> Atme stärker!   Segne mich!

NB: (i) Verbs in *-el* drop the *-e-* of the stem, but keep the ending, e.g. *Kling**l**e laut!* (see (c) above).
    (ii) Verbs which change *-e-* to *-i-* or *-ie-* **never** add *-e*, e.g. *Gib! Nimm!* (see (e) above), except for the form *Siehe!* which is used in the phrase *Siehe da!* 'Behold!' and in references, e.g. *s.S.90* (= *siehe Seite 90*).

(h) Some verbs lack the prefix ge- in the past participle
All these are verbs which are not stressed on the first syllable, i.e.:

(i) Verbs with inseparable prefixes (see 22.4):

bedeuten	'mean'	– bedeutet	*erfinden*	'invent'	– erfunden
gelingen	'succeed'	– gelungen	*mißlingen*	'fail'	– mißlungen
zerbrechen	'smash'	– zerbrochen	*überlegen*	'consider'	– überlegt
unterdrücken	'suppress'	– unterdrückt	*anvertrauen*	'entrust'	– anvertraut

(ii) Verbs in *-ieren*:

> *gratulieren* 'congratulate' – gratuliert   *studieren* 'study' – studiert

(iii) A few others which are not stressed on the first syllable, e.g.:

froh`locken	'rejoice'	*– froh`lockt* (also: *ge`frohlockt*)	*offen`baren* 'reveal' – *offen`bart* (also: *ge`offenbart*)
prophe`zeien	'prophesy' – *prophe`zeit*		*po`saunen* 'bellow' – *po`saunt*
re`cykeln	'recycle' – *re`cykelt*		*schma`rotzen* 'sponge' – *schma`rotzt*

(i) Separable verbs
Separable verbs are made by adding a prefix to a simple verb to form a new verb with a distinctive meaning, as explained in 22.5 and 22.6. In many contexts this prefix is separated from the main verb, and their name is due to this property.

Separable verbs have exactly the same endings and forms, whether weak or strong, as the simple verbs from which they are derived. Thus, *ankommen* 'arrive' conjugates like *kommen, zumachen* 'shut' like *machen*.

(i) In finite forms in main clauses, the prefix is separated from the verb and goes to the end of the clause (i.e. it becomes the final part of the 'verbal bracket' construction, cf. 21.1.2), e.g.:

ankommen 'arrive' : Ich komme morgen um zwei Uhr **an**. Ich kam gestern **an**
ausgehen 'go out' : Sie geht heute abend **aus**
nachahmen 'imitate': Sie ahmten seine Bewegungen **nach**
totschlagen 'kill' : Er schlug das Tier mit einer Keule **tot**

(ii) The prefix remains joined to the verb in the non-finite forms, with the *ge-* of the past participle being inserted after the prefix:

ankommen – ankommend – angekommen
ausgehen – ausgehend – ausgegangen

If the simple verb has no *ge-* in the past participle (see (h) above), it is also lacking in corresponding separable verbs:

einstudieren *rehearse* – einstudiert   anerkennen *recognise* – anerkannt

The *zu* of the expanded infinitive is also added between the prefix and the simple verb (see 13.1.4b):

ankommen – an**zu**kommen   ausgehen – aus**zu**gehen
anerkennen – anzuerkennen

(iii) In subordinate clauses, the prefix rejoins the finite verb in final position and is written together with it, e.g.:

Ich weiß, daß sie heute abend **ausgeht**
Er sah, wie sie seine Bewegungen **nachahmten**

(j) Some verb endings are regularly reduced in everyday speech
Although widely used in speech, these reduced forms are considered to be substandard colloquialisms and they are rarely used in writing.

(i) The ending *-e* tends to be dropped, e.g. *ich kauf, ich fall, ich/es sucht* for *ich kaufe, ich falle, ich/es suchte*.

(ii) The ending *-en* tends to be reduced to *-n*, e.g. *wir kaufn, sie falln, wir kauftn, sie botn, getretn* for standard German *wir kaufen, sie fallen, wir kauften, sie boten, getreten*. This reduction is particularly common in verbs with a stem ending in a long vowel or diphthong, cf. (d) above.

(iii) *brauchen* is sometimes heard without the ending *-t* in the third person singular of the present tense, e.g. *er, sie* **brauch**. This usage is universally considered incorrect, but it is widespread and increasing.

12.2.2 Irregular verbs

The verbs *sein* 'be', *haben* 'have', *werden* 'become', the six 'modal auxiliary' verbs *dürfen, können, mögen, müssen, sollen, wollen* and the verb *wissen* 'know' are wholly irregular in their basic forms. These are all given in Table 12.3 and Table 12.4. A few more specific points about the forms of these verbs, and a few variant forms should be noted, i.e.:

TABLE 12.3 *Simple forms of* sein, haben *and* werden

	sein	**haben**	**werden**
Present tense	ich bin	ich habe	ich werde
	du bist	du hast	du wirst
	es ist	es hat	es wird
	wir sind	wir haben	wir werden
	ihr seid	ihr habt	ihr werdet
	Sie sind	Sie haben	Sie werden
	sie sind	sie haben	sie werden
Past tense	ich war	ich hatte	ich wurde
	du warst	du hattest	du wurdest
	es war	es hatte	es wurde
	wir waren	wir hatten	wir wurden
	ihr wart	ihr hattet	ihr wurdet
	Sie waren	Sie hatten	Sie wurden
	sie waren	sie hatten	sie wurden
Infinitive	sein	haben	werden
Pres. part.	seiend	habend	werdend
Past part.	gewesen	gehabt	geworden
Imperative	sei!	habe!	werde!
	seid!	habt!	werdet!
	seien Sie!	haben Sie!	werden Sie!

TABLE 12.4 *Simple forms of* wissen, dürfen, können, mögen, müssen, sollen *and* wollen

	wissen	**dürfen**	**können**	**mögen**	**müssen**	**sollen**	**wollen**
Present tense	ich weiß	darf	kann	mag	muß	soll	will
	du weißt	darfst	kannst	magst	mußt	sollst	willst
	es weiß	darf	kann	mag	muß	soll	will
	wir wissen	dürfen	können	mögen	müssen	sollen	wollen
	ihr wißt	dürft	könnt	mögt	müßt	sollt	wollt
	Sie wissen	dürfen	können	mögen	müssen	sollen	wollen
	sie wissen	dürfen	können	mögen	müssen	sollen	wollen
Past tense	ich wußte	durfte	konnte	mochte	mußte	sollte	wollte
	du wußtest	durftest	konntest	mochtest	mußtest	solltest	wolltest
	es wußte	durfte	konnte	mochte	mußte	sollte	wollte
	wir wußten	durften	konnten	mochten	mußten	sollten	wollten
	ihr wußtet	durftet	konntet	mochtet	mußtet	solltet	wolltet
	Sie wußten	durften	konnten	mochten	mußten	sollten	wollten
	sie wußten	durften	konnten	mochten	mußten	sollten	wollten
Past part.	gewußt	gedurft	gekonnt	gemocht	gemußt	gesollt	gewollt

(a) Reduced forms of *sein* and *haben* are usual in colloquial speech
For example *es is* for *es ist; wir/sie sin, ham* for *wir/sie sind, haben; simmer, hammer* for *sind wir, haben wir*, etc.

(b) Special forms of *werden*
(i) The old form *ich/es ward* was sometimes used for *ich/es wurde* in elevated styles into the present century, and it is still occasionally found in deliberately archaicising (especially biblical) contexts.
(ii) The past participle of *werden* has no *ge-* when used as an auxiliary to form the passive, see 12.4.2a, e.g.: *Er ist gelobt **worden***. Compare: *Er ist Schauspieler geworden*.

(c) The past participle of the modal auxiliaries is rarely used
When these verbs are used in the perfect tenses in conjunction with a main verb, the infinitive is used rather than the past participle (see 13.3.2):

Ich habe es machen **müssen**   Sie hatte es sehen **können**
Wir haben ihn lehren **sollen**   Sie hatten es uns sagen **wollen**

(d) The present participle and imperative of the modal auxiliaries do not occur in practice
wissen has the following forms:

Present participle: wissend
Imperative: wisse! wißt! wissen Sie!

12.3 The compound tenses

12.3.1 The conjugation of the verb in the compound tenses

(a) The perfect and future are formed with the auxiliary verbs *sein*, *haben* and *werden*
The perfect tenses are formed with the past participle and *haben* or *sein* and the future is constructed using *werden* and the infinitive. Examples of these tenses:

the **perfect**,   e.g. *ich habe gesungen* 'I have sung'
the **pluperfect**,   e.g. *ich hatte gesungen* 'I had sung'
the **future**,   e.g. *ich werde singen* 'I shall sing'
the **future perfect**, e.g. *ich werde gesungen haben* 'I shall have sung'

Full forms of all these tenses are given in Table 12.5 for the weak verb *kaufen* 'buy' and the strong verb *singen* 'sing', which form their perfect tenses with the auxiliary *haben*, and for the strong verb *bleiben* 'remain' which forms its perfect tenses with the auxiliary *sein*. The uses of the tenses are explained in detail in Chapter 14.

(b) The non-finite parts of these compound tenses are placed at the end of the clause in main clauses
i.e. they constitute the final part of the 'verbal bracket', see 21.1.2, e.g. *Ich **habe** sie gestern in der Stadt **gesehen**.*
   In subordinate clauses the auxiliary usually follows the non-finite part at the end of the clause, see 21.1.3, e.g. *Sie wissen, daß ich sie gestern in der Stadt **gesehen habe**.*

TABLE 12.5 *Compound tenses of strong and weak verbs*

	With haben				With sein	
Perfect	ich habe	gekauft	habe	gesungen	bin	geblieben
	du hast	gekauft	hast	gesungen	bist	geblieben
	es hat	gekauft	hat	gesungen	ist	geblieben
	wir haben	gekauft	haben	gesungen	sind	geblieben
	ihr habt	gekauft	habt	gesungen	seid	geblieben
	Sie haben	gekauft	haben	gesungen	sind	geblieben
	sie haben	gekauft	haben	gesungen	sind	geblieben
Pluperfect	ich hatte	gekauft	hatte	gesungen	war	geblieben
	du hattest	gekauft	hattest	gesungen	warst	geblieben
	es hatte	gekauft	hatte	gesungen	war	geblieben
	wir hatten	gekauft	hatten	gesungen	waren	geblieben
	ihr hatten	gekauft	hattet	gesungen	wart	geblieben
	Sie hatten	gekauft	hatten	gesungen	waren	geblieben
	sie haben	gekauft	hatten	gesungen	waren	geblieben
Future	ich werde	kaufen	werde	singen	werde	bleiben
	du wirst	kaufen	wirst	singen	wirst	bleiben
	es wird	kaufen	wird	singen	wird	bleiben
	wir werden	kaufen	werden	singen	werden	bleiben
	ihr werdet	kaufen	werdet	singen	werdet	bleiben
	Sie werden	kaufen	werden	singen	werden	bleiben
	sie werden	kaufen	werden	singen	werden	bleiben
Future perfect	ich werde	gekauft haben	werde	gesungen haben	werde	geblieben sein
	du wirst	gekauft haben	wirst	gesungen haben	wirst	geblieben sein
	es wird	gekauft haben	wird	gesungen haben	wird	geblieben sein
	wir werden	gekauft haben	werden	gesungen haben	werden	geblieben sein
	ihr werdet	gekauft haben	werdet	gesungen haben	werdet	geblieben sein
	Sie werden	gekauft haben	werden	gesungen haben	werden	geblieben sein
	sie werden	gekauft haben	werden	gesungen haben	werden	geblieben sein

12.3.2 *haben* or *sein* in the perfect?

Whether the perfect tense is constructed with *haben* or *sein* depends on the meaning of the verb.

(a) The following groups of verbs form their perfect with *sein*

All these verbs are *intransitive*, i.e. they do not have a direct object in the accusative case (see 18.3):

(i) Intransitive verbs of motion:

> Ich **bin** in die Stadt gegangen   Wir **sind** aus dem Haus entkommen
> Sie **war** zum Boden gefallen   Ihr **wart** auf die Mauer geklettert
> Um die Zeit werden wir schon angekommen **sein**

NB: Some verbs of motion take *sein* or *haben* in different contexts, see (c) below.

(ii) Intransitive verbs expressing a change of state. This group includes a large number of verbs which point to the beginning or end of a process, notably those with the prefixes *er-* and *ver-* (see 22.4):

> Sie **ist** schon eingeschlafen   Die Bombe **ist** um zwei Uhr explodiert
> Das Licht **ist** ausgegangen   Mein Buch **ist** verschwunden

Die Glocke **ist** erklungen   Die Blumen **sind** verwelkt
Der Reifen **war** geplatzt   Der Schnee **war** schon geschmolzen
Sie werden gleich danach ertrunken **sein**

NB: In colloquial north German, *anfangen* and *beginnen* form their perfect with *sein*. One thus hears *ich bin angefangen, begonnen* for standard German *ich habe angefangen, begonnen*.

(iii) Most verbs meaning 'happen', 'succeed', 'fail', i.e.:

begegnen	*meet* (by chance)	glücken	*succeed*	vorgehen	*happen*
fehlschlagen	*fail*	mißglücken	*fail*	vorkommen	*occur*
gelingen	*succeed*	mißlingen	*fail*	zustoßen	*happen*
geschehen	*happen*	passieren	*happen*		

Ich **bin** ihr gestern begegnet   Der Plan **ist** fehlgeschlagen
Es **war** mir gelungen, ihn zu überzeugen   Das **war** schon einmal vorgekommen
Was wird mit ihr passiert **sein**?

NB: The colloquial verb *klappen* 'succeed' takes *haben*, e.g. *Hat's mit den Karten geklappt?* 'Did you manage to get the tickets?'

(iv) The verbs *bleiben* and *sein*:

Sie **ist** früher Lehrerin gewesen   Wir **sind** in Dessau geblieben
War er mal Diplomat gewesen?   Sie wird dort geblieben **sein**

(b) All other verbs form their perfect tenses with *haben*

This includes the majority of German verbs. The most important fall into the following groups:

(i) Transitive verbs, i.e. those taking an accusative object (see 18.3):

Ich **habe** sie gesehen   Sie **hat** ihn geschlagen   Er **hat** die Wohnung geputzt
Der Hund **hatte** die Mülltonne umgeworfen
Ich werde den Brief bis morgen früh geschrieben **haben**

A few compounds of *gehen* and *werden* are exceptions to this rule, e.g.:

Er **ist** die Strecke abgegangen   *He paced the distance*
Sie **ist** die Arbeit mit dem Schüler   *She went through the work with the pupil*
durchgegangen
Er **ist** die Wette eingegangen   *He made the bet*
Ich **bin** ihn endlich losgeworden   *I have finally got rid of him*

(ii) Reflexive verbs

Sie **hat** sich sehr gefreut   Ich **habe** mich schon erholt
Ich **hatte** mich aus dem Zimmer gestohlen   Ich **hatte** mir alles eingebildet
Sie wird sich müde gelaufen **haben**

When verbs which normally form their perfect with *sein* are used with a reciprocal reflexive pronoun in the dative (= 'each other', cf. 3.2.7), the perfect is still constructed with *sein*, e.g.:

Sie sind sich ausgewichen   *They avoided each other*
Wir sind uns in der Stadt begegnet   *We met (each other) in town*

(iii) Intransitive verbs which do not express motion or a change of state, (cf. (a) above). Most of these verbs denote a continuous action, e.g.:

Ich **habe** gestern lange gearbeitet   **Hast** du in der Nacht gut geschlafen?
Dort **hat** jemand auf der Bank gesessen   Oben **hat** vorhin das Licht gebrannt

Sie **hatte** dabei gepfiffen   Sie **hatten** in Münster studiert
Sie wird dort lange gewartet **haben**

The verbs *liegen*, *sitzen* and *stehen* form their perfect tenses with *haben* in standard German, e.g. *ich* **habe** *gelegen, gesessen, gestanden*. However, in south German, *sein* is commonly used (i.e. *ich* **bin** *gelegen*, etc.) and this usage is accepted in writing in Austria and Switzerland.

(iv) Most impersonal verbs:

Es **hat** geregnet, geschneit, gehagelt   An der Tür **hat** es geklopft
Es **hatte** nach Benzin gerochen   Da **hatte** es einen Krach gegeben

Impersonal expressions with verbs which usually form their perfect tenses with *sein* form an exception to this rule, e.g.:

Es **ist** mir kalt geworden   Wie **war** es Ihnen in Berlin gegangen?

(v) The modal auxiliaries:

Ich **habe** es hinnehmen müssen   Sie **hat** ihn besuchen wollen
Wir **haben** es nicht gekonnt   Sie **hat** ihn nie gemocht

(c) The use of *haben* and *sein* with the same verb

(i) The choice of *haben* or *sein* depends on meaning, i.e. it is not an automatic feature of a particular verb. In this way, many verbs which have more than one meaning, or which can be used transitively or intransitively, can be used with *haben* and *sein* in the perfect as their meaning varies between the categories explained in (a) and (b) above. Thus, *fahren*, used as an intransitive verb of motion (= 'go'), forms its perfect with *sein*:

Sie **ist** nach Stuttgart gefahren   Wir **sind** zu schnell gefahren

But when it is used transitively (= 'drive'), it takes *haben*:

Sie **hat** einen neuen Porsche gefahren   Ich **habe** ihn nach Hause gefahren

Selected further examples:

Ich **habe** einen Brief bekommen	*I have received a letter*
Das Essen **ist** mir gut bekommen	*The meal agreed with me*
Er **hat** das Rohr gebrochen	*He has broken the pipe*
Das Rohr **ist** gebrochen	*The pipe has broken*
Sie **hat** auf Zahlung gedrungen	*She has pressed for payment*
Wasser **ist** in das Haus gedrungen	*Water has penetrated into the house*
Er **hat** ihr gefolgt	*He has obeyed her*
Er **ist** ihr gefolgt	*He has followed her*
Es **hat** in der Nacht gefroren	*There was a frost in the night*
Der See **ist** gefroren	*The lake has frozen*
Da **haben** Sie sich geirrt	*You have made a mistake*
Er **ist** durch die Straßen geirrt	*He roamed through the streets*
Sie **hat** ihn zur Seite gestoßen	*She pushed him to one side*
Ich **bin** an den Schrank gestoßen	*I bumped into the cupboard*
Du **hast** mir den Spaß verdorben	*You have spoilt my fun*
Das Fleisch **ist** verdorben	*The meat has gone bad*
Ich **habe** die Vase zerbrochen	*I have broken the vase*
Die Vase **ist** zerbrochen	*The vase has broken*

(ii) A few verbs of motion can form their perfect with *sein* if they express movement from one place to another, but *haben* if they just refer to the activity as such, without any idea of getting somewhere, e.g.:

Ich **habe** als junger Mann viel getanzt	*I danced a lot when I was a young man*
Er **ist** aus dem Zimmer getanzt	*He danced out of the room*
Sie **hat** den ganzen Morgen gesegelt	*She's been sailing the whole morning*
Sie **ist** über den See gesegelt	*She sailed across the lake*

This usage is more frequent in north Germany, and in practice it is now restricted to only a few verbs, i.e. *paddeln* 'paddle', *reiten* 'ride', *rudern* 'row', *schwimmen* 'swim', *segeln* 'sail', *tanzen* 'dance', *treten* 'step'.

12.4 The passive

12.4.1 German has two passives, formed by combining the auxiliary verbs *werden* or *sein* and the past participle

The passive with *werden* is sometimes referred to as the *Vorgangspassiv* in German, and the passive with *sein* as the *Zustandspassiv*. The uses of these two types of passive are dealt with fully in Chapter 15. The forms of both passives which are in current use are given in Table 12.6.

TABLE 12.6 *Forms of the passive*

werden-passive

Present		Past		Perfect	
ich werde	gelobt	wurde	gelobt	bin	gelobt worden
du wirst	gelobt	wurdest	gelobt	bist	gelobt worden
es wird	gelobt	wurde	gelobt	ist	gelobt worden
wir werden	gelobt	wurden	gelobt	sind	gelobt worden
ihr werdet	gelobt	wurdet	gelobt	seid	gelobt worden
Sie werden	gelobt	wurden	gelobt	sind	gelobt worden
sie werden	gelobt	wurden	gelobt	sind	gelobt worden

Pluperfect		Future		Future perfect	
ich war	gelobt worden	werde	gelobt werden	werde	gelobt worden sein
du warst	gelobt worden	wirst	gelobt werden	wirst	gelobt worden sein
es war	gelobt worden	wird	gelobt werden	wird	gelobt worden sein
wir waren	gelobt worden	werden	gelobt werden	werden	gelobt worden sein
ihr wart	gelobt worden	werdet	gelobt werden	werdet	gelobt worden sein
Sie waren	gelobt worden	werden	gelobt werden	werden	gelobt worden sein
sie waren	gelobt worden	werden	gelobt werden	werden	gelobt worden sein

sein-passive

Present		Past		Imperative
ich bin	verletzt	ich war	verletzt	Sei gegrüßt!
du bist	verletzt	du warst	verletzt	Seid gegrüßt!
es ist	verletzt	es war	verletzt	Seien Sie gegrüßt!
wir sind	verletzt	wir waren	verletzt	
ihr seid	verletzt	ihr wart	verletzt	
Sie sind	verletzt	Sie waren	verletzt	
sie sind	verletzt	sie waren	verletzt	

12.4.2 Notes on the formation of the passive

(a) The *werden*-passive
(i) A form of the past participle of *werden* without *ge-*, i.e. *worden*, is used in the perfect tenses of the passive, e.g. *Das Haus ist 1845 gebaut **worden***.

(ii) Imperative forms of the *werden*-passive, e.g. *werde gelobt!* are rare. If a passive imperative is needed, the form with *sein* is used, see (b) below.

(b) The *sein*-passive
In practice, only the present and past tenses of the *sein*-passive, and the imperative, are at all frequently used. Other tenses, e.g. the perfect (*ich bin verletzt gewesen*, etc.) or the future (*ich werde verletzt sein*, etc.) are only used occasionally.

(c) The participle is placed at the end of the clause in main clauses
i.e., as in other compound verb forms, cf. 21.1.1a, e.g.:

Das Haus wurde 1845 **gebaut**   Das Kind war schwer **verletzt**

In subordinate clauses the participle comes at the end, before the auxiliary, cf. 21.1.3, e.g.:

Ich weiß, daß das Haus voriges Jahr **gebaut** wurde

12.5 The subjunctive

Most recent German grammars distinguish two major forms of the subjunctive, i.e. '*Konjunktiv I*' and '*Konjunktiv II*'. Each of these has a simple form, and various compound forms constructed with auxiliary verbs in a similar way to the tenses and the passive forms of the indicative. These forms are traditionally termed 'present subjunctive', 'perfect subjunctive', etc., but they do not express time differences in the same way as the tenses of the indicative, as is explained in Chapter 16.

12.5.1 *Konjunktiv I*

(a) The simple form of *Konjunktiv I* is regular for all verbs except *sein*
The forms of this (traditionally called the 'present subjunctive') are given for a few representative verbs in Table 12.7. Further points to note:

(i) The second person singular and plural forms in *-est* and *-et* (e.g. *du sagest, ihr saget*, are felt to be artificial and are seldom used. This means that for most verbs except *sein*, the only difference in practice between *Konjunktiv I* and the present indicative is in the third person singular.

(ii) There are no vowel changes with any strong or irregular verbs. Compare subjunctive *er gebe, er fahre* with indicative *er gibt, er fährt*.

(iii) The verbs with a stem in *-el* (cf. 12.2.1c) usually drop the *-e-* of the stem before the ending *-e*, e.g. *es segle, es lächle*, etc.

(b) Compound forms of *Konjunktiv I*
Compound perfect and future tenses of *Konjunktiv I*, and *werden-* and *sein-*passives, are constructed in the same way as in the indicative, using the auxiliary

TABLE 12.7 Konjunktiv I

Simple forms	kaufen	bleiben	kommen	können	werden	haben	sein
ich	kaufe	bleibe	komme	könne	werde	habe	sei
du	kaufest	bleibest	kommest	könnest	werdest	habest	sei(e)st
es	kaufe	bleibe	komme	könne	werde	habe	sei
wir	kaufen	bleiben	kommen	können	werden	haben	seien
ihr	kaufet	bleibet	kommet	könnet	werdet	habet	seiet
Sie	kaufen	bleiben	kommen	können	werden	haben	seien
sie	kaufen	bleiben	kommen	können	werden	haben	seien

Compound forms	Perfect (+ *haben*)		Perfect (+ *sein*)		Future		*sein*-passive	
ich	habe	gekauft	sei	geblieben	werde	kaufen	sei	gekauft
du	habest	gekauft	sei(e)st	geblieben	werdest	kaufen	sei(e)st	gekauft
es	habe	gekauft	sei	geblieben	werde	kaufen	sei	gekauft
wir	haben	gekauft	seien	geblieben	werden	kaufen	seien	gekauft
ihr	habet	gekauft	seiet	geblieben	werdet	kaufen	seiet	gekauft
Sie	haben	gekauft	seien	geblieben	werden	kaufen	seien	gekauft
sie	haben	gekauft	seien	geblieben	werden	kaufen	seien	gekauft

	werden-passive (pres.)		*werden*-passive (perf.)		*werden*-passive (future)	
ich	werde	gekauft	sei	gekauft worden	werde	gekauft werden
du	werdest	gekauft	sei(e)st	gekauft worden	werdest	gekauft werden
es	werde	gekauft	sei	gekauft worden	werde	gekauft werden
wir	werden	gekauft	seien	gekauft worden	werden	gekauft werden
ihr	werdet	gekauft	seiet	gekauft worden	werdet	gekauft werden
Sie	werden	gekauft	seien	gekauft worden	werden	gekauft werden
sie	werden	gekauft	seien	gekauft worden	werden	gekauft werden

verbs *haben*, *sein* or *werden* together with the past participle or the infinitive. They are illustrated below for the third person singular, which is the most commonly used form and where the difference from the indicative is clear, with their traditional names:

Simple form of *Konjunktiv I* ('present subjunctive')	*es habe* *es komme*
Perfect form of *Konjunktiv I* ('perfect subjunctive' with *haben* or *sein*)	*es habe gehabt* *es sei gekommen*
Future form of *Konjunktiv I* ('future subjunctive')	*es werde haben* *es werde kommen*

werden-passive of *Konjunktiv I* ('present subjunctive of *werden*-passive')	*es werde gekauft*
Perfect of *werden*-passive of *Konjunktiv I* ('perfect subjunctive of *werden*-passive')	*es sei gekauft worden*
sein-passive of *Konjunktiv I* ('present subjunctive of *sein*-passive')	*es sei gekauft*

12.5.2 *Konjunktiv II*

(a) The forms of *Konjunktiv II*

Konjunktiv II, like *Konjunktiv I* and the indicative, has a simple, one-word form, and compound forms constructed by using auxiliary verbs and the infinitive or the past participle. These are illustrated below, with their traditional names:

Simple form of *Konjunktiv II* ⎱ ('past subjunctive') ⎰	*ich hätte* *ich käme*
Perfect form of *Konjunktiv II* ⎱ ('pluperfect subjunctive' with *haben* or *sein*) ⎰	*ich hätte gehabt* *ich wäre gekommen*
Future form of *Konjunktiv II* ⎱ ('conditional', with *würde*) ⎰	*ich würde haben* *ich würde kommen*
werden-passive of *Konjunktiv II* ('past subjunctive of *werden*-passive')	*es würde gekauft (werden)*
Perfect of *werden*-passive of *Konjunktiv II* ('pluperfect subjunctive of *werden*-passive')	*es wäre gekauft worden*
sein-passive of *Konjunktiv II* ('past subjunctive of *sein*-passive')	*es wäre gekauft*

Full paradigms of these *Konjunktiv II* forms are given for a representative selection of verbs in Table 12.8. Further details on the formation of *Konjunktiv II* are given in the remainder of this section.

TABLE 12.8 Konjunktiv II

Simple forms	kaufen	bleiben	kommen	können	werden	haben	sein
	ich kaufte	bliebe	käme	könnte	würde	hätte	wäre
	du kauftest	bliebest	kämest	könntest	würdest	hättest	wärest
	es kaufte	bliebe	käme	könnte	würde	hätte	wäre
	wir kauften	blieben	kämen	könnten	würden	hätten	wären
	ihr kauftet	bliebet	kämet	könntet	würdet	hättet	wäret
	Sie kauften	blieben	kämen	könnten	würden	hätten	wären
	sie kauften	blieben	kämen	könnten	würden	hätten	wären

Compound forms	Pluperfect (+ *haben*)	Pluperfect (+ *sein*)	Conditional
	ich hätte gekauft	wäre geblieben	würde kaufen
	du hättest gekauft	wärest geblieben	würdest kaufen
	es hätte gekauft	wäre geblieben	würde kaufen
	wir hätten gekauft	wären geblieben	würden kaufen
	ihr hättet gekauft	wäret geblieben	würdet kaufen
	Sie hätten gekauft	wären geblieben	würden kaufen
	sie hätten gekauft	wären geblieben	würden kaufen

	werden-passive		*werden*-passive (Pluperf.)		*sein*-passive	
	ich würde	gekauft	wäre	gekauft worden	wäre	gekauft
	du würdest	gekauft	wärest	gekauft worden	wärest	gekauft
	es würde	gekauft	wäre	gekauft worden	wäre	gekauft
	wir würden	gekauft	wären	gekauft worden	wären	gekauft
	ihr würdet	gekauft	wäret	gekauft worden	wäret	gekauft
	Sie würden	gekauft	wären	gekauft worden	wären	gekauft
	sie würden	gekauft	wären	gekauft worden	wären	gekauft

(b) The simple form of *Konjunktiv II* (traditionally called the 'past subjunctive') is similar to the past tense of the indicative

(i) For most weak verbs it is in fact identical to the past indicative, e.g. *ich kaufte, du kauftest, er kaufte*, etc.

(ii) For strong verbs, it is formed by taking the form of the past indicative, umlauting the vowel if possible, and adding *-e* to the singular endings. Examples for common verbs:

Verb	Past indicative	*Konj. II*	Verb	Past indicative	*Konj. II*
bleiben	blieb	ich bliebe	**kommen**	kam	ich käme
geben	gab	ich gäbe	**lassen**	ließ	ich ließe
gehen	ging	ich ginge	**tun**	tat	ich täte
fahren	fuhr	ich führe	**ziehen**	zog	ich zöge

NB: The *-e* of these endings is often dropped in speech.

The formation of *Konjunktiv II* for all strong verbs is given in Table 12.8. A few strong verbs have an irregular *Konjunktiv II* form with a different vowel from the past indicative. Details are given in Table 12.9; in practice, only the following are commonly used:

helfen	ich hülfe (less common hälfe)
stehen	ich stünde (less common stände)
sterben	ich stürbe

(iii) Some irregular verbs also have *Umlaut* in the simple *Konjunktiv II*. The most frequent are given below:

sein	ich wäre	dürfen	ich dürfte	wissen	ich wüßte
haben	ich hätte	können	ich könnte	bringen	ich brächte
werden	ich würde	mögen	ich möchte	denken	ich dächte
		müssen	ich müßte		

In colloquial (especially south German) speech, *brauchen* 'need' also often has a *Konjunktiv II* form with *Umlaut*, e.g. *ich bräuchte*, etc. DUDEN (1985: 145) considers this usage to be substandard, but it is widespread and increasingly common in writing.

(c) The simple form of *Konjunktiv II* and the compound form with *würde*

The compound 'conditional' form with *würde* is often used rather than the simple ('past subjunctive') form of *Konjunktiv II*, so that, for example, *ich würde kommen* commonly substitutes for *ich käme*. Which form is preferred depends on register and the individual verb involved. Current usage is explained fully in 16.4.4; it can be summarised briefly as follows:

(i) The simple forms of the weak verbs and those of many less frequent strong verbs are only used in formal writing. Indeed, a fair number of simple forms of strong verbs (e.g. *ich flöge, ich röche*) are felt to be stilted and avoided entirely. These are indicated in Table 12.9.

(ii) On the other hand, with the most common verbs, in particular *haben, sein, werden* and the modal auxiliaries, the simple form is much more common than the compound form in *both* writing *and* everyday speech.

Notes on the use of Table 12.9:

This table gives the principal parts, i.e. the infinitive, the past tense and the past participle, of all strong and irregular verbs, with the exception of the wholly irregular verbs (see Table 12.3).

(a) The third person singular of the present tense is given for those verbs which have vowel changes (cf. 12.2.1e/f).
(b) The simple form of *Konjunktiv II* (cf. 12.5.2b) is given for all verbs listed, but it is enclosed in square brackets if it is rarely used (cf. 12.5.2c).
(c) The auxiliary used to form the perfect tenses (cf. 12.3.2b) is indicated by *hat* or *ist* alongside the past participle.
(d) Less common alternative forms are given in brackets after the more common ones.
(e) In principle, simple forms of the verbs (i.e. without prefixes) are given if they exist, even if prefixed forms may be commoner. As a rule, compound verbs conjugate in the same way as the simple verb from which they are derived; apparent exceptions to this are noted.
(f) Where appropriate, notes on the forms are given below the verb.

TABLE 12.9 *Principal parts of strong and irregular verbs*

Infinitive 3rd. sing. pres.	Past indicative *Konjunktiv II*	Past participle
backen *bake* es **bäckt**	**backte** (buk) [büke]	hat **gebacken**

NB: *es backt* is frequent in speech. *buk* is still quite common in writing.

befehlen *command* es **befiehlt**	**befahl** [beföhle (befähle)]	hat **befohlen**

NB: (i) *empfehlen* 'recommend' has similar forms.
(ii) *fehlen* 'lack' is weak, i.e. *fehlte, gefehlt.*

beginnen *begin*	**begann** begänne [(begönne)]	hat **begonnen**
beißen *bite*	**biß** bisse	hat **gebissen**
bergen *rescue; hide* es **birgt**	**barg** [bärge]	hat **geborgen**
bersten *crack, burst* es **birst** (berstet)	**barst** [bärste]	hat **geborsten**
bewegen *induce*	**bewog** [bewöge]	hat **bewogen**

NB: *bewegen* 'move' is weak, i.e. *bewegte, bewegt.*

biegen *bend; turn*	**bog** [böge]	hat/ist **gebogen**
bieten *offer*	**bot** [böte]	hat **geboten**
binden *bind*	**band** bände	hat **gebunden**

TABLE 12.9 *Principal parts of strong and irregular verbs – continued*

Infinitive 3rd. sing. pres.	Past indicative *Konjunktiv II*	Past participle
bitten *ask, request*	**bat** [bäte]	hat **gebeten**
blasen *blow* es bläst	**blies** [bliese]	hat **geblasen**
bleiben *stay, remain*	**blieb** bliebe	ist **geblieben**
braten *fry, roast* es brät (bratet)	**briet** [briete]	hat **gebraten**
brechen *break* es bricht	**brach** bräche	hat/ist **gebrochen**
brennen *burn*	**brannte** [brennte]	hat **gebrannt**
bringen *bring*	**brachte** brächte	hat **gebracht**
denken *think*	**dachte** dächte	hat **gedacht**
dreschen *thresh* es drischt	**drosch** [drösche]	hat **gedroschen**
dingen *hire, engage* (i.e. servant)	**dingte** (dang) [dingte/dänge]	hat **gedungen**

NB: Simple *dingen* is archaic, but the compound *sich (etwas) ausbedingen* 'make (sth.) a condition' is still found in formal registers. It is always strong, with the forms *bedang sich ... aus, ausbedungen.*

dringen *penetrate*	**drang** [dränge]	hat/ist **gedrungen**

empfehlen *recommend* has the same forms as *befehlen*, q.v.

erkiesen *choose*	**erkor** [erköre]	hat **erkoren**

NB: Only the past tense and the past participle are now used, in elevated styles.

erlöschen *go out* (of lights) es erlischt	**erlosch** [erlösche]	ist **erloschen**

NB: Transitive *löschen* 'extinguish' is weak, i.e. *löschte, gelöscht.*

erschrecken *be startled* es erschrickt	**erschrak** [erschräke]	ist **erschrocken**

NB: Transitive *erschrecken* 'frighten' is weak, i.e. *erschreckte, erschreckt.*

essen *eat* es ißt	**aß** äße	hat **gegessen**
fahren *go, drive* es fährt	**fuhr** führe	ist/hat **gefahren**

TABLE 12.9 *Principal parts of strong and irregular verbs – continued*

Infinitive 3rd. sing. pres.	Past indicative *Konjunktiv II*	Past participle
fallen *fall* es fällt	**fiel** fiele	ist **gefallen**
fangen *catch* es fängt	**fing** finge	hat **gefangen**
fechten *fight, fence* es ficht	**focht** [föchte]	hat **gefochten**
finden *find*	**fand** fände	hat **gefunden**
flechten *plait, braid* es flicht	**flocht** [flöchte]	hat **geflochten**
fliegen *fly*	**flog** [flöge]	ist/hat **geflogen**
fliehen *flee*	**floh** [flöhe]	ist **geflohen**
fließen *flow*	**floß** [flösse]	ist **geflossen**
fragen *ask* er fragt (frägt)	**fragte** (frug) fragte	hat **gefragt**

NB: In standard German *fragen* is weak. *frägt* is colloquial South German. *frug* is occasional in literary registers.

fressen *eat* (of animals) es frißt	**fraß** [fräße]	hat **gefressen**
frieren *freeze*	**fror** [fröre]	hat/ist **gefroren**
gären *ferment*	**gor/gärte** [göre/gärte]	hat/ist **gegoren/ gegärt**

NB: The strong forms are more usual when the verb is used in a literal sense, the weak ones when it is used figuratively.

gebären *give birth* es gebärt (gebiert)	**gebar** [gebäre]	hat **geboren**
geben *give* es gibt	**gab** gäbe	hat **gegeben**
gedeihen *thrive*	**gedieh** [gediehe]	ist **gediehen**
gehen *go*	**ging** ginge	ist **gegangen**
gelingen *succeed*	**gelang** gelänge	ist **gelungen**

NB: *mißlingen* 'fail' has similar forms.

gelten *be valid* es gilt	**galt** [gälte (gölte)]	hat **gegolten**

TABLE 12.9 *Principal parts of strong and irregular verbs – continued*

Infinitive 3rd. sing. pres.	Past indicative *Konjunktiv II*	Past participle
genesen *recover* (elev.)	**genas** [genäse]	ist **genesen**
genießen *enjoy*	**genoß** [genösse]	hat **genossen**
geschehen *happen* es geschieht	**geschah** geschähe	ist **geschehen**
gewinnen *win*	**gewann** [gewänne/gewönne]	hat **gewonnen**
gießen *pour*	**goß** [gösse]	hat **gegossen**
gleichen *resemble*	**glich** gliche	hat **geglichen**
gleiten *glide, slide*	**glitt** [glitte]	ist **geglitten**

NB: *begleiten* 'accompany' is weak, i.e. *begleitete, begleitet*.

glimmen *glimmer*	**glomm/glimmte** [glömme/glimmte]	hat **geglommen/** **geglimmt**

NB: This verb is restricted to formal literary language. Strong and weak forms are equally common.

graben *dig* es gräbt	**grub** [grübe]	hat **gegraben**
greifen *grasp*	**griff** griffe	hat **gegriffen**
halten *hold; stop* es hält	**hielt** hielte	hat **gehalten**

NB: The compound verbs *beinhalten* 'comprise' and *haushalten* 'be economical' are weak.

hängen *hang* (intrans.)	**hing** hinge	hat **gehangen**

NB: The transitive verb *hängen* 'hang' is weak, i.e. *hängte, gehängt*.

hauen *hew, cut*	**haute (hieb)** [haute (hiebe)]	hat **gehauen** (gehaut)

NB: The strong past form *hieb* is used, in formal literary German only, in the meaning 'hew', 'cut (with a sword)'. The weak past participle *gehaut* is regional and colloquial.

heben *lift*	**hob (hub)** [höbe (hübe)]	hat **gehoben**

NB: The alternative forms *hub* and *hübe* are archaic, but still occasionally used in formal literary registers, particularly with the compound *anheben* 'commence'.

heißen *be called*	**hieß** hieße	hat **geheißen**

TABLE 12.9 *Principal parts of strong and irregular verbs – continued*

Infinitive 3rd. sing. pres.	Past indicative *Konjunktiv II*	Past participle
helfen *help* es hilft	**half** [hülfe (hälfe)]	hat **geholfen**
kennen *know*	**kannte** kennte	hat **gekannt**
klimmen *climb*	**klomm** (klimmte) [klömme]	hat **geklommen** (geklimmt)

NB: Simple *klimmen* is rarely used, but the compound *erklimmen* 'scale', is still found in literary registers. It only has strong forms.

klingen *sound*	**klang** klänge	hat **geklungen**
kneifen *pinch*	**kniff** kniffe	hat **gekniffen**
kommen *come*	**kam** käme	ist **gekommen**
kriechen *creep, crawl*	**kroch** [kröche]	ist **gekrochen**
küren *choose*	**kürte** (kor) [kürte/köre]	hat **gekürt** (gekoren)

NB: The strong forms are occasionally used in elevated registers.

laden *load; invite* es lädt (ladet)	**lud** [lüde]	hat **geladen**

NB: *ladet* is regional, and only used in the sense 'invite', or with the compound *einladen*.

lassen *leave; let* es läßt	**ließ** ließe	hat **gelassen**

NB: *veranlassen* 'cause' is weak, i.e. *veranlaßte, veranlaßt*.

laufen *run* es läuft	**lief** liefe	ist/hat **gelaufen**
leiden *suffer*	**litt** litte	hat **gelitten**

NB: *verleiden* 'spoil' is weak, i.e. *verleidete, verleidet*.

leihen *lend; borrow*	**lieh** liehe	hat **geliehen**
lesen *read* es liest	**las** [läse]	hat **gelesen**
liegen *lie*	**lag** läge	hat **gelegen**
lügen *tell lies*	**log** [löge]	hat **gelogen**
mahlen *grind*	**mahlte** mahlte	hat **gemahlen**

TABLE 12.9 *Principal parts of strong and irregular verbs – continued*

Infinitive 3rd. sing. pres.	Past indicative *Konjunktiv II*	Past participle
meiden *avoid*	**mied** miede	hat **gemieden**
melken *milk* es melkt (milkt)	**melkte** (molk) [melkte]	hat **gemolken** (gemelkt)
messen *measure* es mißt	**maß** [mäße]	hat **gemessen**
nehmen *take* es nimmt	**nahm** nähme	hat **genommen**
nennen *name, call*	**nannte** [nennte]	hat **genannt**
pfeifen *whistle*	**pfiff** pfiffe	hat **gepfiffen**
preisen *praise*	**pries** priese	hat **gepriesen**
quellen *gush, well up* es quillt	**quoll** [quölle]	ist **gequollen**
raten *advise* es rät	**riet** riete	hat **geraten**
reiben *rub*	**rieb** riebe	hat **gerieben**
reißen *tear*	**riß** risse	hat/ist **gerissen**
reiten *ride* (a horse)	**ritt** ritte	hat/ist **geritten**
rennen *run*	**rannte** [rennte]	hat/ist **gerannt**
riechen *smell*	**roch** [röche]	hat **gerochen**
ringen *wrestle*	**rang** [ränge]	hat **gerungen**
rinnen *flow, trickle*	**rann** [ränne (rönne)]	ist **geronnen**
rufen *call, cry*	**rief** riefe	hat **gerufen**
salzen *salt*	**salzte** [salzte]	hat **gesalzen** (gesalzt)

NB: In a figurative sense, only the form *gesalzen* is used, e.g. *gesalzene Preise*.

saufen *booze;* *drink* (of animals) es säuft	**soff** [söffe]	hat **gesoffen**
saugen *suck*	**saugte/sog** [saugte/söge]	hat **gesaugt/gesogen**

TABLE 12.9 *Principal parts of strong and irregular verbs – continued*

Infinitive 3rd. sing. pres.	Past indicative *Konjunktiv II*	Past participle
NB: In technical language only the weak forms are used, especially in the compound *staubsaugen* 'vacuum'.		
schaffen *create*	**schuf** [schüfe]	hat **geschaffen**
NB: *schaffen* is weak (*schaffte, geschafft*) in the meaning 'manage, work'.		
scheiden *separate; depart*	**schied** schiede	hat/ist **geschieden**
scheinen *seem; shine*	**schien** schiene	hat **geschienen**
scheißen *shit* (vulg.)	**schiß** [schisse]	hat **geschissen**
schelten *scold* es schilt	**schalt** [schölte]	hat **gescholten**
scheren *shear, clip*	**schor** [schöre]	hat **geschoren**
NB: *scheren* is weak (i.e. *scherte, geschert*) in the meaning 'concern', as is the reflexive *sich scheren* 'bother about'; 'clear off'.		
schieben *push, shove*	**schob** [schöbe]	hat **geschoben**
schießen *shoot*	**schoß** [schösse]	hat/ist **geschossen**
schinden *flay, ill-treat*	(schindete)	hat **geschunden**
NB: In practice, this verb is not used in the past tense.		
schlafen *sleep* es schläft	**schlief** schliefe	hat **geschlafen**
schlagen *hit, beat* es schlägt	**schlug** schlüge	hat **geschlagen**
schleichen *creep*	**schlich** schliche	ist **geschlichen**
schleifen *grind, sharpen*	**schliff** schliffe	hat **geschliffen**
NB: *schleifen* is weak (i.e. *schleifte, geschleift*) in the meaning 'drag'.		
schließen *shut*	**schloß** schlösse	hat **geschlossen**
schlingen *wind, wrap*	**schlang** [schlänge]	hat **geschlungen**
schmeißen *chuck* (coll.)	**schmiß** schmisse	hat **geschmissen**
schmelzen *melt* es schmilzt (schmelzt)	**schmolz** (schmelzte) [schmölze]	hat/ist **geschmolzen** (geschmelzt)
NB: The weak forms are only used with transitive *schmelzen*, and are less frequent even then.		

TABLE 12.9 *Principal parts of strong and irregular verbs – continued*

Infinitive 3rd. sing. pres.	Past indicative *Konjunktiv II*	Past participle
schneiden *cut*	**schnitt** schnitte	hat **geschnitten**
schreiben *write*	**schrieb** schriebe	hat **geschrieben**
schreien *shout, scream*	**schrie** [schriee]	hat **geschrie(e)n**
schreiten *stride*	**schritt** schritte	ist **geschritten**
schweigen *be silent*	**schwieg** schwiege	hat **geschwiegen**
schwellen *swell* es schwillt	**schwoll** [schwölle]	ist **geschwollen**

NB: *schwellen* is weak (i.e. *schwellte, geschwellt*) used transitively.

schwimmen *swim*	**schwamm** [schwömme (schwämme)]	ist/hat **geschwommen**
schwinden *disappear*	**schwand** schwände	ist **geschwunden**
schwingen *swing*	**schwang** [schwänge]	hat **geschwungen**
schwören *swear*	**schwor** (schwur) [schwüre (schwöre)]	hat **geschworen**

NB: *schwur* is only found in old-fashioned literary German.

sehen *see* es sieht	**sah** sähe	hat **gesehen**
senden *send*	**sendete/sandte** sendete	hat **gesendet/gesandt**

NB: Only regular forms (*sendete, gesendet*) are used in technical senses, (i.e. = 'broadcast'). Otherwise the irregular forms are commoner.

sieden *boil* (elev.; south German)	**siedete/sott** [siedete (sötte)]	hat **gesotten** (gesiedet)
singen *sing*	**sang** sänge	hat **gesungen**
sinken *sink*	**sank** [sänke]	ist **gesunken**
sinnen *meditate* (elev.)	**sann** [sänne (sönne)]	hat **gesonnen**
sitzen *sit*	**saß** säße	hat **gesessen**
spalten *split, cleave*	**spaltete** spaltete	hat/ist **gespaltet** (gespalten)

NB: The strong past participle *gespalten* is used mainly as an adjective, e.g. *das gespaltene Deutschland*.

TABLE 12.9 *Principal parts of strong and irregular verbs – continued*

Infinitive 3rd. sing. pres.	Past indicative *Konjunktiv II*	Past participle
speien *spit, spew* (elev.)	**spie** [spiee]	hat **gespie(e)n**
spinnen *spin; be stupid*	**spann** [spönne (spänne)]	hat **gesponnen**
sprechen *speak* es spricht	**sprach** spräche	hat **gesprochen**
sprießen *sprout* (elev.)	**sproß** [sprösse]	ist **gesprossen**
springen *jump*	**sprang** spränge	ist **gesprungen**
stechen *prick, sting* es sticht	**stach** [stäche]	hat **gestochen**
stehen *stand*	**stand** stünde (stände)	hat **gestanden**
stehlen *steal* es stiehlt	**stahl** [stähle (stöhle)]	hat **gestohlen**
steigen *climb; rise*	**stieg** stiege	ist **gestiegen**
sterben *die* es stirbt	**starb** stürbe	ist **gestorben**
stieben *fly up* (like dust) (elev.)	**stob** (stiebte) [stöbe]	ist **gestoben** (gestiebt)
stinken *stink*	**stank** [stänke]	hat **gestunken**
stoßen *bump; push* es stößt	**stieß** stieße	ist/hat **gestoßen**
streichen *stroke*	**strich** striche	ist/hat **gestrichen**
streiten *quarrel*	**stritt** stritte	hat **gestritten**
tragen *carry; wear* es trägt	**trug** trüge	hat **getragen**

NB: *beantragen* 'apply' and *beauftragen* 'commission' are weak.

Infinitive 3rd. sing. pres.	Past indicative *Konjunktiv II*	Past participle
treffen *meet; hit* es trifft	**traf** träfe	hat **getroffen**
treiben *drive; drift*	**trieb** triebe	ist/hat **getrieben**
treten *step* es tritt	**trat** träte	ist/hat **getreten**
triefen *drip*	**triefte/troff** [tröffe]	hat **getrieft** (getroffen)

TABLE 12.9 *Principal parts of strong and irregular verbs – continued*

Infinitive 3rd. sing. pres.	Past indicative *Konjunktiv II*	Past participle
trinken *drink*	**trank** tränke	hat **getrunken**
trügen *deceive*	**trog** [tröge]	hat **getrogen**
tun *do*	**tat** täte	hat **getan**
verbleichen *fade*	**verblich** verbliche	ist **verblichen**

NB: Simple *bleichen* 'bleach' is now always weak (i.e. *bleichte, gebleicht*), as is *erbleichen* 'turn pale'.

verderben *spoil* es verdirbt	**verdarb** [verdürbe]	hat/ist **verdorben**
verdrießen *vex* (elev.)	**verdroß** [verdrösse]	hat **verdrossen**
vergessen *forget* es vergißt	**vergaß** vergäße	hat **vergessen**
verlieren *lose*	**verlor** verlöre	hat **verloren**
verschleißen *wear out*	**verschliß** verschlisse	ist/hat **verschlissen**
verzeihen *excuse*	**verzieh** verziehe	hat **verziehen**
wachsen *grow* es wächst	**wuchs** wüchse	ist **gewachsen**
wägen *weigh* (one's words)	**wog/wägte** [wöge]	hat **gewogen/gewägt**

NB: Simple *wägen* is archaic. The more frequent compound *erwägen* 'consider' only has strong forms, i.e. *erwog, erwogen*.

waschen *wash* es wäscht	**wusch** [wüsche]	hat **gewaschen**
weben *weave*	**webte** (wob) webte	hat **gewebt** (gewoben)

NB: Usually weak, but the strong forms are used in literary German in figurative senses.

weichen *yield, give way*	**wich** wiche	ist **gewichen**

NB: The weak verb *weichen* (*weichte, geweicht*) means 'soften'. It has the compounds *einweichen* 'soak' and *aufweichen* 'make soft'.

weisen *point*	**wies** wiese	hat **gewiesen**
wenden *turn*	**wandte/wendete** wendete	hat **gewandt/gewendet**

TABLE 12.9 *Principal parts of strong and irregular verbs – continued*

Infinitive 3rd. sing. pres.	Past indicative *Konjunktiv II*	Past participle
NB: The irregular forms *wandte, gewandt* are generally more frequent, except in the sense 'turn over', 'turn round' (e.g. *das Auto, den Braten, das Heu wenden*) and in the compounds *entwenden* and *verwenden*.		
werben *recruit; advertise* es wirbt	**warb** [würbe]	hat **geworben**
werfen *throw* es wirft	**warf** [würfe]	hat **geworfen**
wiegen *weigh*	**wog** [wöge]	hat **gewogen**
NB: *wiegen* is weak (*wiegte, gewiegt*) in the meaning 'rock (cradle, etc.)'.		
winden *wind, twist* (elev.)	**wand** [wände]	hat **gewunden**
winken *wave*	**winkte** winkte	hat **gewinkt** (**gewunken**)
NB: *gewunken* is very common in regional and colloquial usage.		
wringen *wring* (clothes)	**wrang** [wränge]	hat **gewrungen**
ziehen *pull; move*	**zog** zöge	hat/ist **gezogen**
zwingen *force*	**zwang** [zwänge]	hat **gezwungen**

13

The infinitive and the participles

This chapter deals with the main uses of the infinitive and the present and past participles. These 'non-finite' forms of the verb (cf. 12.1.1e) do not have endings to show agreement with the subject for person and number, or to express other categories of the verb such as tense and mood. Apart from being used to form compound tenses and the passive (see 12.3 and 12.4), they occur in a number of constructions which depend on an element in a full clause with a finite verb. The formation of the infinitive and the participles is shown on Table 12.2.

Despite certain similarities, German differs quite markedly from English in respect of some non-finite constructions and their use, especially those with the present participle.

13.1 Forms of the infinitive

13.1.1 The simple infinitive

The simple infinitive is the basic form under which verbs are usually listed in dictionaries, cf. 12.1. For most verbs it ends in *-en* (e.g. *kommen*, *machen*, *sehen*) but a few verbs have an infinitive ending in *-n*, i.e. *sein*, *tun* and verbs with a stem in *-el* and *-er* (see 12.2.1c).

13.1.2 The compound infinitive

The infinitive of the auxiliaries *haben*, *sein* and *werden* can be combined with the past participle of a verb to form compound infinitives:

perfect – with *haben* or *sein* (see 12.3)   gesehen haben, angekommen sein
passive – with *werden* or *sein* (see 12.4)   verletzt werden, verletzt sein
perfect passive   verletzt worden sein

The German perfect infinitive is used to denote that an action took place *before* that of the main verb. This is similar to English:

Sie muß das Buch **lesen**   *She must **read** the book*
Sie muß das Buch **gelesen haben**   *She must **have read** the book*

13.1.3 The infinitive with and without zu

In some constructions in German, the infinitive is accompanied by the particle *zu*, whilst in others a 'bare' infinitive is used, without *zu*:

Ich riet ihr, zum Arzt **zu gehen**   *I advised her **to go** to the doctor*
Ich konnte nicht zum Arzt **gehen**   *I couldn't **go** to the doctor*

Constructions *with zu* (which are more frequent) are explained in 13.2. Constructions with the bare infinitive are treated in 13.3.

The uses of the German infinitive are well explained in Buscha and Zoch (1988), which has a good range of examples and exercises for the foreign learner. Bech (1983) is still the most detailed survey of infinitive constructions in German.

13.1.4 The form of the infinitive with *zu*

(a) With simple verbs and verbs with inseparable prefixes

zu comes immediately before the verb and is separated from it in writing:

> Sie fing an **zu schreiben**   Ich war bereit **zu verhandeln**
> Es gefiel mir, mich mit ihr **zu unterhalten**

(b) With verbs with a separable prefix

(see 12.2.1i and 22.5) *zu* is placed between the prefix and the verb. The whole is written as a single word:

> Sie hatte vor, ihn **anzurufen**   Es war schön, euch **wiederzusehen**
> Es freut mich, Sie **kennenzulernen**

Similarly, if a separable prefix precedes an inseparable one:

> Es fällt mir nicht ein, mich ihm **anzuvertrauen**

NB: Although *mißverstehen* is inseparable, the *zu* is placed *after* the prefix, i.e *mißzuverstehen*. This is an alternative, if less frequent, possibility with a few other verbs with the prefix *miß-*, e.g. *zu mißachten* or (less commonly) *mißzuachten*, see 22.6.3.

(c) With compound infinitives

zu precedes the auxiliary *haben, sein* or *werden*:

Er verleugnet es, sie betrogen **zu haben**	*He denies having deceived her*
Ihr gefällt es nicht, betrogen **zu werden**	*She doesn't like being deceived*
Sie behauptete, betrogen worden **zu sein**	*She claimed to have been deceived*
Es freut mich, Sie hier begrüßen **zu dürfen**	*It is a pleasure to be able to welcome you here*

13.2 The use of the infinitive with *zu*

13.2.1 The infinitive with *zu* occurs in a reduced clause

In German this is called the *Infinitivsatz*. It can depend on a noun, verb or adjective in a full clause within the same sentence.

The infinitive with *zu* comes at the end of its clause, i.e. in the same position as the finite verb in a subordinate clause (see 21.1.1c):

Er fing an, **heftig zu weinen**	*He began to cry bitterly*
Er gab mir die Erlaubnis, **in Berlin zu bleiben**	*He gave me permission to stay in Berlin*
Es ist nicht schwer, **eine Fremdsprache zu lernen**	*It is not difficult to learn a foreign language*

13.2.2 The position of the infinitive clause with *zu*

(a) The infinitive clause is usually quite separate from the main clause
i.e. it is not normally 'enclosed' within the clause it depends on (cf. 21.9.2), but
follows any part of the verb in final position in the clause. In writing it is marked
off by commas unless it is very short (see 23.5.2):

> Sie hatten beschlossen, **vor dem Rathaus zu warten**
> (NOT: Sie hatten vor dem Rathaus zu warten beschlossen)
> Wir hatten vor, **im Urlaub nach Rom zu fliegen**
> (NOT: Wir hatten im Urlaub nach Rom zu fliegen vor)
> ... weil er sich bemüht hat, **rechtzeitig fertig zu sein**
> (NOT: ... weil er sich rechtzeitig fertig zu sein bemüht hat)

**(b) However, in some constructions enclosure of the infinitive clause is
possible, or even obligatory**
Askedal (1983) and (1991) gives full details on these.

(i) Enclosure is the rule with the 'semi-auxiliary' verbs (see 13.2.5):

> ... bevor sein Duft ihn **zu ersticken drohte** (*Süßkind*)
> Seine Brutalität ist nicht mehr **zu ertragen gewesen** (*Wickert*)

(ii) Enclosure is possible with a number of other common verbs (though it is
more frequent in subordinate clauses than with the compound tenses):

> Daß sie ihn **entdeckt zu haben** glaubte, war ein Beweis dafür, daß ... (*Süßkind*)
> (*or*: Daß sie glaubte, ihn entdeckt zu haben, ...)
> Du hast mir **das zu tun** versprochen
> (*or*: Du hast mir versprochen, das zu tun)

Other verbs which are regularly used in this way are *anfangen, beginnen, hoffen,
meinen, trachten, vermögen, versuchen, wagen, wünschen*. In very formal registers
enclosed infinitive clauses may be found with other verbs and phrases. These
can sound rather stilted.

(c) Incorporation of infinitive clause and main clause
If there is only the finite verb and its subject in the main clause, the infinitive
clause can be incorporated with the main clause by splicing the object of the
infinitive into it, e.g.:

Er wagte **die Reise** aus diesem Grunde nicht **abzubrechen**	*He didn't dare to break his journey for this reason*
Diesen Vorgang wollen wir zu **erklären** versuchen	*We want to try to explain this series of events*

This construction is restricted to formal registers. It is most frequent with verbs
which regularly enclose the infinitive clause, cf. (b) above.

(d) Infinitive clauses depending on relative clauses
The German equivalent of English constructions such as 'a man whom I tried to kill' typically has the infinitive clause incorporated inside the relative clause, e.g. *ein Mann,* **den** ich **zu töten** *versuchte.* Other examples:

... die Person, **deren Gesicht** ich **zu erraten** versucht hatte (*Frisch*)	... *the person whose face I had tried to recognise*
... kein Mann, **den zu beseitigen** eine Revolution gelohnt hätte (*Spiegel*)	... *not a man whom it would have been worth a revolution to get rid of*

Alternatively, a simple infinitive clause (i.e. one consisting only of *zu* plus the infinitive) may follow the finite verb, e.g. *ein Mann, den er versuchte* **zu töten.**

13.2.3 An infinitive clause with *zu* can be the subject of a verb

(a) A German infinitive clause used as the subject of a verb can correspond in English to an infinitive clause or to a clause with an *ing*-form
In many contexts a choice exists in English which is lacking in German, since German does not use present participles in the way the *ing*-form is used in English (see 13.7.1). The finite verb has the endings of the third person singular (see 12.1.4a):

Ihn zu überzeugen wird nicht leicht sein	*To convince him/Convincing him won't be easy*
So etwas zu erlauben ist unerhört	*To allow/Allowing that kind of thing is outrageous*
Ihr Ziel ist einen Roman zu schreiben	*Her aim is to write a novel*

(b) If a subject infinitive clause is short, it may, optionally, lack *zu*
This is most frequent with the verb *sein* and in set phrases:

Lange Auto (zu) fahren ist sehr anstrengend	*Driving a car for long periods is very strenuous*
Irren ist menschlich	*To err is human*

(c) A subject infinitive clause which follows the main verb is often anticipated by *es* in the main clause
(see 3.6.2e for further details):

Es war mir nicht möglich, früher zu kommen	*It wasn't possible for me to come earlier*
Ihm steht (es) nicht zu, ein Urteil zu fällen	*It's not up to him to pass judgement*

13.2.4 Many verbs can have an infinitive clause with *zu* as their object

(a) A German infinitive clause used as the object of a verb can correspond to an English infinitive clause or a clause with an *ing*-form
In English the choice of infinitive or *ing*-form depends on the individual verb used:

Ich hoffe, dich bald wiedersehen zu können	*I hope to be able to see you again soon*
Ich gebe zu, das gesagt zu haben	*I admit having said that*
Ich habe vor, sie morgen zu besuchen	*I intend to visit them/visiting them tomorrow*

(b) Sometimes the subject of the main verb is taken as the subject of the infinitive clause, but in some instances it is the object
Compare:

Christian versprach Ellen, sie mitzunehmen	*Christian promised Ellen to take her with him*

(The **subject** of *versprechen* is understood as the subject of *mitzunehmen*.)

Christian bat Ellen, ihn mitzunehmen	*Christian asked Ellen to take him with her*

(The **object** of *bitten* is understood as the subject of *mitzunehmen*.)

This depends on the sense of the verbs involved and the context (see Eisenberg (1994: 376–82) for more details). In practice English and German generally agree on which complement (subject or object) is to be understood as the subject of the infinitive. More examples:

Er gab zu, sich geirrt zu haben	*He admitted having made a mistake*
Sie hat ihm geraten, die Ausstellung zu besuchen	*She advised him to see the exhibition*

However, there are one or two constructions where there are significant differences between the two languages, i.e.:

(i) Fewer German than English verbs allow an object to be taken as the subject of a following infinitive clause. In particular, it is not possible with verbs of wishing, desiring, saying, knowing, thinking and the like. With these a *daß*-clause has to be used in German, not an infinitive clause:

Sie will, daß ich mit ihr gehe	*She wants me to go with her*
Ich möchte nicht, daß es irgendein Mißverständnis gibt	*I don't want there to be any misunderstanding*
Ich erwarte, daß sie bald nach Flensburg umzieht	*I expect her to move to Flensburg soon*
Mir wäre es lieber, wenn Sie hier nicht rauchen würden	*I would prefer you not to smoke here*
Sage ihm doch, daß er warten soll	*Tell him to wait, though*
Ich wußte, daß es ein Irrtum war	*I knew it to be a mistake*

It is not possible, either, to use these verbs in the passive voice with a following infinitive clause. Thus, there is no direct equivalent in German for English constructions of the type 'She is expected to move to Flensburg soon', 'We were told to wait'. A subordinate clause is required for these in German, e.g. *Man erwartet, daß sie bald nach Flensburg umzieht; Man sagte uns/Uns wurde gesagt, daß wir warten sollten.*

(ii) With some verbs the subject of the infinitive has to be understood as indefinite (i.e. = *man*):

Der Präsident hat angewiesen, alle Universitäten zu schließen	*The president has instructed that all the universities should be closed*
Er ordnete an, die Gefangenen zu entlassen	*He ordered the prisoners to be released*
Helmut befahl, früh aufzubrechen	*Helmut ordered an early start*

Other verbs commonly used this way are *anregen, auffordern, beantragen, befür-
worten, bitten, drängen, eintreten, empfehlen, ersuchen, fordern, plädieren, raten, veranlassen, verlangen, warnen.*

(iii) With a few verbs, the subject *or* the object (or both) can be taken to be the
subject of the infinitive:

Er schlug mir vor, das Zimmer aufzuräumen	*He suggested that I/he/we should tidy the room up*

Other verbs which can be used like this are *anbieten, einreden, zusichern.*

(c) An infinitive clause can be used with some verbs denoting mental processes

The English equivalents usually require a subordinate clause:

Er behauptete (glaubte, meinte, war überzeugt), mich gesehen zu haben	*He maintained (believed, thought, was convinced) that he had seen me*

This construction is more usual in writing than in speech, where a subordinate
clause will frequently be preferred, e.g. *Er meinte, er hätte mich gesehen / daß er mich
gesehen hätte.*

(d) A following object infinitive may be anticipated by *es*
(see 3.6.3a for further details):

Ich konnte es kaum ertragen, ihn so leiden zu sehen	*I could hardly bear to see him suffer like that*
Sie hat (es) versäumt, die Miete zu zahlen	*She failed to pay the rent*

(e) When verbs which govern a prepositional object are followed by an infinitive clause, it is usually anticipated by a prepositional adverb
(i.e. *da(r)* + preposition. See 18.6.14 for further details):

Ich verlasse mich **darauf**, ihn zu Hause zu finden	*I am relying on finding him at home*
Ich erinnere mich (**daran**), sie voriges Jahr in Bremen gesehen zu haben	*I remember having seen her in Bremen last year*

13.2.5 Infinitive clauses with 'semi-auxiliary' verbs

Some verbs have a closer link with a dependent infinitive clause than others.
Their main role is to modify the meaning of the verb used in the infinitive in
some way, like a modal auxiliary verb (see Chapter 17), and it is useful to think
of them as a set of 'semi-auxiliary' verbs.

A feature of these 'semi-auxiliaries' is that they *always* enclose the infinitive in
dependent clauses or compound tenses (see 13.2.2b):

... da er den eben Angekommenen **zu erkennen schien**
... als das Boot **zu kentern drohte**
Sie hat uns **zu verstehen gegeben**, daß sie morgen kommt

These verbs are also often incorporated with a dependent infinitive clause, cf.
13.2.2c, and the infinitive clause with them is not always separated by commas
in writing, cf. 23.5.2d.

English has a much wider range of such 'semi-auxiliary' verbs than German. The natural German equivalent to many of these English verbs is a construction with an adverb, e.g. *Ich spiele gern Tennis* 'I **like** to play tennis', *Ich sah sie zufällig in der Stadt* 'I **happened** to see her in town'. A survey of these equivalences is given in 7.3.4.

The most important verbs which can be used as semi-auxiliaries in German are listed below. Many of them have other uses and meanings.

bekommen 'get':

> Und wenn ich dich **zu fassen**   *And if I get my hands on you, ...*
> **bekomme** ...

belieben 'like', 'wish'. Nowadays archaic except in an ironic sense:

> Sie **belieben zu scherzen**   *You must be joking*

bleiben 'remain'. The following infinitive has a passive force:

> Die Gesetzesvorlage **bleibt** noch **zu**   *The draft bill still remains to*
> **diskutieren**   *be discussed*

NB: For the use of *bleiben* with a bare infinitive, see 13.3.1f.

brauchen 'need'. In this sense it only occurs with a negative (or with *nur* or *bloß*). In practice, *nicht brauchen* is the most common negative to *müssen* (see 17.5.1c):

> Du **brauchst** nur **anzurufen**, und ich   *You only need to call and I'll come*
> komme sofort   *straight away*
> eine Sprache, die sie nie **zu**   *a language which they never needed*
> **erlernen brauchten** (*Spiegel*)   *to learn*

NB: (i) In colloquial speech, *brauchen* is commonly used without *zu* (see 13.3.1a): *Ich brauche nicht hingehen*.
    (ii) The infinitive is used rather than the past participle in the perfect tenses (see 13.3.2a): *Du hättest nicht hinzugehen brauchen*.

drohen 'threaten'. The subject is usually inanimate in this use:

> Oskars Herz **drohte** zu Stein **zu**   *Oskar's heart threatened to turn to*
> **werden** (*Grass*)   *stone*

geben 'give'. Used mainly with *denken, erkennen, verstehen*:

> ... weil sie uns **zu verstehen gab,**   *... because she gave us to understand*
> daß sie bald kommen würde   *that she would be coming soon*

NB: *es gibt* 'there is' (see 18.2.5) is also used as a semi-auxiliary, e.g. ... *weil es hier wenig zu trinken gibt*.

gedenken 'propose'. It is restricted to elevated, formal registers:

> die Zahl der Truppen, die die Nato   *the number of troops which NATO*
> nach Bosnien **zu schicken gedenkt**   *proposes to send to Bosnia*
> (*Presse*)

gehen The use of *gehen* as a semi-auxiliary is colloquial. It expresses a possibility and the infinitive has passive force (see 15.4.5):

> Die Uhr **geht zu reparieren**   *The clock can be repaired*

NB: For the use of *gehen* with a bare infinitive, see 13.3.1e.

haben 'have' expresses necessity or obligation. It is a (rather less frequent) alternative to *müssen* or *sollen*:

Was **habe** ich **zu bezahlen?**	*What have I got to pay?*
Ich **habe** mehrere Briefe **zu schreiben**	*I have several letters to write*
Sie **haben** hier nichts **zu suchen**	*You have no business here*

With some verbs (especially *tun*), this use of *haben* is idiomatic and there is little sense of obligation or necessity:

Das **hat** mit dieser Sache nichts **zu tun**	*That's got nothing to do with this matter*
Das **hat** wenig **zu bedeuten**	*That doesn't mean very much*

NB: For the use of *haben* with a bare infinitive, see 13.3.1f.

kommen 'come' expresses a (chance) result:

Es war nicht meine Absicht, daß wir auf dieses Thema **zu sprechen kamen**	*It was not my intention for us to get onto this subject*
Wir arrangierten es so, daß ich neben ihr **zu sitzen kam**	*We arranged it so that I came to sit next to her*

NB: For the use of *kommen* with a bare infinitive, see 13.3.1e.

pflegen 'be accustomed to' is restricted to literary registers:

Dann **pflegte** ich öfters zwischen den schweren Eisenstangen hindurch in Katharinas Stall **einzutreten** (*Grzimek*)	*Then I often used to go through the heavy iron bars into Katharina's pen*

scheinen 'seem'

Ihm **schien** es **zu gefallen**	*He seemed to like it*
Das Dorf Lidiče, wohin die Spuren der beiden Attentäter **zu führen schienen**, wurde zerstört (*Presse*)	*The village of Lidiče, where the tracks of the two assassins seemed to lead, was destroyed*

sein 'be', as a semi-auxiliary, is the equivalent of *können* (or sometimes *müssen* or *sollen*). The following infinitive has passive force, cf. 15.4.5:

Ist der Direktor heute **zu sprechen?**	*Can I see the manager today?*
Die Fahrausweise **sind** auf Verlangen **vorzuzeigen**	*The tickets are to be shown on demand*
Das Haus **ist zu verkaufen**	*The house is for sale*

NB: For the use of *sein* with a bare infinitive, see 13.3.1e.

stehen has a similar sense to *sein*, and the following infinitive also has passive force. It is used chiefly with *befürchten*, *erwarten* and *hoffen*:

Es **steht zu erwarten**, daß er bald nachgibt	*It can be expected that he will soon give in*

suchen 'try', 'seek' is restricted to formal registers:

eine Ordnung, die die selbständige militärische Betätigung des Adels **einzuschränken suchte** (*Bumke*)	*a decree which sought to limit the independent military activities of the nobility*

versprechen 'promise'. In this sense, *versprechen* refers to an involuntary action with something desirable in the offing. The subject is normally inanimate:

Das Wetter **verspricht** schön **zu werden**	*The weather promises to be nice*
Wir sind froh, weil das Unternehmen **zu gedeihen verspricht**	*We are happy because the enterprise promises to prosper*

NB: As a full verb, in the sense of 'make a promise', *versprechen* is used with a separated infinitive clause and the subject is always *animate*, e.g. *Der Arzt versprach mir, sofort zu kommen.*

verstehen 'be able to', 'know how to':

Sie war in Verhältnisse geschleudert worden, mit denen sie nicht **umzugehen verstand** (*Fleißer*)	*She had been catapulted into circumstances which she didn't know how to cope with*

wissen 'know how to'. In this sense *wissen* is similar to *verstehen*:

Er weiß mit den Leuten umzugehen	*He knows how to deal with people*
Wie soll zurechtkommen, wer sich in das Gegebene nicht **zu schicken weiß**? (*Wolf*)	*How is anyone going to manage who doesn't know how to come to terms with reality?*

13.2.6 The infinitive with *zu* after adjectives

In some infinitive constructions after *sein* used with an adjective the subject of *sein* must be understood as the object of the infinitive:

Diese Aufgabe ist **einfach zu lösen**	*This problem is simple to solve*
Er ist **leicht zu überzeugen**	*He is easy to convince*
Diese Frage ist **schwer zu beantworten**	*This question is difficult to answer*

This construction can be used with many adjectives in English, but with only very few in German, i.e.: *einfach, interessant, leicht, schwer, schwierig*. In German, too, the construction is only possible if the verb takes an accusative object, i.e. it cannot occur with verbs like *helfen*. These other English constructions have different German equivalents:

Es war schön, sie zu kennen (i.e. NOT: *Sie war schön zu kennen*)	*She was nice to know*
Meiner Schwester zu helfen war schwierig (i.e. NOT: *Meine Schwester war schwierig zu helfen*)	*My sister was difficult to help*
Zum Trinken war der Kaffee zu heiß (i.e. NOT: *Der Kaffee war zu heiß zu trinken*)	*The coffee was too hot to drink*

In English we can also use these adjectives attributively (i.e. in front of a noun), with an infinitive depending on them, e.g. 'That is a **difficult** question **to answer**'. This construction does not exist in German, cf.:

Diese Frage zu beantworten ist schwer / Das ist eine schwer zu beantwortende Frage	*That is a difficult question to answer*
Es ist ein leicht erreichbarer Ort	*It's an easy place to reach*
Es war dumm, diese Frage gestellt zu haben	*That was a silly question to have asked*

13.2.7 The infinitive with *zu* after prepositions

An infinitive with *zu* can be used after a few prepositions, i.e. *um, ohne, (an)statt* and (to a more limited extent) *außer*. Such constructions have special meanings and are the equivalent of adverbial clauses.

(a) The construction *um ... zu*

This has a number of different uses:

(i) It can express purpose, often corresponding to English 'in order to'. It is the equivalent of a clause introduced by *damit* (see 19.5.1a):

Ich konnte nichts tun, **um** ihn **zu** beruhigen	*I couldn't do anything to reassure him*
Er zündete das Haus an, **um** die Versicherung **zu** kassieren	*He set fire to the house (in order) to collect on the insurance*
Da war kein Wasser, **um** das Feuer **zu** löschen	*There was no water to put the fire out*

NB: The *um* is sometimes omitted, in elevated and colloquial registers, e.g. *Ich konnte nichts tun, ihn zu beruhigen.*

(ii) It is used after an adjective qualified by *zu* or *genug*:

Er ist **zu jung, um** alles **zu** verstehen	*He is too young to understand everything*
Er ist alt **genug, um** alles **zu** verstehen	*He is old enough to understand everything*

NB: *um* is sometimes omitted, especially in colloquial speech, e.g. *Er ist zu jung, alles zu verstehen.*

If the subject of the two clauses is different, the conjunction *als daß* is used, e.g. *Er ist zu jung/nicht alt genug, als daß wir es ihm erklären könnten.* See 19.5.3 for further details.

(iii) It can be used simply to link clauses, as an equivalent to *und*:

Er betrat die Gaststätte, **um** sie nach kurzer Zeit wieder **zu** verlassen	*He went into the restaurant, only to leave it again after a short time*

NB: This construction is limited to formal writing and has been criticised by stylists, e.g. DUDEN (1985: 583–4), which advises against using it, as it might be misunderstood to imply purpose, e.g. *Karl ging nach Australien, um dort von einem Auto überfahren zu werden.*

(b) *ohne ...zu*

This corresponds to English *without* followed by an *ing*-form:

Wir konnten nie mehr Karten spielen, **ohne** an Henriette **zu** denken (*Böll*)	*We could never play cards again without thinking of Henriette*
Er verließ das Haus, **ohne** gesehen **zu** werden	*He left the house without being seen*

With a change of subject, the conjunction *ohne daß* (cf. 19.7.7) is used:

Er verließ das Haus, ohne daß ich ihn sah	*He left the house without me seeing him*

(c) *(an)statt . . . zu*

This corresponds to English *instead of* followed by an *ing*-form:

Er hat gespielt, **(an)statt zu** arbeiten   *He played instead of working*

A clause with *(an)statt daß*, e.g. *Er hat gespielt, (an)statt daß er gearbeitet hat* is an alternative to this construction. No change of subject is possible with either *(an)statt zu* or *(an)statt daß*.

(d) *außer . . . zu*

This corresponds to English *except* or *besides* with an infinitive:

Was konnten sie tun, **außer zu**   *What could they do except protest?*
protestieren? *(Zeit)*

The use of *außer* with an infinitive is quite recent. A common alternative is with the preposition *außer* with an infinitive noun, e.g. *Sie tat nichts außer Schlafen.* With a different subject, a clause with the conjunction *außer daß* is used (see 19.7.2a):

Alle Folgen des Unwetters waren   *All the effects of the storm had*
beseitigt, außer daß bei ihnen   *been cleared away, except that*
noch Wasser im Keller stand   *they still had water in their cellar*

(e) German equivalents for other English constructions with prepositions and a following infinitive

In German only the prepositions given in (a) to (d) above can be used with a following infinitive. English can use other prepositions, notably *for* and *with*, with a following infinitive. These correspond to different constructions in German.

(i) English *for* + noun/pronoun + infinitive

In a few contexts this corresponds to a noun with *für* or a noun in the dative in the main clause in German:

Es ist Zeit für uns loszugehen   *It is time for us to leave*
Es war ihm unmöglich, das auch nur   *It was impossible for him even to*
zu verstehen   *understand that*

However, the most usual German equivalent is a construction with a subordinate clause, with the conjunction used depending on the sense:

Ihr lag es sehr daran, daß er die   *She was very keen for him to take*
Stelle annahm   *the job*
Hier sind ein paar Formulare, die   *Here are a few forms for you to fill*
Sie ausfüllen sollen   *in*
Er wartete darauf, daß sie ankam   *He was waiting for her to arrive*
Sie bringt die Fotos, damit wir sie   *She's bringing the photographs for*
uns ansehen können   *us to look at*
Sie muß schon sehr krank sein, wenn   *She must be very ill for her mother*
ihre Mutter ein Telegramm schickt   *to send a telegram*

(ii) English *with* + noun/pronoun + infinitive
Depending on the sense, the German equivalent for this can be a subordinate
clause with *da* or *weil*, a main clause with *und*, or a relative clause:

Da ich so viele Briefe schreiben muß, werde ich wohl nicht ins Kino gehen können	*With so many letters to write, I probably shan't be able to go to the cinema*
Sie waren nur auf der Durchreise in München und konnten dort nur ein paar Stunden verbringen	*They were just passing through Munich, with no more than an hour or two to spend*
Auch der Sonntag, an dem sie nicht ins Büro ging, verging irgendwie	*Even Sunday, with no office to go to, passed somehow*

13.2.8 English uses infinitives in a number of constructions where an infinitive with *zu* is not used in German

Some of these are explained in 13.2.4 and 13.2.6–7, but there are others.

(a) English infinitives in indirect questions
e.g. *He told me how to do it.* In German a subordinate clause (often with *sollen*,
müssen or *können*) is used:

Er sagte mir, **wie ich es machen soll**	*He told me how to do it*
Ich weiß nicht, **was ich tun soll/muß**	*I don't know what to do*
Woher weiß man, **welchen Knopf man drücken soll?**	*How do you tell which button to press?*

(b) English infinitives used after a noun as attributes
e.g. *the person to apply to.* A relative clause is used in German:

Ich möchte ein Paar Handschuhe, **die zu meinem Wintermantel passen**	*I want a pair of gloves to go with my winter coat*
das einzige, **was man tun kann**	*the only thing to do*

These constructions are especially common after superlatives:

Er war der erste (der letzte, der beste Spieler), **der gekommen ist**	*He was the first (the last, the best player) to come*

13.2.9 Other uses of the infinitive with *zu*

(a) In comparative phrases with *als*
zu can be omitted, although it is more usual for it to be included:

Du kannst nichts Besseres tun, als zu Hause (zu) bleiben
Man sollte lieber erst alles gründlich besprechen, als sofort (zu) streiten

(b) In exclamations
These are very similar to the corresponding English constructions:

Und zu denken, daß es ihr nichts bedeutet hat!	*And to think it didn't mean anything to her!*
Ach, immer hier zu bleiben!	*Oh, to stay here for ever!*

(c) In small ads

Zwei-Zimmer-Wohnung ab 1. Mai zu vermieten	*Two-room-flat to let from May 1st*

13.3 The infinitive without *zu*

The 'bare' infinitive, without *zu*, is used in fewer constructions than the infinitive with *zu*, but many of these are very frequent.

13.3.1 A few verbs are followed by an infinitive without *zu*

Such infinitives usually come at the end of the clause: *Sie will diese Briefe morgen schreiben*. They are enclosed in subordinate clauses and compound tenses: *Ich weiß, daß sie diese Briefe morgen schreiben will* or *Sie hat diese Briefe heute schreiben wollen*. For further details see 21.1.

The infinitive without *zu* is used with the following verbs:

(a) The modal auxiliaries
i.e. *dürfen, können, mögen, müssen, sollen, wollen* (see Chapter 17):

Sie darf heute nicht **ausgehen**	Ich mußte heute früh **aufstehen**
Wir können es nicht **verhindern**	Er wird mir nicht **helfen** wollen

There is a tendency is colloquial German to treat *brauchen* as a modal auxiliary and use it with a bare infinitive, e.g. *Sie brauchen heute nicht hingehen*. However, many German speakers consider this to be substandard, and *brauchen* is normally used *with zu* in writing.

(b) A few verbs of perception
i.e. *fühlen, hören, sehen, spüren*, e.g.:

Ich **sah** ihn ins Zimmer **kommen**	*I saw him come into the room*
Sie **hörte** das Kind **weinen**	*She heard the child crying*
Er **fühlte** sein Herz **klopfen**	*He felt his heart beat(ing)*
Ich **spürte** seinen Einfluß **wachsen**	*I sensed how his influence was growing*

With these verbs, a clause with *wie* is an alternative to the infinitive construction, e.g.:

Ich **hörte, wie** das Kind weinte	Ich **spürte, wie** sein Einfluß wuchs
Ich **sah, wie** der Polizist sich nach dem alten Mann umsah	

This tends to be more frequent than the infinitive construction in certain contexts, i.e. if the sentence is long or complex, with the verbs *fühlen* and *spüren*, and in colloquial registers.

(c) *lassen*
lassen with a bare infinitive has two principal meanings:

(i) 'let', 'allow':

Er **ließ** mich das Buch **behalten**	*He let me keep the book*
Laß sie doch **hereinkommen!**	*Do let her come in!*

In this sense *lassen* is often used reflexively with a similar force to a passive construction (cf. 15.4.6):

Das **läßt sich** leicht **ändern**	*That can easily be changed*
Das Buch **läßt sich** leicht **lesen**	*The book is easy to read*

(ii) 'cause', 'make':

Sie **ließ** den Schlosser die Tür **reparieren**	*She had the locksmith fix the door*
Die Nachricht **ließ** ihn **erblassen**	*The news made him turn pale*
Er **ließ** sich die Haare **schneiden**	*He had his hair cut*

lassen is never followed by a passive infinitive, but in both meanings the infinitive after *lassen* can have passive force:

Er **läßt** die Bäume **fällen**	*He has the trees felled*
Er **ließ** sich **sehen**	*He allowed himself to be seen*
Er **ließ** die Brücke **von den Gefangenen bauen**	*He had the bridge built by the prisoners*

NB: Some combinations with *lassen* have developed into separable compounds, e.g. *fallenlassen* 'drop', *stehenlassen*, *liegenlassen* 'leave behind'.

(d) *tun*

The use of *tun* with a bare infinitive is typical of colloquial speech:

Er **tut** ja immer noch **essen**	*He's still eating*
Tust du mich auch **verstehen**?	*Do you understand me?*
Ich **täte** gern ins Kino **gehen**	*I would like to go to the cinema*

This usage is generally considered substandard and not normally acceptable in writing. It is, however, permissible in written German to use *tun* in order to allow an emphasised verb to be placed first in the sentence:

Bewundern tu ich ihn nicht, aber er imponiert mir doch	*I don't admire him, but he does impress me*
Aber **schmerzen tat** es darum nicht weniger (*Reuter*)	*But it was no less painful for all that*

(e) Certain verbs of motion

i.e. *gehen, kommen, fahren, schicken*. The verb in the infinitive expresses the purpose of going:

Während ich **öffnen ging**, ... (*Andersch*)	*While I went to open the door, ...*
Kommst du heute **schwimmen**?	*Are you coming swimming today?*
Er **fährt** immer vormittags **einkaufen**	*He always goes shopping in the mornings*
Sie hat den Großvater **einkaufen geschickt**	*She sent grandfather shopping*

This usage is typically (but not only) colloquial. In everyday speech, too, the past tenses of *sein* can be used with a bare infinitive to mean 'go':

Ich **war** heute morgen **schwimmen**	*I went swimming this morning*
Er **ist einkaufen gewesen**	*He went/has been shopping*

NB: (i) *schicken* can alternatively be used with *zu* and an infinitive: *Sie hat den Großvater geschickt, Kartoffeln und Gemüse zu kaufen*. This is most usual if the infinitive clause is fairly long.

  (ii) *spazieren* forms separable compounds with *gehen* and *fahren*, i.e. *spazierengehen, spazierenfahren*.

(f) *bleiben, finden* and *haben* followed by a verb of position

Er **blieb** im Zimmer **sitzen**	*He stayed sitting in the room*
Sie **ist** an den Ampeln **stehengeblieben**	*She stopped at the lights*
Er **hat** sein Auto vor der Tür **stehen**	*He's got his car at the door*
Sie **hat** einen Bruder in Köln **wohnen**	*She's got a brother living in Cologne*
Sie **fand** das Buch auf dem Boden **liegen**	*She found the book lying on the floor*

NB: (i) *stehenbleiben* 'stop' and *sitzenbleiben* 'repeat a year' (at school) have become established separable compounds.
   (ii) For *finden* with the present participle, see 13.7.5c.
   (iii) *haben* is used with a bare infinitive in a few set constructions with adjectives, i.e.
       Du hast gut / leicht reden 'It's all very well for you to talk'.

(g) *heißen* 'command', *helfen, lehren, lernen*

These verbs can be followed by a bare infinitive or an infinitive with *zu*:

Sie **hieß** ihn **schweigen**	*She bade him be silent*
Er **hieß** seine Truppen, die Burg bis zum letzten Mann **zu verteidigen**	*He ordered his troops to defend the castle to the last man*
... und jetzt **hilf** mir **anpacken** (Remarque)	*... and now give me a hand*
Er **half** Carla, die Weinflaschen **zu öffnen** (Horbach)	*He helped Carla to open the wine bottles*
Sie **lehrte** mich **kochen**	*She taught me to cook*
Sie **lehrte** mich, Suppe **zu kochen**	*She taught me how to make soup*
Er **lernte** beim Militär Russisch **sprechen/zu sprechen**	*He learnt to speak Russian in the army*

NB: (i) This sense of *heißen*, i.e. 'command', is restricted to older literary language. In the sense 'mean', *heißen* is always followed by an infinitive without *zu*, see (h) below.
   (ii) *kennenlernen* 'meet', 'get to know' is an established separable compound.

The construction with *zu* tends to be used with longer and more complex infinitive clauses. However, the bare infinitive will naturally be preferred if the alternative is an awkward construction, e.g.:

Es geht darum, die seit vierzig Jahren geforderte Freiheit der osteuropäischen Völker verwirklichen zu helfen (FR) (i.e. NOT: *zu verwirklichen zu helfen*)	*It is a matter of helping the peoples of Eastern Europe to realise the freedom which they have been demanding for forty years*

(h) A few other verbs in certain constructions or idioms

(i) With *machen* in a couple of idioms, i.e. *von sich reden machen* 'become a talking point' and *jemanden etwas glauben machen* 'convince someone of something', and with a few verbs, i.e. *jdn. gruseln, lachen, schwindeln, weinen, zittern machen* 'make sb. have the creeps, laugh, feel dizzy, cry, tremble'.

(ii) A bare infinitive is used as the complement of *heißen* 'be (the equivalent of)', 'mean' and *nennen* 'call', e.g.:

Das **heißt lügen**	*That amounts to lying*
Das **hieße** wieder von vorne **anfangen**	*That would mean starting from scratch again*
Das **nennst** du höflich **sein!**	*You call that being polite!*

NB: *heißen* in the meaning 'command' is followed by a bare infinitive or an infinitive with *zu*, see (g) above.

(iii) *legen* is followed by a bare infinitive in the idiom *sich schlafen legen* 'go to bed', e.g. *Ich legte mich schlafen.*

13.3.2 The use of the infinitive for a past participle

The infinitive is used rather than a past participle in the perfect tenses of some verbs used with a bare infinitive, e.g. *Sie hat kommen **wollen*** (not *gewollt*). This is the case with the following verbs:

(a) the modal auxiliaries

Er hat heute ausgehen **dürfen**	Wir hätten Ihnen helfen **können**
Er hat ihn sehen **müssen**	Sie hätte es machen **sollen**
Karl hatte Sie sehen **wollen**	

brauchen also forms its perfect tenses with the infinitive rather than the past participle, whether used with an infinitive with or without *zu* (see 13.3.1a), e.g.: *Wir haben nicht (zu) warten brauchen.*

NB: The past participle is occasionally used with these verbs in spoken German, e.g. *Sie hat arbeiten gemußt, gekonnt, gewollt* etc. These forms are substandard.

(b) *lassen*

Sie hat den Schlosser die Tür **reparieren lassen**
Er hat sich die Haare **schneiden lassen**
Er hat sie in das Zimmer **kommen lassen**

The infinitive of *lassen* is generally used rather than the past participle in the sense 'cause', 'make' (cf. 13.3.1c) or in the meaning 'let, allow'. The past participle is most usual in the sense of 'leaving something somewhere', e.g. *Ich habe Kaffee und Kuchen stehen gelassen* (more usual *stehen lassen*), and with the compounds *fallenlassen, liegenlassen*, etc.

(c) *sehen, hören* and other verbs of perception

Ich habe sie hereinkommen **sehen**	*I have seen her come in*
Sie hatte ihn nicht kommen **hören**	*She hadn't heard him come*

In colloquial speech, the past participle is sometimes used with these verbs, e.g. *Sie hatte ihn nicht kommen gehört.* This is usually regarded as substandard, but it is occasionally encountered in writing.

On the other hand, *fühlen* and *spüren* are now used almost exclusively with a past participle, e.g. *Sie hat die Katastrophe kommen gefühlt.*

(d) *helfen, heißen* and other verbs used with a bare infinitive
(i) With *helfen* the infinitive is now more usual than the past participle:

Sie hat ihm den Koffer **tragen helfen** (less common: **tragen geholfen**)

(ii) With *heißen* the infinitive and the past participle are equally common:

Wer hat dich kommen **heißen/geheißen**?

(iii) With other verbs, i.e. *lehren, lernen, machen*, the infinitive is now very rarely used, and the past participle is the norm:

> Er hat sie **lachen gemacht** (unusual: **lachen machen**)

NB: In subordinate clauses the auxiliary precedes these double infinitives: *Er sagte, daß sie es hätte machen sollen/. . ., daß sie den Koffer hat tragen helfen*, etc. (see also 17.1.3c and 21.1.3).

13.3.3 Other uses of the bare infinitive

(a) In commands, in place of an imperative

The use of the infinitive with the force of a command is particularly frequent in official language and instructions, see also 16.2.2a:

> Nicht rauchen! Bitte anschnallen!   *No smoking. Fasten seat-belts*

(b) In isolation, especially in elliptical questions, wishes and the like

> Wie? Alles vergessen und vergeben?   *What? (Am I supposed to) forgive and forget?*
> Wozu sich weiter bemühen?   *Why (should we) bother further?*
> Was möchtest du jetzt? – Schlafen   *What would you like to do now? –*
> bis Mittag!   *Sleep till lunchtime!*

13.4 Infinitives used as nouns

13.4.1 The infinitive of almost any verb can be used as a noun in German

(a) Infinitival nouns often correspond to English *ing*-forms used as nouns

Such nouns from infinitives are neuter, cf. 1.1.3e, and they are spelled with a capital letter:

> Ich hörte das laute Bellen eines Hundes   *I heard the loud barking of a dog*
> Nach monatelangem Warten erhielt sie die Nachricht von seinem Erfolg   *After waiting for months she received news of his success*
> Das Mitnehmen von Hunden ist polizeilich verboten   *Bringing dogs in is forbidden by law*
> die Kunst des Schreibens   *the art of writing*

(b) With reflexive verbs, the pronoun *sich* is usually omitted

This is especially the case if the use of the infinitive as a noun is established, e.g. *das Benehmen* 'behaviour' (from *sich benehmen* 'behave').

However, it may be included to avoid ambiguity, e.g. *die Kunst des Sichäußerns* 'the art of expressing oneself', where *das Äußern* could mean something different. Increasingly, too, *sich* tends to be included with forms which have not yet become established usage, e.g. *dieses ständige Sichumschauen* 'this continual looking round', *das meditative Sichannähern an Gott* 'coming closer to God through meditation', *das Sichnichtbegnügenkönnen* (*Süßkind*) 'not being able to be satisfied'.

NB: The spelling of nouns from reflexive verbs produces uncertainties, and spellings like *das sich Äußern* are not unusual, if incorrect.

(c) Infinitival nouns cannot normally be used in the plural

This is because, like the English *ing*-form, they simply express the action denoted by the verb. However, one or two established forms, with extended meanings, are commonly used in the plural, see 13.4.4.

(d) They can be compounded with the object or another part of the clause

e.g. *das Zeitunglesen* 'reading the newspaper', *das Rückwärtsfahren* 'reversing', *das Schlafengehen* 'going to bed'.

If there are several words in these additional elements, they are normally written with hyphens, e.g. *dieses ständige Mit-sich-selbst-Beschäftigen* (SWF), *das Mit-der-Faust-auf-den-Tisch-Schlagen*. The first word, the infinitive, and any nouns in the combination are all spelled with capital letters.

13.4.2 Wide use of infinitival nouns is typical of written German

They are especially frequent in technical registers, e.g.:

In der Bundesrepublik beginnt sich diese Basis humanen **Miteinanderlebens**, **Untereinanderaussprechens** und **Miteinanderwirkens** aufzulösen (*FAZ*)	*In the Federal Republic this foundation of humane living together, freely exchanging ideas and cooperating is beginning to dissolve*

But they are used in literary prose, too, e.g.:

Dann kam das Schiff, und ich beobachtete, wie so viele Male schon, das vorsichtige **Längsfahren**, **Stoppen**, **Zurückweichen** in dem **Sprudeln** und **Rauschen** und **Räderklatschen**, das **Taueschleudern** und **Festbinden** (*Emil Strauß*).

13.4.3 Infinitival nouns used with prepositions

(a) *beim* + infinitival noun

This usually corresponds to English *on* with an *ing*-form, or a clause with *when* or *as*:

Beim Erwachen am Morgen erschrak ich eine Sekunde lang (*Frisch*) Die Brücke war so dicht mit vierstöckigen Häusern bebaut, daß man **beim Überschreiten** den Fluß nicht zu Gesicht bekam (*Süßkind*)	*On waking up/When I woke up in the morning I was frightened for an instant The bridge was so densely built up with four-storey houses that you couldn't see the river as you crossed it*

(b) *zum* + infinitival noun

(i) This combination expresses purpose. It often corresponds to English *for* with an *ing*-form or an infinitive with *to*:

Zum Fußballspielen ist der Garten viel zu klein Ich gebrauche das Messer **zum Kartoffelschälen** Der Kaffee ist zu heiß **zum Trinken**	*The garden is much too small for playing football in I use the knife for peeling potatoes The coffee is too hot to drink*

(ii) Some combinations of infinitival nouns with *zum* are idiomatic:

Das ist doch **zum Lachen**, **zum Kotzen**, **zum Verrücktwerden**	*But that's laughable, enough to make you sick, enough to drive you mad*

(iii) *bis zum* with an infinitival noun is used for 'until':

Bitte bewahren Sie den Fahrschein *Please retain your ticket until*
bis zum Verlassen des Bahnhofs *you leave the station*

(iv) Combinations of infinitival nouns with *zum* are used with *bringen* or *kommen* to form phrasal verbs expressing the completion of an action:

zum Halten bringen/kommen *bring/come to a stop*
zum Kochen bringen/kommen *bring/come to the boil*

(c) *ins* **+ infinitive**
This combination is frequent with *geraten* or *kommen* to form phrasal verbs denoting the beginning of an action, e.g.:

Der Ball geriet/kam **ins Rollen** *The ball started rolling*
Der Turm kam/geriet **ins Schwanken** *The tower started to sway*
Der Wagen kam **ins Schleudern** *The car went into a skid*

13.4.4 Some infinitival nouns have extended meanings
In effect, they have become independent nouns, isolated from the verb they come from and no longer merely expressing the action denoted by it. The following is a selection of the most frequent:

das Andenken	*souvenir*	das Schrecken	*terror*
das Benehmen	*behaviour*	das Unternehmen	*enterprise*
das Dasein	*existence*	das Verbrechen	*crime*
das Einkommen	*income*	das Vergnügen	*pleasure*
das Essen	*meal*	das Vermögen	*wealth*
das Gutachten	*reference*	das Versprechen	*promise*
das Guthaben	*credit balance*	das Vorhaben	*intention*
das Leben	*life*		

Such nouns are sometimes used in the plural, and plural forms of all the above may be encountered, except for *das Benehmen* and *das Dasein*.

13.5 The present and past participles

Aside from the use of the past participle to form the perfect tenses and the passive (see 12.3–4), the German participles are chiefly employed as adjectives or in participial clauses.

13.5.1 The names and meanings of the participles
The two participles are usually called the 'present participle' (e.g. *lesend, überwältigend*, etc.), and the 'past participle' (e.g. *gestellt, geworfen*, etc.). These terms are rather misleading, as the participles do not necessarily refer to present or past time, and they are often referred to as 'das erste Partizip' and 'das zweite Partizip' in German.

(a) The present participle usually indicates an action which is taking place at the same time as that of the finite verb

Den Schildern **folgend**, fanden sie *Following the signs, they found the hospital*
das Krankenhaus (*Walser*)

(b) The meaning of the past participle differs according to the verb
(i) With intransitive verbs, the past participle has an active (i.e. not passive) sense, and refers to an action which has taken place prior to that indicated by the finite verb:

Der neue Lehrer, in Freiburg **angekommen**, suchte das Humboldt-Gymnasium auf	*Having arrived in Freiburg, the new teacher went to the Humboldt Secondary School*

(ii) With transitive verbs, the past participle has a passive sense. If the verb denotes a continuous action, the participle refers to an action simultaneous with that of the main verb:

Der Zug, von zwei Lokomotiven **gezogen**, fuhr in den Bahnhof ein	*The train, which was being pulled by two engines, came into the station*

With verbs which denote a momentary action, the past participle refers to an action which has taken place before that of the main verb:

Der Flüchtling, von seinen Freunden **gewarnt**, verließ sein Versteck	*The fugitive, who had been warned by his friends, left his hiding-place*

13.5.2 The adjectival use of the participles

(a) Most German present and past participles can be used as adjectives
This is in fact their most frequent type of use outside compound tenses:

die **schreienden** Vögel	mein **verlorener** Schirm
das **kochende** Wasser	der **gehaßte** Feind

(b) Like other adjectives, they can be used as nouns
See 6.4 for more information on the use of adjectives as nouns:

die **Streikenden** *the people on strike*	die **Gehaßte** *the detested woman*
der **Sterbende** *the dying man*	das **Hervorragende** *the outstanding thing*

ein bitterer Kampf zwischen **Habenden** und Habenichtsen, zwischen **Überfütterten** und **Zukurzgekommenen** (*Zeit*)	*a bitter struggle between the haves and the have-nots, between people who are overfed and people who have come off badly*

Many such participles used as nouns have taken on special meanings, e.g. *der/die Abgeordnete* 'member of parliament', *der/die Vorsitzende* 'chairperson', etc. More of these are given in 6.4.3.

(c) Like many other adjectives, they can be used as adverbs
These are chiefly of manner or viewpoint, see 7.3.1c:

Er hat die Sache **überraschend** schnell erledigt	*He settled the matter surprisingly quickly*
Sie rannten **schreiend** davon, als sie ihn sahen (*Süßkind*)	*They ran off screaming when they saw him*
Die alte Frau ging **gebückt** zum Rathaus hin	*The old woman was walking with a stoop towards the town hall*

(d) They are often compounded, especially in written German

These compounds can then also be used as nouns or adverbs in the same way as simple participles:

Vancouver ist eine Stadt von **atemberaubender** Schönheit	*Vancouver is a breathtakingly beautiful city*
die **Arbeitssuchenden**	*the people looking for work*
ein **weichgekochtes** Ei	*a soft-boiled egg*
Tiefgefrorenes	*frozen food*

(e) Present participles can be used adjectivally with an accompanying *zu*

e.g. *das **abzufertigende** Gepäck* 'the baggage for checking'. This is an adjectival form of the construction with *sein* and an infinitive with *zu* expressing possibility or necessity (see 13.2.5). As in that construction the participle has passive force:

ein nicht **zu übersehender** Fehler	*a mistake which cannot be overlooked*
ihre **anzuerkennende** Leistung	*her achievement which must be acknowledged*
ein **Auszubildender**	*a trainee*

As the last example shows, these forms, too, can be used as nouns. This construction is common in official written registers, but it is rare in informal speech.

13.5.3 The extended participial phrase

In German, a participle used adjectivally can be expanded leftwards by adding objects and/or adverbials. In this way, what in English would be a phrase or a subordinate clause placed *after* the noun can appear in German as an extended adjectival phrase placed *before* the noun:

Die **um ihre eigenen Arbeitsplätze fürchtenden** Stahlarbeiter wollten nicht streiken (*FR*)	*The steelworkers, who were afraid for their own jobs, did not want to strike*
Ich habe dieses von meinem Vetter **warm empfohlene** Buch mit Genuß gelesen	*I enjoyed reading this book which was strongly recommended to me by my cousin*
Wegen Überproduktion entlassene Arbeiter demonstrierten im Fabrikhof	*Workers who had been laid off on account of overproduction were demonstrating in the factory yard*
eine **von allen echten Demokraten zu begrüßende** Entwicklung	*a development which must be welcomed by all true democrats*

These extended adjectival phrases can be made into nouns, e.g. *das wirklich Entscheidende* 'what is really decisive', *die soeben Angekommenen* 'the people who have just arrived', etc.

This construction is common in formal written German, especially in non-literary registers (journalism, officialese, non-fiction, etc.), but it is not usual in everyday speech. The following example shows that there can be a considerable distance between article and noun in these phrases:

> Zwar gilt **der** in den vergangenen vier Jahren auf der Basis einer deutsch-amerikanischen Regierungsvereinbarung für bislang 552 Millionen Mark **entwickelte Panzer** als Spitzenmodell seiner Klasse (*Spiegel*)

Although such constructions typically occur with participles, they are used with other adjectives, too: *eine für sie ganz typische **Haltung*** (see 6.6.3).

13.5.4 Lexicalisation of participles used as adjectives

Many participles used as adjectives have become 'lexicalised', i.e. they have developed a meaning distinct from that of the original verb, so that they are now felt to be independent adjectives rather than participles. A clear indication of this happening is that lexicalised participles can be used with the usual comparative and superlative endings, e.g. *spannender, am spannendsten* 'more, most exciting'. With true participles, *mehr* and *meist* are used, see 8.2.7. Another indication of lexicalisation is the possibility of using the prefix *un-* with them, e.g. *(un)bedeutend* '(in)significant', *(un)angebracht* '(in)appropriate', etc. A selection of those most frequently used is given below.

(a) Lexicalised present participles

abstoßend	*repulsive*	beruhigend	*reassuring*	rührend	*touching*
abwesend	*absent*	dringend	*urgent*	spannend	*exciting*
ansteckend	*infectious*	drückend	*oppressive*	überraschend	*surprising*
anstrengend	*strenuous*	einleuchtend	*reasonable*	überzeugend	*convincing*
anwesend	*present*	empörend	*outrageous*	umfassend	*extensive*
auffallend	*conspicuous*	entscheidend	*decisive*	verblüffend	*amazing*
aufregend	*exciting*	glühend	*glowing*	verlockend	*tempting*
bedeutend	*significant*	reizend	*charming*	wütend	*furious*

These can be used not only before an adjective, but also after *sein*:

ein spannender Film	*an exciting film*
der Film war **spannend**	*the film was exciting*

True present participles cannot be used like this in German, and English speakers must beware of confusing these lexicalised participles with the *ing*-forms of the English progressive tenses. Compare:

die brennenden Lichter	*the burning lights*
die Lichter **brennen**	*the lights are burning*

i.e. not *die Lichter sind brennend*. German present participles cannot be used with *sein* to form progressive tenses as can the English *ing*-form with the verb *be* (see also 14.6).

(b) Lexicalised past participles

angebracht	*appropriate*	ausgezeichnet	*excellent*	gelehrt	*scholarly*
angesehen	*respected*	bekannt	*famous*	geschickt	*clever*
aufgebracht	*outraged*	belegt	*occupied*	verliebt	*in love*
aufgeregt	*excited*	erfahren	*experienced*	verrückt	*insane*

Some lexicalised past participles are archaic and are no longer used as the past participle of the verb in question, e.g.:

erhaben	*illustrious*	(*erheben* 'raise'	– modern past part. *erhoben*)
gediegen	*solid, upright*	(*gedeihen* 'prosper'	– modern past part. *gediehen*)
verhohlen	*secret*	(*verhehlen* 'conceal'	– modern past part. *verhehlt*)
verworren	*confused*	(*verwirren* 'confuse'	– modern past part. *verwirrt*)

A few adjectives with the form of past participles are in fact not from verbs at all, e.g. *beleibt* 'portly' and *benachbart* 'neighbouring', which come directly from the nouns *der Leib* 'body' and *der Nachbar* 'neighbour'. There are no such verbs as *beleiben* or *benachbaren*.

13.5.5 Other uses of the past participle

(a) Elliptical use of the past participle

The past participle is sometimes used in isolation as an exclamation or a depersonalised command. Many such forms have become idiomatic:

Verdammt! Verflucht (noch mal)!	*Blast!*
Frisch gewagt!	*Let's get on with it!*
Aufgepaßt!	*Watch out!*

For further details, see 16.2.2b.

(b) The past participle after *finden*

This corresponds closely to the English construction:

Ich fand sie vor dem Ofen **zusammengesunken**	*I found her slumped in front of the stove*
Du wirst ihn dort **aufgebahrt** finden	*You will find him laid out there*

NB: For the use of *finden* with a present participle, see 13.7.5c.

(c) The past participle after *kommen*

This corresponds to an English *ing*-form:

Er kam ins Zimmer **gelaufen**	*He came running into the room*
Sie kam **herbeigeeilt**	*She came hurrying along*

(d) The past participle after *bleiben* and *scheinen*

e.g. *Ihr Brief blieb unbeantwortet; Die Tür schien geschlossen.* The participle with these verbs has a similar force to the *sein*-passive, see 15.2.2e.

13.6 Clauses with participles

13.6.1 Both participles are used to construct non-finite clauses

These can have the force of an adjective, qualifying a noun or pronoun, or of an adverb, giving the circumstances of the action. The participle is usually placed last in the clause, but, exceptionally, it may come earlier:

Ich putzte **auf dem Brett stehend** das Fenster von außen (*Spiegel*)	*I was cleaning the window from the outside, standing on the window-sill*
eine ständige Verbesserung des Automobils nach den Möglichkeiten der Zeit, **doch zugleich immer aufbauend auf das Erreichte** (*Mercedes advert*)	*a continuous improvement of the car according to the possibilities of the time, but at the same time always building on what has been achieved*
Zwar hatte dieses Mal der Dolch, **durch ein seidenes Unterkleid abgelenkt**, das Opfer nicht sogleich tödlich getroffen (*Heyse*)	*Although this time the dagger, deflected by a silk petticoat, had not immediately wounded the victim fatally*

Von der Wucht seiner Rede	*Carried away by the force of his*
hingerissen, brachen die Zuhörer	*speech, the audience continually*
immer wieder in Beifall aus	*broke out into applause*
Da saß eine zarte Dame mit einem	*There sat a delicate lady with a*
zarten Gesicht, **umrahmt von einem**	*delicate face, which was framed by*
blonden Pagenkopf	*blonde hair cut in the page-boy style*

Participial clauses like these are restricted to formal written registers in German. In particular, those with present participles sound stilted and they are used much less frequently than clauses with *ing*-forms in English. In practice, English learners are best advised to avoid them entirely in German and use instead one of the alternatives detailed in 13.7.

13.6.2 Comparative clauses can be formed with *wie* and a past participle

eine Betonburg, **wie** von einem	*a castle made of concrete, as if it*
anderen Stern in diesen Wald	*had fallen into this forest from*
gefallen (*Walser*)	*another star*

In general, this construction is also typical of formal registers, but some have become established idioms and are more widely used:

Also, wie ausgemacht: Wir treffen	*Well, then, as arranged, we'll meet*
uns um acht	*at eight o'clock*
wie gesagt, wie erwartet,	*as I said, as expected,*
wie vorausgesehen	*as foreseen*
wie gehabt (coll.)	*as before, as usual*

13.6.3 A clause with a past participle can be introduced by *obwohl*

This is similar to the English construction with (*al*)*though*:

Obwohl von seinen Kollegen geachtet,	*(Al)though respected by his*
war er nicht sehr beliebt	*colleagues, he was not very popular*

No other conjunction can introduce a participial clause in German.

13.7 German equivalents of English constructions with the *ing*-form

The English *ing*-form is used more widely than the German present participle, which is found mainly as an adjective (see 13.5). In other contexts, different constructions are usually preferred in German.

In particular, the German present participle is not often used in participial clauses (see 13.6.1). English learners are advised to avoid clauses with the present participle entirely in German. In general, the equivalents given below for constructions with the English *ing*-form represent more idiomatic German usage.

13.7.1 English *ing*-form used as a noun

The usual German equivalent is one of the following. Often, more than one alternative is possible:

(a) An infinitive used as a noun, or another noun derived from a verb
(see 13.4 and 22.2):

Aufmerksames **Zuhören** ist wichtig	*Attentive listening is important*
die Freuden des **Skilaufens**	*the pleasures of skiing*
Warum hat man die **Eröffnung** der neuen Schule aufgeschoben?	*Why has the opening of the new school been delayed?*
Er ist einer solchen **Tat** nicht fähig	*He is not capable of doing such a thing*

(b) An infinitive clause with *zu*

Es ist wichtig, **aufmerksam zuzuhören**	*Attentive listening is important*
Er gab zu, **das Fenster zerbrochen zu haben**	*He admitted having broken the window*
Ich verlasse mich darauf, **ihn zu Hause zu finden**	*I rely on finding him at home*

(c) A *daß*-clause

Es ist wichtig, **daß man aufmerksam zuhört**	*Attentive listening is important*
Er gab zu, **daß er das Fenster zerbrochen hatte**	*He admitted having broken the window*
Ich verlasse mich darauf, **daß ich ihn zu Hause finde**	*I rely on finding him at home*

This alternative **must** be used if the English *ing*-form has a different subject from that of the main verb:

Ich kann es mir nicht vorstellen, **daß sie ihren Ring verkauft**	*I can't imagine her selling her ring*
Ich verlasse mich darauf, **daß er alles arrangiert**	*I rely on his/him arranging everything*

NB: After verbs (or nouns and adjectives) governing a preposition, the infinitive clause or *daß*-clause of alternatives (b) and (c) above is usually anticipated by a prepositional adverb (e.g. *darauf*), as the relevant examples show. For details see 6.6.2 and 18.6.14.

(d) A finite verb

Wer **kocht** bei Ihnen zu Hause?	*Who does the cooking at your house?*

The subjectless passive (see 15.1.4) can be used for an English *ing*-form after *there is/are*:

Überall **wurde** laut **gesungen**	*There was loud singing everywhere*

For *there is/are* followed by *no* and an *ing*-form, a construction with *sich lassen* (cf. 15.4.6) is often possible, e.g.:

Das **läßt sich** nicht leugnen	*There's no denying that*

13.7.2 The English *ing*-form after prepositions

(a) *by* (or *through*) + *ing*-form
This construction usually corresponds to a clause with *dadurch, daß* or *indem* (see 19.7.3), or to *durch* followed by an infinitival noun:

Er rettete sich dadurch, daß er aus dem Fenster sprang Er rettete sich, indem er aus dem Fenster sprang Er rettete sich durch einen Sprung aus dem Fenster	*He escaped by jumping out of the window*
Er erreichte sein Ziel dadurch, daß wir ihm geholfen haben	*He attained his goal through our having helped him*

(b) *for* + *ing*-form
The commonest equivalents are *(um) ... zu* (see 13.2.7a), or *zum* with an infinitival noun (see 13.4.3b):

Sie hat keine Zeit mehr, (um) zu üben Sie hat keine Zeit mehr zum Üben	*She no longer has any time for practising*
Es ist zu kalt zum Schwimmen	*It's too cold for swimming*

(c) *instead of* + *ing*-form
For this, *(an)statt ... zu* or *(an)statt daß* is used (see 13.2.7c):

Er spielt,	anstatt zu arbeiten anstatt daß er arbeitet	*He is playing instead of working*

(d) *on* + *ing*-form
This usually corresponds to a clause with *als* or *wenn,* or *beim* followed by an infinitival noun (see 13.4.3a):

Als sie den Brief las, wurde sie rot Beim Lesen des Briefes wurde sie rot	*On reading the letter, she blushed*

(e) *with* + *ing*-form
This construction has a variety of possible equivalents in German, similar to those for adverbial clauses with *ing*-forms (see 13.7.3):

Wenn der Berg nur als ein unbestimmtes Gebilde erscheint, **wobei** sich die Baumgruppen bloß als blasse Schatten zeigen, ...	*If the hill only appears as an indefinite shape with the groups of trees showing only as faint shadows, ...*
Es ist schön hier, **wenn** die Sonne durch die Bäume scheint	*It's lovely here with the sun shining through the trees*
Wir sahen die alte Stadt, **über die** die zerfallene Burg emporragte	*We could see the old town with the ruined castle towering above it*
Da der Fluß rasch stieg, mußten Notmaßnahmen getroffen werden	*With the river rising rapidly, emergency measures had to be taken*
Der Bürgermeister eröffnete die Sitzung **unter** Ausschluß der Öffentlichkeit	*The mayor opened the meeting, with the public being excluded*
Sie eilte durch die Stadt, **und dabei** wehten ihre Haare nach hinten	*She raced through the town with her hair streaming behind her*

(f) *without* + *ing*-form

This corresponds to *ohne ... zu* or *ohne daß* (see 13.2.7b):

Der Zug fuhr durch, **ohne zu halten**	*The train went through without stopping*
Er bot uns seine Hilfe an, **ohne daß wir ihn darum bitten mußten**	*He offered us his help without our/us having to ask him for it*

(g) Other prepositions followed by *ing*-forms

These correspond most often to a German subordinate clause or an appropriate preposition with an infinitival noun:

Nach seiner Ankunft/**Nachdem** er angekommen war, ging er sofort zum Rathaus	*After arriving he went straight to the town hall*
Vor dem Einschlafen/**Bevor** er einschlief las er schnell die Zeitung	*Before going to sleep he read the newspaper quickly*
Trotz seiner Hilfe/**Obwohl** er mir geholfen hatte, kam ich zu spät an	*In spite of his/him having helped me, I arrived late*

NB: *ing*-forms after prepositions governed by nouns, verbs or adjectives (e.g. *I rely on finding him at home*) are dealt with in 13.7.1.

13.7.3 Participial clauses with *ing*-forms

The German equivalent depends on the sense of the clause.

(a) The participial clause and the main verb refer to consecutive or simultaneous actions

(i) The simplest German equivalent is to use main clauses joined by *und*; *dabei* can be used in the second to stress the simultaneity of the actions:

Sie öffnete die Schublade **und** nahm das Testament heraus	*Opening the drawer, she took out the will*
Ich saß an seinem Tisch **und** schrieb einen Brief	*I was sitting at his table writing a letter*
Er erzählte seine Geschichte **und** machte (**dabei**) nach jedem Satz eine Pause	*He told his story, pausing after each sentence*

NB: In modern German, clauses with *indem* do *not* correspond to English participial clauses like those above, despite what some English handbooks of German claim. For the use of *indem*, see 19.7.3.

(ii) A clause introduced by *wobei* can be used if the actions in the two clauses are simultaneous: *Er erzählte seine Geschichte, **wobei** er nach jedem Satz eine Pause machte.*

(iii) If the action of the English participial clause precedes that of the main clause, the German equivalent is a clause with *als*, *wenn* or *nachdem*:

Als wir zum Fenster hinausschauten, sahen wir einen Polizeiwagen heranfahren	*Looking out of the window, we saw a police car approaching*
Wenn man oben auf dem Kirchturm steht, sieht man das ganze Dorf	*Standing on top of the church tower, you can see the whole village*
Nachdem ich die Briefe beantwortet hatte, ging ich spazieren	*Having answered the letters, I went for a walk*

(b) Participial clauses which give a reason or cause

In German, a subordinate clause with *da* or *weil* can be used:

Da es schon spät war, gingen wir nach Hause	*It being late, we went home*
Weil ich wußte, daß sie verreist war, habe ich sie nicht angerufen	*Knowing that she was away, I didn't call her*

(c) Participial clauses introduced by a conjunction

Subordinate clauses with the appropriate conjunction are used in German:

Während ich auf dich wartete, habe ich einen schweren Unfall gesehen	*While waiting for you, I saw a bad accident*

13.7.4 Clauses with *ing*-forms used to qualify nouns

These correspond in German to a relative clause or, especially in formal written German, to an extended participial phrase (see 13.5.3):

Er sah **ein in entgegengesetzter Richtung kommendes** Auto Er sah ein Auto, **das in entgegengesetzter Richtung kam**	*He saw a car coming in the opposite direction*
Einige Minuten später eilte der Arzt, **der einen kleinen Koffer trug**, zum Krankenhaus hin	*A few minutes later the doctor, carrying a small suitcase, was hurrying towards the hospital*

13.7.5 English *ing*-forms after some verbs

The usual German equivalent of English *ing*-forms after verbs is an infinitive with *zu* or a clause, cf. 13.7.1. However, a few verbs are special cases.

(a) Verbs of perception

i.e. *see, hear, feel*. The English *ing*-form corresponds to a bare infinitive or a clause with *wie* (see 13.3.1b):

Ich höre die Vögel laut **singen** Ich höre, wie die Vögel laut **singen**	*I can hear the birds singing loudly*

(b) Verbs of motion

e.g. *go, come, send*, etc. If the *ing*-form expresses purpose, a bare infinitive is used in German (cf. 13.3.1e):

Wir gehen heute **schwimmen**	*We're going swimming today*
Kommst du heute mit **schwimmen**?	*Are you coming swimming with us today?*
Sie schickte ihn **einkaufen**	*She sent him shopping*

The *past* participle is used after *kommen*, e.g. *Sie kam herangelaufen* 'She came running up', see 13.5.5c.

(c) *ing*-form expressing position

i.e. *standing, sitting*, etc. after *find, have, remain, stay*.

(i) German uses a bare infinitive after *bleiben, finden, haben* and *lassen* (see 13.3.1):

Sie blieb neben dem Ofen **sitzen**	*She remained sitting by the stove*
Ich fand ihn am Fenster **stehen**	*I found him standing by the window*
Haben Sie einen Mantel in der Garderobe **hängen**?	*Have you got a coat hanging in the cloakroom?*
Sie ließ ihre Sachen **herumliegen**	*She left her things lying about*

(ii) *finden* can also be used with the present participle of most verbs, e.g. *Sie fand ihn schlafend. Er fand sie Pilze suchend im Wald.* This construction is also possible with verbs of place, as an alternative to the infinitive (cf. (i) above): *Sie fand das Buch auf dem Boden liegend.*

(d) keep + ing-form
A frequent equivalent is *lassen* with a bare infinitive, cf. 13.3.1:

Sie ließ uns warten	*She kept us waiting*

(e) keep/go on + ing-form
The simplest idiomatic equivalent is *weiter* with the verb (see also 7.3.4):

Sie sang weiter	*She kept/went on singing*

(f) need, want + ing-form
These most often correspond to *müssen*, cf. 17.5.1b:

Das muß noch erklärt werden	*That still needs/wants explaining*
Man muß sich um sie kümmern	*She needs/wants looking after*

(g) can't help + ing-form
einfach müssen is the commonest German equivalent, see also 17.3.6:

Sie mußte einfach lachen	*She couldn't help laughing*

14

Uses of the tenses

This chapter deals with the uses of the tenses of the indicative in German. German and English agree in many aspects of tense use, and, in the main, detailed explanations are only given for those where German usage differs in such a way from English as to present difficulties for English learners.

A great deal has been written on the German tenses. Thieroff (1992) is an excellent comprehensive recent survey of both tense and mood. Dieling and Kempter (1989) give full and useful details for the foreign learner from a practical point of view, with exercises. Comrie (1985) is an informative introduction to tense in general.

14.1 The German tenses: general

14.1.1 German has six tenses in the indicative mood of the active voice

i.e. two simple tenses (the **present** and the **past**) and four compound tenses (the **perfect**, the **pluperfect**, the **future** and the **future perfect**).

The formation of these tenses is explained in Chapter 12 and shown in full in Tables 12.2 (for regular verbs), 12.3 and 12.4 (for irregular verbs) and 12.5 (for the compound tenses). Table 14.1 gives a brief resumee of the six tenses of German by way of illustration, giving the first person singular forms for the verbs *machen* and *bleiben*.

14.1.2 What is called the German 'past tense' in this book is sometimes referred to as the 'imperfect tense'

However, unlike the 'imperfect tense' of some other languages (e.g. French or Latin), but like the English 'past tense', this German tense does not necessarily convey the idea of an incomplete or continuous action. For this reason, the less misleading term 'past tense' is to be preferred.

TABLE 14.1 *The tenses of German*

Present	ich mache	ich bleibe
Past	ich machte	ich blieb
Perfect	ich habe gemacht	ich bin geblieben
Pluperfect	ich hatte gemacht	ich war geblieben
Future	ich werde machen	ich werde bleiben
Future perfect	ich werde gemacht haben	ich werde geblieben sein

14.1.3 The *werden*-passive has the same range of tenses as the active, but in the *sein*-passive, only the present and past are commonly used

Full details are given in 15.2.1.

14.1.4 There is a rather different range of tenses in the subjunctive

Full details are given in 16.1.

14.1.5 There are no progressive tenses in German

ich singe, for instance, usually corresponds to both English *I sing* and *I am singing*. However, in some contexts the difference in meaning between these English forms can (or must) be expressed in a different way in German. Details are given in 14.6.

14.2 The present tense

14.2.1 The present tense is used to relate present, habitual or 'timeless' actions or events

This corresponds in general to the use of the present tense (simple or progressive) in English:

Sie **singt** gut	*She sings/is singing well*
Ich **lese** die Zeitung von gestern	*I'm reading yesterday's newspaper*
Dankend **bestätigen** wir den Empfang	*We gratefully acknowledge receipt of*
Ihres Schreibens vom 30. Juni	*your letter of June 30th*
Ursula **spricht** ein wenig Spanisch	*Ursula speaks a little Spanish*
In Irland **regnet** es viel	*It rains a lot in Ireland*

14.2.2 The present tense is commonly used to relate an action or state which began in the past and is still going on at the moment of speaking

Such sentences usually contain an adverb (*schon* or *bisher*), an adverbial phrase with *seit*, or an adverbial clause with *seit(dem)* or *solange* expressing the idea of 'up to now'.

(a) In such 'up-to-now' sentences the German present tense usually corresponds to an English perfect, most often a perfect progressive

Ich **stehe** schon lange hier vor dem Bahnhof	*I've been standing in front of the station for a long time*
Seit wann **wohnen** Sie in Rendsburg?	*How long have you been living in Rendsburg?*
Hier im Ngorongoro-Krater **darf** schon seit Jahrzehnten nicht mehr geschossen werden (*Grzimek*)	*Shooting hasn't been allowed here in the Ngorongoro crater for decades*
Seitdem die Europäer Tanganjika **verwalten**, hat sich eine solche Hungersnot nur noch in Kriegszeiten ereignet (*Grzimek*)	*Since the Europeans have been governing Tanganyika a famine like that has only occurred in wartime*
Er **wohnt** in Hamburg, solange ich ihn kenne	*He's been living in Hamburg as long as I've known him*

(b) The perfect tense is used in some 'up-to-now' sentences
There are two main types of context where this is so, i.e.:

(i) In negative statements:

Ich **habe** ihn seit Jahren nicht **gesehen**	*I haven't seen him for years*
Seitdem ich ihn kenne, **haben** wir uns nie **gestritten**	*Since I've known him, we have never quarrelled*

However, the present is used *if* there has been a continuous action or state lasting up to the present time:

Seit Weihnachten **arbeitet** er nicht mehr	*He hasn't worked since Christmas*
Seitdem ich im Dorf wohne, **bin** ich nie einsam	*Since I've been living in the village, I've never been lonely*

(ii) When referring to a series of actions or states

Er **ist** seit Weihnachten mehrmals krank **gewesen**	*He's been ill several times since Christmas*
Seit ihrer Erkrankung/Seitdem sie krank ist, **hat** sie viele Bücher **gelesen**	*Since she's been ill, she has read a lot of books*

However, the present tense *is* used to refer to a habit or state which has continued up to the present (note the difference in tense in English to the previous example):

Seit ihrer Erkrankung/Seitdem sie krank ist, **liest** sie viele Bücher	*Since she's been ill, she's been reading a lot of books*

NB: In sentences with a *seit(dem)* clause, the verb in the *seit(dem)* clause is *always* in the present. The variation between present and perfect explained above only affects the tense in the main clause.

(c) The present of *kommen* is often used to refer to the immediate past
Again, the idea is of an action continuing up to the present moment. English normally uses the perfect:

Ich **komme**, die Miete zu bezahlen	*I've come to pay the rent*

14.2.3 The present tense used to refer to future time

(a) A present tense is often quite usual in German in contexts where a future is needed in English
This applies whether English uses a future with *will/shall* or *be going to*:

In zwei Stunden **bin** ich wieder da	*I'll be back in two hours*
Wir **finden** es nie	*We're never going to find it*

In practice, the present is more frequent than the future in German to refer to future time as long as future reference is clear from the context:

Sigrid **holt** uns von der Bahn ab	*Sigrid is going to meet us from the station*
Ich erwarte, daß sie **kommt**	*I expect she'll come*
Weitere Einzelheiten **erteilt** Ihnen unser Fachpersonal	*Our specialist staff will give you further information*
Vielleicht **sage** ich es ihm	*Perhaps I'll tell him*
Ich **schreibe** den Brief heute abend	*I'll write the letter tonight*
Morgen um diese Zeit **bin** ich in Wien	*This time tomorrow I'll be in Vienna*

This means we only need to use the future tense in German to express future time *if* the present tense could be taken simply to refer to the present, i.e. if the context does not make it clear that reference is to the future, as in the following sentences:

Er **wird** wieder bei der Post **arbeiten**	*He's going to work for the post office again*
Ich **werde** auf sie **warten**	*I'll be waiting for them*
Sie weiß, was **geschehen wird**	*She knows what will happen*

In the absence of further clues, the corresponding German sentences with the present tense must be taken to refer to the present:

Er **arbeitet** wieder bei der Post	*He's working for the post office again*
Ich **warte** auf euch	*I'm waiting for you*
Sie weiß, was **geschieht**	*She knows what is happening*

(b) If the future is used where it would be possible to use the present, it emphasises the idea of a prediction, an intention or a supposition

This is particularly the case where reference to the future is clear, e.g. through adverbials:

Es **wird** morgen wieder **regnen**	*It is going to rain again tomorrow*
Ich **werde** den Brief heute abend **schreiben**	*I shall write the letter tonight*
Wir aber fliegen dorthin, wo die Sonne scheint, und keine Wolken **werden** uns jetzt noch **stoppen** (*Grzimek*)	*But we're flying to where the sun shines, and no clouds are going to stop us now*

14.2.4 The present tense is sometimes used to refer to the past

This so-called 'historic present' is used more often in writing in German than English. It makes the past seem more immediate and is a common stylistic device in narrative fiction and historical writing:

Mit zuckenden Nerven **marschieren** sie näher, noch immer **versuchen** sie sich gegenseitig zu täuschen, so sehr sie alle schon die Wahrheit **wissen**: daß die Norweger, daß Amundsen ihnen zuvorgekommen **ist**. Bald **zerbricht** der letzte Zweifel ... (*Zweig*)

Similarly in newspaper headlines:

40-Tonner **zermalmt** Trabi – 2 starben (*BILD*)	*Forty-ton lorry squashes Trabi – two dead*

It is also a typical feature of colloquial speech, as in English:

Gestern abend **geh'** ich ins Café und **seh'** den Horst Brunner dort an der Theke sitzen	*Last night I go down the pub and see Horst Brunner sitting there at the bar*

14.3 The past and the perfect

14.3.1 The uses of the past and the perfect tenses in German: summary

(a) In English there is a clear difference in meaning between the past and the perfect tenses

Thus, *I **broke** my leg* and *I **have broken** my leg* are quite distinct in meaning. The difference between the deceptively similar German forms *Ich **brach** mir das Bein* and *Ich **habe** mir das Bein **gebrochen**,* on the other hand, is much less clear-cut, and they can quite often replace one another in context. However, this is a matter of tendency rather than simply of grammatical rules, as there is a great deal of stylistic and regional variation. The main features of current usage are sketched here as simply as possible, following the detailed account in Latzel (1977).

(b) The main differences between the past and perfect tenses in German
These differences can be summarised as follows:

(i) The perfect tense is used:

- to refer to a past action or event which has relevance to the present.
- in spoken German, to refer to past actions and events.

(ii) The past tense is used:

- in written German, to refer to past actions and events.

More details are given in the rest of this section, with examples. It is important to remember that, despite what has often been claimed, the idea of completed or uncompleted action has no relevance whatsoever to the use of these tenses in German.

14.3.2 The use of the perfect and past tenses to refer to a past action or event which has continuing relevance in the present

(a) The perfect tense is usual in spoken and written German to indicate a past action or event whose effect is relevant at the moment of speaking
Linking the past with the present is the typical function of the perfect, and, in general, English and German agree in using the perfect in such contexts. Specifically, we find the perfect used in German:

(i) Where the result of an action or event is still evident at the moment of speaking:

Es **hat** in der Nacht **geschneit** (there's snow on the ground)	*It has snowed in the night*
Sie **hat** sich das Bein **gebrochen** (her leg is still in plaster)	*She's broken her leg*
Meine Tante **ist** gestern **angekommen** (and she's still here)	*My aunt arrived last night*

NB: As the last example above shows, the perfect can be used in German to express the present relevance of a past action even if there is a past time expression in the sentence. In such contexts, with an adverb expressing past time, English always uses the past tense.

(ii) To refer to something which happened in the immediate past:

Jetzt **hat** Klinsmann den Ball **eingeworfen**	*Klinsmann has just thrown the ball in*
Damit **haben** wir diese kleine Führung **beendet**	*With this we have come to the end of this short guided tour*

(iii) To refer to states or repeated actions which have lasted up to the moment of speaking:

Ich **habe** immer **gefunden**, daß es nützlich ist, viel zu wissen	*I've always found it useful to know a lot*
Ich **habe** ihm wiederholt **gesagt**, daß er ihr schreiben sollte	*I've told him repeatedly that he ought to write to her*
Das Paket **ist** noch nicht **angekommen**	*The parcel hasn't arrived yet*

NB: The present tense is used to refer to activities or states which began in the past and continue into the present, i.e. in cases where English typically uses a perfect progressive, cf. 14.2.2.

(b) The past tense is occasionally used to indicate a past action or event which has relevance for the present

i.e. in the kind of contexts given under (a) above. This use of the past tense in these typically 'perfect' meanings is mainly restricted to the following contexts, predominantly in written German:

(i) In newspaper headlines and short announcements. In such cases the one-word form of the past tense has the merit of greater brevity:

Lastwagenfahrer **gaben** Blockade am Brenner nach einer Woche auf (*FR*)	*Lorry drivers give up their blockade on the Brenner pass after a week*
Sie **sahen** soeben einen Bericht von unserem Korrespondenten in Moskau	*You have just been watching a report from our Moscow correspondent*

(ii) With common verbs, especially the auxiliaries, and in the passive:

In der letzten Zeit **war** sie sehr krank	*She has been very ill recently*
Er **mußte** heute kommen	*He has had to come today*
Noch nie **wurde** ein Auto so oft gebaut (*VW advert*)	*No car has ever been produced in such numbers*

(iii) In relative clauses:

Das sind die ersten Bilder der Unruhen in Beijing, die uns **erreichten**	*These are the first pictures which have reached us of the disturbances in Beijing*

In all the above examples the perfect would be equally possible.

14.3.3 The use of the past and perfect tenses to relate actions or events which lie wholly in the past and have no link to the present

(a) In general, narrations of past actions and events are in the past tense in written German and in the perfect tense in spoken German

In English, we typically use the past tense to indicate that an action or event occurred entirely before the moment of speaking. In German, however, while the past tense is usual in such contexts in the written language, the perfect predominates in speech. This is especially the case in south Germany, where the past tense is not used at all in everyday speech.

The normal use of the past tense for a written narrative can be seen in the following passage from Böll's novel 'Billiard um halb zehn':

Aber ich **hatte** Angst, **wartete**, bis auch die Putzfrau **ging**, und **ließ** mich in die Schule einschließen; es **gelang** mir nicht immer, denn meistens **warf** mich die Putzfrau hinaus, bevor sie **abschloß**, aber wenn es mir **gelang**, eingeschlossen zu werden, **war** ich froh.

In Franz Xaver Kroetz's *Chiemgauer Gschichten*, by contrast, where ordinary people (from south Germany) are telling their stories to the author, the narrative is almost entirely in the perfect tense:

> Ja, und dann **hats** wieder ein bißchen **gedauert**, bis sie wieder eine Arbeit **gekriegt hat**, also Lohn von ihr **ist** praktisch nichts **eingegangen**. **Hab** ich alles selbst verdienen **müssen**. Da wo wir dann **geheiratet haben**, da **hab** ich zwei Monate so noch **gearbeitet** auf Montage, und dann **bin** ich gekündigt **worden**.

This general tendency for the past tense to be used for written narratives and the perfect for spoken narratives is subject to certain qualifications, as outlined in (b) to (d) below.

(b) The past tense is not uncommon in spoken north German in some contexts
The main ones are:

(i) With some common verbs, i.e. with *sein, haben, bleiben, gehen, kommen* and *stehen*, with the modal auxiliaries, with verbs of saying, thinking and feeling, and in the passive. In practice, the following are equally frequent in north German speech (to about as far south as Frankfurt/Main):

Ich **war** vorige Woche in Bremen	– Ich **bin** vorige Woche in Bremen **gewesen**
Sie **konnte** gestern nicht kommen	– Sie **hat** gestern nicht kommen **können**
Was **sagten** Sie?	– Was **haben** Sie **gesagt**?
Das alte Haus **wurde** abgerissen	– Das alte Haus **ist** abgerissen **worden**

The past tense of other verbs can be heard in spoken north German, but, in general, less frequently than the perfect.

(ii) In clauses introduced by *als* or *wie*, and in any clause with *damals*:

Ich habe sie gemerkt, als sie aus der Straßenbahn **ausstieg**	*I noticed her when she got out of the tram*
Ich habe gehört, wie sie die Treppe **herunterkam**	*I heard her coming down the stairs*
Damals **mußten** wir alle Ersatzkaffee trinken	*At that time we all had to drink coffee substitute*

(iii) To record a state, or a habitual or repeated action in the past:

Die Rechnung **lag** auf dem Balkon	*The bill was lying on the balcony*
Bei uns in der alten Heimat **dauerten** die Sommerferien länger als hier	*In our old homeland the summer holidays used to last longer than they do here*
Ich habe gewußt, daß sein Vater **trank**	*I knew his father used to drink*

(c) There is a tendency for a longer narrative to start with a perfect, and then continue in the past
The perfect is used to set the scene, as it were. This usage is not only found in speech, but also in writing, especially in newspaper reports:

> 10 Tage nach der Jumbo-Katastrophe in Japan **ist** schon wieder eine Boeing **explodiert**. 54 Urlauber **starben** gestern in einem flammenden Inferno auf dem Flughafen Manchester (England). Als ihr Jet nach Korfu (Griechenland) starten **wollte, wurde** das linke Triebwerk krachend zerfetzt. Sofort **brannte** die Maschine wie eine Reisenfackel. Im Rumpf eingeschlossene Urlauber **trampelten** andere tot. (*BILD*)

(d) The perfect is sometimes used as a narrative tense in written German

The perfect may be used deliberately to give a more colloquial tone. However, particularly outside fiction, it is often treated simply as an alternative to the past and used for reasons relating to style, emphasis and sentence rhythm, as in the following text from Grzimek's *Serengeti darf nicht sterben*:

> Ein tüchtiger Mann namens Rothe, der Verwalter bei den Siedentopfs **war**, **hat** 1913 die Reste einer uralten Siedlung und eines Friedhofs aus der Jungsteinzeit am Nordende des Kraters **entdeckt**. Schon diese Leute, die einige Jahrhunderte vor Christus **gelebt haben**, **weideten** als Hirten ihr Vieh wie heute die Massai. Rothe **hieß** eigentlich anders, er war 1905 bei der ersten finnischen Revolution kurze Zeit Minister **gewesen**, ... In Ägypten **stellte** ihm die russische Geheimpolizei nach, und so **kam** er als Tierpfleger mit Maultieren nach Deutsch-Ostafrika.

In practice, the past could be substituted for any of the perfect tenses in this passage, or vice-versa, without any real difference in meaning.

NB: For stylistic reasons the *du* and *ihr* forms of many verbs in the past tense tend to be avoided, since they can sound clumsy. Thus, *du hast gearbeitet, du hast geschossen, ihr habt gebadet* will often be preferred to *du arbeitetest, du schossest, ihr badetet*, etc.

14.3.4 Other uses of the past tense

The perfect cannot replace the past tense in any of these uses.

(a) To relate a state or activity which began in the past and is still in progress at a more recent point in the past

This is the equivalent in past time of the use of the present with *seit* phrases etc. (cf. 14.2.2). In English a pluperfect (especially pluperfect progressive) is used in such contexts:

Seitdem ich ihn **kannte, besuchte** ich ihn jeden Sonntag	*Since I had known him, I had visited him every Sunday*
Ich **wartete** schon zwei Stunden/seit zwei Stunden auf sie	*I had been waiting for her for two hours*

Similar exceptions to those for the present apply here, too, in that the pluperfect, not the past, is used in negative statements or when referring to a series of actions or states:

Seitdem ich ihn kannte, **hatten** wir uns nie **gestritten**	*Since I had known him, we had never quarrelled*
Ich **hatte** ihm seit Jahren **zugeredet**, sein Haus zu verkaufen	*I had been urging him for years to sell his house*

(b) With the sense of a future-in-the-past

Here, the past is a much less frequent alternative to the *würde*-form of *Konjunktiv II* (the 'conditional', see 16.4.5):

Nachdem er sicher war, daß der Vorgang nicht mehr **hochging**, verließ er das Theater	*When he was sure that the curtain would not go up again, he left the theatre*

(c) To refer to the present

This is a rather special usage to recall information which has already been given in the past:

Wie **war** ihr Name doch gleich?	*What was your name again?*
Wer **erhielt** das Eisbein?	*Who is getting the knuckle of pork?*
Herr Ober, ich **bekam** noch ein Bier	*Waiter, I did order another beer*

14.3.5 Further uses of the perfect

The past tense cannot replace the perfect in any of these uses.

(a) As an alternative to the future perfect

The perfect is commonly used with the sense of a future perfect as long as it is clear from the context (e.g. from a time adverb) that reference is to the future:

Bis morgen um diese Zeit **habe** ich alles **geregelt**	*By this time tomorrow I shall have settled everything*
Bald **habe** ich den Brief **geschrieben**	*I'll have written the letter soon*

If the future perfect is used in such sentences, e.g. *Bis morgen um diese Zeit **werde** ich alles **geregelt haben***, there is often an additional sense of a prediction or a supposition, cf. 14.4.2.

The perfect is the usual tense in subordinate time clauses with future reference in *both* English *and* German:

Wenn ich von ihm **gehört habe**, werde ich dir schreiben	*When I've heard from him, I shall write to you*

Very occasionally, a future perfect is used in such sentences in German:

Ich will fortgehen, wenn ich genug **gelesen haben werde** (*Andersch*)	*I intend to leave when I have read enough*

(b) To indicate a characteristic state

Because the perfect can signal the present result of a past action, it can be used in German to indicate an action whose completion can be taken to define a particular person or thing. This usage has no direct equivalent in English. It is particularly common in technical and legal language:

Ein Unglück **ist** schnell **geschehen** (i.e. they are finished before you've realised it)	*Accidents happen quickly*
Ein Akademiker **hat studiert**	*A graduate is a person who has completed a course of studies*
Die Mannschaft, die zuerst 50 Punkte **erreicht hat**, ist Sieger	*The first team to reach 50 points is the winner*

14.4 The future and the future perfect

14.4.1 Both the future and the future perfect are used less frequently in German than in English simply to refer to future time

If the time reference is clear from the context, German tends to prefer the present tense to the future and the perfect to the future perfect (see 14.2.3 and 14.3.5a). However, there are instances where these tenses *must* be used simply to indicate futurity, since the present or the perfect would have a quite different meaning:

Ich mag sie nicht und **werde** sie nie **mögen**	*I don't like her and I'll never like her*
Hat er Ihnen nicht gesagt, daß er	*Didn't he tell you that he's going*
Sie **besuchen wird?**	*to visit you?*
Am Montag **wird** sie den Gipfel **erreicht**	*On Monday she'll have reached the*
haben	*summit*

14.4.2 The future and future perfect often convey the idea of an intention or an assumption in addition to futurity

This is generally the case when future time reference is otherwise clear from the context, and the present or the perfect could be used rather than the future tenses:

Morgen **wird** es bestimmt **schneien**	*It will definitely snow tomorrow*
Ich **werde** es heute abend noch **erledigen**	*I am going to finish it tonight*
Morgen **wird** er die Arbeit **beendet haben**	*He'll have finished the work tomorrow*

14.4.3 The future tenses often do not refer to the future at all, but simply express an assumption

In these contexts the future refers to the present and the future perfect to the past:

Sie **wird** bereits zu Hause **sein**	*She'll be home already*
Er ist nicht gekommen. Er **wird**	*He hasn't come. He'll have too much to*
wieder zu viel zu tun **haben**	*do again*
Sie **wird** den Zug **verpaßt haben**	*She'll have missed the train*
Er **wird** sich gestern einen neuen	*He'll have bought a new hat yesterday*
Hut **gekauft haben**	

When used in this way, these tenses are often accompanied by the particle *wohl* (see 10.35.1):

Sie wird **wohl** bereits zu Hause sein	Sie wird **wohl** den Zug verpaßt haben

NB: This sense of the future and future perfect is very similar to the meaning of *dürfte* (cf. 17.2.2), so that *Sie wird wohl bereits zu Hause sein* means much the same as *Sie dürfte bereits zu Hause sein.*

14.5 The pluperfect

14.5.1 The German pluperfect mainly indicates a past within the past

(a) **The use of the German pluperfect corresponds closely to that of the English pluperfect**

Wir warteten, bis der Zug **abgefahren war**	*We waited until the train had left*
Sie kamen zu spät, denn das	*They came too late, as the high*
Hochwasser **hatte** den Damm schon	*water had already flooded over the*
überflutet	*embankment*
Das bemerkte man erst, nachdem man	*You only noticed that after you had*
Platz **genommen hatte** (*Morgner*)	*sat down*

(b) **The perfect is occasionally used where one would expect a pluperfect**
This may emphasise the immediacy of a state or an action. The effect is rather similar to that of the 'historic present', cf. 14.2.4, e.g.:

Dann seufzte sie auf eine Weise,	*Then she sighed in a way which made it clear*
die mir deutlich machte, wie alt	*to me how old she had become*
sie **geworden ist** (*Böll*)	

This usage is fairly frequent in writing, and increasingly common in everyday speech.

(c) The past is sometimes used for an expected pluperfect

This usage is predominantly literary and is usually motivated by stylistic reasons, the one-word form being preferred in context:

> ... doch ergab der Befund jene hoffnunglose Krankheit, die man **vermutete** (*Dürrenmatt*)
> ... *but the investigation revealed the terminal disease which had been suspected*

14.5.2 The pluperfect is sometimes used in colloquial German simply to refer to the past

i.e. the pluperfect occurs where a past or perfect tense would be expected:

> Eva hatte dich gesucht
> Wer war das gewesen?
> *Eva was looking for you*
> *Who was that?*

This 'pseudo-pluperfect', as Lockwood (1987: 241) calls it, is a fairly recent development, but it is increasingly common in everyday speech. DUDEN (1995: 150) considers it to be substandard.

14.5.3 Complex pluperfect forms

In south Germany the past tense is not used in speech, and the pluperfect is commonly formed with the *perfect* of *haben*. Thus, one hears, for example, *Ich habe ihn gesehen gehabt* for standard German *Ich hatte ihn gesehen*.

Forms like this are now widespread in speech and not restricted to the south. If an extra dimension of remoteness in time is needed, the *pluperfect* tense of the auxiliary is sometimes used, e.g.: *Sie hatte ihn gesehen gehabt, bevor er sie bemerkt hatte*. This form is particularly common in speech if the action has been reversed again, e.g.:

> Sie **hatte** ihren Schlüssel **vergessen gehabt**
> *She had forgotten her key*
> (but she's remembered it again now)

These complex pluperfects are primarily colloquial and generally regarded as non-standard e.g. by DUDEN (1985: 283) and Weinrich (1993: 238). However, they have a long history and they are not unknown in formal writing:

> Er dachte: Du kannst jetzt nichts gesehen haben, du kannst wegdrücken ... und **hast** bloß den Anschluß **verloren gehabt** und bist kein Jäger (*Gaiser*).
> Wir **haben** uns alle schon daran **gewöhnt gehabt**, daß nichts geschieht, aber immer etwas geschehen soll (*Musil*).

14.6 German equivalents for the English progressive tenses

14.6.1 There are no progressive tenses in German

Thus, the distinction between, say, the progressive *He is singing well* (i.e. at the moment) and the habitual *He sings well* (i.e. usually) cannot be expressed by using different forms of the verb. In many contexts this distinction is ignored in German, which uses *Er singt gut* in both cases.

NB: The English perfect progressive can indicate that an action beginning in the past is still going on at the moment of speaking, e.g. *I have been waiting here for an hour*. German uses the simple present tense in these contexts, cf. 14.2.2.

14.6.2 Ways of indicating continuous action in German

Nevertheless, there are contexts where we need to make it clear in German that we are dealing with a continuous action. For instance, an English sentence like *He was reading 'War and Peace' yesterday* implies that he didn't finish reading it, whereas to say in German *Gestern las er „Krieg und Frieden"* or *Gestern hat er „Krieg und Frieden" gelesen* could imply that he <u>did</u> finish it. In such contexts, German has a number of possibilities for indicating that the action was continuous or unfinished, i.e.:

(a) By using an appropriate adverb
(i) Especially *eben* or *gerade*:

Ich schreibe **eben** Briefe	*I'm writing letters*
Er rasiert sich **gerade**	*He's shaving*

(ii) With verbs of motion, *schon* or *gleich* can often be used:

Ich fahre **schon**	*I'm leaving*
Sie kommt **gleich**	*She's coming*

(iii) Other adverbs may serve in other contexts:

Ich habe ihn **letzthin** zweimal in der Woche gesehen	*I've been meeting him twice a week (recently)*
Ich kümmere mich **eben mal** darum	*I'm seeing to it now*

(iv) Conversely, the sense of habitual or repeated action expressed by a simple tense in English can be indicated by an adverb in German:

Damals stand ich **immer** um sechs auf	*In those days I got up at six*
Sie spielt **meistens** gut	*She (usually) plays well*

(b) By using (*gerade/eben*) *dabei sein* followed by an infinitive with *zu*

Ich bin **gerade dabei**, das Zimmer ein bißchen aufzuräumen	*I'm just tidying the room up a bit*
Gestern war er **gerade dabei**, „Krieg und Frieden" zu lesen	*He was reading 'War and Peace' yesterday*

(c) By using a construction with an infinitival noun
(i) In standard German *beim* is used with an infinitival noun (cf. 13.4.3a):

Als seine Frau zurückkam, war er **beim Kochen**	*When his wife returned, he was cooking*
Wir waren **beim Kartenspielen**, als er klingelte	*We were playing cards when he rang the bell*

(ii) In the Rhineland, *am* is often used with an infinitival noun to express continuous action:

Wir sind **am Arbeiten**	*We are working*
In Köln ist es immer **am Regnen**	*It's always raining in Cologne*

This originally regional usage has recently become much more widely used in colloquial speech, but DUDEN (1985: 44) still considers it substandard.

(d) By using a noun with a prepositional phrase

Wir sind **an der Arbeit**	*We're working*
Er liest **in der Zeitung**	*He's reading the newspaper*
Sie strickte **an einem Strumpf**	*She was knitting a stocking*

(e) By using a different verb

Some German verbs, especially those with prefixes, imply the completion of an action. The corresponding unprefixed verbs do not necessarily imply that the action has finished and can in certain contexts correspond more closely to the sense of the English progressive:

Sie **erkämpften** die Freiheit ihres Landes (i.e. they were successful)	*They fought for their country's freedom*
Sie **kämpften** für die Freiheit ihres Landes	*They were fighting for their country's freedom*
Wir **aßen** die Würste **auf**	*We ate the sausages (up)*
Wir **aßen** die Würste	*We were eating the sausages*
Sie **erstiegen** den Berg	*They climbed the mountain*
Sie **stiegen** auf den Berg	*They were climbing the mountain (i.e. in the process of climbing, or only part of the way)*

15

The passive

The active and the passive voice differ in presenting a different perspective on an action. Using the passive allows us to talk about an activity without mentioning who is doing it (the 'agent'). An active sentence like *Meine Frau liest das Buch* informs us what is happening and who is doing it. The corresponding passive sentence *Das Buch wird gelesen* only gives us information about what is going on, not who is doing it.

There are two passives in German, using the auxiliary verbs *werden* or *sein* together with the past participle:

- The *werden*-passive expresses a process and is closely related to the corresponding active voice. Its use is explained in 15.1.
- The *sein*-passive expresses a state. Its use is more restricted than that of the *werden*-passive (which is three or four times more frequent). Its use, and the difference in meaning between the two passives, are explained in 15.2.

German also has a wide range of alternative ways of expressing passives. Many of these are common, and they are treated in 15.4. In general, the passive is used rather less frequently in German than in English, with the active often being preferred if possible; this is explained in 15.5.

15.1 The *werden*-passive

15.1.1 The *werden*-passive has the same range of tenses and moods as the active voice

For the conjugation of these in the indicative see Table 12.6, for the subjunctive see Table 12.7 and Table 12.8.

(a) The use of the passive tenses is in general the same as in the active
(cf. Chapter 14). There is slight variation in use in a few instances:

(i) The future tense is even less frequent in the passive than in the active. The present is always preferred unless there is a serious risk of being misunderstood (cf. 14.4):

Das Buch **wird** nächste Woche **gelesen**	*The book will be read next week*
Es **werden** große Anforderungen an Sie gestellt werden (*Kafka*)	*Great demands will be placed on you*

In the first example above, the present tense can be used, as the time reference is clear from the phrase *nächste Woche*. In the second example, however, only the use of the future tense shows unambiguously that reference is to the future.

(ii) The past tense of the passive is commonly used rather than the perfect in *both* written *and* spoken German (see 14.3.2b and 14.3.3b).

(b) Imperative forms of the *werden-***passive are scarcely ever used**
However, the imperative of the *sein*-passive is quite frequent (see 15.2.1).

15.1.2 The werden-passive can be formed from most transitive verbs
i.e those which govern a direct object in the accusative, see 18.3.1.

(a) The direct object of the active verb becomes the subject of the corresponding passive construction

Mein Vater liest **das Buch**	*My father is reading the book*
→**Das Buch** wird (von meinem Vater) gelesen	*The book is being read (by my father)*
Der starke Verkehr hielt **mich** auf	*The heavy traffic held me up*
→**Ich** wurde (durch den starken Verkehr) aufgehalten	*I was held up (by the heavy traffic)*
Meine Schwester hat **diesen Brief** geschrieben	*My sister has written this letter*
→**Dieser Brief** ist (von meiner Schwester) geschrieben worden	*This letter has been written by my sister*

(b) A few transitive verbs cannot be used in the *werden-***passive**
With most such verbs, e.g. *dauern* 'last', *schwitzen* 'sweat', *stinken* 'stink', the corresponding English verbs do not have passives, either.

However, no passive is possible in German with verbs of knowing, containing, possessing and receiving, i.e. *bekommen, besitzen, enthalten, erhalten, haben, kennen, kriegen, umfassen, wissen*. German uses other constructions as the equivalent of English passives with such verbs, in particular active forms of another verb or a construction with *man*:

Dieses Schloß gehört dem Grafen von Libowitz	*This palace is owned by Count von Libowitz*
(i.e. NOT: *wird . . . besessen*)	
Ihr Brief traf gestern ein	*Your letter was received yesterday*
(i.e. NOT: *wurde . . . erhalten*)	
Man wußte nicht, wie viele Kinder kommen würden	*It was not known how many children would come*

NB: *enthalten* can be used with *sein*, e.g. *Wieviel Essig ist in diesem Gefäß enthalten?* However, this is not really a passive construction, cf. Helbig and Buscha (1986: 179).

(c) No passive can be formed with the verbs of perception followed by a bare infinitive
(See 13.3.1.) These verbs can be used in the passive with an *ing*-form in English, but the equivalent sentences in German must use alternative constructions, usually with the active voice:

Man hörte ihn singen	*He was heard singing*
Ein Vorbeigehender sah ihn in das Haus einbrechen	*He was seen breaking into the house by a passer-by*

(d) Reflexive verbs are not normally used in the passive
As their direct object is the reflexive pronoun, the possibility of a passive is
excluded. However, the subjectless passive of reflexive verbs occurs occasionally
in spoken German, e.g. *Jetzt wird sich gewaschen* 'It's time to get washed'. This
usage is not widely accepted as standard.

15.1.3 Only the accusative object of an active verb can become the subject of the corresponding passive construction in German

This is an important restriction which does not apply in English. It means that
the dative object, the genitive object or the prepositional object of a verb can *never*
become the subject of a passive construction.

**(a) If a verb which governs a dative is used in the passive, the dative object
remains in the dative case**

Greta dankte **ihm** für seine Hilfe	*Greta thanked him for his help*
→**Ihm** wurde für seine Hilfe gedankt	*He was thanked for his help*

As the dative object stays in the dative, the verbs in these passive constructions
are 'subjectless' or 'impersonal' and the verb has the endings of the third person
singular. Further examples:

Die Zigeuner können **Ihnen** helfen	*The gypsies can help you*
→**Ihnen** kann geholfen werden	*You can be helped*
Er hat **mir** empfohlen, eine Kur zu nehmen	*He has recommended me to take a course of treatment at a spa*
→**Mir** ist empfohlen worden, eine Kur zu nehmen	*I have been recommended to take a course of treatment at a spa*

The pronoun *es* (see 3.6.2a) is inserted if no other element (e.g. the dative or an
adverbial) comes before the verb in a main clause:

> **Es** kann Ihnen geholfen werden
> **Es** ist mir empfohlen worden, eine Kur zu nehmen

**(b) 'Subjectless' passives are also used with verbs which govern a genitive
object or a prepositional object**
Like dative objects, these objects remain in the same form in the passive:

Sie gedachten **der Toten**	*They remembered the dead*
→**Der Toten** wurde gedacht	*The dead were remembered*
Meine Mutter sorgt **für die Kinder**	*My mother is taking care of the childen*
→**Für die Kinder** wird gesorgt	*The children are being taken care of*

es is used with these verbs, too, if no other element comes first:

> **Es** wurde der Toten gedacht   **Es** wird für die Kinder gesorgt

NB: In practice, *gedenken* is the only verb governing the genitive which is used in the passive in modern German.

**(c) With verbs which take a direct (accusative) and an indirect (dative) object,
the indirect object must remain in the dative in the passive**
In German, only the direct object of the active construction can become the subject in the passive in German. This differs from English, where, with many verbs,

either the direct or the indirect object can become the subject of the passive:

Er gab **dem alten Mann** ein Paar Schuhe	*He gave the old man a pair of shoes*
→**Dem alten Mann** wurde ein Paar Schuhe gegeben	*The old man was given a pair of shoes*
Seine Eltern hatten **ihm** ein neues Fahrrad versprochen	*His parents had promised him a new bike*
→**Ihm** war ein neues Fahrrad versprochen worden	*He had been promised a new bike*

NB: An indirect object can become the subject of a passive construction with *bekommen* or *kriegen*, see 15.4.2.

(d) An infinitive clause with *zu* cannot be constructed containing the passive infinitive of a verb which governs the dative

The (understood) subject of an infinitive clause with *zu* must be the same as either the subject or the object of the verb in the main clause (cf. 13.2.4b). But the passive of a verb governing the dative is 'subjectless'. This precludes the use of the passive infinitive of such verbs, and a separate clause with a finite verb is necessary in German. In English, which does not have such restrictions, a non-finite clause is possible:

Er konnte nicht hoffen, daß ihm geholfen wurde	*He could not hope to be helped*
Er besteht darauf, daß ihm geantwortet wird	*He insists on being answered*

15.1.4 The 'subjectless' *werden*-passive

(a) The *werden*-passive can be used without a subject to denote an activity in general

This construction is widely used in spoken and written German. The agent is unspecified, so that there is no indication of who is performing the action. The verb has the third person singular endings. No comparable construction exists in English:

Sie hörten, wie im Nebenzimmer **geredet wurde**	*They heard someone talking in the next room*
Hier darf nicht **geraucht werden**	*Smoking is not allowed here*
Vor Hunden **wird gewarnt**	*Beware of dogs*
Heute ist mit den Bauarbeiten **begonnen worden** (*ARD*)	*They started building today*

(b) A subjectless passive can be formed from any verb which expresses an activity by an agent, whether the verb is transitive or intransitive

This construction thus forms a notable exception to the general rule that the passive is restricted to transitive verbs. Examples with intransitive verbs:

Dann **wurde** auf den Straßen **getanzt**	*Then there was dancing in the streets*
An dem Abend **wurde** viel **gesungen**	*There was a lot of singing that evening*
Hier **wird gelegen, gestöhnt, geliebt, gestorben** (*Goes*)	*Here men lie, moan, love, die*

NB: This is in essence the same construction as that used with verbs which do not govern a direct object in the accusative case, (and which, strictly speaking, are also intransitive), cf. 15.1.3.

(c) The pronoun *es* is inserted if no other element comes before the verb in a main clause
(see 3.6.2a for further details on this use of *es*):

Es wurde auf den Straßen getanzt	*There was dancing in the streets*
Es wird besonders rücksichtslos geparkt (*ARD*)	*People are parking in a particularly inconsiderate way*

(d) The subjectless passive is often used to give commands
(see 16.2 for further details on commands):

Jetzt wird gearbeitet!	*Let's get down to work now*
Jetzt wird nicht gelacht!	*No laughing now!*

15.2 The *sein*-passive

15.2.1 Forms of the *sein*-passive

The conjugation of verbs in the *sein*-passive is given in Table 12.6 (for the indicative) and Table 12.7 and Table 12.8 (for the subjunctive). In practice, only a restricted range of tenses and moods is in use:

Present	ich **bin** verletzt	**Past**	ich **war** verletzt
Konjunktiv I	ich **sei** verletzt	**Konjunktiv II**	ich **wäre** verletzt
Imperative	**Sei** gegrüßt!		

The future tense (e.g. *Die Bilder **werden** morgen entwickelt **sein***) is rare. The past tends to be used rather than the perfect, although the perfect is sometimes heard in spoken German and may occasionally be found in writing:

Die Finnen **sind** nie von sowjetischen Truppen **besetzt gewesen** (*Zeit*)	*The Finns were never occupied by Soviet troops*

15.2.2 The *sein*-passive and the *werden*-passive

(a) The *sein*-passive indicates the *state* which the subject of the verb is in as the *result* of a previous action
This is reflected in its German name: *Zustandspassiv*. The *werden*-passive, on the other hand, relates an action or process, hence its German name: *Vorgangspassiv*.

(i) The following sentence, from Andersen (1990: 196), illustrates the difference between the two passives:

Als ich um fünf kam, **war** die Tür **geschlossen**, aber ich weiß nicht, wann sie **geschlossen wurde**	*When I came at five the door was shut, but I don't know when it was shut*

In the first case, someone had already shut the door by the time I arrived, i.e. it was in a shut *state*, and for this reason the *sein*-passive is used. In the second case I am referring to the time when the *action* of shutting the door occurred, and the *werden*-passive has to be used.

(ii) As with the *werden*-passive, cf. 15.1.3, only the accusative object of a transitive verb can become the subject of a *sein*-passive. With verbs which take a dative, genitive or prepositional object, a 'subjectless' construction must be used in the *sein*-passive, too:

Damit ist den Kranken nicht geholfen	*The patients have not been helped by that*
Für die Verletzten ist gesorgt	*The wounded have been taken care of*

NB: In practice few intransitive verbs are used in the *sein*-passive, viz.: *dienen, helfen, nützen, schaden, sorgen für.*

(iii) The *werden*-passive is used more widely than the *sein*-passive. It can occur with more verbs (see (f) below), and, overall, it is three or four times more frequent in both speech and writing. Nevertheless, the *sein*-passive can be quite common in some registers, e.g. in newspaper reports, which often have reason to refer to *states* or to the *results* of actions:

Deutschland **ist** fest in die NATO **eingebunden** (*Welt*)
Daß die Wahlergebnisse in der DDR **gefälscht waren**, bestreitet auch Modrow nicht (*Spiegel*)

(b) Examples of the difference between the *sein*-passive and the *werden*-passive

A source of confusion for English learners is that the English passive, which uses the auxiliary *be*, looks like the *sein*-passive. The examples below show that the two passives have distinct meanings and are rarely interchangeable (although the distinction is not always upheld in speech):

Der Tisch **wird gedeckt**	*The table is being laid*
(i.e. someone is performing the action of laying the table)	
Der Tisch **ist gedeckt**	*The table is laid*
(i.e. someone has already laid it)	
Das Pferd **wird** an den Baum **gebunden**	*The horse is being tied to the tree*
(i.e. someone is carrying out the action at this very moment, or does it regularly)	
Das Pferd **ist** an den Baum **gebunden**	*The horse is tied to the tree*
(i.e. someone has tied the horse to the tree)	
Die Stadt **wurde** 1944 **zerstört**	*The town was destroyed in 1944*
(i.e. the action took place in 1944)	
Die Stadt **war zerstört**	*The town was destroyed*
(i.e. someone had already destroyed it)	
Die Stadt **wurde** allmählich von Truppen **umringt**	*The town was gradually (being) surrounded by troops*
(i.e. the troops were in the process of surrounding it)	
Die Stadt **war** von Truppen **umringt**	*The town was surrounded by troops*
(i.e. the troops are already in position round the town)	

Sections (c) to (f) below give a number of indicators which are helpful in establishing whether to use the *sein*-passive or the *werden*-passive.

(c) The *werden*-passive often corresponds to an English progressive form, whilst this is never the case with the *sein*-passive

As the examples in (b) above show, this is especially the case in the present tense.

(d) As the *sein*-passive relates the state resulting from a previous action, its meaning is close to that of the perfect tense

The perfect tense often presents a result (see 14.3.2). This means, for example, that the difference between the following pairs of sentences is slight:

Das Haus **ist gebaut** – Das Haus **ist gebaut worden**
Die Stadt **war zerstört** – Die Stadt **war zerstört worden**

As a consequence, the idiomatic English equivalent of a German *sein*-passive is often a perfect or pluperfect rather than a present or a past:

Das Auto **ist repariert**	*The car has been repaired*
Rund 2500 Polizeibeamte riegelten die Stadt ab, über die ein umfassendes Demonstrationsverbot **verhängt war** (*Welt*)	*About 2500 police officers cordoned off the city, which had been made subject to a comprehensive ban on demonstrations*

(e) In the *sein*-passive, the past participle is essentially descriptive
It is used with the force of an adjective describing the state of the subject of the verb.

(i) For example, *geöffnet* in the sentence *Die Tür ist geöffnet* is used with much the same function as *offen* in *Die Tür ist offen*. Compare also:

Der Brief **ist geschrieben** – Der Brief ist fertig
Die Stadt **war zerstört**   – Die Stadt war kaputt

(ii) The past participles of many reflexive verbs (which cannot form a passive) can similarly be used with *sein* with the force of an adjective:

Das Mädchen **ist verliebt**	(cf. Das Mädchen hat sich verliebt)
Ich **bin erholt**	(cf. Ich habe mich erholt)

Helbig and Buscha (1986: 220) term this construction the '*Zustandsreflexiv*'.

(iii) The past participle can be used in a similar manner, with the force of an adjective, with the verbs *bleiben* and *scheinen*:

Ihr Brief **blieb unbeantwortet**	*Her letter remained unanswered*
Der Bau **schien** noch **unvollendet**	*The building still seemed incomplete*

(f) As the *sein*-perfect expresses a state resulting from a previous action, it can only be used with verbs whose action produces a clear result
e.g. *bauen, begraben, beunruhigen, brechen, öffnen, reparieren, schreiben, verletzen, waschen, zerstören*, etc. Compare the following examples:

Meine Hand **ist verletzt** (and you can see the resulting injury)	*My hand is injured*
Mein Wagen **ist beschädigt** (and you can see the resulting damage)	*My car is damaged*

By contrast, verbs whose action does not involve some kind of tangible or visible result, like *bewundern* or *zeigen*, cannot be used in the *sein*-passive at all, as admiring or showing do not produce a result. Other common verbs which similarly cannot be used in the *sein*-passive are:

anbieten	*offer*	bemerken	*notice*	brauchen	*need*	loben	*praise*
befragen	*question*	betrachten	*look at*	erinnern	*remind*	sehen	*see*
begegnen	*meet*			lachen	*laugh*		

(g) The *sein*- and *werden*-passive with *geboren*
Current usage with this verb is most often as follows:

(i) *Ich bin geboren* is used when no other circumstances or only the place of birth are mentioned:

> Wann sind Sie geboren?   Ich bin in Hamburg geboren

(ii) *Ich wurde geboren* is used if further circumstances, or the date, are mentioned:

> Ich wurde im Jahre 1965 in Hamburg geboren.
> Als ich geboren wurde, schneite es.

(iii) Referring to people who are dead, either passive may be used:

> Goethe wurde/war im Jahre 1749 in Frankfurt geboren

15.2.3 The *sein*-passive can indicate a continuing state

Diese Insel **ist** von Kannibalen **bewohnt**	*The island is inhabited by cannibals*
Die Oberrheinebene **ist** durch ihre Randgebirge vor rauhen Winden **geschützt** (*Brinkmann*)	*The Upper Rhine plain is protected from harsh winds by the hills which fringe it*
Die Häuser **sind** nur durch einen Drahtzaun von der Müllverbrennungsanlage **getrennt**	*The houses are only separated from the incinerating plant by a wire fence*
Das Eßzimmer **ist** von einem großen Kronleuchter **beleuchtet**	*The dining-room is lit by a large chandelier*
Die Bücher in der alten Bibliothek **sind** mit Staub **bedeckt**	*The books in the old library are covered with dust*

Here we are not dealing with the result of a process, but with a lasting state, often a permanent one. In such sentences, and *only* in such sentences, the *werden*-passive and the *sein*-passive are interchangeable as long as the *werden*-passive cannot be interpreted as referring to an action. Thus, the following are alternatives to the first four examples above:

> Diese Insel **wird** von Kannibalen bewohnt
> Die Oberrheinebene **wird** durch ihre Randgebirge vor rauhen Winde geschützt
> Die Häuser **werden** nur durch einen Drahtzaun von der Müllverbrennungsanlage getrennt
> Das Eßzimmer **wird** von einem großen Kronleuchter beleuchtet

But not *Die Bücher in der alten Bibliothek* **werden** *mit Staub bedeckt*, as this would mean someone is covering them with dust!

15.3 *von* or *durch* with the passive

A major motivation for using the passive rather than the active is to avoid mentioning who is performing the action. However, if required, the agent can be included in a passive construction by adding a prepositional phrase introduced by *von* or *durch*, which correspond to English *by*. These occur chiefly with the *werden*-passive. With the *sein*-passive they usually only occur when it is a matter of a continuing state, as in 15.2.3.

The traditional rule of thumb is that *von* is used with persons, *durch* with things. This can be useful as a guideline, but it is not fully reliable, as it simplifies the real meaning of the two prepositions in passive contexts, and usage is not wholly consistent.

15.3.1 *von* indicates the agent performing the action

This is usually a person, but can be an inanimate force:

Ich war **von meinem Onkel** gewarnt worden	*I had been warned by my uncle*
Sie wurde **von zwei Polizeibeamten** verhaftet	*She was arrested by two police officers*
Die Stadt wurde **von dem großen Waldbrand** bedroht	*The city was being threatened by the huge forest fire*

15.3.2 *durch* indicates the means by which the action is carried out

This is most often a thing which is the involuntary cause of the occurrence, but it can be a person acting as an intermediary:

Die Ernte wurde **durch den Hagel** vernichtet	*The crop was destroyed by hail*
Ich wurde **durch den starken Verkehr** aufgehalten	*I was held up by the heavy traffic*
Die Hühnerpest wird **durch ein mikroskopisch nicht nachweisbares Virus** verursacht (*ND*)	*Fowl pest is caused by a virus which is not detectable under the microscope*
Ich wurde **durch einen Boten** benachrichtigt	*I was informed by a messenger*

(the messenger was an intermediary for someone else's message)

Die Provinz wurde **durch Flüchtlinge** neu besiedelt	*The province was resettled by refugees*

(*durch* can be used because it was ultimately some other, unnamed person(s) who instigated the resettlement of the province)

durch, not *von*, is used after a noun with verbal force:

die Entdeckung Amerikas **durch Kolumbus**	*the discovery of America by Columbus*
der Ersatz der Muskelkraft **durch die Maschine**	*the replacement of muscle power by machines*

15.3.3 The distinction between *von* and *durch* is not always upheld

(a) In practice there is considerable hesitation between *von* and *durch*

It is often not wholly clear whether we are dealing with the 'agent' or the 'means'. *von* is always usual for persons who obviously carried out the action themselves. However, when this might be a matter of interpretation, or with 'things' (like storms and earthquakes) which people might think of as actually carrying out an action, either *von* or *durch* can be acceptable. Helbig and Heinrich (1983: 31) consider that 'most native speakers' would accept either alternative in the following instances:

Die Brücke ist **von Pionieren/durch Pioniere** gesprengt worden	*The bridge has been demolished by sappers*
Der Baum ist **von dem Blitz/durch den Blitz** getroffen worden	*The tree has been struck by lightning*

The degree of uncertainty in current usage is shown by the fact that DUDEN (1985: 515) says exactly the opposite and claims that 'Man kann nicht sagen: *Der Baum ist durch den Blitz getroffen worden*'. In practice, unless we need to make it *absolutely* clear that one is dealing with the 'doer' or the 'means', *von* and *durch* are effectively interchangeable in modern German.

(b) The difference between *von* and *durch* is most clear when both are used in the same sentence

Ich war **von meinem Onkel durch**   *I had been warned by my uncle through*
seinen Sohn gewarnt worden   *his son*
(My uncle is doing the warning, his son is the intermediary)

Die Kaserne wurde **von Terroristen**   *The barracks were destroyed by terrorists*
durch einen Sprengstoffanschlag *in a bomb attack*
zerstört
(Terrorists destroyed it, the bombs were the means)

15.3.4 A phrase with *mit* is used to indicate the instrument used to perform an action

Das Schiff wurde **mit einem Torpedo**   *The ship was sunk by a torpedo*
versenkt
Das Schloß mußte **mit einem Hammer** *The lock had to be opened with a*
geöffnet werden   *hammer*
Dieser Brief ist **mit der Hand**   *This letter was written by hand*
geschrieben

durch can replace *mit* when inanimate instruments are involved, so that, for instance, *Das Schiff wurde **durch ein Torpedo** versenkt* is a possible alternative for the first example above.

15.4 Other passive constructions

German has a wide range of alternative means of expressing the passive.

15.4.1 *man* is often used in German where English naturally uses a passive

See 5.5.18 for details on the use of *man*.

Man sagt, daß …   *It is said that …*
Man hatte ihn davor **gewarnt** *He had been warned about it*
Das **macht man** nicht   *That's not done*

15.4.2 A passive construction is possible with *bekommen* and *kriegen*

(a) By using the verbs *bekommen* or *kriegen* a dative object can be made into the subject of a passive construction

As explained in 15.1.3, dative objects cannot become the subjects of the *werden*-passive. Compare, however:

Ich schenke **meinem Bruder** das Buch
→**Mein Bruder kriegt/bekommt** das Buch (von mir) **geschenkt**
Ich widerspreche **meinem Bruder**
→**Mein Bruder kriegt/bekommt** (von mir) **widersprochen**

This construction is chiefly found in speech (especially with *kriegen*), and not all Germans accept it as standard. However, it is increasingly frequent in writing. The conditions under which it is possible are still not fully clear, but in general it appears that it can only be used with verbs which express an action and where the original dative object can be interpreted in some way as receiving something.

NB: Less commonly, the verb *erhalten* is used rather than *bekommen* or *kriegen*, e.g. *Sie erhält die Kosten erstattet*.

(b) The *bekommen/kriegen*-passive can be formed from various kinds of dative

Specifically:

(i) From the indirect dative object of a verb which governs both a direct and an indirect object (see 18.4.2). The English equivalent may be a passive, or a construction with *have* and a past participle:

Ich **bekomme/kriege** das Geld regelmäßig **ausgezahlt**	*I am paid the money regularly/I have the money paid to me regularly*
Wir haben viel **gezeigt bekommen/gekriegt**	*We were shown a lot/We had a lot shown to us*
Dort wartet die Oma, um **erzählt zu bekommen**, was sie in den nächsten Tagen sehen wird (*Böll*)	*Granny is waiting there to be told what she is going to see in the next few days*

This construction is possible with most such verbs, except *geben*.

(ii) From the dative object of verbs which only govern a dative object (cf. 18.4.1):

Sie **bekam gratuliert**	*She was congratulated*
Vera **bekommt** von dir **geholfen**	*Vera is being helped by you*
Er **bekam** von niemandem **widersprochen**	*He was contradicted by nobody*

For the reasons given under (a), this construction is not possible with verbs which do not denote an activity or whose dative object cannot be interpreted as a recipient, e.g. *ähneln*, *begegnen*, *gefallen*, *gehören* or *schaden*.

(iii) From the dative of advantage or the dative of possession (cf. 2.5.3 and 2.5.4). This often corresponds to an English construction with 'get':

Sie **kriegte** den Wagen **repariert**	*She got her car repaired*
Man **bekommt** den Schlips **abgeschnitten** (*Grzimek*)	*You get your tie cut off*
Er **bekam** von mir die Wohnung **renoviert**	*He got his flat renovated by me*
Das Haus **bekam** einen Balkon **angebaut**	*The house got a balcony built on*

(c) In a few instances, the subject of a construction with *kriegen/bekommen* does not relate to a dative

(i) It can be used with verbs which take two accusatives, e.g. *lehren* 'teach' and *schimpfen* 'tell off', 'bawl out' (cf. 18.3.3). The conditions are the same, i.e. that the verb denotes an action and the subject of the *kriegen/bekommen* construction is a recipient:

Er **bekommt** (von mir) **geschimpft**	*He's getting told off (by me)*
Der Junge **bekommt** die Vokabeln **gelehrt**	*The boy is getting the words taught him*

(ii) It can be used in other contexts where English can use a construction with 'get':

Ich **kriege** den Brief bis heute abend **geschrieben**	*I'll get the letter written by tonight*

15.4.3 A reflexive verb can often be an alternative to a passive

This is typically possible with verbs which denote accomplishments or activities. A sense of ability (= *können*) is often implied, but not with all verbs. Fagan (1992) gives a detailed account of these constructions.

(a) Reflexive constructions from transitive verbs
In most instances an adverbial of manner is needed to complete the sense:

Das **lernt sich** rasch	*That is/can be quickly learned*
Das **erklärt sich** leicht	*That is/can be easily explained*
Das Buch **verkaufte sich** in Rekordauflagen	*The book was sold in record numbers*
Mein Verdacht **hat sich bestätigt**	*My suspicions have been confirmed*

(b) Reflexive constructions from intransitive verbs
An adverbial of manner and an adverbial of place or time are usually needed to complete the sense. These are impersonal constructions, and *es* can be deleted if it is not in first position in a main clause, cf. 3.6.2a:

Es fährt sich gut auf der Autobahn	*You can drive well on the motorway*
In der Hauptstadt **lebt es sich** besser als anderswo (*Zeit*)	*You can live better in the capital than anywhere else*

(c) A reflexive verb is the natural German equivalent of many English passives or constructions which look like passives

sich ärgern	*be annoyed*	sich schämen	*be ashamed*
sich freuen	*be pleased*	sich verbinden	*be associated*

15.4.4 Many phrasal verbs have a passive meaning

Such phrasal verbs comprise a verbal noun (especially in *-ung*) and a verb which has little real meaning in the context. The following verbs are frequently used to form such complex verb phrases with a passive sense: *erfahren, erhalten, finden, gehen, gelangen, kommen, stehen*:

eine große Vereinfachung erfahren (= sehr vereinfacht werden)	*be greatly simplified*
seine Vollendung finden (= vollendet werden)	*be completed*
in Vergessenheit geraten (= vergessen werden)	*be forgotten*
zur Anwendung kommen (= angewendet werden)	*be used*
Unsere Arbeit hat Anerkennung gefunden	*Our work was appreciated*
Der Wunsch ging in Erfüllung	*The wish was fulfilled*
Das Stück gelangte/kam zur Aufführung	*The play was performed*
Diese Frage steht zur Diskussion	*This question is being discussed*

Such phrasal verbs are characteristic of modern written German. They have been criticised by stylists as verbose, but as DUDEN (1985: 496) points out, they have nuances lacking in the simple verb. For example, *Das Stück gelangte zur Aufführung* emphasises the start of the action, whilst *Das Stück wurde aufgeführt* simply records that the action took place.

15.4.5 The infinitive with *zu* with some semi-auxiliary verbs has the force of a passive

See 13.2.5 for further details on these verbs. Depending on the verb, this construction expresses possibility, obligation or necessity, i.e. it has the sense of *können*, *müssen* or *sollen* followed by a passive infinitive. The following verbs occur in this construction:

(a) *sein*: the construction has the sense of *können*, *müssen* or *sollen*

Die Anträge **sind** im Rathaus **abzuholen** (= Die Anträge können/müssen im Rathaus abgeholt werden)	*The applications may/must be collected from the town hall/are to be collected from the town hall*
Diese Frage ist noch **zu erörtern** (= Diese Frage muß/soll noch erörtert werden	*This question must still be discussed/is still to be discussed*
Dieser Text **ist** bis morgen **zu übersetzen** (= Dieser Text muß/soll bis morgen übersetzt werden)	*This text must be translated by tomorrow/This text is to be translated by tomorrow*

This construction can be turned into an extended adjective using a present participle, e.g. *diese noch zu erörternde Frage* (see 13.5.2e).

(b) *bleiben*: the construction has the sense of *müssen*

Vieles **bleibt** noch **zu erledigen** (= Vieles muß noch erledigt werden)	*Much still remains to be done*

(c) *gehen*: the construction has the sense of *können*

Das Bild **geht** nicht **zu befestigen** (= Das Bild kann nicht befestigt werden)	*The picture cannot be secured*

This construction is colloquial and considered substandard.

(d) *stehen*: the construction has the sense of *müssen*

It is only used impersonally, with a limited number of verbs, principally *befürchten* and *erwarten*:

Es **steht zu befürchten**, daß sich diese Vorfälle häufen (= Es muß befürchtet werden, daß sich diese Vorfälle häufen)	*It is to be feared that these incidents will occur increasingly*

(e) *es gibt*: the construction has the sense of *müssen*

Es **gibt** noch vieles **zu tun** (= Vieles muß noch getan werden)	*There's still a lot to be done*

15.4.6 *sich lassen* with a following infinitive can have the force of a passive and expresses possibility

i.e. it means much the same as *können* with a passive infinitive. This construction is frequent in all registers, with most types of verb:

Das **läßt sich** aber **erklären**	*But that can be explained*
(= Das kann aber erklärt werden)	
Das Problem **läßt sich** leicht **lösen**	*The problem can be solved easily*
(= Das Problem kann leicht gelöst werden)	
Das **ließe sich** aber **ändern**	*That might be altered, though*
(= Das könnte geändert werden)	
Ein Ende **läßt sich** nicht **absehen**	*The end is not in sight*
(*Lenz*)	

This construction can also be used impersonally. The impersonal subject *es* can be omitted if it is not in initial position in a main clause:

Es **läßt sich** dort gut **leben**	*It's a good life there*
Darüber **läßt** (es) **sich streiten**	*We can argue about that*

In general, this construction is only possible if the subject is a thing rather than a person. Reflexive *lassen* with a person as subject usually has the sense of 'cause' or 'permit', see 13.3.1c.

15.4.7 *gehören* with a past participle has passive force and the sense of obligation or necessity

This construction is mainly colloquial and southern:

Dieser Kerl **gehört eingesperrt**	*That bloke ought to be locked up*
(= Dieser Kerl sollte eingesperrt werden)	
Dem **gehört** das deutlich **gesagt**	*He ought to be told that clearly*
(= Ihm sollte das deutlich gesagt werden)	

15.4.8 Adjectives in *-bar* from verbs can be used with *sein* to express a possibility with a passive sense

They correspond to English adjectives in *-able/-ible*, cf. 22.3.1a:

Diese Muscheln sind nicht **eßbar**	*These shellfish are not edible/cannot be eaten*
(= Diese Muscheln können nicht gegessen werden)	
Das Argument ist nicht **widerlegbar**	*The argument is irrefutable/cannot be refuted*
(= Dieses Argument kann nicht widerlegt werden	
Man ist einfach **unerreichbar** (*Frisch*)	*One simply cannot be reached*

Adjectives with the suffixes *-lich* (from some verbs, see 22.3.1f) or *-fähig* (from some verbal nouns) can have similar force:

Seine Antwort war **unverständlich**	*His answer was incomprehensible/could not be understood*
(= Seine Antwort konnte nicht verstanden werden)	
Dieser Apparat ist nicht weiter **entwicklungsfähig**	*This apparatus cannot be developed further*
(= Dieser Apparat kann nicht weiter entwickelt werden)	

15.5 The use of active and passive in German

The passive is common in German, particularly in formal writing (especially in technical registers and journalism), and it is certainly not to be 'avoided' as a matter of course, as some English manuals and handbooks of German suggest. However, it does tend to be rather less frequent than in English. A reason for this is that we often use a passive in English to manoeuvre something other than the subject to the beginning of the sentence. In German, with its more flexible word-order, this can be achieved simply by shifting the elements in the sentence round. Thus, the following sentences probably represent the most natural equivalents in the two languages:

Diesen Roman hat Thomas Mann *This novel was written by Thomas Mann*
während eines Aufenthaltes in Italien *during a stay in Italy*
geschrieben

In German, the accusative object can be placed before the verb and the subject after it, in order to change the emphasis of the sentence, without needing to use a passive construction, as in English. Clearly, this is only possible if the agent (i.e. the subject of the verb in the active) is mentioned. For a more detailed explanation, see 21.2.3b.

16

Mood
The imperative and the subjunctive

In German, as in many languages, speakers can signal their attitude to what they are saying by using different 'moods' of the verb, which are shown by special endings or forms.

16.1 German has three moods: indicative, imperative and subjunctive

The forms of the indicative and the imperative in the simple tenses are given in Table 12.2 (for the strong and weak verbs) and Table 12.3 and 12.4 (for the irregular verbs). Indicative forms for compound tenses are to be found in Table 12.5, and for the passive in Table 12.6. All forms of the subjunctive are shown in Table 12.7 and Table 12.8.

16.1.1 The 'indicative' mood presents what the speaker is saying as a fact

The indicative is the most frequent mood, used in all kinds of statements and in questions – in effect in all contexts where the speaker does not want to give a command or to draw the listener's attention to the fact that what s/he is saying may not be the fact. As it is the 'normal' mood, its use does not need to be treated specifically.

16.1.2 The 'imperative' mood is used in commands and requests

As we normally address these to the person we are talking to, the imperative mood is restricted to the second person (i.e. the 'you'-form). The uses of the imperative in German are treated in section 16.2, together with the other ways of giving commands and requests in German.

16.1.3 The 'subjunctive' mood presents what the speaker is saying as not necessarily true

If we use the subjunctive, we are characterising an activity, an event or a state as unreal, possible or, at best, not necessarily true (hence the old German name of *Möglichkeitsform*). English has largely lost its distinct subjunctive forms, and we express these ideas in other ways, most often by using a 'modal auxiliary' verb like *may* or *should*, or an adverb of attitude like *perhaps* or *presumably*. German has these possibilities too, with modal auxiliaries like *können* or *müssen* (see Chapter 17) or adverbs of attitude like *vielleicht* and *vermutlich* (see 7.3.2). But the subjunctive is still widely used in German, in particular to signal a hypothetical possibility and in reported speech. Full information on the use of the subjunctive in German is given in sections 16.3 to 16.7.

16.2 Commands and the imperative

16.2.1 The imperative mood is used in all kinds of commands and requests

(a) The imperative mood only has special forms for the second person
i.e. the person to whom the request or command is being directly addressed. For the forms for regular and irregular verbs, see Tables 12.2 and 12.3:

> Hans, **sei** doch nicht so dumm!   Angela, **stell(e)** dich nicht so an!
> Kinder, **bringt** mal die Stühle zu uns in den Garten!
> **Kommen Sie** doch bitte herein und **nehmen Sie** Platz, Frau Meier!

In colloquial speech the imperative is characteristically used with the modal particles *mal* (see 10.22.1) and/or *doch* (see 10.7.3). Without one of these, a spoken command can sound insistent or harsh. Other modal particles which are commonly used with the imperative and alter the tone of a command are *ja* (10.19.3), *nur* (10.26.1a), *ruhig* (10.28) and *schon* (10.30.4).

(b) Stressed *du* or *ihr* are sometimes added to the simple imperative form
A pronoun is normally only present in the *Sie* form of the imperative, but the other pronouns are occasionally added to give strong emphasis:

> **Bestell du** inzwischen das Frühstück!   *Meanwhile, you order breakfast*
> (*Wendt*)
> Kinder, wir kommen gleich. **Geht ihr**   *Children, we're just coming. You go first*
> schon vor!

16.2.2 Other ways of expressing commands and requests

German has a range of constructions besides the imperative which express commands, requests, instructions and the like.

(a) The infinitive is commonly used in official commands and instructions
Using the infinitive makes the command sound more general and less directed at a particular person or group:

> Nicht **rauchen**! Bitte **anschnallen**!   *No smoking. Fasten seat-belts*
> Erst **gurten**, dann **starten**!   *Fasten your safety-belt before*
> (official advice to motorists)   *setting off*
> Bitte **einsteigen** und die Türen   *Please get in and close the doors*
> **schließen**! (railway announcement)
> 4 Eiweiß zu sehr steifem Schnee   *Beat 4 egg-whites until stiff*
> **schlagen** (cooking instruction)

With reflexive verbs, the reflexive pronoun is usually omitted:

> Nicht **hinauslehnen**!   *Do not lean out of the window*
> (*sich hinauslehnen* 'lean out')

(b) The past participle is sometimes used for depersonalised commands

See also 13.5.5a. In practice, this construction is limited to idiomatic usage with a small number of verbs:

Abgemacht!	*Agreed!*
Aufgepaßt!	*Look out!*
Stillgestanden!	*Attention!* (military command)

(c) The subjectless passive can have the force of a command

See also 15.1.4d. The speaker can include him/herself in the instruction:

| Jetzt wird gearbeitet! | *Let's get down to work now* |
| Hier wird nicht geraucht! | *No smoking here!* |

(d) Statements or questions in the present or future can serve as commands

i.e. by being given the characteristic intonation of a command, as in English. These always sound more blunt than the simple imperative. In this way, any of the following could be used for English 'Are you going to listen now?!' or 'You're going to listen now!':

| Hörst du jetzt zu?! | Du hörst jetzt zu! |
| Wirst du jetzt zuhören?! | Du wirst jetzt zuhören! |

(e) The modal auxiliary *sollen* can be used with the force of a command

This usage is linked to the basic meaning of *sollen*, which expresses obligation, see 17.6.1b:

| Du **sollst** das Fenster zumachen | *(I want you to) shut the window* |
| Sie **sollen** ihr sofort schreiben | *(You should) write to her at once* |

sollen is often used to repeat a command to someone who appears not to have heard the first time: *Du sollst* <u>sofort</u> *nach Hause kommen!*

Commands in indirect speech are nowadays also most often formulated with *sollen*, e.g. *Sie sagte ihm, daß er sie am Dienstag anrufen **sollte*** 'She told him to call her on Tuesday'. For details see 16.6.4b.

sollen is also commonly used in third person commands, see (g) below.

(f) Commands and requests in the first person plural

In English, these are typically in the form *Let's . . .* German has a number of equivalents for this, i.e.:

(i) The first person plural form of *Konjunktiv I*, with the verb first:

Na, also, **gehen wir** ganz langsam (*Fallada*)	*Well then, let's walk quite slowly*
Seien wir dankbar, daß nichts passiert ist!	*Let's be thankful that nothing happened*
Also, **trinken wir** doch noch ein Glas Wein!	*All right, let's have another glass of wine then*

Note that it is only the form of the verb *sein* which shows us that a subjunctive is used in this construction, as this is the only verb with a distinctive first person plural *Konjunktiv I* form.

(ii) The imperative of *lassen*. This construction is rather formal:

Laß uns jetzt ganz langsam gehen!   **Laßt uns** dankbar sein!
Lassen Sie uns doch noch ein Glas Wein trinken!

(iii) The modal auxiliary *wollen*:

Wir wollen doch noch ein Glas Wein trinken!

Questions with *wollen*, e.g. *Wollen wir jetzt nach Hause gehen?* have the force of a suggestion, rather like English *Shall we ..?* (see 17.7.1b).

(g) Commands and requests in the third person
We use these, for instance, to ask someone else to tell a third person to do something, cf. English *Let her come in*, or when issuing general instructions to anyone concerned.

(i) In modern German, third person commands are most often expressed by means of the modal auxiliary *sollen*, cf. 17.6.1b:

Er **soll** hereinkommen	*Let him come in/Tell him to come in*
Das **soll** dir eine Warnung sein	*Let this be a warning to you*
Sie **sollen** draußen bleiben	*Tell them to stay outside*
Man **soll** hier nicht parken	*There's no parking here*

(ii) *Konjunktiv I* is sometimes used in third person commands (see 16.7.6d):

Es **sage** uns niemand, es **gebe** keine	*Let nobody tell us that there is no longer*
Alternative mehr (*Augstein*)	*any alternative*
Er **komme** sofort	*Let him come at once*

A generalised command (i.e. 'to whom it may concern') can be expressed by using *Konjunktiv I* with the pronoun *man*:

Man **schlage** 4 Eiweiß zu sehr steifem	*Beat 4 egg-whites until stiff*
Schnee	

These constructions with *Konjunktiv I* sound stilted and old-fashioned nowadays: *sollen* is preferred for third person commands, and the infinitive for generalised commands and instructions (see (a) above).

(iii) *Konjunktiv I* of the modal auxiliary *mögen* can also express a command to a third person: *Er **möge** sofort kommen*. This usage is formal and rather old-fashioned.

(h) A *daß*-clause in isolation can be used as a command
These are emotive in tone and are normally heard exclusively with the particle *ja* (see 10.19.3) and/or with an 'ethic' dative (see 2.5.3d):

Daß du mir (ja) gut aufpaßt!	*Be careful for my sake*
Daß ihr ja der Mutter nichts davon erzählt!	*Just don't tell your mother anything about it*

16.3 The subjunctive mood: general

Although the subjunctive mood is widely used in modern German, some forms and uses are nowadays restricted to formal written German, whilst others have become obsolete. Even educated native speakers are often uncertain about what is 'good' or 'correct' usage, and there is often a gulf between what people think they ought to say or write and what they actually do say or write. This does not make it easy to give clear rules for the foreign learner, but we concentrate here on those usages which are most likely to be encountered in practice or needed when speaking and writing German. The forms and tenses of the subjunctive in German are explained in section 16.4. Its use in conditional sentences is treated in 16.5, and in reported speech in 16.6. Other uses of the subjunctive are covered in 16.7.

Much has been written on the subjunctive, and no other aspect of German grammar has attracted so much attention from self-appointed guardians of the language and sundry pedants. Bausch (1979) gives a balanced account of modern usage, Jäger (1970) provides helpful recommendations based on current usage, and Buscha and Zoch (1984) is a detailed survey with exercises for foreign learners.

16.4 Forms and tenses of the subjunctive

16.4.1 The subjunctive mood in German has two main sets of forms, called *Konjunktiv I* and *Konjunktiv II*

The forms of the subjunctive are traditionally referred to by the names of the tenses, e.g. 'present subjunctive' (*er komme*), 'past subjunctive' (*er käme*), 'perfect subjunctive' (*er sei gekommen*), etc. However, the six forms of the subjunctive do not correspond to time differences in the same way as the tenses of the indicative, and these traditional terms are misleading. Most modern German grammars group the six subjunctive forms into two sets which they call *Konjunktiv I* and *Konjunktiv II* as set out in Table 16.1. This makes it easier to explain how the subjunctive is used in German, and these terms will be adopted here.

TABLE 16.1 *Tenses of* Konjunktiv I *and* Konjunktiv II

Konjunktiv I	'present' subjunctive	*es schlafe*
	'perfect' subjunctive	*es habe geschlafen*
	'future' subjunctive	*es werde schlafen*
Konjunktiv II	'past' subjunctive	*es schliefe*
	'pluperfect' subjunctive	*es hätte geschlafen*
	'conditional'	*es würde schlafen*

16.4.2 *Konjunktiv I* and *Konjunktiv II* have largely distinct uses

These have nothing to do with time or tense, and the 'present subjunctive' and the 'past subjunctive' can both refer to the present time, as the following examples demonstrate:

(a) 'present' subjunctive

> Gisela sagt ihrer Mutter, sie **komme**   *Gisela is telling her mother that she is*
> um sechs in Berlin an   *arriving in Berlin at six*

The main use of the 'present subjunctive' – and all the other *Konjunktiv I* forms – is to mark indirect speech, see 16.6.

(b) 'past' subjunctive

> Wenn ich es jetzt **wüßte, könnte** ich   *If I knew it now, I would be able to tell you*
> es dir sagen

The main use of the 'past subjunctive' – and all the other *Konjunktiv II* forms – is to indicate an unreal condition or a possibility, see 16.5.

16.4.3 We can indicate time differences within both *Konjunktiv I* and *Konjunktiv II* by using compound forms

(a) The 'perfect subjunctive' serves as the past tense of *Konjunktiv I*

> Gisela sagt ihrer Mutter, sie **sei** um   *Gisela is telling her mother that she arrived*
> sechs in Berlin **angekommen**   *in Berlin at six*

(b) The 'pluperfect subjunctive' serves as the past tense of *Konjunktiv II*

> Wenn ich es damals **gewußt hätte,**   *If I had known it then, I would have been able*
> **hätte** ich es dir sagen **können**   *to tell you*

16.4.4 *Konjunktiv II*: the 'conditional' with *würde* is often used rather than the simple 'past subjunctive'

The compound 'conditional' form, e.g. *ich würde bleiben*, is frequently preferred to the simple form of the 'past subjunctive', e.g. *ich bliebe*. Whether the one or the other is used depends on the individual verb involved and on register. The use of the simple forms is often encouraged as a mark of good formal written style, as in Berger (1982: 65–9), but many are felt in practice to be stilted or archaic and avoided. The following summary of usage is based on Bausch (1979).

(a) With the weak verbs the simple form can be used in formal German, but only if the subjunctive meaning is otherwise clear from the context

This is because the simple form of *Konjunktiv II* of weak verbs is exactly the same as the past indicative. For example:

> Wenn ich das Fenster **aufmachte,**   *If I opened the window, we would*
> **hätten** wir frische Luft im Zimmer   *have some fresh air in the room*

Although the form *aufmachte* could be ambiguous (in isolation we would have no way of knowing whether it is indicative or subjunctive), the clear *Konjunktiv II* form *hätte* in the other half of the sentence makes it clear that the whole sentence is to be understood as expressing possibility.

However, the simple forms of *Konjunktiv II* of weak verbs are not used in everyday speech, which usually prefers the compound form with *würde*:

> Wenn ich das Fenster **aufmachen würde,** hätten wir frische Luft im Zimmer

Even in writing, the compound form is used if subjunctive meaning is not otherwise clear from the context:

In diesem Fall **würde** ich das Fenster **aufmachen** *In that case I would open the window*

(b) With the common irregular verbs only the simple form is usual

This applies to *sein, haben, werden* and the modal auxiliaries. With these, the simple forms *wäre, hätte, würde, könnte, müßte,* etc. are used, in <u>both</u> spoken <u>and</u> written German, almost to the exclusion of the compound forms *würde sein, würde haben,* etc.

(c) The simple forms of a few other strong or irregular verbs are roughly as frequent in written German as the compound forms with *würde*

This applies to the following verbs:

finden   geben   gehen   halten   heißen   kommen   lassen   stehen   tun   wissen

The simple forms of *kommen, tun* and *wissen* (i.e. *käme, täte, wüßte*) are also quite common in spoken German, as well as in writing, and those of the others in this group are sometimes heard, too.

(d) The simple forms of the other strong or irregular verbs are restricted to formal written German

However, even there they are less frequent than the compound forms with *würde*. Several, in particular most of the irregular ones and others in -ö- and -ü- (e.g. *begönne, flösse, verdürbe*), are felt to be impossibly archaic and stilted, and they are generally avoided even in writing. The verbs to which this applies are indicated in Table 12.9.

(e) Pluperfect forms with *würde … haben/sein* are unusual

They do occasionally occur, e.g.:

Es **würde** nichts mehr **verändert haben**, wenn ich im gleichen Ton auch noch von Napoleon erzählt hätte (*Frisch*) *It wouldn't have changed anything if I had told stories in the same tones about Napoleon*

However, they are much less common than the forms with *hätte* or *wäre*, especially in writing.

16.4.5 The 'conditional' form with *würde* is often used in the sense of a 'future-in-the-past'

i.e. where the writer is looking forward within a narrative in the past tense, e.g.:

Er wußte viel besser als Chénier, daß er keine Eingebung **haben würde**; er hatte nämlich noch nie eine gehabt (*Süßkind*) *He knew much better than Chénier that he would not have an inspiration; because he had never had one*

Ich beschloß, sobald ich groß **sein würde**, Spengler zu lesen (*Dönhoff*) *I decided I would read Spengler as soon as I was grown-up*

Mein Hauptgedanke war gewesen, ob ich jemals wieder meine Gesangstunden **aufnehmen würde können** (*Bernhard*)	*My main consideration was whether I would ever be able to take up my singing lessons again*
Ich dachte auch an die Gossen, in denen ich einmal **liegen würde** (*Böll*)	*I thought also of the gutters I would some day lie in*

The simple 'past subjunctive' form of *Konjunktiv II* cannot be substituted for the 'conditional' in contexts of this type. Thieroff (1992) gives detailed information on this usage.

16.5 Conditional sentences

Conditional sentences typically have the form of a subordinate clause introduced by the conjunction *wenn*, expressing a condition, and a main clause, expressing the consequence, e.g.:

Wenn ich Zeit hätte, käme ich gern mit

16.5.1 *Konjunktiv II* is used in sentences which express unreal conditions

(a) The simple or compound (*würde-*) form of *Konjunktiv II* is used to express an unreal condition relating to the present or the immediate future

Wenn wir Zeit **hätten**, **könnten** wir einen Ausflug machen	*If we had time, we would be able to go on an excursion*
Die Europäer **wären** erleichtert, wenn England wieder **austreten würde** (*Zeit*)	*The Europeans would be relieved if England pulled out again*
Die Dinge, die ich ihr **kaufen würde**, wenn ich Geld **hätte** (*Böll*)	*The things I would buy her if I had any money*
Wenn ich 20 000 Mark im Lotto **gewinnen würde**, **würde** ich sofort nach Teneriffa **fliegen**	*If I won 20,000 marks in the lottery I would fly to Tenerife immediately*

Note that a form of *Konjunktiv II* is used in *both* the *wenn*-clause *and* the main clause in German. This is different from English, which uses the past tense in the *if*-clause, and the conditional in the main clause.

Either the simple form or the compound form (with *würde*) of *Konjunktiv II* may be used in *both* the *wenn*-clause *and* the main clause. Which one is used depends on register and on the individual verb used, as explained in 16.4.4.

Stylists have long recommended that sentences with a *würde*-form in *both* clauses should be avoided. However, it is common in spoken German and not unusual in writing, especially if the simple forms of the verbs involved are obsolete, as in the last example above and the following:

Mein Vater **würde** sich im Grabe **umdrehen**, wenn ich jetzt nicht seine Ansprüche **weiterfolgen würde** (*Spiegel*)	*My father would turn in his grave if I didn't continue to keep to the standards he set*

(b) Conditional sentences with the pluperfect subjunctive express a hypothetical possibility in the past

The pluperfect subjunctive form of *Konjunktiv II* is used in both the *wenn*-clause *and* the main clause:

Wenn ich es nicht mit eigenen Augen **gesehen hätte, hätte** ich es nicht **geglaubt**	*If I hadn't seen it with my own eyes, I wouldn't have believed it*
Wenn mich jener Anruf nicht mehr **erreicht hätte, wären** wir einander nie **begegnet** (*Frisch*)	*If that call hadn't reached me, we would never have met*
Es **wäre** besser für mich **gewesen,** wenn ich **hätte** absagen **können** (*Böll*)	*It would have been better for me if I had been able to refuse*

(c) Time differences between the main clause and the *wenn*-clause can be indicated by using the simple or pluperfect forms as appropriate

Wäre de Gaulle schon im ersten Wahlgang **gewählt worden, würde** die französische Bevölkerung schon jetzt das Datum **kennen** (*FAZ*)	*If de Gaulle had been elected on the first ballot the French people would already know the date*
Ich **säße** hier nicht auf demselben Stuhl, wenn wir bisher diesen Punkt nicht **erreicht hätten** (*Zeit*)	*I wouldn't be sitting here in the same chair if we hadn't already reached this point*

(d) Other auxiliary verbs used in sentences expressing unreal conditions

(i) The *Konjunktiv II* of *sollen* is often used in the *wenn*-clause. This is similar to the use of *should* or *were to* in English:

Wenn sie mich **fragen sollte,** würde ich ihr alles sagen	*If she were to ask me, I would tell her everything*
Er hält sich bereit, aus der Bodenluke zu springen, wenn sich nachts ein Auto der Sägemühle **nähern sollte** (*Strittmatter*)	*He is ready to jump out of the skylight if a car should approach the sawmill at night*

(ii) The *Konjunktiv II* of *wollen* also occurs frequently in the *wenn*-clause, often with only a faint suggestion of its basic meaning of 'want', 'intend':

Wenn du schneller **arbeiten wolltest,** könntest du mehr verdienen	*If you worked a bit faster you could earn more*
Wie wäre es, wenn wir ihr **helfen wollten**?	*What about us helping her?*

It is particularly common in formal written German if the conjunction *wenn* is omitted (cf. 16.5.3a):

Es würde uns zu lange aufhalten, **wollten wir** alle diese Probleme ausführlich behandeln	*It would detain us too long if we were to treat all these problems in detail*

(iii) Especially in south Germany, the *Konjunktiv II* of *tun* is common in substandard colloquial speech instead of *würde*, cf. 13.3.1d:

Wenn ich jetzt **losfahren täte,** so könnte ich schon vor zwölf in Augsburg sein	*If I set off now, I could be in Augsburg by twelve*

16.5.2 The indicative is used in conditional sentences which express 'open' conditions

i.e. where there is a real possibility of the conditions being met. These correspond to conditional sentences without *would* in English:

Wenn sie immer noch krank **ist, muß** ich morgen allein kommen	*If she's still ill, I'll have to come on my own tomorrow*
Wenn ich ihr jetzt **schreibe, bekommt** sie den Brief morgen	*If I write to her now, she'll get the letter tomorrow*
Wenn wir jetzt **losfahren, werden** wir schon vor zwölf in Augsburg **sein**	*If we set off now, we'll be in Augsburg by twelve*

With the past tense, the sense is that the conditions have been met:

Wenn meine Eltern mir Geld **schickten, kaufte** ich mir sofort etwas zum Anziehen	*If my parents sent me money I immediately bought something to wear*

16.5.3 Alternative forms for conditional sentences

A typical conditional sentence has a *wenn*-clause and a main clause, as shown in 16.5. There are a few variations on this pattern, i.e.:

(a) The conjunction *wenn* can be omitted

If this is done, the subordinate clause begins with the verb:

Hätte ich Zeit, käme ich gern mit	*If I had time, I should like to come with you*
Ist sie krank, muß ich morgen allein kommen	*If she's ill, I'll have to come on my own tomorrow*
Sollte ich nach Berlin kommen, würde ich sie sicher besuchen	*If I should get to Berlin I'd be sure to visit her*

This construction can be compared to the similar, rather old-fashioned English construction, e.g. 'Had I time, . . .'. In German it is commoner in formal writing than in speech. Occasionally, the main clause comes first:

Das Bild wäre unvollständig, **würden** nicht die vielen Gruppen erwähnt, die den Einwanderern das Leben leichter machen (*FR*)	*The picture would be incomplete if the many groups were not mentioned who make life easier for the immigrants*

(b) If the *wenn*-clause comes first in the sentence, it can be picked up by *so* or *dann* at the start of the main clause

This 'correlating' *so* or *dann* is optional, but quite common:

Wenn ich Zeit hätte, (**so/dann**) käme ich gern mit
Wenn ich ihr heute schreibe, (**so/dann**) bekommt sie den Brief morgen

It is particularly frequent if *wenn* is omitted, cf. (a) above:

Hätte ich Zeit, (**so**) käme ich gern mit
Ist sie krank, (**so**) muß ich morgen allein kommen
Sollte ich nach Berlin kommen, (**so**) würde ich sie sicher besuchen

(c) The condition may appear in another form than in a *wenn*-clause
e.g. in an adverbial or another kind of clause. A form of *Konjunktiv II* is used to
signal a hypothetical condition:

Dieser Unbekannte würde mich **wahrscheinlich** besser verstehen (*Böll*)	*This stranger would probably understand me better*
Ohne die Notlandung in Tamaulipas wäre alles anders gekommen (*Frisch*)	*But for the emergency landing in Tamaulipas everything would have turned out different*
Wer diese Entwicklung vorausgesehen hätte, hätte viel Geld verdienen können	*Anyone foreseeing this development would have been able to make a lot of money*

In some sentences the condition may be wholly implicit:

Lieber bliebe ich zu Hause (i.e. wenn ich die Wahl hätte)	*I would rather stay at home*
Ich hätte dasselbe getan (i.e. wenn ich an deiner Stelle gewesen wäre)	*I would have done the same*

(d) Other conjunctions used in conditional sentences
wenn is the predominant conjunction in conditional sentences, but there are one
or two other possibilities:

(i) *falls* 'if' unambiguously introduces a condition, unlike *wenn*, which can also
mean 'when(ever)' (see 19.3.1d). In contexts where a misunderstanding would
be possible it can be useful to make the sense clear. Compare:

Wenn ich nach Berlin komme, besuche ich sie	*When(ever) I get to Berlin I visit her* or *If I get to Berlin I shall visit her*
Falls ich nach Berlin komme, besuche ich sie	*If I get to Berlin I shall visit her*

It is most often used to introduce 'open' conditions, with the indicative (cf.
16.5.2), although it does occasionally occur with *Konjunktiv II*, and it is particularly frequent with *sollte*:

Sie kann niemanden ins Oberhaus befördern lassen, **falls** er einen unsicheren Wahlkreis vertritt (*FAZ*)	*She cannot elevate anybody into the Upper House if he hasn't got a safe seat*
Falls diese Hinweise zuträfen, wäre das eine eindeutige Verletzung der Abmachungen (*MM*)	*If these indications were correct, that would be a clear infringement of the agreements*
Man hielt eine Ratskonferenz für denkbar, jedoch nur, **falls** Frankreich dem Haushalt die Zustimmung verweigern sollte (*FAZ*)	*A meeting of the Council was considered conceivable, but only if France should refuse to give its consent to the budget*

Even if it is used with the subjunctive, it still leaves the possibility open that the
consequence can be realised – unlike *wenn*, which can indicate a completely
hypothetical and unfulfillable condition.

(ii) *angenommen, daß ...*, *vorausgesetzt, daß ...* 'assuming that', 'provided
that'. These mainly introduce 'open' conditions. The *daß* can be omitted, and
then the following clause has the word order of a main clause:

Angenommen, daß er den Brief erhalten hat/**Angenommen,** er hat den Brief erhalten, wird er bald hier sein	*Assuming he got the letter, he'll be here soon*
Vorausgesetzt, daß nichts dazwischen kommt/**Vorausgesetzt,** es kommt nichts dazwischen, ziehen wir im Frühjahr nach Graz um	*Provided that all goes well, we'll be moving to Graz in the spring*

(iii) *sofern* and *soweit* are often used in the sense of 'if' or 'provided that' in open conditions, cf. 19.7.4:

Sofern/Soweit es die Witterungsbedingungen erlauben, findet die Aufführung im Freien vor der alten Abtei statt	*If weather conditions permit, the performance will take place in the open air in front of the old abbey*

(iv) *selbst wenn, auch wenn, sogar wenn, wenn . . . auch*

These can all correspond to English 'even if', so that, for example, the German equivalent of 'Even if I wrote him today, he wouldn't get the letter until Tuesday', could be any of the following:

Selbst wenn ich ihm heute schriebe, **Auch wenn** ich ihm heute schriebe, **Sogar wenn** ich ihm heute schriebe, **Wenn** ich ihm **auch** heute schriebe,	würde er den Brief erst Dienstag bekommen

or with *wenn* omitted, in formal written German only (and commonly with an optional *doch* in the main clause):

Schriebe ich ihm **auch** heute, würde er den Brief (**doch**) erst Dienstag bekommen

(v) *es sei denn, (daß) . . .* 'unless' is chiefly used in 'open' conditions. The *daß* can be omitted, and then the following clause has the word order of a main clause:

Ich komme um zwei, **es sei denn,** { ich werde aufgehalten { daß ich aufgehalten werde	*I'll come at two, unless I'm held up*

In old-fashioned literary usage *denn* on its own can have this meaning:

„Ich lasse dich nicht fort", rief sie, „du sagst mir **denn**, was du im Sinn hast" (*Wiechert*)	*'I shan't let you go', she cried, 'unless you tell me what you have in mind'*

wenn . . . nicht is the most frequent equivalent for English 'unless'. It is used with open or unreal conditions, in the latter case with *Konjunktiv II*:

Wenn er **nicht** bald kommt, wird es zu spät sein	*Unless he comes soon, it will be too late*
Er hätte es nicht gesagt, **wenn** er **nicht** schuldig wäre	*He wouldn't have said it unless he was guilty*

In some contexts, though, *wenn . . . nicht* can have a different meaning (i.e. 'if not'). Compare:

Du brauchst die Suppe nicht zu essen, wenn du sie wirklich nicht magst	*You needn't eat the soup if you really don't like it*

16.6 Indirect speech

16.6.1 Indirect and direct speech

(a) By means of 'indirect' (or 'reported') speech we report what someone said by incorporating it into a sentence of our own

This contrasts with 'direct' speech, where we quote what someone said in the original spoken form. Compare the following English examples:

Direct speech: She said, **'I am writing a letter'**
Indirect speech: She said **that she was writing a letter**

There are marked differences in English between direct and indirect speech. In particular, we put what was said in a subordinate clause of its own, often introduced by *that*, the pronoun is altered (in the example, from first to third person) and the tense is shifted to the past.

(b) In German, instead of shifting the tense, we use forms of *Konjunktiv I* to mark indirect speech

Direct speech: Sie sagte: **„Ich schreibe einen Brief"**
Indirect speech: Sie sagte, **daß sie einen Brief <u>schreibe</u>**

This is the most important use of *Konjunktiv I* nowadays – so much so that **Konjunktiv *I* on its own is often enough to indicate indirect speech.**

However, the use of the subjunctive to mark indirect speech varies considerably; it is much less used in informal registers, and there is much uncertainty among native speakers. The remainder of this section explains current usage, which is summarised for quick reference in Table 16.2.

The conjunction *daß*, like English *that*, can be omitted after the verb of saying, see 19.2.1b. If this is done, the following dependent clause has the order of a main clause, with the verb second, e.g. *Sie sagte, sie* **schreibe** *einen Brief.*

16.6.2 Standard rules for the use of the subjunctive in indirect speech

All modern grammars of German prescribe the following rules as correct usage for formal writing. They are summarised in Table 16.2.

(a) *Konjunktiv I* **is used to mark indirect speech wherever possible**
i.e. as long as the forms of *Konjunktiv I* are clearly distinct from those of the present indicative. In practice, for all verbs except *sein*, this is the case *only* in the third person singular, where the *-e* ending of *Konjunktiv I* contrasts with the present indicative ending *-t* (compare subjunctive *sie schreibe*, but present indicative *sie schreibt*).

(i) In most cases the indirect speech keeps the same tense in the subjunctive as was used in the indicative in the original direct speech:

Direct Speech	Indirect Speech
present indicative	→ **present subjunctive**
„Ich weiß es nicht"	Sie sagte, sie **wisse** es nicht
future indicative	→ **future subjunctive**
„Ich werde morgen kommen"	Sie sagte, sie **werde** morgen kommen
perfect indicative	→ **perfect subjunctive**
„Ich habe ihn gesehen"	Sie sagte, sie **habe** ihn gesehen

TABLE 16.2 *Rules for indirect speech in formal written German*

RULE 1: Use *Konjunktiv I*, keeping the same tense as in the original direct speech	*Present tense* Ich schreibe den Brief *I am writing the letter*	→ *Present subjunctive* Sie sagte, sie **schreibe** den Brief *She said she was writing the letter*
	Future tense Ich werde den Brief schreiben *I shall write the letter*	→ *Future subjunctive* Sie sagte, sie **werde** den Brief **schreiben** *She said she would write the letter*
	Past tense Ich schrieb den Brief *I wrote the letter*	→ *Perfect subjunctive* Sie sagte, sie **habe** den Brief **geschrieben** *She said she had written the letter*
	Perfect tense Ich habe den Brief geschrieben *I have written the letter*	→ *Perfect subjunctive* Sie sagte, sie **habe** den Brief **geschrieben** *She said she had written the letter*
	Pluperfect tense Ich hatte den Brief geschrieben *I had written the letter*	→ *Perfect subjunctive* Sie sagte, sie **habe** den Brief **geschrieben** *She said she had written the letter*
RULE 2: BUT if the *Konjunktiv I* form is the same as the indicative, use *Konjunktiv II*	*Present tense* Wir schreiben den Brief *We are writing the letter*	→ *Past subjunctive* Sie sagten, sie **schrieben** den Brief *They said they were writing the letter*
	Future tense Wir werden den Brief schreiben *We shall write the letter*	→ *Conditional* Sie sagten, sie **würden** den Brief **schreiben** *They said they would write the letter*
	Past tense Wir schrieben den Brief *We wrote the letter*	→ *Pluperfect subjunctive* Sie sagten, sie **hätten** den Brief **geschrieben** *They said they had written the letter*
	Perfect tense Wir haben den Brief geschrieben *We have written the letter*	→ *Pluperfect subjunctive* Sie sagten, sie **hätten** den Brief **geschrieben** *They said they had written the letter*

If the present tense of the original direct speech refers to the future (cf. 14.2.3), the future subjunctive is often used in indirect speech as an alternative to the present subjunctive:

Sie heiratet bald → Sie sagte, sie **werde** bald heiraten

(ii) If the original direct speech was in the past or the pluperfect tense, the perfect subjunctive is used in indirect speech:

past indicative	→ **perfect subjunctive**
„Ich wußte es nicht"	Sie sagte, sie **habe** es nicht gewußt
pluperfect indicative	→ **perfect subjunctive**
„Ich hatte es nicht gewußt"	Sie sagte, sie **habe** es nicht gewußt

Complex pluperfect forms are sometimes used if the original direct speech was in the pluperfect, e.g. (as an alternative to the last example above): *Sie sagte, sie habe es nicht gewußt gehabt.*

(b) If the form of *Konjunktiv I* is the same as that of the indicative, then *Konjunktiv II* is used

The principle underlying this 'replacement rule' is that indirect speech should be marked by a distinct subjunctive form if possible. This is typically needed in the third person plural, where only *sein* has a *Konjunktiv I* form (*sie seien*) which differs from the form of the present indicative:

Direct Speech	Indirect Speech
present indicative	→ **past subjunctive**
„Wir wissen es nicht"	Sie sagten, sie **wüßten** es nicht
future indicative	→ **conditional**
„Wir werden morgen kommen"	Sie sagten, sie **würden** morgen kommen
past or perfect indicative	→ **pluperfect subjunctive**
„Wir sahen ihn nicht"	Sie sagten, sie **hätten** ihn nicht gesehen
„Wir haben ihn nicht gesehen"	

In these examples, the *Konjunktiv I* forms *sie wissen, sie werden kommen* and *sie haben gesehen* are no different from those of the present indicative, and they are replaced by *Konjunktiv II* forms.

(c) The standard rules for the use of the subjunctive in indirect speech are adhered to with particular consistency in newspapers

By using *Konjunktiv I* we can indicate that we are simply reporting what someone else said, without committing ourselves to saying whether we think it is true or not. This makes it a handy device for journalists (especially when reporting politicians?!) and newspapers make wide use of it:

Der Bundespressechef verwies darauf, daß in den kommenden Gesprächen noch manches verfeinert werden **könne** (*FAZ*)	*The Federal information officer pointed out that some things could be refined in future discussions*
Auf seine Eindrücke über den Stand des Bürgerkrieges – der besser **verliefe**, als es die Presse **darstelle**, erklärte Johnson – sollen sich die Beschlüsse stützen (*Welt*)	*The decisions ought to be based on his impressions of the state of the civil war – which, Johnson declared, was going better than portrayed by the press*

Konjunktiv I is such a clear indication of reported speech that it can be used on its own to show that a statement is simply reported. This means that in German we can often dispense with the repeated cues like *He said that . . ., He went on to say that . . .* which we usually need in English. Almost any report in a serious newspaper will provide examples of how this possibility is exploited to the full:

> Die Bundesregierung **verhalte** sich „widerrechtlich", wenn sie DDR-Bürgern in ihrer Botschaft Aufenthalt **gewähre**, sagte der Sprecher des Ostberliner Ministeriums am Abend. Diese „grobe Einmischung in die souveränen Angelegenheiten der DDR" **könne** ebenso wie „Kampagnen, die bis zur versuchten Erpressung anderer Staaten ausarten, zu folgenreichen Konsequenzen führen". Bundesdeutsche Medien **führten** eine Kampagne, in die sich Berichten zufolge nun auch das Auswärtige Amt in Bonn **eingeschaltet habe**. (*Süddeutsche Zeitung 8.8.1989*)

Note the alternation of *Konjunktiv I* and *Konjunktiv II* forms and that, even in a main clause without any verb of saying, as in the last sentence above, the subjunctive on its own is enough to signal reported speech.

16.6.3 Alternative current usage in indirect speech

The standard rules given in 16.6.2 still represent dominant usage in formal writing, and recent surveys, e.g. Sommerfeldt (1990), have confirmed that they are still adhered to pretty consistently in that register. However, there is a fair range of alternative usage, particularly in colloquial speech. This section surveys these alternatives and explains where they occur most commonly.

(a) *Konjunktiv II* is used rather than *Konjunktiv I*, even where a distinct *Konjunktiv I* form is available

i.e. in contexts – notably in the third person singular of most verbs except *sein* – where it is not required by the 'replacement rule' explained in 16.6.2b. This occurs:

(i) in everyday speech:

Sie hat gesagt, sie **käme** heute nicht	*She said she wasn't coming today*
Sie hat gesagt, sie **hätte** es verstanden	*She said she had understood it*
Sie hat gesagt, sie **würde** den Brief noch heute schreiben	*She said she'd get the letter written today*

Konjunktiv II is an alternative in speech to the indicative, (see (c) below), but it sounds more formal and it may be preferred when the main verb is in the past tense. *Konjunktiv II* also tends to be used if there is a longer stretch of reported speech covering more than one sentence:

Er sagt, er hat eben einen neuen Wagen gekauft. Der **hätte** über 80 000 Mark gekostet und **hätte** eine Klimaanlage	*He says he's just bought a new car. It cost more than 80,000 marks and it's got air-conditioning*

Konjunktiv I is rarely used in indirect speech in colloquial German, as it sounds stilted and affected in informal registers. However, forms of *sein* are occasionally heard, but usually implying that the speaker has doubts, e.g. *Gertrud hat mir gesagt, sie **sei** heute krank* (but I think that she might not have been telling the truth!).

(ii) In writing *Konjunktiv II* is less usual than *Konjunktiv I*, but it does occur occasionally:

Sie sagte, ihr Vater **schliefe** erst gegen morgen richtig ein und **würde** bis neun im Bett **bleiben**, und sie müsse ... den Laden aufmachen (*Böll*)	*She said that her father didn't get to sleep properly till the morning and he would stay in bed till nine and that she had to open the shop*
Tante Sissi schrieb uns, es gehe Onkel Heinrich nicht gut und sie **säße** oft an seinem Bett (*Dönhoff*)	*Aunt Sissi wrote telling us that Uncle Heinrich wasn't well and she often sat at his bedside*
('Standard' usage here would be *schlafe, bleibe* and *sitze*)	

NB: There is no consistent distinction in meaning between *Konjunktiv I* and *Konjunktiv II* in indirect speech, and they are quite often used interchangeably, as in the two examples above. Cf. also (d) below.

(b) The compound form with *würde* is used in place of the simple form of *Konjunktiv II*

For English speakers, the use of *würde* in indirect speech as a substitute for *Konjunktiv II* is potentially confusing, and they need to be careful not to interpret it as equivalent to an English conditional with 'would'.

(i) The use of *würde* is particularly common in colloquial spoken German, especially since the use of the simple form of *Konjunktiv II* is restricted to a few common verbs (cf. 16.4.4):

Er sagte, ich **würde** zu schnell **reden**	*He said I talk too fast*
Sie sagte, ihr Hund **würde** kein Fleisch **fressen**	*She said that her dog didn't eat meat*

(ii) In writing the use of the conditional is frowned on by purists, but it does occur, most often with those strong verbs whose simple *Konjunktiv II* forms are obsolete, or with weak verbs (cf. 16.4.4).

It can be used for a *Konjunktiv II* required by the 'replacement rule':

Immer häufiger, berichtet Professor N. von der Uni Hamburg, **würden** Studenten abends oder nachts **jobben**. Tagsüber seien sie dann furchtbar erschöpft (*Spiegel*)	*Professor N. from the University of Hamburg reports that more and more often students take on casual work in the evenings or at night. During the day they are then terribly exhausted, he said*
Sieben Leser gaben an, sie **würden** regelmäßig Fachzeitschriften **lesen** (*MM*)	*Seven readers declared that they regularly read specialist journals*

The conditionals are being used here rather than the ambiguous simple *Konjunktiv II* of *jobben* or the obsolescent form *läsen*.

It can be used even where a distinct *Konjunktiv I* form is available:

Gleichzeitig informierte man die Presse, die Polizei **würde** auch die Namen zweier Komplizen **kennen** (*Horizont*)	*At the same time the press was informed that the police also knew the names of two accomplices*

The *Konjunktiv II* form *kennte* is obsolete, but by the standard rule one would expect the unambiguous *Konjunktiv I* form *kenne*

It can be used in place of the *Konjunktiv I* form *werde* if the meaning is 'future-in-the-past' (cf. 16.4.5):

Er glaubte, er **würde** schon eine Lösung **finden**	*He thought he would surely find a solution*

In practice, this last usage is frequent, and it is accepted in formal writing even by the most fastidious stylists.

(c) The indicative is used rather than the subjunctive

(i) This is the case in spoken German. The tense of the original direct speech is usually retained:

Sie hat gesagt, sie **weiß** es schon	*She said she knew it already*
Sie hat gesagt, sie **hat** es verstanden	*She said she had understood it*
Sie hat gesagt, sie **wird** den Brief noch heute schreiben	*She said she'd write the letter today*

In practice, the indicative is the most frequent alternative in informal registers, although *Konjunktiv II* also occurs (see (a) above).

(ii) This is the case in writing. There are a few contexts where the indicative is fairly regular in indirect speech in written German, as a permissible alternative to the subjunctive, i.e.:

– If the indirect speech is in a clause introduced by *daß*:

Der Kanzler erklärte, daß er zu weiteren Verhandlungen bereit **ist/war**	*The Chancellor declared that he was prepared to enter into further negotiations*
Es wurde erzählt, daß der Verwalter ihnen persönlich das Mittagessen **auftrug** (*Wiechert*)	*It was recounted that the administrator served them lunch in person*

– If *daß* is included, the indicative is almost as frequent as the subjunctive even in written German. However, if *daß* is omitted (cf. 19.2.1b), then the subjunctive is essential: *Der Kanzler erklärte, er sei zu weiteren Verhandlungen bereit.*

NB: If the main verb is in the past tense, the verb in indirect speech is usually in the tense of the original direct speech. However, it is sometimes shifted, as in English, as the second example shows.

– If a first or second person is involved:

Er sagte ihr, von wo ich gekommen **bin**	*He told her where I had come from*
Ich habe ihm erzählt, daß der Fluß hier tief **ist**	*I told him that the river was deep here*
In deinem letzten Brief hast du mir geschrieben, seine Tochter **studiert** schon vier Semester in Hamburg	*In your last letter you wrote that his daughter had already been studying in Hamburg for four semesters*

The function of *Konjunktiv I* is to distance the speaker from what is being reported, i.e. to make it clear that s/he isn't willing to vouch for whether it is true or not. For this reason it may not make sense to use it in contexts in which the speaker or the listener is directly involved.

If the 'replacement rule' (cf. 16.6.2b) is ignored:

Die Verfügung des letzten deutschen Kaisers besagte, daß im Ruhrgebiet weder Universitäten noch Kasernen gebaut werden **dürfen** (*v.d. Grün*)	*The decree by the last German emperor declared that neither universities nor barracks were allowed to be built in the Ruhr*

The standard rule would require *dürften*, as the form *dürfen* is identical with the indicative and not a clear subjunctive. However, these ambiguous third person plurals are not unusual. They are sometimes used, too, if the 'replacement rule' produces an archaic *Konjunktiv II* form, as in the following newspaper example given by Lockwood (1987: 272):

Der Unterhändler sagte, er hoffe, daß die Vernunft siege und Verhandlungen **beginnen**	*The negotiator said he hoped that reason would prevail and talks would begin*

Applying the replacement rule would result in the obsolete form *begönnen*.

– For stylistic reasons, to render the flavour of colloquial speech:

Seit der Wende denken die Nazis, uns **bestraft** ja eh keiner (*Spiegel*)	*Since the Wall came down the Nazis have thought that nobody would punish them anyway*

(d) There is no consistent distinction in meaning between *Konjunktiv I*, *Konjunktiv II* and the indicative when used in indirect speech

It is sometimes claimed that there is a difference between the three possible forms, i.e.:

    (i)   Manfred sagte, daß er krank **gewesen sei**
    (ii) Manfred sagte, daß er krank **gewesen wäre**
    (iii) Manfred sagte, daß er krank **gewesen ist**

According to this theory, **(i)** *Konjunktiv I* is used merely to report Manfred's statement neutrally, without offering any personal opinion as to whether it is true or false. Using **(ii)** *Konjunktiv II*, on the other hand, would make it clear that the speaker does not believe Manfred, whilst in **(iii)** the speaker's use of the indicative would acknowledge that it is a fact that he had been ill.

However, although some writers may try to operate with such a distinction, it has never been consistently maintained. In practice the use of the three forms is determined not by meaning, but by register, stylistic considerations and norms of usage, as outlined in this section.

16.6.4 Indirect questions and commands

(a) Usage in indirect questions follows the same norms as in indirect statements

i.e. as outlined in 16.6.2 and 16.6.3, viz.:

(i) In written German *Konjunktiv I* (or *Konjunktiv II*, by the 'replacement rule') is used:

Sie fragte ihn, wie alt sein Vater **sei**	*She asked him how old his father was*
Der Lehrer fragte uns, ob wir **wüßten**, was das **bedeute** (*Böll*)	*The teacher asked us if we knew what that meant*
Die Dame fragte, ob denn die Typen einer bestimmten Sorte von Schreibmaschinen alle ununterscheidbar gleich **wären** (*Johnson*)	*The lady asked whether the characters of a particular make of typewriter were all the same and indistinguishable from each other*

As in statements, *Konjunktiv II* is sometimes used even if a distinct *Konjunktiv I* form is available: *Sie fragte ihn, wie alt sein Vater* **wäre**. The indicative occasionally occurs in indirect questions in formal writing:

Warum ich nicht fragte, ob Hanna noch lebt, weiß ich nicht (*Frisch*)	*I don't know why I didn't ask whether Hanna was still alive*

But it is less frequent than the subjunctive, even though the conjunction (*ob, wie, was*, etc. cf. 19.2) cannot be deleted.

(ii) In spoken German either the indicative or *Konjunktiv II* is used:

    Sie hat ihn gefragt, wie alt sein Vater **ist/wäre**
    Tante Emma hat sie gefragt, ob sie Hunger **hat/hätte**
    Der Lehrer hat gefragt, ob sie es **wissen/wüßten**

(b) Commands are reported in indirect speech by using a modal verb

Konjunktiv I can be used in writing, but both *Konjunktiv II* and the indicative are quite frequent, and they are usual in spoken German.

(i) *sollen* is the verb used most often in indirect commands. Thus the direct command:

> Rufe mich morgen im Büro an!   *Call me at the office tomorrow*

would correspond to the indirect command:

> Herr Hempel sagte ihr, sie **solle/**   *Mr Hempel told her to call him at the*
> **sollte/soll** ihn morgen im Büro   *office tomorrow*
> anrufen

(ii) *müssen* indicates a rather more forceful command, e.g. *Herr Hempel sagte ihr, sie **müsse/müßte/muß** ihn (unbedingt) morgen im Büro anrufen.*

(iii) *mögen* sounds less peremptory. It is most often used now in the *Konjunktiv II* form *möchte: Herr Hempel sagte ihr, sie **möchte** ihn morgen im Büro anrufen.* The *Konjunktiv I* form *möge* is occasionally still found, but it can sound old-fashioned and stilted (or facetious):

> Bitte richten Sie Herrn Schnier aus,   *Please inform Mr. Schnier that his brother's*
> die Seele seines Bruders sei in   *soul is in peril and he should call as soon*
> Gefahr, und er **möge**, sobald er mit   *as he has finished his meal*
> dem Essen fertig ist, anrufen (*Böll*)

16.7 Other uses of the subjunctive

16.7.1 Hypothetical comparisons: *as if*-clauses

(a) Clauses expressing a hypothetical comparison are typically introduced by *als ob* in German
This corresponds to English clauses with *as if*:

> Er tat, **als ob** er krank wäre   *He acted as if he was/were ill*
> Das Kind weint, **als ob** es Schmerzen hätte   *The child is crying as if it is in pain*

There are one or two alternatives to using *als ob*:

(i) The *ob* of *als ob* can be left out. The finite verb then moves into the position immediately after the *als*:

> Er tat, **als wäre** er krank   Das Kind weint, **als hätte** es Schmerzen

> Sie sprach Deutsch, **als wäre** es ihre   *She spoke German as if it was her native*
> Muttersprache (*Bednarz*)   *language*

This is more frequent than *als ob* in writing, but it is rare in speech.

(ii) *als wenn* or *wie wenn* are less frequent alternatives to *als ob*:

> Er tat, **als wenn/wie wenn** er krank wäre
> Das Kind weint, **als wenn/wie wenn** es Schmerzen hätte

(b) The verb in German *as if*-clauses is usually in a form of *Konjunktiv II*
(i) If the action in the *as if*-clause is simultaneous with the action in the main clause, the simple form of *Konjunktiv II* is used:

> Er tat, als ob er krank **wäre**   *He acted as if he was/were ill*
> Das Kind weint, als ob es Schmerzen   *The child is crying as if it is in pain*
> **hätte**

The *würde*-form of *Konjunktiv II* can be used if the simple form is obsolete or unusual (cf. 16.4.4. See also (c) below):

Sie hatten den Eindruck, als **würde**   *They got the impression that Diana*
sich Diana um die Rolle in einem   *was trying for a part in a period film*
Kostümfilm **bewerben** (*Spiegel*)
(Simple *bewürbe* is obsolete)

(ii) If the action in the *as if*-clause took place before the action in the main clause, the pluperfect subjunctive is used:

Sie sieht aus, als ob sie seit Tagen   *She looks as if she hasn't eaten for days*
nicht **gegessen hätte**
Er tat, als ob nichts **passiert wäre**   *He acted as if nothing had happened*

(iii) If the action in the *as if*-clause will take place after the action in the main clause, the *würde*-form of *Konjunktiv II* is used:

Es sieht aus, als ob es **regnen würde**   *It looks as if it will rain*
Es sah aus, als ob er gleich   *It looked as if he was about to fall down*
hinfallen würde

(c) In written German *Konjunktiv I* can be used in *as if*-clauses

It is less frequent than *Konjunktiv II* even in writing, and some Germans even consider it incorrect. It can be used *if* its form is distinct from that of the present indicative:

Er tat, als ob er krank **sei**   Es sah aus, als **werde** er hinfallen
Sie sieht aus, als ob sie seit Tagen nicht gegessen **habe**

Es klang, als **beklage** sie sich bei   *It sounded as if she was complaining*
Klaus Buch über Helmut (*Walser*)   *to Klaus Buch about Helmut*

There is no difference in meaning between *Konjunktiv I* and *Konjunktiv II* in *as if*-clauses. *Konjunktiv I* can sometimes be used, rather than a *würde*-form (see (b) above), to avoid an obsolete or unusual simple form of *Konjunktiv II* (cf. 16.4.4):

Der Eindruck, als **befände** sich die   *The impression that the party was on*
Partei auf dem Weg zurück in ihre   *the road back to its problematic past,*
beschwerliche Vergangenheit – als   *that it wasn't fighting to overcome*
kämpfe sie nicht für die   *immediate problems*
Überwindung akuter Probleme (*Zeit*)

The *Konjunktiv II* form *kämpfte* is not distinguishable from the past tense, and so the writer has preferred to use *Konjunktiv I* – although he has used a *Konjunktiv II* (*befände*) earlier in the same sentence.

(d) In spoken German the indicative is commonly used in *as if*-clauses

The indicative is probably at least as frequent as the subjunctive in spoken German, but it is much less common in writing:

Er tat, als ob er krank **war**   Es ist mir, als ob ich hinfallen **werde**
Sie sieht aus, als ob sie seit Tagen nicht gegessen **hat**

NB: The *ob* of *als ob* is not omitted if the verb is in the indicative.

16.7.2 The subjunctive in clauses of purpose

(a) Clauses with *damit* 'so that' sometimes have a verb in the subjunctive
Konjunktiv I or *Konjunktiv II* are used without any difference in meaning:

Konstantin mußte als erster über den Graben, um die Flinte in Empfang zu nehmen, damit sie nicht womöglich mir ins Wasser **fiele** (*Dönhoff*)	*Konstantin had to cross the ditch first to take hold of the shotgun so that I shouldn't let it drop into the water*
Einmal schickte Dionysos dem Aristippos drei Mädchen, damit er sich eine davon als Geliebte aussuchen **könne** (*SZ*)	*Dionysus once sent three girls to Aristippos so that he could choose one of them as a lover*

This usage is now restricted to formal German and can sound old-fashioned. The indicative is nowadays more frequent in all registers, e.g.:

Ich habe ihm auch Bücher gebracht, damit er sich nicht **langweilte** und nicht immer gezwungen **war**, an seine Verschwörungen zu denken (*Bergengruen*)	*I brought him some books too, so that he didn't get bored and wasn't always compelled to be thinking of his plots*

The modal verbs *können* or *sollen* are often used in *damit*-clauses, especially (but not only) in spoken German:

Er zog sich zurück, damit wir ihn nicht sehen **konnten/sollten**

(b) The conjunction *auf daß* 'so that'
auf daß is an alternative to *damit* used only in formal written German. It sounds archaic and solemn and is in practice always followed by a subjunctive (usually *Konjunktiv I* if the form is unambiguous):

Der Häuptling eines Eingeborenenstammes verfluchte sie, auf daß ihnen nichts von allem, was sie dem Boden und den Gewässern abgewinnen würde, je zum Nutzen **gereiche** (*Spiegel*)	*The chief of a native tribe cursed them, that they might never derive benefit from anything they gained from the soil or the waters*

16.7.3 *Konjunktiv II* can moderate the tone of an assertion, a statement, a request or a question and make it sound less blunt

This usage is very frequent, especially in spoken German. The simple form of the common verbs is used, or the *würde*-form of others (cf. 16.4.4):

Ich wüßte wohl, was zu tun **wäre**	*I think I know what's to be done*
Eine Frage **hätte** ich doch noch (*Valentin*)	*There's one more thing I'd like to ask*
Da **wäre** er nun aufgewacht (*Dürrenmatt*)	*He seems to have woken up*
Ich **würde** auch **meinen**, daß es jetzt zu spät ist	*It seems a little late to me, too*
Diese Sache **hätten** wir also geregelt	*That would appear to be sorted out*
Das **wär**'s für heute	*I think that's enough for today*
Hätten Sie sonst noch einen Wunsch?	*Is there anything else you would like?*
Würden Sie bitte das Fenster **zumachen**?	*Would you be so kind as to shut the window?*
Könnten Sie mir bitte sagen, wie ich zum Bahnhof komme?	*Could you please tell me how to get to the station?*

16.7.4 *Konjunktiv II* is sometimes used in time clauses introduced by *bis*, *bevor* or *ehe*

This use is restricted to formal written German and is an optional alternative to the indicative. It can stress that it was still in doubt whether the action or event in question would actually take place:

Sie beschlossen zu warten, bis er **käme**	*They decided to wait till he came*
Er weigerte sich, den Vertrag zu unterzeichnen, bevor wir ihm weitere Zugeständnisse **gemacht hätten**	*He refused to sign the contract before we had made further concessions* ·

16.7.5 The subjunctive in negative contexts

Konjunktiv II can be used in contexts where an event, action or state was possible, but in fact did not take place or was not the case. The indicative is in most cases a possible alternative, especially in speech, but it can sound less tentative. Such contexts are:

(a) After the conjunctions *nicht daß*, *ohne daß* and *als daß*

Nicht, daß er faul **wäre** (*or*: ist), aber er kommt in seinem Beruf nicht voran	*Not that he's lazy, but he's not getting on in his career*
Vukovar ist in den letzten drei Monaten pausenlos beschossen worden, ohne daß klar geworden **wäre**, warum dies geschah (*NZZ*) (*ist* would sound more definite)	*Vukovar has been shelled incessantly over the last three months without it becoming clear why this was happening*
Die Auswahl war zu klein, als daß ich mich **hätte** schnell entscheiden mögen (*Grass*)	*The choice was too small for me to have wanted to decide quickly*

NB: The set phrase *nicht daß ich (es) wüßte* 'not that I know of' is always used with a subjunctive.

(b) In other subordinate clauses where the main clause and/or the subordinate clause have a negative element

So gab es keine menschliche Tätigkeit, die nicht von Gestank begleitet gewesen **wäre** (*Süßkind*)	*So there was no human activity which was not accompanied by the stench*
Es gibt nichts, was schwieriger **wäre** (*or*: ist), als der Gebrauch des Konjunktivs	*There's nothing more difficult than the use of the subjunctive*
nicht eine einzige Großstadt, die nicht ihr Gesicht in zwei Jahrzehnten gründlich gewandelt **hätte** (*Zeit*) (*hat* would sound much more positive)	*Not a single city that has not changed its appearance totally in twenty years*

(c) In sentences with *fast* or *beinahe*

In these the pluperfect subjunctive can be used to emphasise that something almost happened, but didn't:

Er wäre (*or*: ist) beinahe hingefallen	*He almost fell down*
Ich wäre (*or*: bin) fast nicht gekommen	*I nearly didn't come*
Wir hätten (*or*: haben) das Spiel beinahe gewonnen	*We almost won the match*

16.7.6 The subjunctive in wishes, instructions and commands

(a) Konjunktiv I can be used in the third person to express a wish

In modern German this is largely restricted to set phrases, e.g.:

Gott **segne** dich/dieses Haus!	*God bless you/this house!*
Es **lebe** die Freiheit!	*Long live freedom!*
Gott **sei** Dank!	*Thank God!*
Behüte dich Gott!	*God protect you!*

NB: (i) *Behüte dich Gott* is often heard in Bavaria and Austria in the contracted form *Pfiati (Gott)!* 'goodbye'.

(ii) The use of the *Konjunktiv I* of *mögen* in wishes, e.g. *Möge er glücklich sein!* 'May he be happy!' is now archaic.

(b) A conditional clause with Konjunktiv II can express a wish

The clause can have the form with or without *wenn*, cf. 16.5.3a. The force of the wish is often strengthened by adding *doch* and/or *nur* or *bloß* (cf. 10.7.6 and 10.26.1c):

Wenn er doch nur **käme!**	*If only he would come*
Wenn er bloß fleißiger **arbeiten würde!**	*If only he would work harder!*
Wenn ich bloß/nur/doch zu Hause geblieben **wäre!**	*If only I'd stayed at home!*
Hätte mein Vater doch dieses Haus nie gekauft!	*If only my father hadn't bought this house!*

(c) The Konjunktiv I of sein or the sein-passive is sometimes used in technical German to express a proposition

Gegeben **sei** ein Dreieck ABC	*Given a triangle ABC*
In diesem Zusammenhang **sei** nur darauf verwiesen, daß diese Hypothese auf Einstein zurückgeht	*In this context we merely wish to point out that this hypothesis goes back to Einstein*

NB: In mathematical contexts the indicative is nowadays at least as common as the subjunctive, e.g. *Gegeben **ist** ein Dreieck ABC.*

(d) Konjunktiv I is used for commands or instructions in the third person and the first person plural

Also, spielen wir jetzt Karten!	*Well, let's play cards*
Im Notfall wende man sich an den Hausmeister!	*In case of emergency please apply to the caretaker*

Details are given in 16.2.2f–g.

17

The modal auxiliaries

The six modal auxiliary verbs _dürfen, können, mögen, müssen, sollen, wollen_ indicate the standpoint of the speaker with regard to what is being said. Their meaning is similar to that of the category of mood (see 16.1), which is why they are known as 'modal' auxiliaries. They are used with other verbs to express ability, possibility, permission, necessity, obligation, volition, and the like. However, each verb has a wide range of meaning which is not always easy to pin down, and they all have a number of elusive idiomatic uses.

All these verbs have a number of features in common, which are dealt with in 17.1. Each individual verb is then treated, in alphabetical order, in sections 17.2 to 17.7. They are all highly irregular in their conjugation, and their forms in the simple tenses are given in Table 12.4. Öhlschläger (1989) provides a modern detailed account of the German modal auxiliaries.

17.1 The modal auxiliaries: common features of form and syntax

17.1.1 The German modal auxiliaries have a full range of tense and mood forms

In this they differ from the corresponding English verbs (_can, may, must_, etc.), which have at most only a present tense and a past tense (often with conditional meaning). Thus, German _können_ can be used in the future tense:

Er **wird** es morgen nicht machen können   _He won't be able to do it tomorrow_

English _can_ is impossible here, as it has no future, and we have to use the paraphrase 'be able to'. Similarly, there is a clear difference in German between the past tense _konnte_, which always means 'was able to', and the subjunctive _könnte_, which always means 'would be able to'. English _could_, on the other hand, can often be used in either sense, depending on the context.

Because of this, the German modals can seem difficult for the English learner. But they are easy to master if the various combinations of tense and mood with a following simple or compound infinitive are treated independently and learned with their usual English equivalents. The examples in sections 17.2 to 17.7 are set out to facilitate this, and Table 17.1 illustrates the various possible combinations with _können_.

TABLE 17.1 *The tenses of* können *with an infinitive*

> *Present tense + simple infinitive*
> Sie **kann** es **machen**   *She can do it*
>
> *Present tense + compound infinitive*
> Sie **kann** es **gemacht haben**   *She may have done it*
>
> *Future tense + simple infinitive*
> Sie **wird** es **machen können**   *She will be able to do it*
>
> *Past tense + simple infinitive*
> Sie **konnte** es **machen**   *She was able to do it*
>
> *Perfect tense + simple infinitive*
> Sie **hat** es **machen können**   *She was/has been able to do it*
>
> *Past subjunctive + simple infinitive*
> Sie **könnte** es **machen**   *She could/might do it*
>
> *Past subjunctive + compound infinitive*
> Sie **könnte** es **gemacht haben**   *She might have done it*
>
> *Pluperfect subjunctive + simple infinitive*
> Sie **hätte** es **machen können**   *She would have been able to do it*

17.1.2 The modal verbs are followed by a 'bare' infinitive, without *zu*

(see 13.3.1a). As Table 17.1 shows, they can be followed by a simple or a compound infinitive (see 13.1):

    Ich kann **schwimmen**   Sie möchte **gehen**   Sie kann es **gesehen haben**

17.1.3 The position of the modal auxiliary and the infinitive

For more detailed information on word order and the modals, see 21.1.

(a) In main clauses the infinitive of the main verb is in final position

    Darf ich heute Tennis **spielen**?   *May I play tennis today?*
    Ich möchte das Buch gern **lesen**   *I would like to read that book*

In compound tenses, the infinitive of the modal verb comes after the infinitive of the main verb at the end of the clause:

    Sie wird morgen nicht **kommen können**   *She won't be able to come tomorrow*
    Sie hätte ihrem Mann doch **helfen sollen**   *She really ought to have helped her*
                                                   husband

(b) In infinitive clauses with *zu*, the modal verb comes after the infinitive of the main verb at the end of the infinitive clause

The infinitive particle *zu* comes between the main verb and the modal verb:

    Es scheint **regnen zu wollen**   *It looks as if it's going to rain*
    Sie gab vor, meine Handschrift nicht   *She claimed not to be able to read my*
    lesen zu können   *handwriting*

(c) In subordinate clauses, the modal verb comes after the infinitive of the main verb at the end of the clause

Wenn Sie diesen Ring nicht **kaufen wollen**, . . .	*If you don't want to buy this ring, . . .*
Obwohl ich gestern abend **ausgehen durfte**, . . .	*Although I was allowed to go out last night, . . .*
die Frau, die ich **besuchen sollte**, . . .	*the woman I ought to visit . . .*

If a modal verb is used in a compound tense in a subordinate clause, the tense auxiliary *werden* or *haben* comes *before* the two infinitives:

Obwohl ich ihn morgen **werde** besuchen können, . . .	*Although I'll be able to visit him tomorrow . . .*
Es war klar, daß er sich **würde** anstrengen müssen	*It was clear that he would have to exert himself*
Das Buch, das ich **hätte** kaufen sollen, kostete dreißig Mark	*The book I ought to have bought cost thirty marks*
Sie hat mir gesagt, daß sie es **hat** machen müssen	*She told me she had had to do it*

17.1.4 In the perfect tenses, the infinitive of the modal verbs is used, not the past participle, if they are followed by a dependent infinitive

Wir haben meinen Onkel nicht besuchen **können**	*We weren't able to visit my uncle*
Ich habe es ihr versprechen **müssen**	*I had to promise her*
Sie hätte das Buch lesen **sollen**	*She ought to have read the book*

The past participle is used if they have no dependent infinitive, cf. 17.1.5, e.g. *Ich habe es nicht gewollt.*

NB: The use of the past participle in such contexts, e.g. *Herbert hat arbeiten gemußt*, is not unknown in colloquial speech, but it is considered substandard.

17.1.5 The omission of the infinitive after the modal verbs

In certain contexts the main verb can be left understood and omitted, i.e.:

(a) A verb of motion
(i) If there is an adverb, an adverb phrase or, very commonly, a separable prefix in the sentence which conveys the idea of movement, a specific verb of motion can be omitted after the modal verbs. This usage is predominantly colloquial, but it is by no means restricted to the spoken register:

Wo wollen Sie morgen hin?	*Where do you want to go tomorrow?*
Ich will nach Frankfurt	*I want to go to Frankfurt*
Ich sollte zu meinem Onkel	*I ought to go to my uncle's*
Ich kann heute abend nicht ins Kino	*I can't go to the cinema tonight*
Sie will ihm nach	*She wants to go after him*
Er kletterte über die Mauer, aber er konnte nicht zurück	*He climbed over the wall, but he couldn't get back*
Ich möchte jetzt fort	*I'd like to leave now*

If the modal is at the end of the clause, a separable prefix is written together with it, e.g. *Wir werden bald zurückmüssen.*

(ii) The verb understood is usually *gehen*, *kommen* or *fahren*, as in the above examples, but other verbs can be omitted if the idea of movement is sufficiently clear from the adverbial or the prefix:

Er wollte über die Mauer [klettern]	*He wanted to climb over the wall*
Die Strömung war so stark, daß er	*The current was so strong that*
nicht bis ans Ufer [schwimmen] konnte	*he couldn't swim to the bank*
Er mußte in den Krieg [ziehen] (*Böll*)	*He had to go to the war*

(iii) The omission of a verb of motion is most common with simple tenses of the modals, but the future and perfect of *können* and *müssen* do occur:

Er hat ins Geschäft gemußt	*He's had to go to work*
Ich glaube, ich werde vorbeikönnen	*I think I'll be able to get past*

(b) The verb *tun*

Das kann ich nicht	*I can't do that*
Das darfst/sollst du nicht	*You mustn't/ought not to do that*
Was soll ich damit?	*What am I supposed to do with it?*
Ich kann nichts dafür	*I can't help it*
Er kann was	*He is very able*

(c) A verb just mentioned

This usually corresponds to English usage. Optionally, *es* can be added to make it clear that a previous phrase is being referred to, cf. 3.6.1a:

Ich wollte Tennis spielen, aber ich	*I wanted to play tennis, but I*
konnte/durfte (es) nicht	*couldn't/wasn't allowed to*
Soll ich?	*Shall I?*
Der junge Herr Leutnant könnte	*The young lieutenant couldn't recognise*
niemanden erkennen, auch wenn er es	*anyone even if he wanted to*
wollte (*Wolf*)	

(d) In some idiomatic phrases

Ich kann nicht mehr [weitermachen]	*I can't go on*
Was soll das eigentlich [bedeuten]?	*What's the point of that?*
Sie hat nicht mehr gewollt	*She didn't want to go on*
Er kann mich [am Arsch lecken] (vulg.)	*He can get stuffed*
Mir kann keiner [was antun]	*No-one can touch me*

17.1.6 In German two modals can be used in the same sentence

This is not usual in standard English:

Rechnen **muß** doch jeder **können**	*But everyone has to be able to add up*
Wir **müßten** hier spielen **dürfen**	*We should be allowed to play here*
Wie **kannst** du das nur machen **wollen**?	*How can you want to do that?*

17.2 dürfen

17.2.1 dürfen most often expresses permission

(a) In this sense it corresponds to English 'be allowed to' or 'may'

Sie **dürfen** hereinkommen	*They may/can come in* *They are allowed to come in*
Sie **durfte** ausgehen, wenn sie wollte	*She was allowed to go out when she wanted to*
Endlich **durfte** er die Augen wieder aufmachen	*At last he could open his eyes again*
Sie **wird** erst heute nachmittag mit uns spielen **dürfen**	*She won't be allowed to play with us till this afternoon*

In English, 'can' often expresses permission and is often preferred to 'may', which can sound affected. *können* can be heard for *dürfen* in everyday speech (see 17.3.4), but it is less common in this sense than English 'can'.

(b) Negative *dürfen* has the sense of English 'must not'
i.e. it expresses a prohibition (= 'not be allowed to'):

Sie **dürfen nicht** hereinkommen	*They mustn't come in* *They're not allowed to come in*
Aber ich **darf** mich **nicht** loben (*Langgässer*)	*But I mustn't praise myself*
Wir **dürfen** es uns **nicht** zu leicht machen (*Brecht*)	*We mustn't make it too easy for ourselves*

NB: *nicht müssen* usually means 'doesn't have to', 'needn't', cf. 17.5.1b.

Konjunktiv II forms of *nicht dürfen* can correspond to English 'shouldn't', 'ought not to'. As *dürfen* keeps its basic sense of permission in such contexts, it sounds more incisive than *sollen*, cf. 17.6.4a:

Das **dürfte** sie doch gar **nicht** wissen (it shouldn't be allowed)	*She ought not to know that*
Er **hätte** so etwas **nicht** machen **dürfen** (someone should have forbidden it)	*He ought not to have done anything like that*

(c) *dürfen* is commonly used in polite formulae
It usually corresponds to English 'can' in such contexts. The tone is that of a polite request or a tentative suggestion:

Das **darf** als Vorteil betrachtet werden	*That can/may be seen as an advantage*
Was **darf** sein? (in shop)	*How can/may I help you?*
Der Wein **dürfte** etwas trockener sein	*The wine could just be a bit drier*
Dürfte ich Sie um das Salz bitten?	*Could I ask you to pass the salt?*
Wir freuen uns, Sie hier begrüßen zu **dürfen**	*We are pleased to be able to welcome you here*

17.2.2 *dürfen* can express probability

The *Konjunktiv II* of *dürfen* expresses an assumption that something is likely:

Das dürfte reichen	*That'll be enough*
Rapid dürfte unser bisher schwerster Gegner im Europacup werden (*BILD*)	*Rapid will probably be our most difficult opponent so far in the European Cup*
Das dürfte ein Vermögen gekostet haben	*That'll have cost a fortune*

This sense of *dürfen* is very close to that of the future tense with *werden* (see 14.4), or that of the modal particle *wohl* (see 10.35.1).

17.3 *können*

17.3.1 *können* is most often used to express ability

Its usual English equivalents are 'can' or 'be able to':

Sie **kann** ihn heute besuchen	*She can/is able to visit him today*
Ich **konnte** sie nicht besuchen	*I couldn't visit her/I wasn't able to*
Ich **habe** sie nicht besuchen **können**	*visit her*
Ich **werde** sie morgen besuchen **können**	*I'll be able to visit her tomorrow*
Ich **könnte** sie morgen besuchen, wenn ich Zeit hätte	*I could visit her tomorrow if I had time*
Ich **hätte** sie gestern besuchen **können**, wenn ich Zeit gehabt hätte	*I would have been able to/could have visited her yesterday, if I'd had time*

17.3.2 *können* can have the sense of possibility

In this sense *können* usually corresponds to English 'may':

Das **kann** sein	*That may be*
Ich **kann** mich irren	*I may be wrong*
Er **kann** krank sein	*He may be ill*

(a) The use of *können* to express possibility is limited
In general *können* can only be used in this sense in contexts where it cannot be interpreted in the sense 'be able to'. This is most frequently the case:

(i) With a compound infinitive:

Er **kann** den Schlüssel **verloren haben**	*He may have lost the key*
Die Straße **kann gesperrt sein**	*The road may be blocked*
Er **kann** krank **gewesen sein**	*He may have been ill*

(ii) In the *Konjunktiv II* form **könnte** (= English 'might' or 'could'), to indicate a remote possibility:

Sie **könnte** jetzt in Wien sein	*She could be in Vienna now*
Wir **hätten** umkommen **können**	*We might/could have been killed*
Er **könnte** krank sein	*He might/could be ill*
Er **könnte** krank gewesen sein	*He might/could have been ill*

könnte can also be used to express a tentative request (cf. 16.7.3):

Könnten Sie mir bitte helfen?	*Could you please help me?*

(b) Other German equivalents for English 'may', 'might'
Since *können* can only be used in the sense of possibility in contexts where it could not be taken to mean 'be able to', we often need to express the idea of possibility in other ways, i.e.:

(i) The adverbs *vielleicht* or *möglicherweise*, or a paraphrase (e.g. *Es ist möglich, daß ...*) are often possible alternatives:

Vielleicht arbeitet er im Garten	*He may be working in the garden*
cf. Er kann im Garten arbeiten	*He is able to work in the garden*
Es ist möglich, daß er jetzt im	*He may be working in the garden now*
Garten arbeitet	
cf. Er kann jetzt im Garten arbeiten	*He can work in the garden now*
Möglicherweise kommt sie heute abend	*She may come tonight*
cf. Sie kann heute abend kommen	*She can come tonight*

(ii) In sentences with a negative, the phrasings given under (i) above can be used, or the sense of possibility can be made clear by adding *auch* to *nicht können* (cf. 10.4.1). *nicht* is stressed in such contexts:

Sie **kann auch** <u>nicht</u> kommen	
Möglicherweise kommt sie nicht	*She may not come*
Er **kann auch** <u>nicht</u> krank gewesen sein	
Vielleicht ist er gar nicht krank gewesen	*He may not have been ill*
Sie **kann** das Auto **auch** <u>nicht</u>	
gesehen haben	
Vielleicht hat sie den Wagen gar	*She may not have seen the car*
nicht gesehen	

17.3.3 *können* is used in the meaning 'know' of things learnt

This applies especially to languages, school subjects, the rules of games, etc.:

Er **kann** Spanisch	*He can speak Spanish*
Ich **kann** die Melodie der	*I know the tune of the Austrian*
österreichischen Nationalhymne	*national anthem*
(i.e. I've learnt it)	
Kann der Manfred Skat?	*Does Manfred know how to play Skat?*
Ich **kann** den Trick	*I know that trick*
(i.e. 'I can do it'. Compare *Ich kenne den Trick* 'I've seen it before')	

17.3.4 *können* is used colloquially for *dürfen* to express permission

Kann ich herein?	*Can I come in?*
Du **kannst** den Bleistift behalten	*You can keep the pencil*

Even in colloquial German *können* is less frequent in this sense than is 'can' in English, cf. 17.2.1.

17.3.5 *können* is used less often than English 'can' with verbs of sensation

The verbs *see, hear, feel* and *smell* are often used with 'can' in English without any real idea of being able. In such contexts *können* is frequently not felt to be necessary in German:

Ich sehe die Kirche	*I can see the church*
Ich höre Musik	*I can hear music*
Sie sahen die Stadt im Tal liegen	*They could see the town lying in the valley*

17.3.6 German equivalents for English 'I couldn't help . . .'

There are a number of alternative possibilities in German for this English construction, e.g., for English *I couldn't help laughing*:

(i)   Ich **mußte einfach** lachen
(ii) Ich **konnte nicht anders, ich mußte** lachen
(iii) Ich **konnte nichts dafür, ich mußte** lachen
(iv) Ich **konnte nicht umhin zu** lachen

Alternative (i) is the simplest and most usual in speech, although (ii) and (iii) are quite current. Alternative (iv) is restricted to formal registers.

17.3.7 *könnte . . . gemacht haben* and *hätte . . . machen können*

These two constructions have quite different meanings in German. The English equivalents for both are 'could have done' or 'might have done', but German makes distinctions here which we ignore in English, e.g.:

Sie **könnte** den Brief nicht **geschrieben haben** — *She couldn't have written the letter*
(i.e. it isn't possible that it was she who wrote it)

Sie **hätte** den Brief nicht **schreiben können** — *She couldn't have written the letter*
(i.e. she wouldn't have been able to)

Er **könnte umgekommen sein** — *He might have been killed*
(i.e. it is possible that he was killed)

Er **hätte umkommen können** — *He might have been killed*
(i.e. it was possible, but he wasn't)

17.4 *mögen*

17.4.1 The most frequent sense of *mögen* is to express liking

(a) It most commonly occurs in the *Konjunktiv II* form *möchte*
This expresses a polite request and usually corresponds to English 'would like' or 'want'. It is often linked with the adverb *gern*:

Sie **möchte** (gern) nach Rom fahren — *She would like to go to Rome*
Ich **möchte** nichts mehr davon hören — *I don't want to hear any more about it*
Ich **möchte** ihr Gesicht gesehen haben — *I would have liked to see her face*
Ich **möchte** nicht, daß er heute kommt — *I don't want him to come today*

The pluperfect subjunctive is also used occasionally in this sense, e.g.:

Baldini **hätte** ihn erwürgen **mögen** — *Baldini would have liked to strangle him*
(*Süßkind*)

In general, though, German more often uses *gern* with the pluperfect subjunctive of the verb e.g., for 'I would have liked to read the book', Ich **hätte gern** dieses Buch **gelesen**.

(b) Other tenses of *mögen* are used in the sense of English 'like'
(i) It occurs most often (although not exclusively) in the negative, chiefly with reference to people, places and food:

Sie **mag** keinen Tee	*She doesn't like tea*
Mögt ihr den neuen Lehrer?	*Do you like the new teacher?*
Ich **mag** ihn nicht	*I don't like him*
Er **mochte** nicht allein an der Straße stehen (*Johnson*)	*He didn't want to stand on the street alone*
Sie **hat** ihn nie **gemocht**	*She never liked him*

(ii) With a following infinitive it is only used in the negative:

Wie es im Winter werden soll, daran **mag** er noch gar nicht denken (*Zeit*)	*He doesn't want to think about what it's going to be like in winter*
Ich **mag** das Wort gar nicht aussprechen	*I don't even like saying that word out loud*
Ich **mag** diese Fragen nicht beantworten (*BILD*)	*I don't want to answer these questions*

17.4.2 *mögen* sometimes expresses possibility or probability

The use of *mögen* to express possibility is largely limited to formal written registers and set phrases (although it is more widely used in spoken south German). When it is used it tends to express a rather higher degree of probability than *können*, see 17.3.2.

(a) When indicating possibility *mögen* often has a concessive sense
i.e. there is an expected qualification by a following *aber* (which may or may not be present). This usage is similar to English *That may well be (, but . . .)*:

Das **mag** vielen nicht einleuchten, (aber . . .)	*That may not be clear to many, (but . . .)*
Das Tief **mag** über Italien weiterwandern und den Balkan einnässen. Wir aber fliegen dorthin, wo die Sonne scheint (*Grzimek*)	*The low may drift over Italy and make the Balkans wet. But we're flying to where the sun shines*
Eine Zeitlang **mochte** es scheinen, daß es gelänge, das Absinken der deutschen Währung abzubremsen, doch schien es nur so (*Heuss*)	*For a time it might have appeared that the attempt to stop the German currency falling would be successful, but that appearance was deceptive*

(b) In other contexts *mögen* indicates a reasonable degree of probability
i.e. somewhere between 'possible' and 'probable':

Sie **mag/mochte** etwa sechzig sein	*She is/was probably about sixty*
Jetzt **mögen** über 1000 DDR-Bürger sich in der Botschaft aufhalten (*ARD*)	*There are now probably more than a thousand GDR citizens in the embassy*
An einem Sonntag im März – es **mochte** etwa ein Jahr seit seiner Ankunft in Grasse vergangen sein (*Süßkind*)	*On a Sunday in March – it was probably about a year after his arrival in Grasse*

(c) Some idiomatic phrases with *mögen* express possibility
The following are used in spoken German as well as in formal writing:

Das mag (wohl) sein	*That may well be*
Wer mag das (schon) sein?	*Who can that be?*
Wie mag das (nur) gekommen sein?	*How can that have happened?*

A few phrases with *möchte* convey a doubt or a supposition:

Ich möchte meinen, daß ...	*I should think that ...*
Dabei möchte man verrückt werden	*It's enough to drive you mad*

könnte can be used for *möchte* in such contexts, but it sounds less tentative.

17.4.3 *mögen* in concessive clauses

i.e. the German equivalent of English clauses like *whatever/whoever that may be*, etc. (see also 19.6.2). *mögen* can be used in such clauses in German:

Wann er auch ankommen mag, ...	*Whenever he may arrive ...*
Was auch immer geschehen mag, ...	*Whatever happens ...*
Wer er auch sein mag, ...	*Whoever he may be ...*

Alternatively, the main verb can simply be used on its own, and in practice this is more frequent in less formal registers, especially in spoken German:

Wann er auch **ankommt**, ...   Was auch immer **geschieht**, ...   Wer er auch **ist**, ...

However, *mögen* is *always* used in the set phrase *Wie dem auch sein mag* 'However that may be'.

17.4.4 *mögen* in wishes and commands

(a) *Konjunktiv I* of *mögen* can express a wish or a command in the third person

Möge er glücklich sein!	*May he be happy!*
Die Herren **mögen** bitte unten warten	*Would the gentlemen be so kind as to wait downstairs*

This usage is limited to formal German and sounds old-fashioned, see 16.2.2g.

(b) The subjunctive of *mögen* is used in indirect commands

Sagen Sie ihr, sie **möchte** zu mir kommen	*Ask her to be kind enough to come and see me*
Er sagte mir, ich **möchte** einen Augenblick auf ihn warten	*He asked me to wait for him a moment*

The *Konjunktiv I* of *mögen* (e.g.: ... *sie möge zu mir kommen*) is nowadays rather old-fashioned in indirect commands. For further details, see 16.6.4b.

17.5 *müssen*

17.5.1 *müssen* most often expresses necessity or compulsion

(a) The most frequent English equivalent is 'must', 'have (got) to'

Wir **müssen** jetzt abfahren	*We must leave now* / *We have (got) to leave now*
Wir **werden** bald abfahren **müssen**	*We'll have to leave soon*
Ich **mußte** um acht abfahren / Ich **habe** um acht abfahren **müssen**	*I had to leave at eight*
Ich **muß** den Brief bis heute abend **geschrieben haben**	*I've got to have the letter written by tonight*
Wir **mußten** die Anträge bis zum 15. Januar **abgegeben haben**	*We had to have the applications handed in by the 15th of January*
Sie **muß** sich beeilen, wenn sie den Zug erreichen will	*She'll have to hurry if she wants to catch the train*

(b) With a passive infinitive or a passive equivalent, 'need' is sometimes a more natural English equivalent for *müssen*

Das muß gut überlegt werden	*That needs thinking about properly*
Man muß sich um sie kümmern	*She needs looking after*

(c) Negative *müssen* retains the sense of necessity
(i) This normally corresponds to English 'needn't' or 'don't have to':

Wir **müssen** noch **nicht** gehen	{ *We needn't go yet* { *We don't have to go yet*
Er **hat** es **nicht** tun **müssen**	*He didn't need to/didn't have to do it*
Du **mußt nicht** hierbleiben, du kannst auch gehen	*You needn't stay here, you can leave*

In practice *nicht brauchen* (see 13.2.5) is more frequent than *nicht müssen* in this meaning, e.g. *Du brauchst nicht hierzubleiben*.

(ii) English 'mustn't' expresses a prohibition, and usually corresponds in German to *nicht dürfen*, see 17.2.1b. *nicht müssen* is sometimes used in this sense in speech, e.g. *Sie müssen hier nicht parken* 'You mustn't park here', but this is usually considered to be non-standard and regional (northern).

17.5.2 *müssen* can express a logical deduction

(a) This corresponds to English 'must' or 'have to'

Sie spielt heute Tennis, also **muß** es ihr besser gehen	*She's playing tennis today, so she must be better*
Das **muß** ein Fehler sein	*That must/has to be a mistake*
Sie **muß** den Unfall gesehen haben	*She must have seen the accident*

If *müssen* could be taken in context to express necessity where logical deduction is intended, the meaning can be made clear by using the adverb *sicher* rather than *müssen*, e.g.:

Er ist heute **sicher** in Frankfurt	*He must be in Frankfurt today*

Er muß heute in Frankfurt sein would naturally be understood as 'He has to be in Frankfurt today'.

(b) German uses the past tense *mußte* with a simple infinitive to express a logical deduction in the past
In such contexts English uses *must* with a compound infinitive:

Er schuftete, daß ihm heiß sein **mußte** (Grass)	*He was working hard, so he must have been hot*

(c) A logical deduction can be queried by *nicht brauchen*
This is commoner than *nicht müssen*, e.g.: *Er war heute nicht im Büro, aber er* **braucht nicht** *deshalb krank zu sein* (less often: ... *aber er muß nicht* ...)

(d) A negative logical deduction is expressed by *nicht können*
This corresponds to English 'can't':

Sie spielt heute Tennis, also **kann** sie **nicht** krank sein	*She's playing tennis today, so she can't be ill*

17.5.3 The *Konjunktiv II* of *müssen*

(a) *müßte* can express a possible compulsion or necessity
In this sense it can correspond to English 'would have to/need to':

Er weiß ja nicht, was er tut – ich **müßte** ja sonst meine Hand von ihm zurückziehen (*Böll*)	*He doesn't know what he's doing – otherwise I would have to disown him*
Es sind Felsen, Gestein, wahrscheinlich vulkanisch, das **müßte** man nachsehen und feststellen (*Frisch*)	*They are rocks and stones, probably volcanic, that would need to be checked and established*

In negative sentences the *Konjunktiv II* of *nicht brauchen* is more usual than that of *nicht müssen*, cf. 17.5.2:

Du hättest nicht hinzugehen brauchen, wenn ...	*You wouldn't have had to go there if ...*

(b) *müßte* can express a possible logical deduction
(i) In this sense, 'should' or 'ought to' are the usual English equivalents:

Deutschlands Kohle ist teurer, als sie sein **müßte** (*Zeit*)	*Coal in Germany is dearer than it ought to be/should be*
Das **müßte** eigentlich reichen	*That really ought to be enough*
Es **müßte** viel mehr Prügel in der Schule geben (*Böll*)	*There should be a lot more beatings in school*
Ich **hätte** mich vielleicht anders ausdrücken **müssen**	*Perhaps I ought to/should have expressed myself differently*

(ii) This sense of *müßte* is close to that of *sollte*, which also corresponds to English 'should', 'ought to', cf. 17.6.4. There is a difference, though, as *sollte* always expresses an obligation (often laid on a person by someone else), whereas *müßte* expresses a logical probability or necessity. Compare:

Sie **sollte** heute im Büro sein	*She ought to be at the office today*
(i.e. she is obliged to if she doesn't want to get wrong with the boss)	
Sie **müßte** heute im Büro sein	*She ought to be at the office today*
(i.e. I assume that is the most likely place for her to be)	
Das **hätte** er eigentlich wissen **sollen**	*He ought to have known that*
(i.e. he was obliged to – it could have stopped him making a mistake)	
Das **hätte** er eigentlich wissen **müssen**	*He ought to have known that*
(i.e. I would have thought it was a pretty fair assumption that he did)	
Wo ist der Brief? – Er **müßte** in dieser Schublade sein	*Where's the letter? – It ought to be/should be in this drawer*
(A logical deduction: *sollte* would not be possible)	

müßte nicht is seldom used as an equivalent for English 'shouldn't', 'ought not to'; we usually find *sollte nicht* or *dürfte nicht*, cf. 17.6.4.

(c) *müßte ... gemacht haben* and *hätte ... machen müssen*
The English equivalent for both these constructions is usually 'should/ought to have done', but there is normally a clear distinction between them in German. Compare, for English *He ought to have written the letter yesterday*:

Er **müßte** den Brief schon gestern **geschrieben haben**
(i.e. it is a fair deduction that he did)
Er **hätte** den Brief schon gestern **schreiben müssen**
(i.e. he had to, but he didn't)

17.6 *sollen*

17.6.1 *sollen* most commonly expresses an obligation

(a) This corresponds to 'be to', 'be supposed to' or (occasionally) 'shall'

Um wieviel Uhr **soll** ich kommen?	*What time am I to/shall I come?*
Ich **soll** nicht so viel rauchen	*I'm not supposed to smoke so much*
Was **soll** ich in Greifswald tun?	*What am I (supposed) to do in Greifswald?*
Sie wußte nicht, was sie tun **sollte**	*She didn't know what to do*
Wir **sollten** uns gestern treffen	*We were (supposed) to meet yesterday*

The meaning of *sollen* is close to that of *müssen*, and 'must', 'have to' is often a possible English equivalent. However, *sollen* always conveys the idea that some other person is making an obligation. Compare:

Ich **soll** hier bleiben	*I am to/have (got) to stay here*
	(i.e. someone's told me to)
Ich **muß** hier bleiben	*I've got to stay here*
	(i.e. it is necessary for me)

In questions, the past tense of *sollen* can be used to prompt a strong reaction (negative or positive, depending on the context). It can sound ironic:

Wie **sollte** ich das wissen?	*How was I (supposed) to know that?*
Sollte das nun fertig sein?	*Is that supposed to be finished?* (ironic)
Sollte er wirklich nichts davon wissen?	*Is he really supposed not to know anything about it?*

(b) *sollen* often has the force of a command

See also 16.2.2e. This use is related to the basic sense of obligation:

Du **sollst** nicht stehlen	*Thou shalt not steal*
Du **sollst** das Fenster zumachen	*(I want you to) shut the window*
Man **soll** sofort den Saal verlassen	*Everyone has to leave the room immediately*
Das **soll** dir eine Warnung sein	*Let that be a warning to you*
Er **soll** sofort kommen	*He is to/has got to come at once* *Tell him to come at once*

sollen is the most frequent modal in indirect commands (see 16.6.4b):

Er sagte ihr, sie **solle/sollte** unten warten	*He told her to wait downstairs*
Ich habe ihm gesagt, er **soll** seinem Vater helfen	*I told him to help his father*

17.6.2 *sollen* can express an intention or prediction

(a) In this sense *sollen* corresponds to 'be to', 'be supposed/meant to'

Eine zweite Fabrik **soll** bald hier gebaut werden	*A second factory is to be built here soon*
Soll das ein Kompliment sein?	*Is that meant as a compliment?*
Es **sollte** eine Überraschung sein	*It was intended to be a surprise*
Was **soll** das heißen?	*What's that supposed to mean?*
Es **soll** nicht wieder vorkommen	*It won't happen again*
Das **sollst** du noch bereuen	*You're going to regret that*

(b) The sense of intention is common in first person plural questions
In such contexts *sollen* is an alternative to *wollen*, although there is a slight difference of meaning, see 17.7.1b:

Was **sollen wir** uns heute in der Stadt ansehen?	*What are we going to look at in town today?*
Sollen wir heute abend ins Kino gehen?	*Shall we go to the cinema tonight?*

(c) The past tense of *sollen* can indicate what was destined to happen
This sense is essentially that of a 'future-in-the-past':

Diese Meinung **sollte** sie noch oft zu hören bekommen	*She would often hear this opinion again*
Er **sollte** früh sterben	*He would/was (destined) to die young*
Er **sollte** niemals nach Deutschland zurückkehren	*He would never return to Germany*

In these contexts *sollte* differs slightly from *würde* (see 16.4.5), since it indicates that this is a prediction by the speaker.

17.6.3 *sollen* can express a rumour or report

i.e. 'It is said that . . .'. Only the present tense of *sollen* is used in this sense, with a compound infinitive to refer to past time if necessary:

Er **soll** steinreich (gewesen) sein	*He is said to be (have been) enormously rich*
Bei den Unruhen **soll** es bisher vier Tote gegeben haben (*FAZ*)	*So far four people are reported to have been killed in the course of the riots*
Eine solche Bombe **soll** die Katastrophe von Lockerbie ausgelöst haben (*ARD*)	*A similar bomb is assumed to have caused the Lockerbie disaster*

17.6.4 The *Konjunktiv II* of *sollen*

(a) The *Konjunktiv II* of *sollen* conveys the idea of a possible obligation
This is related to its basic sense, but these forms have the clear English equivalents 'should (have)', 'ought to (have)':

Warum **sollte** ich denn nicht ins Theater gehen?	*Why shouldn't I go to the theatre?*
Das **solltest** du mal probieren	*You ought just to try that*
Das **sollte** ihm inzwischen klar geworden sein	*He ought to have realised that by now*
Das **hätten** Sie mir aber gestern sagen **sollen**	*You ought to have told me that yesterday*

NB: (i) For negative 'shouldn't', 'ought not to', *dürfte nicht* can be used as a more incisive alternative to *sollte nicht*, see 17.2.1b.
(ii) For the distinction between *sollte* and *müßte* as equivalents of English 'should/ought to', see 17.5.3b.

(b) *sollte . . . gemacht haben* and *hätte . . . machen sollen*
The English equivalent for both these constructions is usually 'should/ought to have done', but German can make a distinction between them. Thus, for English *He ought to have written the letter yesterday*:

Er **sollte** den Brief gestern **geschrieben haben**
(i.e. I would expect him to have done so)
Er **hätte** den Brief gestern **schreiben sollen**
(i.e. he ought to have done, but he didn't)

(c) In questions, *sollte* is often used as an alternative to *könnte*

There is no real difference in meaning:

Wie **sollte/könnte** ich das wissen?	*How could I know that?*
Warum **sollte/könnte** er nicht einmal in London gewesen sein?	*Why shouldn't he have been to London some time?*

(d) *sollte* is often used in conditional sentences and clauses of purpose

(i) In *if*-sentences it corresponds to 'should' or 'were to', see 16.5.1d:

Wenn/Falls es regnen **sollte**, so komme ich nicht	*If it should rain, I shan't come*
Sollten Sie ihn sehen, dann grüßen Sie ihn bitte von mir	*If you were to see him, please give him my regards*

(ii) *sollen* is commonly used in clauses of purpose with *damit* (cf. 19.5.1a):

Ich trat zurück, damit sie mich nicht sehen **sollten**	*I stepped back, so that they shouldn't see me*

For alternative usage in clauses of purpose see 16.7.2.

17.7 *wollen*

17.7.1 *wollen* most often expresses desire or intention

(a) In many contexts it expresses a wish

(i) It usually corresponds to English 'want/wish (to)':

Sie **will** ihn um Geld bitten	*She wants to ask him for money*
Sie **wollte** ihn um Geld bitten	
Sie **hat** ihn um Geld bitten **wollen**	*She wanted to ask him for money*
Hättest du kommen **wollen**?	*Would you have wanted to come?*
Willst du nicht deinem Vater helfen?	*Don't you want to help your father?*

(ii) In this sense, *wollen* is often used without a dependent infinitive:

Was **wollen** Sie von mir	*What do you want from me?*
Der Arzt **will**, daß ich mehr Bewegung mache	*The doctor wants me to take more exercise*
Mach, was du **willst**	*Do what you like*

(iii) The sense of 'wish' is often given by *Konjunktiv II*:

Ich **wollte**, ich hätte sie nicht so beleidigt	*I wish I hadn't offended her like that*
Ich **wollte**, ich wäre zu Hause	*I wish I was at home*

(iv) *wollen* can correspond to English 'will', 'would':

Er **will** es nicht zugeben	*He won't admit it*
Ich bat sie, es zu tun, aber sie **wollte** nicht	*I asked her to do it, but she wouldn't*
Willst du mir helfen?	*Will you help me?*
– Ja, ich **will** dir helfen	*– Yes, I will help you*

wollen in this sense must be distinguished from the future tense. The future, i.e. *Wirst du mir helfen? – Ja, ich werde dir helfen*, sounds more impersonal and lacks the sense of active willingness on the part of the speaker conveyed by *wollen*.

(v) *wollen* is common in second person questions with the sense of an insistent request:

Willst du bitte nochmal nachsehen?	*Will you have another look, please?*
Wollen Sie bitte die Frage wiederholen?	*Will you repeat the question, please?*

In such requests, *Konjunktiv II* (e.g. *Würden Sie bitte nochmal nachsehen?*, see 16.7.3) sounds less blunt and direct than *wollen*.

(b) *wollen* can express intention

(i) In such contexts it often corresponds to English 'be going to', but *wollen* stresses the notion of intention more forcefully than the future with *werden*:

Wir **wollen** uns bald einen neuen Fernseher anschaffen	*We're going to buy ourselves a new TV set soon*

(The future *Wir werden uns bald einen neuen Fernseher anschaffen* would have more the sense of a prediction than a definite intention)

Wie **wollen** Sie ihm das klarmachen?	*How are you going to explain that to him?*
Ich **wollte** Sie darüber fragen	*I was going to ask you about it*
Was **wollen** Sie damit sagen?	*What do you mean by that?*
Das **will** nicht viel sagen	*That doesn't mean much*
Ich **will** sie erst morgen anrufen	*I don't intend phoning her till tomorrow*
Es scheint regnen zu **wollen**	*It looks as if it's going to rain*

(ii) In first person plural questions *wollen* has the sense of English 'Shall we. . .?':

Wollen wir eine Tasse Kaffee trinken?	*Shall we have a cup of coffee/ Let's have a cup of coffee*
Was **wollen wir** heute machen?	*What shall we do today?*
Na, dann **wollen wir** mal (anfangen)?	*Well then, let's get on with it!*

sollen is an alternative to *wollen* in such constructions, see 17.6.2b. However, there is a slight difference in meaning: *wollen* clearly indicates that the speaker is in favour of the proposal, but *sollen* leaves the decision entirely to the other person(s).

(c) With an inanimate subject, *wollen* corresponds to English 'need'

The sense of *wollen* in these contexts is similar to that in (a) and (b) above, but English 'want' and 'wish' are not normally used with an inanimate subject:

Tomaten **wollen** viel Sonne	*Tomatoes need a lot of sun*
Eine solche Arbeit **will** Zeit haben	*A piece of work like that needs time*
Das **will** gut überlegt werden	*That needs proper consideration*
Solche Dolmetscherarbeit **will** gelernt sein, das darf man mir glauben (Frisch)	*Working like that as an interpreter needs to be learnt, believe me*

Negative *wollen* with an inanimate subject has the sense of 'refuse':

Der Koffer **wollte** nicht zugehen	*The suitcase refused to/wouldn't close*
Meine Beine **wollen** nicht mehr	*My legs won't carry me any further*
Das **will** mir nicht in den Kopf	*I can't grasp that*

17.7.2 *wollen* can be used in the sense of 'claim'

In this use, the present tense of *wollen* is commonly linked with a compound infinitive. The implication is usually that the claim is false:

Er **will** eine Mosquito **abgeschossen haben** (*Gaiser*)	*He claims to have shot down a Mosquito*
Sie **wollen** dich in Berlin **gesehen haben**	*They say they saw you in Berlin*
Zur gleichen Zeit, da ich das Judenauto **gesehen haben wollte**, ... (*Führmann*)	*At the same time at which I said I had seen the car with the Jews, ...*

A few set phrases are an extension of this sense of *wollen*:

Keiner will es getan haben	*No-one admits doing it*
Ich will nichts gesagt haben	*Go on as if I hadn't said anything*
Ich will nichts gehört/gesehen/ gemerkt haben	*I'll go on as if I hadn't heard/ seen/noticed anything*

18

Verbs: Valency

The term 'valency' is borrowed from chemistry, where the 'valency' of a chemical element determines the number of atoms of that element needed to form a compound. In grammar, it refers to the construction required by a particular verb (i.e. whether a verb governs the dative, the accusative, the accusative and the dative, etc.). The term has been widely used in German grammar, e.g. DUDEN (1995: 650–81) and good recent surveys are to be found in Fox (1990: 218ff.) and Storrer (1992).

In this chapter we first (18.1) explain what is meant by 'valency' and then (18.2 – 18.8) deal with the different valency patterns, with lists of verbs, paying attention to those verbs and constructions which are most different from their nearest English equivalents.

Details on valency in German are given in two 'valency dictionaries': Helbig and Schenkel (1983) and Engel and Schuhmacher (1978). In addition, the dictionary by Wahrig (1978) is useful for the foreign learner because it indicates clearly the valency of each verb in its various meanings.

18.1 Valency, complements and sentence patterns

18.1.1 The 'complements' of the verb are the elements which are needed by a particular verb in order to construct a grammatical sentence

Different verbs require different elements to make a grammatical sentence. For example, the action of giving necessarily involves a person handing a thing over to another person. The verb *geben*, therefore, needs three elements to form a sentence: a subject (in the nominative), a direct object (in the accusative) and an indirect object (in the dative):

> Gestern hat **mein Vater** (Nom.) **seinem Bruder** (Dat.) **das Geld** (Acc.) gegeben

If we omitted any of these, the sentence would be ungrammatical. Other verbs, like *telefonieren*, only need one element, i.e. a subject:

> **Ich** habe eben telefoniert   *I've just made a phone call*

Many verbs, like *schlagen*, need two, i.e. a subject and a direct object:

> **Sie** hat **den Ball** geschlagen   *She hit the ball*

Some verbs have other types of construction, for example with a subject and a phrase with a particular preposition, like *warten*:

> **Ich** habe lange **auf dich** gewartet   *I waited a long time for you*

The elements a verb needs to form a grammatical sentence are called the 'complements' of the verb (in German *Ergänzungen*). Typical complements are the subject and the objects of the verb – and in German the objects can be in the accusative, dative or (less frequently) the genitive case. But there are other types of complement, too, for instance the prepositional phrase with *warten*, which we can call a 'prepositional object'. And since verbs of motion necessarily imply a place to be reached, the word or phrase indicating that goal is a 'complement', too. Thus, if someone (the subject) *fährt*, it must be *irgendwohin*, and this is the 'direction complement'.

All the complements of German are shown, with examples, in Table 18.1. Each of them is explained further, in detail, in sections 18.2 to 18.8.

18.1.2 The type and number of complements required by a particular verb to construct a grammatical sentence are the 'valency' of the verb

Every German verb 'governs' a number of complements. Thus, *geben* has three: a subject, an accusative object and a dative object. *warten*, on the other hand, has two: a subject and a prepositional object. And *telefonieren* has only one: a subject. This property of each verb to govern a specific number of complements of a specific type is the 'valency' of the verb.

In order to use a German verb correctly, we have to know its valency. This can often be different from that of what may seem to be the equivalent English verb:

Das hat er **mir** gestern mitgeteilt	*He informed me of that yesterday*
Ich fürchte **mich vor dem Zahnarzt**	*I'm afraid of the dentist*
Er riet **ihr von dieser Reise** ab	*He advised her against (making) this journey*

TABLE 18.1 *Complements in German*

		Example
Subject	a noun or pronoun in the nominative	**Der Bäcker** trank zu viel Das hast **du** mir versprochen!
Accusative object	a noun or pronoun in the accusative case (direct object)	Er trinkt **viel Kaffee** **Diesen Mann** sah ich in der Stadt
Dative object	a noun or pronoun in the dative	**Ihrem Sohn** hat sie das Geld gegeben Er nahm **ihr** den Ring
Genitive object	a noun or pronoun in the genitive	Sie bedarf **meiner Hilfe** Er erinnerte sich **des Vorfalls**
Prepositional object	a phrase introduced by a preposition determined by the individual verb	Sie wartete **auf ihre Freundin** Ich dankte ihr sehr **dafür**
Place complement	a phrase indicating place with a verb of position	Sie wohnte lange **in Hildesheim** Ich blieb **dort**
Direction complement	a phrase indicating direction with a verb of motion	Gestern ging sie **in die Stadt** Ich folgte ihr **hinein**
Predicate complement	a noun in the nominative or an adjective with verbs like *sein* and *werden*	Er ist **ihr Betreuer** Das Heft ist **teuer**

For this reason it is important to learn German verbs by memorising typical sentences which show the valency of the verb clearly.

A number of verbs, especially the most frequent, are used with different valencies. This is often associated with differences in meaning:

| jemanden achten | *respect somebody* |
| auf jemanden achten | *pay attention to somebody* |

Further examples are given in the remainder of this chapter.

18.1.3 German sentence patterns

In principle, all German verbs require one, two or three of the complements listed in Table 18.1 to form a complete clause or sentence. How many there are, and of what type, is determined by the valency of the verb.

There are a limited number of combinations of complements which occur commonly with German verbs, since many verbs have the same valency. In this way, we can say that German possesses a restricted number of possible sentence structure types or 'sentence patterns' (the German term is *Satzbaupläne*). For example, many verbs are 'einem etwas' verbs, like *geben*, requiring an accusative object and a dative object besides a subject.

The most frequent sentence patterns of German are given in Table 18.2. More detail can be found in DUDEN (1995: 650–81) and Engel (1991: 200–17). The various patterns are treated fully in sections 18.2 to 18.8 under the heading of the chief complements.

18.1.4 Complements are different from adverbials

The complements are those elements which are *required* by the verb to form a complete sentence. However, a sentence can contain other elements:

Mein Vater hat seinem Bruder **gestern** das Geld gegeben
Heute habe ich diesen Mann **in der Stadt** gesehen
Sie wohnte **lange** in Halle
Gestern ging sie **schnell** in die Stadt

Words and phrases like those in bold type provide additional information or circumstantial detail, often about the time, manner or place of the action or event. They may be important in context, but they are not an essential component of the sentence and not closely bound up with the basic meaning of the verb in the way that complements are. If we leave them out, the sentence is still grammatical:

| Mein Vater hat seinem Bruder das Geld gegeben | Sie wohnte in Halle |
| Ich habe diesen Mann gesehen | Sie ging in die Stadt |

The German term for these elements is *freie Angaben*, which indicates their function in the sentence. In English they are usually called 'adverbials', since they can be adverbs or adverb phrases. Whether they are single words or phrases, they can be classified into types as outlined in Chapter 7.

As a rule, complements are necessary to make a complete grammatical sentence, whilst adverbials are optional and, as long as they make sense, they can be added to any sentence with any verb. But the distinction is not always clear cut or easy to draw. Certain complements of some verbs can be omitted without this resulting in an ungrammatical sentence. Compare:

| Er trinkt **viel Kaffee** | – Er trinkt |
| Sie fährt **in die Stadt** | – Sie fährt |

TABLE 18.2 *German sentence patterns*

A	Subject + verb	**Mein Vater** (subj.) schwimmt gern
B	Subject + verb + accusative object	**Sie** (subj.) bauten **ein Haus** (acc.)
C	Subject + verb + dative object	**Der Polizist** (subj.) hilft **der alten Frau** (dat.)
D	Subject + verb + accusative object + dative object	**Mein Vater** (subj.) schreibt **ihr** (dat.) **einen Brief** (acc.)
E	Subject + verb + genitive object	**Sie** (subj.) bedarf **der Ruhe** (gen.)
F	Subject + verb + accusative object + genitive object	**Man** (subj.) klagte **ihn** (acc.) **des Diebstahls** (gen.) an
G	Subject + verb + prepositional object	**Sie** (subj.) suchte **nach ihrem Taschentuch** (prep.)
H	Subject + verb + accusative object + prepositional object	**Ich** (subj.) konnte **ihn** (acc.) **davon** (prep.) überzeugen
I	Subject + verb + dative object + prepositional object	**Sie** (subj.) dankte **ihm** (dat.) **für seine Mühe** (prep.)
J	Subject + verb + place complement	**Das Bild** (subj.) hängt **über seinem Arbeitstisch** (place)
K	Subject + verb + direction complement	**Der Junge** (subj.) fiel **in den Brunnen** (dir.)
L	Subject + verb + accusative object + direction complement	**Sie** (subj.) steckte **den Schlüssel** (acc.) **in ihre Tasche** (dir.)
M	Subject + verb + predicate complement	**Helga** (subj.) ist **Lehrerin** (pred.) geworden

We still have grammatical sentences even when the phrases in bold are left out. However, the action of *trinken* necessarily involves consuming some liquid (the direct object), and the action of *fahren* must entail going somewhere (the direction complement). These elements are so closely bound up in meaning with the action of the verb that, even if we can leave them out in some contexts, they must be taken as complements rather than as adverbials, i.e. optional extra pieces of information.

It can happen that the same word or phrase functions as a complement in some contexts, but as an adverbial in others. Compare:

Sie wohnte **in Köln**	*in Köln* is a place complement to the verb of position *wohnen*; it cannot be omitted
Sie starb **in Köln**	*in Köln* can be omitted; it is an adverbial adding extra information to the sentence

18.2 The subject

18.2.1 Most German verbs require a subject complement

Characteristically, the subject of most verbs in the active voice is the 'agent', i.e. the animate being carrying out the action, e.g. *der Räuber hat das Geld gestohlen, die Soldaten singen, der Bär frißt das Fleisch*.

(a) If the subject is a noun or pronoun, it is in the nominative case

A finite verb agrees with the subject for person and number, see 12.1.4:

Ich reise nach Italien	Das hat uns **die Geschichte** gelehrt
Wer ruft mich?	Kommen **deine Geschwister** morgen?

For the use of *es* as a 'dummy subject' in order to permit the real subject to occur later, e.g. *Es saß eine alte Frau am Fenster*, see 3.6.2d.

(b) The subject can be a subordinate clause or an infinitive clause

The finite verb has the third person singular ending, see 12.1.4a.

> **Daß du hier bist**, freut mich   **Dich wiederzusehen**, hat mich gefreut

Subordinate subject clauses are introduced by *daß* or an interrogative, see 19.2. For further information on subject infinitive clauses see 13.2.3.

If such a clause is not in first position in the sentence, it may be anticipated by *es*, e.g. *Es freut mich, daß du hier bist*, see 3.6.2e.

18.2.2 A few verbs do not need a subject complement

i.e. they just have an accusative or a dative object (depending on the verb), but no subject. The verb is in the third person singular form, e.g. *mich hungert, mir bangt*. Most of these verbs express an emotion or a sensation, and almost all are now limited to formal or literary registers, or to regional usage (especially southern). A selection of those still used is given below (with more currently used equivalents where appropriate):

Mich **hungert, dürstet**	*I am hungry, thirsty*
(More usual *Ich habe Hunger, Durst*)	
Mich **friert**	*I am cold*
(More usual *Es friert mich* or, more colloquially *Ich friere*)	
Mich **wundert**, daß ...	*I am surprised that ...*
(This is still frequent in all registers, but there are commonly used alternatives, i.e. *Es wundert mich/Ich wundere mich, daß ...*)	
Mich/Mir **schaudert** vor etwas (dat.)	*I shudder at sth.*
(More usual *Es schaudert mich vor etwas*)	
Mich/Mir **ekelt** vor etwas (dat.)	*I am disgusted at sth.*
(More usual *Es ekelt mich/Ich ekele mich vor etw.* or *Etwas ekelt mich*)	
Mich/Mir **schwindelt**	*I feel dizzy*
(More usual *Mir ist schwindlig*)	
Mir **träumt** von etwas (dat.)	*I dream of sth.*
(More usual *Ich träume von etw.*)	
Mir **graut** vor jdm./etw. (dat.)	*I have a horror of sb./sth.*
(More usual *Es graut mir vor etw.*)	
Mir **bangt** vor etw. (dat.)	*I am afraid of sth.*
(More usual *Ich habe Angst vor etw.*)	

18.2.3 German is more restrictive than English in respect of the type of noun which can occur as the subject of the verb

In English nouns can often be used as the subject of the verb which do not denote the agent. This is not normally possible in German, which requires the subject of the verb to be the agent who is actually performing the action. Typically the noun which is the subject in English appears in a prepositional phrase in German. The following examples are taken from Hawkins (1986: 57–61), who gives more detail about this:

In diesem Hotel sind Hunde verboten	*This hotel forbids dogs*
In diesem Zelt können vier schlafen	*This tent sleeps four*
Mit dieser Anzeige verkaufen wir viel	*This advertisement will sell us a lot*
Wir können **mit dem Prozeß** nicht fortfahren	*The trial cannot proceed*
Damit haben wir den besten Mittelstürmer verloren	*This loses us the best centre-forward*
In Berlin wird es wieder ziemlich heiß sein	*Berlin will be rather hot again*

Logically, things like 'hotels' cannot really 'forbid'. Neither do 'tents' actually 'sleep' or 'advertisements' do any 'selling', etc., and, in the last example, Berlin is *where* 'it' is hot rather than a person or thing feeling the heat. The German constructions reflect this more clearly than do the corresponding English sentences.

18.2.4 The impersonal subject *es*

A large number of verbs are exclusively or commonly used impersonally, with the indefinite subject *es* (see also 3.6.2a). The *es* cannot be omitted in these constructions except for the cases indicated under (e) and (f) below.

(a) Verbs referring to weather

Es regnet, hagelt, schneit	*It is raining, hailing, snowing*
Es blitzte	*There were flashes of lightning*
Es dämmert	*It is growing light/dusk*

These verbs are *only* used impersonally.

(b) Verbs used with impersonal *es* to refer to an indefinite agent

These are verbs which can be used with a specific subject, but are used impersonally if the agent is vague or unknown:

(i) Verbs referring to natural phenomena:

Es zieht	*There's a draught*
Es brennt	*Something's burning*
Da riecht es nach Teer	*There's a smell of tar there*

(ii) Verbs denoting noises:

Es läutet, klingelt	*Someone's ringing the bell*
Es klopfte an der Tür	*There was a knock at the door*
Es kracht, zischt, knallt	*There is a crashing, hissing, banging noise*

Many other verbs can be used with an impersonal *es* to bring out the idea of a vague impersonal agent, see 3.6.2a.

(c) Verbs denoting sensations and emotions

Many verbs denoting sensations can be used with an impersonal *es* as subject to bring out the idea of an unspecified force causing the sensation. The person involved appears as an accusative object:

Es juckt mich	*I itch*
Es überlief mich kalt	*A cold shiver ran up my back*
Es zog mich zu ihr	*I was drawn to her*
Es hält mich hier nicht länger	*Nothing's keeping me here any more*

Most of the verbs which can be used without a subject in formal or older German are now more usually constructed like this, e.g.: *Es friert mich, Es wundert mich*, etc. See 18.2.2 for details.

(d) Impersonal *es* with *sein* or *werden* followed by a noun or an adjective

This usually corresponds to English *it*:

Es ist, wurde spät	*It is, got late*
Es ist dein Vater	*It's your father*

Further details on this use of *es* are given in 3.6.2b. The use of *es ist* in the sense of English 'there is/are' is treated in detail in 18.2.5.

(e) *sein* and *werden* can be used impersonally with a personal dative and some adjectives expressing a sensation

Es ist mir heiß, kalt, schwindlig, übel, warm, etc.

For details see 2.5.5c. *es* is usually omitted if it is not in initial position in a main clause:

Ist (es) dir kalt? – Ja, mir ist (es) kalt
Ich merkte, daß (es) mir schwindlig wurde

(f) Impersonal passive and reflexive constructions

Es lebt sich gut in dieser Stadt   Es wurde im Nebenzimmer geredet

es is usually deleted unless it is in initial position in a main clause. For details see 3.6.2a, 15.1.3–4 and 15.4.3b.

(g) Other impersonal verbs and constructions

Many of these are idiomatic and the verbs involved are also used in other constructions with a definite subject. A selection of the most common:

Es bedurfte keiner anonymen Briefe	*No anonymous letters were needed*
(*Th. Mann*)	
Es fehlt mir an etwas (dat.)	*I lack sth.*
(see also 18.4.1d)	
Es gefällt mir in Heidelberg	*I like it in Heidelberg*
(see also 18.4.1d)	
Es gibt	*There is/are*
(For *es gibt* and *es ist* as equivalents of 'there is/are', see 18.2.5)	
Es geht	*It can be done; OK* (in answer to
	Wie geht es (dir/Ihnen)?)
Wie geht es (dir/Ihnen)?	*How are you?*

Es geht um Leben und Tod	*It's a matter of life and death*
Es gilt, etwas zu tun	*The thing is to do something*
Es geschah ihm recht	*It served him right*
Es handelt sich um etwas (acc.)	*It is a question of sth.*
Es heißt, daß ...	*It is said that ...*
Es kommt auf etwas (acc.) an	*It depends on sth.*
Es kommt zu etwas (dat.)	*Something occurs*
e.g. Am Abend **kam es zu** neuen Zusammenstößen	*There were fresh clashes in the evening*
Es liegt an etwas (dat.)	*It is due to sth.*
e.g. **Woran liegt es**, daß ...?	*Why is it that ...?*
Es macht/tut nichts	*It doesn't matter*
Es steht schlecht/besser um ihn	*Things look bad/better for him*
Wie steht es mit ihr?	*How's she doing?*
Es verhält sich so	*Things are like that*
e.g. Ähnlich **verhält es sich** an der Universität Münster	*Things are similar at the University of Münster*

18.2.5 *es ist/sind* and *es gibt* as equivalents of English 'there is/are'

es ist/sind and *es gibt* have rather different meanings. The following is a guide to choosing the correct one for the context.

(a) *es gibt* indicates existence in general
It is a real impersonal construction, and the *es* is never omitted.

(i) *es gibt* is typically used in broad, general statements, denoting existence in general, without necessarily referring to a particular place:

Es gibt Tage, wo alles schiefgeht	*There are days when everything goes wrong*
So etwas **gibt es** nicht	*There's no such thing*
Es gibt verschiedene Gründe dafür	*There are various reasons for that*
Es **hat** immer Kriege **gegeben** (*Valentin*)	*There have always been wars*
Unglückliche **gibt es** in allen Häusern, in jedem Stand (*Walser*)	*There are unhappy people in every kind of home, in every walk of life*

(ii) *es gibt* is used to point in a general way to permanent existence in a large area (i.e. a city or a country):

Es gibt drei alte Kirchen in unserer Stadt	*There are three old churches in our town*
In Trier **gibt es** ja so viel zu sehen	*There's so much to see in Trier*
Es dürfte in der Bundesrepublik wenige **geben**, die so gut wie er informiert sind (*Zeit*)	*There are probably not many people in the Federal Republic who are as well informed as he is*

(iii) *es gibt* records the consequences of some event:

Wenn du das tust, **gibt's** ein Unglück	*If you do that, there'll be an accident*
Bei den Unruhen **soll es** bisher vier Tote **gegeben haben** (*FAZ*)	*It is reported that there have been four killed in the disturbances so far*

NB: In everyday speech in south-west Germany, *es hat* is used for *es gibt*. This is a substandard regionalism.

(b) *es ist/sind* **indicates the presence of something at a particular time and place**

The *es* of *es ist/sind* is a 'dummy' subject (see 3.6.2e), allowing the real subject of the verb to occur later in the sentence, and it drops out when it is not in initial position in a main clause. Compare:

Es war eine Maus in der Küche	*There was a mouse in the kitchen*
BUT: In der Küche **war** eine Maus	*In the kitchen there was a mouse*
Er hat gemerkt, daß eine Maus in der Küche **war**	*He noticed that there was a mouse in the kitchen*

Given this, *es ist/sind* is used in the following cases:

(i) To refer to permanent or temporary presence in a definite and limited place, or temporary presence in a large area, e.g.:

Es war eine kleine Gastwirtschaft im Keller (*Baum*)	*There was a little bar in the cellar*
Schade, daß hier im Haushalt keine Nähmaschine **ist** (*Fallada*)	*It's a shame there isn't a sewing machine here in the house*
Es ist irgendjemand an der Tür	*There's someone at the door*
Es waren noch viele Menschen auf den Straßen	*There were still a lot of people in the streets*
Es waren Wolken am Himmel	*There were clouds in the sky*

Sentences with *es ist/sind must* contain an indication of place. This is often simply *da*:

Es ist ein Brief für Sie **da**	*There's a letter for you*

es gibt is occasionally used in such contexts. It emphasises the thing rather than the place and underlines its distinctive character:

In dieser Diele gab es gegenüber der Tür einen offenen Kamin (*Wendt*)	*In this lounge there was an open fireplace opposite the door*

(ii) To record events and when speaking of weather conditions:

Letzte Woche **war** in Hamburg ein Streik	*There was a strike in Hamburg last week*
Im Fernsehen **war** eine Diskussion darüber (*Valentin*)	*There was a discussion about that on the television*
In Mainz **war** ein Aufenthalt von fünf Minuten	*There was a five minute stop in Mainz*
Am nächsten Morgen **war** dichter Nebel	*Next morning there was thick fog*
Gestern **war** ein Gewitter in Füssen	*There was a thunderstorm in Füssen yesterday*

Usage varies in this type of context, and *es gibt* is often used:

Letzte Woche gab es einen Streik in Hamburg
In Mainz gab es einen Aufenthalt von fünf Minuten
Gestern gab es ein Gewitter in Füssen

es gibt is particularly frequent when a need is felt to emphasise the exceptional nature of the event or to refer to the future:

Es gab eine Explosion in der Fabrik	*There was an explosion in the factory*
Morgen wird es wieder schönes Wetter geben	*It will be fine again tomorrow*

18.3 The accusative object

18.3.1 Transitive verbs govern a direct object in the accusative as one of their complements

With many verbs, the accusative is the only complement apart from the subject (sentence pattern **B** on Table 18.2):

Er schlug **sie**
Seine Worte haben **mich** verletzt

Christian hat **seine Freundin** besucht
Sie hat **den Arzt** gesehen

As Table 18.2 shows, transitive verbs can also have, in addition to the accusative object, a dative object (sentence pattern **D**), a genitive object (sentence pattern **F**), a prepositional object (sentence pattern **H**) or a direction complement (sentence pattern **L**). Details about verbs with these sentence patterns are in the sections dealing with these other complements.

NB: The accusative is used in some time and place phrases, e.g.: *Es hat **den ganzen Tag** geschneit* (see 2.2.5). These are not accusative complements, but adverbials.

18.3.2 The direct object can have the form of a clause

(a) **Many verbs can have a clause as their direct object**
(i) A subordinate clause with *daß*, *ob* or an interrogative (see 19.2):

Ich bedauerte, **daß ich nicht kommen konnte**
Sie fragte mich, **ob ich dort übernachten wollte**

(ii) An infinitive clause with *zu* (see 13.2.4):

Ich hoffe, **dich bald wiedersehen zu können**
Ich habe vor, **sie morgen zu besuchen**

Many verbs which have a clause as object permit either a subordinate clause or an infinitive clause, depending on context. However, a few verbs only allow an infinitive clause (especially verbs denoting an intended action, e.g. *versuchen, vorhaben, wagen, sich weigern, zögern*), whereas others only allow a subordinate clause (especially verbs of saying and hearing, e.g. *erleben, fragen, mitteilen, verfügen*). In practice, usage in German is similar to that with the nearest English equivalents; exceptions are detailed in 13.2.4.

(b) **A direct object clause is sometimes anticipated by** *es*
This can be the case whether the complement is a subordinate clause or an infinitive clause, e.g.:

Sie sah **es** als gutes Zeichen an, daß keine Leute mehr vorbeikamen
Ich konnte **es** kaum ertragen, ihn so leiden zu sehen

Details on the use of this 'anticipatory' *es* are given in 3.6.3a.

18.3.3 A handful of verbs are used with two accusatives

In general, only one accusative (direct) object is possible in a sentence. However, a small number of verbs allow two accusative complements.

(a) Verbs with two accusative objects

(i) *kosten* and *lehren* are normally used with two accusatives:

Der Flug hat **meinen Vater 5000 Mark** gekostet	*The flight cost my father 5000 marks*
Sie hat **mich Deutsch** gelehrt	*She taught me German*

In colloquial German both these verbs are commonly used with a dative of the person, e.g. *Sie hat **mir** Deutsch gelehrt; Das hat **mir** viel Geld gekostet*. This is considered substandard, but DUDEN (1985: 435) allows it for *kosten*, as an alternative to the accusative, in figurative contexts:

Das kann **ihn/ihm** das Hals kosten	*That may cost him his life*

(ii) *abfragen* and *abhören* 'to test orally' can be used either with two accusative objects or a dative of the person and an accusative:

Der Lehrer hat **ihn/ihm** die englischen Vokabeln abgefragt/abgehört	*The teacher gave him a test on his English vocabulary*

If only the person is mentioned in the sentence, only the accusative is used, e.g. *Der Lehrer hat **ihn** abgefragt/abgehört*.

(iii) *bitten* and *fragen* can be used with two accusatives. One denotes the person asked, the other is an indefinite pronoun or a subordinate clause:

Hast du **ihn etwas** gefragt?	*Did you ask him something?*
Das möchte ich **dich** bitten	*I would like to request that of you*
Sie fragte **ihn, ob er mitkommen wollte**	*She asked him if he wanted to come with her*

NB: (i) *bitten* is more commonly used with a prepositional object introduced by *um*, see 18.6.10, e.g. *Ich möchte dich **darum** bitten*.
    (ii) In the passive the indefinite pronoun remains in the accusative, e.g. *Das bin ich gebeten/gefragt worden*.

(iv) *angehen* is used with an accusative of the person involved and an indefinite expression of quantity, e.g.:

Das geht **dich nichts** an	*That doesn't concern you at all*

Similarly, *Das geht mich viel, wenig, einen Dreck an*. The use of *angehen* with a dative of the person (e.g. *Das geht **dir** nichts an*) is a substandard north German regionalism.

(b) A few verbs have a predicate complement in the accusative

i.e. an additional element which relates back to the accusative object, describing or identifying it, e.g.:

Er nannte **mich einen Lügner**	*He called me a liar*

This construction is restricted in German to verbs of calling, i.e. *heißen*, *nennen* and *schimpfen*. It is used with more verbs in English; in corresponding contexts German usually has a phrase with *als* in apposition (cf. 2.6) or a prepositional complement, most often introduced by *zu*:

Ich sehe es als eine Schande an	*I consider it a shame*
Er bewies sich als Feigling	*He proved himself a coward*
Er machte sie zu seiner Frau	*He made her his wife*
Man erklärte ihn zum Verräter	*He was declared a traitor*
Wir hielten ihn für einen Idioten	*We considered/thought him an idiot*

18.3.4 Some German transitive verbs have English equivalents with different constructions

etwas beantragen	*apply for sth.*
jemanden beerben	*inherit from sb.*
etwas bezahlen	*pay for sth.*
etwas ekelt mich (see also 18.2.2)	*I am disgusted at sth.*
etwas dauert mich	*I regret sth.*
etwas freut mich	*I am pleased/glad about sth.*
jemanden/etwas fürchten	*be afraid of sb./sth.*

18.3.5 Fewer verbs can be used both transitively and intransitively in German than in English

German verbs are often less flexible syntactically than their nearest English counterparts and more restricted to use in certain constructions only. A few German verbs can be used transitively and intransitively, e.g.:

Ich brach den Zweig	*I broke the branch*
Der Zweig brach	*The branch broke*

However, far fewer German than English verbs have this facility, and the transitive and intransitive uses of many English verbs have different German equivalents. These can take a number of forms:

(a) The transitive and intransitive uses of some English verbs can correspond to quite different verbs in German

grow
Er **züchtet** Blumen	*He grows flowers*
Die Blumen **wachsen** im Garten	*The flowers grow in the garden*

leave
Sie **verließ** das Haus	*She left the house*
Ich **ließ** den Brief im Fach (**liegen**)	*I left the letter in the pigeonhole*
Der Zug **fährt** schon **ab**	*The train is already leaving*
Er **ging** früher als ich (**weg**)	*He left before me*

open
Ich **machte** die Tür **auf**	*I opened the door*
Die Tür **ging auf**	*The door opened*
(See also (c) below)	

(b) The transitive and intransitive uses of some English verbs may correspond to related verbs in German

The prefix *be-* (cf. 22.4.1) often forms transitive verbs from intransitive verbs, but other prefixes (e.g. *er-* and *ver-*) can sometimes have this function, and there are some pairs of verbs with vowel changes:

answer
Sie **beantwortete** die Frage	*She answered the question*
Sie **antwortete**	*She answered*

climb
Ich **bestieg** den Berg	*I climbed the mountain*
Ich **erstieg** den Berg	*I climbed the mountain (to the top)*
Die Maschine **stieg**	*The plane climbed*

drown
Man **ertränkte** die Hexe	*The witch was drowned*
Die Matrosen **ertranken**	*The sailors drowned*

sink
Wir **versenkten** das Schiff
Das Schiff **sank**

> *We sank the ship*
> *The ship sank*

(c) Some transitive German verbs can be used reflexively as the equivalent of the intransitive use of the corresponding English verb

change
Das hat nichts **geändert**
Das hat **sich geändert**
feel
Sie **fühlte** etwas unter ihren Füßen
Sie **fühlte sich** unwohl
open
Ich **öffnete** die Tür
Die Tür **öffnete sich**
(See also (a) above)
turn
Ich drehte das Rad
Das Rad drehte sich

> *That has changed nothing*
> *That has changed*
>
> *She felt something under her feet*
> *She felt unwell*
>
> *I opened the door*
> *The door opened*
>
> *I turned the wheel*
> *The wheel turned*

(d) In some cases a construction with *lassen* and a German intransitive verb corresponds to the transitive use of the verb in English

For this 'causative' use of *lassen*, see 13.3.1c:

drop
Ich **ließ** den Stein **fallen**
Der Stein **fiel**
fail
Sie **haben** den Kandidaten **durchfallen lassen**
Der Kandidat **ist durchgefallen**
run
Ich **habe** das Wasser in die Badewanne **laufen lassen**
Der Wasserhahn **läuft**

> *I dropped the stone*
> *The stone dropped*
>
> *They failed the candidate*
> *The candidate failed*
>
> *I've run the bathwater*
> *The tap's running*

(e) In some cases a construction with *sich lassen* and a German transitive verb corresponds to the intransitive use of the verb in English

For this construction with *sich lassen*, see 15.4.6:

cut
Sie **hat** das Papier **geschnitten**
Das Papier **läßt sich** leicht **schneiden**

> *She cut the paper*
> *The paper cuts easily*

18.3.6 Verbs used with an accusative reflexive

For the form of the reflexive pronoun, see 3.2. The 'reflexive' verbs of German have no direct equivalent in English, and they can correspond to a variety of English verb constructions and verb types. Many have English equivalents which are quite distinct from those of the simple verb (and the English equivalent is often an intransitive verb), e.g. *sich fragen* 'wonder' (cf. *fragen* 'ask'), *sich setzen* 'sit down' (cf. *setzen* 'put'), etc. In a significant number of other instances the nearest English equivalent is a passive (or passive-like) construction (cf. 15.4.3).

Many verbs used with a reflexive accusative also have other complements, e.g. a dative, genitive or prepositional object. They are treated in the sections dealing with these other complements.

It is helpful to distinguish two types of reflexive verb in German:

(a) 'True' reflexive verbs, which are only used with a reflexive pronoun
With these, the reflexive pronoun is an integral part of the verb:

sich bedanken	*say 'thank you'*	sich erholen	*recover*
sich beeilen	*hurry*	sich erkälten	*catch a cold*
sich befinden	*be (situated)*	sich irren	*be mistaken*
sich benehmen	*behave*	sich verabschieden	*say goodbye*
sich eignen	*be suited*	sich verneigen	*bow*
sich entschließen	*decide*	sich weigern	*refuse*

(b) Other transitive verbs used reflexively, with the accusative object appearing as a reflexive pronoun
(i) Many transitive verbs can be used with a reflexive pronoun, with the action of the verb thereby being related back to the subject. Effectively the agent is performing the action on him/herself. Compare:

Das habe ich **meinen Bruder** gefragt	Das habe ich **mich** gefragt
Ich setzte **den Koffer** auf den Stuhl	Ich setzte **mich** auf den Stuhl
Ich habe **den Hund** gewaschen	Ich habe **mich** gewaschen
Ich habe **ihn** nicht überzeugen können	Ich habe **mich** nicht überzeugen können

(ii) Many transitive verbs denoting activities and accomplishments can be used reflexively with a subject which is not the person carrying out the action. These usually correspond to English passive constructions:

Das **erklärt sich** leicht	*That is easily explained*
Mein Verdacht **hat sich bestätigt**	*My suspicions were confirmed*

Intransitive verbs denoting activities and accomplishments can also be used in a similar way with a reflexive pronoun. These constructions are always impersonal and have a sense similar to a construction with *man*:

Dort **wohnt** es **sich** gut	*One can live well there*
Hier **arbeitet** es **sich** bequem	*One can work comfortably here*

Further details on this construction are given in 15.4.3.

(iii) A few verbs have reflexive and non-reflexive forms where the reflexive variant is a 'true' reflexive, with a rather different meaning:

Das erinnert mich an etwas	*That reminds me of something*
Ich erinnere mich an etwas	*I remember something*
Das hat mich gefreut	*That pleased me*
Ich habe mich gefreut	*I was pleased*
Das habe ich ihr versprochen	*I promised her that*
Ich habe mich versprochen	*I made a slip of the tongue*

18.4 The dative object

A dative object occurs in three main sentence patterns, cf. Table 18.2:

- C: Subject + verb + dative object
- D: Subject + verb + accusative object + dative object
- I: Subject + verb + dative object + prepositional object

Verbs with the patterns **C** and **I** are treated together in 18.4.1 (for the prepositional objects in the relevant cases, see 18.6). Verbs governing both a dative (indirect) and an accusative (direct) object are explained in 18.4.2. Verbs with a dative reflexive are dealt with in 18.4.3.

The dative has a wide range of other uses in German, as explained in 2.5, in particular the so-called 'free' dative, which can occur with many verbs. These are not generally regarded as complements since they occur freely and are not bound closely to particular verbs, but for an alternative view, see Wegener (1985).

NB: As explained in 15.1.3, the dative object of an active construction can *never* become the subject of the corresponding passive sentence.

18.4.1 Verbs governing the dative

A fair number of verbs in German have a dative object, but no accusative object. These have no direct equivalent in English, which does not distinguish accusative and dative cases by endings, and English learners need to devote some attention to these verbs. In essence, governing a dative is a peculiarity of individual verbs, since no general rules can be given as to which verbs govern a dative. Nevertheless, it is helpful to be aware that these dative objects often relate to persons who are advantaged or disadvantaged in some way through the action expressed by the verb.

(a) Common verbs which govern a dative object

abraten *advise against*
Sie hat **ihm** davon abgeraten — *She advised him against it*

ähneln *resemble, look like*
Er ähnelt **seinem Bruder** — *He looks like his brother*

ausweichen *get out of the way of, evade, avoid*
Er ist **der Gefahr** ausgewichen — *He avoided the danger*

begegnen *meet (by chance)*
Ich bin **ihr** in der Stadt begegnet — *I met her in town*

bekommen *agree with one (of food)*
Fleisch bekommt **mir** nicht — *Meat doesn't agree with me*

NB: *bekommen* with an accusative object means 'receive', e.g. *Er bekam einen langen Brief von seinem Vater.*

danken *thank*
Ich dankte **ihnen** sehr dafür — *I thanked them very much for it*

dienen *serve*
Er diente **dem König von Italien** — *He served the king of Italy*

drohen *threaten*
Sie drohte **ihm** mit einem Stock — *She threatened him with a stick*

einfallen *occur*
Das ist **mir** nicht eingefallen — *That didn't occur to me*

folgen *follow*
Er ist **ihr** ins Exil gefolgt — *He followed her into exile*

NB: *folgen* is used with *auf* (acc.) in the sense 'succeed', 'come after' e.g. **Auf den Sturm** *folgten drei sonnige Tage.*

gehorchen *obey*
Sie gehorcht **ihrem Vater** — *She obeys her father*

gehören *belong*
Der Mercedes gehört **mir** nicht — *The Mercedes doesn't belong to me*

NB: (i) In the sense 'be part of', 'be one of', *gehören* is used with *zu*: *Das Feld gehört zu unserem Garten. Das gehört zu meinen Aufgaben.*
(ii) In the sense 'belong' (i.e. 'be a member of'), *angehören* is used. It also takes a dative: *Ich gehöre diesem Verein an.*

gelten *be meant for, be aimed at, be for*
Gilt diese Bemerkung **mir**? — *Is that comment meant for me?*
Sein letzter Gedanke galt **seinem Volk** — *His last thought was for his people*

gleichen *be equal to, resemble*
Jeder Tag glich **dem anderen** — *One day was like the next*

gratulieren *congratulate*
Sie haben **ihr** zum Geburtstag gratuliert — *They congratulated her on her birthday*

helfen *help*
Er half **seinem Vater** in der Küche — *He helped his father in the kitchen*

imponieren *impress*
Sie hat **ihm** sehr imponiert — *She impressed him a lot*

kündigen *fire, give notice*
Der Chef hat **ihm** gestern gekündigt — *The boss gave him notice yesterday*

NB: In colloquial German, *kündigen* is used with an accusative object, e.g. *Der Chef hat **ihn** gekündigt.* When used to mean 'cancel', it is *always* used with an accusative, e.g. *Er hat den Vertrag gekündigt.*

nutzen/nützen *be of use*
Das nutzt **mir** doch gar nichts — *But that's no use to me*

passen *suit*
Das neue Kleid paßt **dir** gut — *The new dress suits you*

schaden *harm*
Rauchen schadet **der Gesundheit** — *Smoking is harmful to your health*

schmeicheln *flatter*
Der Student wollte **dem Professor** schmeicheln — *The student wanted to flatter the professor*

trauen *trust*
Ich traute **meinen Augen** nicht — *I couldn't believe my eyes*

NB: *mißtrauen* 'distrust' also governs a dative object.

trotzen *defy*
Er trotzte **der Gefahr** — *He defied/braved the danger*

unterliegen *be defeated by, be subject to*
Er unterlag **seinem Gegner** — *He lost to his opponent*

vertrauen *have trust in*
jemandem blind vertrauen — *have a blind trust in somebody*

wehtun *hurt*
Der Wespenstich hat **ihm** wehgetan — *The wasp sting hurt him*

(b) Most verbs with the meaning 'happen', 'occur' govern a dative

Es wird **dir** doch nichts geschehen	*But nothing will happen to you*
Was ist **ihm** gestern passiert?	*What happened to him yesterday?*
So etwas ist **mir** noch nie vorgekommen	*Nothing like that has ever happened to me*

Similarly, *bevorstehen, widerfahren, zustoßen*, etc.

(c) Verbs with certain prefixes usually take a dative

i.e. those with *bei-, ent-, entgegen-, nach-, wider-, zu-*, e.g.:

Er ist **der SPD** beigetreten	*He joined the SPD*
Das entsprach **meinen Erwartungen**	*That came up to my expectations*
Sie kam **mir** entgegen	*She approached me*
Er eilte **ihr** nach	*He hurried after her*
Das Kind widersprach **seiner Mutter**	*The child contradicted its mother*
Er hat **dem Gespräch** zugehört	*He listened to the conversation*

Similarly (among many others):

beistehen	*give support to*	nachlaufen	*run after*
beiwohnen	*be present at*	nachstellen	*follow, pester*
entsagen	*renounce*	nachstreben	*emulate*
entstammen	*originate from*	sich widersetzen	*oppose*
entgegengehen	*go to meet*	widerstehen	*resist*
entgegenwirken	*counteract*	zulaufen	*run up to*
nachahmen	*imitate*	zulächeln	*smile at*
nachgeben	*give way to*	zustimmen	*agree with*
nachkommen	*follow*	zuvorkommen	*anticipate*

The verbs prefixed with *ent-* meaning 'escape' (*entgehen, entfliehen, entkommen, entrinnen, entwischen*, etc.) also all govern a dative.

NB: A few verbs with these prefixes have a dative and an accusative object (see 18.4.2), e.g. *jemandem etwas beibringen* 'teach somebody something', *jemandem etwas zutrauen* 'credit somebody with something'.

(d) The dative object of some verbs corresponds to the subject of the usual English equivalent

Etwas fällt **mir** auf	*I notice something*
Etwas entfällt **mir**	*I forget something*
Es fällt **mir** leicht, schwer	*I find something easy, difficult*
Etwas fehlt, mangelt **mir** ⎱	*I lack something*
Es fehlt, mangelt **mir** an etwas ⎰	
Etwas gefällt **mir**	*I like something*
Etwas geht **mir** auf	*I realise something*
Etwas gelingt **mir**	*I succeed in something*
Etwas tut **mir** leid	*I am sorry about something*
Das leuchtet **mir** nicht ein	*I don't understand that*
Es liegt **mir** viel an etwas (dat.)	*I am keen on something*
Etwas liegt **mir**	*I fancy something*
Das genügt, reicht **mir**	*I have had enough of that*
Etwas schmeckt **mir**	*I like something* (i.e. food)

NB: With these verbs, there is a marked tendency for the dative object to precede the verb in main clauses, e.g. *Mir hat das nicht gefallen*.

18.4.2 Verbs governing a dative and an accusative object

These are transitive verbs with two complements aside from the subject, i.e. an accusative (direct) object, which is usually a thing, and a dative (indirect) object, which is usually a person. It is helpful to remember them as *einem etwas* verbs. The German dative commonly corresponds to an English prepositional phrase with *to* or *from*, or to an English indirect object (e.g. *He gave me the book*). English learners should be aware that the indirect object is marked solely by using the dative case in German. Contrary to the case in English, **no preposition is required**.

With many verbs (e.g. *geben*) the dative object is obligatory to construct a grammatical sentence, with others (e.g. *beweisen*) it can be suppressed in some contexts.

(a) Verbs of giving and taking (in the widest sense) govern a dative and an accusative object
There are a large number of such verbs, e.g.:

Sie haben **mir eine Stelle** angeboten	*They offered me a job*
Das wollte er (**mir**) beweisen	*He wanted to prove that (to me)*
Er brachte (**ihr**) **einen Blumenstrauß**	*He brought (her) a bunch of flowers*
Ich kann (**dir**) **diesen Roman** empfehlen	*I can recommend this novel (to you)*
Er hat **dem Lehrer einen Bleistift** gegeben	*He gave the teacher a pencil*
Sie will **mir** jetzt **etwas Ruhe** gönnen	*She is now willing to let me have some peace and quiet*
Kannst du **mir zehn Mark** leihen?	*Can you lend me ten marks?*
Wir haben (**ihr**) **die Tasche** genommen	*We took the bag (from her)*
Ich habe (**ihr**) **das Paket** geschickt	*I've sent (her) the parcel*
Du schuldest **mir** noch **hundert Mark**	*You still owe me a hundred marks*
Er verkaufte (**mir**) **seinen alten Opel**	*He sold (me) his old Opel*
Er zeigte **ihr seine Kupferstiche**	*He showed her his etchings*

(b) Most verbs involving an act of speaking are used with a dative and an accusative object
(i) With many of these the accusative object can only be either a neuter or indefinite pronoun (e.g. *es, das, etwas, nichts*) or a clause (a subordinate clause introduced by *daß, ob* etc., or an infinitive clause). There are often differences from the constructions with the equivalent English verbs:

Sie hat (**mir**) geantwortet, daß sie morgen kommen wollte	*She replied that she was going to come tomorrow*
Wer hat (**dir**) befohlen, die Geiseln zu erschießen?	*Who ordered you to shoot the hostages?*
Das habe ich ihm schon gestern erzählt	*I already told him that yesterday*
Er hat mir geraten, mein Haus zu verkaufen	*He advised me to sell my house*
Er versicherte mir, daß er alles erledigt hätte	*He assured me he had taken care of everything*
Das wird er (**dir**) nie verzeihen können	*He'll never be able to forgive you that*

NB: With *antworten*, the dative is only used for *persons*. Compare: *Er hat **auf** meinen Brief, auf meine Frage geantwortet.*

sagen is normally used in this way, with an optional dative of the person:

Was wollen Sie (ihm) sagen?	*What do you want to say (to him)?*
Sie sagte mir, daß sie es auf keinen	*She told me that on no account would*
Fall machen würde	*she do that*

However, it is used with *zu* when introducing direct speech or addressing oneself:

„Nun komm doch!" sagte sie zu	*'Come along now,' she said to Christian*
Christian	
„Wie kannst du das nur machen?"	*'How on earth can you do that?,' he*
sagte er zu sich selbst	*said to himself*

(ii) With a few verbs the accusative object or the dative object can be omitted, as the context requires:

Die irakische Regierung erlaubte	*The Iraqi government allowed the*
(der Delegation) die Einreise	*delegation into the country*
Sie hat mir (einen langen Brief) geschrieben	*She wrote me (a long letter)*

(iii) *glauben* has a dative of the person and/or an accusative of the thing:

Er glaubt **dem Lehrer**	Er glaubt **jedes Wort**
Er glaubt **dem Lehrer jedes Wort**	

NB: *glauben an* (acc.), cf. 18.6.2b, is used for 'believe in', e.g. *Ich **glaube an** seinen Erfolg.*

(c) With some verbs the German dative and accusative construction differs from the construction used with the nearest equivalent English verb

Man merkt ihm die Anstrengung an	*One notices the effort he's making*
Sie fügte es dem Brief bei	*She enclosed it with the letter*
Das hat ihm das Studium ermöglicht,	*That made it possible, difficult for*
erschwert	*him to study*
Das hat sie mir gestern mitgeteilt	*She informed me of that yesterday*
Die Polizei konnte ihm nichts	*The police couldn't prove anything*
nachweisen	*against him*
Das hat sie mir aber verschwiegen	*She didn't tell me about that, though*
Das hätte ich ihr nicht zugetraut	*I wouldn't have believed her capable of that*

(d) With verbs of sending or transferring a phrase with *an* may be a common alternative to the dative
The effect is to emphasise the recipient more strongly:

Ich habe ein Paket **an meinen Vater** geschickt
Ich habe einen Brief **an deinen Vater** geschrieben
Er hat seinen alten Opel **an seinen Vater** verkauft

(e) A few reflexive verbs have a dative object
With these the reflexive pronoun is the accusative object:

Sie mußten sich **dem Feind** ergeben	*They had to surrender to the enemy*
Sie näherten sich **der Stadt**	*They approached the city*

18.4.3 A number of verbs are used with a dative reflexive pronouon

(a) Many verbs governing a dative may be used with a dative reflexive pronoun if the action refers back to the subject
Both types of verbs governing the dative can be used in this way, i.e.:

(i) Verbs where the dative is the sole object (cf. 18.4.1):

Ich habe **mir** mehrmals widersprochen	*I contradicted myself several times*
Du schadest **dir** mit dem Rauchen	*You're harming yourself by smoking*

(ii) *einem etwas* verbs (cf. 18.4.2):

Ich erlaubte **mir**, ihm zu widersprechen	*I allowed myself to contradict him*
Ich muß **mir** Arbeit verschaffen	*I must find work*
Ich habe **mir** zu viel zugemutet	*I've taken on too much*

(b) A few other verbs occur with a dative reflexive pronoun

These are 'true' reflexive verbs (cf. 18.3.6), where the reflexive pronoun is an integral part of the verb. All also have an accusative object:

Das habe ich **mir** angeeignet	*I acquired that*
Das habe ich **mir** eingebildet	*I imagined that*
Das verbitte ich **mir**	*I refuse to tolerate that*
Ich habe **mir** vorgenommen, das zu tun	*I have resolved to do that*
Das kann ich **mir** gut vorstellen	*I can imagine that well*
Ich habe **mir** eine Grippe zugezogen	*I contracted flu*

Similarly, *sich etwas anmaßen* 'claim sth. for oneself', *sich etwas ausbedingen* 'make sth. a condition'.

18.5 Genitive objects

A genitive object occurs in two main sentence patterns, cf. Table 18.2:

E: Subject + verb + genitive object
F: Subject + verb + accusative object + genitive object

Both are uncommon and restricted in practice to formal written (especially official) German. Some more are used only in set phrases. In listing those verbs which are still encountered with a genitive more widely used alternatives are given wherever possible.

18.5.1 Non-reflexive verbs which require a genitive as the only object

bedürfen *need* (more common: *brauchen, benötigen*)
Er bedurfte **meiner Hilfe** nicht   *He didn't need my help*

entbehren *lack* (more commonly used with an accusative object)

Der Staat konnte **eines kraftvollen**	*The state could not do without a*
Monarchen nicht entbehren	*powerful monarch*
(*v. Rimscha*)	

gedenken *remember* (elev. for *denken an* (acc.), with reference to the dead)

Lech Walensa hat **der Opfer** des	*Lech Walensa remembered the victims*
Nationalsozialismus gedacht (*FR*)	*of National Socialism*

harren *await* (elev. for *warten auf* (acc.). It has a biblical ring)
Wir harren **einer Antwort** (*Zeit*)   *We are awaiting an answer*

18.5.2 Reflexive verbs with a genitive object

Most of these are 'true' reflexive verbs, with an accusative reflexive pronoun (cf. 18.3.6):

sich annehmen *look after, take care of* (more usual *sich kümmern um*)
Er hätte sich **dieses Kindes** *He would have looked after this child*
angenommen (*Walser*)

sich bedienen *use* (more usual *benutzen, gebrauchen, verwenden*)
Die Firma bediente sich nur *The firm only used dirty ships*
schmutziger Schiffe (*Böll*)

sich bemächtigen *seize* (various alternatives, e.g. *ergreifen, nehmen*)
Sie bemächtigten sich **des** *They seized the mayor of Le Mans*
Bürgermeisters von Le Mans (*Zeit*)

sich entsinnen *remember* (more usual *sich erinnern an* (acc.), see 18.6.2b)
Ich entsann mich **des Anblicks** der *I remembered the sight of the long huts*
langgestreckte Baracken (*Andersch*)

sich erfreuen *enjoy* (more usual *genießen, sich freuen über* (acc.))
Sie erfreuten sich **des schönen** *They were enjoying the fine summer*
Sommerwetters (*OH*) *weather*

sich erinnern *remember* (more usual *sich erinnern an* (acc.), see 18.6.2b)
Ich erinnere mich **bestimmter Details** *I still remember certain details*
noch (*Böll*)

sich erwehren *refrain from* (more usual *abwehren*)
Ich konnte mich **eines Lächelns** kaum *I could scarcely refrain from a smile*
erwehren

sich rühmen *boast about/of* (more usual *stolz sein über*)
Die meisten Länder Europas rühmen *Most European countries can boast of*
sich **einer tausendjährigen** *a thousand years of history*
Geschichte (*Haffner*)

sich schämen *be ashamed of* (more usual *sich schämen für/wegen*, cf. 18.6.5)
Er schämte sich **seines Betragens** *He was ashamed of his behaviour*

sich vergewissern *make sure* (more usual *nachprüfen, überprüfen*)
Sie vergewisserte sich **der** *She made sure about this man's reliability*
Zuverlässigkeit dieses Mannes

18.5.3 Verbs used with a genitive and an accusative object

anklagen *accuse* (outside formal legal parlance: *anklagen wegen*)
Man klagte **ihn der fahrlässigen** *He was accused of manslaughter through*
Tötung an *culpable negligence*

berauben *rob* (more commonly *einem etwas rauben*)
Er beraubte **ihn der Freiheit** *He robbed him of his freedom*

versichern *assure* (more commonly *einem etwas zusichern*)
Ich versichere **Sie meines** *I assure you of my absolute trust*
uneingeschränkten Vertrauens

The following verbs are used with a genitive in legal language, but with a following clause in everyday speech:

jemanden einer Sache beschuldigen ⎱	*accuse sb. of sth.*
jemanden einer Sache bezichtigen ⎰	
jemanden einer Sache überführen	*convict sb. of sth.*
jemanden einer Sache verdächtigen	*suspect sb. of sth.*

18.5.4 Set phrases with the genitive

Many more verbs were used with a genitive in older German, and some of these still occur in idiomatic phrases:

der Gefahr nicht achten	*pay no heed to danger*
jemanden eines Besseren belehren	*teach someone better*
sich eines Besseren besinnen	*think better of something*
jeder Beschreibung spotten	*beggar description*
jemanden des Landes verweisen	*expel sb. from a country*
seines Amtes walten	*discharge one's duties*
jemanden keines Blickes würdigen	*not to deign to look at sb.*

18.6 Prepositional objects

18.6.1 Many verbs are followed by an object introduced by a preposition

The preposition used in these prepositional objects is idiomatic and determined by the individual verb. The fact that German has *Ich warte* **auf** *Sie* for English 'I am waiting **for** you', for instance, is arbitrary; it is not connected in any way with the usual meaning of the preposition *auf*. For this reason, the foreign learner has to treat each combination of verb and preposition separately and remember them as an idiomatic whole.

Three main sentence patterns involve prepositional objects, cf. Table 18.2. Some verbs govern a prepositional object as their only object (sentence pattern **G**), others have an accusative or a dative object beside the prepositional object (sentence patterns **H** and **I** respectively). A few verbs even have two prepositional objects. All prepositional objects are treated in this section under the individual prepositions, with other complements governed by the verb indicated in appropriate cases.

18.6.2 *an* most often occurs with a following dative in prepositional objects, but a few verbs govern *an* with the accusative

(a) Used in prepositional objects with the dative case, *an* often conveys the idea of 'in respect of', 'in connection with'

Ich erkannte sie **an ihrem knallroten Haar**	*I recognised her by her bright red hair*
Er ist **an einer Lungenentzündung** gestorben	*He died of pneumonia*
Ich zweifle **an seiner Ehrlichkeit**	*I doubt his honesty*

A selection of other verbs:

arbeiten an	*work at*	mitwirken an	*play a part in*
erkranken an	*fall ill with*	teilnehmen an	*take part in*
gewinnen an	*gain (in)*	verlieren an	*lose (some)*
(e.g.: *an Bedeutung gewinnen*)		(e.g.: *an Boden verlieren*)	
leiden an	*suffer from*		
sich an jemandem/etwas freuen	*take pleasure in sb./sth.*		

NB: *sich freuen auf* (acc.) 'look forward to' (18.6.3a), *sich freuen über* 'be glad/pleased about' (18.6.9).

jemanden an etwas hindern	*prevent sb. from (doing) sth.*
Es fehlt mir an etwas	*I lack sth.* (cf. 18.4.1d)
Es liegt mir viel an etwas	*I am very keen on sth.* (cf. 18.4.1d)
sich an etwas orientieren	*orientate oneself by sth.*
etwas an jemandem rächen	*avenge sth. on sb.*
sich an jemandem für etwas rächen	*take revenge on sb. for sth.*

(b) Most of the few verbs which govern a prepositional object with *an* and a following accusative denote mental processes

Du erinnerst mich **an ihn**	*You remind me of him*
Ich erinnere mich **an ihn**	*I remember him* (cf. 18.5.2)
Ich glaube **an den Fortschritt**	*I believe in progress* (cf. 18.4.2b)

Also:

denken an	*think of*	sich gewöhnen an *get used to*
sich an etwas halten *stick to sth.*		

18.6.3 *auf* most often occurs with the accusative in prepositional objects; only very few verbs govern *auf* with the dative

(a) *auf* + accusative is the commonest preposition in prepositional objects

Ich werde auf deine Kinder aufpassen	*I'll mind your children*
Seine Bemerkung bezog sich auf dich	*His comment related to you*
Das läuft auf das gleiche hinaus	*It amounts to the same thing*
Er wies (mich) auf die Schwierigkeiten hin	*He pointed the difficulties out (to me)*

Other verbs:

achten auf	*pay attention to*	schimpfen/auf	*curse about*
achtgeben	*pay attention to*	schwören auf	*swear on/by*
sich berufen auf	*refer to*	sich spezialisieren auf	*specialise in*
drängen auf	*press for*	sich stützen auf	*lean on, count on*
sich erstrecken auf	*extend to*	sich verlassen auf	*rely on*
folgen auf	*follow* (cf. 18.4.1a)	sich verstehen auf	*be expert in*
sich freuen auf	*look forward to*	(jemanden) verweisen auf	
(cf. 18.6.2a)		*refer (sb.) to*	
hoffen auf	*hope for*	verzichten auf	*do without*
sich konzentrieren auf	*concentrate on*	warten auf	*wait for*
pfeifen auf (coll.)	*not care less about*	zählen auf	*count on*
pochen auf	*insist on*	zurückkommen auf	*come back to, refer to*
reagieren auf	*react to*		

Es kommt (mir) auf etwas an	*Sth. matters (to me)*
etwas auf etwas beschränken	*limit/restrict/confine sth. to sth.*
sich auf etwas beschränken	*limit oneself/be limited to sth.*
etwas auf etwas zurückführen	*put sth. down to sth.*

(b) A few verbs which convey the idea of not moving govern *auf* + dative

Er beharrte **auf seiner Meinung**	*He didn't shift from his opinion*
Ich bestehe **auf meinem Recht**	*I insist on my right*

NB: *bestehen aus* 'consist of' (18.6.4), *bestehen in* 'consist in' (18.6.6).

Similarly, *basieren auf, beruhen auf, fußen auf*, which all mean 'be based on', 'rest on'. Note, however, *sich gründen auf* (**acc.**) 'be based on', e.g. *Der Vorschlag gründet sich **auf diese Annahme.***

18.6.4 *aus* usually has the meaning 'of', 'from' in prepositional objects

Ihr Essen bestand **aus trockenem Brot**   *Their food consisted of dry bread*

Other verbs:

etwas aus etwas entnehmen, ersehen	*infer, gather sth. from sth.*
sich aus etwas ergeben	*result from sth.*
etwas aus etwas folgern, schließen	*conclude sth. from sth.*

NB: (i) *entnehmen* can alternatively be constructed with a dative, e.g. *Ich entnehme (aus) ihrem Brief, daß Sie das Geschäft aufgeben wollen.*
(ii) *sich in etwas ergeben* 'submit to sth.' (cf. 18.6.6), *sich jemandem/etwas ergeben* 'surrender to sb./sth.' (cf. 18.4.2e).

18.6.5 *für* usually has the meaning 'for' in prepositional objects

Ich habe ihm **für seine Mühe** gedankt   *I thanked him for his trouble*
Ich habe mich **für den Audi** entschieden   *I decided on the Audi*
Ich halte deine Freundin **für hochbegabt**   *I consider your friend to be very gifted*

Other verbs:

sich (bei jemandem) für etwas bedanken	*give thanks for sth. (to sb.)*
sich für etwas begeistern	*be enthusiastic about sth.*
sich für jemanden/etwas eignen	*be suitable for sb./sth.*
sich für jemanden/etwas interessieren	*be interested in sb./sth.*
sich für jemanden/etwas schämen	*be ashamed for sb./of sth.*
für jemanden/etwas sorgen	*take care of/look after sb./sth.*

NB: (i) Non-reflexive *interessieren* may be used with *für* or *an* (dat.), e.g. *Er hat sie für das/an dem Unternehmen interessiert.*
(ii) *sich eignen zu/als* means 'be suitable as'.
(iii) *sich (wegen) jemandes/etwas schämen* (cf. 18.5.2) 'be ashamed of sb./sth.', *sich vor jemandem schämen* 'feel ashamed in front of sb.' (cf. 18.6.12a).
(iv) *sich um jemanden/etwas sorgen* 'be worried about sb./sth.'.

18.6.6 *in* is more often used with the accusative in prepositional objects

Sie willigte **in die Scheidung** ein   *She agreed to the divorce*
Er verliebte sich **in sie**   *He fell in love with her*

Other verbs:

jemanden in etwas einführen	*introduce sb. to sth.*
sich ergeben in	*submit to (cf. 18.6.4)*
sich mischen in	*meddle in*
sich vertiefen in	*become engrossed in*

A very few verbs govern *in* with the dative, i.e.:

Meine Aufgabe besteht **in der Erledigung** der Korrespondenz	*My duties consist in dealing with the correspondence (cf. 18.6.3b)*
Ich habe mich nicht **in ihr** getäuscht	*I was not mistaken in (my judgement of) her*

18.6.7 *mit* usually has the sense of 'with' in prepositional objects

Sie hat **mit ihrer Arbeit** angefangen	*She made a start on her work*
Willst du bitte **damit** aufhören?	*Please stop doing that*
Sie hat ihm **mit der Faust** gedroht	*She threatened him with her fist*
Ich habe gestern **mit ihm** telephoniert	*I spoke to him on the telephone yesterday*

sich abfinden mit	*be satisfied with*	übereinstimmen mit	*agree with*
sich befassen mit	*deal with*	sich unterhalten mit	*converse with*
sich begnügen mit	*be satisfied with*	vergleichen mit	*compare with*
sich beschäftigen mit	*occupy o.s. with*	sich verheiraten mit	*marry*
rechnen mit	*count on*	versehen mit	*provide with*
sprechen mit	*speak to/with*	zusammenstoßen mit	*collide with*
(*or*: jemanden sprechen)			

18.6.8 *nach*

(a) *nach* **often has the sense of English 'after ', 'for' with verbs of calling, enquiring, longing, reaching, etc.**

Haben Sie sich **nach seinem Befinden** erkundigt?	*Have you enquired how he is?*
Plötzlich griff das Kind **nach der Katze**	*Suddenly the child made a grab for the cat*
Sie schrie **nach ihrem Cousin**	*She yelled for her cousin*
Ich telephonierte **nach einem Arzt**	*I rang for a doctor*

Other verbs:

fragen nach	*ask after, for*	streben nach	*strive for*
hungern nach	*hunger after, for*	suchen nach	*search for*
rufen nach	*call after, for*	verlangen nach	*ask, long for; crave*
sich sehnen nach	*long for*		

NB: *sich erkundigen über* 'enquire about'; *fragen über* 'ask about'.

(b) *nach* **often has the sense of English 'of' with verbs of smelling, etc.**

Es riecht **nach Teer**	*It smells of tar*
Es schmeckte **nach Fisch**	*It tasted of fish*

Similarly, *duften nach, stinken nach*, etc. cf. also: *Es sieht nach Regen aus* 'It looks like rain'.

18.6.9 *über* always governs the accusative in prepositional objects

(a) *über* **corresponds to English 'about' with verbs of saying, etc.**

Ich habe mich sehr **über sein Benehmen** geärgert	*I was very annoyed at his behaviour*
Sie mußte lange **darüber** nachdenken	*She had to think it over for a long time*
Ich sprach gestern mit dem Chef **über diese Bewerbung**	*I talked to the boss about this application yesterday*

Many verbs can be used with *über* in this sense. A selection of others:

sich bei jemandem über etwas beklagen, beschweren	*complain to sb. about sth.*
sich über jemanden/etwas freuen	*be pleased about sth.* (cf. 18.6.2a)
jemanden über etwas informieren	*inform sb. about sth.*
über jemanden/etwas spotten	*mock sb./sth.*
sich täuschen über etwas	*be mistaken about sth.* (cf. 18.6.6)
über etwas urteilen	*judge sth.*
sich über jemanden/etwas wundern	*be surprised at sb./sth.*

Some verbs, i.e. *denken, erzählen, hören, lesen, sagen, schreiben, sprechen* and *wissen*, can be used with *über* or *von* in the sense of 'about'. *über* tends to refer to something more extensive than *von*. Compare:

Was denken Sie darüber?	*What is your view of that?*
Was denken Sie von ihm?	*What do you think of him?*
Er wußte viel über Flugzeuge	*He knew a lot about aeroplanes*
Er wußte nichts von ihrem Tod	*He knew nothing of her death*

(b) Other verbs governing a prepositional object with *über*

es über sich bringen, etwas zu tun	*bring o.s. to do sth.*
sich über etwas hinwegsetzen	*disregard sth.*
über etwas verfügen	*have sth. at one's disposal*

18.6.10 *um* usually has the meaning 'concerning', 'in respect of' in prepositional objects

Sie hat sich **um ihre Schwester** in Dresden geängstigt	*She was worried about her sister in Dresden*
Es handelte sich **um eine Wette**	*It was a question of a bet*
Ich kümmerte mich **um meine Enkelkinder**	*I took care of my grandchildren*

Other verbs:

sich um etwas bemühen	*take trouble over sth.*
jemanden um etwas beneiden	*envy sb. sth.*
jemanden um etwas betrügen	*cheat sb. out of sth.*
jemanden um etwas bitten, ersuchen (elev.)	*ask sb. for sth., request sth. from sb.*
jemanden um etwas bringen	*make sb. lose sth.*
Es geht um etwas (cf. 18.2.4f)	*Something is at stake*
um etwas kommen	*lose sth., be deprived of sth.*
sich um jemanden/etwas sorgen	*be worried about sth.*
sich um etwas streiten	*argue about/over sth.*

18.6.11 *von* usually has the sense of English 'of' or 'from' in prepositional objects

Ich will dich nicht **von der Arbeit** abhalten	*I don't want to keep you from your work*
Wir müssen **davon** ausgehen, daß ...	*We must start by assuming that ...*
Ich muß mich **von meinem Kollegen** distanzieren	*I have to dissociate myself from my colleague*
Das Kind träumte **von einer schönen Prinzessin**	*The child was dreaming of a beautiful princess*

Other verbs:

Etwas hängt von jemandem/etwas ab	*Something depends on sb./sth.*
jemandem von etwas abraten	*advise sb. against sth.*
von etwas absehen	*refrain from sth., disregard sth.*
jemanden von etwas befreien	*liberate sb. from sth.*
sich von etwas erholen	*recover from sth.*
von etwas herrühren	*stem from sth.*
jemanden von etwas überzeugen	*convince sb. of sth.*
jemanden von etwas verständigen	*inform sb. of sth.*
von etwas zeugen	*show, demonstrate sth.*

18.6.12 *vor* is always used with the dative in prepositional objects

(a) *vor* often corresponds to English 'of' with verbs of fearing, etc.

Ich ekele mich **vor diesen großen Spinnen**	*I have a horror of these big spiders* (cf. 18.2.2)
Er fürchtete sich **vor dem Rottweiler**	*He was afraid of the Rottweiler*
Er warnte mich **vor dem Treibsand**	*He warned me about the quicksand*

Other verbs:

sich vor jemandem/etwas ängstigen	*be afraid of sb./sth.* (cf. 18.6.10)
Angst vor jemandem/etwas haben	*be afraid, scared of sb./sth.*
sich vor etwas drücken (coll.)	*dodge sth.*
vor jemandem/etwas erschrecken	*be scared by sb./sth.*
sich vor jemandem/etwas hüten	*beware of sb./sth., be on one's guard against sb./sth.*
sich vor jemandem schämen	*feel ashamed in front of sb.* (cf. 18.6.5)
sich vor etwas scheuen	*be afraid of, shrink from sth.*

(b) *vor* often corresponds to English 'from' with verbs of protecting, etc.

Sie bewahrte ihn **vor der Gefahr**	*She protected him from danger*
Sie flohen **vor der Polizei**	*They fled from the police*

Other verbs:

jemanden vor jemandem/etwas beschützen, beschirmen (elev.)	*protect sb. from sb./sth.*
jemanden vor etwas retten	*save sb. from sth.*
sich vor jemandem/etwas verbergen	*hide from sb./sth.*

18.6.13 *zu*

(a) *zu* commonly corresponds to English '(in)to' with verbs of empowering, leading, persuading, etc.

All these verbs are transitive, i.e. they have an accusative object besides the prepositional object with *zu*:

Er ermutigte sie **zum Widerstand**	*He encouraged them to resist*
Er trieb sie **zur Verzweiflung**	*He drove her to despair*
Er überredete mich **zu einem Glas Wein**	*He talked me into having a glass of wine*
Er zwang mich **zu einer Entscheidung**	*He forced me into a decision*

Other verbs used similarly:

autorisieren	*authorise*	herausfordern	*challenge*
berechtigen	*entitle*	nötigen	*compel*
bewegen	*induce*	provozieren	*provoke*
einladen	*invite*	veranlassen	*cause*
ermächtigen	*empower*	verführen	*seduce*

(b) Some other verbs have a prepositional object with *zu*

Das hat **zu seinem Erfolg** sehr beigetragen	*That contributed a lot to his success*
Sie entschloß sich **zur Teilnahme**	*She decided to take part*
Ich rechne, zähle ihn **zu meinen Freunden**	*I count him among my friends*

Other verbs:

es zu etwas bringen	*attain sth. (cf. 3.6.3c)*
zu etwas dienen	*serve as sth.*
sich zu etwas eignen	*be suitable as sth. (cf. 18.6.5)*
zu etwas führen	*lead to sth.*
zu etwas gehören	*be part of sth., be one of sth. (cf. 18.4.1a)*
jemandem zu etwas gratulieren	*congratulate sb. on sth.*
zu etwas neigen	*tend to sth.*
zu jemandem/etwas passen	*go with sb./sth. (cf. 18.4.1a)*
jemandem zu etwas raten	*advise sb. to (do) sth.*
sich zu etwas verhalten	*stand in a relationship to sth.*
jemandem zu etwas verhelfen	*help sb. to (do) sth.*

18.6.14 A prepositional object can take the form of a clause, and it is then usually anticipated by a prepositional adverb

i.e. the form *da(r)* + preposition, cf. 3.5. The prepositional object may be a subordinate clause (usually introduced by *daß*), or an infinitive clause with *zu*, for example:

Sie hat ihm **dafür** gedankt, **daß er ihr geholfen hatte**
Ich verlasse mich **darauf, daß er alles arrangiert**
Er hinderte mich **daran, den Brief zu schreiben**
Ich verlasse mich **darauf, ihn zu Hause zu finden**

The prepositional adverb is optional with some verbs, e.g.:

Ich ärgerte mich (**darüber**), daß er so wenig getan hatte
Sie haben (**damit**) angefangen, die Ernte hereinzubringen

It is impossible to give precise rules for contexts when the prepositional adverb is used or not. In practice, there are a number of verbs with which it is omitted frequently. If it is used with these, it tends to throw rather more emphasis on the following clause. In general, it is more commonly included than omitted in written German, whilst omission is more typical of everyday speech. The following list includes most common verbs with which the prepositional adverb can be omitted:

abhalten von	sich ekeln vor	raten zu
abraten von	sich entscheiden für	sich schämen über
achtgeben auf	sich entschließen zu	sich scheuen vor
anfangen mit	sich erinnern an	sich sehnen nach
(sich) ärgern über	fragen nach	sorgen für
aufhören mit	sich freuen auf/über	sich sorgen um
aufpassen auf	sich fürchten vor	sich streiten über
beginnen mit	glauben an	träumen von
sich beklagen über	hindern an	überzeugen von
sich bemühen um	hoffen auf	urteilen über
sich beschweren über	sich hüten vor	sich wundern über
bitten um	klagen über	zweifeln an
sich einigen über		

In addition, the prepositional adverb can be omitted with all the transitive verbs which govern *zu* (see 18.6.13a).

18.7 Place and direction complements

In traditional grammars, place and direction complements were treated as adverbials. However, although the distinction is not always clear-cut, place and direction complements differ from adverbials in being more closely linked with the meaning of the verb, as explained in 18.1.4. The difference is particularly important in respect of word order, see 21.8.1.

18.7.1 A few verbs denoting position have a complement indicating place

i.e. sentence pattern J in Table 18.2. The place complements often have the form of a prepositional phrase or an equivalent word:

Sie wohnte lange **in der Pfeilgasse**	*She lived a long time in the Pfeilgasse*
Der Brief befand sich **dort**	*The letter was there*
Nach der Party übernachtete er **bei ihr**	*He spent the night with her after the party*
Sie hielt sich **in Hamm** auf	*She stayed in Hamm*

In these examples, the highlighted place phrases are clearly complements, since the sentences would be ungrammatical or meaningless if they were omitted. Common verbs which require place complements are:

sich aufhalten	*stay*	parken	*park*	übernachten	*spend the night*
bleiben	*stay, remain*	sitzen	*sit*	sich verlieren	*get lost*
hängen	*hang*	stattfinden	*take place*	wohnen	*live, dwell*
leben	*live*	stehen	*stand*	zelten	*camp*
liegen	*lie, be lying*				

18.7.2 Verbs which denote motion can occur with a direction complement

A direction complement usually takes the form of a prepositional phrase or an equivalent word (e.g. a prepositional adverb with *da(r)-*, cf. 3.5, or a direction compound with *hin-/her-*, see 7.2). Direction complements occur in two sentence patterns, depending on whether the verb is transitive or intransitive, cf. Table 18.2:

(i) sentence pattern **K** – subject + verb + direction complement:

Gestern fuhr sie **nach Italien**   Der Junge fiel **hinein**

(ii) sentence pattern **L** – subject + verb + accusative object + direction complement:

Ich stürzte mich **darauf**   Sie legte das Buch **auf den Tisch**

Since motion implies a goal, direction complements are clearly linked with the action expressed by the verb, and they are often essential to complete the meaning of the sentence. Thus, *Gestern fuhr sie* and *Sie legte das Buch* are meaningless without the direction complements. In principle, *all* verbs of motion can be used with a direction complement, although it may be suppressed in certain contexts with some verbs.

18.8 Predicate complements

A very few verbs have a predicate complement, normally in the form of either a noun or pronoun in the nominative case or an adjective. This is shown as sentence pattern **M** in Table 18.2. The following verbs are used with a predicate complement:

bleiben *remain*	scheinen *seem*	werden *become*
heißen *be called*	sein *be*	

Er ist **mein Freund**	*He is my friend*
Das Buch ist **rot**	*The book is red*
Das schien mir **ratsam**	*That seemed advisable to me*
Sie wurde **blaß**	*She went pale*

The complement describes the subject or identifies it more closely. The verb may be seen as linking the subject with the complement and these verbs are known as 'copular' (i.e. 'linking' verbs). English learners need to pay attention to the fact that, because these verbs simply link the subject and the predicate complement, the complement is in the **nominative** case if it is a noun, just like the subject.

werden is used in two sentence patterns. When used with the predicate complement it has the meaning 'become' and is typically used with nouns denoting professions and beliefs, etc. (e.g. *Er wurde Katholik, Kommunist; Sie werden Soldaten*). When used with a prepositional object introduced by *zu*, it means 'change', 'develop', 'turn into', e.g.:

Die Felder waren zu Seen geworden	*The fields had turned into lakes*
Das ist mir zur Gewohnheit geworden	*That has become a habit of mine*
Es wurde zur Mode	*It became a fashion*
Er wurde zum Verbrecher	*He became a criminal*

19

Conjunctions and subordination

In complex sentences containing more than one clause, the clauses can be related to one another in two ways. There may be two (or more) parallel clauses of equal status. Typically, 'main' clauses (German *Hauptsätze*) with, in German, the finite verb in second position, can be linked by a 'coordinating' conjunction like *und* or *aber*. Coordination of clauses in German and coordinating conjunctions are dealt with in 19.1.

Alternatively, one or more clauses can be embedded inside another. These are 'subordinate' clauses (sometimes also called 'embedded clauses' or 'dependent clauses': German *Nebensätze*) with, in German, the finite verb in final position and introduced by a 'subordinating' conjunction. In this way, subordinate clauses form part of another clause, and we can distinguish three main types of subordinate clause according to their function in the clause of which they form a part:

1 **Noun clauses**, which play the same part as a noun, for instance as the subject or object of a verb, e.g. *Ich weiß, **daß sie morgen kommt***. As they are typically used as complements to the verb they are sometimes termed 'complement clauses'. They are explained in section 19.2.
2 **Adjective clauses**, which have the function of adjectives, e.g. *die Frau, **die morgen kommt***. They are introduced by relative pronouns and are often called 'relative clauses'. Details about relative clauses and relative pronouns in German are given in section 5.4.
3 **Adverbial clauses**, which have the same function as adverbs, i.e. they indicate time, place, reason, etc., e.g. *Die Frau kam, **als die Sonne aufging***. They can be categorised according to their meaning in the same way as adverbs (see Table 7.1), and they are dealt with in this way in sections 19.3–7.

Buscha (1989) provides a useful survey of German conjunctions.

19.1 Coordinating conjunctions

Coordinating conjunctions link clauses of the same kind. If both the clauses they join are main clauses, they are followed by regular main clause word order, i.e. the verb is the second element, see 21.1:

> Er ist gestern abend angekommen, **aber** ich **habe** ihn noch nicht gesehen

They can also join two subordinate clauses:

> Ich weiß, daß sie morgen kommt **und** daß sie mich sehen möchte

Most of them can also link single words or phrases:

> Ich finde diese Compact-Disc schön, **aber** etwas zu teuer
> Sie hat ein Buch **und** zwei Zeitschriften gekauft

A few, like *sowie*, are only used like this, i.e. they cannot link clauses.

The coordinating conjunctions of German, which are all treated in this section, are shown in Table 19.1.

TABLE 19.1 *Coordinating conjunctions*

aber	*but*	nämlich	*as*
allein	*but*	oder	*or*
bald ... bald	*now ... now*	sondern	*but*
beziehungsweise	*or*	sowie	*as well as*
denn	*as, for*	sowohl als/wie	*as well as*
doch	*but*	teils ... teils	*partly ... partly*
entweder ... oder	*either ... or*	und	*and*
jedoch	*but*	weder ... noch	*neither ... nor*

19.1.1 *aber, allein, doch, jedoch, sondern* 'but'

(a) *aber* **is the usual equivalent of English 'but'**

> Er runzelte die Stirn, **aber** sie sagte   *He frowned, but she still didn't say*
> noch nichts   *anything*

NB: For *aber* with *zwar* in the preceding clause, see 19.5.1b.

(b) *allein, doch* **and** *jedoch* **are mainly literary alternatives to** *aber*

(i) *allein* is only used in formal literary German. It usually introduces a restriction which is unwelcome or unexpected:

> Ich hatte gehofft, ihn nach der Sitzung   *I had hoped to speak to him after*
> zu sprechen, **allein** er war nicht zugegen   *the meeting, but he wasn't present*

(ii) *jedoch* is rather more emphatic than *doch*:

> Der Lohn ist karg, **doch** man genießt   *The wages are meagre, but one enjoys*
> die abendlichen Stunden (*Jens*)   *the evening hours*
> Im allgemeinen war er kein guter   *In general he was not a good pupil,*
> Schüler, **jedoch** in Latein war er   *but he was better than any in Latin*
> allen überlegen

(c) *aber, doch* **and** *jedoch* **are also used as modal particles or adverbs**
(For *aber*, see 10.1.2, for *doch*, see 10.7.1.) They have much the same meaning when used like this as when they are used as conjunctions, but they form part of the clause rather than introduce it, and the word order is different. Compare these alternatives to the sentences in (a) and (b):

> Er runzelte die Stirn, <u>sie</u> **aber** sagte noch nichts ⎱
> Er runzelte die Stirn, sie sagte **aber** noch nichts ⎰
> Der Lohn ist karg, **doch** genießt man die abendlichen Stunden ⎱
> Der Lohn ist karg, man genießt **doch** die abendlichen Stunden ⎰
> ..., in Latein **jedoch** war er allen überlegen ⎱
> ..., in Latein war er **jedoch** allen überlegen ⎰

In constructions like this the second clause can lack an introductory conjunction. This highlights the contrast rather more. If the verbs in the two clauses have the same subject, *aber* is often used like this, placed after the second verb: *Er runzelte die Stirn, sagte aber noch nichts.*

(d) *sondern* **'but'**

(i) *sondern* contradicts a preceding negative

Er ist nicht reich, **sondern** arm	*He is not rich, but poor*
Wir sind nicht ins Kino gegangen, **sondern** wir haben im Garten gearbeitet	*We didn't go to the cinema, but worked in the garden*

sondern is distinct from *aber*, which can only be used after a negative if it doesn't contradict, i.e. if *both* the linked concepts are valid:

Er ist nicht reich, **aber** ehrlich	*He is not rich, but honest*
(i.e. he is *both* 'not rich' *and* 'honest')	

(ii) *nicht nur . . . sondern auch* corresponds to 'not only . . . but also':

Er ist **nicht nur** reich, **sondern auch** großzügig	*He is not only rich, but generous, too*
Sie besorgt **nicht nur** ihren Haushalt, **sondern** sie ist **auch** berufstätig	*She doesn't only run the household, she's got a job, too*

NB: (i) See 12.1.4d–e for the agreement of the finite verb if the subject consists of more than one noun or pronoun linked by *nicht nur . . . sondern auch*.
  (ii) Initial *nicht nur* is followed immediately by the finite verb, e.g. **Nicht nur hat Helmut kräftig mitgeholfen, sondern Franziska hat auch ihren Teil dazu beigetragen.**

19.1.2 *denn, nämlich* **'as', 'because'**

denn and *nämlich* are *coordinating*, not subordinating conjunctions, i.e. they are used with main clauses, with the verb in second position. Clauses with them give the reason for the event or action in the preceding clause, so clauses with them are never in first position in the sentence.

(a) *denn*

Karsch räusperte sich, **denn** anderes fiel ihm nicht ein (*Johnson*)	*Karsch cleared his throat because he couldn't think of anything else to do*

denn is now infrequent in colloquial speech, and *weil* is often heard in its place as a coordinating conjunction, followed by a main clause, even though this is regarded as substandard, cf. 19.4.1.

(b) *nämlich*

nämlich is always placed within the clause, after the verb:

Er konnte sie nicht verstehen, er war **nämlich** taub	*He couldn't understand her, as he was deaf*

19.1.3 *oder, beziehungsweise* **'or',** *entweder . . . oder* **'either . . . or',** *weder . . . noch* **'neither . . . nor'**

See 12.1.4d–e for the agreement of the finite verb if the subject consists of two or more nouns or pronouns linked by these conjunctions.

(a) *oder* **is the most usual equivalent for English 'or'**

Ich weiß, was passiert, wenn eine Warmfront **oder** eine Kaltfront vorbeiziehen (*Grzimek*)	*I know what happens when a warm front or a cold front go past*
Morgen können wir zu Hause bleiben, **oder** wir können einen Spaziergang machen, wenn du willst	*Tomorrow we can stay at home, or we can go for a walk if you want to*
Wir können in Heidelberg **oder** in Mannheim umsteigen	*We can change trains in Heidelberg or Mannheim*
Sie wollten das Haus aus- **oder** umbauen	*They wanted to extend or alter the house*

As with English 'or', the alternatives linked by *oder* can be exclusive (one or the other, but not both) or inclusive (i.e. 'and/or', as in the last example above). In order to stress that exclusion is meant, *aber* (*auch*) can be added to *oder* (see 10.1.2), e.g.: *Wir können in Heidelberg, **oder aber (auch)** in Mannheim umsteigen.* Alternatively, *beziehungsweise* or *entweder . . . oder* can be used to signal exclusion (cf. (b) and (c) below).

(b) *beziehungsweise* **indicates mutually exclusive alternatives**
In writing it is usually abbreviated to *bzw.*:

Sie haben lange in Deutschland gewohnt, **bzw.** sie haben dort oft Urlaub gemacht	*They lived a long time in Germany, or (else) they often took their holidays there*
Es kostet 300 Mark, **bzw.** 250 Mark mit Rabatt	*It costs 300 marks, or 250 marks with the discount*

beziehungsweise was originally restricted to formal registers, but it is now common both in speech and writing.

(c) *entweder . . . oder* **'either . . . or' signals mutually exclusive alternatives**

Entweder er wird entlassen, **oder** er findet gar keine Stellung (*BILD*)	*He will either be dismissed or not find a job at all*

Rather less commonly, *entweder* may be immediately followed by the verb, e.g. *Entweder wird er entlassen . . .*

(d) *weder . . . noch* **'neither . . . nor'**

Er liest **weder** Bücher **noch** Zeitungen	*He reads neither books nor newspapers*
Ich habe **weder** seinen Brief bekommen, **noch** habe ich sonst von ihm gehört	*Neither have I received his letter, nor have I heard from him in any other way*

A common alternative to *weder . . . noch* is to use *und auch nicht/kein*. This is often felt to be less clumsy and more natural, especially in spoken German:

Er liest keine Bücher **und auch keine** Zeitungen.
Ich habe seinen Brief nicht bekommen, **und** ich habe **auch nicht** sonst von ihm gehört.

noch cannot be used on its own in the sense of 'nor' without a preceding *weder*. *und auch nicht/kein* can be used as the equivalent of English 'nor' without a preceding 'neither', or of 'or' preceded by a negative:

Sie hat mir noch nicht geschrieben, **und** ich erwarte **auch nicht**, daß ich bald von ihr höre	*She hasn't written to me yet, nor do I expect to hear from her soon*
Ich höre die Nachrichten im Radio nicht **und** kaufe **auch keine** Zeitungen	*I don't listen to the news on the radio or buy newspapers*

19.1.4 *und* 'and'; *sowie, sowohl ... als/wie* 'as well as'

(a) *und* **is the common equivalent for English 'and'**

Angela **und** Gudrun wollen auch kommen	*Angela and Gudrun want to come too*
Einer der Verdächtigen durchbrach eine Straßensperre **und** konnte erst nach einer Verfolgungsjagd gestoppt werden (NZZ)	*One of the suspects broke through a road block and could only be stopped after a chase*

(b) *sowie, sowohl ... als* **'both ... and', 'as well as'**

These are in practice frequent stylistic alternatives to *und*, especially in written German, though they are by no means unknown in speech. They emphasise the connection between the elements more than *und*, and they are often used with a following *auch*:

Dürrenmatt hat **sowohl** Dramen **als (auch)** Kriminalromane geschrieben	*Dürrenmatt wrote both plays and detective novels*

NB: Less commonly, *wie* is used for *als* with *sowohl*.

sowie puts rather more stress on the second element, e.g.:

Dürrenmatt hat Dramen **sowie (auch)** Kriminalromane geschrieben

NB: See 12.1.4d–e for the agreement of the finite verb if the subject consists of more than one noun or pronoun linked by *sowohl ... als* or *sowie*.

19.1.5 Less frequent coordinators

(a) *bald ... bald* **'one moment ... the next', 'now ... now'**

This is mainly found in formal writing. *bald* is followed immediately by the verb in both clauses:

Bald weinte das Kind, **bald** lachte es	*One moment the child was crying, the next it was laughing*

(b) *teils ... teils* **'partly ... partly'**

Wir haben unseren Urlaub **teils** in Italien verbracht, **teils** in der Schweiz	*We spent our holiday partly in Italy, partly in Switzerland*
teils heiter, **teils** wolkig	*cloudy with sunny intervals*

When linking clauses, the verb follows *teils* in both clauses:

Teils war man sehr zuvorkommend, **teils** hat man mich völlig ignoriert	*Sometimes people were very helpful, at others I was completely ignored*

19.2 Complement clauses

Complement clauses have the same function in the sentence as nouns or noun phrases, i.e. they can be the subject (*Daß sie kommt, freut mich*), direct object (*Sie* *sah, **wie er sich anstrengte***) or one of the other complements of a verb (cf. Table 18.1). They can also depend on adjectives, or on nouns related to verbs, e.g.:

> Ich bin froh, **daß du kommen konntest**
> Ihn quälte die Angst, **daß etwas passieren könnte**

Complement clauses in German can be introduced by *daß, ob, wenn* or the interrogative *w*-words (see 7.5). Which one(s) are used depends on the function of the clause (subject, object, etc.) and the individual verb.

NB: If a complement clause is the subject of a verb, the verb has the third person singular endings, see 12.1.4a.

19.2.1 *daß* 'that'

(a) *daß* is the commonest conjunction used to introduce complement clauses
In this respect it corresponds closely to English 'that':

subject:	**Daß sie morgen kommt**, erstaunt mich
accusative object:	Sie versicherte mir, **daß alles in Ordnung war**
genitive object:	Man klagt ihn an, **daß er das Geld gestohlen hat**
prepositional object:	Er wartete darauf, **daß Peter ihn grüßte**
predicate complement:	Tatsache ist, **daß er gelogen hat**

(b) The omission of *daß*
The conjunction *daß* can be omitted in some contexts and some types of complement clause, in which case the dependent clause has the order of a main clause, with the verb second. Compare the following alternatives:

> Sie sagte, **daß** sie einen Brief **schreibe**
> Sie sagte, sie **schreibe** einen Brief

However, it is far less frequent for *daß* to be omitted in German than is the case for English *that*. It is possible to drop *daß*:

(i) After verbs (and other expressions) of saying, when introducing indirect speech (cf. 16.6):

Ich sagte, sie sei das einzige Mädchen, mit dem ich „diese Sache" tun wollte (*Böll*)	*I said she was the only girl I wanted to do "that" with*
Bei denen herrscht die Meinung vor, die Universitäten litten an der Überlast ungeeigneter Studenten (*Spiegel*)	*With these people the idea is dominant that universities are suffering from being overloaded with unsuitable students*

In practice, the alternative without *daß* is rather more frequent in both spoken and written German. However, *daß* is usually included if the main verb is negative. Thus *Er sagte nicht, daß er sie nach Hause fahren werde* is more usual than *Er sagte nicht, er werde sie nach Hause fahren*.

In the alternative without *daß*, in written German, the verb in the dependent clause is usually in the subjunctive, see 16.6.3c.

(ii) After verbs (and other expressions) of perceiving, feeling, hoping, thinking and believing (in the widest sense). With these, the omission of *daß* is more frequent in spoken German than in formal writing

Ich hatte gehofft, er würde es auf zehn Mark abrunden (*Böll*)	*I had hoped he would round it down to ten marks*
die Ahnung, sie könnte noch unterwegs sein	*the idea that she could still be on her way*

(c) Initial *daß*-clauses are more frequent in German than in English

In German, especially in writing, it is much more usual to find sentences which begin with a subject or object *daß*-clause than is the case in English, where we tend to provide a noun (especially, *the fact* ...) for the *that*-clause to link to. Compare:

Daß die Wahlergebnisse der DDR gefälscht waren, bestreitet auch Modrow nicht (*Spiegel*)	*The fact that the election results in the GDR were falsified is not disputed even by Modrow*
Daß die SED-Führung da mauert, muß nicht überraschen (*Zeit*)	*The fact that the SED leadership is stalling shouldn't surprise us*
Daß er einmal nicht mehr wollen würde, wagte er nicht zu hoffen (*Walser*)	*The possibility that at some time he wouldn't want to any more, was something he didn't dare to hope*

(d) *daß* should not be followed immediately by another conjunction

It is considered poor style for another conjunction to come straight after *daß*, so that the following constructions:

(i) Sie sagte, **daß** er, **wenn** er am Wochenende kommen sollte, bei ihrer Mutter übernachten könnte

(ii) Sie sagte, **daß** er bei ihrer Mutter übernachten könnte, **wenn** er am Wochenende kommen sollte

are considered preferable to:

(iii) Sie sagte, **daß**, **wenn** er am Wochenende kommen sollte, er bei ihrer Mutter übernachten könnte

although this construction does occur in colloquial speech and occasionally in writing. In English, though, an adverbial clause (especially one introduced by *as*, *if* or *when*) often follows straight after *that*, e.g.: *She said that if he were to come at the weekend he would be able to stay with her mother*. It is advisable for English learners to avoid this type of construction in German, and to use only type **(i)** or **(ii)**.

(e) Isolated *daß*-clauses

daß-clauses can be used elliptically, i.e. on their own

(i) In commands or wishes:

Daß du (mir) rechtzeitig nach Haus kommst! *Make sure you're not too late home!*

These are often used with an 'ethic' dative, see 2.5.3d.

(ii) In exclamations:

Daß die es heute so eilig haben! *They <u>are</u> in a hurry today!*

19.2.2 *ob* 'whether', 'if'

(a) *ob* typically indicates a question or a doubt
ob-clauses are all, in the widest sense, indirect questions of one kind or another.
They can have the following functions:

subject:	**Ob sie morgen kommt**, ist mir gleich
accusative object:	Sie vergaß, **ob sie eine Karte gekauft hatte**
prepositional object:	Ich erinnere mich nicht, **ob ich eine gekauft habe**
predicate complement:	Die Frage ist, **ob wir eine Tankstelle erreichen**

(b) Isolated *ob*-clauses
ob-clauses are quite often used elliptically, especially in spoken German. They
can be used to ask a question:

> Ob es in Schwerin noch Glocken gibt?   *Are there still bells in Schwerin?*
> (*Surminski*)

They are particularly frequent to pick up or repeat a question. They are also often
used to express a general query or supposition:

> Ja, ob das wirklich stimmt?   *I wonder whether that's really right*

19.2.3 *wenn* 'when', 'if'

Complement clauses introduced by *wenn* can function as:

subject:	Mir ist es recht, **wenn sie heute nicht kommt**
accusative object:	Sie mag es nicht, **wenn ich sie bei der Arbeit störe**

As with adverbial conditional sentences, the verb in a complement *wenn*-clause
can be in the *Konjunktiv II* form if an unreal condition is involved, cf. 16.5.1, e.g.
Mir wäre es recht, wenn sie heute nicht käme.

   Complement clauses with *wenn* are *always* associated with a correlating *es* in
the main clause, cf. 19.2.5.

19.2.4 Interrogatives

All the *w*-words which can be used as interrogative adverbs to ask questions (see
7.5) can also be used as conjunctions to introduce complement clauses. These can
all be considered, in the widest sense, as indirect questions. Clauses with these
can function as:

subject:	**Was sie dort macht**, ist mir gleich
accusative object:	Sie vergaß, **wie man es macht**
prepositional object:	Ich erinnere mich nicht daran, **wann ich es hörte**
predicate complement:	Die Frage ist, **wo sie es gekauft hat**

19.2.5 Correlates to complement clauses

In German, complement clauses are often linked to a pronoun in the main clause
which anticipates the complement clause. Such pronouns are called correlates,
and their form differs depending on the function of the clause. Sonnenberg
(1992) gives a comprehensive account of correlates in German.

(a) The pronoun *es* functions as a correlate to subject and object clauses

Dann fiel **es** mir auf, daß sie plötzlich fehlte	*Then I noticed that all at once she wasn't there*
Ich bedaure **es**, daß sie nicht kommen konnte	*I regret that she couldn't come*

Further details on this 'correlating' *es* are given in 3.6.2e and 3.6.3a.

(b) The prepositional adverb can have the role of a correlate to complement clauses functioning as prepositional objects

i.e. the form *da(r)* + preposition (see 3.5) can appear in the main clause:

die Angst **davor**, daß er vielleicht nicht entkommen könnte	*the fear of perhaps not being able to escape*
Er verläßt sich **darauf**, daß wir rechtzeitig kommen	*He's relying on us arriving on time*

With many nouns, adjectives and verbs this use of the prepositional adverb is optional, and it is impossible to give comprehensive rules for usage. For further details, see 6.6.2 and 18.6.14.

(c) The pronoun *dessen* can function as a correlate to complement clauses with the function of a genitive object

These constructions are in practice infrequent in modern German, and *dessen* is in all cases optional:

Ich bin mir (**dessen**) bewußt, daß ich ihn strafen sollte	*I am aware that I should punish him*

19.3 Conjunctions of time

Table 19.2 lists the main conjunctions referring to time in German.

19.3.1 *als, indem, wann, wenn, wie* 'when', 'as'

(a) Clauses with *als* refer to a **single** event in the past

als corresponds to English 'when' or 'as':

Als ich in Passau ankam, habe ich sie auf dem Bahnsteig gesehen	*When I arrived in Passau, I saw her on the platform*
Als ich weiterging, wurde ich immer müder	*As I went on, I grew more and more tired*
Als die Frau später ihre Arbeitspapiere vorlegen mußte, kam die Wahrheit an den Tag (*BILD*)	*When, later on, the woman had to show her work documents, the truth came to light*

TABLE 19.2 *Conjunctions of time*

als	*when*	indes, indessen	*while, whilst*
bevor, ehe	*before*	sooft	*as often as, whenever*
seit(dem)	*since*	kaum daß	*hardly, scarcely*
bis	*until, till; by the time*	während	*while, whilst*
sobald, sowie	*as soon as*	nachdem	*after*
indem	*as*	wenn	*when(ever)*
solange	*as long as*	wie	*as*

NB: A main clause following an *als*-clause is often introduced by a correlating *da*, e.g. *Als ich in Passau ankam, da habe ich sie auf dem Bahnstieg gesehen.* This *da* is always optional.

da is a literary (and rather old-fashioned) alternative to *als*:

Die Sonne schien an einem wolkenlosen Himmel, **da** er seinen Heimatort verließ (*Dürrenmatt*)	*The sun was shining in a cloudless sky as/when he left his home village*

(b) *wie* can be used for 'when' with a verb in the present tense referring to a past action

i.e. with a 'historic' present (cf. 14.2.4). *wie* is an alternative to *als* in such contexts:

Als/Wie ich das Fenster öffne, schlägt mir heftiger Lärm entgegen	*As/When I opened the window, I was confronted by an intense noise*

The use of *wie* in place of *als* with a past or perfect tense is common in colloquial spoken German, especially in the south, e.g. *Wie ich in Passau ankam/angekommen bin, . . .* This usage is occasionally found in writing, but it is generally considered substandard.

(c) *wann* is used in questions

wann is an interrogative adverb (= 'when?'), cf. 7.5. As such, it is used to introduce *questions* in direct speech, e.g. *Wann kommst du heute abend nach Hause?* or in indirect speech (cf. 19.2.4), e.g. *Er fragte mich, wann ich heute abend nach Hause komme.*

(d) *wenn* introduces clauses referring to the present, the future, or to repeated actions in the past

Ich bringe es, **wenn** ich morgen vorbeikomme	*I'll bring it when I drop by tomorrow*

A main clause following a *wenn*-clause is often introduced by *dann*. This *dann* is always optional:

Wenn das Wasser ausgelaufen ist, (**dann**) schließt sich die Klappe automatisch	*When the water has run out, the valve shuts off automatically*

Wenn often conveys the sense of English 'whenever', especially in the past, where *als* must be used if a single action is involved (cf. (a) above):

Er empfand eine Art Ekel, **wenn** er daran dachte, mit wieviel Vergangenheit er schon angefüllt war (*Walser*)	*He felt a kind of disgust when(ever) he thought about how full of the past he was*

wenn, not *als*, is used if there is a sense of a future-in-the-past:

Ich wollte zu Hause sein, **wenn** Karl ankam	*I wanted to be at home when Karl arrived*

wenn is also used in conditional clauses, i.e. = 'if' (cf. 16.5). If there is a possibility of ambiguity, *immer wenn* can be used to emphasise that the sense is that of 'whenever'. Alternatively, *falls* can be used to make it clear that 'if' is meant (cf. 16.5.3d).

(e) *indem* **'as'**
indem can only link simultaneous actions:

Anna küßte ihre Mutter, **indem** sie die Palette und den nassen Pinsel in ihren Händen weit von ihr abhielt (*Th. Mann*)	*Anna kissed her mother, holding the palette and the wet brush well away from her in her hands*

This use of *indem*, where the *indem*-clause corresponds to an English participial phrase, now sounds old-fashioned. See 13.7 for German equivalents of English phrases with an ing-form. In modern German, *indem* is mainly used in the sense of English 'by + . . .ing', see 19.7.3.

(f) Equivalents of English 'when' introducing relative clauses
e.g. *zu einer Zeit, wo* . . . 'at a time **when** . . .'. For these, see 5.4.6b.

19.3.2 *bevor, ehe* 'before'; *bis* 'until, till', 'by the time'

For the occasional use of the subjunctive in clauses introduced by these conjunctions, see 16.7.4.

(a) *bevor* **and** *ehe* **'before'**
There is no real difference in meaning between these. *bevor* is far more frequent; *ehe* is typical of more formal registers, although it does occasionally occur in speech.

die Großmutter hatte angefangen Achim zu fragen, **bevor** sie etwas kaufte (*Johnson*)	*Grandmother had started asking Achim before she bought anything*
Es bestand, **ehe** die Erde geschieden war von den Himmeln (*Heym*)	*It existed before the earth was separated from the heavens*

bevor or *ehe* can be strengthenend by *noch* to give the sense of '**even** before', e.g.
Noch bevor/ehe sie zurückkam 'Even before she got back'.

(b) German equivalents for English 'not . . . before', 'not . . . until'
(i) The most straightforward equivalent is usually . . . *erst* . . ., *wenn/als*:

Ich will **erst** nach Hause gehen, **wenn** Mutter wieder da ist	*I don't want to go home before/until mother gets back*
Das Kind hörte **erst** zu weinen auf, **als** es vor Müdigkeit einschlief	*The child didn't stop crying until it was so tired that it fell asleep*

(ii) *nicht . . . bevor* (or *ehe*) and *nicht . . . bis* are only used if the dependent clause implies a condition. An extra (redundant) *nicht* is often added:

Bevor er sich (nicht) entschuldigt hatte, wollte sie das Zimmer nicht verlassen	*She didn't want to leave the room before/until he had apologised*
Du darfst nicht gehen, **bis** du (nicht) deine Hausaufgaben fertig hast	*You can't go out until you've finished your homework*

DUDEN (1985: 489f.) claims that this second *nicht* is only added if the subordinate clause precedes. This rule is not always followed in practice.

(c) *bis* **has two main English equivalents**
(i) 'until', 'till':

Ich warte hier, **bis** du zurückkommst	*I'll wait here till you get back*

(ii) 'by the time (when)', e.g.:

Bis du zurückkommst, habe ich das Fenster repariert	*I'll have fixed the window by the time you get back*

19.3.3 *kaum (daß)*, etc. 'hardly/scarcely ... when', 'no sooner ... than'

The most usual German equivalent for these English combinations is to use two main clauses, the first introduced by *kaum*, the second by *so* or *da*:

Kaum hatten wir das Wirtshaus erreicht, **so/da** begann es zu regnen	*We had hardly reached the inn/No sooner had we reached the inn, when it began to rain*

Alternatively, a main clause introduced by *kaum* followed by a subordinate clause with *als* can be used: *Kaum hatten wir das Wirtshaus erreicht, **als** es zu regnen begann.*

In formal written German, the phrasal conjunction *kaum daß* is sometimes used, e.g. *Kaum daß wir das Wirtshaus erreicht hatten, begann es zu regnen.* This alternative now sounds rather old-fashioned.

19.3.4 *nachdem* 'after'

Genau eine Woche **nachdem** er die Bergeinsamkeit verlassen hatte, fand sich Grenouille auf einem Podest in der großen Aula der Universität von Montpellier (*Süßkind*)	*Exactly a week after he had left his mountain fastness Grenouille found himself on a platform in the great hall of the University of Montpellier*

nachdem is sometimes used in a causal sense, as an alternative to *da* (= 'as, since', cf. 19.4.1):

Er mußte zurücktreten, **nachdem** ihm verschiedene Delikte nachgewiesen wurden	*He had to resign, as various offences had been proved against him*

This usage is now restricted to south Germany and Austria.

NB: For *je nachdem* 'according as', see 19.7.5.

19.3.5 *seit, seitdem* 'since'

The shorter form *seit* was formerly restricted to colloquial registers, but it is at least as frequent as *seitdem* nowadays, even in writing:

Seitdem er sein Haus verkauft hat, wohnt er in einem Hotel	*Since he sold his house, he's been living in a hotel*
Seit ich warte, sind mindestens dreißig Leute 'reingegangen (*Fallada*)	*Since I've been waiting, at least thirty people have gone in*

NB: For the use of tenses in sentences with *seit(dem)*, see 14.2.2 and 14.3.4a.

19.3.6 *sobald* 'as soon as', *solange* 'as long as', *sooft* 'as often as'

None of these conjunctions is normally followed by *als* or *wie*. They are always spelled as single words, cf. 23.2.3.

(a) *sobald* 'as soon as'

Sobald ich merkte, daß er gar nicht zuhörte, griff ich ihn am Ärmel (*Frisch*)	*As soon as I noticed he wasn't listening I grabbed him by the sleeve*

NB: *sowie* is commonly used for *sobald* in colloquial registers, e.g. *Das tat sie auch, sowie sie nach Hause kam.*

(b) *solange* 'as long as'
(i) *solange* can refer purely to time:

Wir haben gewartet, **solange** wir konnten	*We waited as long as we could*
Solange es Menschen auf der Erde gibt, haben sie immer in der Natur zwischen ihren Mitgeschöpfen gelebt (*Grzimek*)	*As long as there have been people on earth they have lived amongst their fellow-creatures in natural surroundings*

NB: The sense of *solange* may approach that of *seit(dem)*, as in the second example, and tense use is similar, see 14.2.2 and 14.3.4a.

(ii) It may also have a conditional sense (= 'provided that'), e.g.:

Solange er sein Bestes tut, bin ich zufrieden	*As long as he does his best, I shall be satisfied*

(iii) The conjunction *solange* should be distinguished from the phrase *so lange* 'so long':

Du hast uns **so lange** warten lassen, daß wir den Zug verpaßt haben	*You kept us waiting so long that we missed the train*
So lange er auch wartete, es kam kein Zug mehr	*However long he waited, no more trains came*

(c) *sooft* corresponds to English 'as often as' or 'whenever'

Du kannst kommen, **sooft** du willst	*You can come as often as you want to*
Sooft er kam, brachte er uns immer Geschenke mit	*Whenever he came, he always brought us presents*

19.3.7 *während* 'while', 'whilst' and alternatives

(a) *während* is the usual equivalent of English 'while', 'whilst'
Like 'while', it can express time or a contrast (i.e. = 'whereas'):

Die Zollprobleme löste Boris, **während** wir in Urlaub waren (*Bednarz*)	*Boris solved the problems with the customs while we were on holiday*
Klaus Buch müßte auch sechsundvierzig sein, **während** der vor ihm Stehende doch eher sechsundzwanzig war (*Walser*)	*Klaus Buch ought to be forty-six as well, whereas the man standing in front of him was more like twenty-six*

NB: (i) *noch während* is used for 'even as/whilst', e.g. *Noch während sie schlief . . .* 'Even as she slept . . .'
(ii) *während* is sometimes used with main clause word order (i.e. with the verb second) in colloquial speech. This usage is substandard.

(b) *indes* and *indessen* are alternatives to *während* in both senses

They are restricted to rather old-fashioned literary styles:

> Du kannst mich füttern, indes ich   *You can feed me while I'm plucking*
> die Ente rupfe (*Langgässer*)   *the duck*

(c) *wohingegen* is an alternative to *während* to signal a contrast

It occurs mainly in formal writing and stresses the contrast more strongly:

> Er ist sehr zuvorkommend, **wohingegen**   *He is very obliging, whilst/whereas*
> sein Bruder oft einen recht   *his brother often makes a very*
> unfreundlichen Eindruck macht   *unpleasant impression*

19.4 Causal conjunctions

German conjunctions signalling a cause or a reason:

da	*as, since*
nun (da/wo)	*now that, seeing that*
um so mehr als	*all the more because*
weil	*because*
zumal	*especially as*

19.4.1 *da* and *weil*

The distinction between *da* and *weil* parallels that between English 'as' (or 'since') and 'because'. *da*-clauses, like those with 'as' or 'since', usually precede the main clause and typically indicate a reason which is already known.

> Ich mußte zu Fuß nach Hause gehen,   *I had to walk home because I had*
> **weil** ich die letzte Straßenbahn   *missed the last tram*
> verpaßt hatte
> **Da** er getrunken hatte, wollte er   *As he'd had something to drink, he*
> nicht fahren   *didn't want to drive*

A *weil*-clause can be anticipated by *darum*, *deshalb* or *deswegen* in the preceding main clause. This is particularly common in spoken German. The effect is to give greater emphasis to the reason given in the *weil*-clause:

> Er konnte **darum/deshalb/deswegen**   *He wasn't able to come because*
> nicht kommen, **weil** er krank war   *he was ill*

In colloquial German *weil* is frequently heard with a main clause word order i.e. with the finite verb second rather than at the end of the clause:

> Du mußt langsam sprechen, **weil** der   *You'll have to speak more slowly because*
> **versteht** nicht viel   *he doesn't understand a lot*

This usage is increasingly common, but it is universally regarded as substandard and felt to be quite unacceptable in written German.

NB: *denn* and *nämlich* are also used to indicate a cause or a reason (i.e. in the sense of English 'because'). They are, however, *coordinating* conjunctions, with main clause word order, cf. 19.1.2.

19.4.2 *nun da*, etc. 'now that', 'seeing that'

nun da is the usual equivalent for these English conjunctions:

Nun da wir alle wieder versammelt
sind, können wir das Problem weiter
besprechen

*Seeing/Now that we're all gathered
together again, we can carry on
talking about the problem*

There are a number of alternatives to *nun da*. Simple *nun* is occasionally found in formal written registers:

Nun alles geschehen ist, bleibt nur
zu wünschen, daß ... (*FAZ*)

*Now that everything has been done,
one can only wish that ...*

Other alternatives, i.e. *nun wo, wo ... (doch), da ... nun (mal)*, are in the main more typical of colloquial registers:

Nun wo du sowieso in die Stadt
fährst, kannst du uns wohl
mitnehmen, oder?
Ich muß es wohl tun, **wo** ich es dir
(**doch**) versprochen habe
Da er das **nun (mal)** schon weiß, (so)
muß ich ihm wohl das weitere erzählen

*Seeing as you're going into town
anyway, you'll be able to take us
with you, won't you?*
*I'll have to do it, seeing that I
promised you*
*Seeing that he already knows that,
I'll have to tell him the rest*

19.4.3 Other causal conjunctions

(a) *zumal* is a stronger alternative to *da*
It corresponds to English 'especially as':

Sie wird uns sicher helfen, **zumal**
sie dich so gern hat
Mehr verriet sie nicht, **zumal** es
Stiller gar nicht wunderte, warum
sie dieses Bedürfnis hatte (*Frisch*)

*She's sure to help us, especially as she's
so fond of you*
*She didn't reveal any more, especially
as Stiller was not at all surprised
why she felt this need*

(b) *um so mehr ..., als/da/weil* correspond to 'all the more ... because'

Ich freute mich **um so mehr** über
seinen Erfolg, **als/da/weil** er
völlig unerwartet war
Jetzt rechnet die Nato **um so mehr**
mit französischer Zurückhaltung,
als sich de Gaulle unmittelbar nach
der Konferenz einer Stichwahl
stellen muß (*FAZ*)

*I was all the more pleased about
his success because it was totally
unexpected*
*NATO is now counting all the more on
French caution because de Gaulle
has got to face elections
immediately after the conference*

The construction with *um so ..., als* can be used with other comparatives:

Die Sache ist **um so** dringlicher, **als/da**
die Iraker den Ölhahn zudrehen könnten

*The matter is all the more urgent because
the Iraqis could turn off the oil tap*

19.5 Conjunctions of purpose and result

German conjunctions indicating purpose or result (also called 'final' and 'consecutive' conjunctions respectively):

als daß
damit, auf daß
so daß, derart daß

for ... to
so that, in order that
so that, such that

English learners need to be aware that 'so that' has two distinct senses, with different German equivalents, i.e.:

(i) Final 'so that' expresses purpose and is an alternative to 'in order that'. The usual German equivalent is *damit*, cf. 19.5.1.

(ii) Consecutive 'so that' expresses a result and has the sense of '(in) such (a way) that'. It corresponds to German *so daß*, cf. 19.5.2.

19.5.1 Clauses of purpose

(a) ***damit* is the most widely employed conjunction in final clauses**

Diese Tüte ist aus Papier, **damit** sie nicht aus Kunststoff ist	*This bag is made of paper so that it shouldn't be made of plastic*
König Ludwig ließ Wagner 40 000 Gulden auszahlen, **damit** sich der total verschuldete Meister bei seinen Gläubigern freikaufen konnte (*SZ*)	*King Ludwig had 40,000 guilders paid to Wagner so that the totally debt-ridden maestro could pay off his creditors*

NB: (i) The verb in *damit*-clauses is usually in the indicative in modern German. For the occasional use of the subjunctive, see 16.7.2a.
(ii) Infinitive clauses with *um . . . zu* have a final meaning (= 'in order to'), see 13.2.7a.

(b) ***auf daß* is an old-fashioned sounding alternative to *damit***
It has a formal and biblical ring and is used principally for stylistic effect. It is always followed by a subjunctive, cf. 16.7.2b:

. . . schenke du ihr ein reines Herz, **auf daß** sie einstmals eingehe in die Wohnungen des ewigen Friedens (*Th. Mann*)	*. . . give her a pure heart, so that she may some day enter into the dwellings of eternal peace*

(c) Simple *daß* is sometimes used for *damit*
This usage is most often encountered in colloquial speech, but it is not unknown in formal writing, where it is sometimes used with a subjunctive:

Ich mache dir noch ein paar Stullen, **daß** du unterwegs auch was zu essen hast	*I'll make you a couple of sandwiches so that you've got something to eat on the journey*
Er entfernte sich leise, **daß** niemand ihn sehe, niemand ihn höre (*Süßkind*)	*He withdrew quietly, so that no-one should see him, no-one should hear him*

NB: In colloquial German *so daß* is sometimes used to introduce clauses of purpose. This usage is considered substandard.

19.5.2 Clauses of result

(a) *so daß* is the most frequent conjunction introducing clauses of result

Sein Bein war steif, **so daß** er kaum gehen konnte	*His leg was stiff, so that he could hardly walk*
Das Wetter war schlecht, **so daß** wir wenig wandern konnten	*The weather was bad, so that we couldn't do much hiking*
Er schob den Ärmel zurück, **so daß** wir die Narbe sehen konnten	*He pushed his sleeve back, so that we were able to see the scar*

The difference between consecutive clauses and final clauses is clear if we replace *so daß* by *damit* in the last example. *Er schob die Ärmel zurück, **damit** wir die Narbe sehen konnten* implies that he did it with the express purpose that we should see the scar. With *so daß*, the fact that we could see the scar is only the (possibly unintentional) result of his action.

NB: *so daß* is written as a single word (i.e. *sodaß*) in Austrian usage.

(b) In clauses with adjectives or adverbs, the *so* can precede these
These correspond to similar constructions in English. Compare the examples below to the first two examples in (a) above:

Sein Bein war **so** steif, **daß** er kaum gehen konnte	*His leg was so stiff that he could hardly walk*
Das Wetter war **so** schlecht, **daß** wir wenig wandern konnten	*The weather was so bad that we weren't able to do much hiking*

derart and (in some contexts) *dermaßen* are more emphatic alternatives to *so* in such contexts:

Er fuhr **so/derart/dermaßen** langsam, daß Frieda uns leicht einholte	*He drove so slowly that Frieda caught us up easily*
Es hat **so/derart/dermaßen** geregnet, daß wir schon Montag nach Hause gefahren sind	*It rained so much that we came home on Monday*

dermaßen is only possible if some idea of quantity is involved. Thus, only *derart* could replace *so* in: *Er hat den Ärmel **so/derart** zurückgeschoben, daß wir die Narbe sehen konnten.*

19.5.3 *als daß* only occurs after adjectives modifed by *zu*, *nicht genug* or *nicht so*

The equivalent English sentences usually have an infinitive with *for*:

Er ist zu vernünftig, **als daß** ich das von ihm erwartet hätte	*He's too sensible for me to have expected that of him*
Es ist noch nicht so kalt, **als daß** wir jetzt schon die Heizung einschalten müßten	*It's not so cold for us to have to turn the heating on yet*
Das Kind ist nicht alt genug, **als daß** wir es auf einer so langen Reise mitnehmen könnten	*The child is not old enough for us to be able to take it with us on such a long journey*

In everyday speech, simpler constructions are preferred to sentences with *als daß*, e.g. *Es ist noch nicht so kalt, also brauchen wir die Heizung noch nicht einschalten.*

NB: (i) If the subject of the two clauses is the same, an infinitive clause with *um ... zu* is used (see 13.2.7a).
(ii) *Konjunktiv II*, particularly of a modal verb, is commonly used in *als daß* clauses, cf. 16.7.5a.

19.6 Concessive conjunctions

Concessive conjunctions include the equivalents for '(al)though' (19.6.1), and the forms which correspond to English 'however', 'where(so)ever', etc. (19.6.2). Conditional concessive conjunctions (= English 'even if') are treated in 16.5.3d.

19.6.1 German equivalents for English '(al)though'

(a) *obwohl* is the commonest concessive conjunction in current usage

Obwohl sie Schwierigkeiten mit dem Reißverschluß hatte, stand ich nicht auf, ihr zu helfen (*Böll*)	*Although she was having difficulties with her zipper, I didn't stand up to help her*

If the *obwohl*-clause comes first, the contrast can be emphasised by using *(so)* ... *doch* in the main clause:

Obwohl ich unterschrieben hatte, (**so**) blieb sie **doch** sehr skeptisch	*Although I had signed, she still remained very sceptical*

Less commonly, the contrast may be stressed by putting the verb second in the following main clause:

Obwohl er mein Vetter ist, ich **kann** nichts für ihn tun	*Although he is my cousin, I can't do anything for him*

(b) Other concessive conjunctions

(i) *obschon* is quite common in Swiss usage:

Ivy hatte drei Stunden lang auf mich eingeschwätzt, **obschon** sie wußte, daß ich grundsätzlich nicht heirate (*Frisch*)	*Ivy had kept on at me for three hours although she knew that I wasn't getting married on principle*

(ii) *trotzdem* is sometimes used as a conjunction to mean 'although':

Trotzdem ich mich auf alle mögliche Weise anstrengte, ernst zu sein, kam das Lachen stoßweise immer wieder (*Rilke*)	*Although I made every possible effort to be serious, the laughing kept coming back spasmodically*

The use of *trotzdem* as a conjunction is chiefly colloquial, and many Germans consider it unacceptable in writing. However, DUDEN (1985: 665f.), which gives the example above, and Engel (1991: 728f.) state that it can no longer be regarded as incorrect.

(iii) A common alternative way to express concession is a construction with *zwar* ... *aber*, i.e. with two main clauses. The first one contains the particle *zwar* (cf. 10.36.1), and the second is introduced by *aber*:

Offenbar war ihr meine Existenz **zwar** bekannt, **aber** sie hatte keine klaren Anweisungen mich betreffend (*Böll*)	*Although evidently she was aware of my existence, she didn't have any clear instructions in respect of me*

(iv) A few other alternatives to *obwohl* occur in written German, roughly in the following descending order of frequency:

> *obgleich*   *wenngleich*   *wiewohl*   *obzwar*

19.6.2 Clauses of the type 'however', 'whoever', 'whenever', etc.

(a) The usual German equivalent for these is *wie ... auch*, *wer ... auch*, etc.

i.e. the clause is introduced by one of the interrogative pronouns (cf. 5.3) or the interrogative adverbs (cf. 7.5), and the particle *auch* is placed later in the clause:

Wer er **auch** ist, ich kann nichts für ihn tun	*Whoever he is, I can't do anything for him*
Wann sie **auch** ankommt, ich will sie sofort sprechen	*Whenever she arrives, I want to speak to her immediately*
Wohin sie **auch** hingeht, ich werde ihr folgen	*Wherever she may go, I shall follow her*
Wo er sich **auch** zeigte, er wurde mit Beifall begrüßt	*Wherever he showed himself, he was greeted with applause*

As the examples show, a main clause following these concessive clauses usually has normal word order, with the verb second, cf. 21.2.1c. Other features of this type of concessive clause:

(i) The modal verb *mögen* often occurs in these clauses in more formal registers, e.g. *Wer er auch sein **mag**, . . .; Wann sie auch ankommen **mag**, . . .* etc. (cf. 17.4.3).

(ii) In modern German, the indicative mood is used in clauses of this type. The subjunctive still occurs occasionally, but it can sound affected, except in the set phrase *Wie dem auch sei* 'However that may be'.

(iii) *auch* can be strengthened by adding *immer*, e.g. *Wo er sich auch **immer** zeigte, ...* Alternatively, *immer* can be used on its own. It always follows the interrogative, e.g.: *Wo **immer** er sich zeigte . . .*

(b) *so/wie . . . auch* **corresponds to English 'however' followed by an adjective or an adverb**

So/Wie gescheit er **auch** sein mag, für diese Stelle paßt er nicht	*However clever he may be, he's not right for this job*
So/Wie teuer das Bild **auch** ist/sein mag, ich will es doch kaufen	*However dear the picture is, I'm still going to buy it*
So höhnisch die Antwort Vittlars **auch** sein mochte, gab sie mir dennoch mehr Gewißheit (*Grass*)	*However scornful Vittlar's answer may have been, it still gave me more certainty*

Similarly, *sosehr . . . auch* is usual for 'however much':

Sosehr ich es **auch** bedaure, es wird mir nicht möglich sein	*However much I regret it, I shan't be able to do it*

noch so can be used in a concessive sense with a following adjective. Compare the following alternative to the first example above:

Er mag **noch so** gescheit sein, für diese Stelle paßt er nicht.

(c) *was für (ein)* or *welcher . . . auch* **correspond to 'whatever' with a noun**

Was für Schwierigkeiten du **auch** hast, es ist der Mühe wert	*Whatever difficulties you may have, it's worth the trouble*
. . . diese Vorgänge, von **weicher** Seite man sie **auch** betrachtet (*SZ*)	*these events, from whatever side one considers them*
aus **welchem** Land **auch immer**	*from whatever country*
aus **welchem** Grund **auch immer**	*for whatever reason*

19.7 Conjunctions of manner and degree

Table 19.3 gives the principal conjunctions of manner and degree.

TABLE 19.3 *Conjunctions of manner and degree*

als	*than*	je … um so/	*the more … the*
als ob/wenn	*as if*	desto mehr	*more*
(an)statt daß	*instead of*	je nachdem (ob/wie)	*according to,*
außer daß	*except that*		*depending on*
außer wenn	*except when*	nur daß	*only that*
dadurch daß, indem	*by + … ing*	ohne daß	*without + … ing*
insofern (als),	*inasmuch as, (in)*	sofern	*provided that*
insoweit (als)	*so far as*	soweit	*as/so far as*
		wie	*as, like*

19.7.1 *als* and *wie* are used to introduce comparative clauses

For the use of *als* and *wie* generally in comparatives, see 8.3:

> Wir fahren schneller, **als** du denkst · *We're travelling faster than you think*
> Der Vortrag war nicht so · *The lecture was not as interesting*
> interessant, **wie** ich erwartet hatte · *as I had expected*

NB: For clauses expressing unreal comparisons (i.e. = 'as if'), see 16.7.1, for *je … um so/desto* 'the more…the more', see 8.3.5.

19.7.2 *außer daß* and *außer wenn*

(a) *außer daß* corresponds to English 'except that'

> Ich habe nichts herausfinden können, · *I didn't find anything out, except that*
> **außer daß** er erst im April · *he's not coming back till April*
> zurückkommt

NB: An infinitive clause with *außer…zu* can be used if the subjects of the two clauses are the same, cf. 13.2.7d.

(b) *außer wenn* usually corresponds to English 'except when' or 'unless'

> Wir gingen oft im Gebirge wandern, · *We often used to go hiking in the*
> **außer wenn** es regnete · *mountains, except when/unless*
> · *it was raining*
> Du brauchst die Suppe nicht zu · *You don't need to eat the soup,*
> essen, **außer wenn** du sie wirklich · *unless you really like it*
> magst

Especially in colloquial speech, *außer* can be used for *außer wenn*. It is followed by normal word order, with the verb second, e.g. *Wir gehen morgen im Gebirge wandern, außer es regnet.*

NB: (i) For other equivalents for English 'unless', see 16.5.3d.
(ii) For *anstatt daß* 'instead of', see 13.2.7c.

19.7.3 *dadurch daß* and *indem* have instrumental meaning

Their usual English equivalent is *by* followed by the *ing*-form of the verb, see also 13.7.2a:

Er hat sich **dadurch** gerettet, **daß**
er aus dem Fenster sprang
Er hat sich gerettet, **indem** er aus
dem Fenster sprang

*He saved himself by jumping out of
the window*

Man kann **dadurch** Unfälle vermeiden
helfen, **daß** man die Verkehrsvorschriften
beachtet
Man kann Unfälle vermeiden helfen,
indem man die Verkehrsvorschriften
beachtet

*One can help to avoid accidents by
observing the highway code*

NB: This is the *only* current use of *indem* in modern German. Its use in time clauses, see 19.3.1e, is now obsolete.

19.7.4 *insofern (als)*, *insoweit (als)*, *sofern*, *soweit*

These are all quite close in meaning.

(a) *insofern (als)* **and** *insoweit (als)* **correspond to English '(in) so/as far as' or 'inasmuch as'**

Ich werde dir helfen,
insofern (als) ich kann/
insoweit (als) ich kann

I'll help you in so far as I'm able to

insofern and *insoweit* can be placed within a preceding main clause, especially qualifying an adjective or adverb. In this case they *must* be used with a following *als*:

Diese Verhandlungen werden **insofern**/
insoweit schwierig sein, **als** es
sich um ein ausgesprochen heikles
Problem handelt

*These negotiations will be difficult,
inasmuch as we're dealing with
an extremely delicate problem*

(b) *soweit* **usually has the sense of '(in) so/as far as'**
In this sense it is an alternative to *insofern/insoweit (als)*:

Ich werde dir helfen, **soweit** ich kann
Soweit ich die Lage beurteilen kann,
muß ich ihm recht geben

I'll help you as far as I can
*In so far as I can judge the situation,
I've got to admit he's right*

It can sometimes be used with a conditional sense. In such contexts it is an alternative to *sofern*, see (c) below and 16.5.3d:

Soweit/Sofern noch Interesse besteht,
wollen wir schon morgen damit anfangen

*Provided there's still interest we're
going to make a start tomorrow*

NB: *soviel ich weiß* 'as far as I know'.

(c) *sofern* **usually has a clear conditional sense, corresponding to English 'provided that' or 'if'**

Sofern wir es im Stadtrat durchsetzen
können, wird die neue Straße bald
gebaut

*Provided (that)/If we can get it through
the town council, the new road will
soon be built*

19.7.5 *je nachdem* 'according to', 'depending on'

je nachdem is normally used with a following *ob* or an interrogative:

Je nachdem ob es ihm besser geht oder nicht, wird er morgen verreisen	*Depending on whether he's better or not, he'll leave tomorrow*
Je nachdem wann wir fertig sind, werden wir hier oder in der Stadt essen	*Depending on when we get finished, we'll eat here or in town*
Je nachdem wie das Wetter wird, werden wir am Montag oder am Dienstag segeln gehen	*According to what the weather is like, we'll go sailing on Monday or Tuesday*

je nachdem often occurs in isolation, e.g.:

Kommst du morgen mit? – Na, je nachdem	*Are you coming tomorrow? – Well, it depends*

19.7.6 *nur daß* 'only (that)'

In der neuen Schule hat er sich gut eingelebt, **nur daß** seine Noten etwas besser sein könnten	*He's settled down well at his new school, only his marks could be a bit better*

Especially in spoken German, a construction with a main clause is often preferred to *nur daß*, e.g. ..., *nur könnten seine Noten etwas besser sein.*

19.7.7 *ohne daß* 'without'

ohne daß must be used for English 'without' followed by an *ing*-form if the subordinate clause has a different subject from the main clause:

Er verließ das Zimmer, **ohne daß** wir es merkten	*He left the room without us noticing*
Sie haben mir sofort geholfen, **ohne daß** ich sie darum bitten mußte	*They helped me immediately without my having to ask them*

If the subjects of the two clauses are the same, an infinitive clause with *ohne* ... *zu* can be used for English 'without' + *ing*, see 13.2.7b.

NB: The subjunctive is often used in *ohne daß* clauses, cf. 16.7.5a.

20

Prepositions

All the prepositions of German are dealt with in this chapter, ordered according to the case they govern, i.e. the accusative (20.1), the dative (20.2), the dative or the accusative (20.3) and the genitive (20.4). The most important literal and figurative senses of each preposition are treated together, with an indication where necessary of where further information may be found in other parts of the book. Some uses of prepositions are dealt with in more detail elsewhere: the use of prepositions in time phrases is treated in 11.5, the use of prepositions after adjectives in 6.6, after verbs (the 'prepositional object') in 18.6, the contraction of some prepositions with the definite article (e.g. *am*, *ins*) in 4.1.1c, and the use of the prepositional adverb (e.g. *darauf*, *damit*) in 3.5. The German equivalents for English 'to', which are often confusing for English learners, are explained in 20.5. Table 20.1 lists the most frequent German prepositions for convenient reference.

Schmitz (1964) and Schröder (1990) are useful introductions to the use of German prepositions, specifically written for the foreign learner.

TABLE 20.1 *Common German prepositions*

Prepositions followed by the:			
Accusative	bis gegen	durch ohne	für um
Dative	aus gegenüber seit	außer mit von	bei nach zu
Accusative or Dative	an hinter über zwischen	auf in unter	entlang neben vor
Genitive	statt wegen	trotz während	

20.1 Prepositions taking the accusative

Six common prepositions are used with the accusative:

bis   durch   für   gegen   ohne   um

The following are less frequent and are treated together in 20.1.7:

à   betreffend   eingerechnet   per   pro   wider

20.1.1 *bis*

In practice, *bis* is rarely used as a preposition in its own right. It is *never* followed by an article (or any determiner) and it is used on its own only with names, adverbs and a few time words. Otherwise it is followed by another preposition which determines the case of the following noun.

(a) Referring to place, *bis* means 'as far as', '(up) to'

(i) Followed by names of places and adverbs *bis* is used without an article. In practice the case of the following noun is never obvious:

Ich fahre nur **bis** Frankfurt	*I'm only going as far as Frankfurt*
Bis dahin gehe ich mit	*I'll go that far with you*
bis hierher und nicht weiter	*so far and no further*

(ii) If the following noun has an article, an appropriate preposition must follow, usually the appropriate equivalent of English 'to', cf. 20.5:

Wir gingen **bis zum** Waldrand	*We went as far as the edge of the forest*
Sie ging **bis zur** Tür	*She went up to the door*
Sie ging **bis an** die Tür	*She went right up to the door*
Wir fuhren **bis an** die Grenze	*We went as far as/up to the border*
Sie standen im Wasser **bis an** die Knöchel (*H. Mann*)	*They were standing in water up to their ankles*
(Compare: Sie standen in Wasser **bis über** die Knöchel)	
bis hin zu den Warzen im Gesicht (*Borst*)	*right down to the warts on his face*
Er stieg **bis aufs** Dach	*He climbed right onto the roof*
bis über die Ohren verschuldet	*up to one's ears in debt*

(iii) With names of towns, cities and countries, *bis* or *bis nach* can be used. The latter is rather more emphatic:

Wir fahren bis (nach) Freiburg, von Köln bis (nach) Bonn

(b) Referring to time, *bis* means 'until' or 'by'

See 11.5.4. If the noun is used with a determiner, *zu* (or another appropriate preposition) is inserted: *bis zum Abend, bis zum 4. Mai, bis zu seinem Tod, bis zu diesem Augenblick, bis auf den heutigen Tag.*

(c) *bis auf* (+ acc.) means 'down to (and including)' or 'all but', 'except'

Die Kabinen waren mit 447 Passagieren **bis auf** das letzte Klappbett belegt (*Zeit*)	*With 447 passengers, the cabins were full down to the last camp bed*
Die Insassen kamen alle um **bis auf** drei	*All but three of the passengers were killed*

bis auf can be ambiguous in some contexts. Thus, *Der Bus war bis auf den letzten Platz besetzt* could mean 'The bus was full down to the last seat' or 'The bus was full except for the last seat'.

20.1.2 *durch*

(a) *durch* means 'through', referring to place

Sie ging **durch** die Stadt	*She went through the city*
Et atmete **durch** den Mund	*He was breathing through his mouth*
mitten **durch** den Park (cf. 7.1.3)	*through the middle of the park*

durch is often strengthened by adding *hindurch*, cf. 7.2.4, e.g.:

Wir gingen **durch** den Wald **hindurch**	*We went (right) through the forest*

It can also be used for English 'across', especially with a preceding *quer*. This can give the sense of 'crosswise', 'diagonally', but it is often used simply to strengthen *durch* (i.e. = 'right through'):

Wir wateten (**quer**) **durch** den Fluß	*We waded across the river*
Neulich wurde ein Junge gebracht,	*Not long ago a boy was brought in; a*
dem ein Speer **quer durch** den Bauch	*spear had gone right through his belly*
gegangen war (*Grzimek*)	

(b) *durch* can also be used for English 'throughout'

(i) This is its usual sense when it refers to time, in which case it may be strengthened by adding *hindurch*, e.g. *durch viele Generationen* (*hindurch*) 'throughout many generations'.

(ii) *hindurch* can be used without a preceding *durch* for 'throughout' after an accusative phrase of time with *ganz*, cf. 11.4.1a:

den ganzen Winter **hindurch**	*throughout the winter*
die ganze Nacht **hindurch**	*throughout the whole night*

A phrase with *ganz* and an appropriate preposition is needed to give the sense of English 'throughout' referring to place, e.g.:

im **ganzen** Land	*throughout the country*
durch die **ganze** Stadt	*throughout the town*

(c) *durch* is used to express means

(i) It introduces the agent or means through whom or which an action is carried out, e.g.:

Durch harte Arbeit hat er sein Ziel erreicht	*He attained his aim by (means of) hard work*
Er ist **durch** einen Unfall ums Leben gekommen	*He was killed through an accident*
durch seine eigene Schuld	*through his own fault*
Ich habe es **durch** Zufall erfahren	*I learnt of it by chance*

This use of *durch* is related to its use for *by* in passive sentences, see 15.3.

(ii) *durch* in this sense corresponds to 'by' with a verbal noun:

die Annahme des Kaisertitels **durch** den König	*the assumption of the title of emperor by the king*
die Erfindung des Verbrennungsmotors **durch** Benz und Daimler	*the invention of the internal combustion engine by Benz and Daimler*

(iii) *durch* with a verbal noun often corresponds to English *by* with an *ing*-form, see 13.7.2a, e.g.: *durch Betätigung des Mechanismus* 'by activating the mechanism'.

(iv) The prepositional adverb *dadurch* often has the sense of 'thereby':

Was willst du **dadurch** erreichen?	*What do you hope to gain by that?*
Meinst du, **dadurch** wird alles wieder gut?	*Do you think that will make everything all right again?*

NB: For the compound conjunction *dadurch, daß*, see 19.7.3.

20.1.3 *für*

(a) *für* **corresponds to English 'for' in a wide range of senses**
i.e. where 'for' has the meaning of 'on behalf of' and the like, e.g.:

Er hat viel **für** mich getan	Das ist kein Buch **für** Kinder
Das wäre genug **für** heute	Ich habe es **für** zehn Mark gekriegt
Das war sehr unangenehm **für** mich (cf. 6.5.1a)	
Für einen Ausländer spricht er recht gut Deutsch	

für is used idiomatically in *ein Sinn, ein Beispiel für etwas* 'a sense, an example **of** sth'.

NB: Where English 'for' expresses purpose, its usual German equivalent is *zu*, see 20.2.9d.

(b) *für* **is used to indicate a period of time**
e.g. *für sechs Wochen* 'for six weeks'. For this, and other German equivalents for English 'for' referring to time, see 11.5.5.

20.1.4 *gegen*

(a) **Referring to place or opposition,** *gegen* **means 'against'**

Er warf den Ball **gegen** die Mauer	*He threw the ball against the wall*
gegen den Strom schwimmen	*swim against the current (in literal and figurative senses)*
Er verteidigte sich **gegen** diese Leute	*He defended himself against those people*

The prepositional adverb *dagegen* is frequent to indicate opposition, e.g.:

Hast du was **dagegen**, wenn wir früher anfangen?	*Do you have any objection to us starting earlier?*

Note the different idiomatic usage between German and English in *Ich brauche Tabletten gegen Kopfschmerzen* 'I need tablets **for** a headache'.

(b) *gegen* **can indicate direction**
(i) It then often corresponds to 'into':

Er fuhr **gegen** einen Baum	*He drove into a tree*
Wir müssen aufpassen, daß wir nicht **gegen** die Kraterwände fliegen (*Grzimek*)	*We've got to watch out that we don't fly into the sides of the crater*

(ii) In some contexts it can have the sense of 'towards':

Michael will die Maschine mit dem Propeller **gegen** die flache Böschung am Seeufer drehen (*Grzimek*)	*Michael wants to turn the aeroplane with the propellor towards the slight incline on the lake shore*

The use of *gegen* in the sense of 'towards' with the points of the compass is now old-fashioned. For *gegen Norden fahren* one now finds **nach** *Norden fahren*, see 20.2.6. The form *gen* (e.g. *gen Norden fahren*) is even more restricted to elevated literary registers and sounds archaic and biblical.

NB: Note the difference from English usage in *etwas* **gegen** *das Licht halten* 'to hold sth. up to the light'.

(c) *gegen* **can express a contrast (= 'contrary to', 'compared with')**

Ich handelte **gegen** seinen Befehl	*I acted against/contrary to his orders*
gegen alle Erwartungen	*against/contrary to all expectations*
Gegen meine Schwester bin ich groß	*I'm tall compared with my sister*
gegen früher	*compared with formerly*

(d) *gegen* **can have the sense of '(in exchange/return) for'**

Er gab mir das Geld **gegen** eine Quittung	*He gave me the money in exchange for a receipt*
Ich will meine Kamera **gegen** einen Camcorder eintauschen	*I want to exchange my camera for a camcorder*

(e) *gegen* **can express approximation (= 'about')**

Es waren **gegen** 500 Zuschauer im Saal	*There were about 500 spectators in the hall*

(f) *gegen* **is used after a number of nouns and adjectives**
See also 6.6.1. These nouns or adjectives mostly involve a mental attitude 'towards' something or someone, e.g.:

die Abneigung gegen	*aversion for*	die Grausamkeit gegen	*cruelty towards*
der Haß gegen	*hatred of*	das Mißtrauen gegen	*distrust of*
argwöhnisch gegen	*suspicious of*	gleichgültig gegen	*indifferent to*
gesichert gegen	*secure against*		

seine Pflicht gegen seine Eltern	*his duty towards his parents*
sein Verhalten gegen seinen Chef	*his attitude to(wards) his boss*
rücksichtslos/rücksichtsvoll gegen	*(in)considerate towards*

With these nouns and adjectives *gegenüber* is often a possible alternative to *gegen*, see 20.2.4d, and some adjectives can be followed by *zu* or *gegen*, see 20.2.9g.

(g) Referring to time, *gegen* **means 'about', 'towards'**
e.g. *Sie kam* **gegen** *Abend,* **gegen** *vier Uhr an.* For details, see 11.5.6.

20.1.5 *ohne*

In most contexts *ohne* corresponds almost exactly to English 'without':

Das tat er **ohne** mein Wissen	Er geht selten **ohne** Hut
Das haben wir **ohne** große Schwierigkeiten erledigt	

ohne can be used idiomatically on its own in colloquial speech:

Der Wein ist nicht **ohne**	*The wine's got quite a kick*
Er ist gar nicht so **ohne**	*He's got what it takes*

NB: (i) *ohne* is used with no determiner in many contexts where English has an indefinite article or a possessive, see 4.9.3b.

  (ii) For the use of *ohne* in infinitive clauses (i.e. *ohne . . . zu*), see 13.2.7b; for the conjunction *ohne daß*, see 19.7.7.

20.1.6 *um*

(a) Referring to place, *um* means '(a)round', 'about'

Wir standen **um** den Teich	*We were standing (a)round the pond*
Er kam **um** die Ecke	*He came (a)round the corner*
Sie sah **um** sich	*She looked round (in all directions)*
Er hat gern viele Mädchen **um** sich	*He likes having a lot of girls about him*

um is often strengthened by adding *rund*, *rings* or *herum* (cf. 7.2.4b), e.g.:

Wir standen **rings/rund um** den Tisch or **um** den Tisch **herum**	
Er kam **um** die Ecke **herum** Sie sah um sich **herum**	

(b) *um* means 'at' with clock times, but 'about' with other time expressions
e.g. *Ich komme um zwei Uhr*. See 11.5.11 for more details.

um can also be used adverbially with numerals in the sense of 'about', 'approximately', see 9.1.6. It is then often followed by a definite article, but a following adjective has *strong* endings, e.g. *um die vierzig ausländische Gäste*.

(c) *um* is used to denote the degree of difference
This often corresponds to English 'by':

Ich werde meinen Aufenthalt **um** zwei Tage verlängern	*I shall extend my stay by two days*
Sie hat sich **um** 20 Mark verrechnet	*She was 20 marks out in her calculations*
um die Hälfte mehr	*half as much again*
eine Erweiterung der EWG **um** England (*SZ*)	*an expansion of the EEC by the inclusion of England*

When *um* is used in this sense with a comparative adjective and a measurement phrase (see 8.3.1b), an alternative to *um* is simply to put the measurement phrase in the accusative case, e.g.: *Er ist (um) einen Kopf größer als ich.*

(d) *um* can convey the idea of 'in respect of', 'concerning'
This sense is common when *um* is used as a prepositional object, see 18.6.10, but it occurs in other constructions, especially after some nouns and adjectives, e.g.:

der Kampf **ums** Dasein	*the struggle for existence*
Er tat es nur **um** das Geld	*He only did it for the money*
Er wandte sich an mich **um** Rat	*He turned to me for advice*
Es ist schade **um** den Verlust	*It's a pity about the loss*
Es steht schlecht **um** ihren Bruder	*Her brother's in a bad way*
ein Streit **um** etwas	*an argument about sth.*
die Angst **ums** Leben	*fear for one's life*
Es ist recht still **um** ihn geworden	*You don't hear anything about him now*

Idiomatically also:

Auge um Auge, Zahn um Zahn	*an eye for an eye, a tooth for a tooth*

(e) The prepositional adverb *darum* is used in the meaning 'therefore', 'that's why'

It is an alternative to *deshalb*:

Darum habe ich nicht schreiben können	*That's why I couldn't write*
Sie hatte eine Panne, **darum** ist sie	*She had a breakdown, that's why*
so spät gekommen	*she was so late coming*

20.1.7 Less frequent prepositions which govern the accusative

(a) *à* is used in the sense of 'at' (i.e. @), with prices

e.g.: *zehn Paar Schuhe à 150 Mark.* This usage is now rather old-fashioned, and *zu* is now more frequent than *à*, see 20.2.9h.

(b) *betreffend* 'with regard to' is used mainly in commercial German

It is an alternative to *betreffs* (+ gen.) and may precede or follow the noun it governs: *betreffend Ihr Schreiben vom 23. Mai* or *Ihr Schreiben vom 23. Mai betreffend*.

(c) *eingerechnet* 'including' is limited to commercial language

It follows the noun it governs: *meine Unkosten eingerechnet* 'including my expenses'.

(d) *per* 'per', 'by'

per was originally only used in commercial language, but it has increasingly come to be used in spoken registers. When used with a means of transport it is an alternative to more usual *mit*, cf. 20.2.5b:

per Post (= mit der Post)	*by post*	per Bahn (= mit der Bahn)	*by rail*
per Luftfracht	*by air*	per Einschreiben	*by recorded mail*
per Adresse (p.A.)	*c/o*	per Anhalter fahren	*hitchhike*

mit jemandem per du sein	*be on first-name terms with sb.*
Sie bezahlen erst per 31. Dezember	*You do not pay until December 31st*
Die Waren sind per 1. Mai bestellt	*The goods are ordered for May 1st*

As *per* is used predominantly without a following determiner, the case it governs is often not discernible. This has given rise to uncertainty, and in practice, when a case is clear, *per* is seen to be used as often with the dative as with the accusative, e.g. *per zweitem Bildungsweg* (*Spiegel*).

(e) *pro* 'per'

pro was originally restricted to commercial language, but, like *per*, it has increasingly come to be used in spoken registers. A common alternative is *je*, see 9.4.1:

Die Pfirsiche kosten 80 Pfennig **pro** Stück	*The peaches cost 80 pfennigs each*
Was ist der Preis **pro** Tag?	*What is the cost per day?*
zwanzig Mark **pro** Person	*twenty marks per person*
Unsere Reisekosten betragen 3000	*Our travel expenses amount to 3000*
Mark **pro/je** Vertreter **pro/je** Monat	*marks per representative per month*

As with *per*, when the case of a following noun is clear, *pro* is seen to be used as frequently with the dative as with the accusative.

(f) *wider* 'against' is an obsolete alternative to *gegen*

It is occasionally used in elevated registers, but most often in a few set phrases:

Diese Unterlassung relativiert alle	*This omission qualifies all the*
markigen Worte **wider** den	*vigorous speeches against*
Terrorismus (*Zeit*)	*terrorism*
wider (alles) Erwarten	*against (all) expectations*
wider Willen	*against my (his, her, etc.) will*
wider besseres Wissen (*MM*)	*against my (his, her, etc.) better judgement*

20.2 Prepositions taking the dative

Nine common prepositions are used with the dative:

aus	außer	bei	gegenüber	mit	nach	seit	von	zu

The following are less frequent and are treated together in 20.2.10:

ab	(mit)samt
binnen	nahe
dank	nebst
entgegen	zufolge
entsprechend	zuliebe
fern	zuwider

20.2.1 *aus*

(a) *aus* most commonly denotes direction 'out of' or 'from' a place

(i) Examples of the use of *aus* in the sense of 'out of':

Er kam **aus** dem Haus	*He was coming out of the house*
Ich sah **aus** dem Fenster	*I looked out of the window*
(*or*: zum Fenster hinaus)	
Er trank **aus** einer Tasse	*He was drinking out of a cup*
Sie ging mir **aus** dem Weg	*She avoided me*
aus der Mode kommen/sein	*go/be out of fashion*
aus der Übung kommen	*get out of practice*

(ii) In practice, *aus* more often corresponds to English 'from', and English learners need to distinguish it carefully from *von*, which can also mean 'from' (see 20.2.8a). *aus* is used with reference to places one has been **in**, with the idea of origin. Its opposite is *in* (+ acc.). *von*, by contrast, is used for 'from' with reference to places one has been **at**, i.e. it expresses the idea of direction. Its opposite is *zu*. Examples of *aus*:

Er kommt **aus** Hamburg	*He comes from Hamburg*
(i.e. *Er wohnt in Hamburg. Er kommt von Hamburg* means 'He is travelling from Hamburg' (on this occasion)).	
aus dieser Richtung	*from that direction*
Compare *in diese(r) Richtung* 'in that direction'	
Dieser Schrank ist **aus** dem 18.	*This cupboard is from the 18th*
Jahrhundert	*century*
(i.e. it was made *in* the 18th century)	
ein Mädchen **aus** unserer Klasse	*a girl from our class*
(i.e. she is *in* our class)	

(b) *aus* denotes 'made of' referring to materials

Die Kaffeekanne war **aus** Silber	*The coffee pot was made of silver*
aus Holz, Stahl, Eisen	*made of wood, steel, iron*
ein Kleid **aus** Wolle	*a woollen dress*

(c) *aus* is used to denote a cause, a reason or a motive

Sie tat es **aus** Dankbarkeit,	*She did it out of gratitude,*
aus Mitleid, **aus** Überzeugung	*out of sympathy, from conviction*
Ich weiß es **aus** (der) Erfahrung	*I know it from experience*
Ich frage nur **aus** Interesse	*I'm only asking out of interest*
aus Furcht vor, Liebe zu etwas	*for fear, love of sth.*
aus diesem Grund(e)	*for that reason*

NB: For the distinction between *aus* and *vor* (+ dat.) to indicate cause, see 20.3.15d.

(d) Some idiomatic uses of *aus*

aus erster Hand	*at first hand*
Daraus werde ich nicht klug	*I can't make it out*
Aus dir wird nichts werden	*You'll never come to anything*

20.2.2 *außer*

(a) *außer* usually expresses a restriction (= 'except (for)', 'besides')

Niemand hat ihn gesehen **außer** dem Nachtwächter	*No-one saw him except for the night-watchman*
Niemand wird es machen können **außer** mir	*No-one will be able to do it except for me*
Ich konnte nichts sehen **außer** Straßenlichtern	*I couldn't see anything besides street-lights*

außer can also be used with the same case as the word to which it refers back, rather than with the dative. The following are acceptable alternatives to the examples above:

Ich konnte **nichts** sehen außer **Lichter**
Niemand wird es machen können außer **ich**

In effect *außer* is here being used to introduce a phrase in apposition (see 2.6) rather than as a preposition. It can also be used in a similar way to introduce another preposition, e.g.: *Außer bei Regen kann man hier spielen.*

(b) *außer* is used in the meaning 'out of', 'outside'

This sense now occurs chiefly in set phrases, in most of which *außer* is used without a following article:

Die Maschine ist **außer** Betrieb	*The machine is out of service*
außer Kontrolle sein/geraten	*be/get out of control*
etwas **außer** acht lassen	*disregard sth.*
Ich war **außer** mir	*I was beside myself*
Aber dies war etwas, was ganz **außer** seiner Macht lag (*Musil*)	*This was something which lay completely beyond his power*

Similarly:

außer Atem	*out of breath*	außer Gefahr	*out of danger*
außer Reichweite	*out of range*	außer Sicht	*out of sight*
außer Übung	*out of practice*	außer Zweifel	*beyond doubt*

In one or two obsolescent phrases *außer* is used with a genitive, notably in *außer Landes gehen* 'leave the country'. More usual for this would be *ins Ausland gehen*, or simply *auswandern*.

With verbs of motion, *außer* is used with the accusative, although this is only obvious in those rare contexts where a determiner or an adjective is used, e.g. *etwas außer jeden Zweifel setzen*.

20.2.3 *bei*

(a) Referring to place, *bei* usually corresponds to English 'by' or 'at'

(i) In this sense *bei* is rather less precise than *an* (+ dat.), see 20.3.2a, meaning 'in the vicinity of' rather than 'adjacent to':

Er stand **bei** mir	*He was standing by/near me*
(= Er stand in meiner Nähe)	
Bad Homburg liegt **bei** Frankfurt	*Bad Homburg is by/near Frankfurt*
(dicht) **bei** der Kirche	*(right) by the church*
Ich habe ihn neulich **beim**	*I saw him recently at the football*
Fußballspiel gesehen	*match*
Er saß **beim** Feuer	*He was sitting by the fire*

NB: *bei* is always used with battles, e.g. *die Schlacht bei Hastings*.

(ii) Used with reference to people, *bei* usually means 'at (the house of)'. It is also used to indicate place of employment:

Sie wohnt **bei** ihrer Tante	*She lives at her aunt's*
Ich habe dieses Fleisch **beim** neuen	*I bought this meat at the new butcher's*
Metzger gekauft	
Sie arbeitet **bei** der Post, **bei** Bayer	*She works at the post office, at Bayer's*
bei uns	*at our house*
bei uns in der Fabrik	*at our works*

Unlike French *chez*, *bei* cannot be used to indicate motion *to* somebody's house, cf. *Sie geht zu ihrer Tante* 'She's going to her aunt's house'.

(iii) *bei* can also be used in a number of extended senses with reference to people. This often corresponds to English 'with':

Das hat ihm **bei** den Amerikanern sehr	*That did him a lot of harm with the*
geschadet	*Americans*
Ich habe mich **bei** ihm entschuldigt,	*I apologised, complained to him*
beschwert	
Er hat großen Einfluß **beim** Minister	*He has a lot of influence with the minister*
Mathe haben wir **bei** Frau Gerstner	*We have Frau Gerstner for maths*
Hast du deinen Ausweis **bei** dir/dabei?	*Have you got your identity card on you?*
Bei Goethe liest man ...	*In Goethe's works one reads ...*

(b) *bei* is frequently used to indicate attendant circumstances

This usage has a wide range of English equivalents, i.e.:

(i) *bei* can mean 'in view of', 'with', etc., e.g.:

bei den immer steigenden Preisen	*in view of the constantly rising prices*
Bei diesem Gehalt kann ich mir keinen neuen Wagen leisten	*With this salary I can't afford a new car*
Bei all seinen Verlusten bleibt er ein Optimist	*Despite all his losses he remains an optimist*

(ii) *bei* can mean 'on the occasion of', 'at'. This sense is related to its use in time expressions, see 11.5.3:

bei dieser Gelegenheit	*on this occasion*
bei dem bloßen Gedanken	*at the very thought*
Sie erblaßte bei der Nachricht	*She turned pale at the news*
Acht Menschen kamen bei diesem Verkehrsunfall ums Leben (*FAZ*)	*Eight people were killed in this road accident*
bei diesem Anblick	*at the sight of this*
bei einem Glas Wein	*over a glass of wine*

Similarly:

bei der Arbeit	*at work*	beim Fußball	*when playing football*
bei Tisch	*at table*	bei seinem Tod	*at his death*
bei schönem Wetter	*if it's fine*	bei diesen Worten	*at these words*

Both *bei* and *auf* (see 20.3.4b) can be used for English 'at', referring to formal occasions, functions and the like, e.g.:

Ich habe sie bei/auf ihrer Hochzeit kennengelernt	*I met her at their wedding*

The difference of meaning is often slight but in general *bei* points more clearly to the *time*, rather than the *place*, of the event in question.

(iii) *bei* is used with the infinitive or other verbal nouns in the sense of English 'on + . . .ing' or a subordinate time clause, see 13.4.3a and 13.7.2d. This usage is very frequent in non-literary written German, but it is not restricted to that register:

beim Schließen der Türen	*on shutting the doors*
beim Schlafen, beim Essen	*whilst sleeping, eating*
bei seiner Ankunft	*on arrival/when he arrived*
bei näherer Überlegung	*on closer consideration*

(c) Some idiomatic uses of *bei*

Sie war bei guter/schlechter Laune	*She was in a good/bad mood*
Sie nannte mich beim Vornamen	*She called me by my first name*
Sie nahm mich beim Wort	*She took me at my word*
Sie nahm mich bei der Hand	*She took me by the hand*

20.2.4 *gegenüber*

(a) The position of *gegenüber* before or after the noun or pronoun

(i) *gegenüber always* follows a pronoun, e.g.:

Sie saß mir gegenüber	Ihr gegenüber stand ein alter Herr

(ii) *gegenüber* can come before *or* after a noun. It tends to follow words denoting people, otherwise it is commoner for it to precede, e.g.:

Alten Menschen **gegenüber** soll man immer hilfsbereit sein	*One ought always to be ready to help old people*
(Less common: Gegenüber alten Menschen ...)	
Gegenüber dem Rathaus liegt ein Krankenhaus	*Opposite the town hall there is a hospital*
(Less common: Dem Rathaus gegenüber ...)	

(b) Referring to place, *gegenüber* means 'opposite'

Ich setzte mich ihr **gegenüber**	*I sat down opposite her*
Ich wohne **gegenüber** dem Krankenhaus	*I live opposite the hospital*

In this sense, *gegenüber* is often used with a following *von*, especially in speech: *Ich saß gegenüber von ihr. Ich wohne gegenüber vom Krankenhaus.*

gegenüber is often used on its own, as an adverb, e.g. *Sie wohnt gegenüber; das Haus gegenüber; die Leute von gegenüber.*

(c) *gegenüber* can express a comparison (= 'compared with')

Depending on the context, *gegen*, see 20.1.4c, or *neben*, see 20.3.10d, may be alternatives to *gegenüber* in this sense:

Gegenüber meiner Schwester bin ich groß	*I'm tall compared with my sister*
gegenüber dem Vorjahr	*compared with last year*

(d) *gegenüber* can mean 'in relation to', 'in respect of', 'towards'

mein Verhalten Astrid **gegenüber**	*my attitude towards Astrid*
Heinrich war vollkommen hilflos Maries Ängsten **gegenüber** (*Böll*)	*Heinrich was completely helpless in the face of Marie's fears*

In this sense, *gegenüber* is particularly common after nouns and adjectives, where it is an (often more common) alternative to *gegen*, see 20.1.4f, or, in some cases, *zu*, see 20.2.9g:

Er handelte durchaus gerecht mir **gegenüber** (*or*: gegen mich)	*He acted absolutely fairly towards me*
Seine Güte mir **gegenüber** (*or*: zu mir) war rührend	*His kindness towards me was touching*

Similarly:

das Mißtrauen gegenüber/gegen	*distrust of*
eine Pflicht gegenüber/gegen	*a duty towards*
gleichgültig gegenüber/gegen	*indifferent towards*
rücksichtsvoll/-los gegenüber/gegen	*(in)considerate to*
freundlich gegenüber/zu	*kind to(wards)*

20.2.5 *mit*

(a) In most uses *mit* corresponds to English 'with'

ein Paar Würstchen **mit** Kartoffelsalat	*a pair of sausages with potato salad*
Mit ihr spiele ich oft Tennis	*I often play tennis with her*
Was ist **mit** dir los?	*What's up with you?*
mit großer Freude	*with great pleasure*
mit meinem Bruder zusammen	*together with my brother*

(b) *mit* indicates the instrument with which an action is performed

This usually corresponds to English 'with':

Er schrieb **mit** einem Filzstift	*He wrote with a felt-tip*
Er hat sie **mit** einem Messer getötet	*He killed her with a knife*

However, German usage is sometimes at variance with English:

mit Tinte schreiben	*write in ink*
mit leiser Stimme	*in a low voice*
mit der Maschine schreiben	*type*

To refer to a means of transport German has *mit* for English 'by':

mit der Bahn/dem Zug	*by rail/train*	mit dem Auto	*by car*
mit dem Flugzeug	*by plane*	mit der Post	*by post*

Ich bin mit dem Fahrrad gekommen	*I came by bike/on a bike*

NB: Whereas *mit* indicates the *instrument*, the *means* by which an action is carried out is usually given by *durch*, see 20.1.2c.

(c) *mit* is common in phrases involving parts of the body, where English does not have a preposition or uses a simple verb

Sie hat mich **mit** dem Fuß gestoßen	*She kicked me*
mit den Achseln zucken	*shrug one's shoulders*

(d) Selected common idiomatic uses of *mit*

mit vierzig Jahren	*at the age of forty*
mit der Zeit	*in (the course of) time*
etwas mit Absicht tun	*do sth. on purpose*
mit anderen Worten (m.a.W.)	*in other words*
Her damit! (coll.)	*Give it here!*
Schluß damit!	*That's enough!*

20.2.6 *nach*

(a) *nach* is used to denote direction, in the sense of English 'to'

See also 20.5.3. In this sense *nach* is only used as follows:

(i) With neuter names of countries and towns used without an article:

Er ging **nach** Amerika, **nach** Irland, **nach** Bacharach

NB: *in* is used with names of countries which have an article, see 4.4.1: *Sie ging in die Schweiz*.

(ii) With points of the compass used without an article:

Wir fuhren **nach** Norden, Süden, Westen, Osten

NB: If an article is present (normally when the noun is also qualified by an adjective), *in* is used: *Wir fuhren in den sonnigen Süden.*

(iii) With adverbs of place:

Sie ging **nach** oben, **nach** unten, **nach** vorne, **nach** rechts, links

NB: also *nach Hause gehen* 'go home'.

(iv) In north German usage, where *nach* is used for *zu, an, auf* or *in*:

> Ich gehe nach (standard German: zu) meiner Schwester
> Wir gingen nach dem (standard German: auf den, zum) Bahnhof

This usage is regional and colloquial and considered to be non-standard, but north Germans sometimes use it in writing.

(b) *nach* can be used in the sense of 'towards', 'in the direction of'
It is frequently strengthened by adding *hin*, see 7.2.3, e.g.:

Er bewegte sich langsam **nach** der Tür	*He moved slowly towards the door*
Ich sah **nach** der Tür (hin)	*I looked towards the door*
Er richtete seine Schritte **nach** der alten Brücke	*He turned his steps in the direction of the old bridge*
nach allen Seiten (hin)	*in all directions*

NB: *auf . . . zu* is a more frequent equivalent for 'towards', see 20.3.5a.

(c) Referring to time, *nach* means 'after'
e.g. *nach vier Uhr, nach dem Sommer*, etc. Full details are given in 11.5.8. The prepositional adverb *danach* can be used to mean 'after(wards)' or 'later', cf. 11.6.4b.

(d) *nach* can be used in the sense of 'according to', 'judging by'

Nach meiner Uhr ist es schon halb elf	*According to/By my watch, it's already half past ten*
nach italienischer Art	*in the Italian manner*
nach Ansicht meines Bruders	*in my brother's view*
etwas **nach** dem Gewicht verkaufen	*sell sth. by weight*
nach besten Kräften	*to the best of one's ability*
nach Wunsch	*just as I (he, she, etc.) wanted*

In this sense, *nach* can follow the noun. In general, this is usual only with certain nouns (most of which it may precede or follow), in set phrases, and in the meaning 'judging by':

allem Anschein **nach**	*to all appearances*
diesem Bericht **nach**	*according to this report*
(in less formal language usually: nach diesem Bericht)	
der Größe **nach**	*according to size*
(also commonly nach der Größe)	
meiner Meinung **nach**	*in my opinion*
(also nach meiner Meinung)	
Ich kenne sie nur dem Namen **nach**	*I only know her by name*
der Reihe **nach**	*in turns*
Ihrer Aussprache **nach** kommt sie aus Schwaben	*Judging by her accent she comes from Swabia*

NB: A number of other prepositions are used in the meaning 'according to' in formal registers, i.e. *entsprechend, gemäß, laut* and *zufolge*. These are dealt with in 20.2.10e.

20.2.7 *seit*

seit is only used with reference to time, in the meaning of English 'since' (e.g. *seit dem achtzehnten Jahrhundert*) or 'for' (e.g. *Ich warte seit einer halben Stunde auf meine Schwester*). For full details, see 11.5.9. For the use of tenses in *seit* phrases, see 14.2.2 and 14.3.4a.

20.2.8 *von*

(a) *von* indicates direction 'from' a place

(i) In this sense, *von* is the opposite of *zu*, which indicates direction towards, cf. 20.2.9. For the difference between *von* and *aus* as equivalents of English 'from', see 20.2.1a:

Ich fuhr **von** Frankfurt nach München	*I travelled from Frankfurt to Munich*
Sie bekam einen Brief **von** mir	*She received a letter from me*
Sie kommt **von** ihrer Schwester	*She's coming from her sister's*
Ich wohne zehn Minuten **vom** Bahnhof (entfernt)	*I live ten minutes from the station*
Die Blätter fallen **von** den Bäumen	*The leaves are falling from the trees*

(ii) *von* can be strengthened by adding *aus* after the noun to emphasise the point of origin, e.g.:

Von meinem Fenster (**aus**) kann ich die Paulskirche sehen	*I can see St Paul's church from my window*
Wir sind **von** Madrid (**aus**) mit der Bahn nach Barcelona gefahren	*We travelled by train from Madrid to Barcelona*

von . . . aus also occurs in a few idiomatic phrases:

Er war **von** Haus **aus** Lehrer	*He was originally a teacher*
von mir **aus**	*as far as I'm concerned*
von Natur **aus**	*by nature*
Das ist **von** Grund **aus** falsch	*That is completely wrong*

(iii) Direction from a point can be emphasised by adding *her* (cf. 7.2.3):

Eine Stimme kam **von** oben **her**	*A voice came from above*
Ich komme **von** meiner Schwester **her**	*I am coming from my sister's*

von . . . her is now commonly (and fashionably) used in the sense 'in respect of', 'from the point of view of', 'regarding'. In practice this represents a contraction of the phrase *von . . . her betrachtet*, cf. Lehmann (1991):

Von Beruf **her** ist er Schlosser	*As for his job, he's a mechanic*
Wir sind **von** der Technik **her** schon viel weiter	*We're now a lot further on from the point of view of the technology*
Besonders raffiniert **von** der Farbe **her**	*Particularly subtle in respect of the colouring*
Von der Zielsetzung **her** sind wir der gleichen Meinung	*We're of the same opinion in respect of our objectives*

Occasionally, *her* is omitted in these contexts, e.g.: *Von der Zielsetzung sind wir der gleichen Meinung*.

(b) *von* also usually has the sense of 'from' referring to time

In this case it is often strengthened by *an* following the noun, e.g. *von neun Uhr (an)*. Details are given in 11.5.12.

(c) *von* **is used to introduce the agent in passive constructions**
Details about the use of *von* with the passive, and on the distinction between *von* and *durch* as equivalents of English 'by', are given in 15.3.

(d) A phrase with *von* is often used in place of a genitive
i.e. for English 'of', e.g. *ein Ereignis von weltgeschichtlicher Bedeutung*. This usage is fully treated in 2.4.

(e) *von* **has a wide range of figurative uses**
(i) It often corresponds to English 'of' in the sense of 'on the part of':

Das war sehr nett, liebenswürdig, vernünftig von ihr	*That was very nice, kind, sensible of her*
Das war doch dumm von mir	*That was silly of me, wasn't it?*
Er tat es von selbst	*He did it of his own accord*

(ii) A selection of other common idiomatic phrases with *von*:

Das ist nicht von ungefähr passiert	*It didn't happen by accident*
Das kommt davon	*That's what comes of it*
Das gilt nicht von ihm	*That's not true of him*
Ich kenne sie nur vom Sehen	*I only know her by sight*
von ganzem Herzen	*with all one's heart*

20.2.9 *zu*

(a) *zu* **expresses direction**
It is a common equivalent for English 'to', particularly:

(i) For going to a person('s house):

Er ging **zu** seinem Onkel, **zu** Müllers, **zum** Frisör.

NB: For '*at*' (a person's house), *bei* is used, see 20.2.3.

(ii) For going to a place or an occasion:

Dieser Bus fährt **zum** Bahnhof	*This bus goes to the station*
Ich ging **zur** Kirche und wartete dort auf sie	*I went to the church and waited for her there*
Wir machten einen Ausflug **zum** Dorf	*We went on an outing to the village*
Ich war auf dem Weg **zu** einem einsamen Tal	*I was on my way to a secluded valley*
Sie kehrte **zu** ihrer Arbeit zurück	*She returned to her work*
Der Rauch stieg **zur** Decke	*The smoke rose to the ceiling*
eine Expedition **zum** Mond	*an expedition to the moon*
Sie geht morgen **zu** einem Kongreß	*She's going to a conference tomorrow*
Wir alle trotten hinter den Eseln her **zu** einer Wellblechhütte (*Grzimek*)	*We're all trotting behind the donkeys towards a corrugated iron hut*

zu is the opposite of *von*, see 20.2.8a and puts the emphasis on the general direction rather than reaching the destination (and it can thus sometimes correspond to English 'towards' as much as to 'to', as in the last example). For the distinction between it and the more specific prepositions *an*, *auf* or *in* (with the accusative) as an equivalent of 'to', see 20.5.

zu can be strengthened by adding *hin* after the noun, cf. 7.2.3, e.g. *Sie ging zur Post (hin); Er blickte zur Decke (hin).* The effect is to emphasise the direction, with the effect that *zu ... hin* is a common equivalent for English 'towards'.

(iii) In some idiomatic phrases:

Sie sah **zum** Fenster, **zur** Tür **hinaus**	*She looked out of the window, the door*
Setzen Sie sich doch **zu** uns!	*Do come and join us*

(b) *zu* **sometimes refers to a place**
i.e. with the meaning of English 'at' or 'in'. This sense of *zu* used to be common, especially with names of towns, but it is now only used in elevated styles, as modern German prefers *in*:

J.S.Bach wurde **zu** (usually: *in*) Eisenach geboren	*J.S. Bach was born in Eisenach*
der Dom **zu** Köln	*Cologne cathedral*
(more usually: *der Kölner Dom*)	

However, *zu* still occurs in this sense in some set phrases, e.g.:

zu Hause	*at home*
zu beiden Seiten	*on either side*

(c) *zu* **is used in certain time expressions**
It usually corresponds to English 'at', e.g. *zu Ostern, zu dieser Zeit.* Details are given in 11.5.15.

(d) *zu* **is the usual equivalent of English 'for' to express purpose**
(i) Examples of this usage:

zu diesem Zweck	*for this purpose*
Das ist kein Anlaß **zur** Klage	*That is no cause for complaint*
Was gibt es heute **zum** Nachtisch?	*What's for dessert today?*
Stoff **zu** einem neuen Anzug	*material for a new suit*
Zum Geburtstag hat er mir eine Uhr geschenkt	*He bought me a watch for my birthday*
Wir hatten keine Gelegenheit **zu** einem Gespräch	*We didn't have a chance for a talk*

The prepositional adverb *dazu* is commonly used in the sense of 'for that purpose', e.g. **Dazu** *soll man ein scharfes Messer gebrauchen.* Cf. also *Wozu?* 'To what purpose?', 'What for?'.

(ii) In this sense, *zu* is very common with an infinitive used as a noun, or with other verbal nouns, where English uses *for + ...ing* or an infinitive with *to.* More details on this usage are given in 13.4.3b and 13.7.2b. It is particulary frequent in written non-literary German, but it is by no means confined to that register. Examples:

Wozu gebraucht man dieses Messer? – **Zum** Kartoffelschälen.	*What do you use this knife for? – For peeling potatoes/To peel potatoes*
Hier gibt es viele Möglichkeiten **zum** Schilaufen	*There are lots of possibilities for skiing here*
Ich sage dir das **zu** deiner Beruhigung	*I'm telling you this to reassure you*

(iii) In certain contexts, this sense of *zu* approaches that of *als*, i.e. 'by way of', 'as':

Er murmelte etwas **zur** Antwort	*He muttered something by way of reply*
Er tat es mir **zu** Gefallen	*He did it as a favour to me*

Similarly:

zur Abwechslung	*for a change*	zum Scherz	*as a joke*
zum Andenken an	*in memory of*	zum Spaß	*as a joke*
zum Beispiel	*for example*	zur Strafe	*as a punishment*
zur Not	*if necessary, at a pinch*	zum Vergnügen	*for pleasure*

(e) In some contexts *zu* can indicate a result or an effect
The English equivalent is most often 'to':

Zu meinem Erstaunen hat sie das Examen bestanden	*To my surprise she passed her finals*

Similarly:

zu meinem Ärger	*to my annoyance*
zu meiner Befriedigung	*to my satisfaction*
zu meiner großen Freude	*to my great pleasure*
Es ist zum Lachen, zum Heulen,	*It is laughable, enough to make one*
zum Verrücktwerden	*weep, enough to drive one mad*

NB: *zu* commonly occurs in this sense in the prepositional object of a number of verbs, see 18.6.13a.

(f) *zu* can express a change of state
This usage is associated with a small number of verbs or nouns with appropriate meanings:

Sie wählten ihn **zum** Präsidenten	*They elected him President*
Er wurde **zum** Major befördert	*He was promoted to major*
Ich habe es mir **zur** Regel gemacht, dies zu tun	*I've made it a rule to do this*
etwas **zu** Brei kochen	*cook sth. to a pulp*

Similarly with *bestimmen* 'destine to be', *degradieren* 'demote', *ernennen* 'appoint', *krönen* 'crown', *weihen* 'ordain', *werden* 'become' (see 18.8), etc. and the nouns *die Beförderung* 'promotion', *die Ernennung* 'appointment', *die Wahl* 'election', etc.

(g) *zu* can express a mental attitude towards someone or something
(i) This is frequent with adjectives, see 6.6.1, e.g.:

Sie war sehr freundlich **zu** mir	*She was very kind to me*

Similarly:

frech zu	*impudent towards*	nett zu	*nice to*
gut zu	*good, kind to*	respektvoll zu	*respectful to*
(un)höflich zu	*(im)polite to*	unfreundlich zu	*unkind to*

(ii) Also with a number of nouns, e.g.:

Wir haben freundliche Beziehungen **zu** Müllers	*We're on friendly terms with the Müllers*
ihre Einstellung **zur** Wiedervereinigung	*her attitude to reunification*
seine Liebe **zu** ihr	*his love for her*
das Verhältnis des Einzelnen **zum** Staat	*the relationship of the individual to the state*

gegen (cf. 20.1.4f) and *gegenüber* (cf. 20.2.4d) can also denote attitude towards or relations with someone or something. Whether *gegen* or *zu* is used depends largely on the particular noun or adjective, though *gegen* tends to occur with those which denote hostile attitudes, *zu* with those which denote friendly attitudes. A few adjectives can be used with either, e.g.:

gerecht zu/gegen *fair, just to* hart zu/gegen *hard towards*
grausam zu/gegen *cruel to*

gegen is used with some nouns although the related adjective has *zu*, e.g.: *die Frechheit, Gerechtigkeit, Grausamkeit, Härte, (Un)höflichkeit gegen jdn. gegenüber* is a common alternative to *gegen* or *zu* with most adjectives or nouns which occur with these prepositions, cf. 20.2.4.

(h) Uses of *zu* with numbers
(i) To indicate price or measure:

10 Stück Seife **zu** je 2 Mark	*10 pieces of soap at 2 marks each*
5 Päckchen Kaffee **zu** hundert Gramm	*5 hundred gram packs of coffee*
zum halben Preis	*at half price*

Also with fractions, etc.: *zur Hälfte, zum Teil, zu einem Drittel fertig.*

(ii) With the dative of the cardinal or the stem of the ordinal to indicate groups, e.g *zu zweien, zu zweit*, cf. 9.1.3b.

(iii) With the declined ordinal number for 'first(ly)', 'secondly', etc., e.g. *zum ersten, zum zweiten*, etc., cf. 9.2.3.

(i) Selected idiomatic uses of *zu*

jemanden zum besten haben	*make a fool of somebody*
zu Boden fallen	*fall to the ground*
sich (dat.) etwas zu eigen machen	*adopt sth.*
zu Ende gehen	*draw to a close*
zu Fuß	*on foot*
jemanden zu Rate ziehen	*ask somebody's advice*
jemanden zur Rechenschaft ziehen	*call somebody to account*
zur Sache kommen	*come to the point*
jemandem zur Seite stehen	*give somebody one's support*
zur Welt kommen	*be born*

20.2.10 Less frequent prepositions taking the dative

(a) *ab* **'from'**
ab was originally restricted to commercial and official German, but it is now quite common in colloquial registers.

(i) Referring to place, it is an alternative to *von*, but it emphasises the starting point more strongly:

Ab Jericho folgten wir einer langen Kolonne israelischer Touristenbusse (*Zeit*)	*From Jericho we followed a long convoy of Israeli tourist buses*
Dieser Sondertarif gilt **ab** allen deutschen Flughäfen	*This special fare applies from all airports in Germany*
ab Fabrik	*ex works*

(ii) Referring to time, it is an alternative to *von ... an*, see 11.5.12. If is used without a following determiner (as is usually the case, cf. 4.9.3c), it can take the dative or (rather more frequently) the accusative:

ab neun Uhr, **ab** heute	*from nine o'clock, from today*
ab sofort	*with immediate effect*
ab ersten (erstem) Mai	*from the first of May*
ab nächste(r) Woche	*from next week*
ab meinem 21. Lebensjahr	*from the age of 21*

(b) *binnen* **indicates a period of time (= 'within')**

It is used mainly in formal registers to avoid the potential ambiguity of *in*, cf. 11.5.7:

binnen einem Jahr, drei Jahren	*within a year, three years*
binnen kurzem	*shortly*

In elevated literary usage *binnen* may still occasionally be found with a following genitive, e.g. *binnen eines Jahres*.

In Switzerland *innert* is commonly used for *binnen*, with a following dative or (occasionally) a genitive, e.g. *innert einem/eines Jahres*.

(c) *dank* **'thanks to'**

It is mainly found in formal German and is often used with a genitive, especially with a following plural noun:

dank seinem Einfluß/seines Einflusses	*thanks to his influence*
dank seiner Sprachkenntnisse (*Goes*)	*thanks to his knowledge of languages*

(d) *entgegen* **'contrary to'**

It can occur before or (rather less frequently) after the noun:

entgegen allen Erwartungen allen Erwartungen **entgegen**	*contrary to all expectations*

(e) *entsprechend, gemäß, laut, zufolge* **'according to'**

These prepositions are used chiefly in formal German. They all mean 'according to', as does the more frequent *nach*, see. 20.2.6d, but they are not interchangeable in all contexts:

(i) *entsprechend* means 'in accordance with'. It can precede or (more commonly) follow the noun:

unseren Anordnungen **entsprechend** **entsprechend** unseren Anordnungen	*in accordance with our instructions*

(ii) *gemäß* usually follows the noun, but occasionally precedes it. It has the sense of 'in accordance with':

Die Maschine wurde den Anweisungen **gemäß** in Betrieb gesetzt	*The machine was put into operation in accordance with the instructions*

gemäß is occasionally heard with a genitive in spoken German. This usage is substandard.

(iii) *laut* introduces a verbatim report of something said or written. It is commonly used without a following article, cf. 4.9.3:

Laut Berichten soll Saddam Hussein neue Verhandlungen vorgeschlagen haben	*According to reports Saddam Hussein has proposed fresh negotiations*
laut Gesetz	*according to the law*
laut Helmut Kohl	*according to Helmut Kohl*

If the following noun has an article (or an adjective) with it, it is often in the genitive rather than the dative:

laut des Berichtes/dem Bericht aus Bonn	*according to the report from Bonn*
laut neuer Berichte/neuen Berichten	*according to recent reports*
laut ämtlichem Nachweis/ämtlichen Nachweises	*according to an official attestation*

(iv) *zufolge* follows the noun. In accepted usage it indicates a consequence:

Dem Vertrag **zufolge** werden nun große Mengen von Rohöl geliefert	*In accordance with the contract large quantities of crude oil are now being delivered*

It is also used where there is no sense of a consequence or a result. This usage has been frowned on by purists, but it is very widespread:

unbestätigen Berichten **zufolge**	*according to unconfirmed reports*
einem Regierungssprecher **zufolge**	*according to a government spokesman*

The use of *zufolge* with a following noun in the genitive, e.g. *zufolge des Vertrages*, is now obsolete and *infolge* (+ gen.) is used in its stead.

(f) *fern* 'far from' is restricted to elevated registers
It can occur before or (rather less frequently) after the noun:

Sie blieben **fern** der Heimat/ der Heimat **fern**	*They remained far from home*
Europa liegt immer noch **fern** dem britischen Horizont (*Zeit*)	*Europe is still far removed from British horizons*

In practice, *fern von* or *weit von* are more frequent for English 'far from'.

(g) *mitsamt* and *samt* 'together with'
These are restricted to elevated styles. The usual equivalent for 'together with' is *zusammen mit*, or often simply *mit*:

Das große Krögersche Haus stand **mitsamt** seiner würdigen Geschichte zum Verkaufe (*Th. Mann*)	*The great Kröger house, together with its stately history, was up for sale*

(h) *nahe* 'near (to)' is used chiefly in formal registers

ein altes Haus **nahe** dem freien Feld (FR)   *an old house near the open field*

When used in an abstract sense it commonly follows the noun:

Sie war der Verzweiflung **nahe**   *She was close to despair*

(i) *nebst* 'together with', 'in addition to' occurs in formal registers

Sie hatten das Haus **nebst** Obstgarten   *They had rented the house together*
gemietet   *with the orchard*

(j) *zuliebe* 'for the sake of' follows the noun it governs

Ich habe es meiner Mutter **zuliebe** getan   *I did it for my mother's sake*
Dir **zuliebe** gibt es Spargel   *Just for you, we're having asparagus*
wahrscheinlich dem Wald **zuliebe**   *probably for the sake of the forest*
(*Walser*)

(k) *zuwider* 'contrary to' follows the noun it governs
It is an emphatic alternative to *gegen* in formal registers:

Karl handelte seinem Befehl **zuwider**   *Karl acted contrary to his order*

20.3 Prepositions taking the accusative or the dative

Ten prepositions govern the accusative or the dative, i.e.:

an	auf	entlang	hinter	in
neben	über	unter	vor	zwischen

General rules governing the use of the two cases are given in 20.3.1, and the individual prepositions are dealt with in the following sections. For the commoner ones (i.e. *an, auf, in, über, unter* and *vor*) the use with the accusative and the dative is treated separately.

20.3.1 These prepositions govern the accusative if they express direction, but the dative if they express rest

Ich hänge das Bild an **die** Wand   *I'm hanging the picture on the wall*
Das Bild hängt an **der** Wand   *The picture is hanging on the wall*
Wir gingen in **dieses** Zimmer hinein   *We went into this room*
Wir essen in **diesem** Zimmer   *We eat in this room*

However, there are contexts where the reason for the choice of case is less obvious, or where usage varies, i.e.:

(a) Even if direction is involved, the dative is still used if there is no movement in relation to the person or thing denoted by the following noun

Er ging neben **seiner** Frau   *He was walking next to his wife*
Er ging zwischen **seinen** Eltern   *He was walking between his parents*
(His position is constant in relation to his wife or his parents)
Ein Flugzeug kreiste über **der** Stadt   *A plane was circling over the town*
(Though it was moving, it stayed over the town)

Usage where two prepositional phrases occur in the same sentence with a verb of motion follows the basic principle, e.g.: *Elke legte sich auf eine Bank im Schatten hin*. Elke is moving in relation to the bench, but the bench is not moving in respect of the shadow.

(b) The dative is usual with verbs of arriving, appearing and disappearing
German does not consider that such verbs indicate movement or direction:

Sie kamen **am** Bahnhof an	*They arrived at the station*
Wir trafen in **der** Hauptstadt ein	*We arrived in the capital*
Sie kehrten in **einer** Gaststätte ein	*They turned in at an inn*
Sie landeten auf **dem** Mond	*They landed on the moon*
Er kroch unter **dem** Tisch hervor	*He crept out from under the table*
Sie erschien hinter **der** Theke	*She appeared behind the counter*
Der Reiter verschwand hinter **dem** Berg	*The horseman disappeared behind the hill*
Sie verbarg sich unter **der** Decke	*She hid under the blanket*

Occasionally with these verbs the sense of movement in a particular direction may be felt so strongly that the accusative is used, e.g. *Er verschwand über das Dach*. Nevertheless, this is quite infrequent.

(c) In a few contexts, these prepositions are used with the accusative after a simple verb, but with the dative after a related prefixed verb
With the prefixed verbs, the action is seen as already completed, whereas with the simple verbs it is visualised as continuing:

(an/fest)binden *tie, fasten*
Das Pferd war an **einen** Baum gebunden
Das Pferd war an **einem** Baum an-/festgebunden

(vor)fahren *drive up*
Der Wagen fuhr vor **den** Bahnhof
Der Wagen fuhr vor **dem** Schloß vor

(auf)hängen *hang (up)*
Sie hängte das Bild an **die** Wand
Sie hängte das Bild an **der** Wand auf

sich (fest)klammern *cling to*
Er klammerte sich an **sie**
Er klammerte sich an **ihr** fest

sich (nieder)legen, -setzen *lie down, sit down*
Sie legte/setzte sich auf **die** Bank
Sie legte/setzte sich auf **der** Bank nieder

(auf)schreiben *write (down)*
Ich schrieb ihre Adresse in **mein** Notizbuch
Ich schrieb ihre Adresse in **meinem** Notizbuch auf

(d) Usage with verbs with the prefix *ein-*
(i) These verbs are often used with *in*, usually followed by the accusative:

Sie stieg in **den** Zug ein	Wir weihten ihn in **das** Geheimnis ein
Ich trug den Namen in **die** Liste ein	Er wickelte sich in **eine** Decke ein

(ii) The accusative is used even in the *sein*-passive, although here usage is rather variable:

> Er war in **eine** Reisedecke eingehüllt   Sie ist in **das** Geheimnis eingeweiht
> Sein Name war in **die/der** Liste eingetragen

(iii) *sich einschließen* is used with either case depending on whether the actual movement is emphasised: *Sie schloß sich in **ihr/ihrem** Zimmer.*

(iv) *sich einfinden, einkehren* and *eintreffen* are followed by a preposition with the dative, as they denote arrival, see (a) above.

(e) With a few verbs usage is idiomatic

In the main these are verbs which do not denote movement as such. The choice of case depends on how native speakers envisage the action, and it can vary. If no preposition is indicated the verb is commonly used with more than one (e.g. *sehen* occurs with *an, auf, in,* etc.)

(i) The dative is usual in conjunction with the following verbs:

> anbringen *fix*   befestigen an *fasten*   drucken *print*   notieren *note*

(ii) The accusative is usual in conjunction with the following verbs:

anbauen an	*build on to*	kleiden in	*clothe in*	verteilen	*distribute*
anschließen	*add on*	münden in	*flow into*	vertieft in	*engrossed in*
gebeugt über	*bent over*	sehen, schauen	*look*	verwickelt in	*involved in*
grenzen an	*border on*	stützen auf	*support*		

(f) The dative and the accusative have different meanings with a few verbs

aufnehmen The accusative implies complete acceptance, the dative that the acceptance is temporary:

> Er ist in **den** Chor aufgenommen worden   *He was admitted into the choir*
> Ich wurde in **seiner** Familie sehr   *I was amiably received in his family*
> freundlich aufgenommen

einführen If there is an idea of direction, the accusative is used, whereas the dative puts the stress on the place:

> Waren in **ein** Land einführen   *import goods into a country*
> (i.e. **nach** Italien)
> Er will die Sitte in **diesem** Land   *He wants to introduce the custom*
> einführen (i.e. **in** Italien)   *in that country*

halten If the gesture is emphasised, the accusative is used, if the position, the dative:

> Er hielt das Buch in **die** Höhe   *He held the book up in the air*
> Er hielt das Buch in **der** Hand   *He held the book in his hand*

klopfen The accusative is the norm, but in the context of knocking on doors, etc., the dative can be used if the emphasis is on the place rather than the action:

> Er klopfte **an die** Tür, **auf den** Tisch   *He knocked on the door, the table*
> Da klopfte es **an der** Haustür   *There was a knock at the front door*
> (i.e. the front door rather than somewhere else)

schreiben   The accusative is used to refer to the action of writing, the dative if the place where something is written is foremost:

Er schrieb es **in sein** Heft	*He wrote it (down) in his notebook*
In seinem Brief schreibt er, daß ...	*He writes in his letter that ...*

(g) In contexts where there is no reference to place, these prepositions are used only or predominantly with one of the two cases
In such idiomatic uses, *auf* and *über* are used with the accusative, all the other prepositions predominantly with the dative. This is particularly evident where these prepositions are used to refer to time, see 11.5, where they are used in prepositional objects, see 18.6, with adjectives, see 6.6, and in all other contexts where they are not used in their literal senses.

20.3.2 *an* (+ dative)

(a) The basic meaning of *an* with the dative is 'on (the side of)'
(i) In this way it contrasts with *auf* (+ dat.), which means 'on (top of)'. *an* (+ dat.) can correspond to English 'on', or, if the person or thing is not actually touching, 'at', 'by' or 'along'. See 20.2.3a for the distinction between *an* (+ dat.) and *bei* in the sense of 'at':

Das Bild hing **an** der Wand	*The picture was hanging on the wall*
am Berg	*on the mountain(side)*
(Compare *auf dem Berg* 'on the mountain top')	
An der Grenze wird kontrolliert	*There's a check at the border*
Wir warteten **an** der Bushaltestelle	*We were waiting at/by the bus-stop*
am Fluß	*on the river(side)*
(Compare *auf dem Fluß* 'on the river' (i.e. in a boat))	
Wir standen **an** der Kirche	*We were standing by the church*
Ich stand **am** Fenster	*I was standing by/at the window*
Sie wohnt **am** See	*She lives by the lake*
die Bäume **am** Flußtal (*Grzimek*)	*The trees along the river valley*

(ii) *an* (+ dat.) is also used for 'on (the underside of)':

Die Lampe hängt **an** der Decke	*The lamp is hanging from the ceiling*
am Himmel	*in the sky*
(Compare *im Himmel* 'in heaven')	

(iii) In older German, *an* was commonly used in the sense of 'down on', and this is still apparent in phrases like *am Boden, an der Erde* 'on the ground', where *auf* is a possible alternative. Compare also *am Strand* 'on the beach', *am Ufer* 'on the bank', etc.

(iv) *an* (+ dat.) is used in three phrases in conjunction with an adverb following the noun. In all these the dative is used since, although movement is involved, there is no indication of direction.

With a following *hin*, see 7.2.3, *an* expresses movement alongside:

Sie gingen **an** der Mauer **hin**	*They were walking along the wall*

an (+ dat.) ... *vorbei* means 'past':

Wir gingen **an** seinem Haus **vorbei**	*We walked past his house*

an (+ dat.) ... *entlang* means 'along', see 20.3.6c.

(b) *an* **(+ dat.) is used with academic and other institutions at which a person is employed**

Sie lehrt **an** der Universität Augsburg	*She teaches at the University of Augsburg*
Er ist Intendant **am** Staatstheater	*He is director at the State Theatre*
Er ist Pfarrer **an** der Peterskirche	*He is the pastor at St Peter's*

(c) *an* **(+ dat.) is used in a number of time expressions**
In particular with dates and days of the week, e.g. *am Dienstag, am 31. August.*
Full details are given in 11.5.1.

(d) *an* **(+ dat.) is used with many nouns, adjectives and verbs meaning 'in respect of', 'in connection with'**
Further details of the use of *an* in this sense with adjectives are given in 6.6.1. For its use in the prepositional object of verbs, see 18.6.2a.

Der Bedarf **an** Arbeitskräften verringert sich	*The demand for labour is decreasing*
Wir haben mehrere Millionen Mark **an** Aufträgen vorliegen	*We have several million marks worth of orders on the books*
Sie hat etwas Eigenartiges **an** sich	*There's something strange about her*
Das Schönste **an** der Sache ist, daß ...	*The best thing about it is that ...*
Sie waren siebzig **an** der Zahl	*They were seventy in number*
Das Land ist arm, reich **an** Bodenschätzen	*The country is poor, rich in natural resources*

an (+ dat.) often indicates the feature *by* which one recognises or notices something:

Ich bemerkte **an** seinem Benehmen, daß ...	*I noticed from his behaviour that ...*
Sie erkannte ihn **an** seinem Bart	*She recognised him by his beard*

(e) *an* **(+ dat.) indicates a partially completed action**
This often provides a way of indicating progressive action, see 14.6.2d:

Sie strickt **an** einem Pullover	*She's knitting a pullover*
Er arbeitet **an** seiner Dissertation	*He's working on his thesis*

(f) Other uses of *an* **(+ dat.)**
(i) *am* is used to form the superlative of adverbs and predicate adjectives, e.g. *am schönsten, am einfachsten*, see 8.4.1.

(ii) In colloquial German *am* is used with the infinitive to express a continuous action, e.g. *Sie ist am Schreiben*, cf. 14.6.2c.

20.3.3 *an* (+ accusative)

(a) *an* **(+ acc.) indicates direction if the destination is** *an* **(+ dat.)**
i.e. in contexts where the ultimate goal of the person or thing will be a position 'on', 'at' or 'by' something.

(i) It most often corresponds to English 'to' (see 20.5.1c) or 'on':

Sie hängte ein Bild **an** die Wand	*She hung the picture on the wall*
Wir gingen **an** die Kirche	*We went to the church*
Sie fuhr **an** die Küste	*She drove to the coast*

Similarly:

> Ich ging **ans** Fenster, **an** die Tür, **an** seinen Platz
> Er kam **an** die Bushaltestelle, **an** den Waldrand

(ii) The idea of *right up to* somebody or something can be indicated by adding *heran*, cf. 7.2.4b, e.g.:

> Sie trat **an** mich **an** den Tisch **heran**   *She walked up to me, to the table*

(iii) *an* occurs commonly with the person to whom one addresses something:

> Er richtete diese Frage **an** mich   *He addressed this question to me*
> eine Bitte **an** den Bundeskanzler   *a request to the Federal Chancellor*
> Ich werde mich **an** ihn um Rat wenden   *I shall turn to him for advice*

(b) Verbal nouns from verbs which take a dative usually govern *an* (+ acc.)
Cf. 18.4. The dative object of the verb appears in the prepositional phrase with *an*:

> die Anpassung **an** die neuen Verhältnisse   *adaptation to new circumstances*
> (Compare: *Er paßt sich **den neuen Verhältnissen** an*.)
> sein Befehl **an** die Truppen   *his order to the troops*
> (Compare: *Er befahl **den Truppen** . . .*)

Similarly:

> eine Antwort **an** mich   ein Bericht **an** die Akademie
> viele Grüße **an** Onkel Robert   die Kriegserklärung **an** Japan
> der Verkauf des Hauses **an** meinen Sohn   sein Vermächtnis **an** seine Tochter
> der Verrat von Geheimnissen **an** den Feind

NB: For the use of *an* (+ acc.) in this sense with verbs in place of a dative, see 18.4.2d.

(c) *an* (+ acc.) is used to indicate indefinite quantity

> Er verdient **an die** 5000 im Monat   *He earns getting on for 5000 a month*

an in this sense is often followed by the definite article. A following adjective has strong endings: *an die vierzig **ausländische** Gäste*.

(d) Some idiomatic uses of *an* (+ acc.)

> etwas ans Licht, an den Tag bringen   *bring sth. to light*
> an (und für) sich   *actually*
> die Erinnerung an seine Jugend   *the memory of his youth*
> der Glaube an den Sieg   *the belief in victory*

NB: For the use of *an* (+ acc.) in prepositional objects with verbs denoting mental processes, see 18.6.2b.

20.3.4 *auf* (+ dative)

(a) The basic meaning of *auf* (+ dat.) is 'on (top of)'
For the distinction between this and *an* (+ dat.), see 20.3.2a.

> Das Buch liegt **auf** dem Tisch   *The book is lying on the table*
> Sie sind **auf** dem Mond gelandet   *They landed on the moon*
> Die Katze spielt **auf** dem Rasen   *The cat is playing on the lawn*
> **auf** dem Weg nach Stuttgart   *on the way to Stuttgart*

(b) *auf* **(+ dat.) is used for English 'at' or 'in' in some contexts**
(i) For formal occasions, e.g. weddings, conferences, parties, etc.:

Ich traf sie **auf** einem Empfang	*I met her at a reception*
Wir lernten uns **auf** ihrer Hochzeit kennen	*We met at their wedding*
Sie ist **auf** einer Tagung	*She's at a conference*

bei is a common alternative to *auf* in this sense, but there may be a slight difference in meaning, cf. 20.2.3b

(ii) With few other nouns, where idiomatic usage may differ from English:

Die Schafe sind **auf** der Wiese	*The sheep are in the meadow*
Er ist **auf** seinem Zimmer	*He is (up) in his room*
auf dem Land(e)	*in the country*
Die Kinder spielten **auf** der Straße	*The children were playing in the street*

NB: *in* (+ dat.) is used to refer to a particular street, e.g. *Wir wohnen in der Schillerstraße. Das Unglück ereignete sich in unserer Straße.*

Similarly:

auf dem (Bauern)hof	*on the farm*	auf dem Gang	*in the corridor*
auf ihrer Bude	*in her digs*	auf seinem Gut	*on his estate*
auf dem Feld	*in the field*	auf dem Hof	*in the yard*
auf dem Flur	*in the (entrance-)hall*	auf der Toilette	*on the toilet*

(iii) With a few nouns denoting public buildings and places. With several of these *auf* is obsolescent, especially in spoken German. In this case, the preposition which is more frequently used nowadays is given in brackets:

auf dem Bahnhof (an)	auf dem Markt(platz)	auf dem Rathaus (in)
auf der Bank (in)	auf der Post	auf der Universität (an)
auf der Bibliothek (in)		

(c) Some idiomatic uses of *auf* **(+ dat.)**

blind auf einem Auge	*blind in one eye*
Das hat nichts, viel auf sich	*There's nothing, a lot to that*
etwas auf dem Herzen haben	*have sth. on one's mind*
Sie liefen auf dem Feld herum	*They were running all over the field*
auf der Jagd sein	*be hunting*
auf der anderen Seite	*on the other hand*
auf der Stelle	*immediately*

20.3.5 *auf* (+ accusative)

(a) *auf* **(+ acc.) indicates direction if the destination is** *auf* **(+ dat.)**
i.e. in contexts where the ultimate goal of the person or thing will be a position 'on (top of)' or 'at' something.

(i) *auf* (+ acc.) usually corresponds to English 'on(to)':

Sie legte das Buch **auf** den Tisch	*She put the book on the table*
Die Katze sprang **auf** das Dach	*The cat leapt onto the roof*

(ii) Where German uses *auf* (+ dat.) for English 'at' or 'in', *auf* (+ acc.) usually corresponds to English 'into' or 'to':

Wir gingen **auf** das Feld	*We went into the field*
Er ging **auf** sein Zimmer	*He went (up) to his room*
Er geht **auf** die Toilette	*He's going to the toilet*

This use of *auf* (+ acc.) is rather restricted in modern German. More details are given in 20.5.1b.

(iii) *auf* (+ acc.) ... *zu* indicates direction (i.e. = 'towards'):

Sie kam **auf** mich **zu**	*She came towards me/approached me*
Sie ging **auf** die Tore des Friedhofs **zu**	*She went towards the cemetery gates*

(b) *auf* (+ acc.) indicates a period of time extending from 'now'
e.g. *Ich fahre auf vier Wochen in die Schweiz*. For details see 11.5.2. The prepositional adverb *darauf* is used in the sense of 'after(wards)', cf. 11.6.4b, e.g. *am Tag darauf* 'the day after'.

NB: *auf* (+ acc.) is similarly used to indicate a distance <u>from</u> here, e.g.: *Kurven auf fünf Kilometer* 'bends for 5 kilometres'.

(c) *auf* (+ acc.) is used after a large number of adjectives and verbs
e.g.: *Sie ist neidisch **auf** ihn. Ich wartete vor dem Bahnhof **auf** sie.*
For the use of *auf* with adjectives, see 6.6.1, with verbs in prepositional objects, see 18.6.3a.

(d) *auf* (+ acc.) can denote 'in response to', 'as a result of'
In this sense it is often strengthened by a following *hin*, cf. 7.2.3c:

Auf meine Bitte (**hin**) hat er die Sache für sich behalten	*At my request he kept the matter to himself*
Er hat sofort **auf** meinen Brief **hin** gehandelt	*He acted immediately following my letter*

Similarly:

auf Anfrage	*on application*
auf meine Empfehlung (hin)	*on my recommendation*
auf einen Verdacht hin	*on the strength of a suspicion*
auf Wunsch, auf meinen Wunsch (hin)	*by request, at my request*
daraufhin	*as a result, thereupon*

(e) Other uses of *auf* (+ acc.)
(i) With languages:

Sie hat mir **auf deutsch** geantwortet	*She answered me in German*

but *in* (+ dat.) is also used, especially with extended phrases:

Er hält seine Vorlesungen **in Deutsch** /**auf deutsch**	*He gives his lectures in German*
Er sagte es **in gebrochenem Deutsch**	*He said it in broken German*
Wie heißt das **in Ihrer Sprache**?	*What's that called in your language?*

(ii) To form absolute superlatives, e.g. *aufs angenehmste, aufs peinlichste*. See 8.4.3 for further details.

(iii) Some common idiomatic expressions with *auf*:

jemanden auf den Arm, auf die Schippe (north German) nehmen	*pull somebody's leg*
etwas auf die lange Bank schieben	*put sth. off*
auf den ersten Blick	*at first sight*
Das kommt, läuft auf dasselbe hinaus	*It comes down to the same thing*
auf jeden Fall, auf alle Fälle	*in any case*
auf eigene Gefahr	*at one's own risk*
auf eigene Kosten	*at one's own expense*
jemandem auf die Nerven gehen, auf den Wecker gehen, fallen	*get on somebody's nerves*
Das geht auf meine Rechnung	*This one's on me*
auf diese Weise	*in this way*

20.3.6 *entlang*

entlang (often shortened to *lang* in colloquial speech) corresponds to English 'along'. There is much variation in its use, both in respect of the position of the noun and the case used, see Durrell (1993), but predominant usage in modern German makes it appropriate to deal with it under this group of prepositions.

(a) To indicate position alongside an extended object, *entlang* precedes a noun in the dative

im Sommer, wenn **entlang den** Boulevards und in den Vorgärten Rosen blühen (*Zeit*)	*in summer when roses are blooming along the boulevards and in the front gardens*
die Männer, die **entlang der** Küchenwand saßen (*Welt*)	*the men sitting along the kitchen wall*
Bäume standen **entlang der** Bahnlinie	*Trees stood along the railway line*

As an alternative, *entlang* is quite frequently used in formal written German with a following *genitive* to express position:

die Uferpromenade **entlang des** Rheins (*MM*)	*the promenade along the bank of the Rhine*

entlang is very occasionally used with a *preceding* dative or accusative to express position:

die Straße, die Mussolini **der Küste entlang** gebaut hat (*Grzimek*)	*the road which Mussolini built along the coast*
Flaschen und Gläser standen **die lange Tafel entlang** (*Welt*)	*Bottles and glasses were standing along the long table*

(b) To indicate movement alongside an extended object, or down the middle of a road or river, *entlang* follows a noun in the accusative

Gehst du die Reihen der Maschinen **entlang** (*ND*)	*If you walk along the rows of machines*
Sie gingen den Bach **entlang**	*They were walking along the stream*
Sie hastete den Flur **entlang** bis zum Ende des Ganges (*Johnson*)	*She hurried along the entrance-hall to the end of the corridor*
Sie laufen die Feldwege **entlang** (*Strittmatter*)	*They are running along the tracks through the fields*

Occasionally, *entlang* is used with a preceding *dative* to indicate movement alongside:

> Wir flogen gar nicht der Küste **entlang** (*Frisch*)
>
> *We were not flying along the coast at all*

(c) *an* **(+ dat.)** *entlang* **is a common alternative to simple** *entlang*
It can be used with reference to position or movement alongside an extended object, but not for 'down the middle' of roads, rivers, etc.:

> Da gab es **an** der nördlichen Friedhofsmauer **entlang** den Bittweg (*Grass*)
>
> *Along the north wall of the cemetery was the Bittweg*
>
> Er steuerte **am** Ufer **entlang**, bis die Stelle gefunden war (*Frisch*)
>
> *He steered along the bank until he had found the spot*

(d) Alternatives to *entlang* **in the meaning 'along'**
(i) *längs*, cf. 20.4.3, only expresses position. It governs a following genitive or (less commonly) a dative, e.g. *längs der Küste, längs des Flusses/dem Fluß*.

(ii) *an* (+ dat.), see 20.3.2a, often appears in contexts where English could naturally use 'along', e.g.:

> **An der Küste** war das Wetter schön
>
> *The weather was fine along the coast*

an (+ dat.) ... *hin* can refer to movement alongside something, especially when one is very close to it or in contact with it:

> Sie ging **an der Mauer hin**
>
> *She went along the wall*
>
> Er rutschte **am Boden hin**
>
> *He slid along the floor*

20.3.7 *hinter*

(a) *hinter* **is used almost exclusively with reference to place and usually corresponds to English 'behind'**
(i) Used with a following dative, *hinter* indicates position:

> Der Wagen steht **hinter** der Garage
>
> *The car is behind the garage*
>
> Ich habe das Schlimmste **hinter** mir
>
> *I've got the worst behind me*
>
> 100 Kilometer **hinter** der Grenze
>
> *100 kilometres beyond the border*

(ii) Used with a following accusative, *hinter* indicates direction:

> Er fuhr den Wagen **hinter** die Garage
>
> *He drove the car round the back of the garage*
>
> Sie trieben ihn **hinter** die Kirche
>
> *They drove him round the back of the church*

(b) To indicate movement in relation to another person or thing, *hinter* **is used with a following** *her*
See also 7.2.3b. The noun is always in the dative:

> Er rannte **hinter** ihr **her**
>
> *He was running after her*
>
> Ich ging **hinter** meinen Eltern **her**
>
> *I was walking behind my parents*

(c) *hinter* **is used in a few idiomatic expressions**

Ich konnte nicht dahinter kommen	*I couldn't get to the bottom of it*
Es muß etwas dahinter stecken	*There must be something in it*
Schreib dir das hinter die Ohren!	*Will you get that into your thick head!*

20.3.8 *in* (+ dative)

(a) The basic meaning of *in* (+ dat.) is 'in(side)'

Sie ist im Haus, im Freien, in der	*She is in the house, in the open air, in*
Kirche, im Kino, in der Stadt,	*the church, in the cinema, in town, in*
im Wald, im Tal, in ihrem Zimmer	*the forest, in the valley, in her room*
Sie sind in Bremen, in Deutschland,	*They are in Bremen, in Germany, in*
in der Schweiz, im Ausland	*Switzerland, abroad*
Die Milch ist im Kühlschrank	*The milk is in the fridge*
Die Sonne geht im Westen unter	*The sun sets in the west*

NB: In colloquial German *in* is often strengthened by adding *drin*, e.g.: *Die sind in der Hütte drin*.

In a few contexts, German usage is at variance with English, e.g.:

Ihr Büro ist im vierten Stock	*Her office is on the fourth floor*
Das habe ich im Fernsehen gesehen,	*I saw it on the television, heard it*
im Radio gehört	*on the radio*

In particular, German uses *in* with reference to attendance at public buildings and the like, where English often uses 'at':

Die Kinder sind heute in der Schule	*The children are at school today*
Meine Eltern sind in der Kirche	*My parents are at church*
Elke ist im Kino, im Theater, in	*Elke is at the cinema, at the*
einem Konzert, im Rathaus, in der	*theatre, at a concert, at the*
Bibliothek	*town hall, at the library*

(b) *in* **(+ dat.) indicates a period of time**
e.g. *In drei Wochen sind wir wieder da.* Full details are given in 11.5.7.

(c) Some common idiomatic phrases with *in* (+ dat.)

in der Absicht, etwas zu tun	*with the intention of doing something*
im allgemeinen	*in general*
Ist dein Chef im Bilde?	*Is your boss in the picture?*
im Durchschnitt	*on average*
nicht im geringsten/entferntesten	*not in the slightest*
in dieser Hinsicht	*in this respect*
in gewissem Maße	*to a certain extent*
in dieser Weise	*in this way*
(also: **auf diese** Weise)	
in diesem Zusammenhang	*in this context*

20.3.9 *in* (+ accusative)

(a) *in* **(+ acc.) indicates direction if the destination is *in* (+ dat.)**
i.e. in contexts where the ultimate goal of the person or thing will be a position 'in(side)' something.

(i) It often corresponds to English 'into':

Sie ging **ins** Haus, **in** die Kirche, **in** den Wald, **in** das Tal, **in** ihr Zimmer	*She went into the house, the church, the forest, the valley, her room*
Ich habe die Milch **in** den Kühlschrank gestellt	*I put the milk in the fridge*

NB: With *Richtung* the accusative or the dative are equally acceptable alternatives, e.g. *in diese/dieser Richtung.*

(ii) It is a common equivalent of English 'to', if, on arrival, one will be *in* the place concerned, cf. 20.5.1a:

Sie ging **in** ein Konzert, **ins** Kino, **in** den vierten Stock	*She went to a concert, to the cinema, to the fourth floor*
Wir sind **in** die Schweiz, **ins** Ausland gefahren	*We went to Switzerland, abroad*
Die Kinder gehen heute **in** die Schule	*The children are going to school today*
Die Kinder gehen **in** die Schule	*The children go to school*

(b) Some frequent idiomatic phrases with *in* (+ acc.)

Der Vorteil springt ins Auge	*The advantage is obvious*
sich in Bewegung setzen	*begin to move*
mit jemandem ins Gespräch kommen	*get into conversation with sb.*
aus dem Französischen ins Deutsche übersetzen	*translate from French into German*
die Verhandlungen in die Länge ziehen	*drag the negotiations out*

20.3.10 *neben*

(a) *neben* **is most often used with reference to place**

It usually corresponds to English 'next to' or 'beside':

(i) Used with a following dative, *neben* indicates position:

Die Blumen standen **neben** dem Schrank	*The flowers were next to the cupboard*
Das Geschäft ist **neben** dem Verkehrsverein	*The shop is next to the tourist information office*
Er saß **neben** seiner Frau	*He was sitting next to his wife*

(ii) Used with a following accusative, *neben* indicates direction. It can be strengthened by adding *hin*, cf. 7.2.3a:

Er stellte die Blumen **neben** den Schrank (hin)	*He put the flowers (down) next to the cupboard*
Er setzte sich **neben** seine Frau (hin)	*He sat down next to his wife*

(b) To indicate movement in relation to another person or thing, *neben* is used with a following *her*

See also 7.2.3b. The noun is always in the dative:

Er ging **neben** seiner Frau **her**	*He was walking by the side of his wife*

(c) *neben* **(+ dat.) can be used in the sense of 'besides', 'apart from'**

Its sense is close to that of *außer*, cf. 20.2.2a:

Neben zwei Franzosen waren alle Anwesenden aus Deuschland	*Apart from two Frenchmen all those present were from Germany*

(d) *neben* **(+ dat.) can be used to express a comparison**

It is a common alternative to *gegen* or *gegenüber*, cf. 20.2.4c:

Neben ihrer Mutter ist sie groß	*She's tall compared with her mother*

(e) The prepositional adverb *daneben* is often used with verbs to express the idea of failing to hit a target

It is usually interpreted as a separable prefix, see 22.5.2, and written together with the verb:

Er hat danebengeschossen	*He shot wide of the mark*
Sie hat sich danebenbenommen	*She behaved quite abominably*

20.3.11 *über* (+ dative)

With a dative, *über* is only used to refer to position. It corresponds to English 'over', 'above' or, in certain contexts, 'across' or 'beyond':

Das Bild hängt **über** meinem Tisch	*The picture hangs over my desk*
Briançon liegt 1400 Meter **über** dem Meeresspiegel	*Briançon lies 1400 metres above sea level*
Der Baum lag mir (quer) **über** dem Weg	*The tree lay across my path*
Er wohnt **über** der Grenze	*He lives over/across the border*
Sie wohnt **über** dem See	*She lives across/beyond the lake*

20.3.12 *über* (+ accusative)

(a) *über* **(+ acc.) indicates movement over a person or object**

It can correspond to English 'above', 'over', 'across' or (with reference to a journey) 'via':

Sie hängte das Bild **über** meinen Tisch	*She hung the picture over/above my desk*
Wir gingen **über** die Straße	*We crossed the road*
die neue Brücke **über** den Inn	*the new bridge over/across the Inn*
Der Baum fiel uns (quer) **über** den Weg	*The tree fell across our path*
Er ist **über** die Grenze geflüchtet	*He fled over the border*
Es lief mir eiskalt **über** den Rücken	*An ice-cold shiver went down my back*
Wir sind **über** die Schweiz nach Italien gefahren	*We drove to Italy through Switzerland*
Dieser Zug fährt nach Mannheim **über** Heidelberg	*This train goes to Mannheim via Heidelberg*

More idiomatic:

Der Kaiser herrschte **über** viele Länder	*The emperor ruled over many countries*

If the movement involved is parallel to a surface, *über* (+ acc.) can be strengthened by adding *hin*, cf. 7.2.3a:

Die Wildenten flogen **über** den See (**hin**)	*The wild ducks were flying over the lake*

(b) *über* **(+ acc.) is used in more abstract senses of 'above' or 'beyond'**

In the sense of going 'beyond' a limitation it can be strengthened by adding *hinaus*:

Diese Aufgabe geht **über** meine Fähigkeiten (**hinaus**)	*This task goes beyond my capabilities*
Er liebt die Ruhe **über** alles **darüber hinaus**	*He likes quiet above all things over and above that*

(c) *über* **(+ acc.) occurs in a few time expressions in the sense of 'over'**
For details, see 11.5.10.

(d) *über* **(+ acc.) has the sense of 'over', 'more than' with quantities**
e.g. *Es hat über tausend Mark gekostet; Kinder über zehn Jahre*, etc. See 9.1.6 for
further details of this usage and the distinction between the adverbial and
prepositional usage of *über* with quantities.

(e) *über* **(+ acc.) is used in the sense of 'about', 'concerning'**

seine Ansicht **über** eine mögliche Wiedervereinigung	*his views concerning a possible reunification*
ein Buch **über** die europäischen Vögelarten	*a book about European bird species*
meine Freude **über** ihren Erfolg	*my delight at her success*
Er beschwerte sich **über** den kaputten Fernsehapparat	*He complained about the broken television set*
Sie war ärgerlich **über** ihn	*She was annoyed at him*

NB: This usage is particularly frequent with nouns, adjectives (see 6.6.1) and in the
prepositional object of verbs of saying, etc. (see 18.6.9a).

20.3.13 *unter* (+ dative)

(a) With reference to place, *unter* **(+ dat.) corresponds to English
'under(neath)', 'beneath', 'below'**

Manfred lag **unter** dem Tisch	*Manfred was lying under(neath) the table*
200 Meter **unter** dem Gipfel	*200 metres below the summit*
Das Land steht **unter** Wasser	*The land is under water*
unter Tage	*below ground / underground (of miners)*
Sie trug die Tasche **unter** dem Arm	*She was carrying her bag under her arm*
unter dem Schutz der Dunkelheit	*under cover of darkness*
unter Zwang handeln	*act under duress*

(b) *unter* **(+ dat.) is a common equivalent for English 'among(st)'**

Hier bist du **unter** Freunden	*You're among friends here*
Ich fand das Rezept **unter** meinen Papieren	*I found the prescription among my papers*
Es waren viele Ausländer **unter** den Zuschauern	*There were a lot of foreigners among the spectators*
unter uns gesagt	*between ourselves*
unter vier Augen	*in private*
unter anderem (u.a.)	*amongst other things*

zwischen can also correspond to English 'among', cf. 20.3.17a. It is preferred if
unter could be understood to mean 'under'. Compare:

Das Haus steht **unter Bäumen**	*The house stands under some trees*
Das Haus steht **zwischen Bäumen**	*The house stands amongst some trees*

(c) *unter* **(+ dat.) is used to indicate circumstances**

unter diesen Umständen	*under these circumstances*
unter allen Umständen	*in any case*
unter den größten Schwierigkeiten	*with the greatest difficulty*

unter dieser Bedingung	*on this condition*
unter diesem Vorwand	*on this pretext*
Sie starb **unter** großen Schmerzen	*She died in great pain*
Er gestand **unter** Tränen	*He confessed amid tears*
unter Vorspiegelung falscher Tatsachen	*on false pretences*

(d) *unter* **(+ dat.) has the sense of 'under', 'below' with reference to quantity**

e.g. *Es hat unter tausend Mark gekostet.* See 9.1.6 for further details of this usage and the distinction between the adverbial and prepositional usage of *unter* with quantities.

20.3.14 *unter* (+ accusative)

(a) *unter* **(+ acc.) indicates direction if the destination is *unter* (+ dat.)**
i.e. where English has 'under(neath)', 'below', 'among':

Manfred kroch **unter** den Tisch	*Manfred crawled under the table*
Sie steckte die Tasche **unter** ihren Arm	*She put her bag under her arm*
Er tauchte den Kopf **unter** das Wasser	*He dipped his head under the water*
Wir gingen **unter** die Brücke hindurch	*We walked under the bridge*
Sie ging **unter** die Menge	*She went among the crowd*

(b) **Some common idiomatic expressions with *unter* (+ acc.)**

jemanden unter die Arme greifen	*come to somebody's assistance*
sein Licht unter den Scheffel stellen	*hide one's light under a bushel*
etwas unter den Tisch fallen lassen	*let sth. go by the board*

20.3.15 *vor* (+ dative)

(a) **With reference to place, *vor* (+ dat.) means 'in front of', 'ahead of'**

Das Auto steht **vor** der Garage	*The car is in front of the garage*
Der Himalaja lag **vor** uns	*The Himalayas lay before us*
Der Nashorn hatte ein paar Meter **vor** dem Wagen gestoppt (*Grzimek*)	*The rhinoceros had stopped within a few yards of the car*
vor ihm in einiger Entfernung	*some distance ahead of him*
vor Gericht erscheinen	*appear in court*
Die Insel liegt **vor** der deutschen Ostseeküste	*The island lies off the Baltic coast of Germany*

(b) **To indicate movement in relation to another person or thing, *vor* (+ dat.) is used with a following *her***
See also 7.2.3b:

Vor uns **her** fuhr ein roter BMW	*A red BMW was driving along ahead of us*

(c) *vor* **is used in time expressions with the sense of 'ago' or 'before'**
e.g. *vor zwei Jahren, vor Weihnachten.* For details, see 11.5.13.

(d) *vor* **can be used to indicate cause or reason**
In this sense, *vor* (+ dat.) normally occurs without a following article:

Man konnte **vor** Lärm nichts hören	*You couldn't hear anything for the noise*
Ich war außer mir **vor** Wut	*I was beside myself with rage*
Ich konnte **vor** Aufregung nicht einschlafen	*I couldn't get to sleep with the excitement*

Vor Nebel war nichts zu sehen	*You couldn't see anything for the fog*
Sie gähnte **vor** Langeweile	*She yawned from boredom*
Sie warnte mich **vor** dem Hund	*She warned me of the dog*
blaß **vor** Furcht, gelb **vor** Neid	*pale with fear, green with envy*

In contrast to *aus*, cf. 20.2.1c, which points to a voluntary cause or reason, *vor* (+ dat.) always expresses a cause which is *involuntary*.

This use of *vor* (+ dat.) is very common with adjectives, cf. 6.6.1, and in the prepositional object of verbs, see 18.6.12.

20.3.16 *vor* (+ accusative)

(a) *vor* (+ acc.) **indicates direction if the destination is** *vor* **(+ dat.)**

Ich fuhr den Wagen **vor** die Garage	*I drove up in front of the garage*
Sie stellte sich **vor** mich	*She stood in front of me*
Alle traten **vor** den Vorhang	*Everyone stepped out in front of the curtain*
Die Sache kommt **vor** Gericht	*The case is coming to court*

(b) *vor sich hin* **means 'to oneself'**

Cf. 7.2.5, e.g.:

Sie las **vor** sich **hin**	*She was reading to herself*
Ich murmelte etwas **vor** mich **hin**	*I muttered something to myself*

20.3.17 *zwischen*

(a) *zwischen* **is used with reference to place or time in the sense of English 'between'**

(i) *zwischen* (+ dat.) indicates position:

Ich saß **zwischen** dem Minister und seiner Frau	*I was sitting between the minister and his wife*
Das Geschäft liegt **zwischen** dem Kino und der Post	*The shop is between the cinema and the post office*
Die Tagung fand **zwischen** dem 4. und dem 11. Oktober statt	*The conference took place between the 4th and the 11th of October*
zwischen den Zeilen lesen	*read between the lines*

zwischen can also correspond to English 'among(st)' if more than two objects are involved:

Pilze wuchsen zwischen den Bäumen	*Toadstools were growing among(st) the trees*

NB: See 20.3.13b for the distinction between *unter* and *zwischen* to mean 'among'.

(ii) *zwischen* (+ acc.) indicates direction:

Ich setzte mich **zwischen** den Minister und seine Frau	*I sat down between the minister and his wife*
Wir legen die Tagung **zwischen** den 4. und den 11. Oktober	*We are arranging the conference for the 4th and the 11th of October*

(b) To indicate movement in relation to another person or thing, *zwischen* (+ dat.) is used with a following *her*

See also 7.2.3b. The noun is always in the dative:

Ich ging **zwischen** meinen Eltern **her**	*I was walking between my parents*

(c) *zwischen* **(+ dat.) has the sense of 'between' with reference to quantity**
e.g. *Kinder zwischen dem 10. und dem 15. Lebensjahr.* See 9.1.6 for further details of
this usage and the distinction between the adverbial and prepositional usage of
zwischen with expressions of quantity.

20.4 Prepositions taking the genitive

The prepositions governing the genitive fall into three main groups, i.e.:

(i) Four common prepositions, dealt with in 20.4.1:

> (an)statt   trotz   während   wegen

These are normally used with the genitive in formal German, but are often found
with a dative in colloquial speech.

(ii) Eight prepositions expressing place relationships, see 20.4.2:

> außerhalb   oberhalb   diesseits   unweit
> innerhalb   unterhalb   jenseits
> beid(er)seits

These are often used with a following *von* rather than a genitive.

(iii) A large number of prepositions with rather specialised meanings which are
hardly used outside very formal (often official) registers. They are listed and
explained in 20.4.3.

20.4.1 The four common prepositions which govern the genitive

(a) *(an)statt* **'instead of'**

(i) Examples of the use of *statt*:

Statt eines Fernsehers hat sie sich eine neue Stereoanlage gekauft	*Instead of a television she bought herself a new stereo system*
Statt eines Briefes schickte er ihr eine Postkarte	*Instead of a letter he sent her a postcard*
statt dessen	*instead (of that)*

(ii) *(an)statt* can be used as a conjunction rather than a preposition, i.e. as an
alternative to *und nicht*. In this construction the noun has the same case as the
noun immediately preceding *statt* with which it is linked:

Ich besuchte meinen Onkel **statt** (= und nicht) meinen Bruder	*I visited my uncle instead of my brother*
Ihr Haus hat sie mir **statt** (= und nicht) ihm vermacht	*She left her house to me instead of to him*

statt is always used in this way if it links prepositional phrases or personal pronouns:

Ich schreibe jetzt mit einem Filzstift **statt** mit einem Füller	*I write with a felt-tip now instead of with a fountain-pen*

(iii) *anstelle von* is a common alternative to *(an)statt*. It often sounds less stilted:

Wir gebrauchen jetzt Margarine **anstelle von** Butter	*We use margarine instead of butter now*

NB: (i) The longer form *anstatt* is less frequent; it occurs chiefly in formal written German.

(ii) For infinitive phrases with *(an)statt … zu* and the conjunction *(an)statt daß* see 13.2.7c.

(b) *trotz* 'despite', 'in spite of'

Wir sind am Sonntag **trotz** des starken Regens nach Eulbach gewandert	*We walked to Eulbach on Sunday despite the heavy rain*

(c) *während* 'during'

e.g. *während des Sommers* 'during the summer'. Details on the use of *während* are given in 11.5.14.

(d) *wegen* 'because of', 'for the sake of'

(i) *wegen* normally precedes the noun it governs, but it sometimes follows in formal registers:

Wir konnten **wegen** des Regens nicht kommen	*We couldn't come because of the rain*
Er mußte **wegen** zu schnellen Fahrens eine Geldstrafe bezahlen	*He had to pay a fine because he had been driving too fast*
Er wich jeder Schafherde aus, nicht der Schafe **wegen**, sondern um den Geruch der Hirten zu umgehen (*Süßkind*)	*He avoided all the flocks of sheep, not because of the sheep, but to avoid the smell of the shepherds*

(ii) *wegen* is sometimes used in the sense of 'about', 'concerning':

Wegen deiner Reise muß ich noch mit der Astrid sprechen	*I've still got to talk to Astrid about your trip*

(iii) The combination *von* (+ gen.) *wegen* occurs in a few set phrases:

von Amts wegen	*ex officio*
von Berufs wegen	*by virtue of one's profession*
von Rechts wegen	*legally, by rights*

(iv) The combination *von wegen* (+ dat.) is common in colloquial German to mean 'because of' or 'concerning'. It is regarded as substandard:

Jetzt hört mir nur auf **von wegen** Idealismus (*Valentin*)	*For goodness' sake stop talking about idealism*

It is very frequent in isolation to challenge a previous statement:

Also, heute abend bezahlst du alles – **Von wegen!**	*So, you're paying for everything tonight – No way!*

NB: For the forms of personal pronouns with *wegen* (*meinetwegen, ihretwegen*, etc.), see 3.1.2c.

(e) The use of *(an)statt, trotz, während* and *wegen* with a dative

Although these prepositions are normally followed by the genitive case in standard German, in certain conditions they are used with a dative.

(i) They are very commonly used with a following dative in everyday colloquial speech. This reflects the general avoidance of the genitive in informal registers, cf. 2.3. Examples:

> Ich konnte **wegen dem Regen** nicht kommen
> **Während dem Mittagessen** hat sie uns etwas über ihren Urlaub erzählt

(ii) Although the use of the dative with these prepositions is generally considered substandard and avoided in writing, it is accepted (or at least tolerated) in a number of constructions, i.e.:

If they are followed by a plural noun which is not accompanied by a declined determiner or adjective:

> während fünf **Jahren**   wegen ein paar **Hindernissen**

If the noun they govern is preceded by a possessive genitive:

> während Vaters **kurzem Urlaub**   wegen des Kanzlers **langem Schweigen**

To avoid the use of the genitive of the personal pronouns, cf. 3.1.2:

> Langsam fahren – **wegen uns**! (on a road sign outside a Kindergarten)

To avoid consecutive genitives in *-(e)s*, cf. 2.4.2a:

> **trotz dem Rollen** des Zuges (*Th. Mann*)

If the following noun has no determiner with it. In this construction the omission of the genitive ending is optional, see 1.3.7e:

> **trotz Geldmangel(s)**   wegen **Amtsmißbrauch(s)**

To achieve a particular stylistic effect:

> Freies Denken **statt starrem Lenken** (slogan on an election poster)

A following relative pronoun may be in the dative:

> seit dem Ende des zweiten Weltkriegs, während **dem** die Stadt Salzburg zahlreiche Bombenangriffe erleiden mußte (*Baedeker*)

(iii) The use of the dative is the norm with *trotz* in written Swiss and Austrian usage:

Die Koalition wird deshalb vorerst wahrscheinlich trotz **dem neuerlichen Scheitern** überleben (NZZ)	*For this reason the coalition will probably survive for the moment despite its recent failures*

NB: Dative forms are standard in the adverb *trotzdem* 'nevertheless' and the phrase *trotz alledem* 'for all that'.

20.4.2 The eight prepositions denoting position

(a) Meaning and use

(i) *außerhalb* 'outside' and *innerhalb* 'inside', 'within' can be used with reference to place or time:

Sie wohnt **außerhalb** der Stadt	*She lives outside the city*
Das liegt **außerhalb/innerhalb** meines Fachgebietes	*That lies outside/within my specialist field*
Das kann sie **außerhalb** der Arbeitszeit erledigen	*She can finish that outside working hours*
Das wird **innerhalb** eines Jahres geändert werden	*That will be changed within a year*

NB: (i) *außerhalb* and *innerhalb* only denote rest, cf. *Wir gingen aus der Hütte hinaus, in die Hütte hinein* 'We went outside, inside the hut'.
   (ii) Like *binnen* (see 20.2.10b), *innerhalb* can be used to avoid any potential ambiguity with *in*, cf. 11.5.7c.

(ii) *oberhalb* 'above' and *unterhalb* 'below', 'underneath' refer to position and are more specific in meaning than *über* and *unter*:

Oberhalb der Straße war ein Felsenvorsprung	*Above the road there was a rocky ledge*
Ich habe mich **unterhalb** des Knies verletzt	*I injured myself below the knee*
der Rhein **oberhalb/unterhalb** der Stadt Basel	*the Rhine above/below the city of Basle*

(iii) *beid(er)seits* 'on either side of', *diesseits* 'on this side of', *jenseits* 'beyond', 'on the other side of':

in den Bauten **beidseits** des Flusses (FR)	*in the buildings on either side of the river*
diesseits, jenseits der niederländischen Grenze	*on this side, the other side of the Dutch border*

NB: *hinter* is more commonly used for 'beyond' than *jenseits*, especially in everyday German, e.g. *Das Dorf liegt hinter der Grenze, hinter Hannover.*

(iv) *unweit* 'not far from'

Wir standen auf einer Höhe **unweit** des Dorfes	*We were standing on a hill not far from the village*

NB: *unfern*, with the same meaning as *unweit*, is now obsolete. It could be used with the genitive or the dative

(b) All these prepositions are often used with *von* rather than the genitive
(i) This usage is usual in colloquial speech, but it is quite common in writing, too, although many Germans feel the genitive to be more appropriate in formal registers:

Sie wohnt **außerhalb von** der Stadt
Innerhalb von einem Jahr wird alles anders werden
Jenseits von der Grenze standen vier Vopos
ein Dorf **unweit von** Moskau (*Bednarz*)

(ii) The use of *von* is the norm even in written German in those contexts where the common prepositions taking the genitive can be used with a dative (see 20.4.1e), e.g. *innerhalb von drei Jahren.* A following relative pronoun is often in the dative, e.g. *die Zone, innerhalb der* (less commonly: *derer*) *Autos verboten sind.*

20.4.3 Other prepositions governing the genitive

The large number of other prepositions with the genitive are effectively limited to use in formal written German, the majority in official and commercial language. Outside this register, they can sound very stilted. Many of them were originally adverbs, participles or phrases which have come to be used as prepositions, and similar new ones are constantly entering the language. With this proviso, the following list is as complete as possible.

NB: The asterisked prepositions can be used with a dative in the same contexts as with the common prepositions, cf. 20.4.1e:

abseits 'away from'
eine Speisekarte abseits jeglicher Tradition (*Presse*)

*abzüglich 'deducting', 'less':
abzüglich der Unkosten

anfangs 'at the beginning of':
anfangs dieses Jahres (or with the acc. *anfangs nächsten Monat*)

angesichts 'in view of':
angesichts der gegenwärtigen massenhaften Auswanderung von DDR-Bürgern (*Spiegel*)

anhand 'with the aid of', 'from':
anhand einiger Beispiele

NB: *anhand* is sometimes spelled *an Hand*, and is often used with *von*, e.g. *anhand von einigen Beispielen.*

anläßlich 'on the occasion of':
anläßlich seines siebzigsten Geburtstages

anstelle 'in place of', 'instead of':
anstelle einer Antwort

NB: *anstelle* is often used with *von* e.g.: *anstelle von einer Antwort.* In this form it is common in speech, see 20.4.1a.

aufgrund 'on the strength of':
aufgrund seiner juristischen Ausbildung

NB: *aufgrund* is perhaps more often spelled *auf Grund*, and is often used with *von*, especially in speech: *aufgrund von diesen Erkenntnissen.*

*ausschließlich 'exclusive of'
die Miete ausschließlich der Heizungskosten

ausweislich 'according to'
Im Lesen sind die Deutschen ausweislich dieser Studie keineswegs Spitze (*SZ*)

behufs 'for the purpose of'
behufs einer Verhandlung

betreffs, bezüglich 'with regard to'
betreffs, bezüglich Ihres Angebotes

NB: These prepositions are officialese. In everyday German, the usual equivalent for 'with regard to' is *was etwas/jemanden betrifft/anbelangt.*

eingangs 'at the beginning of'
eingangs dieses Jahres

eingedenk 'bearing in mind' (It may precede or follow the noun)
eingedenk seiner beruflichen Fehlschläge

*einschließlich 'including'
einschließlich der Angehörigen (*SZ*)

*exklusive 'excluding'
exklusive Versandkosten

fernab 'far from'
fernab des Lärms der Städte

gelegentlich 'on the occasion of'
  gelegentlich seines Besuches
halber (following the noun) 'for the sake of'
  der Wahrheit halber

NB: (i) *halber* is compounded with a few nouns to form adverbs, e.g. *sicherheitshalber* 'for safety's sake', *vorsichtshalber* 'as a precaution'.
  (ii) When used with pronouns *halber* appears as *-halben* and is compounded with forms of the pronoun in *-t*, e.g. *meinethalben* 'for my sake', 'for all me', see 3.1.2c.

hinsichtlich 'with regard to'
  hinsichtlich Ihrer Anfrage
infolge 'as a result of' (often with *von* rather than a genitive)
  infolge der neuen Steuergesetze (or *infolge von den Steuergesetzen*)
*inklusive 'including'
  inklusive Bedienung
inmitten 'in the middle of'
  inmitten üppiger Blütenpracht (*HA*)
kraft 'in virtue of'
  kraft seines Amtes
längs 'along(side)'
  längs des Flusses (also [less frequently]: *längs dem Fluß*)
links 'on/to the left of'
  links der Donau
*mangels 'for want of'
  Freispruch mangels Beweises
*mittels 'by means of'
  mittels eines gefälschten Passes
namens 'in the name of'
  Ich möchte Sie namens unseres Betriebes einladen
ob 'on account of'
  die Besorgnisse des sowjetischen Staatspräsidenten ob der deutschen Frage
  (*Zeit*)

NB: *ob* with a following dative, meaning 'above', is now only found in place names, e.g.
  Rothenburg ob der Tauber, Österreich ob der Enns.

rechts 'to/on the right of'
  rechts der Isar
seitens 'on the part of'
  seitens der Bezirksverwaltung
seitlich 'to/at the side of'
  seitlich der Hauptstraße
um ... willen 'for the sake of'
  um meiner Mutter willen

NB: *um ... willen* forms compounds with special forms of the personal pronouns, e.g. *um meinetwillen*, see 3.1.2c.

unbeschadet 'regardless of' (It may precede or follow the noun)
  Heute ist London das kulturelle Zentrum der Welt, unbeachtet des Außenhandelsdefizits und des kränklichen Pfund Sterling (*Zeit*)

ungeachtet 'notwithstanding' (It may precede or follow the noun)
   ungeachtet unserer üblichen Skepsis (*Dönhoff*)
vermöge 'by dint of'
   vermöge seines unermüdlichen Fleißes
vorbehaltlich 'subject to'
   vorbehaltlich seiner Zustimmung
zeit 'during' is only used in set phrases with *das Leben*:
   zeit seines Lebens
zugunsten 'for the benefit of'
   eine Sammlung zugunsten der Opfer des Faschismus
zuungunsten 'to the disadvantage of'
   Die Luftanschläge der Nato haben die Gegebenheiten auf dem Terrain zuungunsten der bosnischen Serben geändert (*NZZ*)
*zuzüglich 'plus'
   Es kostet 2000 Mark zuzüglich der Versandkosten
*zwecks 'for the purpose of'
   Er besuchte sie zwecks einer gründlichen Erörterung der Situation

20.5 German equivalents for English 'to'

English 'to' has a number of possible German equivalents depending on context, and the use of each of these is summarised here. Fuller details and further examples can be found in earlier sections under the relevant German prepositions.

20.5.1 *an, auf* or *in* (+ accusative) are frequent equivalents for 'to'

The choice of *an, auf* or *in* with the accusative to mean 'to' depends on which one would be used with the dative to express position 'in' or 'at' the place concerned after you arrive. Thus:

(a) *in* **(+ accusative) is used for going 'to' places which one will then be inside, i.e. (*in* + dative)**

> Sie ging ins Büro, ins Dorf, ins Kino, in die Kirche, in ein Museum, ins Restaurant, in die Schule, in die Stadt, in den Zoo, etc.

In this way, *Ich gehe in die Kirche* means 'I am going to church' in the sense of going in to a service. If one is just going up to the church, one says *Ich gehe an die Kirche* or *Ich gehe zur Kirche*.

(b) *auf* **(+ accusative) is used for going 'to' certain places and events, presence 'at' which is indicated by *auf* (+ dative)**
(i) The use of *auf* is fixed with a number of nouns:

Die Schafe gingen **auf** die Wiese	*The sheep went into the meadow*
Wir fuhren **aufs** Land	*We went into the countryside*
Die Kinder gingen **auf** die Straße	*The children went into the street*

Similarly:

auf den Berg	*up the mountain*	auf sein Gut	*to his estate*
auf den (Bauern)hof	*to the farm*	auf den Hof	*into the yard*
auf ihre Bude	*to her digs*	auf die Jagd gehen	*go hunting*
auf den Flur	*into the (entrance-) hall*	auf die Toilette	*to the toilet*
auf den Gang	*into the corridor*		

With all these, *auf* (+ dative) is used to denote presence 'in' or 'on' them, cf. 20.3.4b.

(ii) *auf* (+ accusative) is also sometimes used for going 'to' formal occasions (e.g. weddings, conferences, parties, etc.):

Sie ging auf einen Empfang, auf eine Hochzeit, auf eine Party, auf eine Tagung

Although *auf* (+ dative) (or *bei*, cf. 20.2.3b) is still used to denote presence 'at' such functions, cf. 20.3.4b, *zu* is now more frequent than *auf* (+ acc.) for going 'to' them, especially in less formal registers.

(iii) *auf* (+ accusative) is used for going 'to' certain public buildings:

Sie ging auf den Bahnhof, auf die Bank, auf die Bibliothek, auf die Post, auf das Rathaus, auf die Universität

With many of these words, *auf* now tends to occur chiefly in more formal registers (see 20.3.4b and 20.3.5a). *zu* is regularly used in its place, although *an* (+ accusative) is frequent with *Universität*.

(c) *an* **expresses direction 'to' a precise spot or objects which extend lengthways (i.e. rivers, shores, etc.)**
an expresses movement to a point adjacent to the object concerned. One is then *an* (+ dative) that point, i.e. 'at' it, cf. 20.3.2a. Examples:

Er ging **an den** Tisch → Er steht an dem Tisch
Sie kam **an die** Bushaltestelle → Sie traf ihn an der Haltestelle
Sie ging **an die** Grenze → An der Grenze wurde kontrolliert
Wir fahren **ans** Meer → Wir verbringen unseren Urlaub am Meer

Similarly:

Er eilte ans Fenster   Er ging an die Kasse
Wir kamen an die Front   Sie ging ans Ufer
Sie geht ans Mikrophon, an ihren Platz, an die Straßenkreuzung, an die Tür, an die Tafel, an die Stelle, wo der Tote aufgefunden wurde
Sie gingen an den Fluß, an die Mosel, an den Strand, an den See, an die Theke, an den Zaun

20.5.2 *zu* commonly has the meaning of English 'to'

(a) *zu* **is used in many contexts rather than the more precise prepositions** *an*, *auf* **and** *in*
(cf. 20.5.1.) It is rather vaguer than these three prepositions and tends to emphasise general direction rather than reaching the objective. It is particularly frequent in colloquial registers.

(i) *zu* is used rather than *in* if one is just going up to the place involved (but not necessarily going inside), or to emphasise the general direction rather than reaching the place:

> Ich ging **zum** neuen Kino und wartete auf ihn
> Die Straßenbahn fährt **zum** Zoo

(ii) *zu* is in practice more common than *auf* in current (especially informal) usage with reference to functions and public buildings:

> Er geht zu einem Empfang, zu einer Tagung, zu einer Party
> Wir gehen zum Bahnhof, zur Bank, zur Post, zum Rathaus, zur Universität

(iii) *zu* can be used rather than *an* if the emphasis is on general direction rather than arriving adjacent to the place concerned:

> Ich begleitete sie zur Fabrik   Er ging zum Fenster, zur Tür
> Sie ging zu ihrem Platz   Er schlenderte zur Theke

(b) ***zu* is always used with reference to people**
i.e. going up to someone, or to their house or shop

> Sie ging zu ihrem Onkel, zu ihrer Freundin
> Er ging zu Fleischers, zu seinem Chef
> Wir gehen zum Bäcker frische Semmeln kaufen

20.5.3 Equivalents for English 'to' with geographical names

(a) ***nach* is used with neuter names of continents, countries and towns which are used without an article**
(cf. 20.2.6a):

> Wir fahren nach Amerika, nach Frankreich, nach Duisburg

(b) *in* **(+ accusative) is used with names of countries, etc. which are used with an article**
Most of these are feminine, but a few are masculine, neuter or plural, see 4.4.1:

> Sie reist morgen in die Schweiz, in den Jemen (*or* nach Jemen), in das Elsaß, in die USA

(c) Various prepositions are used with other geographical names
In particular *in*, *an* or *auf* (+ acc.) are used in the same way as with other nouns, cf. 20.5.1, depending on whether one will be *in*, *an* or *auf* (+ dat.) on arrival:

> Wir fahren in die Alpen, in den Harz
> Wir gingen auf den Feldberg, auf die Jungfrau
> Wir wollen im Sommer an den Bodensee, an die Riviera fahren

21
Word order

German word order is rather more flexible than English. A main reason is that English uses word order to identify the subject and the object(s) of the verb: the subject *must* come before the verb in English, the objects after it, in the order indirect object + direct object. In a sentence like *My father lent our neighbour the old lawn-mower* we cannot move the elements round without saying something quite different: *Our neighbour lent my father the old lawn-mower* has another meaning. In a comparable German sentence, though, a number of permutations are possible, e.g.:

(i)   Mein Vater hat unserem Nachbarn den alten Rasenmäher geliehen
(ii) Unserem Nachbarn hat mein Vater den alten Rasenmäher geliehen
(iii) Den alten Rasenmäher hat mein Vater unserem Nachbarn geliehen
(iv) Mein Vater hat den alten Rasenmäher unserem Nachbarn geliehen

In German, it is the case endings, not the word order, which tell us who is doing what to whom, i.e. what is the subject and what are the objects. Because of this, the order of the words and phrases can be changed round to give a slightly different emphasis to the elements without altering the basic meaning. Sentence (iv), for example, stresses *who* is being lent the lawnmower.

For this reason, it is misleading to think in terms of 'rules' for word order in German, as if every type of element had its own special place in the sentence. In practice, only the position of the verb is absolutely fixed, and the other elements are relatively free to move in order to show different emphases.

Nevertheless, the various types of element do tend, in general, to come in a particular order, and in this chapter we aim to concentrate on showing this 'neutral' order (as the one which the foreign learner will find most useful to follow initially), and then to show what effect variations on this can have in terms of giving different emphases in the sentence. In particular, we explain

- in 21.1 the three basic clause structures, each with the finite verb in a different position, i.e. main clause statements (verb second); questions and commands (verb first), subordinate clauses (verb last).
- in 21.2 how the position before the verb in main clause statements is used to highlight an important element in the sentence.
- in 21.3 to 21.8 the order of all the other elements in the sentence except the verb, i.e. pronouns (21.4), noun subject and objects (21.5), adverbials (21.6), *nicht* (21.7) and the other complements of the verb (21.8).
- in 21.9 what can be placed after the verb at the end of the clause.

Although we usually speak of 'word' order, what we are dealing with in practice is often a phrase of some kind rather than single words. For example, a time adverbial tends to come in a particular place in the sentence, whether it is a single word, like *heute*, a phrase like *den ganzen Tag* or a prepositional construction like *am kommenden Dienstag*. In order to cover these possibilities, it is useful to refer to the 'bits' of the clause whose position we are explaining as 'elements'.

A great deal has been written on German word order. This account draws in particular on the very full treatments in Engel (1991: 303–55) and Heidolph *et al.* (1981: 702–64). Fox (1990: 244–56) gives a useful outline in English of the principles of German word order.

21.1 Clause structure and the position of the verb

A fundamental feature of German word order is that the various parts of the verb (i.e. the finite verb and any infinitives, participles or separable prefixes) have a fixed position in the clause.

21.1.1 The three basic clause structures of German

The three clause types of German differ in the place of the finite verb:

(i) Main clause statements, e.g. *Petra kommt aus Erfurt*
the finite verb is the *second* element
(ii) Questions and commands, e.g. *Kommt Petra aus Erfurt?*
the finite verb is the *first* element
(iii) Subordinate clauses, e.g. *Ich weiß, daß Petra aus Erfurt kommt*
the finite verb is the *last* element

(a) Main clause statements: the finite verb is *the second element*

Only *one* element can normally precede the finite verb in main clause statements (for details see 21.2). All other parts of the verb, i.e. an infinitive or a past participle (in a compound tense or with an auxiliary verb) or a separable prefix are in final position, e.g.:

Initial position	Verb¹	Other elements	Verb²
Helga	kommt	eben aus der Bäckerei	
Morgen	muß	ich mit dem Zug nach Trier	fahren
Dann	blickte	sie zum Fenster	hinaus
In der Stadt	habe	ich eine neue Compact-Disc	gekauft
Als er klein war,	hat	er oft mit Werner	gespielt

Complement clauses with *daß* omitted (see 19.2.1b) have the same structure as main clause statements, e.g.: *Sie glaubt, sie hat ihn gestern in der Stadt gesehen.*

NB: (i) Exceptions to the rule that the finite verb must be the second element are explained in 21.2.1c.
(ii) The order of infinitives and participles at the end of the clause when there is more than one of these is explained in 21.1.3.

(b) Questions and commands: the finite verb is *the first element*

As in main clause statements, any other parts of the verb are in final position. In some types of question (equivalent to English *wh*-questions), the verb is preceded by an interrogative (e.g. *was, was für ein . . .*, etc.):

	Verb¹	Other elements	Verb²
	Kommt	sie bald?	
	Mußt	du schon	gehen?
	Hat	dich Peter schon	gesprochen?
	Fangen	Sie sofort	an!
	Paß	doch an der Kreuzung	auf!
Was	hast	du da schon wieder	angestellt?
Welches Buch	sollen	wir zuerst	lesen?
Was für eine Stadt	ist	Bochum?	

Conditional clauses with no *wenn* (see 16.5.3a), and comparative clauses introduced simply by *als*, cf. 16.7.1a, have a similar structure, with the finite verb in first position, e.g.: *Hätte ich Zeit, so würde ich gern mit Ihnen nach Italien fahren; Es war mir, als wäre ich hoch in der Luft.*

(c) Subordinate clauses: the finite verb is *the last element*

The clause is introduced by a conjunction in first position, see Chapter 19. Other parts of the verb usually come immediately before the finite verb at the end of the clause (for details, see 21.1.3), e.g.:

	Conj.	Other elements	Verb²	Verb¹
Ich konnte es nicht,	weil	ich gestern krank		war
Der Mann,	der	in der Ecke allein		steht
Weißt du,	ob	sie eine neue Bluse	gekauft	hat?
Hast du ihr gesagt,	daß	sie den Brief sofort	tippen	soll?
Bist du sicher,	daß	er morgen		kommt?

Non-finite clauses with a participle or an infinitive with *zu* (see 13.2.1 and 13.6.1) have a similar structure, with the verb last, e.g.: *Den Schildern folgend, fanden sie das Krankenhaus (Walser); eine Betonburg, wie von einem anderen Stern in diesen Wald gefallen (Walser); Gibt es eine Möglichkeit, ihm zu helfen?*

NB: Exclamations introduced by an interrogative word may have the form of questions or subordinate clauses, e.g.: *Wie der Chef darüber geschimpft hat!* or: *Wie hat der Chef darüber geschimpft!*

21.1.2 The 'verbal bracket'

A typical feature of German is that most of the elements in the clause are sandwiched between the various parts of the verb in main clauses, or between the conjunction and the parts of the verb in subordinate clauses. This construction is known as the 'verbal bracket' (in German *Verbalklammer* or *Satzklammer*). This 'bracket' forms a framework for German clauses, and we can relate the order of all the other elements in the clause to it:

Initial position	Bracket¹ [	Other elements	Bracket²]
Heute	darf	sie mit uns ins Kino	kommen
Ich	habe	sie zufällig in der Stadt	gesehen
Ich	komme	morgen gegen zwei Uhr noch einmal	vorbei
	Darf	sie heute mit uns ins Kino	kommen?
	Hast	du sie zufällig in der Stadt	gesehen?
	Komm	doch morgen gegen zwei Uhr noch einmal	vorbei!
...,	ob	sie heute mit uns ins Kino	kommen darf
...,	weil	ich sie heute zufällig in der Stadt	gesehen habe
...,	daß	du morgen gegen zwei Uhr noch einmal	vorbeikommst

More examples of verbal brackets can be seen in the examples in 21.1.1. This construction has a number of characteristic features:

(i)   In main clause statements there is one (*and only one*) element outside the 'bracket', in initial position before the verb. This is called the *Vorfeld* in German; its use is explained in 21.2.

(ii) All other elements (and this means *all* elements in questions, commands and subordinate clauses) are positioned inside the 'bracket'In German, this is called the *Mittelfeld*. As the examples above show, the order of elements in the *Mittelfeld* is **exactly the same for all clause types**; it is explained in 21.3 to 21.8.

(iii) Under certain conditions elements can be positioned after the closing bracket, i.e. after the part of the verb which is at the end, e.g. *Ich rufe an* **aus London**; *Hat sie dich angerufen* **aus London?**; *Ich weiß, daß sie dich angerufen hat* **aus London**. This position is called the *Nachfeld* in German; its use is explained in section 21.9.

21.1.3 The order of verbs at the end of the clause

If there is more than one part of the verb at the end of the clause, e.g. a finite verb, a past participle and/or one or more infinitives, their order is fixed.

(a) In main clauses the auxiliary verb comes after the full verb
This applies equally to statements, questions and commands:

	Finite verb	Other elements	Full verb	Auxiliary
Ich	**werde**	es ihr doch	**sagen**	**müssen**
Sie	**hat**	ihn voriges Jahr	**schwimmen**	**gelehrt**
	Ist	dir das schon	**erklärt**	**worden?**
	Soll	dieser Brief heute noch	**geschrieben**	**werden?**

(b) In subordinate clauses the finite verb usually follows all infinitives and participles
The full verb precedes the auxiliary as in main clauses (cf. (a) above):

	Conj.	Other elements	Full verb	Aux.	Finite vb
	Da	ich sie zufällig	gesehen		**habe**, ...
...,	daß	er mir das Geld	leihen		**wird**
...,	daß	sie mit uns ins Kino	gehen		**darf**
...,	wie	sie den Brief	fallen		**ließ**
Das Haus,	das	sie	verkaufen		**sollte**, ...
...,	daß	mir das schon	erklärt	worden	**ist**
Dar Brief,	des	heute noch	verkauft	werden	**muß**

However, if there are two infinitives at the end of the clause, the finite auxiliary comes before them both:

	Conj.	Other elements	Finite vb	Full verb	Aux.
Ich weiß,	daß	ich es bald	**werde**	erledigen	müssen
der Brief,	den	sie	**hat**	fallen	lassen
...,	weil	er die Probleme	**soll**	unterscheiden	können
das Haus,	das	sie	**hätte**	verkaufen	sollen
...,	daß	Paul ihn	**hat**	kommen	hören

NB: This rule only applies with *lassen, sehen* and *hören* if the infinitive is being used in place of the past participle (cf. 13.3.2), as in the examples. Otherwise auxiliaries follow *lassen*, e.g. *Weil Norwegen die Isländer in einem Stück internationalen Gewässers nicht fischen lassen will*, ... (*Presse*).

21.1.4 Coordinated clauses have the same structure

Coordinated clauses are typically linked by a coordinating conjunction such as *aber, oder* or *und* (see 19.1).

(a) In coordinated main clause statements, the verb is in second position in both

Zu Hause **schreibt** Mutter Briefe, und Vater **arbeitet** im Garten
Am Abend **blieb** ich in meinem Zimmer, aber ich **konnte** nicht arbeiten
Du **kannst** mit uns ins Kino kommen, oder du **kannst** zu deiner Freundin gehen

If the subject of clauses linked by *sondern* or *und* is identical, it can be omitted ('understood'):

Wir **gingen** nicht ins Kino, sondern **arbeiteten** im Garten
Jürgen **kam** um vier Uhr in Soest an und **ging** sofort zu seiner Tante

However, if the second clause has another element in initial position, the subject *must* be inserted after the verb and cannot be omitted. This is a common error for English learners, since in English the subject can still be understood even if another element precedes the verb. Compare:

Ich schrieb ein paar Briefe, und dann   *I wrote a few letters and then went*
ging **ich** zu meiner Tante   *to my aunt's*

If an element other than the subject comes before the verb, it can be omitted (and taken as understood) in following coordinated clauses. The following clauses begin with the verb, and the subject is repeated after it. In this way it can be stressed that the initial element applies equally to all the clauses:

Schon im April demonstrierten die   *As early as April the farmers*
Bauern, blockierten **sie** Straßen in   *demonstrated, blocked streets*
Ost-Berlin und protestierten **sie**   *in East Berlin and protested in*
vor der Volkskammer (*Zeit*)   *front of the Volkskammer*
(*Schon im April* is taken to apply to all three coordinated clauses.)

However, if the connection is felt to be less strong, the second clause has its own initial element (most commonly the subject). In practice this is more usual, especially outside formal written German:

Am Abend blieb ich zu Hause, und **meine**   *That night I stayed at home and my*
Schwester ging ins Kino   *sister went to the cinema*

(b) In parallel subordinate clauses linked by coordinating conjunctions the verb is in final position

Ich weiß, daß sie gestern krank **war**   *I know that she was ill yesterday*
und daß ihr Mann deswegen zu Hause   *and that her husband stayed at home*
geblieben **ist**   *because of that*
Wenn deine Familie dagegen **ist** oder   *If your family is against it or you*
wenn du keine Zeit **hast**, dann   *don't have time, then we'll drop*
wollen wir den Plan fallen lassen   *the plan*

If the two clauses have compound tenses with the same auxiliary, it can be omitted in the first one, e.g.:

Nachdem ich Tee **getrunken** und eine Weile **gelesen hatte**, machte ich einen kurzen Spaziergang

After I had had tea and read for a while, I went for a short walk

21.2 Initial position in main clause statements

21.2.1 Only one element comes before the finite verb in main clause statements

This means that the finite verb is normally the second element in a main clause, forming the first part of the 'verbal bracket', cf. 21.1.1a and 21.1.2.

(a) This clause structure is quite different from the English equivalent

As explained at the beginning of the chapter, the subject of the verb must come before the verb in English, as this is the only way we can tell what the subject is. And in English, other elements can come before the subject, so that there can be several elements in front of the verb, e.g.:

Then she began to read the letter
Then, unwillingly, she began to read the letter
Then, unwillingly, when she had shut the door, she began to read the letter

In the corresponding German sentences, all but one of these elements has to be moved to another position, so that the verb stays in second place, e.g. (among numerous other possible permutations):

Dann begann sie den Brief zu lesen/**Sie** begann dann den Brief zu lesen.
Widerwillig begann sie dann den Brief zu lesen/**Dann** begann sie widerwillig den Brief zu lesen
Nachdem sie die Tür geschlossen hatte, begann sie dann widerwillig den Brief zu lesen/**Dann** begann sie widerwillig den Brief zu lesen, nachdem sie die Tür geschlossen hatte

Because of this fundamental difference in clause structure, corresponding sentences in English and German often have a very different form, as is shown further in 21.2.3.

(b) Many types of element can occur in initial position

The subject is often the most natural element to occur in initial position, and it has been estimated that two-thirds of main clause statements in German in all registers begin with the subject (cf. Engel (1991: 331)), e.g.:

Tobias zog heftig an seiner Pfeife. **Die Spucke im Mundstück** prasselte; **man** hörte es, obwohl jetzt, immer deutlicher, auch noch das Schießen der anderen hinzukam. . . . **Sie** waren am Kahn. **Tobias** bückte sich und ließ das Kettenschloß aufschnappen. **Die Luft überm See** flimmerte. **Der Milan hoch oben** tat keinen Flügelschlag. (*Schnurre*)

However, it is quite wrong to think of the order **subject + finite verb** as the 'normal' order (as it is in English), and thus imply that it is 'abnormal' for something else to come before the verb. Almost all types of element except the negative *nicht* and the modal particles (cf. Chapter 10) can quite naturally come first in a main clause. To demonstrate this, examples are given below of those elements, apart from the subject, which are common at the start of a main clause.

(i) An accusative or dative object. This is occasionally a (stressed) pronoun, more usually a noun phrase:

> **Ihn** nahm er zuletzt nach Prag mit (*Hildesheimer*)
> **Ihr** war das Bett viel zu klein
> **Das Verfahren gegen ihn** deutet er als weiterer Beleg für die politische Verfolgung (*Spiegel*)
> **Mariken** hat es sehr leid getan (*Surminski*)

(ii) An adverbial (a single adverb or a phrase):

> **Natürlich** kannte er sämtliche Parfum- und Drogenhandlungen der Stadt (*Süßkind*)
> **Trotz den feierlichen Londoner Erklärungen** wird weiter gekämpft (*NZZ*)

Time and place adverbials are especially frequent in initial position:

> **An dem Abend** kam ich mit Mahler in den „Kronenkeller" (*Bachmann*)
> **Am steilen Kreidefelsen** bricht sich das Meer (*Wiechert*)

(iii) Another complement of the verb, i.e. a genitive object, a prepositional object, a place or direction complement or a predicate complement (cf. Table 18.1)

> **Zu einem bedauerlichen Zwischenfall** kam es, als ... (*Zwerenz*)
> **Ins Theater/Dahin** komme ich jetzt nur sehr selten
> **Ein guter Kerl** ist er trotz alledem

(iv) A prepositional phrase qualifying a noun later in the clause

> **Über den Ernst der Lage** hat aber auch er keinen Zweifel (*FR*)

(v) The non-finite part of a compound tense. This construction gives particularly strong emphasis to the verb:

> **Anzeigen** wird sie ihn (*Fallada*)
> **Abgefunden mit ihrer Lage** haben sich 16,6 Prozent der Frauen (*LV*)

(vi) A noun belonging with a quantifying determiner later in the clause. This construction gives particular emphasis to the noun:

> **Personen** wurden nach Polizeiangaben keine verletzt (*NZZ*)
> **Menschen** sind um diese Zeit wenige unterwegs (*Gaiser*)

Occasionally this construction is found with adjectives, e.g.:

> **Beweise** hat er äußerst triftige gebracht

(vii) Part of a phrasal verb

> **Sehr leid** hat es mir getan
> **Zur Abstimmung** ist dieser Vorschlag nicht gekommen

(viii) A subordinate clause. This can be a finite or non-finite clause.

> **Wohin sie dich gebracht haben**, weiß ich nicht (*Surminski*)
> **Den Schildern folgend**, fanden sie das Krankenhaus (*Walser*)
> **Ihr Geld zu leihen**, habe ich doch nie versprochen

(c) Constructions with more than one element in initial position

There are a few possible exceptions to the strict 'verb second' rule in main clauses. In the main, they are only apparent exceptions in special kinds of construction, i.e.:

(i) Interjections, the particles *ja* and *nein*, and names of persons addressed are regarded as standing outside the clause proper and are placed before the initial element and followed by a comma, e.g.:

Ach, es regnet schon wieder   **Du liebe Zeit**, da ist sie ja auch
Ja, du hast recht   **Nein**, das darfst du nicht
Karl, ich habe dein Buch gefunden   **Lieber Freund**, ich kann nichts dafür

(ii) Some other words or phrases link a clause up with what has just been said or the general context. They are also regarded as standing outside the clause and placed before the initial element and separated from it by a comma, e.g.:

Kurzum, die Lage ist nun kritisch
Wissen Sie, ich habe sie nie richtig kennengelernt

The most frequent of these words and phrases are:

das heißt (d.h.)	*that is (i.e.)*	so	*well now, well then*
im Gegenteil	*on the contrary*	unter uns gesagt	*between ourselves*
kurz, kurzum, kurzgesagt, kurz und gut	*in short*	weiß Gott	*Heaven knows*
mit anderen Worten	*in other words*	wie gesagt	*as I said*
nun, na	*well*	wissen Sie, weißt du	*you know*
sehen Sie, siehst du	*d'you see*	zugegeben	*admittedly*

A few such words or phrases can be used like the group above, or (more commonly) on their own in initial position as part of the clause, e.g.:

Er ist unzuverlässig. **Zum Beispiel**, er kommt immer spät *or* **Zum Beispiel** kommt er immer spät.

The following words and phrases can be used like this:

zum Beispiel	*for instance*	natürlich	*of course*
erstens, zweitens, etc. (cf. 9.2.3)	*first, secondly*, etc.	offen gesagt	*to be frank*

(iii) A few adverbs and particles can be used together with another element in initial position, i.e.:

Am Ende **freilich** ist etwas Unerwartetes und etwas Neues da (*Borst*)	*To be sure at the end something new and unexpected was there*
Der Buchfink **jedoch** ist nur in den ersten Lebensmonaten lernfähig (*NZZ*)	*Chaffinches, on the other hand, are only able to learn in the first months of their life*
Selbst in den Chroniken der Städter **schließlich** hat sich die Stadt als revolutionäre Neuheit in die Feudalwelt gestellt (*Borst*)	*After all, even in the chronicles of the burghers the city appears as a revolutionary innovation in feudal society*

The following adverbs can be used in this way:

allerdings	*to be sure, admittedly*	jedenfalls	*at any rate*
also	*thus*	jedoch	*however*
freilich	*to be sure, admittedly*	wenigstens	*at least*
höchstens	*at most*	sozusagen	*so to speak*
immerhin	*all the same*	übrigens	*incidentally*

Alternatively, they can occur on their own in initial position in the usual way, e.g. *Freilich ist am Ende etwas Unerwartetes und etwas Neues da.*

NB: The function of these adverbs is like that of a coordinating conjunction in such constructions, and the conjunctions *aber* and *doch* have a similar flexibility in their positioning, see 19.1.1c.

(iv) Some types of subordinate clause are seen as separate from the main clause and are followed by another element before the finite verb, in particular:

a *was*-clause which relates to the following clause as a whole:

> **Was so wichtig ist**, das Buch verkauft   *What is so important, the book is*
> sich gut   *selling well*

concessive clauses of the 'whatever' type, cf. 19.6.2:

> **Es mag noch so kalt sein**, die Post muß ausgetragen werden
> **Wer er auch ist**, ich kann nichts für ihn tun
> **Wie schnell er auch lief**, der Polizist holte ihn ein

(v) Two (or more) elements of the same kind can occur together in initial position if they complement or extend one another, so that, in effect, they are being seen as a single element. This is most frequent with adverbials of time and place, e.g.:

> **Gestern um zwei Uhr** wurde mein Mann operiert
> **Auf dem alten Marktplatz in der Marburger Stadtmitte** findet diese Woche ein Fest statt
> **Gestern abend in Leipzig** fand eine große Demonstration statt

(vi) A highlighted element can occur in isolation from the clause and dislocated from it. It is usually picked up by a pronoun or the like in initial position in the clause proper, e.g.:

> **Nach Kanada auswandern**, das haben sie ja immer gewollt
> **Die Gudrun**, der traue ich ja alles zu
> **Der Nachbar**, der hat uns ja immer davon abhalten wollen
> **Als ich davon hörte**, da war es schon zu spät
> **Mit Andreas**, da wird es bald Ärger geben

Alternatively, the highlighted element may be placed after the clause, with a pronoun, etc. within the clause referring forward to it, e.g. *Der traue ich doch alles zu, der Gudrun*. These constructions are typical of everyday colloquial language and are rarely encountered in formal writing.

21.2.2 The initial element functions as the 'topic' of the clause

i.e. it is an element which we mention first in order to say something further about it, e.g.:

> **Der Kranke** hat die ganze Nacht nicht geschlafen
> (Information is being given about the patient)
> **In Frankfurt** findet jedes Jahr die internationale Buchmesse statt
> (We are being told what happens in Frankfurt)
> **In diesem Zimmer** kannst du dich nicht richtig konzentrieren
> (We are given information about this room)
> **In zwei Tagen** wird die Reparatur fertig sein
> (We are informed about what will be happening in two days)

Whatever comes first (whether the subject or not) operates as a starting-point for the clause. It comes first because it is the thing about which we want to give our listener some piece of new information. Consequently, we can make the following general observations about the element in initial position in a German main clause statement.

(a) The element in initial position is often known or familiar to both speaker and listener

A clause often starts off with something which is 'known' in this way, and some piece of new information is given about it later in the clause. This is shown by the examples above and the following:

> **Trotz des Poststreiks** ist der Brief rechtzeitig angekommen
> (You knew about the postal strike, but it's news to you that the letter still got there on time)

> **An den meisten deutschen Gymnasien** ist Englisch die erste Fremdsprache
> (You are aware of German schools but this is something you didn't know about the curriculum)

The fact that a clause often begins with an element which is familiar to both speaker and listener is a reason why time phrases are so common in initial position.

(b) The initial element often refers back to something just mentioned

Very often we want to pick up something which has just been referred to and give further information about it. The initial element often takes up a preceding word or phrase, especially in continuous texts or dialogue:

> Wir haben ihn im Garten gesucht, aber **im Garten** war niemand zu sehen
> Ich sehe ihn oft. **Seinen Bruder** aber sehe ich jetzt recht selten
> Ich war drei Wochen auf Sylt. – **Darum** siehst du auch so gut aus.

The answer to a question often repeats an element in the question and gives the answer later in the clause. Compare:

> Was ist gegen Kriegsende geschehen? – **Gegen Kriegsende** wurden viele
> Städte zerstört
> Wann wurden diese Städte zerstört? – **Diese Städte** wurden gegen Kriegsende
> zerstört

(c) The element in initial position is seldom the main piece of new information in the clause

This follows from (a) and (b) above. Most main clauses begin with something familiar and the new information appears later. In this way, the following sentences sound odd because they start off with an important piece of new information:

> ?? **In einem kleinen Dorf** in Bohmen ist Stifter im Jahre 1805 geboren
> ?? **Ein neues Schloß** kaufte dieser Mann gestern
> ?? **Scharlachrot** ist ihr neues Kleid

These examples also show that it is not true that 'any' element can be used in initial position in German 'for emphasis', as is often asserted. The first element is simply the 'topic' or starting-point of the clause, and the strongest emphasis is normally on the most important piece of new information later in the clause, cf. 21.3.

(d) In many clauses, the subject may not be suitable for use in initial position

The subject is often a natural choice as 'topic' of a clause. However, if the subject imparts new information, it is often more natural to begin with something 'known' and delay the subject until later in the clause, according to the principle explained in (c) above:

Vor deiner Tür steht doch **ein neues Auto**	*But there's a new car by your front door*

(With strong emphasis on the surprise at seeing the new car)

Zwei Tage darauf wurde gegen die Streikenden **Militär** eingesetzt (*Brecht*)	*Two days later the military was deployed against the strikers*

(*Militär* is the crucial new information; it would sound odd to begin the sentence with it)

It is particularly unusual for a sentence to begin with an indefinite noun, as they normally involve new pieces of information.

For similar reasons, the subject rarely occurs in initial position with verbs of happening, since the event is usually the main new information (cf. also 21.5.3), e.g.: *Gestern ereignete sich **ein schwerer Unfall** in der Kärntner Straße.*

A 'dummy subject' *es* (cf. 3.6.2d) is often used to allow the subject to occur later in the clause and give it heavier emphasis as important new information, e.g.:

Es kamen **viele Gäste**	*There were many guests*
Es möchte Sie **jemand** am Telephon sprechen	*There's somebody who wants to speak to you on the telephone*

(e) The 'topic' of the sentence can be changed quite readily

Since almost any element can be placed before the verb in German and act as the 'topic' of the clause, the emphasis of the clause can be altered quite easily by changing the element in initial position. The element we select to occur in first position depends on precisely how we want to present the information and what we assume the listener already knows. Thus, if we say:

Das Konzert findet heute abend im Rathaus statt

we assume the listener knows that there is a concert on, and we are telling him or her where it is. On the other hand, if we say:

Heute abend findet ein Konzert im Rathaus statt

we are telling the listener what's happening tonight. We are assuming that he or she doesn't know that there's a concert on in the town hall, and we are giving him or her this information. We can begin with *heute abend,* because that is information which the speaker and the listener share. Finally, if we say:

Im Rathaus findet heute abend ein Konzert statt

we are telling the listener something about the town hall, i.e. that there's a concert on there tonight.

21.2.3 English equivalents for German constructions with an element other than the subject in initial position

The ease with which German can move an element into initial position to serve as the 'topic' of the clause, as shown in 21.2.2e, is not shared by English, where the order subject + verb is fixed. For this reason, if we need to make something other than the subject the 'topic' of a main clause in English we have to use more complex constructions for which German has no need. For example:

(a) 'Cleft sentence' constructions
In order to bring an element other than the subject into first position English often places it in a clause of its own, usually with *it* and the verb *be*, e.g. *It was Angela (who) I gave the book to.* These so-called 'cleft sentences' are not used in German; all we need to do is to put the relevant element first, e.g.:

Erst gestern habe ich es ihr gesagt	*It was only yesterday that I told her*
Dort habe ich sie getroffen	*It was there that I met her*
Weil sie oft schwimmt, ist sie fit	*It's because she swims a lot that she's fit*
Was man sagt, zählt	*It's what you say that counts*

There are many variants of this construction, all with simpler equivalents in German, e.g.:

Diesen Wagen da muß ich kaufen	*That's the car I've got to buy*
Dort/Hier wohnt sie	*That/This is where she lives*
Das meine ich (auch)	*That's what I mean*
So macht man das	*That's the way to do it*
Dann ist es passiert	*That's when it happened*
Dem gehört es	*That's whose it is*
Im Frühjahr ist es hier am schönsten	*Spring is when it's loveliest here*
Zu diesem Schluß gelangt Haas in ihrer neusten Arbeit	*This is the conclusion reached by Haas in her most recent work*

With the exception of the type *Er war es, der mich davon abhielt*, cf. 3.6.2c, cleft sentence constructions sound unnatural in German and should be avoided.

(b) English often uses a passive where an active is possible or preferable in German
Passives are often used in English to allow the object of the verb to come first in the clause (as the subject) and be its topic. Although passives are by no means unusual in German, the active construction, with the object in first position, is often preferred, cf. also 15.5. For example:

Meinem Vater hat der Chef sehr freundlich gratuliert	*My father was congratulated by the boss in a very kind manner*
Auf diese Worte müssen nun Taten folgen (*Zeit*)	*These words must now be followed by deeds*

(c) English uses a construction with *have* and a participle which has no direct equivalent in German
This construction is a device to bring the relevant element to the beginning of the sentence by making it the subject of *have*. In German all that is necessary is to place the relevant element first:

In diesem Buch fehlen zwanzig Seiten	*This book has (got) twenty pages missing*
In diesem Wald haben voriges Jahr	*This wood had a lot of nightingales*
viele Nachtigalle genistet	*nesting in it last year*
Ihm wurde eine Golduhr gestohlen	*He had a gold watch stolen*
Ihnen wurden die Fenster eingeworfen	*They had their windows smashed*

21.3 The order of other elements in the sentence: general principles

Most elements in all clause types come within the verbal 'bracket', i.e. between the finite verb and any other parts of the verb in main clauses, or between the conjunction and the verb in subordinate clauses (the so-called *Mittelfeld*, see 21.1.2). The relative order of these elements inside the verbal bracket is the same for *all* clause types, as is shown by the examples in 21.1 and the following:

[   ]

Main cl.: Gestern hat **er auf der Terrasse vergeblich auf das Mädchen** gewartet
Question: Hat **er auf der Terrasse vergeblich auf das Mädchen** gewartet?
Sub. cl.: ..., ob **er auf der Terrasse vergeblich auf das Mädchen** gewartet hat

This order is determined by two main underlying principles:

(i) Elements which are more heavily stressed and convey important new information tend to follow elements which are less stressed

The elements in the *Mittelfeld* usually appear in order of increasing importance, passing from unstressed elements, like pronouns, which are known or familiar to both speaker and listener, to those elements which represent the main new information which the speaker wants to communicate to the listener. In general, the element nearest the end of the bracket is the most important piece of information and naturally carries the heaviest stress, especially in writing, where emphasis cannot be indicated by tone of voice.

(ii) Elements which are more closely linked to the verb tend to come after elements with a less strong link

For instance, most verb complements usually appear immediately before the final part of the verbal 'bracket'. And direct objects, if they are nouns, normally come after the indirect objects whose link with the verb is less 'direct'.

(iii) Following these general principles, the elements within the verbal bracket tend to occur in the order given in Table 21.1

Further details on the position of each of the groups of elements are outlined in sections 21.4 to 21.8. The order given in Table 21.1 is intended as a general guideline to help the English-speaking learner, and it must not be thought of as reflecting some absolute, rigid rule. As explained at the beginning of this chapter, German word order is relatively flexible and can be varied considerably to mark different emphases.

NB: This does mean that English-speaking learners need to be alert to the effect, in terms of emphasis, of changing the position of elements in a sentence. It is quite possible to end up saying something rather different to what you mean! Compare the following:

In Deutschland wird im fünften Schuljahr Englisch unterrichtet
In Deutschland wird Englisch im fünften Schuljahr unterrichtet

TABLE 21.1 *Basic order of the elements in the German sentence*

Vorfeld	Bracket¹	Pronouns N A D	Noun subject	Dative noun	Most adverbials	Accusative noun	nicht	Adverbials of manner	Complements	Bracket²
Gestern	hat	ihm	mein Vater		am Lagerfeuer	ein Märchen				erzählt
	Hat	sie es ihm			schon					gegeben?
...	weil		der Lehrer	dem Schüler					für seine Hilfe	gedankt hat
Sie	will			den Kindern	jetzt	die Geschenke				bringen
	Haben	sie			trotzdem	das Angebot				angenommen?
	Soll	er Ihnen				das Geld				bringen?
...	da		mein Freund		oft		nicht	vorsichtig	nach Berlin	fährt
Trotzdem	möchte	mich	der Chef				nicht	höflich	daran	erinnert
Wir	wurden				nachher		nicht	schnell		schicken
Dann	hat	sie				das Tuch			in ihre Tasche	gesteckt

21.4 The position of the pronouns

21.4.1 Pronouns normally follow immediately after the finite verb or the conjunction

Pronouns refer to persons and things already mentioned, or well known to the speaker and listener. They are typically unstressed and occupy the least prominent position in the *Mittelfeld*, before everything else:

> Gestern hat **ihn** mein Mann in der Stadt gesehen
> Hat **ihn** dein Mann gestern in der Stadt gesehen?
> Da **ihn** mein Mann gestern in der Stadt gesehen hat, ...
> Dann hat **es** mein Bruder meinem Vater gegeben
> Dann hat **mir** mein Bruder den Brief gegeben

> In Taiwan überwacht die Crew die   *In Taiwan the crew supervises the*
> Entladung ihres Jets, dann führt   *unloading of their jet, then their*
> **sie** der Dienst nach Hong Kong   *tour of duty takes them to Hong Kong*
> (*Spiegel*)

The only exception to this rule is that a pronoun can precede or follow a noun subject. In general it is more common for them to come first, but the following are quite usual alternatives to the first three examples above:

> Gestern hat mein Mann **ihn** in der Stadt gesehen
> Hat dein Mann **ihn** gestern in der Stadt gesehen?
> Da dein Mann **ihn** gestern in der Stadt gesehen hat, ...

However, a pronoun does more usually follow a noun subject if the endings do not show nominative and accusative case unambiguously:

> Gestern hat meine Mutter **sie** in der   *My mother saw her in town yesterday*
> Stadt gesehen
> Da das Mädchen **sie** in der Stadt   *As the girl has seen her in town ...*
> gesehen hat, ...

(*Da sie das Mädchen in der Stadt gesehen hat* would normally be taken to mean 'As she has seen the girl in town'.)

If there are two pronoun objects, it is more usual for them to follow a noun subject, e.g.:

> Weil der Lehrer **es ihnen** gezeigt hat, ...   *Because the teacher has shown it to them*

Nevertheless, putting them in another order is also quite possible, e.g.:

> Weil **es** der Lehrer **ihnen** gezeigt hat, ...
> Weil **es ihnen** der Lehrer gezeigt hat, ...

21.4.2 Personal pronouns precede other pronouns

Thus, *er, dir, Ihnen, ihm*, etc. (and *man*) come before demonstrative pronouns such as *der, das, dieser*, etc., irrespective of case, e.g.:

> Wollen **Sie die** gleich mitnehmen?   *Do you want to take those away with you?*
> Hat **ihn dieser** denn nicht erkannt?   *Didn't that person recognise him, then?*
> Eben hat sie **mir das** gezeigt   *She's just shown me that*

21.4.3 Personal pronouns occur in the order *nominative + accusative + dative*

This order is usual if there is more than one personal pronoun in the *Mittelfeld*, e.g.:

Da **sie dich ihm** nicht vorstellen wollte, ...	*As she didn't want to introduce you to him ...*
Hast **du es uns** nicht schon gesagt?	*Haven't you already told us that?*
Gestern hat **er sie ihm** gegeben	*He gave them to him yesterday*
Heute will **sie ihm** helfen	*She's going to help him today*
Heinz hat **es mir** gezeigt	*Heinz showed it to me*

This order is relatively fixed. The only common variation on it is that the pronoun *es*, in the reduced form *'s*, often follows a dative pronoun in colloquial speech, e.g. *Heinz hat mir's gezeigt*.

21.4.4 The position of the reflexive pronoun *sich*

In principle, *sich* occurs in the same position as other accusative or dative pronouns, i.e. in first position in the *Mittelfeld*, immediately after the finite verb or the conjunction:

> Gestern hat **sich** der Deutsche über das Essen beschwert
> Gestern hat **sich** jemand darüber beschwert
> Gestern hat er **sich** darüber beschwert
> Er hatte es **sich** (dat.!) so vorgestellt
> Er hat **sich** (acc.!) mir vorgestellt

However, it is occasionally placed after a noun subject, e.g.:

> Gestern hat der Deutsche **sich** über das Essen beschwert

And very occasionally, it may occur later in the clause, e.g.:

> Gestern hat der Deutsche über das Essen **sich** beschwert

In general, this is only possible with 'true' reflexive verbs used with an accusative reflexive, cf. 18.3.6a.

21.5 The position of noun subject and objects

21.5.1 The usual order for noun subject and objects in the *Mittelfeld* is *nominative + dative + accusative*

This group of elements includes not only noun phrases in the nominative, accusative or dative case but also indefinite pronouns such as *etwas*, *jemand*, *niemand*, *nichts*, etc. As Table 21.1 shows, they usually follow personal and demonstrative pronouns (but see 21.4.1 for exceptions), and precede other verb complements. The position of adverbials in relation to them is explained in 21.6.1. Examples:

> Gestern hat **jemand meinem Vater eine Kettensäge** geliehen
> Warum hat **Manfred seiner Freundin nichts** gebracht?
> Ich weiß, daß **mein Freund seiner Frau diese Bitte** nicht verweigern konnte
> Heute hat **der Chef den Mitarbeitern** für ihre Mühe gedankt

Variations on this order usually involve special circumstances of some kind, as explained in 21.5.2 and 21.5.3.

21.5.2 The dative object can sometimes follow the accusative object

(a) If the dative object refers to a person, this order indicates it is much more important in context and emphasises it very strongly
It is used sparingly:

Er hat sein ganzes Vermögen **seinem Neffen** vermacht	*He left his whole fortune to his nephew*

(We already know about the fortune, what is surprising is who he left it to; *Neffen* is heavily stressed to indicate this)

Er stellte seinen Neffen **dem Pfarrer** vor	*He introduced his nephew to the parson*

(*Who* the nephew was introduced to is the important fact. Compare *Er stellte dem Pfarrer seinen Neffen vor*)

..., als mein Vater diese merkwürdige Geschichte **einem ihm völlig unbekannten Herrn** erzählte	*... when my father told this remarkable story to a gentleman whom he didn't know at all*

(The dative object is indefinite and thus previously unknown to the listener. It is more newsworthy and significant in context than 'this story', which must have been mentioned before)

(b) If both accusative and dative objects refer to things, the more important of them in context is placed second

... daß er uns nicht alle zwingt, unsere höheren Zwecke **seinem Interesse** zu unterwerfen (*Wolf*)	*... that he's not forcing us all to subject our higher aims to his personal interest*
Er hat sein Glück **seiner Karriere** geopfert	*He sacrificed his happiness to his career*

(Compare the quite different emphasis in *Er hat seiner Karriere sein ganzes Glück geopfert*)

(c) A dative object referring to a thing usually follows an accusative object referring to a person
In practice, it is rarely possible for the dative object to come first in such contexts:

Sie überantworteten den Verbrecher **der Justiz**	*They delivered up the criminal to justice*
Sie haben den armen Jungen **der Lächerlichkeit** preisgegeben	*They exposed the poor boy to ridicule*

21.5.3 The noun subject can follow an accusative and/or a dative object (and other elements) if it constitutes the major piece of new information

See also 21.2.2d. In practice the subject is in such contexts usually a noun with an indefinite article or zero article, or an indefinite pronoun:

Glücklicherweise wartet nun in Wien an jeder Ecke **ein Kaffeehaus** (*Zweig*)	*Luckily there is a cafe waiting for you on every corner in Vienna*
Nun begrüßte den Dirigenten und den Virtuosen **lautes Händeklatschen** (*Kapp*)	*Now the conductor and the virtuoso were met with loud applause*
Gestern hat meinen Bruder Gott sei dank **niemand** gestört	*Thank goodness nobody disturbed my brother yesterday*
Er wußte, daß dieser Gruppe **etwas Unangenehmes** bevorstand	*He knew that something unpleasant was in store for this group*

Occasionally a subject with a definite article is placed late in the clause if it needs strong emphasis:

Die Tatsache, daß der EG unausweichlich 1994 **das Geld** ausgeht (*Zeit*) — *The fact that the EC's money will inevitably run out in 1994*

The late position of an indefinite subject is almost regular with verbs of happening and the like, and it is also frequent in passive sentences:

Er wußte, daß seinem Chef **eine große Ehre** zuteil geworden war — *He knew that a great honour had been bestowed on his boss*

Zum Glück ist meinem Bruder da **nichts** passiert — *Luckily nothing happened to my brother*

Deshalb können den Asylbewerbern **keine Personalausweise** ausgestellt werden — *For this reason no identity cards can be issued to the asylum-seekers*

21.6 The place and order of adverbials

An 'adverbial' can be a single word (e.g. *trotzdem*, *heute*), or a phrase with or without a preposition (e.g. *den ganzen Tag*, *mit großer Mühe*). This difference in form has no effect on word order. In practice, the classification of adverbs in Chapter 7 applies equally to all adverbials.

The placing of adverbials is more flexible than that of any other element in the clause. This reflects their general freedom of occurrence as elements optionally added to give additional 'circumstantial' information, cf. 18.1.4. In this section we deal first with the placing of adverbials in relation to other elements (chiefly the noun subject and objects), and then explain the ordering of adverbials where more than one is present.

21.6.1 The placing of adverbials in relation to the noun subject and objects

As shown in Table 21.1, most adverbials occur after a noun subject and dative object, but before an accusative object. However, a number of refinements are necessary to this general guideline, notably because the relative position of adverbials and noun subjects and objects depends on their relative importance in the clause. Specifically, that element appears later in the clause which needs to be emphasised most strongly or conveys the most important new information. Thus:

(a) Unemphatic adverbials (usually single words) can precede the noun subject and/or the dative object
This applies in particular to adverbs of attitude (and modal particles, see Chapter 10), e.g. *bestimmt*, *sicher*, *vielleicht*, etc. Unstressed short adverbs of time and place like *da*, *dort*, *hier*, *gestern*, *heute*, *morgen*, *dann*, *damals*, *daher* also often occur early in the clause, immediately after the personal pronouns, e.g.:

Sie wird es **wohl** ihrem Mann sagen — *She'll probably tell her husband*

Ich weiß, daß sie es **sicher** meinem Vater empfehlen wird — *I know she'll be sure to recommend it to my father*

Sie ist **heute** ihrem Freund aus Bonn begegnet — *She met her friend from Bonn today*

Hat sie **schon damals** ihrem Großvater die ganze Geschichte erzählt? — *Did she tell her grandfather the whole story at that time?*

In most of the above contexts the adverb can follow the noun subject or objects. It is then more strongly emphasised, e.g. *Hat sie ihrem Großvater schon damals die ganze Geschichte erzählt?*

Such permutation is, however, scarcely possible in contexts where the noun subject or object is a vital piece of new information (e.g. if it is indefinite) and needs to be placed where it carries most stress, e.g.:

Das hat bisher keiner gemerkt	*Nobody's noticed it up to now*
Da war doch niemand	*Nobody was there, though*
Ich bin da einem Freund von deinem Bruder begegnet	*I ran into a friend of your brother's there*

A sentence like *Da war niemand doch* would sound quite odd.

(b) The order of adverbials and noun objects (accusative or dative) most frequently depends on emphasis

i.e. how important they are in the context of the whole clause or sentence. The element which is being presented as more important comes later. Compare the following:

Er hat diesen neuen Wagen **im Sommer** gekauft
(The stress is on *when* he bought the new car)
Er hat im Sommer **diesen neuen Wagen** gekauft
(The emphasis is on *what* he bought)
Sie haben Fußball **im Park** gespielt
(This tells us *where* they were playing)
Sie haben im Park **Fußball** gespielt
(This tells us *what* they were playing)
Das hat **gestern** ihr Kollege meinem Verlobten erzählt
(Who was told is the point at issue)
Das hat ihr Kollege **gestern** meinem Verlobten erzählt
(Who did the telling is seen as relatively unimportant)
Das hat ihr Kollege meinem Verlobten **gestern** erzählt
(Prominence is given to the time when the fiance was told)

It should be noted that, although from a grammatical point of view there is flexibility in the order of these elements, in a particular context only one may be appropriate. Thus, in answer to the question *Wann hat er diesen neuen Wagen gekauft?* one would most naturally use the first of the alternatives above, and the second would sound weird.

(c) Adverbials of manner follow the noun objects and all other adverbials

(cf. 21.6.2). This is because they usually convey the most important new information:

Meiner Meinung nach hat das Quartett dieses Stück **viel zu schnell** gespielt	*In my opinion the quartet played that piece much too fast*
Er warf den Ball **sehr vorsichtig** über den Gartenzaun	*He threw the ball very carefully over the garden fence*

21.6.2 The relative order of adverbials

(a) If a clause contains more than one adverbial, they most frequently occur in the following order

attitude – time – reason – viewpoint – place – manner

More detail is given about these groups, which corresponds to the classification in Chapter 7:

(i) Adverbials of attitude. This group includes all the modal particles (see Chapter 10) and other adverbials which express some attitude on the part of the speaker towards what is being said (see 7.3.2), e.g. *angeblich, leider, vermutlich, zum Glück, zweifellos*, etc.:

> Sie wollte **doch** vor zwei Uhr in Magdeburg sein
> Er ist **vielleicht** schon am Montag abgereist

(ii) Time adverbials. As explained in 11.6 these can indicate a point in time (e.g. *bald, voriges Jahr, am kommenden Sonntag*), frequency (e.g. *stündlich, jeden Tag*) or duration (e.g. *lange, seit Montag, ein ganzes Jahr*). If more than one time adverbial occurs in a clause, they are usually be placed in the order 'point of time' – 'duration' – 'frequency'. Within these categories the general precedes the particular, e.g. *jeden Tag um vier Uhr*. Examples:

> Sie ist **vor zwei Tagen** trotz des Sturms nach Reutte gewandert
> Die Streikenden blieben **vier Stunden lang** vor dem Rathaus versammelt

(iii) Adverbials of reason, i.e. adverbials expressing circumstance (e.g. *zu unserem Erstaunen*), condition (e.g. *gegebenenfalls*), purpose (e.g. *zur Durchsicht*) or reason (e.g. *wegen des Unfalls*), see 7.3.3. The passive agent introduced by *von* or *durch* (cf. 15.3), also occurs in this position:

> Sie hat den Brief **trotzdem** mit der Maschine geschrieben
> Der Brand wurde **von der freiwilligen Feuerwehr** schnell gelöscht

(iv) Viewpoint adverbials, e.g. *finanziell* 'from a financial point of view', cf. 7.3.1b. Phrases with *mit* and *ohne* also occur in this position:

> Deutschland ist in den letzten Jahren **wirtschaftlich** stärker geworden
> Der Oberst hat sie **mit dem Beil** in der Küche erschlagen

(v) Place adverbials, see 7.1. Place adverbials should be distinguished from place and direction complements, see (c) below.

> Der Oberst hat sie mit dem Beil **in der Küche** erschlagen
> Ich habe bis 18 Uhr **im Büro** gearbeitet

(vi) Manner adverbials, i.e. those which indicate *how* an action is carried out, cf. 7.3.1. Adverbs of manner are almost always the final element in the clause before the complement, e.g.:

> Sie ist heute mit ihrem Porsche **viel zu schnell** in die Kurve gefahren
> Der Vorschlag wurde von den Anwesenden **einstimmig** angenommen

(b) The order of adverbials is subject to variation for reasons of emphasis

The relative order given in (a) is only a guide to a 'neutral' order of the adverbs, assuming they all have roughly similar emphasis, and it is in no way a rigid grammatical rule. As in the case of the relative order of adverbials and the noun subject and objects, variation in the order of adverbials follows the general principle given in 21.3, in that an adverbial can be given more or less emphasis by being placed later or earlier in the clause. This often depends on what is regarded as the main new information in context, which needs to be emphasised, e.g.:

> Paula ist zum Glück **gestern** nicht zu schnell gefahren
> Paula ist gestern **zum Glück** nicht zu schnell gefahren

The adverbial in bold is made rather more prominent in each case by being placed later. Note that the manner adverbial, as the major information, is the last element in both cases.

> Viele deutsche Städte wurden gegen Kriegsende **von den Allierten** zerstört
> Viele deutsche Städte wurden von den Allierten **gegen Kriegsende** zerstört

Placing the time adverbial after the *von*-phrase in the second example gives it particular prominence, possibly in reply to a question about when it happened.

> Sie hat sehr lange **dort** auf ihre Mutter gewartet
> Sie hat dort **sehr lange** auf ihre Mutter gewartet

Although time adverbials usually precede place adverbials, they can follow if it is felt necessary to give them particular prominence. Note that the prepositional object always follows both adverbials.

(c) The traditional rule that adverbials occur in the order *time – manner – place* can be misleading

As shown in (a) above, adverbials normally occur in the order *time – place – manner*:

> Der junge Tenor hat gestern in Berlin **gut** gesungen
> Die Kinder wollten heute auf der Wiese **ungestört** spielen

Elements indicating place and direction at the end of the *Mittelfeld*, immediately before the final part of the verb, are complements of the verb, not adverbials, cf. 18.7 and 21.8.1. These complements follow *all* adverbials, including those of manner:

> Paula ist gestern viel zu schnell **in die Kurve** gefahren
> Andreas wollte gestern mit seiner Freundin gemütlich **nach Freising** wandern
> Sie hat die schöne Vase sehr vorsichtig **auf den Tisch** gestellt
> Müllers wohnen einsam in einem großen Haus **im Wald**
> Astrid lag erschöpft **auf der Couch**
> Sie sind wegen des schlechten Wetters widerwillig **zu Hause** geblieben

The elements in bold in the above examples are complements, not adverbials. They are either direction complements depending on verbs of motion, or place complements depending on verbs of position. As explained in 18.1.4, where the difference between adverbials and complements is treated, complements are much more closely linked to the verb than adverbials, which simply give additional circumstantial information. Following the principles given in 21.3, they are placed at the end of the *Mittelfeld*, immediately before the second part of the verbal bracket.

21.7 The position of *nicht* and other negative elements

Other negative elements like *nie* 'never' and *kaum* 'hardly', 'scarcely' occupy much the same position in the clause as *nicht*, and the following applies equally to them.

21.7.1 If *nicht* **negates the content of the whole clause it is placed near the end of the clause, just before adverbs of manner and verb complements**

Nicht is in practice an adverb of manner, and this determines its position if it relates globally to the whole content of the clause. However, it usually precedes other manner adverbials. Thus:

(a) *nicht* **follows any noun objects**

Er hat seinen Zweck **nicht** erwähnt	*He didn't mention his purpose*
Er hat mir das Buch **nicht** gegeben	*He didn't give me the book*
Verkaufe die Bücher **nicht**!	*Don't sell the books*
Ich weiß, daß sie ihren Bruder gestern **nicht** gesehen hat	*I know she didn't see her brother yesterday*

However, *nicht* precedes objects used with no article which are part of the verb phrase, e.g.:

Sie hatte damals **nicht** Klavier gespielt   *She didn't play the piano then*
(*Klavier spielen* is essentially a fixed verb phrase, cf. 21.8.2)

(b) *nicht* **follows all adverbials except those of manner**

Sie haben sich seit langem **nicht** gesehen	*They haven't seen each other for a long time*
Den Turm sieht man von hier aus **nicht**	*You can't see the tower from here*
Ich wollte es ihr trotzdem **nicht** geben	*I didn't want to give it to her all the same*
Das ist mir in diesem Zusammenhang **nicht** aufgefallen	*That didn't occur to me in that context*
Wir sind wegen des Regens **nicht** nach Füssen gewandert	*We didn't walk to Füssen because it was raining*
Sie haben gestern **nicht** gut gespielt	*They didn't play well yesterday*
Ich weiß es **nicht** ausführlich	*I don't know it in detail*

(c) *nicht* **precedes most verb complements**

i.e. all complements of the verb except the subject and the objects, cf. 21.8.

Sie sind gestern **nicht** nach Aalen gefahren	*They didn't go to Aalen yesterday*
Sie legte das Buch **nicht** auf den Tisch	*She didn't put the book on the table*
Wir konnten uns **nicht** an diesen Vorfall erinnern	*We couldn't remember the incident*
Er blieb **nicht** in Rostock	*He didn't stay in Rostock*
Sie ist sicher **nicht** dumm	*She's certainly not stupid*
Sie war heute **nicht** im Büro	*She wasn't at the office today*

nicht can follow prepositional objects or place and direction complements if it is relatively unstressed and the complement itself is to be emphasised. Compare:

Das kann ich doch **nicht von ihm** verlangen	*I can't ask that of him*
Das kann ich doch **von ihm nicht** verlangen	*I can 't ask that of him*

21.7.2 If *nicht* applies to one particular element in the clause rather than the clause as a whole, then it precedes that element

As *nicht* in such cases only applies to part of the clause, this is often referred to as 'partial' negation, in contrast to the 'global' negation treated in 21.7.1. The sense is usually 'not that one (, but another one)':

Sie hat mir **nicht** das Buch gegeben (not the book, but something else)	*She didn't give me the book*
Sie sind **nicht** am Freitag nach Teneriffa geflogen (not Friday, but some other day)	*They didn't fly to Tenerife on Friday*
Nicht mir hat er das Buch gegeben, sondern meiner Schwester	*It wasn't me he gave the book to, it was my sister*

NB: Alternatively, the stressed element can appear on its own in initial position, with the *nicht* later in the clause, e.g. *Mir hat er das Buch **nicht** gegeben.* This is common if the contrast is implicit, i.e. if there is no following *sondern* clause.

Unstressed *nicht* is often used in this way in tentative or rhetorical questions or exclamations, e.g.:

Hast du **nicht** die Königin gesehen?	*Didn't you see the Queen?*
War **nicht** dein Vater eigentlich etwas enttäuscht?	*Wasn't your father really a bit disappointed?*
Was du **nicht** alles weißt!	*Don't you know a lot!*

21.8 The position of complements

Of the complements of the verb, the subject and the objects, whether pronouns or nouns, have their own position within the clause and are dealt with separately, see 21.4–6. The other complements, following the general principle given in 21.3, invariably come towards the end of the *Mittelfeld*, immediately before the second part of the verbal bracket. This position for the complements is relatively fixed, irrespective of emphasis, and only very exceptionally are they found earlier in the clause.

21.8.1 The following complements are placed at the end of the *Mittelfeld*

Details about each of these complements are to be found in 18.5–8.

(a) Genitive objects

. . . weil der Verletzte dringend **eines Arztes** bedurfte	*. . . because the injured man needed a doctor urgently*

(b) Prepositional objects

Nun wird er sich sicher **um seine beiden Kinder** kümmern können	*Now he will certainly be able to look after his two children*
Sie hat in der Ankunftshalle lange **auf ihren Mann** gewartet	*She waited for her husband in the arrivals hall for a long time*
Wir haben uns vorgestern lange und ausführlich **darüber** unterhalten	*We talked about it in detail for a long time the day before yesterday*

(c) Place complements with verbs of position

Er befand sich plötzlich **in einem dunklen Saal**	*He suddenly found himself in a dark room*
Er wollte unter keinen Umständen **in Wuppertal** bleiben	*He didn't want to remain in Wuppertal under any circumstances*
Sie haben lange **in dieser Hütte** gewohnt	*They lived in that hut for a long time*

(d) Direction complements with verbs of motion

Warum hat Peter den Stein plötzlich **in den Bach** geworfen?	*Why did Peter suddenly throw the stone in the water?*
Sie ist mit ihrem Porsche zu schnell **in die Kurve** gefahren	*She took the bend too fast in her Porsche*
Wir möchten nächste Woche **nach Emden zu meinen Eltern** fahren	*We want to go to my parents' in Emden next week*

(e) The predicate complement of copular verbs

i.e. *sein, werden, bleiben, scheinen, heißen,* cf. 18.8. This complement may be a noun or an adjective:

Herbert war immerhin längere Zeit **der beste Schüler in unserer Klasse**	*All the same, Herbert was top of our class for a long time*
Sie wurde plötzlich **blaß**	*She suddenly turned pale*
Dann scheinen mir diese Bedingungen jedoch **etwas hart**	*In that case these conditions seem rather hard to me, though*

21.8.2 The noun portions of phrasal verbs also come in the last position in the *Mittelfeld*, immediately before the second part of the verbal bracket

Such extended verb phrases usually consist of a noun (often an infinitive or other verbal noun) used in a set phrase with a verb, e.g. *Abstand halten, Abschied nehmen, ins Rollen geraten.* In respect of their position in the clause such noun portions of phrasal verbs are similar to separable prefixes, and they could be considered as forming part of the final portion of the verb bracket rather than as elements within the clause.

Er hat sie durch seine Unvorsichtigkeit **in die größte Gefahr** gebracht	*He put her in the greatest danger through his carelessness*
Ich habe ihr alle meine Bücher **zur Verfügung** gestellt	*I put all my books at her disposal*
Gestern hat uns der Minister von seinem Entschluß **in Kenntnis** gesetzt	*The Minister informed us of his decision yesterday*
Sein Chef hat ihn vorige Woche sehr **unter Druck** gesetzt	*The boss put him under a lot of pressure last week*
Ich merkte, wie der Wagen langsam **ins Rollen** kam	*I noticed the car slowly starting to roll forwards*

21.9 The placing of elements after the final portions of the verb

As a general rule, the last element in a German clause is the final 'bit' of the verb, whether this is a separable prefix, an infinitive or a past participle (in main clause statements, questions and commands) or the finite verb (in subordinate clauses). This is the second part of the verbal 'bracket', as explained in 21.1.2.

However, there are a number of contexts where it is usual or possible to place an element after this final bracket. This construction is called *Ausklammerung* in German, and it is becoming increasingly frequent, even in formal writing. The following sections explain where *Ausklammerung* is preferable or acceptable in modern German.

21.9.1 Subordinate clauses are normally not enclosed within the verbal bracket

Sentences with clauses enclosed within one another and a cluster of verbs at the end (called *Schachtelsätze*, because they are like sets of boxes inside each other) can be cumbersome and are best avoided. Taken to extremes, as in the following sentence from Lutzeier (1985: 7), they can be almost impenetrable:

> Das „Vorsicht-Glatteis"-Verkehrszeichen, das letzte Nacht, die Frostbildung, was für den Autofahrer, der etwas getrunken und ein Auto, das abgefahrene Reifen hat, hat, erhöhte Gefahren mit sich bringt, brachte, total beschädigt wurde, wird nicht mehr aufgestellt.

As a general rule it is preferable to finish off one clause, with its final 'bit' of verb, before another is begun. In the following pair of sentences, the second alternative, though not ungrammatical, is regarded as clumsier:

> Ich konnte den Gedanken nicht loswerden, **daß wir ihn betrogen hatten**
> Ich konnte den Gedanken, **daß wir ihn betrogen hatten**, nicht loswerden

A relative clause can be separated from the noun it refers to in order to avoid enclosing it:

> Und wie dürfte man eine Zeitung verbieten, **die sich wiederholt und nachhaltig für die Wahl der staatstragenden Partei eingesetzt hat**? (*Spiegel*)

Enclosing the relative clause would result in an unwieldy sentence:

> Und wie dürfte man eine Zeitung, **die sich wiederholt und nachhaltig für die Wahl der staatstragenden Partei eingesetzt hat**, verbieten?

21.9.2 Infinitive clauses

In general, infinitive clauses are not enclosed within the verbal bracket:

> Sie haben beschlossen, **vor dem Rathaus zu warten**
> Er hat versucht, **sein Geschäft zu verkaufen**

However, enclosure is usual or possible in some constructions, notably with some 'semi-auxiliary' verbs. Details are given in 13.2.2.

21.9.3 Comparative phrases introduced by *als* or *wie* are commonly placed outside the verbal bracket

Gestern haben wir einen besseren Wein getrunken **als diesen**	*Yesterday we drank a better wine than this one*
Ich wußte, daß sie ebenso ärgerlich war **wie ich**	*I knew she was just as annoyed as me*

Although this is especially frequent if the *als* or *wie* phrase is the second element in a comparison, enclosure is still not unusual, e.g.:

Die Volkstracht hat sich in Oberbayern stärker **als anderswo in Deutschland** erhalten (*Baedeker*)	*Local costumes have been retained in Upper Bavaria longer than elsewhere in Germany*
ein Mann, der **wie ein Italiener** aussah	*a man who looked like an Italian*

Enclosure is quite frequent within longer clauses, especially in writing:

> da die Orangen und Zitronen von den Kindern **wie Schneebälle** über die Gartenmauern geworfen wurden (*Andres*)

21.9.4 Other elements are sometimes placed after the verbal bracket

There are three main reasons for such *Ausklammerung*, i.e.:

(i) To emphasise the element placed last:

> Du hebst das auf **bis nach dem Abendessen** (*Baum*)

(ii) As an afterthought:

> Ich habe sie doch heute gesehen **in der Stadt**

(iii) In order not to overstretch the verbal bracket, e.g.:

> Seitdem Rodrigue seine Chronik begonnen hatte, freute er sich darauf, sie zu beschließen **mit der Darstellung der Regierung dieses seines lieben Schülers und Beichtkindes**

The following elements are commonly placed outside the verbal bracket:

(a) Adverbials which have the form of prepositional phrases

These are commonly excluded for the reasons given above:

> Vieles hatte Glum schon gesehen **auf seinem Weg von seiner Heimat bis über den Rhein hinweg** (*Böll*)
> Hallo, ich rufe an **aus London** (*Telecom advert*)

In general, these constructions are more typical of colloquial speech than formal writing. However, *Ausklammerung* is not uncommon in writing, especially if the prepositional phrase is lengthy or if a further clause (usually a relative clause) depends on the element excluded, e.g.: *Von hier aus konnte man noch wenig sehen von der kleinen Stadt, die am anderen Ufer im Nebel lag.*

(b) Prepositional objects

Prepositional objects are the only complement of the verb to be regularly excluded in standard German:

> Er hätte das merken können **an den gelegentlichen Rückblicken und dem Arm,** der entspannt auf der freien Vorderlehne lag (*Johnson*)
> Er darf sich entschädigt fühlen **für ganze Jahre Underdog-Dasein im Straßen- verkehr** (*Zeit*)
> Du solltest dich nicht zu sehr freuen **auf diese Entwicklung**

Engel (1991: 316) points out that not all prepositional objects can be excluded in this way and a sentence like, e.g., *Ich habe vor dem Bahnhof gewartet auf meine Freundin* is unacceptable to many native speakers. As no clear rules have yet been established as to which which prepositional objects can be excluded and which not, it is advisable for the English learner to avoid these constructions in cases of doubt.

(c) Other verb complements

i.e. the subject or the accusative and dative objects, place and direction complements. These are not usually excluded in standard German, although *Ausklammerung* of lengthy elements is occasionally encountered in the written language, cf. the following example from Engel (1994: 233):

> Wir haben aus Steuergeldern gebaut **Wohnungen für nahezu zwanzigtausend Menschen**

Otherwise, such exclusions are restricted to substandard colloquial speech (and then only nouns, never pronouns), e.g.:

> Gestern habe ich gesehen **Manfred Schuhmacher und Angela Hartmann**

(d) Adverbs

Exclusion of simple adverbs is common in colloquial speech, but rare in formal written German, e.g.:

> Bei uns hat es Spätzle gegeben **heute**   Sie sollen leise reden **hier**
> Ich bin nach Trier gefahren **deshalb**   Hat es euch gefallen **dort?**

22

Word formation

Knowing how complex words are made up in German is invaluable for extending the foreign learner's vocabulary. The importance of being able to deduce the meaning of a whole word from its parts, or to recognise patterns like *Dank – danken – dankbar – Dankbarkeit – Undankbarkeit* cannot be overestimated. Such series of words are often more transparent in German, as we see when we compare the above with English *thanks – to thank – grateful – gratitude – ingratitude*.

This chapter deals with the most common means of word formation in German. A short general introduction to the methods of word formation is given in 22.1, then the main individual parts of speech are treated in turn, i.e. the nouns (22.2), adjectives (22.3) and verbs (22.4–7). Fleischer and Barz (1995) is a reliable and full account of all aspects of modern German word formation and their material has been widely drawn on.

22.1 Methods of word formation

22.1.1 Complex words are formed from simpler words in three main ways

(a) By means of a prefix or a suffix
In general, prefixes and suffixes do not occur as words in their own right, but are only used with root-words to form other words, e.g.:

(i) Prefixes:

die Sprache → die **Ur**sprache	schön → **un**schön
stehen → **be**stehen	besser → **ver**bessern

(ii) Suffixes:

gemein → die Gemein**heit**	bedeuten → die Bedeu**tung**
der Freund → freund**lich**	denken → denk**bar**
der Motor → motor**isieren**	die Kontrolle → kontroll**ieren**

Prefixes are most often used to create nouns from nouns, adjectives from adjectives, or verbs from other verbs or from nouns and adjectives. Suffixes are most common to make nouns from adjectives or verbs or adjectives from nouns or verbs; they are little used to form verbs.

(b) By means of vowel changes
These vowel changes are often linked with particular suffixes, but they can occur on their own. The following vowel changes are used in word formation:

(i) *Umlaut*:

der Arzt → die Ärztin   der Bart → bärtig
der Druck → drücken   scharf → schärfen

(ii) *Ablaut*, i.e. vowel changes like those of the strong verbs, see 12.1.2. *Ablaut* in word formation is chiefly restricted to use with strong verb roots:

aufsteigen → der Aufst**ie**g   werfen → der W**u**rf
b**ei**ßen → b**i**ssig   schl**ie**ßen → schl**ü**ssig

These vowel changes, especially *Ablaut*, are barely still productive (cf. 22.1.2) in modern German.

(c) By forming compound words

In compounding, a new word is made up from two (or more) existing words:

der Staub + saugen → der Staubsauger   hell + blau → hellblau
der Rat + das Haus → das Rathaus   die Brust + schwimmen →
                                                          brustschwimmen

Sometimes there is a linking sound between the two words, e.g.:

der Bauer + der Hof → der Bauernhof   das Land + der Mann → der
                                                          Landsmann

The ease with which compounds may be formed is a distinctive feature of German, compared to, say, French, Italian or Russian, and the extensive use of compounds is typical of modern German, especially in technical registers.

22.1.2 'Productive' and 'unproductive' word formation patterns

If new words are still being created by means of a particular pattern (e.g. by adding a particular prefix or suffix), that pattern is called 'productive'. For example, the suffix -*bar* is very commonly used to make adjectives from nouns (= English -*able*, -*ible*, cf. 22.3.1a), and new words in -*bar* are regularly encountered, e.g. *eßbar*.

On the other hand, many abstract nouns from adjectives are found with the suffix -*e*, and *Umlaut* of the vowel where possible, cf. 22.2.1b, e.g.:

groß → die Größe   gut → die Güte   hoch → die Höhe   lang → die Länge

but no new nouns are being created in this way; the pattern is 'unproductive'. However, many words which were formed according to this pattern at a time when it was productive remain in the language.

The later sections of this chapter deal in the main with those types of word formation which are still productive in modern German, but attention will also be paid to those which, although no longer productive, still account for a significant number of words in the modern language.

22.2 The formation of nouns

22.2.1 Noun derivation by means of suffixes

The following suffixes are common, but not all of them are fully productive. Most are linked to a particular gender, see 1.1.

(a) *-chen, -lein* (neuter)

These suffixes are very productive and used to form diminutives from nouns:

das Auge → das Äug**lein** *little eye*	die Karte → das Kärt**chen** *little card*
das Buch → das Büch**lein** *little book*	die Stadt → das Städt**chen** *little town*

The vowel of the stressed syllable usually has *Umlaut* if possible, although exceptions are common, especially with names, e.g. *Kurtchen*. *-chen* is commoner than *-lein*, which is used most often with words ending in *-ch, -g* or *-ng*, in a few set instances (like *Fräulein*), and in archaic or poetic language. It was originally south German, but, in practice, colloquial south German speech now uses other forms from the local dialects, e.g. *-li* (Switzerland), *-(e)le* (Baden), *-la* (Franconia), *-(er)l* (Austria and Bavaria).

In some cases, derivations with both *-chen* and *-lein* from the same noun are used with a difference in meaning, e.g. *Fräulein* 'girl', *Frauchen* 'mistress' (e.g. of a dog).

NB: In substandard colloquial speech, *-chen* is sometimes added to plurals in *-er*, e.g. *Kinderchen*.

(b) *-e* (feminine)

(i) Nouns in *-e* from verbs may denote an action or an instrument. The latter is still productive, especially in technical registers:

absagen → die Absage *refusal*	bremsen → die Bremse *brake*
pflegen → die Pflege *care*	leuchten → die Leuchte *light*

(ii) Nouns in *-e* from adjectives denote a quality. The vowel has *Umlaut* if possible. This pattern is no longer productive, having been replaced by *-heit* or *-(ig)keit*, see (e) below:

groß → die Größe *size*   stark → die Stärke *strength*

(c) *-ei, -erei* (feminine)

These suffixes are productive and form nouns from verbs or from other nouns.

(i) Nouns in *-erei* from verbs are mainly pejorative, indicating a repeated, irritating action:

fragen → die Frage**rei** *lots of annoying questions*

The basis may be a whole phrase, e.g.:

Rekorde haschen → die Rekordhasch**erei** *record hunting*

-ei is used in the same sense from verbs in *-eln* and *-ern*:

lieben → die Liebe**lei** *flirtation*

(ii) Nouns in *-ei* from nouns denote the place where something is done. The basis is often a noun in *-er*:

die Auskunft → die Auskunft**ei** *information bureau*
der Bäcker → die Bäcker**ei** *bakery*

The associated forms *-elei* and *-erei*, used with a noun base, have pejorative meanings of various kinds:

Fremdwörter → die Fremdwört**elei** *using (too) many foreign words*
die Sklave → die Sklav**erei** *slavery*

(d) -er, -ler, -ner (masculine)
These productive suffixes form nouns from verbs or nouns. The root vowel occasionally has *Umlaut*, though this is rare with recent formations:

(i) Most nouns in *-er* from verbs denote the person who does something, often indicating a profession:

einbrechen → der Einbrecher *burglar*   lehren → der Lehrer *teacher*
schreiben → der Schreiber *writer*   betteln → der Bettler *beggar*

The base may be a whole phrase:

einen Auftrag geben → der Auftraggeber *client, customer*

(ii) *-ler* (less commonly *-ner*) is used to derive nouns from other nouns to indicate the person who does something. Some are pejorative:

das Bühnenbild → der   die Rente → der Rentner *pensioner*
  Bühnenbildner *stage designer*
die Kunst → der Künstler *artist*   der Sport → der Sportler *sportsman*
der Profit → der Profitler *profiteer*   die Wissenschaft →
      der Wissenschaftler *scientist*

In some instances *-er* is used rather than *-ler* to form nouns from other nouns:

die Eisenbahn → der Eisenbahner *railway worker*
die Taktik → der Taktiker *tactician*

(iii) Some nouns in *-er* from verbs denote an instrument:

bohren → der Bohrer *drill*   empfangen → der Empfänger *receiver*

The base is often a whole phrase, especially in technical language:

Staub saugen → der Staubsauger *vacuum cleaner*

(iv) Nouns in -er from place names designate the inhabitants:

Frankfurt → der Frankfurter   Österreich → der Österreicher
Hamburg → der Hamburger   Wien → der Wiener

Some of these are rather irregular, e.g.:

Hannover → der Hannoveraner   Zürich → der Zürcher

(e) -heit, -(ig)keit (feminine)
These suffixes are used productively to form abstract nouns from adjectives denoting a quality:

bitter → die Bitterkeit *bitterness*   heftig → die Heftigkeit *violence*
gleich → die Gleichheit *similarity*   geschwind → die Geschwindigkeit *speed*
eitel → die Eitelkeit *vanity*   genau → die Genauigkeit *precision*

The distribution of the forms *-heit*, *-keit* and *-igkeit* is not wholly regular. In general, *-heit* is the most common form. *-keit* is used with adjectives ending in *-bar*, *-ig*, *-lich* and *-sam* and with most in *-el* and *-er* (but not all, e.g. *die Dunkelheit*, *die Sicherheit*). *-igkeit* is used with adjectives ending in *-haft* and *-los* (e.g. *die Glaubhaftigkeit*) and a number of others, especially those which end in *-e* (e.g. *müde → die Müdigkeit*).

(f) -*in* (feminine)

The productive suffix -*in* forms nouns denoting the feminine of persons and animals. The root vowel usually has *Umlaut*:

> der Arzt → die Ärztin *woman doctor*   der Fuchs → die Füchsin *vixen*

NB: For the use of these feminine forms in modern German, see 1.1.4a.

(g) -*ling* (masculine)

This productive suffix is used to form nouns from verbs or adjectives.

(i) Nouns in -*ling* from verbs denote persons who are the object of the verbal action:

> prüfen → der Prüfling *examinee*   strafen → der Sträfling *prisoner*

(ii) Nouns in -*ling* from adjectives designate persons possessing that quality, often (but not always) with a pejorative sense:

> feige → der Feigling *coward*   fremd → der Fremdling *stranger*

Similar formations denoting plants and animals are common, e.g. *der Grünling* 'greenfinch', but they are no longer productive.

(h) -*nis* (neuter or feminine)

Nouns in -*nis* are abstract nouns from verbs or adjectives. Those from verbs (which often have irregular forms or use the past participle as a base) often denote the result of the verbal action. The suffix is no longer productive:

> erleben → das Erlebnis *experience*   finster → die Finsternis *darkness*
> ersparen → das Ersparnis *savings*   geheim → das Geheimnis *secret*
> gestehen → das Geständnis *confession*   wild → die Wildnis *wilderness*

(i) -*schaft* (feminine)

The productive use of this suffix is to form nouns from other nouns designating a collective or a state:

> der Student → die Studentenschaft *student body*
> der Freund → die Freundschaft *friendship*

Other derivational patterns with -*schaft*, i.e. from adjectives (e.g. *die Schwangerschaft* 'pregnancy') or from participles (e.g. *die Errungenschaft* 'achievement') are no longer productive.

(j) -*tum* (neuter)

-*tum* is used productively in modern German with nouns referring to persons to form nouns denoting institutions, collectives or characteristic features:

> der Beamte → das Beamtentum *civil servants*   der Papst → das Papsttum *papacy*
> der Deutsche → das Deutschtum *German ethos*   das Volk → das Volkstum *national traditions*
> der König → das Königtum *monarchy*

(k) *-ung* **(feminine)**
This is the most frequent productive suffix to form nouns from verbs referring simply to the action of the verb, e.g.:

> bedeuten *mean* → die Bedeut**ung** *meaning*   landen *land* → die Land**ung** *landing*
> bilden *form* → die Bild**ung** *formation*   töten *kill* → die Töt**ung** *killing*

22.2.2 Noun derivation by means of prefixes

All these prefixes except *Ge-* are stressed. The gender of nouns with prefixes is the same as that of the root noun, with the exception of those in *Ge-*, which are mostly neuter, cf. 1.1.8c.

(a) *Erz-* = 'arch-', 'out and out'

> der Bischof → der **Erz**bischof *archbishop*
> der Gauner → der **Erz**gauner *out and out scoundrel*

(b) *Ge-*
Nouns in *Ge-* (often with the suffix *-e* in addition) can be formed from verbs or from other nouns:

(i) Nouns in *Ge-* from verbs denote a repeated or protracted activity. They often have a pejorative sense, like nouns in *-erei*, cf. 22.2.1c, to which *Ge-* is often an alternative:

> laufen → das **Ge**laufe *running about, bustle* (esp. to no real purpose)
> schwätzen → das **Ge**schwätz *idle talk, gossip*

(ii) Nouns in *Ge-* from other nouns are collectives. The root vowel has *Umlaut* if possible (and *-e-* changes to *-i-*):

> der Ast → das **Ge**äst *branches*   der Berg → das **Ge**birge *mountain range*

(c) *Grund-* = 'basic', 'essential '

> die Tendenz → die **Grund**tendenz *basic tendency*

(d) *Haupt-* = 'main'

> der Bahnhof → der **Haupt**bahnhof *main station*

(e) *Miß-* **designates an opposite or a negative**
It sometimes has a pejorative sense:

> der Brauch → der **Miß**brauch *misuse*   der Erfolg → der **Miß**erfolg *failure*

Fehl- is now probably more productive than *Miß-* to express an opposite or a negative, e.g.:

> die Einschätzung → die **Fehl**einschätzung *miscalculation*

(f) *Mit-* = 'co-', etc.

> der Arbeiter → der **Mit**arbeiter *colleague, collaborator*
> der Reisende → der **Mit**reisende *fellow traveller*

(g) *Nicht-* = 'non-'

    der Raucher → der **Nicht**raucher *non-smoker*

(h) *Riesen-* has an augmentative sense

    der Erfolg → der **Riesen**erfolg *enormous success*

Riesen- is particularly common in speech, and colloquial German is rich in other augmentative prefixes, e.g.: **Superhit, Spitzenbelastung, Bombengeschäft, Heidenlärm, Höllendurst, Mordsapparat, Teufelskerl, Topmanager**, etc.

(i) *Rück-* occurs with many nouns related to verbs in *zurück-*

    die Fahrt → die **Rück**fahrt *return journey* (cf. *zurückfahren*)

The full form *Zurück-* is usually kept with nouns in *-ung* from verbs, e.g. *zurückhalten* → *die* **Zurückhaltung**.

(j) *Un-* = opposite, abnormal

der Mensch → der **Un**mensch *inhuman*	die Summe → die **Un**summe *vast*
person	*sum*
die Ruhe → die **Un**ruhe *unrest*	das Wetter → das **Un**wetter *bad*
	weather

(k) *Ur-* = 'original'

    die Sprache → die **Ur**sprache *original language*

22.2.3 Other methods of noun formation

(a) Many nouns are formed from verb stems without a suffix
Most of these are masculine, cf. 1.1.5b. This means of derivation is no longer productive. It is most common with strong verbs (which may themselves be prefixed), and the root vowel is often changed:

ausgehen → der Ausgang *exit*	schließen → der Schluß *close*
brechen → der Bruch *break*	stechen → der Stich *stab, sting*
ersetzen → der Ersatz *replacement*	zurückfallen → der Rückfall *relapse*

(b) Verb infinitives can be used as nouns
e.g. *das Aufstehen* 'getting up', *das Reiten* 'riding'. These often correspond to English *ing*-forms used as nouns and refer to the action as such. They are all neuter (see 1.1.3e) and further details about them are given in 13.4.

(c) Adjectives and participles can be used as nouns
e.g. *der/die Fremde* 'stranger', *der/die Vorsitzende* 'chair(person)'. This is the most straightforward way of indicating a person carrying out a particular action, and further details on adjectives used as nouns are given in 6.4. Such nouns from adjectives often co-exist with derived nouns:

    fremd → der Fremde *and* der Fremdling
    einbrechen → der Einbrechende *and* der Einbrecher

In these cases the noun derived by means of a suffix has a more developed sense than the adjective used as a noun. Both *der Fremde* and *der Fremdling* mean 'stranger', but the latter is rather pejorative. *der Einbrecher* means, specifically, 'burglar', but *der Einbrechende* simply means 'the person presently breaking in' (who may not necessarily be a criminal).

22.2.4 Compound nouns

The ease with which compound nouns can be formed is a characteristic feature of German, and the use of compounds has increased significantly in recent years. In particular, while two-part compounds like *Krankenhaus* and *Schreibtisch* have always been common, there has been an extension in the use of compounds with three or more elements in the present century, especially in technical language, e.g. *Fahrpreisermäßigung, Autobahnraststätte, Roggenvollkornbrot.* Even so, compounds with more than four elements are (thankfully) still unusual.

NB: Compound nouns usually take the gender of the last part, see 1.1.9a.

(a) Types of noun compound

Almost any part of speech can combine with a noun to form a compound, e.g.:

- noun + noun: das Haar + die Bürste → die Haarbürste *hairbrush*
- adjective + noun: edel + der Stein → der Edelstein *gem*
- numeral + noun: drei + der Fuß → der Dreifuß *tripod*
- verb + noun: hören + der Saal → der Hörsaal *lecture theatre*
- preposition + noun: unter + die Tasse → die Untertasse *saucer*
- adverb + noun: jetzt + die Zeit → die Jetztzeit *the present day*

(b) A linking element is inserted in many noun + noun compounds

e.g.: *die Lieblingsfarbe, die Straßenecke.* These linking elements (called *Fugenelemente* in German), which occur in about a third of all compounds, are notoriously unpredictable. A few words form some compounds with a link and some without one, e.g. *das Lobgesang* but *die Lobeshymne.* Other words form some compounds with one link and others with a different one, e.g. *das Tagebuch* but *die Tageszeitung.* And Austrian and Swiss usage often differs from that in Germany, e.g. Austrian *der Zugsführer* for German *der Zugführer.* In practice, each compound needs to be learnt with its link. These linking elements depend on the *first* part of the compound, and the following are found:

(i) *-e-* occurs with a few nouns, especially those with a plural in *-e*. The root vowel often has *Umlaut* if the plural has *Umlaut*, e.g. *der Pferdestall, der Gänsebraten.*

(ii) *-(e)s-* (i.e. the ending of the genitive) occurs with many masculine and neuter nouns (and a few feminines), e.g. *die Windeseile, das Kalbsleder, der Liebesbrief.*

(iii) *-(e)n-* is used with many feminine nouns, with 'weak' masculine nouns (see 1.3.2) and with adjectives used as nouns, e.g. *der Scheibenwischer, die Heldentat.*

(iv) *-er-* is found with some nouns which have a plural in *-er. Umlaut* is usually present if possible, e.g. *die Männerstimme, die Rinderzucht.*

(c) Restrictions on the formation of compound nouns

Despite the apparent ease with which compound nouns can be formed in German, there are certain restrictions on this. These restrictions are not fully understood and it is not possible to give clear rules. A few hints are given here to guide the foreign learner, but it is good practice to be cautious in forming compounds which one has not actually seen or heard used.

(i) In a German compound noun the first element carries the main stress and usually defines the second. Thus, *Rathaus* is a type of *Haus* and *Tiefkühltruhe* is a kind of *Truhe*.

On the other hand, a compound like *Blauhimmel* for 'blue sky' is not possible, because it is not a 'type' of sky. We must say *der blaue Himmel*. In particular, compounds whose first element is an individual person or place are not usually possible for this reason. We cannot say *Vatermitarbeiter* or *Ulmbesuch* because they are not 'types' of colleague or visit, we have to use a full phrase: *der Mitarbeiter meines Vaters* or *sein Besuch in Ulm*.

(ii) Adjective + noun compounds tend to be very limited. In practice they always mean something rather different from when the relevant adjective is used as an epithet with the noun. Thus, *eine Großstadt* is more than *eine große Stadt*, and *ein Junggeselle* is not simply *ein junger Geselle*.

22.3 The formation of adjectives

22.3.1 Adjective derivation by means of suffixes

(a) -bar
This very productive suffix forms adjectives from verbs with the sense of English *-able, -ible*:

> brauchen → brauch**bar** *usable*   essen → eß**bar** *edible*

Adjectives in *-bar* are a frequent alternative to passive constructions, cf. 15.4.8.

(b) -(e)n, -ern
These suffixes are formed from nouns denoting a material, and the adjective indicates that the qualified noun is made from that material. The form *-ern* is normally associated with *Umlaut*:

> das Gold → gold**en** *golden*   das Silber → silb**ern** *silver*
> das Holz → hölz**ern** *wooden*   der Stahl → stähl**ern** *steel*

NB: Note the difference between adjectives in *-(e)n* or *-ern* and those in *-ig* from the same noun, e.g. *silbern* '(made of) silver', *silbrig* 'silvery' (i.e. like silver), cf. (d) below.

(c) -haft
Adjectives formed from nouns with the suffix *-haft* indicate a quality like the person or thing denoted by the noun, e.g.:

> der Greis → greisen**haft** *senile*   der Held → helden**haft** *heroic*

(d) -ig
This is a common and productive suffix, often associated with *Umlaut*. It is mainly used to form adjectives from nouns:

(i) With the idea of possessing what is denoted by the noun, e.g.:

> das Haar → haar**ig** *hairy*   der Staub → staub**ig** *dusty*

(ii) Indicating a quality like the person or thing denoted by the noun:

> die Milch → milch**ig** *milky*   der Riese → ries**ig** *gigantic*

Adjectives in *-ig* are often formed from whole phrases, e.g. *blauäugig* 'blue-eyed', *heißblütig* 'hot-blooded'.

(iii) Indicating duration (from time expressions):

> zwei Stunden → zweistünd**ig** *lasting two hours*

Note the difference between these adjectives in *-ig* (which express duration) and those in *-lich* (which express frequency), e.g. *zweistündlich* 'every two hours', cf. (f) below.

(iv) *-ig* forms adjectives from adverbs, e.g.:

> dort → dort**ig**   hier → hies**ig**   morgen → morg**ig**
> ehemals → ehemal**ig**   heute → heut**ig**   sonst → sonst**ig**

(e) *-isch*

This is a productive suffix, sometimes associated with *Umlaut*, used mainly to form adjectives from nouns, i.e.:

(i) To form adjectives from proper names and geographical names:

> England → engl**isch** *English*   Homer → homer**isch** *Homeric*
> Europa → europä**isch** *European*   Sachsen → sächs**isch** *Saxon*

(ii) To form adjectives which indicate a quality like that of the person or thing denoted by the noun. They are often pejorative:

> der Held → held**isch** *heroic*   das Kind → kind**isch** *puerile*
> der Herr → herr**isch** *imperious*   der Wähler → wähler**isch** *fastidious*

Compare the pejorative *kindisch* with the neutral *kindlich* 'childlike'.

(iii) To form adjectives from foreign words:

> die Biologie → biolog**isch** *biological*   die Musik → musikal**isch** *musical*
> die Mode → mod**isch** *fashionable*   der Nomade → nomad**isch** *nomadic*

(f) *-lich*

A common suffix with a wide range of functions. Adjectives formed with *-lich* often have *Umlaut*:

(i) Adjectives from nouns in *-lich* indicate a relationship to that person or thing, or indicate the possession of the quality denoted by it:

> der Arzt → ärzt**lich** *medical*   der Preis → preis**lich** *in respect of price*
> der Buchstabe → buchstäb**lich** *literal*   der Tod → töd**lich** *fatal, deadly*
> der Fürst → fürst**lich** *princely*

This is the only use of *-lich* which is still productive in modern German.

(ii) Adjectives in -*lich* from time expressions denote frequency:

> zwei Stunden → zwei**stündlich** *every two hours*

NB: For the difference between adjectives in -*ig* and -*lich* from time expressions, see (d) above.

(iii) Adjectives in -*lich* from verbs indicate ability:

> bestechen → bestech**lich** *corruptible*   verkaufen → verkäuf**lich** *saleable*

This use of -*lich* is no longer productive, having been replaced by -*bar*, see (a) above.

(iv) Adjectives in -*lich* from other adjectives usually indicate a lesser degree of the relevant quality:

> arm → ärm**lich** *shabby; humble*   krank → kränk**lich** *sickly*
> klein → klein**lich** *petty*   rot → röt**lich** *reddish*

(g) -*los*

-*los* is used to form adjectives from nouns and corresponds to English -*less*:

> die Hoffnung → hoffnungs**los** *hopeless*   die Wahl → wahl**los** *indiscriminate*

(h) -*mäßig*

This suffix is very productive in modern German, especially in formal registers, to derive adjectives from nouns:

(i) With the sense of 'in accordance with':

> die Gewohnheit → gewohnheits**mäßig** *habitual*
> der Plan → plan**mäßig** *according to plan*

-*gemäß* is an alternative to -*mäßig* in this sense, but it is less common, e.g. *plangemäß, ordnungsgemäß.*

(ii) With the sense of 'in respect of something':

> der Instinkt → instinkt**mäßig** *instinctive*
> der Verkehr → verkehrs**mäßig** *relating to traffic*

(iii) With the sense of 'like someone or something':

> der Fürst → fürsten**mäßig** *princely*
> das Lehrbuch → lehrbuch**mäßig** *like a textbook*

(i) -*sam*

This suffix is barely productive in modern German. Adjectives in -*sam* have two main sources:

(i) From verbs (especially reflexive verbs), expressing a possibility or a tendency:

> sich biegen → bieg**sam** *flexible*   sparen → spar**sam** *thrifty*

(ii) From nouns, indicating a quality:

> die Furcht → furcht**sam** *timid*   die Gewalt → gewalt**sam** *violent*

22.3.2 Adjective derivation by means of prefixes

These prefixes are usually stressed and form adjectives from other adjectives.

(a) *erz-, grund-, hoch-* **have intensifying meaning**

erz- is mainly used with a rather negative sense, whereas *grund-* and *hoch-* tend to be more positive. Both *erz-* and *grund-* are rather limited in use:

reaktionär → **erz**reaktionär *very reactionary*
ehrlich → **grund**ehrlich *thoroughly honest*
verschieden → **grund**verschieden *totally different*
begabt → **hoch**begabt *highly talented*
intelligent → **hoch**intelligent *very intelligent*

(b) *un-* **negates and/or produces an opposite meaning**

It closely resembles English *un-*. It is not always stressed.

artig → **un**artig *naughty*   wahrscheinlich → **un**wahrscheinlich *improbable*

vorsichtig → **un**vorsichtig *incautious*

If an adjective already has a simple word as its opposite (e.g. *klug – dumm*), the form in *un-* gives a negative rather than an opposite. Thus, whilst *dumm* means 'stupid', *unklug* means 'unwise'.

In general, only adjectives with a positive meaning can form an opposite with *un-*. Thus, whilst *unschön* (← *schön*) is fairly common, one does not find *unhäßlich* from *häßlich*.

(c) *ur-* **with adjectives usually intensifies the sense**

alt → **ur**alt *very old*   komisch → **ur**komisch *very comical*

Sometimes, it gives the idea of 'original' or 'typical', e.g. *urdeutsch* 'typically German'.

22.3.3 Adjective compounding

In general, adjective compounding is similar to noun compounding, see 22.2.4.

(a) Types of adjective compounds

In practice only the following are at all common:

(i)   noun + adjective: die Pflicht + treu → pflichttreu *dutiful*
(ii) verb + adjective: trinken + fest → trinkfest *able to hold one's drink*
(iii) adjective + adjective: klein + laut → kleinlaut *meek*

Adjective + adjective compounds are often 'additive', i.e. the qualities of both adjectives apply, e.g. *naßkalt* 'cold and wet'.

(b) Many noun + adjective compounds have a linking element

These are similar to those in noun + noun compounds, see 22.2.4b. *-s-* and *-n-* are the most common, e.g. *geisteskrank, gesundheitsschädlich, seitenverkehrt*.

22.4 The formation of verbs: inseparable prefixes

Verbs can be formed from nouns, adjectives or from other verbs by means of the prefixes *be-*, *emp-*, *ent-*, *er-*, *ge-*, *ver-* and *zer-*. They are called 'inseparable' prefixes because they always remain attached to the root. They are always unstressed, whereas separable prefixes are stressed, see 22.5.

Many patterns of word formation with inseparable prefixes are common or productive, and the most important are given in the following sections, arranged according to the individual prefixes.

NB: Some prefixes, e.g. *durch-*, *über-*, *um-*, *unter-*, may be separable or inseparable. They are treated in 22.6.

22.4.1 be-

(a) be- makes intransitive verbs transitive
Cf. 18.3.5b. The simple intransitive verb may be used with a dative object or a prepositional object. This becomes the accusative object of the prefixed verb with *be-*, e.g.:

> jemanden **be**dienen *serve sb.* (← jemandem dienen)
> eine Frage **be**antworten *answer a question* (← auf eine Frage antworten)

(b) With transitive verbs be- can change the action to a different object

> jemanden mit etwas **be**liefern *supply sb. with sth.*
> (← jemandem etwas liefern *deliver sth. to sb.*)

(c) be- forms verbs from nouns with the idea of providing with something
In some cases the suffix *-ig-* is added:

> das Wasser → **be**wässern *irrigate*   die Nachricht → **be**nachrichtigen *notify*
> der Reifen → **be**reifen *put tyres on*

(d) be- make verbs from adjectives with the sense of giving someone or something that quality
In some cases the suffix *-ig-* is added:

> feucht → **be**feuchten *moisten*   gerade → **be**gradigen *straighten*
> frei → **be**freien *liberate*   ruhig → **be**ruhigen *calm*

22.4.2 ent-

The prefix *emp-* is a variant of *ent-*, used before some roots beginning with *f*, e.g. *empfehlen*, *empfinden*.

(a) Verbs in ent- from verbs of motion have the idea of escaping or going away
What is being escaped from usually appears as a dative object with these verbs, cf. 18.4.1c, e.g.:

> gleiten → jemandem **ent**gleiten *slip away from sb.* (e.g. glass from hand)
> laufen → jemandem/etwas **ent**laufen *run away/escape from sb./sth.*
> reißen → jemandem etwas **ent**reißen *snatch sth. from sb.*

(b) Verbs in *ent-* from nouns, adjectives or other verbs often have the sense of removing something
In this sense, *ent-* often corresponds to the English prefixes *de-* or *dis-*:

das Gift → **ent**giften *decontaminate*   scharf → **ent**schärfen *tone down*
der Mut → **ent**mutigen *discourage*   spannen → **ent**spannen *relax*

22.4.3 er-

(a) Verbs in *er-* from other verbs often express the achievement or conclusion of an action

bitten → **er**bitten *get (sth.) by asking for it*
schießen → **er**schießen *shoot (sb.) dead*

A distinctive and productive use of *er-* is to form verbs from verbs or nouns with the idea of acquiring something by the action expressed by the simple verb or implied in the noun, cf. *erbitten* above and the following:

arbeiten → Er hat etwas **er**arbeitet *He got sth. by working for it*
die List → Er hat etwas **er**listet *He got sth. through cunning*

A handful of verbs in *er-* from other verbs point to the start of an action, e.g. *erklingen* 'ring out', *erbeben* 'tremble'.

(b) Verbs in *er-* formed from adjectives express a change of state
i.e. either intransitive verbs with the idea of becoming something, or transitive verbs with the idea of making somebody or something have the quality expressed by the adjective, e.g.:

blind → **er**blinden *become blind*   frisch → **er**frischen *refresh*
rot → **er**röten *turn red, blush*   leichter → **er**leichtern *make easier*

22.4.4 ver-

This is the most widely used of these prefixes, and it has a range of different uses. The following are the most frequent or productive:

(a) Many verbs in *ver-* from verbs express the idea of finishing or 'away'

blühen → **ver**blühen *fade (flowers)*   hungern → **ver**hungern *starve to death*
brauchen → **ver**brauchen *consume*   klingen → **ver**klingen *fade away*
                                                                            (sounds)

(b) Some verbs in *ver-* from other verbs convey the notion of 'wrongly' or 'to excess'

biegen → **ver**biegen *bend out of shape*   salzen → **ver**salzen *put too much salt in sth.*
lernen → **ver**lernen *unlearn, forget*

Some reflexive verbs in *ver-* have the idea of making a mistake, e.g.:

fahren → sich **ver**fahren *get lost, take a wrong turning*
wählen → sich **ver**wählen *misdial*

A few verbs in *ver-* are opposites, e.g.:

achten → **ver**achten *despise*   kaufen → **ver**kaufen *sell*

(c) Verbs in *ver-* formed from adjectives often express a change of state

As with *er-* (22.4.3), these may be intransitive verbs with the idea of becoming something, or transitive verbs with the idea of making somebody or something have the quality expressed by the adjective, e.g.:

arm → **ver**armen *become poor*   einfach → **ver**einfachen *simplify*
stumm → **ver**stummen *become silent*   länger → **ver**längern *make longer*

Some verbs in *ver-* from nouns have a similar meaning, e.g.:

das Unglück → **ver**unglücken *have an accident*
der Sklave → **ver**sklaven *enslave*

(d) Many verbs formed from nouns with *ver-* convey the idea of providing with something

das Glas → **ver**glasen *glaze*   der Körper → **ver**körpern *embody*
das Gold → **ver**golden *gild*   der Zauber → **ver**zaubern *enchant*

22.4.5 zer-

Verbs in *zer-*, which are usually formed from other verbs, always convey the notion of 'in pieces', e.g.:

beißen → **zer**beißen *bite into pieces*   fallen → **zer**fallen *disintegrate*
brechen → **zer**brechen *smash*   streuen → **zer**streuen *disperse*

22.5 The formation of verbs: separable prefixes

Most separable prefixes also exist as independent words, chiefly as adverbs, prepositions, nouns or adjectives. The forms of separable verbs, in particular the position of the prefix, are explained in 12.2.1i. Separable prefixes are always stressed.

22.5.1 Simple separable prefixes

The majority of these derive from prepositions or adverbs and their meanings are often transparent. The examples below illustrate some common and productive patterns of derivation.

NB: Prefixes from prepositions expressing direction (e.g. *ab-, an-, auf-*) often have a less transparent or figurative sense because direction can be indicated by using a prefix with *her-* or *hin-*, cf. 7.2.4d.

(a) *ab-*
(i) = 'away':

abfahren *depart, leave*   **ab**fliegen *take off*

(ii) = 'down':

absteigen *get down*   **ab**setzen *put, set down*

(iii) Indicating finishing, achieving or completing an action:

abdrehen *switch off*   **ab**laufen *wear out* (i.e. shoes)

(b) *an-*
(i) With the idea of approaching:

ankommen *arrive*   anreden *address (sb.)*

(ii) Indicating the start of an action, or doing something partially:

andrehen *switch on*   anbrennen *catch fire*

(c) *auf-*
(i) = 'up' or 'on'

aufbleiben *stay up*   aufsetzen *put on* (e.g. hat, water)

(ii) With the idea of a sudden start:

auflachen *burst out laughing*   aufklingen *ring out*

(d) *aus-* = 'out', often pointing to the completion of an action

ausbrennen *burn out*   ausdorren *dry up*

(e) *ein-* is related to the preposition *in*
It often conveys the idea of becoming used to something:

einfahren *run in* (i.e. new car)   sich einleben *settle down*

(f) *los-* most often has the meaning of beginning something

losgehen *set off; start*   losreißen *tear off, tear away*

(g) *mit-* usually has the idea of accompanying or cooperating

mitgehen *go with sb.*   mitarbeiten *cooperate*

(h) *vor-*
(i) With the idea of going forward or preceding:

vorgehen *go ahead; be fast* (clock)   vorstoßen *push forward; attack*

(ii) With the idea of demonstrating something:

vorlesen *read out aloud*   vormachen *show sb. how to do sth.*

(i) *weg-* = 'away'

wegbleiben *stay away*   weglaufen *run away*

fort- is a rather less common alternative to *weg-* with some verbs, e.g. *fortbleiben, fortlaufen.*

(j) Other simple prefixes are less frequent or no longer productive
A few examples:

bei-	beitreten	*join* (e.g. club)	beitragen	*contribute*
da-	dableiben	*stay on/behind*	dastehen	*stand there*
dar-	darstellen	*depict, represent*	darlegen	*explain, expound*
fehl-	fehlgehen	*miss one's way*	fehlgreifen	*miss one's hold*

inne-	innehaben	*occupy* (position)	innehalten	*pause*
nach-	nachahmen	*imitate*	nachgehen	*follow*
nieder-	niederbrennen	*burn down*	niederlassen	*lower, let down*
zu-	zudrehen	*turn off* (tap)	zusteigen	*get on, board* (train)

22.5.2 Compound separable prefixes

(a) Some compound elements, mainly from adverbs, are widely used as separable prefixes

Selected examples:

dabei-	(indicating proximity)	dabeistehen	*stand close by*
daneben-	(indicating missing sth.)	danebenschießen	*miss* (a shot)
davon-	('away')	davoneilen	*hurry away*
dazu-	(indicating an addition)	dazukommen	*be added*
empor-	('upwards')	emporblicken	*look up*
entgegen-	('towards')	entgegennehmen	*receive, accept*
überein-	(indicating agreement)	übereinkommen	*agree*
voraus-	(= 'in advance')	voraussagen	*foretell, predict*
vorbei-, vorüber-	(= 'past,)	vorbeigehen	*pass*
zurück-	(= 'back')	zurückfahren	*drive back, return*
zusammen-	(= 'together' or 'up')	zusammenrücken	*move together*
		zusammenfalten	*fold up*

Other compound elements, e.g. *drauf-, hintan-, vorweg-, zuvor-* are used with one or two verbs only, e.g. *vorwegnehmen* 'anticipate'.

NB: The very frequent compound directional prefixes in *hin-* and *her-* (e.g. *hinausgehen, herunterkommen*) are dealt with in 7.2.4.

(b) Compound prefixes consisting of a preposition with *einander*

Compounds of a preposition with *einander* (cf. 3.2.7) are written together with the verb if the whole can be understood as expressing a single idea:

aneinandergrenzende Grundstücke	*adjacent plots of land*
Es hat sich gezeigt, daß die	*It has become evident that opinions*
Meinungen hierüber **auseinandergehen**	*differ about this*

However, if *einander* clearly means 'each other', or if the compound with *einander* is the equivalent of an adverb, it is written separately:

Wir haben **aneinander** gedacht	*We thought of each other*
Die beiden Läufer sind **nacheinander**	*The two runners set off one after*
gestartet	*the other*

NB: In the spelling reform, see 23.7.2, this difficult rule has been abandoned, and compounds of a preposition + *einander* will *in all cases* be written separately, e.g. *aneinander grenzende Grundstücke*.

22.5.3 Other parts of speech can be used as separable prefixes

(a) Many nouns, adjectives, adverbs, etc. are used as separable prefixes

Most of these are used in one or two combinations only. Examples:

(i) With a noun:

teilnehmen *participate*   **acht**geben *pay heed*

(ii) With an adjective:

    liebgewinnen *grow fond of*   **offen**lassen *leave open*

(iii) With an adverb:

    fernsehen *watch television*   **schwarz**arbeiten *moonlight*

(iv) With a participle:

    gefangennehmen *take prisoner*   **verloren**gehen *get lost*

(v) With an infinitive:

    kennenlernen *meet, get to know*   **spazieren**gehen *go for a walk*

Some verbs look as if they have prefixes, but they are formed from compound nouns and the first element does not separate, e.g. *frühstücken* 'breakfast': *Ich frühstücke, ich habe gefrühstückt*, etc. Similarly:

    handhaben *manipulate*   langweilen *bore*   liebkosen *caress*   wetteifern *compete*

(b) In some instances there is doubt as to whether a combination is a separable verb or two separate verbs
The general rule is that these elements are treated as separable prefixes if the resulting combination has a distinctive new meaning, as illustrated by the examples in (a) above. On the other hand, if the element concerned and the verb retain their literal meanings, they are not written together and the element is not treated as a separable prefix. In such cases, the element concerned and the verb are stressed separately. Compare:

Sie hat es mir ʼleichtgemacht, die Stelle zu bekommen	*She made it easy for me to get the job*
Das hat sie mir sehr ʼleicht geʼmacht	*She made that very easy for me*

ʼfallenlassen	*drop (figuratively, i.e. plan, member of team, remark)*
ʼfallen ʼlassen	*drop (literally, i.e. book, plate, cup, etc.)*
ʼstehenbleiben	*stop*
ʼstehen ʼbleiben	*remain standing*

Compounds of *sein* and *werden* are written together only in their non-finite forms, e.g.:

    dasein: wenn wir **da sind** BUT Wir sind **dagewesen**
    loswerden: wenn ich es **los werde** BUT um es **loszuwerden**

This rule has resulted in a number of uncertainties and anomalies, notably *radfahren* 'cycle' and *maschineschreiben* 'type', where the prefix is spelled as a noun, with a capital letter, when it is separated, but with a small letter when written together with a part of the verb, e.g.:

Wir wollen **radfahren**	Wir sind **radgefahren**	Da ich gern **radfahre**, ...
Ich habe früher nicht **maschinegeschrieben**		ein **maschinegeschriebener** Brief
BUT: Ich **fahre** gern **Rad**	Ich **schreibe** nicht **Maschine**	

NB: This difficult rule will been abandoned in the reformed spelling (see 23.7.2). In future, spelling as separate words will be the rule for all such doubtful cases, which will in practice include *all* separable verbs with infinitives and participles, e.g. *kennen lernen, gefangen nehmen, stehen bleiben* and those which had double forms, e.g. *leicht machen, übrig bleiben, abwärts gehen.* Compounds with *sein* and *werden* will always be spelled separately: *Wir sind da gewesen, um es los zu werden. Rad fahren* and *Maschine schreiben* will be the norm in all contexts.

(c) Some compounds are restricted to non-finite forms of the verb

Such defective compound verbs are frequent in technical German.

(i) Some compounds only exist in the infinitive form, e.g.:

brustschwimmen	*swim breast-stroke*	segelfliegen	*glide*
kettenrauchen	*chain-smoke*	wettlaufen	*race*

(ii) Some are only used in the infinitive and the past participle:

seiltanzen *walk the tightrope*   uraufführen *perform for the first time*

22.6 The formation of verbs: variable prefixes

A small number of prefixes can form *both* separable *and* inseparable verbs. The verb is separable if the prefix is stressed; if it is inseparable, the prefix is unstressed.

22.6.1 *durch-*

durch always expresses the idea of 'through', whether separable or inseparable.

(a) A few compounds with *durch-* are only inseparable

durch`denken *think through*     durch`löchern *make holes in*
durch`leben *experience*

NB: Separable `durchdenken* is also found with the identical meaning to *durch`denken*, but it is less common.

(b) A large number of compounds with *durch-* are only separable

`durchblicken	*look through*	`durchkommen	*get through, succeed*
`durchfallen	*fall through; fail*	`durchkriechen	*crawl through*
`durchführen	*carry out*	`durchrosten	*rust through*
`durchhalten	*hold out, survive*	`durchsehen	*look through*

(c) Many verbs form separable and inseparable compounds with *durch-*

The separable compounds always mean 'right the way through'. The inseparable verbs emphasise penetration without necessarily reaching the other side. However, the distinction may be fine, especially with verbs of motion. Compare:

Er **eilte** durch die Vorhalle **durch**	*He hurried through the vestibule*
Er **durcheilte** die Vorhalle	*He hurried across the vestibule*
Er **ritt** durch den Wald **durch**	*He crossed the forest on horseback*
Er **durchritt** den Wald	*He rode through the forest*

Similarly:

durchbrechen	*break through*	durchschauen	*see through*
durchdringen	*penetrate*	`durchsetzen	*carry through*
durchfahren	*travel through*	durch`setzen	*infiltrate*
durchlaufen	*run through*	durchstoßen	*break through*
durchreisen	*travel through*	durchwachen	*stay awake*

22.6.2 *hinter-* normally forms inseparable compounds

hinter`gehen *deceive*
hinter`fragen *analyse*
hinter`lassen *leave, bequeath*

hinter`legen *deposit*
hinter`treiben *foil, thwart*

Separable compounds with *hinter-* are substandard colloquial regionalisms:

`hinterbringen *take to the back*   `hintergehen *go to the back*

22.6.3 *miß-* is generally inseparable

It has two main senses, i.e.:

(i) 'opposite', e.g.:

mißachten *despise, disdain*   mißtrauen *distrust*

(ii) 'badly', 'wrongly', e.g.:

mißdeuten *misinterpret*   mißhandeln *ill-treat*

With a few verbs *miß-* can be treated as separable in the past participle and the infinitive with *zu*, e.g. *mißgeachtet, mißzuachten*, cf. 13.1.4b. These forms are alternatives to the regular inseparable forms *mißachtet, zu mißachten* and are generally less frequent, with the exception of *mißverstehen*, where the extended infinitive most commonly has the form *mißzuverstehen*.

22.6.4 *über-*

(a) A few compounds with *über-* are only separable

They are all intransitive and have the literal meaning 'over', e.g.:

`uberhängen *overhang*   `überkochen *boil over*
`überkippen *keel over*

(b) A large number of compounds with *über-* are only inseparable

They are all transitive and have a variety of meanings, i.e.:

(i)	repetition:	über`arbeiten *rework*	über`prüfen *check*
(ii)	more than enough:	über`fordern *overtax*	über`treiben *exaggerate*
(iii)	failing to notice:	über`hören *fail to hear*	über`sehen *overlook*
(iv)	'over':	über`denken *think over*	über`fallen *attack*

(c) Many verbs form both separable and inseparable compounds with *über-*

The separable compounds are mostly intransitive. They all have the literal meaning 'over'. The inseparable verbs are mostly transitive, with a more figurative meaning often similar to those given under (b) above:

	Separable	Inseparable
überfahren	*cross over*	*knock down*
überführen	*transfer*	*convict*
übergehen	*turn into sth.*	*leave out*
überlaufen	*overflow; desert*	*overrun*
überlegen	*put sth. over sb./sth.*	*consider*
übersetzen	*ferry over*	*translate*
überspringen	*jump over*	*skip*
übertreten	*change over*	*infringe*
überziehen	*put on*	*cover*

22.6.5 *um-*

(a) A large number of compounds in *um-* are only separable

Most express the idea of turning or changing a state:

`umblicken	*look round*	`umfallen	*fall over*
`umbringen	*kill*	`umschalten	*switch*
`umdrehen	*turn round*	`umsteigen	*change* (trains, etc.)

(b) Many compounds in *um-* are only inseparable

They all express encirclement or surrounding:

um`armen	*embrace*	um`ringen	*surround*
um`fassen	*embrace, encircle*	um`segeln	*sail round, circumnavigate*
um`geben	*surround*	um`zingeln	*surround, encircle*

(c) Many verbs form separable and inseparable compounds in *um-*

The difference in meaning corresponds to that given in (a) and (b) above:

	Separable	Inseparable
umbauen	*rebuild*	*enclose*
umbrechen	*break up*	*set* (i.e. type)
umfahren	*run over, knock down*	*travel round*
umgehen	*circulate*	*avoid*
umreißen	*tear down*	*outline*
umschreiben	*rewrite*	*paraphrase*
umstellen	*rearrange*	*surround*

22.6.6 *unter-*

(a) A large number of compounds in *unter-* are only separable

They generally have a literal meaning, i.e. 'under', e.g.:

`unterbringen	*accommodate*	`unterkommen	*find accommodation*
`untergehen	*sink, decline*	`untersetzen	*put underneath*

(b) Many compounds in *unter-* are only inseparable

They have a variety of meanings, i.e.:

(i) Less than enough:

unter`bieten	*undercut*	unter`schreiten	*fall short*
unter`schätzen	*underestimate*	unter`steuern	*understeer*

(ii) 'under':

unter`drücken	*suppress; oppress*	unter`schreiben	*sign*
unter`liegen	*be defeated*	unter`stützen	*support*

(iii) Other, miscellaneous meanings:

unter`bleiben	*cease*	unter`richten	*teach*
unter`brechen	*interrupt*	unter`sagen	*forbid, prohibit*
unter`lassen	*refrain from*	unter`suchen	*investigate*
unter`laufen	*occur*		

(c) Many verbs form separable and inseparable compounds with *unter-*

The separable verbs are mostly intransitive and have the meaning 'under'. The inseparable compounds are all transitive. Most have a more figurative meaning:

	Separable	**Inseparable**
unterbinden	*tie underneath*	*prevent*
untergraben	*dig in*	*undermine*
unterhalten	*hold underneath*	*entertain*
unterlegen	*put underneath*	*underlay*
unterschieben	*foist*	*insinuate*
unterschlagen	*cross (e.g. legs)*	*embezzle*
unterstellen	*keep, store*	*assume*
unterziehen	*put on underneath*	*undergo*

22.6.7 *voll-*

(a) Many verbs form compounds with *voll-* which are only separable
They all have the meaning 'full', e.g.:

`vollbekommen *manage to fill*  `vollschreiben *fill with writing*
`vollstopfen   *cram full*       `volltanken   *fill up* (car)

(b) A few compounds with *voll-* are only inseparable
Most of these are words of formal registers with the meaning 'complete', 'finish'
or 'accomplish', e.g.:

voll`bringen *achieve, accomplish*   voll`strecken *execute, carry out*
voll`enden   *complete*              voll`ziehen   *execute, carry out*
voll`führen *execute, perform*

22.6.8 *wider-* is in most cases used to form inseparable verbs

wider`legen *refute*   wider`stehen *resist*

Only two verbs in *wider-* are separable, i.e.:

`widerhallen *echo, reverberate*   `widerspiegeln *reflect*

22.6.9 *wieder-* normally forms separable verbs

`wiederkehren *return*   `wiedersehen *see again*

<u>One</u> verb prefixed with *wieder-* is inseparable, i.e. *wieder*`holen 'repeat'.

22.7 Verb formation by means other than by prefixes

By far the most productive means of deriving verbs is by means of prefixes, as
explained in 22.4–6. Nevertheless, a few other derivational patterns are frequent
or productive enough to deserve mention.

22.7.1 A number of verbs meaning 'cause to do' have been formed from strong verbs by means of vowel change

This pattern is no longer productive, but its results are still common. In general,
a transitive weak verb has been formed from an intransitive strong verb:

ertrinken *drown* (intr.)   sitzen *sit* → setzen *set*
  → ertränken *drown* (trans.)   springen *jump* → sprengen *blow up*
fallen *fall* → fällen *fell*

22.7.2 Verbs in *-eln* express a weaker form of the action

They usually have *Umlaut*:

husten *cough* → hüsteln *cough slightly*   streichen *stroke* → streicheln *caress*
lachen *laugh* → lächeln *smile*

Some such verbs have a pejorative sense, e.g.:

tanzen *dance* → tänzeln *mince*

This formation is still productive and can be based on nouns or adjectives as well as on other verbs, e.g.:

der Schwabe *Swabian* → schwäbeln *talk like a Swabian*
fromm *pious* → frömmeln *affect piety*

22.7.3 The suffix *-ieren* is mainly used to form verbs from foreign words

The source of most verbs in *-ieren* (and its derivatives *-isieren* and *-ifizieren*) is French or Latin. Some have entered German directly from French verbs in *-er*, e.g. *arranger* → *arrangieren*. Others have been formed in German from foreign roots, e.g. *Tabu* → *tabuisieren*. Only a very few have been created from German roots, e.g. *der Buchstabe* → *buchstabieren*.

23

Spelling and punctuation

German spelling and punctuation are relatively consistent (particularly in contrast to English!), but some rules are quite different to those for English, some can be ambiguous in certain contexts and difficult to apply, and there are a few inexplicable irregularities and anomalies. A selection of these problematic points is dealt with in this chapter, following the guidelines laid down in DUDEN (1985: 314ff., 385ff. and 785ff.). The rulings given there are accepted as authoritative throughout Germany, and variations in the other German-speaking countries are insignificant. Specifically, we deal with the use of capitals (23.1), whether to write one word or two (23.2), the distribution of ß and ss (23.3), other miscellaneous points of spelling (23.4), the use of the comma (23.5) and of other punctuation marks (23.6).

Proposals have now been accepted by the governments of all the countries where German is an official language for a reform of spelling and punctuation. The most important features of this reform are summarised in 23.7.

23.1 The use of capitals

The basic rules are:

(i) The first word in a sentence or a line of poetry is written with an initial capital letter (as in English).

(ii) All nouns are written with an initial capital letter, e.g. *der Sack, die Schwierigkeit, das Bürgertum, die Pfirsiche*.

(iii) All other words begin with a small letter.

There are several exceptions and anomalies relating to these basic rules which are explained in this chapter. As indicated in the relevant places, many of these will be eliminated in the reformed spelling.

23.1.1 Other parts of speech used as nouns are written with an initial capital letter

beim Lesen	das Für und Wider	das Ich	das Entweder-Oder
eine Drei	ein Drittel	der Vorsitzende	Bekanntes
alles Gute	nichts Schlechtes		

There are several inconsistencies in the application of this rule, as there are sometimes doubts as to whether the word is really being used as a noun.

(a) Adjectives used as nouns are written with a small letter in some phrases

im allgemeinen	*in general*	alles mögliche	*everything possible*
jdn. zum besten haben	*have sb. on*	aufs neue	*afresh*
beim alten bleiben	*remain as it was*	des öfteren	*frequently*
im großen und ganzen	*in general*	im stillen	*in secret*
im klaren sein	*be in the picture*	des weiteren	*furthermore*
auf dem laufenden sein	*be up to date*	im wesentlichen	*essentially*

NB: In the spelling reform *all* the above (and similar) idioms will be spelled with a capital letter, e.g. *im Allgemeinen*, etc.

(b) Adjectives are spelled with an initial small letter if a preceding (or following) noun is understood

Das rote Kleid hat mir nicht gepaßt, ich mußte das **blaue** nehmen
Es ist wohl das **schnellste** von diesen drei Autos

(c) Most indefinite determiners and adjectives are always written with a small letter

cf. 5.5. This remains the case even when they appear to be used as nouns, e.g. *ähnliches, etwas anderes, die beiden, jeder einzelne, das gleiche*, etc. This applies in particular to the following:

ähnlich	*similar*	derartig*	*suchlike*	nächst	*next*
ander	*other*	einzeln	*individual*	übrig	*remaining*
beide	*both*	folgend	*following*	verschieden	*various*
beliebig	*any*	gewiß*	*certain*	weiter*	*further*
bestimmt*	*definite*	gleich	*same*		

NB: (i) Those marked with an asterisk do have a capital after *alles* and *nichts*, e.g. *alles Weitere, nichts Derartiges.*
(ii) This rule will be abandoned in the reformed spelling, and capital letters will be used for *all* these words except the determiners *ander* and *beide*, which will continue to have small letters in all contexts.

(d) Usage with geographical and other proper names

(i) Adjectives forming part of geographical or other names referring to something unique have an initial capital letter, e.g.:

das Schwarze Meer	*the Black Sea*	Karl der Erste	*Charles the First*
das Neue Testament	*the New Testament*	die Olympischen Spiele	*the Olympic Games*
das Auswärtige Amt	*the Foreign Office*	die Französische Revolution	*the French Revolution*
der Eiserne Vorhang	*the Iron Curtain*		

However, the following, and others like them, are not names of unique things, and they are spelled with a small letter:

die goldene Hochzeit *golden wedding*   der schwarze Markt *the black market*

(ii) Indeclinable adjectives in *-er* from the names of towns and countries have an initial capital, e.g.:

der Kölner Dom   die Berliner Straßen   das Wiener Rathaus

(iii) Adjectives formed from proper names with the suffix *-isch* (or *-sch*) have a capital letter when they refer directly to the person concerned, but a small letter if they mean 'in the manner of'. Compare the following:

die Einsteinsche Relativitätstheorie	*Einstein's theory of relativity*
einsteinsche Theorien	*theories like those of Einstein*
das Elizabethanische England	*Elizabethan England*
(i.e. during the reign of Elizabeth I)	
das elizabethanische Drama	*Elizabethan drama*
(i.e. drama written during her reign, but she was not the author)	

NB: This distinction will be eliminated in the reformed spelling, and all adjectives from proper names will be spelled with a small letter irrespective of context, e.g. *das ohmsche Gesetz* 'Ohm's Law'.

(e) Usage with *deutsch* and other adjectives of nationality
(i) Adjectives of nationality are written with a capital letter when used as a noun to refer to the language or the school subject (cf. 6.4.6a):

Er kann kein Wort Deutsch	Wir haben Deutsch in der Schule
Das ist (kein) gutes Deutsch	Ich habe eine Drei in Deutsch

Sie spricht, kann, lernt, liest (kein, gut) Deutsch, Russisch, Englisch
Das Buch ist in Deutsch und Englisch erschienen

As an adjective used as a noun (cf. 6.4.3) *der/die Deutsche* 'German' (cf. 6.4.4) is also always spelled with a capital letter.

(ii) When used as adjectives they have a small letter, e.g.:

das deutsche Volk	ein deutsches Lied	italienische Weine
die deutsche Bundesrepublik	ein britisches Schiff	

This runs counter to English usage, which requires a capital letter (*the German people, Italian wines*, etc.). Only in names (cf. (d) above) is a capital used in German, e.g. *die Österreichische Bundesbahn*.

(iii) They have a small letter when used as the equivalent of an adverb, e.g.:

Der Minister hat mit ihr deutsch gesprochen
Redet sie jetzt deutsch oder niederländisch?

They are also spelled with a small letter when used with the preposition *auf*, as the whole is seen as having adverbial force, e.g.:

Wie sagt man das auf deutsch?	*How do you say that in German?*
Sie hat es mir auf spanisch erzählt	*She told me it in Spanish*

NB: In the reformed spelling, capital letters will be used with language adjectives after *auf*, e.g. *auf Deutsch, auf Englisch*.

(f) Superlatives are spelled with a small letter if they are used with *sein* as the equivalent of a form with *am*
cf. 8.4.1, e.g.:

Es ist das beste (= am besten), wenn wir ihr alles sagen
(Compare *das Beste, was ich je gegessen habe*)

NB: In the reformed spelling, capital letters will be used for these superlatives, e.g. *es ist das Beste, wenn wir ihr alles sagen*.

23.1.2 Nouns used as other parts of speech are written with a small letter

This applies in particular to:

(i) Nouns used as prepositions, cf. 20.4, e.g.:

angesichts   kraft   mittels   statt   trotz

NB: Some prepositions from complex phrases have alternative spellings, i.e. *anhand/an Hand, anstelle/an Stelle, aufgrund/auf Grund.*

(ii) Nouns used as adverbs, e.g.:

morgen   heute abend   von morgens bis abends   kreuz und quer   anfangs

NB: In the reformed spelling capitals will be used for words denoting a part of the day used in conjunction with *heute, gestern* and *morgen*, e.g. *gestern Abend, heute Mittag* (cf. 11.6.2).

(iii) Nouns used in indefinite expressions of number, e.g.:

ein bißchen *a little*   ein paar *a few* (see 5.5.6. Compare *ein Paar* 'a pair')

(iv) Nouns used as predicate adjectives with *sein*, i.e.:

Mir ist angst (but: Ich habe Angst)	*I am afraid*
Sie ist schuld daran	*It's her fault*
Es ist schade	*It's a pity/It's too bad*

(v) Nouns used as separable prefixes (cf. 22.5.3), e.g.:

achtgeben	*pay attention*	teilnehmen	*participate*
Es tut jemandem leid	*sb. is sorry*	jemandem wehtun	*hurt sb.*
stattfinden	*take place*		

NB: In the reformed spelling some of these prefixes will revert to being spelled as separate nouns, i.e. *Acht geben, Leid tun.*

(vi) In some other set phrases with verbs the noun does not have a capital:

außer acht lassen   *leave out of account*   recht/unrecht haben *be right/wrong*
sich in acht nehmen *take care*

NB: In the reformed spelling these exceptions will be eliminated and capitals will be used, e.g. *außer Acht lassen, Recht haben.*

23.1.3 Capitalisation of pronouns and related forms

(a) All forms of the 'polite' second person pronoun *Sie* are spelled with a capital letter
e.g. *Sie, Ihnen, Ihre Frau*, etc.

(b) Forms of the other second person pronouns, *du* and *ihr*, are spelled with a capital in letter-writing

Ich danke **Dir** recht herzlich für **Deinen** Brief
Wir wollen **Euch** zu **Eurer** Verlobung gratulieren

NB: Capitalisation of *du* and *ihr* will be eliminated in the reformed spelling.

23.2 One word or two?

The general rule is that compounds are written as a single word if they are felt to be a single concept. On the other hand, where the individual words are still felt to retain full meaning, they are written separately. The word stress often gives a clue to this, as a true fused compound only has one main stress, whereas separate words are still stressed independently. Compare:

`gut `schreiben	*write well*	`gutschreiben	*credit*
`so `weit	*so far*	`soweit	*on the whole*
`stehen `lassen	*leave standing*	`stehenlassen	*leave untouched*

(This rule is similar to English, e.g. `black `bird and `blackbird.)

However, there is in practice considerable uncertainty, variation and inconsistency in the matter of writing single or separate words. DUDEN (1985: 781) recommends that in all cases of doubt one should continue to write words separately. The reformed spelling will follow this systematically and prescribe writing words separately in all uncertain cases. Details of the proposed reforms are given in all relevant sections.

We deal here with selected important groups of words where clear indications can be given. Some problematic instances regarding the spelling of compounds are dealt with in other sections, i.e. for forms in *irgend-* see 5.5.11, and for the spelling of prefixed verbs see 22.5.3.

23.2.1 Combinations of preposition + noun

These are written separately if the words concerned are still felt to have independent meanings, e.g.:

mit Bezug auf, unter Bezug auf	nach Hause gehen, zu Hause sein
zu Ende gehen	in/außer Kraft treten, sein
in Frage kommen, stehen, stellen	zur Zeit

NB: In Austria and Switzerland *zurzeit* is accepted.

In some cases the words are still written separately, but the noun has a small letter (cf. also 23.1.1a):

von seiten	in betreff	in bezug auf	bei weitem

In several combinations the meanings of the individual components are no longer perceived as independent and they are written together, e.g.:

beiseite (stehen)	instand (setzen)
infolge	zugrunde (gehen, richten)
inmitten	zustande (bringen)

NB: The reformed spelling for these phrases varies depending on whether there are analogous forms already written separately. It prescribes changes to *in Bezug auf* and will tolerate alternative forms for *von Seiten* or *vonseiten, instand* or *in Stand, zugrunde* or *zu Grunde* and *zustande* or *zu Stande*.

23.2.2 Combinations of a noun or an adverb with a participle or an adjective

These are often written together, and the following general principles apply.

NB: In the reformed spelling <u>all</u> the combinations below will be written as separate words, e.g. *ein Aufsehen erregendes Ereignis.*

(a) Established combinations with a noun as first element are written together

ein **aufsehenerregendes** Ereignis	*a sensational occurrence*
das **bahnbrechende** Werk	*the pioneering work*

herzerquickend	*heart-warming*	himmelschreiend	*outrageous*
vertrauenerweckend	*inspiring confidence*	zeitraubend	*time-consuming*

Compounds which involve suppressing a preposition are always written together:

staubbedeckt *covered with dust*	freudestrahlend *beaming with joy*
(= mit Staub bedeckt)	(= vor Freude strahlend)

If the noun is qualified, e.g. by an adjective, it is written separately:

ein heimliches Grauen erregender Anblick
ein unser aller Herz erquickendes Wort

(b) Occasional combinations with an adverb as first element may be written together or separately

ein reichgeschmücktes Haus or ein reich geschmücktes Haus
der hellstrahlende Stern or der hell strahlende Stern
ein weichgekochtes Ei or ein weich gekochtes Ei

Which is preferred depends on whether the writer sees the meaning as as a new whole or as still distinct.

(c) Established combinations with an adverb as first element

These are normally written together when they are used with a following noun, but less usually after the verb *sein*. Thus:

eine **leichtverdauliche** Speise but die Speise ist **leicht verdaulich**
der **schwerverletzte** Mann   but der Mann war **schwer verletzt**

However, they are written separately if the adverb is qualified, e.g.:

eine sehr **leicht verdauliche** Speise   ein sehr **schwer verletzter** Mann

Such combinations are always written together, even after *sein*, if they have a figurative sense or a generic sense, referring to a whole class of people or things:

Das Angebot ist **freibleibend**	*The offer is subject to alteration*
Das Kind ist **minderbegabt**	*The child is less gifted*

23.2.3 Compound adverbs with so-, wie- and wo-

Note the difference between the following pairs (see 19.3.6 for details on the conjunctions in *so-*):

sobald	*as soon as*	so bald	*so soon*
solange	*as long as*	so lange	*so long*
sooft	*as often as*	so oft	*so often*
wieweit?	*to what extent?*	wie weit?	*how far?, what distance?*
woanders	*elsewhere* (cf. 7.1.5d)	wo anders?	*where else?*
womöglich	*possibly*	wo möglich	*if possible*

NB: (i) *so daß* 'so that', cf. 19.5.2, is always spelled as two words in Germany, but *sodaß* is accepted in Austria and Switzerland.

(ii) For the spelling of forms with *-viel* and *-wenig*, e.g. *soviel, wieviel, zuwenig*, see 5.5.25e.

23.3 ss or ß?

The distinction between *-ss-* and *-ß-* is now universally observed in Germany and Austria; only in Switzerland is no distinction made and *-ss-* used in all cases. Foreign learners are strongly recommended to follow the majority practice.

NB: *ß* is usually called *scharfes s* or *eszet*.

(a) *-ss-* is used between vowels if the preceding vowel is short

die Flüsse, ein gewisser, lassen, müssen, wissen, das Wasser, etc.

(b) *-ß-* is used in all other contexts

(i) Before consonants, e.g.:

du läßt, ihr laßt, er wußte, wir mußten, der größte

(ii) At the end of a word or part of a compound, e.g.:

das Faß, der Fuß, der Fluß, der Haß, der Maß, groß, gewiß, daß
das Flußbett, flußabwärts, haßerfüllt, der Großbuchstabe

(iii) Between vowels if the preceding vowel is long, e.g.:

die Buße, die Füße, die Maße, die Grüße, beißen, größer

These rules apply without exception. This means that *-ss-* and *-ß-* alternate in the inflectional forms of many words with a short vowel, depending on whether a vowel, a consonant or the end of the word follows, e.g.:

lassen, ich lasse BUT du läßt, wir ließen
müssen BUT ich muß, ich mußte
wissen BUT ich weiß, ihr wißt, ich wußte, gewußt
ein gewisser Herr BUT gewiß
der Fluß, das Faß BUT die Flüsse, die Fässer

NB: (i) A few personal names are spelled with a final *-ss*, e.g.: *Günther Grass, Theodor Heuss, Richard Strauss* (but *Johann Strauß*), *Carl Zeiss*.

(ii) *-ß-* was originally only a small letter, BUT its use as a capital is now tolerated, e.g. *BONNER STRAßE*.

(iii) In the reformed spelling *-ss-* will be written after a short vowel both in the middle and at the end of a word or compound, e.g. *Kuss, Hass, dass, wissbegierig*. This will eliminate most of the above alternations within the declension of individual words, e.g. *du lässt, ich wusste, gewiss*.

23.4. Other points of spelling

23.4.1 The plural of nouns in *-ee* and *-ie*

These nouns do not add an extra *-e* in forming the plural, even if the plural ending is pronounced as a distinct syllable, e.g.:

der See, die Seen [ze:ən]   das Knie, die Knie [kni:ə]
die Industrie, die Industrien [ɪndʊstri:ən]

Similarly in verb forms, cf. 12.2.1d:

knien [kniːən] *kneel*   wir schrien [ʃriːən] *we cried*

23.4.2 Double vowels are simplified under *Umlaut*

(i) In plurals (cf. 1.2.2d): der Saal *room* - die **Säle**.

(ii) In diminutives (cf. 22.2.1a): das Paar *pair* - das **Pärchen**.

23.4.3 Sequences of three identical consonants in compound words

If a vowel follows, one consonant is deleted, e.g.:

das Bett + das Tuch → das Bettuch   brennen + die Nessel → die Brennessel
still + legen → stillegen   das Schiff + die Fahrt → die Schiffahrt
rollen + die Läden → die Rolläden

However, if a further consonant follows, all three are retained, e.g.:

das Fett + der Tropfen → der Fetttropfen
das Bett + die Truhe → die Betttruhe

NB: In the reformed spelling, sequences of three consonants will be permitted in all contexts, e.g. *das Betttuch, stilllegen*.

23.5 The use of the comma

The basic rule for the use of the comma in German is that every clause within a sentence should begin and end with a comma. In this way, the comma in German is used to mark off grammatical units, not to signal a pause when speaking. This rule includes all types of clauses, i.e.:

Main clauses linked by a coordinating conjunction:

Mein Vater arbeitet im Garten, und meine Mutter fährt in die Stadt
Er runzelte die Stirn, aber sie sagte nichts

Subordinate clauses introduced by a conjunction:

Er fragte, ob ich morgen nach Halberstadt fahren wollte
Weil ich morgen arbeiten muß, werde ich keine Zeit haben

Subordinate clauses not introduced by a conjunction:

Sie sagte, sie habe diesen Mann nie vorher gesehen
Unsere Lage wäre unmöglich gewesen, hätte er diesen Plan nicht ausgedacht

Non-finite subordinate clauses (cf. 13.2 and 13.6):

Ich habe sie dringend gebeten, morgen zu uns zu kommen
Ich bin doch nur gekommen, um meinen alten Freund Peter wiederzusehen
Einmal in Zürich angekommen, mußte er sich sofort bei der Polizei anmelden

Major exceptions to this rule and areas of doubt and difficulty are explained in the remainder of this section.

This rule means that, contrary to the case in English, adverbs and adverbial phrases within the sentence are never separated off by commas. Compare:

Er konnte ihr jedoch helfen   *He was, however, able to help her*
Bringen Sie mir bitte eine Zeitung   *Bring me a newspaper, please*

23.5.1 Clauses linked by *und* or *oder*

(a) Main clauses joined by *und* or *oder* do not have a comma if the subject of the second clause is understood

i.e. if it is omitted because it is the same as that of the first clause:

> Er kam herein und sah seine Frau in der Ecke sitzen
> Mein Vater geht ins Theater oder besucht ein Konzert

However, a comma must be inserted if there is a new subject, or if the subject is repeated:

> Christa rief an, und er erzählte ihr, was passiert war
> Er kam herein, und dann sah er seine Frau in der Ecke sitzen

NB: In the reformed spelling the use of commas before *und* and *oder* will no longer be compulsory, irrespective of whether there is a new subject.

(b) Parallel subordinate clauses linked by *und* or *oder* do not have a comma between them

> Er sagte, daß ich sofort kommen müßte und daß er mir etwas sehr
> Wichtiges zu berichten hätte
> Sie wird nicht kommen, weil sie nicht kann oder weil sie einfach keine Lust hat

23.5.2 Infinitive clauses with *zu*

Infinitive clauses with *zu* are usually separated off by commas:

> Sie beschloß, den Betrag möglichst bald zu überweisen, und ging am
> nächsten Morgen zur Bank

There are a few exceptions to this general rule, i.e.:

(a) No comma is used if the clause consists simply of the infinitive with *zu*

> Sie beschloß zu warten   Ich hoffte zu gewinnen

Compare: *Ich hoffte, in der nächsten Runde zu gewinnen*. A comma is also necessary with compound infinitives, e.g. *Sie glaubte, gesiegt zu haben*.

(b) No comma is used if the infinitive clause is conflated with the clause on which it depends

(cf. 13.2.2), e.g.:

> Das bleibt noch abzuwarten   Diesen Vorgang wollen wir zu erklären
>   versuchen

(c) No comma is used if the infinitive clause is the subject of the verb

(cf. 13.2.3), e.g.:

> So etwas zu erlauben ist unerhört

(d) No comma is used after certain verbs even if the infinitive clause contains other elements

This is particularly the case with some of the 'semi-auxiliary' verbs dealt with in 13.2.5 and a few others. With these, the infinitive clause is felt to form a single unit with the main verb and a comma is seen as unnecessary:

Ich brauche heute nicht ins Geschäft zu gehen
Du hast dir jetzt die Hände zu waschen
So ein Apparat ist in London nicht mehr zu bekommen

This is *always* the case with the following semi-auxiliary verbs:

brauchen   haben   pflegen   scheinen   sein   vermögen

With a number of verbs the use of a comma is optional if they have no objects or adverbs with them, e.g.:

Sie hörte auf(,) mich zu belästigen
Sie versuchte(,) ihn telephonisch zu erreichen

This applies to the following:

anfangen	bitten	fürchten	versprechen	wagen
aufhören	denken	glauben	verstehen	wissen
beginnen	drohen	hoffen	versuchen	wünschen

NB: In the reformed spelling commas will no longer need to be used at all with infinitive clauses, but they may be employed at the writer's discretion to make the sense clear.

23.5.3 Longer participial clauses are separated by commas from the remainder of the sentence

Später wanderte er, ein altes Lied summend, durch den Garten
Einmal in seiner Heimatstadt angekommen, ging er sofort zum Haus, wo seine Großmutter gewohnt hatte

Commas are also used with absolute phrases (cf. 2.2.6), e.g.:

Der Polizist trat ins Zimmer, einen Revolver in der Hand

Short phrases, especially those which simply consist of a participle, are not separated by commas if they are felt to be an integral part of the clause, e.g.: *Das Kind lag weinend im Bett; Es war im Grunde genommen bloß ein Scherz.*

NB: In the reformed spelling, commas will no longer be required in any participial clauses, but they may be employed at the writer's discretion to make the sense clear.

23.5.4 Interjections, exclamations, explanatory phrases, phrases in apposition and parenthetical words and phrases

If these are seen as separate from the structure of the clause they are normally divided from it by commas, e.g.:

Ach, kannst du morgen wirklich nicht zu uns kommen?
Kurz und gut, die Lage ist kritisch
Wissen Sie, ich kann Ihnen da leider nicht mehr helfen
Sohn eines reichen Gutsbesitzers, er hat in seiner Eigenschaft als Reserveoffizier mit den Regeln des Ehrenhandels Bekanntschaft geschlossen
Das macht, **grob gerechnet,** vierzig Prozent von unserem Absatz aus
Ich habe jetzt, **wie gesagt,** keine Zeit dazu
Wir wurden durch Herrn Meiring, **den Direktor des Instituts,** aufs herzlichste empfangen

Comparative phrases introduced by *als* or *wie* are not normally separated off by commas, e.g.:

Sie ist jetzt wohl größer als ihre ältere Schwester
Dieser Mann sah aus wie ein Schornsteinfeger

23.5.5 Two or more adjectives qualifying a noun are divided by commas if they are of equal importance

i.e. if they could, alternatively, be linked by *und*, e.g.:

> gute, billige Äpfel (i.e. the apples are good *and* cheap)

No comma is used if the second adjective forms a single idea with the noun:

> gute englische Äpfel (i.e. English apples which are good)

In practice, this rule is not always followed consistently (any more than the similar rule in English is) and many German writers use no commas in any series of adjectives.

23.6 Other punctuation marks

23.6.1 The semi-colon is little used in German

In general, a comma or full stop is preferred, as appropriate. In particular, a comma tends to be used between two main clauses not linked by a conjunction:

> Gehe in die Stadt und kaufe Mehl, unterdessen heize ich schon den Ofen an

23.6.2 A colon, not a comma, is used when direct speech is introduced by a verb of saying

> Dann sagte sie: „Ich kann es nicht".

23.6.3 The first of a set of inverted commas is placed on the line

i.e. not above it as in English. This applies equally to single and double inverted commas:

> Dann sagte sie: „Ich kann ihn überhaupt nicht verstehen".
> Er fragte mich: „Kennen Sie Brechts Stück ‚Mutter Courage und ihre Kinder'?"

23.6.4 The exclamation mark

(a) The exclamation mark is used after interjections and exclamations

> Ach!   Donnerwetter!   Pfui Teufel!   Guten Tag!

(b) Commands are followed by an exclamation mark

> Komm sofort zurück!   Hören Sie sofort auf!
> Seid doch vorsichtig, Kinder!   Einsteigen und die Türen schließen!

Standard usage has traditionally required the use of the exclamation mark with commands in German, but this rule is not always followed nowadays, and many Germans prefer to use a full stop, especially if the command is not felt to be particularly forceful.

(c) An exclamation mark is used after the words of address at the beginning of a letter

> Sehr geehrter Herr Dr. Fleischmann!   Liebe Petra!

This traditional usage is now being supplanted by the use of the comma, as in English. However, if a comma is used, a capital letter is not used for the first word of the letter proper, as, strictly speaking, it is not the beginning of a sentence, e.g.:

> Lieber Martin,
>
> es hat uns sehr gefreut, wieder mal von Dir zu hören ...

23.7 The reform of German spelling and punctuation

The present spelling of German was last regulated for official uses, especially for teaching in schools, as long ago as 1901/1902, and it has long been felt that the rulings made then had still left some unnecessary inconsistencies and anomalies which needed to be eliminated. More radical suggestions, such as the abandonment of capital letters for nouns, were ultimately rejected, and the countries where German is used as an official language agreed in 1994/95 on a set of relatively modest reforms. These will be introduced in schools in 1998. For a transitional period of seven years the old and the new spellings will be permitted, but from the year 2005 only the new spellings will be regarded as correct.

In the following the most important features of the reformed spelling are briefly summarised, following Sitta (1994) and Heller (1995), concentrating on general principles, as detail cannot be given here on individual words which will be affected. Indications of the alterations have also been given in footnotes in relevant sections in this chapter and throughout this book.

23.7.1 *ss* will be used at the end of a word after a short vowel

Cf. 23.3. This ruling extends the general principle of German that short vowels are indicated in the spelling by being followed by double consonants, long vowels by a single consonant. It means that there will no longer be the confusing alternation between *ss* and *ß* in the declension of a number of common words:

Old spelling	New spelling
der Fluß – die Flüsse	der Fluss – die Flüsse (short vowel)
der Fuß – die Füße	der Fuß – die Füße (long vowel)
lassen – sie läßt	lassen – sie lässt
wissen – ich wußte	wissen – ich wusste

23.7.2 Inconsistencies in spelling words together or separately will be eradicated

Cf. 23.2. The present rule that words should be spelled together if they form a single sense unit, but separately if they retained distinct meanings, was impossible to operate in practice and gave rise to much uncertainty and confusion. In all such doubtful cases, particularly with compound verbs (cf. 22.5.3), writing the components separately will become the norm:

Old spelling	New spelling
sitzenbleiben, stehengeblieben	sitzen bleiben, stehen geblieben
gefangennehmen, verlorengehen	gefangen nehmen, verloren gehen
übrigbleiben, fertigbringen	übrig bleiben, fertig bringen
ineinanderfließen (cf. 22.5.3b)	ineinander fließen
radfahren, haltmachen	Rad fahren, Halt machen
maschineschreiben	Maschine schreiben
nahestehend, zartfühlend	nahe stehend, zart fühlend

Compounds with *viel* and *wenig* (cf. 5.5.25e) will be systematised, and all will be spelled separately:

Old spelling	New spelling
soviel, wieviel, zuviel	so viel, wie viel, zu viel
sowenig, zuwenig	so wenig, zu wenig
so viele, wie viele	so viele, wie viele

Compounds with *irgend* (cf. 5.5.11a) will be systematised, and all will be spelled as one word:

Old spelling	New spelling
irgend etwas, irgend jemand	irgendetwas, irgendjemand
irgendwer, irgendwo	irgendwer, irgendwo

23.7.3 Inconsistencies in the use of capital letters will be eliminated

Cf. 23.1. In particular, some nouns (especially adjectival nouns) in set phrases and combinations which have (rather arbitrarily) been spelled with a small letter will henceforward be spelled with a capital, e.g.:

Old spelling	New spelling
der, die, das letzte, nächste	der, die, das Letzte, Nächste
der erste, der dritte	der Erste, der Dritte
alles übrige	alles Übrige
in bezug (auf)	in Bezug (auf)
achtgeben, haltmachen	Acht geben, Halt machen
im folgenden, im nachhinein	im Folgenden, im Nachhinein
ins reine schreiben	ins Reine schreiben
auf dem trockenen sitzen	auf dem Trockenen sitzen
Es ist das beste, wenn . . .	Es ist das Beste, wenn . . .
auf deutsch (cf. 23.1.1e)	auf Deutsch

In addition, superlatives in *aufs* may, optionally, be spelled with a capital letter, e.g. *aufs herzlichste* or *aufs Herzlichste* (see 8.4.3).

The nouns for parts of the day in time phrases will be spelled with a capital in conjunction with *gestern*, *heute* and *morgen*, but written together with the weekdays:

Old spelling	New spelling
gestern abend, morgen mittag	gestern Abend, morgen Mittag
am Dienstag abend	am Dienstagabend
Dienstag abends	dienstagabends

Finally, adjectives from names will be spelled with a small letter (e.g. *das ohmsche Gesetz*, cf. 23.1.1d), and forms of *du* and *ihr* will no longer be capitalised in letters (see 23.1.3).

23.7.4 Revision of comma rules

See 23.5. There are two major revisions, i.e.:

- a comma will no longer need to be used before *und* and *oder*, even if the subject is present in the second clause.
- a comma will no longer be required with infinitive clauses.

Thus:

Old spelling	New spelling
„Das gibt Arbeit", sagte Holger, und er wischte sich den Rasierschaum aus dem Bart	„Das gibt Arbeit", sagte Holger und er wischte sich den Rasierschaum aus dem Bart
Er hatte nicht die Absicht, sie an dem Abend anzurufen	Er hatte nicht die Absicht sie an dem Abend anzurufen

In these contexts a comma can be used at the writer's discretion, in particular to mark a pause clearly or to avoid ambiguities. Heller (1995: 23) gives the following examples:

> Sie begegnete ihrem Trainer, und dessen Mannschaft musste lange auf ihn warten

Inserting a comma makes it clear at first sight that she only met the manager, not the manager *and* his team.

> Ich rate, ihm zu helfen   Ich rate ihm, zu helfen

Inserting the comma in the appropriate place makes the sense quite clear.

Bibliography and references

We list below all the major works which were consulted during the preparation of the revised edition, together with those books and articles on more specialised topics which are cited in the text. Reference is made to them where appropriate by giving author, year of publication and page numbers in the conventional way, e.g. Abraham (1995: 378–90).

Abraham, W. (1995) *Deutsche Syntax im Sprachvergleich: Grundlegung einer typologischen Syntax des Deutschen*. Narr: Tübingen.

Admoni, W. (1982) *Der deutsche Sprachbau*. 4th edn Beck: München.

Andersen, P.K. (1990) 'Typological approaches to the passive'. *Journal of Linguistics* 26, 189-202.

Askedal, J.O. (1983) 'Kohärenz und Inkohärenz in deutschen Infinitfügungen. Vorschlag zur begrifflichen Klärung'. *Lingua* 59, 177–96.

Askedal, J.O. (1990) 'Zur syntaktischen und referentiell–semantischen Typisierung der deutschen Pronominalform *es*'. *Deutsch als Fremdsprache* 27, 213–25.

Askedal, J.O. (1991) '"Ersatzinfinitiv/Partizipersatz" und verwandtes. Zum Aufbau des verbalen Schlußfeldes in der modernen deutschen Standardsprache'. *Zeitschrift für germanistische Linguistik* 19, 1–23.

Bausch, K. (1979) *Modalität und Konjunktivgebrauch in der gesprochenen deutschen Standardssprache. Sprachsystem, Sprachvariation und Sprachwandel im heutigen Deutsch*. Hueber: München.

Bausewein, K. (1990) *Akkusativobjekt, Akkusativobjektsätze und Objektsprädikate im Deutschen*. Niemeyer: Tübingen.

Bech, G. (1983) *Studien über das deutsche Verbum infinitum*. 2nd edn Niemeyer: Tübingen.

Bergenholtz, H. (1985) 'Kasuskongruenz in der Apposition'. *Beiträge zur Geschichte der deutschen Sprache und Literatur (Tübingen)* 107, 21–44.

Berger, D. (1982) *Fehlerfreies Deutsch*. 2nd edn Dudenverlag: Mannheim, Wien, Zürich.

Bethke, I. (1990) *'der', 'die', 'das' als Pronomen*. iudicium-verlag: München.

Bisle-Müller, H. (1991) *Artikelwörter im Deutschen. Semantische und pragmatische Aspekte ihrer Verwendung*. Niemeyer: Tübingen.

Blake, B.J. (1994) *Case*. Cambridge University Press: Cambridge.

Bornstein, M. & Butt, M. (1987) 'Zum Status des s-Plurals im gegenwärtigen Deutsch'. In: W. Abraham & R. Århammar (eds), *Linguistik in Deutschland*.

Akten des 21. Linguistischen Kolloquiums, Groningen 1986. Niemeyer: Tübingen, pp. 135–53.

Bresson, D. (1988) *Grammaire d'usage de l'allemand contemporain*. Hachette: Paris.

Buscha, J. (1988) 'Die Funktionen der Pronominalform ES'. *Deutsch als Fremdsprache* 25, 27–33.

Buscha, J. (1989) *Lexikon deutsche Konjunktionen*. Verlag Enzyklopädie: Leipzig.

Buscha, J. & Zoch, I. (1984) *Der Konjunktiv*. Verlag Enzyklopädie: Leipzig.

Buscha, J. & Zoch, I. (1988) *Der Infinitiv*. Verlag Enzyklopädie: Leipzig.

Butt, J. & Benjamin, C. (1994) *A New Reference Grammar of Modern Spanish*. 2nd edn Edward Arnold: London.

Clyne, M. (1995) *The German Language in a Changing Europe*. Cambridge University Press: Cambridge.

Collinson, W.E. (1953) *The German Language Today: Its Patterns and Historical Background*. Hutchinson's University Library: London.

Comrie, B. (1985) *Tense*. Cambridge University Press: Cambridge.

Corbett, G. (1991) *Gender*. Cambridge University Press: Cambridge.

Curme, O. (1922) *A Grammar of the German Language*. rev. edn Macmillan: New York.

Dieling, K. & Kempter, F. (1989) *Die Tempora*. 2nd edn Verlag Enzyklopädie: Leipzig.

Doleschal, U. (1992) *Movierung im Deutschen. Eine Darstellung der Bildung und Verwendung weiblicher Personenbezeichnungen*. Lincom Europa: Unterschließheim/München.

Dückert, J. & Kempcke, G. (eds) (1984) *Wörterbuch der Sprachschwierigkeiten*. VEB Bibliographisches Institut: Leipzig.

DUDEN (1985) *Richtiges und gutes Deutsch. Wörterbuch der sprachlichen Zweifelsfälle*. 3rd edn Dudenverlag: Mannheim, Wien, Zürich.

DUDEN (1991) *Rechtschreibung der deutschen Sprache und Fremdwörter*. 20th edn Dudenverlag: Mannheim, Wien, Zürich.

DUDEN (1993) *Das große Wörterbuch der deutschen Sprache*. 2nd edn 8 vols Dudenverlag: Mannheim, Leipzig, Wien, Zürich.

DUDEN (1995) *Grammatik der deutschen Gegenwartssprache*. 5th edn Dudenverlag: Mannheim, Leipzig, Wien, Zürich.

Durrell, M. (1993) 'The use of *entlang* in modern standard German'. In J.L. Flood et al. (eds), 'Das unsichtbare Band der Sprache'. *Studies in German Language and Linguistic History in Memory of Leslie Seiffert*. Heinz: Stuttgart, pp. 521–38.

Eichhoff, J. (1977/78) *Wortatlas der deutschen Umgangssprachen*. 2 vols Francke: Bern and München.

Eisenberg, P. (1994) *Grundriß der deutschen Grammatik*. 3rd edn Metzler: Stuttgart and Weimar.

Eisenberg, P. & Gusovius, A. (1985) *Bibliographie zur deutschen Grammatik 1965–1983*. Narr: Tübingen.

Engel, U. (1991) *Deutsche Grammatik*. 2nd edn Groos: Heidelberg.

Engel, U. (1994) *Syntax der deutschen Gegenwartssprache*. 3rd edn Erich Schmidt: Berlin.

Engel, U. & Schuhmacher, H. (1978) *Kleines Valenzlexikon deutscher Verben*. Narr: Tübingen.

Fagan, S.M.B. (1992) *The Syntax and Semantics of Middle Constructions: A Study with Special Reference to German*. Cambridge University Press: Cambridge.

Farrell, R.B. (1977) *Dictionary of German Synonyms*. 3rd edn Cambridge University Press: Cambridge.

Flämig, W. (1991) *Grammatik des Deutschen. Einführung in Struktur- und Wirkungszusammenhänge erarbeitet auf der theoretischen Grundlage der 'Grundzüge einer deutschen Grammatik'*. Akademie-Verlag: Berlin.

Fleischer, W. & Barz, I. (1995) *Wortbildung der deutschen Gegenwartssprache*. rev. edn Niemeyer: Tübingen.

Fourquet, J. (1952) *Grammaire de l'allemand*. Hachette: Paris.

Fox, A. (1990) *The Structure of German*. Clarendon Press: Oxford.

Freund, F. (1989) 'Ich, der ich . . ./Ich der . . . – Bemerkungen zu einer altbekannten Variation in Relativsätzen'. In J. Buscha & J. Schröder (eds), *Linguistische und didaktische Grammatik. Beiträge zu Deutsch als Fremdsprache*. Verlag Enzyklopädie: Leipzig, pp. 128–36.

Freund, F. & Sundqvist, B. (1988) *Tysk grammatik*. Natur och Kultur: Stockholm.

Glück, H. & Sauer, W. (1990) *Gegenwartsdeutsch*. Metzler: Stuttgart.

Götz, D., Haensch, G. & Wellmann, H. (eds) (1993) *Langenscheidts Großwörterbuch Deutsch als Fremdsprache*. Langenscheidt: Berlin.

Götze, L. & Hess-Lüttich, E.W.B. (1989) *Knaurs Grammatik der deutschen Sprache. Sprachsystem und Sprachgebrauch*. Knaur: München.

Gregor, B. (1983) *Genuszuordnung. Das Genus englischer Lehnwörter im Deutschen*. Niemeyer: Tübingen.

Grewendorf, G. (1984) 'Reflexivierungsregeln im Deutschen'. *Deutsche Sprache* 12, 14–30.

Griesbach, H. (1986) *Neue deutsche Grammatik*. Langenscheidt: Berlin.

Grimm, Hans-J. (1986) *Untersuchungen zum Artikelgebrauch im Deutschen*. Verlag Enzyklopädie: Leipzig.

Grimm, Hans-J. (1987) *Lexikon zum Artikelgebrauch*. Verlag Enzyklopädie: Leipzig.

Hartwig, H. (1985) *Besseres Deutsch – größere Chancen*. Heyne: München.

Hawkins, J.A. (1986) *A Comparative Typology of English and German: Unifying the Contrasts*. Croom Helm: London, Sydney.

Heidolph, K.E., Flämig, W. & Motsch, W. (eds) (1981) *Grundzüge einer deutschen Grammatik*. Akademie-Verlag: Berlin.

Helbig, G. (1973) *Die Funktion der substantivischen Kasus in der deutschen Gegenwartssprache*. Niemeyer: Halle/Saale.

Helbig, G. (1982) *Valenz – Satzglieder – semantische Kasus – Satzmodelle*. Verlag Enzyklopädie: Leipzig.

Helbig, G. (1983) *Studien zur deutschen Syntax*. Verlag Enzyklopädie: Leipzig.

Helbig, G. (1988) *Lexikon deutscher Partikeln*. Verlag Enzyklopädie: Leipzig.

Helbig, G. (1993) *Deutsche Grammatik. Grundfragen und Abriß*. 2nd edn iudicium-verlag: München.

Helbig, G. & Buscha, J. (1986) *Deutsche Grammatik. Ein Handbuch für den Ausländerunterricht*. 9th edn Verlag Enzyklopädie: Leipzig.

Helbig, G. & Heinrich, G. (1983) *Das Vorgangspassiv*. 4th edn VEB Bibliographisches Institut: Leipzig.

Helbig, G. & Schenkel, W. (1983) *Wörterbuch zur Valenz und Distribution deutscher Verben*. 6th edn VEB Bibliographisches Institut: Leipzig.

Heller, K. (1995) *Rechtschreibung 2000. Die Reform auf einen Blick. Wörterliste der geänderten Schreibungen*. Klett: Stuttgart.

Hentschel, E. (1993) 'Flexionsverfall im Deutschen?'. *Zeitschrift für germanistische Linguistik* 21, 320–33.

Hentschel, E. & Weydt, H. (1994) *Handbuch der deutschen Grammatik.* 2nd edn de Gruyter: Berlin & New York.

Jaeger, C. (1992) *Probleme der syntaktischen Kongruenz. Theorie und Normvergleich im Deutschen.* Niemeyer: Tübingen.

Jäger, S. (1970) *Empfehlungen zum Gebrauch des Konjunktivs.* Schwann: Düsseldorf.

Kirkwood, H.W. (1969) 'Aspects of word order and its communicative function in English and German'. *Journal of Linguistics* 5, 85–107.

Kohrt, M. (1992) 'Realisierungsvarianten des Genitiv Singular im Neuhochdeutschen. Zur Interdependenz von Phonologie, Morphologie und Orthographie'. *Deutsche Sprache* 20, 127–38.

Köpcke, K.-M. (1982) *Untersuchungen zum Genussystem der deutschen Gegenwartssprache.* Niemeyer: Tübingen.

Kretzenbacher, H.L. & Segebrecht, W. (1991) *Vom Sie zum Du – mehr als eine Konvention?* Luchterhand Literaturverlag: Hamburg, Zürich.

Lamprecht, A. (1977) *Grammatik der englischen Sprache.* 5th edn Cornelsen-Velhagen & Klasing: Berlin.

Latzel, S. (1977) *Die deutschen Tempora Perfekt und Präteritum. Eine Darstellung mit Bezug auf die Erfordernisse des Faches 'Deutsch als Fremdsprache'.* Hueber: München.

Lauterbach, S. (1993) *Genitiv, Komposition und Präpositionalattribut – Zum System nominaler Relationen im Deutschen.* iudicium-verlag: München.

Lehmann, C. (1991) 'Grammaticalization and related changes in contemporary German'. In E.C. Traugott & B. Heine (eds), *Approaches to Grammaticalization.* Benjamins: Amsterdam, Philadelphia, pp. 493–535.

Leirbukt, O. (1995) 'Über Setzung und Nichtsetzung des Korrelats bei Relativsätzen mit *wer*'. In H. Popp (ed.), *Deutsch als Fremdsprache. An den Quellen eines Faches. Festschrift für Gerhard Helbig zum 65. Geburtstag.* iudicium-verlag: München, pp. 151–63.

Lockwood, W.B. (1987) *German Today: The Advanced Learner's Guide.* Clarendon Press: Oxford.

Lutzeier, P. (1985) *Lexikalische Semantik.* Metzler: Stuttgart.

Marx-Moyse, J. (1983) *Untersuchungen zur deutschen Satzsyntax. 'Es' als vorausweisendes Element eines Subjektsatzes.* Steiner: Wiesbaden.

Mills, A.E. (1986) *The Acquisition of Gender: A Study of English and German.* Springer: Berlin, Heidelberg.

Öhlschläger, G. (1989) *Zur Syntax und Semantik der Modalverben des Deutschen.* Niemeyer: Tübingen.

Pfeffer, J.A. & Linder, B. (1982) 'The inflection of adjectives after indefinites in written and spoken German'. In J.A. Pfeffer (ed.), *Probleme der deskriptiven deutschen Grammatik.* Groos: Heidelberg, pp. 135–61.

Pfeffer, J.A. & Lorentz, J.P. (1979) 'Der analytische Genitiv mit "von" in Wort und Schrift'. *Muttersprache* 89, 53–70.

Quirk, R. *et al.* (1985) *A Comprehensive Grammar of the English Language.* Longman: London.

Sanders, W. (1986) *Gutes Deutsch – Besseres Deutsch. Praktische Stillehre der deutschen Gegenwartssprache.* Wissenschaftliche Buchgesellschaft: Darmstadt.

Sanders, W. (1992) *Sprachkritikastereien und was der 'Fachler' dazu sagt*. Wissenschaftliche Buchgesellschaft: Darmstadt.

Schanen, F. & Confais, Jean-P. (1986) *Grammaire de l'allemand. Formes et fonctions*. Nathan: Paris.

Schmitz, W. (1964) *Der Gebrauch der deutschen Präpositionen*. Hueber: München.

Scholze-Stubenrecht, W. & Sykes, J.B. (eds) (1990) *The Oxford Duden German Dictionary*. Clarendon Press: Oxford.

Schröder, J. (1990) *Lexikon deutscher Präpositionen*. Verlag Enzyklopädie: Leipzig.

Sitta, H. (ed.) (1994) *DUDEN. Informationen zur neuen deutschen Rechtschreibung*. Dudenverlag: Mannheim, Leipzig, Wien, Zürich.

Sommerfeldt, K.E. (ed.) (1988) *Entwicklungstendenzen in der deutschen Gegenwartssprache*. Niemeyer: Tübingen.

Sommerfeldt, K.-E. (1990) 'Zum Modusgebrauch in der indirekten Rede – Regel und Realität'. *Deutsch als Fremdsprache* 27, 337–42.

Sommerfeldt, K.-E. & Schreiber, H. (1977) *Wörterbuch zur Valenz und Distribution deutscher Adjektive*. 2nd edn VEB Bibliographisches Institut: Leipzig.

Sommerfeldt, K.-E. & Starke, G. (1992) *Einführung in die Grammatik der deutschen Gegenwartssprache*. 2nd edn Niemeyer: Tübingen.

Sonnenberg, B. (1992) *Korrelate im Deutschen. Beschreibung, Geschichte und Grammatiktheorie*. Niemeyer: Tübingen.

Storrer, A. (1992) *Verbvalenz. Theoretische und methodischer Grundlagen ihrer Beschreibung in Grammatographie und Lexikographie*. Niemeyer: Tübingen.

Swan, M. (1980) *Practical English Usage*. Oxford University Press: Oxford.

Terrell, P. *et al.* (eds) (1991) *Collins German-English English-German Dictionary*. 2nd edn HarperCollins: Glasgow.

Thieroff, R. (1992) *Das finite Verb im Deutschen. Tempus – Modus – Distanz*. Narr: Tübingen.

Toman, J. (ed.) (1984) *Studies in German Grammar*. Foris: Dordrecht.

Trask, R.L. (1993) *A Dictionary of Grammatical Terms in Linguistics*. Routledge: London and New York.

Ulvestad, B. & Bergenholtz, H. (1983) '"Es" als "Vorgreifer" eines Objektsatzes. Teil II'. *Deutsche Sprache* 11, 1–26.

Wahrig, G. (ed.) (1978) *dtv-Wörterbuch der deutschen Sprache*. dtv: München.

Wahrig, G. (1986) *Deutsches Wörterbuch*. rev. edn Betelsman: Gütersloh.

Wegener, H. (1985) *Der Dativ im heutigen Deutsch*. Narr: Tübingen.

Wegener, H. (1995) *Der Nominalflexion des Deutschen – verstanden als Lerngegenstand*. Niemeyer: Tübingen.

Weinrich, H. (1993) *DUDEN – Textgrammatik der deutschen Sprache*. Dudenverlag: Mannheim, Leipzig, Wien, Zürich.

West, J. (1992–94) *Progressive Grammar of German*. 6 vols Authentik: Dublin.

Weydt, H. *et al.* (1983) *Kleine deutsche Partikellehre*. Klett: Stuttgart.

Sources

The examples illustrating points of grammar and usage have been drawn from a wide range of sources and registers, spoken as well as written. Many of the unattributed examples which are new to this revised edition have been simplified or amended from modern texts, from phrases and sentences heard in conversation or on radio and television, etc. and in large number from the computerised corpus of modern spoken and written German set up by the Institut für deutsche Sprache in Mannheim. Longer examples quoted verbatim or with minor simplifications have been attributed wherever possible. The following sources have provided such material:

Authors

A.	Andersch	U. Frevert	G. Kapp	W. Schnurre
S.	Andres	M. Frisch	E. Kästner	A. Seghers
R.	Augstein	F. Fühmann	A. Kolb	E. Strauß
I.	Bachmann	G. Gaiser	F.X. Kroetz	E. Strittmatter
V.	Baum	A. Goes	E. Langgässer	A. Surminski
K.	Bednarz	G. Grass	S. Lenz	P. Süßkind
W.	Bergengruen	B. Grzimek	H. Mann	T. Valentin
T.	Bernhard	S. Haffner	K. Mann	H. von Rimscha
P.	Bichsel	E.W. Heine	Th. Mann	M. von der Grün
H.	Böll	S. Hermlin	I. Morgner	M. Walser
O.	Bollnow	T. Heuss	R. Musil	P. Weiß
K.H.	Borst	S. Heym	T. Pinkwart	I. Wendt
B.	Brecht	P. Heyse	T. Plievier	U. Wickert
S.	Brinkmann	W. Hildesheimer	R. Pörtner	E. Wiechert
J.	Bumke	M. Horbach	E.M. Remarque	G. Wohmann
A.	Döblin	E.H. Jacob	G. Reuter	C. Wolf
M.	Dönhoff	W. Jens	R.M. Rilke	C. Zuckmayer
F.	Dürrenmatt	U. Johnson	J. Roth	S. Zweig
H.	Fallada	E. Jünger	P. Schneider	G. Zwerenz
M.L.	Fleißer	F. Kafka		

Newspapers

The following newspapers or periodicals have provided material. Some titles have been abbreviated as indicated:

BILD	BILD-Zeitung	FR	Frankfurter Rundschau
BZ	Berliner Zeitung	HA	Hamburger Abendblatt
FAZ	Frankfurter Allgemeine Zeitung		Horizont
LV	Leipziger Volkszeitung		Quick
MM	Mannheimer Morgen		(Der) Spiegel
ND	Neues Deutschland		Stern
NZZ	Neue Zürcher Zeitung	SZ	Süddeutsche Zeitung
OH	Odenwälder Heimatzeitung		(Die) Welt
	(Die) Presse		(Die) Zeit

In addition, the Baedeker series of travel guides, Knaur's encyclopedia, and Innsbruck University *Vorlesungsverzeichnis* provided some examples, as did the following radio and television stations: ARD, NDR, SWF, WDR, ZDF.

German word index

The indexes comprise a German word index, an English word index and a topic index. The German word index contains all words about which specific information is given, but it does not include individual personal pronouns or articles, or words which are simply given in lists of examples. Important entries on individual items are in bold. Verbs which can be used reflexively or non-reflexively are indicated as follows: ändern (sich).

English word index

The indexes comprise a German word index, an English word index and a topic index. The English word index contains all those English words where specific information is given about their German equivalents.

Topic index

The indexes comprise a German word index, an English word index and a topic index. The topic index lists all grammatical and other topics covered in the work, but does not list individual words in either language, for which the word-indexes should be consulted.